Babies by the Bay

SECOND EDITION

Babies by the Bay

SECOND EDITION

The Insider's Guide to Everything from Doctors and Diapers to Playgrounds and Preschools in the San Francisco Bay Area

Michelle L. Keene

Stephanie S. Lamarre

WILDCAT CANYON PRESS
An Imprint of Council Oak Books
San Francisco / Tulsa

Wildcat Canyon Press, San Francisco/Tulsa
counciloakbooks.com

First edition published 2002
Second edition published December 2005

The names of many of the products and services mentioned in these pages are registered trademarks and service marks, belonging to their owners. We acknowledge the rights of these owners.

Cover Design: Mary Beth Salmon
Cover Illustration (skyline): Mike Powell
Art Direction: Leyza Yardley
Interior Design & Typesetting: Margaret Copeland/Terragrafix
Typographic Specifications: Body text in Korinna 10/13, headings in Minya-Nouvelle.
Printed in the United States of America
ISBN-10: 1-885171-86-2
ISBN-13: 978-1-885171-86-3

Library of Congress Cataloging-in-Publication Data
Keene, Michelle L., 1965-
  Babies by the bay : the insider's guide to everything from doctors and diapers to playgrounds and preschools in the San Francisco Bay area / Michelle L. Keene, Stephanie S. Lamarre.-- 2nd ed.
    p. cm.
  Includes bibliographical references and index.
  ISBN-13: 978-1-885171-86-3
  ISBN-10: 1-885171-86-2
 1. Infants--Services for--California--San Francisco Bay Area--Directories.
2. Toddlers--Services for--California--San Francisco Bay Area--Directories.
3. Preschool children--Services for--California--San Francisco Bay Area--Directories. 4. Infant health services--California--San Francisco Bay Area--Directories. 5. Maternal health services--California--San Francisco Bay Area--Directories. 6. Infants' supplies--California--San Francisco Bay Area--Directories. 7. Parents--Services for--California--San Francisco Bay Area--Directories. 8. Family recreation--California--San Francisco Bay Area--Directories. I. Lamarre, Stephanie S., 1966- II. Title.

HQ774.K44 2005
362.7029'7946--dc22

2005027545

Dedication

For our own babies by the bay,
Michael, Maximilian, and Mattheus
Jack and Elise

Acknowledgments to the Second Edition

Once again, we were fortunate to have the help of a number of friends and family members in putting together the second edition. First and foremost, we thank our husbands, David Lamarre and Mark Tellini, who showed remarkable patience and single parenting skills as we toiled at our computers. Thank you to all the parents who responded to our second edition surveys with invaluable opinions. For their help with the second edition, particular thanks go to Tanya Alsberg, Pam Bonnie, Sara Duskin, Erin Fish, Monica Friedman, Hope Gelbach, Gretchen Harding, Nancy Held, Jennifer Keohane, Kari Marble, Michele Mason, Jill McNay, Ceres Rutan, Sara Duskin, Gina Tribolet, Sally Van Ingen, Christine Varon, Dr. Donna Wiggins, and the moms of Lone Mountain Children's Center. Our publicist, Sharon Poynor, did a remarkable job of putting the first edition into the right hands. Thank you also to Ja-lene Clark, Sally Dennison, and Paulette Millichap at Council Oak Books, for their continued support.

Acknowledgments to the First Edition

We would like to thank the many people who went above and beyond the call in helping us as we researched and wrote this book: our husbands, Mark Tellini and David Lamarre, for their support and encouragement; all of the parents who responded to our surveys for their invaluable advice and opinions; our entire Wednesday play group—Alix Arndt, Anne Brundige, Christie Carlson, Elizabeth Clark, Amy Culp, Hope Gelbach, Kathy Hoyt, Nicole Klionsky, Anne Nicholson, Amanda Safka, Robyn Sealander, Christine Varon, and Heather Young—for their inspiration; and Mary Asel, Paula Atkinson, Page Barnes, Margaret Bielak, Lesley Brascesco, Sally Brammell, Stephanie Bornstein at Equal Rights Advocates, Wynn Burkett, Genevieve Butcher, Helen Byrne, Irene Byrne, Jeff Byrne, Elizabeth Clark, Pam Clemmons, Dr. Suzanne Cobb-Christie, Susan Condon, Sara Duskin, Carol Egan, Diane Forese, Erin Gilheary, Deborah Klein,

Todd Madalone, Cindy Mall, Monica Canty McCarty, Trigg Robinson McLeod, Amy Metzler, Diane Michelsen, Ashley Paff, Barbara Papini, Heather Pedersen, Nancy Pile, Helen Riley, Bonnie Rose, Nishan Shephard, Vena Skolnick, Juliet Tanner, Rose Titcomb, Ashley Tobin, Anne Waltzer, Dr. Donna Wiggins, Kim Yee, and Heather Young for providing much-needed help with research, surveys, leads, and drafts.

Finally, we would like to thank Tamara Traeder at Wildcat Canyon Press for making this book possible.

A Note from the Authors

Our goal in this book is to present information and, when available, "insider information" about parents' experiences of pregnancy and young child resources in the Bay Area. We collected opinions about such resources from several hundred parents in an unofficial survey. The parents' ratings in this book come from our interpretation of the opinions in those surveys, and/or from our own personal experience of the resource. These ratings are merely personal opinions of the authors and their sources, are not official or factual in nature, and should not be looked at as authoritative! Also, the absence of a parent rating carries no negative connotation; it just means that we received no opinions from our surveys, and we have no personal opinion about a particular resource.

We have tried in each chapter to give you some background material that may help you as you consider the resources in that chapter. Of course, this information is general in nature and should not be construed as medical, legal, or other professional advice. We're not doctors, so it's best to consult with your health care provider before acting on any medical decision. And if you have legal questions, you should consult a lawyer about your specific circumstances.

As you may expect, inclusion in this book should not be regarded as a referral to or an endorsement of particular doctors, midwives, lawyers, or other service providers, nor a guarantee of the quality of the services they each offer. Similarly, we can't guarantee the quality of any of the products described in this book. You must make your own independent evaluation of all goods and services prior to purchasing or using them.

We do not have any ownership in any of the resources listed in this book. We also did not receive any compensation for including any resource here. We will disclose that our friend and photographer, who is listed in the book, took our author photo as a gift to us! (But we would have recommended her anyway.)

All that being said, we hope that this book is helpful to you, and that it makes the experience of being an expectant and new parent a little easier. Enjoy!

Table of Contents

Introduction to the Second Edition

It has been three years since we published the first edition of *Babies by the Bay,* and in doing the research for this second edition we have realized just how much has changed for Bay Area parents! There seem to be more cutting-edge birthing options available in the Bay Area, more strollers, high chairs, and car seats than ever to choose from, as well as a pregnancy and postpartum fitness craze that has taken off like nowhere else in the country. Maternity clothes have been revolutionized—in part by some talented designers in the Bay Area—and the range of classes and outings for young children has expanded more than ever. Child care options and preschools have also increased, affording parents more opportunities to consider.

While we are two moms who experience all of the above on a daily basis, we truly believe that our book is unique in that we draw upon a broad spectrum of parents across the Bay Area to gather their opinions and experiences and bring them to you! We recognize that this is far from a perfect method of research (see authors' note and introduction to the first edition), but we also believe that the intrinsic value of our book lies in the informal parent-to-parent associations and personal feedback via written surveys and individual conversations we have taken the time to have with parents. Thanks to these parents who have taken precious amounts of their time to share their favorite resources and opinions with us, we have more resources listed than before, with more ratings, including many more resources in the East and South Bays as well as in Napa, Sonoma, and Santa Cruz counties. All of this is intended to help *you* save time as a parent and to make your parenting resource choices more wisely and more efficiently. We hope that this book helps you accomplish this goal. As always, we love getting additional feedback and updated information, so please contact us via our website, www.babiesbythebay.com, if you would like to tell us about a particular resource.

Introduction to the First Edition

Becoming a parent in the Bay Area catapults you into a new and mysterious world. As we eagerly awaited our first children more than three years ago, we had so many questions about everything, but didn't know where to turn for answers. We wondered how we could have felt so competent in our professional lives, yet feel so incompetent as expectant, and then new, parents. We asked these questions and more:

- How do I find the best hospitals and doctors in the Bay Area?
- Where can I find great maternity and baby gear at the best prices without driving around the entire Bay Area?
- Where can I work out safely during pregnancy, and do any of these clubs have child care?
- Where can I meet other new parents?
- Which kids' classes are worth the money?
- Where can we take our kids on a rainy day?
- How do I find a competent doula, baby nurse, nanny, babysitter, or day care center near my home?
- How do I find, and more importantly, get into, a good preschool in my area?

As we struggled to adapt to life after our first babies were born, we searched in vain for a local baby guide. The phone book was no help—either it did not list the necessary resources, or we had no way of knowing which places other parents liked. More importantly, as new parents we just did not have time to drive in circles around the Bay Area to investigate—and who wants to take a chance on something as important as a baby? We quickly realized that we needed a guide to parenthood in the Bay Area, found there was none . . . and the idea for this book was born.

Our hope is that our work on this book will spare you some of the time and energy we spent finding great resources, and let you enjoy more hours with your children. As we discovered, the Bay Area is full of great resources for parents—so many, in fact, that the trick is to find time to experience them all. During the journey of writing this book, we logged thousands of miles in our cars and strollers, and hundreds of telephone hours. Together we've searched for maternity clothes, baby gear, hospitals, doctors, and preschools. We're both in search of the Holy Grail of postnatal fitness. We've carted our children to museums, libraries, and parks all over the Bay Area. We are both active in several mothers' groups, which keep us sane. Between us we've lived in almost all the local regions, and we've met wonderful parents everywhere we've gone. Along the way, we both somehow managed to find time to have second children, and we have realized again and again that the Bay Area is a great place to raise kids.

We wanted our guidebook to be filled with parents' opinions—a true insider's guide for new parents. And we certainly could not personally experience every single resource in the Bay Area! So before we sat down to write, we surveyed local parents in all six Bay Area counties (Alameda, Contra Costa, Marin, San Francisco, Santa Clara, and San Mateo) about topics ranging from favorite doctors to favorite parks to favorite shopping haunts. We received several hundred enthusiastic responses, including frank opinions on everything from pregnancy through preschool. These parents' opinions, and our own, formed the basis for the ratings and quotes you'll see in this book.

Throughout the book, you'll find a five-star "parent rating" system. Think of it as a report card for baby resources. For those resources we received parent opinions about or have experienced ourselves, we've assigned a rating, ranging from one star (☆) at the bottom end, to five stars (☆ ☆ ☆ ☆ ☆) at the top. If we have listed no rating, it simply means that we received no comments on the resource from any of the parents surveyed, and have not personally experienced it ourselves. Here is a key to the ratings:

☆ I wouldn't send my worst enemy there.

☆ ☆ Poor to fair reviews; not the worst, but you can do better elsewhere.

☆ ☆ ☆ Satisfactory or mixed reviews.

☆ ☆ ☆ ☆ Good reviews; not perfect, but still a great resource.

☆ ☆ ☆ ☆ ☆ Excellent; our highest rating.

You won't see many one- and two-star ratings in here, because we wanted to focus on the resources most highly rated (and probably the most useful to users). And of course, ratings are inherently biased, and not gospel. Though we gathered as many viewpoints as possible, our survey process was far from scientific, so take it for what it is: unvarnished personal opinion. (And, if you disagree with any ratings, please let us know! See below for contact information.)

A word on how our book is organized: We've tried to lay out the chapters in the order you'll need them, progressing from pregnancy through postpartum, babyhood, and the preschool years. We discuss health care for mom and baby (Chapter 1); fitness and massage (Chapter 2); maternity clothes (Chapter 3); shopping for baby gear (Chapter 4); postpartum help (Chapter 5); play groups and parents' groups (Chapter 6); classes for babies and kids (Chapter 7); fun outings (Chapter 8); child care (Chapter 9); and preschools (Chapter 10). Resources under each topic are divided by locality into San Francisco, the North Bay, the East Bay, and the South Bay (including the Peninsula). Though we've tried to provide up-to-date, complete information about each resource, be sure to call ahead to verify hours, prices, and services, because things always change. Our focus is on the six counties of the Bay Area, but we also discuss some resources in Sonoma (North Bay), Napa (North Bay), and Santa Cruz (South Bay) counties. We had to draw the line somewhere, so we've limited the book to resources for babies through preschoolers, up to about age five. (Talk to us in five years about a guide for older children...)

More than just listing resources, we've endeavored to explain what to look for as a new parent, and how to find it. If we've done our job right, reading this book will be like having a best friend who's gone through everything and who tells it like it is, with no advertising hype or bias. Stick the book in your diaper bag as you explore all the Bay Area has to offer. Keep it by the telephone for those crisis moments when you don't know where to turn for help. Whether you're a new parent or an old hand, we hope this book will help you navigate the unknown, and sometimes surprising, territory of parenthood, while having fun along the way.

We've made every effort to be inclusive, but we may have missed something. Please let us know if you have a new resource, or an opinion on one listed here.

You can email us at jacksonstreetpress@yahoo.com. Look for our website, www.babiesbythebay.com, with updates on the book and more tips for Bay Area parents.

CHAPTER 1

IN THE BEGINNING . . .
Making Smart Pregnancy, Delivery, and Pediatric Health Care Choices

First things first. If you are thinking of having a baby, or if you are already pregnant, you will need to choose a prenatal care provider and a place to have your baby. You will also need to decide who will help you through labor, how you want to deliver your baby, and who will be your child's primary doctor. This chapter explores Bay Area resources for prenatal health care, delivery, and pediatric health care—from obstetricians, family practitioners, pediatricians, and midwives, to hospitals and birthing centers, doulas, prenatal education, and cord blood banking. Plus we will tell you what is customary in local care during pregnancy and childbirth, so you'll know what to expect. If you are having difficulty becoming pregnant, we will also suggest where to find a fertility specialist. If you are interested in surrogacy or adoption, turn to the section on local resources and legalities. We will also cover resources for babies with special needs. And finally, working parents-to-be will want to check out our discussion of pregnancy discrimination and maternity leave laws.

This chapter will answer the following questions and more:

- Where can I find a good obstetrician, family practitioner, pediatrician, or midwife?
- Are midwives licensed in California?
- What's the best hospital in my neighborhood?
- Can I deliver my baby at home?
- What is a doula, and where can I find one?
- How do I arrange for cord blood banking?
- Where can I take prenatal classes?
- Where can I go for fertility assistance?
- How do I find a surrogate or an adoption agency near me?
- Where can I find help for my baby with special needs?
- Now that I'm pregnant, what are my rights in my workplace in California?

Choosing Care Providers

Choosing people to care for you and your baby involves some of the most important decisions you will make. Below we explain the basic choices in prenatal and pediatric care, how to find a care provider, and which local doctors and midwives are parents' favorites according to our surveys.

PRENATAL CHOICES: OB/GYNS, FPS, AND LMS

In California, you have 3 basic choices in prenatal care and delivery: an obstetrician/gynecologist (OB/GYN), a family practitioner (FP), or a licensed midwife (CNM; LM).

Obstetricians are medical doctors who specialize in caring for women and delivering babies. They have completed medical school, residency, and board certification by the American Board of Obstetrics and Gynecology, and they deliver babies in hospitals. The advantages of choosing an obstetrician are obvious: they are specialists trained to deal with whatever contingency may arise, and they deliver babies all the time. Also, an obstetrician is the only one of the 3 types of practitioners who is trained as a surgeon, should you need a C-section or episiotomy. If you have a high-risk pregnancy (previous problematic pregnancies, medical problems, Rh or genetic problems, or are under

2

17 or over 35), you will want to see an obstetrician (and perhaps even a perinatologist—a sub-specialist in high-risk pregnancies).

Family practitioners provide general care for all members of the family. They are medical doctors, have specialty training and board certification in family practice, and practice in hospitals. If you would like one person to care for your entire family, are not high risk, but still want to see a doctor, a family practitioner may be for you.

California licenses 2 types of midwives: certified nurse-midwives (CNMs) and licensed direct entry midwives (LMs). Both are allowed to provide prenatal and postpartum care, to manage and support normal labor, and to deliver babies of normal spontaneous birth (just about everything short of a Caesarean section or vacuum extraction). Both encourage a natural birth process without the use of medical interventions, and they focus on educating the parents for childbirth. Both must arrange for a doctor as a backup in case of emergency, and they practice in hospitals, birthing centers, and homes. The difference is in their training.

Nurse-midwives are registered nurses who also have specialized training in caring for women and babies during the prenatal and immediate postpartum period. A CNM has completed nursing school, hospital training in labor and delivery, a graduate program in nurse-midwifery (from 9 months to 2 years), and a national examination (the American College of Nurse-Midwives certification board exam). Most CNMs practice in hospitals or doctors' offices, although they can establish independent birthing centers or their own practices. They can write limited prescriptions.

In 1993, California also began certifying licensed direct entry midwives. LMs are not RNs, but they have passed the Medical Board's licensing exam. To be eligible to take the exam, they must have either graduated from an approved 3-year midwifery education program, successfully challenged courses of an approved program by passing the exams of that program, or been licensed in another state with equivalent standards. LMs generally apprentice with experienced midwives (as opposed to CNMs, who train in hospitals).

Under the law, LMs must be "supervised" by a licensed OB-GYN. The supervising physician need not be physically present while the

3

LM is caring for the patient, but the LM must make arrangements for medical consultation and referral during the prenatal, delivery, and postpartum periods. Midwives must also tell patients the scope of what they can and cannot do legally, whether or not they carry malpractice insurance, and how to contact the Medical Board if patients have complaints.

If you are healthy, expect a normal, trouble-free pregnancy and delivery, and would like a more natural approach without medication, a midwife may be for you. Local moms report that midwives generally have more time than obstetricians during routine visits and are able to stay with patients during the entire labor and delivery process (and make a number of postpartum visits in many cases). On the other hand, if you expect complications, would like medication, or would like the extra security of a medical doctor, an obstetrician is the way to go.

WHAT KIND OF PEDIATRIC DOCTOR?

Several types of doctors treat children. Pediatricians are medical doctors specializing in children's health. They have completed a 3-year pediatric residency after medical school and passed a board examination making them board-certified in pediatrics. Family practitioners, described above, also care for children. Some parents prefer pediatricians because they specialize in taking care of children, while others prefer family practitioners because they can take care of the entire family. Family practitioners are more common in rural areas but not as popular in metropolitan regions like the Bay Area because of the prevalence of specialists. You may also occasionally see a doctor with the abbreviation "DO" rather than MD. This means "doctor of osteopathic medicine." An osteopathic physician, like an MD, is a licensed doctor. Both attended medical school and completed a residency. But osteopathic medical schools focus on training primary care physicians, osteopathic doctors emphasize a "whole person" approach to medicine rather than treating specific illnesses, and osteopaths are trained to pay special attention to the musculoskeletal system.

4

HOW TO CHOOSE A CARE PROVIDER

Ideally you have found your own care provider before you get pregnant. Start your search for a pediatric doctor well before your due date, in the beginning of your third trimester, to allow time for research and interviews.

Remember that whomever you choose—an OB, FP, midwife, or pediatrician—you will see this person a lot. Be sure you are comfortable with him or her. Changing care providers in the middle of a pregnancy or after your child becomes accustomed to him or her is not ideal. Get a sense of whether your care provider will take the time to answer your questions.

Your care provider's and your child's doctor's offices should be convenient to your home or work. Remember, you will be going to your care provider once a week toward the end of your pregnancy. Given the number of times babies and toddlers are sick, you'll regret choosing a pediatrician whose office is far away. Personally (and probably because we are always running late), we think location is critical. Free, convenient, and available parking is also a top priority. Those parking fees—and tickets, if you are like us—can add up. If you live in San Francisco, driving may be preferable to taking MUNI in the later stages of pregnancy. (We could tell you horror stories about perfectly healthy people refusing to give up disabled seats to women who looked like they were about to give birth right there on the bus.)

Make sure your insurance covers your provider's fees, or that you can afford them if not. Most California insurance plans provide generous coverage for prenatal visits, at no or low cost to the patient, to encourage healthy pregnancies. We know a mom who paid a grand total of $5 out of pocket to have her first baby. Her HMO picked up the rest of the tab—from initial visit through delivery. What a deal! Insurance companies—particularly HMOs—can be notoriously stingy when it comes to home births. If you plan to use a midwife for a home birth, check with your insurance plan to see whether these expenses are covered and who covers transport, physician, and hospital fees in the event of transfer to a hospital. Most insurance, including Medi-Cal, does cover CNM fees for hospital births.

As for pediatric coverage, unfortunately we've heard reports of parents having difficulty finding pediatricians who will accept new HMO patients, particularly in the East Bay. Fortunately, once you have found a physician accepting your insurance, it's likely that your insurance plan will cover well-baby visits at periodic intervals and immunizations. Check to make sure your insurance also covers emergency room visits (without a hefty co-pay), and preferably after-hours clinic care (better than an ER for many reasons, as we'll explain below). You should also make sure the plan includes the hospital to which your physician admits patients (preferably one that specializes in pediatrics), as well as the pediatric specialists to whom you may need referrals. Obviously you can't anticipate all the specialists you may need to see, but make sure the plan includes all the major types of specialties, such as pediatric anesthesiologists, pediatric surgeons, and pediatric ophthalmologists, to name a few. Also, make sure your plan offers good coverage while traveling, such as a nationwide network of physicians.

In searching for a pediatrician, consider whether his or her practice offers access to an after-hours pediatric clinic. As parents, we much prefer pediatric urgent care clinics (except, of course, in life-threatening emergencies, which a clinic is not equipped to handle). At a pediatric clinic, your child will be seen by a pediatrician rather than a generalist. The pediatrician will have the proper child-sized equipment. The clinic visit fees are generally much lower than for an ER visit. And you may actually be able to get an appointment rather than waiting hours in a crowded ER waiting room where your child may be exposed to all sorts of adult diseases. Plus, pediatric clinics are much less frightening places for kids than big ERs. Check with your pediatric doctor for local urgent care clinics. Many pediatricians are affiliated with certain clinics, in which case your insurance is billed for a normal office visit.

WHAT TYPE OF PRACTICE? SOLO VS. GROUPS

In choosing care providers, you also need to decide what type of practice you want to visit. Solo practitioners are reputed to provide more personalized attention to patients, but you may be stuck with a

Prenatal Testing, Newborn Screening, and Immunizations

If you have concerns about the effects of drugs, chemicals, infectious diseases, and other things that may be harmful to an unborn child (called "teratogens"), ask your care provider or contact:

Fetus Pregnancy Risk Information

University of California
San Diego Medical Center
800-532-3749 (hotline)

This is a statewide program operated by the UCSD Medical Center to collect, analyze, and disseminate information on known or potential teratogens. It provides confidential counseling and referrals for pregnant women exposed to harmful agents.

At 16 to 20 weeks of gestation, you may take the California Expanded Alpha Feto-Protein (AFP) test. This is a voluntary, state-administered blood test for spina bifida, Down's syndrome, and certain other birth defects. If results are positive, diagnostic tests will be performed (ultrasound and amniocentesis) and genetic counseling offered. For more information about the AFP test, contact:

California Department of Health Services —Genetic Disease Branch

510-412-1502
www.dhs.ca.gov

In California, newborns must by law undergo a state-administered Newborn Screening Test for certain diseases, including PKU, galactosemia, hypothryoidism, sickle cell disease, and other hemoglobin diseases. For more information, contact the Genetic Disease Branch listed above.

California has also implemented a Newborn Hearing Screening Program, offering hearing tests on newborns before they leave the hospital. For more information, contact:

California Newborn Hearing Screening Program

916-322-5794 or 877-388-5301
www.dhs.ca.gov

For immunization requirements for school and child care entry, see:

California Department of Health Services—Immunization Branch

510-540-2065
www.dhs.ca.gov

stranger—the on-call doctor or the ER—delivering your baby or caring for your child if your doctor is unavailable when you deliver or in an urgent care situation. In a group OB/GYN practice, you typically see each member of the group at different prenatal visits. This can be somewhat disjointed (and frustrating if you prefer one doctor), but at least you are guaranteed to have met the person delivering your baby.

The nature of pediatric care being what it is (unpredictable), many pediatricians practice in groups so patients can be assured of seeing *someone* in the group whenever the need for urgent care arises.

Questions to Ask a Potential Care Provider

Schedule an interview appointment with each candidate, by telephone if not in person. If a candidate objects to an interview, you don't want to see that person anyway. Here are some questions you might ask a candidate. In addition to their answers, also consider *how* they approach your questions. This can be a good indication of how they will respond to you as a patient or parent!

- What is your background, training, and experience?
- (If it is a group practice) How many doctors are in your practice, and how do you divide responsibilities? Who will I see at my regular visits? Who will deliver my baby? Under what circumstances would another member of the practice deliver my baby or see my child? Can I request appointments with you?
- Will nurse practitioners or physician assistants see me at my visits? (If important to you: Can I opt to see a doctor instead?)
- What are your opinions on: (choose any important to you)
  - ✧ Use of pain medication and anesthesia in delivery
  - ✧ Prenatal testing (first-trimester screen vs. chorionic villus sampling vs. "triple screen" vs. amniocentesis)
  - ✧ Episiotomies
  - ✧ Having support persons in the delivery room
  - ✧ Birth plans
  - ✧ Inducing labor
  - ✧ Circumcision (in California, this is usually performed by the obstetrician if done in a hospital)
  - ✧ Breastfeeding
  - ✧ Immunizations
  - ✧ Antibiotics
  - ✧ Child-rearing philosophies in general
- Whom do I call in an emergency? What is the procedure if I think I'm in labor?

◆ What are your after-hours policies? Is there an advice nurse available to answer questions 24/7?

◆ Are you available by telephone if I want to speak with you directly?

◆ Where do you have hospital or birthing center privileges?

◆ (For prenatal care providers) What experience do you have with high-risk pregnancies? How many babies have you delivered/do you deliver per year?

◆ (For midwives) Where and how long did you apprentice? With which doctors and hospitals are you affiliated, in case of complications? What conditions require transport? Do you have current CPR certification, and what medications and equipment do you have for emergencies?

◆ (For pediatric doctors) Will you come to the hospital or home to examine my baby after delivery? What tests do you do at that point? Do you offer same-day appointments for sick children? Do you have special provisions for sick children (e.g., a separate waiting room)?

In the end, your decision probably will come down to a gut feeling. You should not feel rushed or as if you are asking "stupid" questions. Having a baby is a very intimate, personal experience. You need to trust this person with your lives, and you should feel very comfortable with him or her.

How to Find a Care Provider

So now you are thinking: all those questions are great, but how do I actually find this person? We have found the most reliable sources are personal referrals—the good old word-of-mouth method. Start with friends, colleagues, and neighbors. Find out how they like their doctors or midwives. Check out our list of favorite doctors and midwives. Check with nurses, lactation consultants, and staff at your local hospital's perinatal or women's center. They regularly interact with doctors and midwives and their patients, and know which providers are good (and which are not!). Of course, once you have found a doctor or midwife for yourself, he or she will likely be able to recommend a pediatrician for your baby.

If you are not having any luck with the old-fashioned method, here are some good referral sources:

San Francisco Magazine (formerly San Francisco Focus)

PARENT RATING: ☆ ☆ ☆ ☆ ☆

This magazine annually publishes a list of the "best" Bay Area doctors, by type of practice. We have found that this list, while not always comprehensive because it focuses on specialists, includes many popular doctors.

Birthways

570 14th St.
Oakland
510-869-2797
www.birthways.org

PARENT RATING: ☆ ☆ ☆ ☆ ☆

This grassroots, nonprofit, volunteer-supported organization maintains referral lists of hospitals, doctors, midwives, and doulas (accessible in the center, by phone, or on the website).

Blossom Birth Services

1000 Elwell Ct.
Palo Alto
650-964-7380
www.blossombirth.com

This holistically oriented, nonprofit resource center maintains binders of providers such as midwives and doulas (and a few doctors). Information is also accessible via the website.

Natural Resources

816 Diamond St.
San Francisco
415-550-2611
www.naturalresourcesonline.com

PARENT RATING: ☆ ☆ ☆ ☆ ☆

A pregnancy, childbirth, and parenting center in the Noe Valley neighborhood, this store maintains binders of information about doctors, midwives, pediatricians, and doulas (some advertising, and some consumer feedback). Although the feedback on doctors is quite dated, there are many current opinions on local midwives. If you are planning a home birth in San Francisco, this is the place to start your research.

The Nurture Center

3399 Mt. Diablo Blvd.
Lafayette
925-283-1346 or 888-998-BABY
www.nurturecenter.com

PARENT RATING: ☆ ☆ ☆ ☆ ☆

This Contra Costa County parenting center run by 2 local moms features professional listings of obstetricians, midwives, and doulas.

UC Berkeley Parents Network

http://parents.berkeley.edu

PARENT RATING: ☆ ☆ ☆ ☆ ☆

This invaluable website is filled with parents' uncensored opinions about doctors, midwives, hospitals, insurance companies, and just about anything else related to parenting. Though the focus is the East Bay, parents occasionally mention resources in other parts of the Bay Area.

American Academy of Family Physicians

11400 Tomahawk Creek Pkwy.
Leawood, KS 66211-2672
913-906-6000
www.aafp.org

PARENT RATING: ☆ ☆ ☆ ☆ ☆

This national association of family doctors offers a searchable database of family practitioners' websites, as well as a very useful website for family health information.

American Academy of Pediatrics

141 Northwest Point Blvd.
Elk Grove Village, IL 60007-1098
847-434-4000
www.aap.org

PARENT RATING: ☆ ☆ ☆ ☆ ☆

This national association of pediatricians offers an online Pediatrician Referral Service to member pediatricians and specialists. Their website features very useful articles on pediatric health.

American College of Obstetricians and Gynecologists

409 12th St., S.W.
Washington, DC 20090-6920
202-638-5577
www.acog.com

PARENT RATING: ☆ ☆ ☆ ☆

This website provides a physician directory and health information.

Best Doctors

www.bestdoctors.com

PARENT RATING: ☆ ☆ ☆

This private organization polls doctors to come up with a list of its "best doctors" nationwide. You can get a customized list for a fee. Peer review is subjective, but a useful starting point.

Health Grades

www.healthgrades.com

PARENT RATING: ☆ ☆ ☆

This is an online national database of physicians and hospitals. You can search by geographic area, specialty, or name, and for a fee get basic information about a doctor's education and training, licensure, board certification, and disciplinary actions. (Note: you can also get this information for free from the Medical Board of California and the American Board of Medical Specialties, see below.) For some (not all) doctors, you can also view the results of patient satisfaction surveys.

Pacific Business Group on Health

www.healthscope.org

PARENT RATING: ☆ ☆ ☆ ☆

This business group provides a searchable directory of physicians, as well as ratings of health plans, medical groups, and hospitals (based on objective criteria such as mortality rates).

Your insurance plan's referral service

PARENT RATING: ☆ ☆ ☆

Most insurance plans, particularly HMOs and PPOs, have telephone or online referral services. The insurers won't provide subjective information, but they will let you search by objective criteria like neighborhood, specialty, and school attended.

MIDWIVES

For *midwives,* the search may be a bit more difficult. In addition to the foregoing, try the following organizations for referral lists, but bear in mind that inclusion on these lists is largely voluntary and does not reflect any kind of selection process.

California Association of Midwives

P.O. Box 460606
San Francisco, CA 94146
800-829-5791
www.californiamidwives.org

This is a professional organization of California midwives. The website can give you a list of midwives practicing in your area.

California Nurse-Midwives Association

www.cnma.net

The website for this professional organization of California CNMs provides a searchable database of members.

Midwives' Alliance of North America (MANA)

375 Rockbridge Rd., Ste. 172-313
Lilburn, GA 30047
888-923-6262
www.mana.org

PARENT RATING: ☆ ☆ ☆ ☆ ☆

This is a national midwives' organization; call or e-mail (membership@mana.org) for referrals to midwives by state. The useful website is a good place to start your research about midwifery.

Bay Area Birth Information

www.bayareabirthinfo.org

Bay Area Birth Information provides a referral list of South Bay midwives who agree with this nonprofit organization's mission statement to encourage spontaneous birth and reduce medical interventions.

Birth Network of Santa Cruz County

www.birthnet.org

This group favors natural birth and provides a resource directory with a referral list of midwives practicing in the Santa Cruz area.

www.birthwithlove.com

Run by midwives, this is an online directory of midwives and doulas, searchable by zip code.

www.gentlebirth.org

This local midwife's site lists South Bay midwives and other home birth resources and includes anecdotal reviews of South Bay hospitals' attitudes toward midwives and natural childbirth.

CHECKING CREDENTIALS

Once you have several candidates, narrow them down by checking their credentials with the appropriate licensing agencies. Be sure to find out whether the provider is licensed, board certified (in the case of OB/GYNs, pediatricians, family practitioners, and other specialists), and has no history of malpractice claims. Popularity alone provides no assurance of competence.

Medical Board of California

1426 Howe Ave., #54
Sacramento, CA 95825
916-263-2382 (for doctors)
916-263-2393 (for LMs, the Midwifery Licensing Program)
www.medbd.ca.gov

PARENT RATING: ☆ ☆ ☆ ☆

This board can tell you: whether a doctor or LM is licensed, what school he or she attended and the year he or she graduated, whether there are any disciplinary charges pending or any completed disciplinary actions against him or her (if charges have been filed by the Board), and whether any malpractice judgments or felony criminal actions have been reported to the Board. Get a free pamphlet, *Information and Services to Consumers from the Medical Board of California,* on how to choose a doctor or check credentials.

American Board of Medical Specialties (ABMS)
1007 Church St., Ste. 404
Evanston, IL 60201-5913
866-ASK-ABMS (phone verification)
847-491-9091
www.abms.org
PARENT RATING: ☆ ☆ ☆ ☆ ☆

This organization can tell you whether an OB-GYN or other specialist is board certified (the California Medical Board does *not* have this information).

The Official ABMS Directory of Board-Certified Medical Specialists
This directory, updated annually by ABMS, is available in most public libraries.

California Board of Registered Nursing
400 R St., Ste. 4030
Sacramento, CA 95814
916-322-3350
800-838-6828 (phone verification)
www.rn.ca.gov
This board licenses CNMs in California; you can check a CNM's licensure status online.

American College of Nurse-Midwives (ACNM)
8403 Colesville Rd., Ste. 1550
Silver Spring, MD 20910
240-485-1800
www.midwife.org
This group administers board examinations for CNMs and maintains a database of CNMs searchable by zip code.

North American Registry of Midwives (NARM)
5257 Rosestone Dr.
Lilburn, GA 30047
888-842-4784
www.narm.org
This offshoot of MANA (see above) administers an international competency certification program and grants the title Certified Professional Midwife (CPM). However, note that the CPM title does not grant legal status to practice in California; a midwife must still pass the California board exam.

Doctors and Midwives: Survey Favorites

We hesitate to name favorite doctors, practice groups, or midwives. The criteria are often highly subjective, personal reactions can vary widely, and we don't want to create a land rush to certain providers. That said, our survey revealed some consistent favorites, and we thought we should share that information with you. Of course, the fact that a particular person is not on this list does not mean he or she is not a great care provider. As we have said, our survey was far from scientific! See the Introduction for an explanation. And remember, always check credentials with the Medical Board (see above) before selecting a doctor or midwife.

And the top picks from our survey are ...

OBSTETRICIANS

For ease of reference, we have noted the hospitals at which each doctor has privileges.

San Francisco

Maryam Arjomand, Laurie Green, Frederica Lofquist, and Elizabeth Moy, MDs
3838 California St.
415-379-9600
www.pacwomens.com
California Pacific Medical Center

Amy (Meg) Autry and Elena Gates, MDs
UCSF Women's Health Center
2330 Post St., Ste. 220
415-885-7788

Karen Callen, Jane Fang, Katherine (Linieki) Gregory, Fung Lam, and Donna Wiggins, MDs
3838 California St., Ste. 812
415-666-1250
CPMC

Margaret Chen, Cynthia Farner, Bernard Gore, Jordan Horowitz, and Joanne Kim, MDs
• 3625 California St.
• 525 Spruce St.
415-668-1010
CPMC

Kathryn Clark and Holly Holter, MDs
• 3838 California St., 415-668-1560
• 909 Hyde St., 415-673-6522
CPMC

Dorothy Dube, MD
2100 Webster St., Ste. 427
415-923-3128
CPMC

Mary Norton, MD
Director, UCSF Prenatal Diagnosis Center
350 Parnassus, Ste. 810
415-476-4080
Prenatal testing and diagnosis.

Julian Parer, MD, PhD
UCSF Women's Health, Obstetrics
and Perinatology
400 Parnassus, Plaza Level
415-353-2566
Perinatology (high-risk) services.

Perinatal Services
Michael Katz and Elliott Main, MDs
3700 California St., 5th Fl.
415-600-6388
CPMC
Perinatology services.

Prenatal Diagnosis Center
James (Jim) Goldberg, Denise Main, Thomas Musci, and Carl Otto, MDs
3700 California St., #G330
415-600-6400
CPMC, Marin General Hospital,
Peninsula Medical Center
Prenatal testing and diagnosis. Also
offices in Greenbrae, San Mateo, and
Santa Rosa.

Pearl Yee, MD
• 3838 California St., Ste. 412,
  415-379-6800
• 1199 Bush St., Ste. 290, 415-563-9000
CPMC

North Bay

Stephen Bearg, Nona Cunningham, and Sylvia Flores, MDs
1260 S. Eliseo Dr.
Greenbrae
415-461-7800
Marin General Hospital

Brian DeMuth, MD
1000 S. Eliseo Dr., Ste. 101
Greenbrae
415-464-0184
Marin General

David Galland, MD
5 Bon Air Rd., Ste. 117
Larkspur
415-924-4870
Marin General

LizEllen LaFollette, MD
599 Sir Francis Drake Blvd., Ste. 308
Greenbrae
415-461-1949
Marin General

Richard Printz, MD
599 Sir Francis Drake Blvd., Ste. 202
Greenbrae
415-461-8636
Marin General

Gerald Wilner, MD
5 Bon Air Rd., Ste. 117
Larkspur
415-924-9770
Marin General

East Bay

Arzou Ahsan, Eleanore Kim, Elizabeth Kanwit, and Katarina Lanner-Cusin, MDs
2915 Telegraph Ave., Ste. 200
Berkeley
510-845-8047
Alta Bates Summit Medical Center

F. Ryan Anderson, MD
909 San Ramon Valley Blvd., Ste. 214
Danville
925-820-9898
John Muir Medical Center

Robert Cole, MD
110 Tampico, Ste. 210
Walnut Creek
925-935-6952
John Muir

Kimberley Fillmore, MD
- Concord
  2299 Bacon St., Ste. 1
- Walnut Creek
  120 La Casa Via, Ste. 202
925-676-3450
John Muir

Yaron Friedman and Louis Klein, MDs
- Danville
  780 San Ramon Valley Blvd.,
  Ste. 100, 925-820-6500
- Walnut Creek
  112 La Casa Via, Ste. 130
  925-937-0995
John Muir

Jill Foley, John Girard, and Marilyn Honegger, MDs
- Berkeley
  2999 Regent Street, Ste. 701
  510-845-4200
- Orinda
  12 Camino Encinas, Ste. 15
  925-254-9000
Alta Bates

Nadine Hanna, Sandy Hughes, and Gerald Walker, MDs
2021 Ygnacio Valley Rd., Ste. C103
Walnut Creek
925-937-4747
www.muirob.com
John Muir

Judith Hartman, Janine Senior, and Janette Walker, MDs
2121 Ygnacio Valley Rd., Ste. E101
Walnut Creek
925-945-6600
John Muir

Amy Huibonhoa, MD
2999 Regent St., Ste. 201
510-204-0965
Alta Bates

Craig Eastman Johnson, MD
2299 Mowry Ave., Ste. 2
Fremont
510-796-3498
Washington Hospital

Debra Levinsky, MD
895 Moraga Rd., Ste. 11
Lafayette
925-283-5800
Alta Bates

Paula Melone, MD
106 La Casa Via, Ste. 260
Walnut Creek
925-937-5213
John Muir
Perinatology (high-risk) services.

Jim Hisao Nishimine, MD
2507 Ashby Ave.
Berkeley
510-644-3000
Alta Bates

Palo Alto Medical Foundation
3200 Kearney St.
Fremont
510-490-1222
www.pamf.org
Washington Hospital

Richard Rudd, MD
2999 Regent Street, Ste. 301
Berkeley
510-843-7722
Alta Bates

James Sakamoto, MD
Kaiser Permanente Medical Group
3779 Piedmont Ave.
Oakland
510-752-1080
Kaiser Permanente Oakland
Medical Center

Hank Streitfeld, MD
3000 Colby St., Ste. 303
Berkeley
510-644-0110
Alta Bates

Stephen Wells, MD
110 Tampico, Ste. 220
Walnut Creek
925-935-5356
John Muir

Kurt Wharton, MD
970 Dewing Ave., Ste. 201
Lafayette
925-962-0002
Alta Bates

South Bay

Camino Medical Group
• Sunnyvale
301 Old San Francisco Rd.
408-730-4240
• Mountain View
515 South Dr.
650-934-7956
www.caminomedical.org
El Camino Hospital

**C. Andrew Combs and
Alan Fishman, MDs**
Obstetrix Medical Group
900 E. Hamilton Ave., Ste. 200
Campbell
408-371-7111
www.obstetrix.com
Good Samaritan Hospital
Perinatology (high-risk) services.

Maurice Druzin, MD
Chief of Obstetrics and Gynecology
Lucile Packard Children's Hospital
at Stanford, Obstetrics Clinic
770 Welch Rd., Ste. 201
Palo Alto
650-725-8623 or 650-498-4069
Perinatology (high-risk) services.

Nancy Mason, MD
1101 Welch Rd.
Palo Alto
650-329-1293
Stanford Medical Center

Kathryn Matthews, MD
1101 Welch Rd.
Palo Alto
650-328-5141
Stanford

Menlo Medical Clinic
1300 Crane St.
Menlo Park
650-498-6500
www.menloclinic.com
Stanford

**Los Olivos Women's
Medical Group**
15151 National Ave.
Los Gatos
408-356-0431
www.losolivos-obgyn.com
Good Samaritan

17

Palo Alto Medical Foundation, Palo Alto Clinic

795 El Camino Real
Palo Alto
650-321-4121
www.pamf.org
Stanford
This clinic also has offices in Fremont and Los Altos.

Peninsula Women's Health and Medical Group

1828 El Camino Real, Ste. 805
Burlingame
650-692-3818
www.peninsulawomenshealth.com
Peninsula Medical Center
This group also has offices in San Mateo and Half Moon Bay.

Portola Valley Women's Health Center

(affiliated with Palo Alto Medical Foundation)
3250 Alpine Rd.
Portola Valley
650-851-6650
www.pamf.org
Stanford

Jagdip Powar, MD

1101 Welch Rd., Ste. A-7
Palo Alto
650-328-1420
Stanford

Claire Serrato, MD

50 S. San Mateo Dr., Ste. 420
San Mateo
650-344-1114
Peninsula Medical Center

MIDWIVES

Where it is not obvious, we have noted whether the midwife delivers babies at home, in a birth center, or in a hospital.

San Francisco

Bay Area Home Birth Collective

415-273-5185
www.bayareahomebirth.org
Group of midwives, doulas, and childbirth educators

John Fassett, CNP

• 3625 California St.
• 525 Spruce St.
415-668-1010
Practices with a group of OB/GYNs; hospital birth

Maria Iorillo, LM, CPM

816 Diamond St.
415-285-9233
www.wisewomanchildbirth.com
Home birth or hospital labor support

Nancy Myrick, CNM

Rites of Passage
415-454-5804
www.ihomebirth.com

Angelika Nugent, LM, CPM

1447 34th Ave.
415-242-0517
Home birth

Judith Tinkelenberg, CNM

154 A Capp St.
San Francisco
415-552-6600
www.sagefemme.net
Birth center

UCSF Faculty OB/GYN Group
400 Parnassus St.
415-353-2566
Hospital practice includes CNMs.

North Bay

Circle of Life Midwifery Center
145 Bolinas Rd.
Fairfax
415-456-2961
www.circleoflifemidwifery.org
Three midwives offer home birth and tub rentals.

East Bay

Bay Area Home Birth Collective
See listing above under San Francisco.

Hsiu-Li (Sho-Li) Cheng, CNM
East Bay Perinatal Medical Associates
3232 Elm St., Ste. B
510-832-2388
Alta Bates Summit Medical Center

Beah Haber, CNM
4460 Black Ave.
Pleasanton
925-449-7666
Home birth or birth center

Lindy Johnson, CNM
2107 Dwight Way, Ste. 102
Berkeley
510-644-0104
Alta Bates

Jeri Zukoski, CNM
2107 Dwight Way, Ste. 102
Berkeley
510-530-3374
Alta Bates

South Bay

Cedar OB/GYN
455 O'Connor Dr., Ste. 300
San Jose
408-287-4441
www.cedarobgyn.com
Group of 2 OBs and 4 CNMs practice at O'Connor and Good Samaritan hospitals.

Mary Newberry, CNM
1828 El Camino Real, Ste. 805
Burlingame
650-692-3818
Peninsula Medical Center

Kathryn Newburn, CNM
1301 Sanchez Ave.
Burlingame
650-347-6943
www.homebirthcnm.com
Home birth

PEDIATRICIANS

Our survey could not possibly include every wonderful pediatrician in the Bay Area, so we advise not limiting your search to those listed here!

San Francisco

Jane Anderson, Marta Kosinski, and William DeGoff, MDs
UCSF/Mt.Zion Pediatric Primary Practice
2330 Post St., Ste. 320
415-885-7478

Eileen Aicardi, Martin Ernster, William Gonda, Michelle Pepitone, Mary Piel, Laurie Schultz, and Lisa Dana, MDs
- San Francisco
  3641 California St., 415-668-0888
- Mill Valley
  61 Camino Alto, 415-388-6303

Brock Bernsten, Gianna Frazee, Steven Rosenbaum, Robert Saffa, and Carolyn Wright, MDs
Town and Country Pediatrics
- San Francisco
  3838 California St., Ste. 111
  415-666-1860
- Mill Valley
  61 Camino Alto, Ste. 105
  415-383-0918

Yan Chin, MD
San Francisco On Call Medical Professionals
490 Post St., Ste. 710
415-732-7029
Makes house calls! www.SFoncall.com.

Katherine Crosby, Susan Dab, Gary Gin, Alan Johnson, and Margaret Miller, MDs
Spruce Street Pediatrics
- San Francisco
  525 Spruce St.
  415-668-8900
- Tiburon
  21 Main St.
  415-435-3154

Nayana Anne and James Schwanke, MDs
Noe Valley Pediatrics
3700 24th St.
415-641-1019

Yasuko Fukuda, MD
3905 Sacramento St., Ste. 301
415-752-8038

Martin Fung, Colleen Halloran, Mitchell Sollod, and Nanci Tucker, MDs
Stonestown Medical Building
595 Buckingham Way, Ste. 355
415-566-2727

Sonja Huie and Diana Tang, MDs
3905 Sacramento St., Ste. 100
415-379-6700

Daniel Kelly, MD, Barry Rostek, DO, and William Solomon, MD
45 Castro St., Ste. 232
415-565-6810
UCSF Pediatric Primary Care Clinic

Martha Taylor, Carol Miller, Robert Pantell, and Alan Uba, MDs
400 Parnassus St.
415-353-2000

North Bay

See above for San Francisco practices with Marin offices.

Melissa Congdon, Richard Dow, and Michael Harris, MDs
1206 Strawberry Village
Mill Valley
415-388-3364

John Harvey, Erin Heath, Jan Maisel, and Stewart Rowe, MDs
- Greenbrae
  599 Sir Francis Drake Blvd.
  415-461-0440
- Novato
  1615 Hill Rd., Ste. 11, 415-892-0965

Martin Joffee, Kathryn Sexton, and Katrina Urbach, MDs
- Greenbrae
  1000 S. Eliseo Dr., Ste. 1-A
  415-461-5436
- Novato
  505A San Marin Dr., Ste. 260
  415-898-5437

Kara Ornstein and Scott Werner, MDs
1100 S. Eliseo Dr., Ste. 106
Greenbrae
415-461-8828

Pediatric Alternatives Stacia Lansman and Lindy Woodard, MDs
10 Thomas Dr.
Mill Valley
415-380-8448
Traditional and homeopathic medicine.

East Bay

Myles Bruce Abbott, Dorit Bar-Din, Marcia Charles-Mo, Mary Jones, and Richard Oken, MDs
East Bay Pediatrics
- Berkeley
  2999 Regent St., Ste. 325
- Orinda
  96 Davis Rd., Ste. 2
925-438-1100

Ralph Berberich, Jane Hunter, Steve Kowaleski, and Petra Landman, MDs
Pediatric Medical Group
2320 Woolsey St., Ste. 301
Berkeley
510-849-1744

Philip Chamberlain, Kimberly Mar, and Lloyd Takao, MDs
4 Country Club Plaza
Orinda
925-254-9500

James Cuthbertson, Elaine Davenport, Annemary Franks, and Olivia Lang, MDs
Berkeley Pediatrics
1650 Walnut St.
Berkeley
510-848-2566

Bruce Gach, MD
- Livermore
  1131 East Stanley Blvd., Ste. 103
  925-455-5050
- Pleasanton
  5575 W. Las Positas, Ste. 340
  925-847-9777

Juliet Patricia Granberg, MD
2915 Telegraph Ave.
Berkeley
510-843-4077

Colleen Hogan and Tracy Trotter, MDs
San Ramon Valley Primary Care
Medical Group
200 Porter Dr., Ste. 300
San Ramon
925-838-6511

William Jenkins, MD
Richmond Pediatric Medical Group
3619 Cutting Blvd.
Richmond
510-529-1271

David Kittams, Robin Winokur, and Elizabeth Salzburg, MDs
Kiwi Pediatrics
1744 Alcatraz Ave.
Berkeley
510-652-1720

Montgomery Kong, MD
Walnut Creek Pediatrics
1822 San Miguel Dr.
Walnut Creek
925-945-3580

Andrew Nash, Margaret Saltzstein, and Lynne Whyte, MDs
Muir Primary Care
• Alamo
  1505 St. Alphonsus Way
• San Ramon
  5201 N. Canyon Rd., 925-837-4225

Palo Alto Medical Foundation (Fremont office)
Tina Scobel, MD
3200 Kearney St.
Fremont
510-490-1222
www.pamf.org

Daniel Robbins, MD
Lamorinda Pediatrics
930 Dewing Ave.
Lafayette
925-284-1800
www.lamorindapeds.com

South Bay

Bay Area Pediatric Medical Group
• Belmont
  2100 Carlmont Dr., 650-591-3937
• Daly City
  1800 Sullivan Ave., 650-756-4200
• Daly City
  1500 Southgate Ave., 650-992-4200
• San Mateo
  29 Baywood Ave., 650-343-4200
www.bayareapediatrics.com

Raquel Burgos, MD, MPH
The Village Doctor
2979 Woodside Rd.
Woodside
650-851-4747
www.thevillagedoctor.com

Camino Medical Group
301 Old San Francisco Rd.
Sunnyvale
408-730-4251
www.caminomedical.org
Other offices are in Sunnyvale,
Santa Clara, and Cupertino.

Donna Chaet and Penny Loeb, MDs
Altos Pediatrics
842 Altos Oaks Dr.
Los Altos
650-940-7177

Alger Chapman, MD
ABC Pediatrics
50 S. San Mateo Dr., Ste. 260
San Mateo
650-579-6500

Brian Drucker, MD
2577 Samaritan Dr.
San Jose
408-354-7910

22

**Remington Fong, Kim Harvey,
Annette Hwang, Judith Murphy,
and Jelena Vukicevic, MDs**
Welch Road Pediatrics
1101 Welch Rd., Ste. A-1
Palo Alto
650-329-0300

Christine Halaburka, MD
2505 Samaritan Dr., Ste. 607
San Jose
408-356-9900

**Albert Kasuga and Jeffrey Tan,
MDs**
Peninsula Pediatric Medical Group
1720 El Camino Real, Ste. 205
Burlingame
650-259-5050
They also have an office in
San Mateo.

Fernando Mendoza, MD
Lucile Packard Children's Hospital
at Stanford, Primary Care Clinic
730 Welch Rd., 1st Fl.
Palo Alto
650-497-8820

**Menlo Medical Clinic
Nancy Adelman and James Cisco,
MDs**
1300 Crane St.
Menlo Park
650-498-6500
www.menloclinic.com

Palo Alto Medical Foundation
795 El Camino Real
Palo Alto
650-853-2992
www.pamf.org
Other offices are in Fremont, Los
Altos, and Redwood Shores.

David Trager, MD
RAMBLC Pediatric Medical Group
2420 Samaritan Dr.
San Jose
408-371-7777
www.ramblc.com

Pediatric Dentists

Sooner or later, you will have to make that much-feared first dental appointment. The American Academy of Pediatrics recommends that children get regular dental checkups after age 3 or when all 20 baby teeth have come in. If possible, see a pediatric dentist, who has an additional 2 to 3 years of training in treating children. You can find a referral to a pediatric dentist either through the American Dental Association (www.ada.org) or the American Academy of Pediatric Dentistry (www.aapd.org), both of which have useful websites with lots of publications and searchable databases of pediatric dentists.

Health Care Coverage When You Cannot Afford It

Pregnant and uninsured? The State of California administers several programs for families having difficulty getting health insurance. For general information, call the California Baby Cal hotline (800-BABY-999) or visit www.dhs.ca.gov/babycal.

Access for Infants and Mothers (AIM)

P.O. Box 15559
Sacramento, CA 95852-0559
800-433-2611
www.aim.ca.gov

This program provides low-cost health insurance coverage to low- to moderate-income pregnant women (who do not qualify for Medi-Cal). It covers mothers during pregnancy, childbirth, and 60 days postpartum. After a low-cost contribution, you receive health care coverage from one of the participating health plans. It is administered by the California Managed Risk Medical Insurance Board.

Healthy Families Program (HFP)

888-747-1222
www.healthyfamilies.ca.gov

This program provides low-cost health, dental, and vision coverage for children (birth to age 19) in low-wage families who do not qualify for Medi-Cal. There is a choice of several insurance plans.

Major Risk Medical Insurance Program (MRMIP)

800-289-6574
www.mrmib.ca.gov

By contracting with 4 insurance plans, this program provides health insurance to those who are unable to obtain coverage in the individual health insurance market. Participants contribute to the premiums.

Medi-Cal

888-747-1222
www.medi-cal.ca.gov

California's version of the U.S. Government's Medicaid program, eligibility depends on income and family size. Medical, dental, and vision care are provided at no cost. Visit or call your local county's department of health, human, or social services.

Child Health and Disability Prevention Program (CHDP)

California Department
of Health Services
916-327-1400
www.dhs.ca.gov

This program provides regular check-ups, immunizations, and specialist referrals to children in families meeting certain financial eligibility guidelines. Every California local health department has a CHDP program. For more information, contact your county health department or the California Department of Health Services.

County hospitals and health services also run low-cost clinics. Check with your local county.

Problems with Managed Care Health Insurance?

Is your HMO giving you a hard time? California has an innovative program to help patients deal with managed health care. The state created the Department of Managed Health Care (DMHC) in January 2000 to "ensure high quality prevention and health care for Californians enrolled in managed care plans." The DMHC is charged with licensing managed health care plans, enforcing quality of care laws, educating the public on health care rights, providing an annual report card on quality of care under managed care, and implementing a third-party review system for patient grievances and coverage disputes. Contact:

Department of Managed Care
California HMO Help Center
888-HMO-2219 (consumer HMO complaints)
www.hmohelp.ca.gov

Choosing Where You Will Deliver

From hospitals to birthing centers to home birth, the Bay Area offers many delivery options.

HOSPITALS

Over 40 hospitals in the Bay Area deliver babies. But don't be overwhelmed. Use the following list to find a nearby hospital offering the services you want. Within the list you'll find hospitals that received consistent high praise from the Bay Area parents we surveyed, designated with parent comments. If you're deciding between a few hospitals, be *sure* to take a tour to see for yourself and ask questions, and check the following key attributes:

Location. You don't want to be stuck on a bridge or in a tunnel delivering your baby. On the other hand, many suburbanites bypass more convenient hospitals to travel to San Francisco's California Pacific Medical Center (CPMC) because of the highly touted doctors and the Level III nursery.

Level of neonatal intensive care. Hospital nurseries are classified as either Level I, II, or III (according to the American Academy of Pediatrics and the American College of Obstetrics and Gynecology). A Level I nursery is for healthy newborns. A Level II nursery is an intermediate care or "special care" nursery for premature or ill infants. A Level III neonatal intensive care unit (NICU) admits more serious cases (from other hospitals as well) who can't be cared for in the other 2 types of nurseries. In any facility, look for 24/7 coverage by perinatologists (OBs with specialized training in high-risk pregnancies and deliveries) and neonatologists (pediatricians specializing in caring for sick newborns).

Who practices there? No surprise—highly rated doctors seem to congregate at certain highly rated (generally private or university-run) hospitals. Compare our list of doctors to the list of hospitals. (That does not mean there are not some great doctors at other hospitals.) In addition, consider the nursing staff's reputation. Good labor and delivery nurses are critical to your experience since you will likely spend more time with them than with your doctor.

Private postpartum rooms. This may seem like a petty concern. But think about spending the most intimate, physically uncomfortable 48 hours of your life with a total stranger and her family (not to mention 2 screaming newborns) and then take our advice: if you can afford it, get a private room! Sometimes this means paying extra if your insurance does not cover it. You are not going to get much sleep at home during the first few weeks postpartum, so try to get as much as possible at the hospital.

Accreditation, ratings, and awards. The Joint Commission on Accreditation of Healthcare Organizations (JCAHO) evaluates and accredits U.S. hospitals and other health care organizations. A JCAHO accreditation means that the hospital meets certain performance standards. All of the hospitals listed below were accredited as of 2005. The JCAHO's website also allows you to check quality against other accredited organizations using objective criteria such as mortality rates. Also, an independent organization, HCIA-Sachs, annually publishes a list of what it views as the "100 Top Hospitals" nationally. See www.100tophospitals.com. We've noted the Bay Area hospitals making the grade in recent years. However, making this list depends on the entire hospital, not just the labor and delivery department. You can also check hospital ratings by an employer organization (www.healthscope .org) and a consumer organization (www.checkbook.org).

Other amenities. A Jacuzzi tub in the labor and delivery room sounds nice, but like us, you may be too busy during labor to remember it's even there. More important to your husband or partner may be a cot for him or her to spend the night. Most hospitals allow a husband or partner to spend the night in a private room, but not in a semiprivate one. Note that some hospitals do not allow children, even siblings. Also, hospitals are generally flexible about having support people in the delivery room, but if you absolutely must have your entire extended family in the delivery room filming the event, you may want to check the hospital's policy.

The following list provides facts and figures about each hospital, largely supplied by the hospitals themselves. In addition to the key attributes identified above, the list also includes the following information:

Type of hospital: This includes each hospital's size, ownership (private or public), and any affiliation with large health care systems, HMOs, or universities. Bear in mind that teaching hospitals are just that; although they are known for top-notch research, you may work with interns and residents (though supervised).

Number of births annually: All figures are from 2004, unless noted.

Caesarean section rate: A higher rate of Caesarean or "C"-sections does not necessarily indicate poor care. Indeed, many of the best hospitals have higher C-section rates simply because they attract more high-risk patients. If you are looking for a less medically managed orientation, however, be sure to ask about attitudes toward C-sections and VBACs (vaginal birth after Caesareans). Your care provider is the place to start this discussion.

Rooms: An LDR (labor, delivery, and recovery) room is the modern maternity ward standard. It means you will labor, deliver, and spend your initial recovery in the same room. This is very convenient, considering you won't be able to walk if you have an epidural. (Some hospitals have separate ORs or C-section suites for C-section deliveries.)

In an LDRP (LDR plus postpartum) room, you'll also spend the rest of your visit in the same room. This is even more convenient, but most hospitals don't have LDRPs. To facilitate early breastfeeding and mother-baby bonding, most hospitals today allow (and encourage) healthy moms to keep their healthy babies in their rooms ("rooming-in"), rather than whisking them away to the nursery. You may want to take advantage of the nursery to get some shut-eye, however! Since every hospital responding to our survey encouraged rooming-in, we did not include it as a separate item in our list.

Are midwives on staff? What percentage of deliveries do midwives perform? If having a midwife deliver your baby is important to you, find a hospital that has midwives on staff or allows them privileges. Some hospitals have lots of experienced midwives; others don't allow them at all.

Breastfeeding rate: Many hospitals do not keep figures on the number of women breastfeeding (or intending to breastfeed, if their milk has not come in) upon discharge from the hospital. We've given you the hospital-supplied estimates, if no hard figures were available.

Perinatal classes: Most hospitals offer classes for expectant and new parents ("perinatal classes"). We recommend you take a newborn care class, a breastfeeding class, a childbirth preparation class, and an infant CPR class, at the minimum. See additional resources for perinatal classes after the hospital list.

San Francisco Hospitals

California Pacific Medical Center (CPMC)

3700 California St.
415-600-6000
415-600-BABY (Newborn Connections, 3698 California St.)
www.cpmc.org

Type: Large, private, nonprofit medical center and Sutter Health affiliate. Level III nursery.

Births and C-section rate: 6,188; 26% (including repeats); 18% (primary)

Rooms: 19 LDR rooms; 50 (of 54) postpartum rooms are private.

Midwives on staff: Yes. Midwives attend fewer than 10% of deliveries.

Breastfeeding: 94%

Perinatal classes: Pregnancy support group, prenatal fitness, pre-term labor, childbirth preparation, mindfulness-based pain reduction, multiples, newborn parenting, breastfeeding, breastfeeding multiples, father preparation, sibling preparation, choosing child care, infant CPR, new family forum, and many support groups.

Amenities: CPMC has perinatologists and neonatologists on staff and features a prenatal diagnosis and genetic counseling program and an antenatal testing center. Breastfeeding assistance with certified lactation consultants is offered through Newborn Connections. Expectant mothers can define and share their birth plan prior to labor and delivery. There is 24/7 coverage by OB-GYNs, pediatricians, and anesthesiologists. Families receive a celebration dinner after their child's birth and can select from a room service menu. Moms can shop from their beds via the in-room shopping cart.

PARENT RATING: ☆ ☆ ☆ ☆ ☆

CPMC is regarded as the leading private hospital in San Francisco, and parents gave CPMC universally excellent reviews for doctors and advanced care. The labor and delivery nurses were praised as "professional," "knowledgeable" and "top notch." "Great NICU care . . . clean facility, organized operation, and loving nurses." Parents also love the Newborn Connections center with its myriad classes, support groups, and lactation consultants, and called it "a great value." In postpartum care, the nurses received reviews ranging from "I felt well taken care of," "fabulous," and "orderly," to "hit or miss." Some recent patients noted an increase in the level of responsiveness from postpartum nurses since several years ago, and say the hospital has recovered its customer focus.

St. Luke's Hospital

3555 Cesar Chavez St.
415-647-8600
415-626-BABY (maternity services, education, and tours)
www.stlukes-sf.org

Type: Private, nonprofit hospital and Sutter Health affiliate. Level II nursery.

Births and C-section rate: 1,053; 13.5%

Rooms: 3 LDR rooms; 3 labor rooms; 2 ORs; 1 recovery room; 6 (of 28) postpartum rooms are private.

Midwives on staff: Yes. Midwives attend 35% of deliveries.

Breastfeeding: 85%

Perinatal classes: Pregnancy, childbirth preparation, breastfeeding, infant CPR, and free prenatal and mom-baby yoga classes. Classes and materials are also available in Spanish.

Amenities: St. Luke's serves all of San Francisco, but primarily residents from southern San Francisco and northern San Mateo counties. Midwifery care is available 24/7, as is neonatologist and pediatric coverage. The hospital provides access to trained doulas and breastfeeding support services. Staff is multilingual.

San Francisco General Hospital

1001 Potrero Ave.
415-206-8000
415-206-5302 (Women's Health Center)
www.dph.sf.ca.us/chn/SFGH

Type: Large public hospital run by the City and County of San Francisco. Level III nursery.

Births and C-section rate: 1,211; 20%

Rooms: 7 labor and delivery rooms.

Midwives on staff: Yes. Midwives attend 33% of deliveries.

Breastfeeding: 76%

Perinatal classes: Classes are open only to Department of Public Health patients.

Amenities: S.F. General is a public hospital serving all patients needing emergency services regardless of their ability to pay. General services are available to all county residents. It is a teaching hospital for UCSF and a state-designated trauma center.

Seton Medical Center

1900 Sullivan Ave.
Daly City
650-992-4000
650-991-6435 (classes)
www.setonmedicalcenter.org

Type: Private, nonprofit medical center run by Daughters of Charity Health System. Level II nursery.

Births and C-section rate: 500-600; 18%

Rooms: 6 LDR rooms; 2 C-section rooms; 2 (of 20) postpartum rooms are private.

Midwives on staff: No.

Breastfeeding: About 80%

Perinatal classes: Childbirth preparation, breastfeeding, baby care, parenting, women's health issues, postpartum care, and infant CPR.

Amenities: Seton's nursery is staffed by San Francisco Neonatology Services. Before leaving the hospital, parents attend a mom and baby care class. There is a breastfeeding support group once a week.

University of California at San Francisco Medical Center (UCSF)

505 Parnassus St.
415-476-1000
415-353-1787 (Birth Center)
415-353-2667 (classes and tours, Women's Center, 2356 Sutter St.)
415-476-1817 (CPR classes)
www.ucsfhealth.org

Type: Large state university research hospital. Level III nursery.

Births and C-section rate: 1,775; 15%

Rooms: 6 LDR rooms. All 22 (of 22) postpartum rooms are private.

Midwives on staff: Yes.

Breastfeeding: 95%

Perinatal classes: Pregnancy, childbirth preparation, breastfeeding, parenting, baby care, infant health, multiples, and infant CPR.

Amenities: Some of the rooms feature city views. UCSF's Women's Center offers Great Expectations classes, breast pump rentals and sales, and a lending library. UCSF is also home to many highly regarded groups of doctors, including the members of its OB-GYN department, its reproductive endocrinologists specializing in fertility treatments, and its pediatric surgeons and anesthesiologists. The hospital has extensive services for high-risk pregnancies, including a special program for women expecting multiples. UCSF is Northern California's only nationally designated Center of Excellence in Women's Health.

PARENT RATING: ☆ ☆ ☆ ☆ ☆

UCSF—one of the leading academic hospitals on the West Coast—garnered high praise from parents, particularly for C-sections and high-risk deliveries, as well as pediatrics. Patients found the nurses "particularly wonderful," and the level of care excellent. The pediatric surgery ward is "tailored to babies and children, and very welcoming to families. . . . This is definitely the place you want to go if your child needs to see a specialist or have surgery."

North Bay Hospitals

Marin General Hospital
250 Bon Air Rd.
Greenbrae
415-925-7000
415-925-7992 (classes)
www.maringeneral.sutterhealth.org

Type: District hospital (acute-care facility) owned by the publicly elected Marin Healthcare District. A Sutter Health affiliate. Level II nursery.

Births and C-section rate: 1,808; 26%

Rooms: 8 LDR rooms; 1 recovery room. 16 (of 22) postpartum rooms are private.

Midwives on staff: Yes. Midwives perform 33% of all deliveries.

Breastfeeding: 94%+

Perinatal classes: Childbirth preparation (series or intensive), a 5-week series in prenatal education, including parenting, baby safety, breast and bottle feeding, labor and delivery, C-sections, and postpartum care.

Amenities: The labor and delivery rooms were renovated recently and are extremely spacious. Some rooms feature Mt. Tamalpais views. The hospital offers an on-site lactation center, a doula service, and 24/7 OB-GYN coverage, and it is a state-designated trauma center.

PARENT RATING: ☆ ☆ ☆ ☆ ☆
Patients praised the hospital's labor and delivery facilities and nurses, while some cautioned that the postpartum care was "not as great as expected."

Petaluma Valley Hospital
400 N. McDowell Blvd.
Petaluma
707-778-1111
707-778-2502 (classes)
707-778-2780 (tours)
www.stjosephhealth.org

Type: Small, private, nonprofit hospital run by the St. Joseph Health System. No intensive care nursery (ICN).

Births and C-section rate: 580; 16%

Rooms: 3 LDR rooms. All 5 postpartum rooms are semiprivate, but the staff tries to give patients private rooms whenever possible.

Midwives on staff: Yes. Midwives perform 20% of all deliveries.

Breastfeeding: 90%

Perinatal classes: Pregnancy, childbirth preparation, breastfeeding, newborn care, infant CPR, childbirth refresher, and sibling preparation.

Amenities: Petaluma Valley's sister hospital is Santa Rosa Memorial, home of a Level II Intensive Care Nursery affiliated with UCSF and directed by a full-time neonatologist. The hospital offers a neonatal transport service. Lactation services are available. Rooms feature sleeping accommodations for significant others.

Queen of the Valley Hospital

1000 Trancas St.

Napa

707-252-4411

www.thequeen.org

Type: Small, private, nonprofit hospital run by the St. Joseph Health System. Level I nursery.

Births and C-section rate: 950; 24%

Rooms: 5 LDR rooms; 4 (of 5) postpartum rooms are private.

Midwives on staff: No.

Breastfeeding: 94%

Perinatal classes: Childbirth preparation classes are available free or at low cost.

Amenities: The hospital remodel, expected to be complete in 2006, will add 5 LDR rooms and 14 private postpartum rooms.

St. Helena Hospital and Health Center

10 Woodland Rd.

St. Helena

707-963-3611

707-963-1912 (classes, tours)

www.sthelenahospital.org

Type: Small, private, nonprofit hospital run by Adventist Health System. Level I nursery.

Births and C-section rate: 382; 12%

Rooms: 6 LDRP rooms. All are private.

Midwives on staff: Yes. Midwives perform 25% of all deliveries.

Breastfeeding: 90%

Perinatal classes: Most classes are free and cover topics including pregnancy, childbirth preparation, breastfeeding, newborn care, sibling preparation, and infant CPR.

Amenities: St. Helena Hospital's Family Birth Center features views of Napa Valley. Every mother who lives in Napa County receives a postpartum home visit from an RN/lactation consultant, regardless of her ability to pay. There is a child safety seat technician on staff.

Santa Rosa Memorial Hospital

1165 Montgomery Dr.

Santa Rosa

707-546-3210

707-525-5695 (classes, tours)

www.stjosephhealth.org

Type: Private, nonprofit, acute-care hospital run by the St. Joseph Health System. Level II nursery.

Births and C-section rate: 1,406; 21%

Rooms: 7 LDR rooms. 2 C-section rooms. 5 (of 15) postpartum rooms are private.

Midwives on staff: Yes. Midwives attend 14% of all deliveries.

Breastfeeding: 95%

Perinatal classes: Classes include pregnancy, breastfeeding, childbirth preparation, newborn care, sibling preparation, infant CPR, and infant massage.

Amenities: Santa Rosa Hospital's intensive care nursery is affiliated with UCSF. The hospital offers high-risk obstetrical services, a diabetes in pregnancy program, lactation services, a perinatal program for Medi-Cal patients, and an antenatal testing center.

Sonoma Valley Hospital

347 Andrieux St.
Sonoma
707-935-5000
707-938-2063 (classes)
www.svh.com

Type: Small, nonprofit community hospital operated by the Sonoma Valley Healthcare District. Level I nursery.

Births and C-section rate: 275; 10%

Rooms: 3 LDRP rooms, a C-section OR, 4 private postpartum rooms.

Midwives on staff: No.

Breastfeeding: 90% +

Perinatal classes: Lamaze

Amenities: The hospital is affiliated with the UCSF Perinatal/Pediatric Outreach Program. The LDRP rooms have views of the Sonoma hills. The family-centered birthing unit has a bilingual staff (Spanish-English) with a full-time neonatal educator. Plans for a new hospital include 4 LDRP rooms with whirlpool baths or showers, and large postpartum rooms. The Families First program provides 3 home visits during a newborn's first year to support new parents.

Sutter Medical Center Santa Rosa

3325 Chanate Rd.
Santa Rosa
707-576-4000
707-576-4800 (Women's Health Resource Center)
www.suttersantarosa.org

Type: Private, nonprofit medical center and Sutter Health affiliate. Level III nursery.

Births and C-section rate: 1,800; 10-15%

Rooms: 8 LDR rooms. 6 (of 12) postpartum rooms are private.

Midwives on staff: Yes. Midwives perform 15-20% of deliveries.

Breastfeeding: 95%

Perinatal classes: Pregnancy, childbirth preparation, breastfeeding, infant care, multiples, sibling preparation, and infant CPR. Classes are also taught in Spanish.

Amenities: The Women's Health Resource Center offers classes, support groups, lactation consultation, and breast pump rentals Construction of a new hospital facility is scheduled to begin in 2007 and open in 2009 with all new private rooms.

East Bay Hospitals

Alta Bates Summit Medical Center

Alta Bates Campus
2450 Ashby Ave.
Berkeley
510-204-4444
510-204-1334 (classes, tours)
www.altabatessummit.com

Type: Large, private, nonprofit hospital and Sutter Health affiliate. Level III nursery.

Births and C-section rate: 10,700; 26%

Rooms: 24 LDR rooms. Approximately 70 postpartum rooms, 90% of which are private.

Midwives on staff: Yes. Midwives deliver babies at the hospital.

Breastfeeding: 85%

Perinatal classes: Healthy pregnancy, childbirth preparation, pain management, breastfeeding, baby care, sibling preparation, father preparation, and infant CPR/first aid.

Amenities: Alta Bates recently merged with Summit Medical Center and says it delivers "more babies than any other California hospital." The facility offers 24/7 coverage by perinatologists and neonatologists, genetic counseling, a gestational diabetes program, and a respected in vitro fertilization program. A postpartum nurse follows up with a telephone call to the patient.

PARENT RATING: ☆ ☆ ☆ ☆ ☆

Parents responding to our survey gave Alta Bates very positive reviews as a "fantastic" facility, agreeing that the hospital has the reputation as "the best" in the East Bay, with particularly excellent high-risk care. Most found the labor and delivery doctors and nurses to be "superb," "caring," and "professional." Those with difficult deliveries seemed to get the best care. One patient saw a lactation consultant in the hospital who was "excellent." Overall, parents advised shelling out the extra money for the quiet of a private room, being proactive with the nursing staff, and hiring a doula or other experienced support person as an advocate and teacher in the hospital.

Contra Costa Regional Medical Center

2500 Alhambra Ave.
Martinez
925-370-5000
925-370-5200, ext. 5495 (classes)
www.cchealth.org/medical_center/

Type: Public hospital run by Contra Costa County. A teaching hospital for UC Davis Medical School. Level II nursery.

Births and C-section rate: 2,000; 19%

Rooms: 8 LDR rooms; 2 ORs. Postpartum rooms are semiprivate.

Midwives on staff: No.

Breastfeeding: 85%

Perinatal classes: Childbirth preparation, breastfeeding, and newborn safety classes in English and Spanish.

Amenities: Contra Costa Medical Center was completely rebuilt and reopened in January 1998. The majority of patients have health coverage through public sources. An "early labor lounge" offers patients a place to be monitored without being admitted. Lactation educators are on staff.

Doctors Medical Center

2000 Vale Rd.
San Pablo
510-970-5000
800-206-WELL (classes)
www.doctorsmedicalcenter.org

Type: Public hospital run by the West Contra Costa Healthcare District. Level II nursery.

Births and C-section rate: 750; 25%

Rooms: 5 LDR rooms; C-section suite. 8 postpartum rooms are usually private.

Midwives on staff: No.

Breastfeeding: 90%

Perinatal classes: Classes are free for hospital patients and include childbirth preparation, breastfeeding, newborn care, and infant safety.

Amenities: The maternity ward was remodeled recently. When space permits, spouses may room-in on sleeper couches. There is 24/7 coverage by neonatologists, and the staff provides breastfeeding support. The small maternity ward affords personalized attention from the staff.

Eden Medical Center

20103 Lake Chabot Rd.
Castro Valley
510-537-1234
510-727-2715 (classes, tours)
www.edenmedcenter.org

Type: Private, nonprofit hospital and Sutter Health affiliate. Level II nursery.

Births and C-section rate: 945; 22%

Rooms: 3 LDR rooms; 2 labor rooms; 1 C-section room; 3-bed recovery room; 3 (of 11) postpartum rooms are private.

Midwives on staff: None.

Breastfeeding: 87%

Perinatal classes: In addition to a monthly "Pregnancy Forum," the hospital offers classes on childbirth preparation, breastfeeding, baby care, infant and child CPR, and sibling preparation. Tours are available in Spanish.

Amenities: Eden is a state-designated trauma center. Cots are available for spouses/partners. The director of the neonatal ICU is a neonatologist. Newborns requiring advanced care are usually sent to Alta Bates (a Sutter affiliate). A lactation consultant is on staff. The maternity unit was completely renovated in December 2004, adding more private rooms with showers.

Highland Hospital (Alameda County Medical Center)

1411 E. 31st St.
Oakland
510-437-4800
510-437-4792 (Bright Beginnings Family Birthing Center, classes, tours)
www.acmedctr.org

Type: Public hospital owned by Alameda County. Level II nursery.

Births and C-section rate: 1,500; 23%

Rooms: 6 LDR rooms; 1 C-section OR. All 11 postpartum rooms are semiprivate.

Midwives on staff: Yes (24-hour coverage). Midwives perform 54% of deliveries.

Breastfeeding: 65-70%

Perinatal classes: Classes are open only to current patients and include prenatal care, breastfeeding, baby care, and car seat safety.

Amenities: Highland Hospital is part of the Alameda County Medical Center, serving the medically indigent population of the county regardless of their ability to pay. It is a state-designated trauma center and a teaching hospital. The spouse/partner may stay overnight on a cot in the patient's room if space is available. A free doula program is offered (student doulas in training). They provide breastfeeding counselors to assist patients.

John Muir Medical Center

1601 Ygnacio Valley Rd.
Walnut Creek
925-939-3000
925-941-7900 (classes, Women's Health Center, 1656 N. California Blvd., Walnut Creek)
www.johnmuirmtdiablo.com

Type: Large, private, nonprofit acute-care medical center. Part of the John Muir/Mt. Diablo Health System. Level III nursery.

Births and C-section rate: 3,100; 28%

Rooms: 10 LDR rooms; 2 ORs; 2 high-risk labor rooms; 11 antepartum beds for pre-term labor or at-risk patients. All 34 postpartum rooms are private.

Midwives on staff: No.

Breastfeeding: 94%+

Perinatal classes: Pregnancy, childbirth preparation, newborn care and breastfeeding, sibling preparation, father preparation, multiples, grandparenting, car seat safety, infertility, parenting, infant/child CPR, and many other classes and lectures. Register early as the classes fill quickly.

Amenities: The hospital features a Level III nursery, 24/7 coverage by in-house perinatologists and neonatologists, antenatal testing, and lactation consultants on staff for inpatient consultation. The New Women's Health Center in downtown Walnut Creek offers classes, support groups, exercise programs, and a lactation center with inpatient and outpatient services by lactation specialists. The nursing staff is trained to support breastfeeding during postpartum stays, and pump rentals and supplies are available at bedside. The hospital also has a free support line for breastfeeding assistance, and each new mother receives a home visit from a Birth Center nurse. In-room massage therapy is available. The hospital is the only state-designated trauma center for Contra Costa County, and other hospitals send sick infants to John Muir's ICU.

PARENT RATING: ☆ ☆ ☆ ☆ ☆

Parents praised John Muir as being a comfortable place to deliver—with nice amenities and less of a crowd than bigger hospitals. High-risk patients favored John Muir over other Contra Costa County hospitals.

St. Rose Hospital

27200 Calaroga Ave.
Hayward
510-264-4000
510-264-4044 (classes)
www.strosehospital.org

Type: Private, nonprofit acute-care hospital. Part of the Via Christi Health System. Level I nursery.

Births and C-section rate: 1,416 (1999); 17.7%

Rooms: 9 LDRP rooms. 2 ORs. 2 semiprivate postpartum rooms. 9 (of 11) postpartum rooms are private.

Midwives on staff: One midwife on staff; midwives with hospital privileges may deliver babies.

Breastfeeding: 80-85%

Perinatal classes: Natural family planning, childbirth preparation, breastfeeding, infant care, sibling preparation, and infant massage, as well as many classes on specific health issues.

Amenities: St. Rose was founded by an order of Catholic nuns and retains a Christian orientation (according to its website). A large VIP suite is available on a first-come, first-served basis. A Jacuzzi tub is also available. The maternity unit prides itself on providing a "home-like" environment.

San Ramon Regional Medical Center

6001 Norris Canyon Rd.
San Ramon
925-275-9200
925-275-8230 (classes, tours)
www.sanramonmedctr.com

Type: Private acute-care medical center. Part of Tenet Health Systems. Level II nursery.

Births and C-section rate: 838; C-section rate not available.

Rooms: 10 LDRP rooms. 2 ORs. All 18 (of 18) postpartum rooms are private.

Midwives on staff: No.

Breastfeeding: 98%

Perinatal classes: Childbirth preparation, breastfeeding, newborn care, sibling preparation, and infant safety.

Amenities: SRRMC offers 24/7 coverage by neonatologists, anesthesiologists, and a Children's Hospital Oakland pediatrician. A lactation consultant is on staff. The Breastfeeding Resource Center offers consults, support groups, and breast pump rentals.

Sutter Delta Medical Center

3901 Lonetree Way
Antioch
925-779-7200
925-779-7230 (Women's Health Center, classes)
www.sutterdelta.com

Type: Nonprofit hospital and Sutter Health affiliate. Level II nursery.

Births and C-section rate: 1,000; 21%

Rooms: 8 LDR rooms (3 with Jacuzzi tubs). 14 private postpartum rooms.

Midwives on staff: No.

Breastfeeding: 75%

Perinatal classes: Childbirth preparation, breastfeeding, postpartum care, sibling preparation, car seat safety, and infant safety/CPR.

Amenities: Sutter Delta has a lactation nurse on staff and features "hotel-like" rooms.

Sutter Solano Medical Center

300 Hospital Dr.
Vallejo
707-554-4444
707-554-5164 (classes, tours)
www.suttersolano.org

Type: Nonprofit community hospital and Sutter Health affiliate. Level I nursery.

Births and C-section rate: 950; 19%

Rooms: LDR rooms, C-section OR.

Midwives on staff: Yes.

Breastfeeding: 50%

Perinatal classes: Pregnancy, childbirth preparation, breastfeeding, newborn care, sibling preparation, car seat safety, and infant safety. There are also support groups for diabetics and teens, and classes are available in Spanish.

Amenities: Neonatologists and anesthesiologists are available 24/7, and the hospital offers antenatal testing services.

Valleycare Medical Center

5555 W. Las Positas Blvd.
Pleasanton
925-847-3000
800-719-9111 (classes, tours)
www.valleycare.com

Type: Small, nonprofit community hospital. In the process of affiliating with Stanford Medical Center. Level II nursery.

Births and C-section rate: 1,500; C-section rate not available.

Rooms: 9 LDRP rooms. 2 ORs. 8 (of 10) postpartum rooms are private.

Midwives on staff: No.

Breastfeeding: 98%

Perinatal classes: Childbirth preparation, breastfeeding, newborn care, sibling preparation, infant massage, and infant CPR. There is a special class for moms on bed rest.

Amenities: Valleycare was recently remodeled. Neonatologist consultants are available. Lactation educators are on staff. LDRP rooms have whirlpool tubs. A new pediatric unit opened in spring 2002.

Washington Hospital

2000 Mowry Ave.
Fremont
510-797-1111
510-791-3423 (classes, tours)
www.whhs.com

Type: Nonprofit district hospital run by Washington Township Health Care District. Level II nursery.

Births and C-section rate: 2,800; 25%

Rooms: 18 LDR rooms. 18 private postpartum rooms.

Midwives on staff: No.

Breastfeeding: 95%

Perinatal classes: Childbirth preparation, breastfeeding, an infertility lecture, a diabetes and pregnancy program, a parenting workshop, sibling preparation, infant and toddler safety, CPR, and a pediatric asthma class.

Amenities: Washington's ICN is run by Lucile Packard Children's Hospital with a neonatologist and lactation consultants on staff. Lactation consultants visit each patient after delivery to facilitate breastfeeding.

South Bay Hospitals

Community Hospital of Los Gatos

815 Pollard Rd.
Los Gatos
408-378-6131
408-866-3905 (classes, tours)
www.communityhospitallg.com

Type: For-profit acute-care hospital. Part of Tenet Health Systems. Level II nursery.

Births and C-section rate: 975; 25%

Rooms: 6 LDR rooms. All 8 postpartum rooms are private.

Midwives on staff: Yes. Midwives perform 35% of all deliveries.

Breastfeeding: 95%

Perinatal classes: Childbirth preparation, breastfeeding, newborn care, sibling preparation, infant massage, and infant CPR.

Amenities: The hospital has a Jacuzzi available and provides cots for the spouse/partner to spend the night. They offer lactation consultation and pump rentals and sales.

El Camino Hospital

2500 Grant Rd.
Mountain View
650-940-7000
800-216-5556 (Maternal-Child Health Center)
650-940-7302 (classes, tours)
www.elcaminohospital.org

Type: Large, nonprofit district hospital run by the hospital board. Level III nursery.

Births and C-section rate: 4,421; 31%

Rooms: 10 LDR rooms. 28 (of 36) postpartum rooms are private.

Midwives on staff: No, but several midwives have hospital privileges.

Breastfeeding: 95%

Perinatal classes: Childbirth preparation, breastfeeding, newborn care, sibling preparation, infant massage, infant safety, and infant/child CPR.

Amenities: The labor and delivery rooms overlook a garden, and the hospital offers sleep chairs for patients' spouses or partners. The hospital has perinatologists available for consultation in the Prenatal Diagnostic Center (in conjunction with Stanford). Along with the Level III nursery, neonatologists (members of Stanford's neonatology department) are on staff. Two rooms are available in the neonatal intensive care unit for parents to visit and feed newborns. The Maternal Connections lactation center features 11 staff lactation consultants, support groups, a store, and a library. The hospital received a best birthing facility award from *Bay Area Parent* magazine in 2004, and twice made the HCIA-Sachs "100 Top Hospitals" national benchmarks list. See www.100tophospitals.com.

PARENT RATING: ☆ ☆ ☆ ☆ ☆

Parents responding to our survey praised El Camino as a "pleasant, patient-friendly" place to deliver a baby. "The Ritz Carlton of Labor and Delivery . . . excellent nurses, great NICU."

Good Samaritan Hospital of Santa Clara Valley

2425 Samaritan Dr.
San Jose
408-559-2011
408-559-BABY (classes)
www.goodsamsj.org or
www.goodsambabies.com

Type: Large, investor-owned, acute-care hospital run by HCA Health Care. Level III nursery.

Births and C-section rate: 4,400; 25%

Rooms: 17 LDR rooms. 48 private postpartum rooms.

Midwives on staff: Midwives work with affiliated physicians and perform 2% of deliveries.

Breastfeeding: 99%

Perinatal classes: Classes include pregnancy, childbirth preparation, breastfeeding, newborn care, sibling preparation, and infant CPR, as well as new mom support groups.

Amenities: Good Samaritan features 24/7 neonatologist coverage in the NICU and provides high-risk perinatal services and fertility services. Air and ground ambulance service supports maternal and neonatal transport for a

5-county area. Good Samaritan's breastfeeding center is staffed by lactation consultants, sells breastfeeding supplies, and rents and sells breast pumps. LDR rooms have showers and whirlpools, and postpartum rooms are new and spacious with private showers. There are 2 new newborn nurseries. New moms can choose what and when to eat through a room service menu.

PARENT RATING: ☆ ☆ ☆ ☆ ☆

If you are in San Jose or south, this is the place to have a baby. *Bay Area Parent* magazine consistently rates the hospital as the best place to have a baby in the South Bay.

O'Connor Hospital

2105 Forest Ave.
San Jose
408-947-2500
408-947-2699 (classes)
408-947-2743 (lactation center)
www.oconnorhospital.org

Type: Private, nonprofit hospital run by Daughters of Charity Health System. Level II nursery.

Births and C-section rate: 3,600; 30%

Rooms: 12 LDR rooms; 2 C-section suites; all 36 postpartum suites are private.

Midwives on staff: Yes, there are 2 midwives on staff, and midwives deliver babies at the hospital.

Breastfeeding: 70%

Perinatal classes: Natural family planning, childbirth preparation, breastfeeding, parenting, sibling preparation, infant care, and infant CPR.

Amenities: O'Connor offers perinatal consultation for high-risk pregnancies and 24/7 coverage by neonatologists, as well as a diabetes in pregnancy program, outpatient antepartum testing, and staff lactation consultants. The lactation center provides consultation, supplies, support groups, bra fitting, and pump rentals.

Peninsula Medical Center (Mills-Peninsula Health Services)

1783 El Camino Real
Burlingame
650-696-5400
650-696-5600 (Wellness Center, classes, tours)
www.mills-peninsula.org

Type: Nonprofit, community acute-care hospital and Sutter Health affiliate. Level II nursery.

Births and C-section rate: 2,315; 24%

Rooms: 15 LDR rooms; 2 C-section suites. 18 private postpartum rooms.

Midwives on staff: Yes. Midwives attend 33% of deliveries.

Breastfeeding: 95%

Perinatal classes: Childbirth preparation/Lamaze, breastfeeding, newborn care, infant massage, and sibling preparation.

Amenities: The hospital offers staff lactation consultants, neonatologists, and a Prenatal Diagnosis Program in conjunction with CPMC perinatologists, as well as a diabetics and pregnancy program, and many support groups through the Wellness Center. The hospital twice made the HCIA-Sachs "100 Top Hospitals" national benchmark list, and was voted one of the best places to have a baby by *Bay Area Parent* magazine in 2004.

PARENT RATING: ☆ ☆ ☆ ☆ ☆

A perennial favorite for San Mateo County moms, Peninsula is said to provide "lots of amenities," from "nice" private rooms with refrigerators and rocking chairs to sleeper sofas for spouses and partners. Most reported they had a "great experience. . . . It's small so you get lots of personalized service." Parents raved about the many classes and support groups.

Regional Medical Center of San Jose

225 N. Jackson Ave.
San Jose
408-259-5000
www.regionalmedicalsanjose.com

Type: Large, private, for-profit medical center run by HCA Health Care. Level II nursery.

Births and C-section rate: 2,215; 28%

Rooms: 10 LDR rooms. Only 3 (of 32) postpartum rooms are private, but the staff tries to give each patient a private room whenever possible.

Midwives on staff: No.

Breastfeeding: 80%

Perinatal classes: Classes (many in Vietnamese and Spanish) include childbirth preparation, breastfeeding, newborn care, and father preparation.

Amenities: Regional Medical Center was formerly known as Alexian Brothers Hospital. A perinatologist and neonatologist group is associated with the hospital. There are 2 lactation consultants on staff, plus a breastfeeding clinic for postpartum support. Sleep chairs are available for spouses/partners.

St. Louise Regional Hospital

9400 No Name Uno
Gilroy
408-848-2000
408-594-0591 (classes)
www.saintlouisehospital.org

Type: Small, private, nonprofit hospital run by Daughters of Charity Health System. No ICN.

Births and C-section rate: 700; C-section rate not available.

Rooms: 4 LDR rooms. All 9 postpartum rooms are technically semi-private but are usually private when ward is not full.

Midwives on staff: Yes (2). Approximately one-third of deliveries are performed by midwives.

Breastfeeding: Figure not available.

Perinatal classes: Pregnancy, childbirth preparation, breastfeeding, newborn care, infant/child CPR, sibling preparation, breastfeeding support group, parent support groups.

Amenities: St. Louise features a newly remodeled LDR. There is a lactation consultant on staff.

Santa Clara Valley Medical Center

751 S. Bascom Ave.
San Jose
408-885-5000
408-885-6400 (maternity)
www.scvmed.org

Type: Large, public hospital owned and operated by Santa Clara County. Level III nursery.

Births and C-section rate: 5,000; 19%

Rooms: 13 LDR rooms. 3 private postpartum rooms, of 56 postpartum beds.

Midwives on staff: No.

WHAT ABOUT KAISER PERMANENTE?

You may have noticed that Kaiser Permanente Medical Centers are not on our list of hospitals. That is because to deliver at a Kaiser hospital, you must be a member of the Kaiser Permanente HMO. More than likely, if you are a Kaiser member, you made that decision well before you became pregnant. Kaiser is a "closed system" of health care—in exchange for lower insurance premiums, you must stay within the Kaiser managed care network of doctors and hospitals. It started as a health care system for industrial laborers in the 1930s and has evolved into the largest nonprofit HMO in the U.S.

Parents we surveyed varied considerably in their opinions of Kaiser. Some were very happy with the care they received, and applauded the cost savings and the preventive medicine/patient education programs (many classes are free to members). Some were not so happy, particularly with the concept of a large group practice where you don't have your own OB/GYN but get the doctor available at your appointment time. But almost everyone recommended the same thing: since this is a managed care system, you must be very proactive about your patient care and learn how to navigate the system, which can be Byzantine (starting with the phone system for making appointments). We also learned that midwives do most low-risk deliveries in many Kaiser hospitals, so depending on your views of midwives, this may or may not be a benefit for you. Additionally, some Kaiser facilities have weekend pediatric urgent care centers, a most welcome benefit.

If you are a Kaiser member, perhaps you will be more successful than we were in getting information about Kaiser's maternity units. In any event, here is some basic information about Kaiser hospitals delivering babies in the Bay Area. For more information, go to www.kaiserpermanente.org.

Kaiser Permanente San Francisco Medical Center
2425 Geary Blvd.
415-833-2000
Level III nursery. Kaiser-SF also serves many of Kaiser's Marin patients, as there is no Kaiser hospital delivering babies in Marin.

Kaiser Permanente Santa Rosa Medical Center
401 Bicentennial Way
Santa Rosa
707-571-4000
www.kaisersantarosa.org
Level II nursery. Kaiser Santa Rosa is the only Kaiser hospital delivering babies in the North Bay.

Kaiser Permanente Hayward Medical Center
27400 Hesperian Blvd.
Hayward
510-784-4000
www.haykaiser.org
Level III nursery.

Kaiser Permanente Oakland Medical Center
280 W. MacArthur Blvd.
Oakland
510-752-1000
www.kaiseroakland.org
Level III nursery.

Kaiser Permanente Vallejo Medical Center
975 Sereno Dr.
Vallejo
369-651-1000
Level I nursery. Newborns requiring advanced care are transported from Vallejo to Walnut Creek.

Kaiser Permanente Walnut Creek Medical Center
1425 S. Main St.
Walnut Creek
925-295-4000
Level III nursery.

Kaiser Permanente Redwood City Medical Center
1150 Veterans Blvd.
Redwood City
650-299-2000
650-299-2692 (Breastfeeding Center, 610 Walnut St., Redwood City)
Level II nursery.

Kaiser Permanente Santa Clara Medical Center
900 Kiely Blvd.
Santa Clara
408-236-6400
www.kaisersantaclara.org
Level III nursery.

Kaiser Permanente Santa Teresa Medical Center
250 Hospital Pkwy.
San Jose
408-972-3000
Level II nursery.

Breastfeeding: 70-80%

Perinatal classes: Offers a 5-week prenatal class in English and Spanish.

Amenities: Santa Clara Valley Medical Center has an open-door policy, meaning it serves those needing medical care regardless of their ability to pay. It is a state-designated trauma center. There are board-certified lactation consultants on staff.

Sequoia Hospital District

170 Alameda de las Pulgas
Redwood City
650-369-5811
650-368-BABY (birth center, classes, tours)
www.sequoiahospital.org

Type: Community hospital. A Catholic Healthcare West affiliate. Level II nursery.

Births and C-section rate: 1,300; 30%

Rooms: 13 LDRP rooms; 2 C-section rooms. 6 postpartum rooms. All rooms are private.

Midwives on staff: No.

Breastfeeding: 96%

Perinatal classes: Childbirth preparation, breastfeeding, infant care, sibling preparation, infant massage, and pediatric first aid and CPR.

Amenities: Sequoia's remodeled birth center offers private baths and cots for spouses. The NICU is affiliated with Lucile Packard Children's Hospital at Stanford. All new patients receive a Sequoia *Baby's First Months* video as well as a monthly parenting newsletter during the baby's first year. The Lactation Education Center offers in- and out-patient consultations and a "CalmLine" for questions.

Lucile Packard Children's Hospital at Stanford Medical Center

725 Welch Rd.
Palo Alto
650-497-8000
650-723-4600 (classes, tours)
800-690-2282 (Parent Information Referral Center)
www.lpch.org

Type: Large, private university hospital. Levels I, II, and III nurseries.

Births and C-section rate: 5,120; 26%

Rooms: 10 LDR rooms; 1 early labor room; 2 surgical suites. 16 (of 52) postpartum rooms are private.

Midwives on staff: No.

Breastfeeding: Figure not available.

Perinatal classes: Stanford's "Becoming Parents" program is extremely popular, so sign up early. The hospital offers a full set of classes, including childbirth preparation, breastfeeding, newborn care, multiples, grandparenting, sibling preparation, infant safety, infant CPR, infant massage, special issues (NICU), and lectures on many parenting topics.

Amenities: The Johnson Center for Pregnancy and Newborn Services combines the perinatal services of Stanford Hospital with the neonatal medicine services of Lucile Packard Children's Hospital at Stanford. The hospital offers neonatologists and perinatologists on staff, as well as genetic testing, diagnosis, and counseling. The Perinatal Diagnostic Center provides services for high-risk patients. There are 19 physician faculty members (Stanford is a teaching hospital); private practice physicians also deliver babies at Stanford. The

Family Resource Center provides a wealth of information on maternal and child health. Lactation consultants are available, and the prenatal/postnatal education program is highly rated. The Children's Hospital is world-renowned. In 2004, LPCH was ranked 12th in the nation in *U.S. News and World Report*'s annual survey of the nation's best pediatric hospitals.

PARENT RATING: ☆ ☆ ☆ ☆ ☆

Parents rated Stanford as *the* place to have a baby on the Peninsula. Nurses received excellent reviews, as did the level of advanced care for high-risk deliveries. "I had a great experience in delivery," said one patient. Though the level of care was universally praised, the hospital was sometimes criticized in more detailed areas. One parent said that it "can be a bit disorganized" since it is a very large place, and one can easily get "lost in the crowd." "The birthing/recovery rooms were pretty disappointing," noted another parent. As at other hospitals, parents advised patients to be proactive—order your anesthesia early and be a squeaky wheel. Also, if your

child requires pediatric specialist care or surgery and you live in the South Bay, this is the hospital you want.

—∿—

Finally, we would be remiss if we did not mention the largest and most comprehensive pediatric medical center in Northern California, Children's Hospital Oakland. Many parents praised its specialized departments and services, as well as its Family Resource and Information Center (510-428-3549). In 2004, *U.S. News and World Report* rated the hospital as one of the top 25 pediatric hospitals in the nation.

Children's Hospital Oakland
747 52nd St.
Oakland
510-428-3000
www.childrenshospitaloakland.org
PARENT RATING: ☆ ☆ ☆ ☆ ☆

BIRTH CENTERS

Independent birth centers are run by doctors and midwives outside of hospitals. They target low-risk patients who prefer a more natural, minimal intervention, drug-free approach in a home-like environment, but who want the extra security of a birth center. Local birth centers charged about $4,000 per birth in 2005, including prenatal care and delivery. Check with the California Office of Statewide Health Planning and Development, www.oshpd.cahwnet.gov, for a list of licensed birth centers. Be sure to check whether the birth center is accredited according to national standards developed by:

Commission for the Accreditation of Birth Centers
P.O. Box 34
East Greenville, PA 18041
215-679-4833
www.birthcenters.org
Affiliated with the National Association of Childbearing Centers, this website allows you to search for centers in your area.

Bay Area Birth Centers

The Birth Home
4441 Railroad Ave.
Pleasanton
866-639-9915
www.birthhome.com
PARENT RATING: ☆ ☆ ☆
We received largely positive reviews of this center, although one patient complained of not being told ahead of time that a physician rather than a midwife would attend the birth. Since opening in 1997, the center has been the site of hundreds of births. Featuring 3 birthing rooms, a Jacuzzi tub, and water birth facilities, the facility is staffed by both a physician and midwives, and focuses on natural childbirth and nonintervention. Hospital backup is at Valleycare Medical Center 3 miles away. The center accepts insurance.

Women's Health and Birth Center
583 Summerfield Rd.
Santa Rosa
707-539-1544
www.womenshealthandbirthcenter.com
Run by CNMs, this center features 2 birthing rooms and 2 birthing tubs. CNMs perform deliveries. Doulas and lactation consultants are available. Each patient receives a home visit from a nurse. The center is licensed and accredited, and is certified by the Baby-Friendly Hospital Initiative, a breastfeeding initiative of UNICEF/WHO. The center accepts insurance and arranges backup care at Sutter Santa Rosa Medical Center in case of complications. It also offers classes in pregnancy, childbirth preparation, and breastfeeding, as well as a lending library, lactation support, and breast pump rentals and sales.

HOME BIRTH

Contrary to popular myth, home birth is legal in California. People who choose home birth say it increases intimacy, privacy, and control over the birthing experience. They choose it because they want a natural, drug-free childbirth experience. To deliver at home, refer to the section on midwives, above, to find a competent midwife. Check the credentials of your midwife carefully, and make sure he or she is trained in emergency measures and has the right equipment for such an eventuality (typically, a fetal stethoscope or doppler, oxygen, suturing materials, medicine to control bleeding, IVs, and newborn resuscitation equipment). It goes without saying that you must be healthy and expecting a normal delivery to deliver at home (C-sections are only done in hospitals). Make sure you have arranged for medical transport to a nearby hospital in case of emergency.

Midwives' fees for a typical home birth—including prenatal care, delivery, and postpartum visits—averaged about $3,000-4,000 in California in 2005. Many insurance companies, particularly HMOs and including state-subsidized Medi-Cal, will not cover home birth fees, so some patients see a doctor for prenatal care, lab tests, and ultrasounds, and then see the midwife during the third trimester and delivery.

For local water tub rental, home birth information, and referrals, contact Natural Resources in San Francisco, Circle of Life Midwifery Center in the North Bay, Birthways or The Nurture Center in the East Bay, or Blossom Birth Services in the South Bay, all listed above under Choosing Care Providers. For further information, check out the following:

Midwifery Today Magazine

P.O. Box 2672
Eugene, OR 97402
800-743-0974 or 541-344-7438
www.midwiferytoday.com

This magazine and affiliated website provide information about midwifery and home birth.

Waterbirth International

P.O. Box 1400
Wilsonville, OR 97070
503-682-3600
www.waterbirth.org

This group provides water birth information, tub rentals, and referrals to local waterbirth resources.

Prenatal Education

Before you deliver or adopt a baby, you should educate yourself on 3 basic topics, at a minimum: childbirth, breastfeeding, and newborn care. Check out the classes at your local hospital, above, or see the following independent entities for more classes. Note that different organizations have different philosophies, and you will want to ensure you agree with whatever approach they are teaching.

For example, most hospital childbirth courses are "reality based" and will focus on the medical aspects of childbirth, in addition to labor pain management techniques, while "alternative" parent centers may emphasize childbirth as a spiritual experience and not provide much in the way of medical information. If you are considering natural childbirth, you may want to take a combination of basic childbirth preparation classes and specialized labor pain management classes.

For newborn care classes, look at the parenting books recommended by the teacher before you register—they will tell you a lot about the child-rearing philosophies taught in the class. You will see marked differences in approaches to breastfeeding (set intervals vs. on demand) and sleeping (from family beds to letting them cry it out). Though first-timers may not have a clue as to how they will parent, choose the approach that appeals to your fundamental values.

If you are short on time, and money is not an issue, hospitals and parenting centers can also provide lists of nurses or childbirth educators who will give private classes in your home. Parents raved about these private classes.

Look for classes taught by nurses or certified childbirth educators with experience in the field—there are many people out there claiming to be experts who really are not. Note that several organizations provide educator certification, sometimes resulting in a flood of different acronyms after educators' names (CCE, ICCE, LCCE, etc.). Local educators tell us that one of the most well regarded is the ICCE certification bestowed by the International Childbirth Education Association. And for breastfeeding classes, you will want to make sure the educator is appropriately certified, preferably by the International Board of Lactation Consultants (IBCLC, see full explanation in Ch. 5). In all cases, you should check out the certifying organization before you choose an educator to determine whether you agree with their basic philosophy.

You should also take an infant CPR class to learn specialized techniques for emergencies. Hire a private instructor to teach a group of expectant or new parents at a "CPR party" in your home. (This is also a great way for experienced parents to refresh their knowledge of CPR and first aid.) Be sure any child care providers you hire also have CPR training. Some courses provide American Red Cross or American Heart Association certification and some do not; if you need certification for a job, be sure to inquire first. For infant and child CPR and first aid courses, in addition to the resources listed below, try your local fire department. We've heard reports of several fire stations offering free classes!

For all classes, consider the comfort factor of the facility where the classes are taught. It may sound petty, but a pregnant woman will be very uncomfortable sitting in a metal folding chair for any length of time—and some of the one-day intensive classes go on for 7 hours!

For more parenting classes and groups after you have the baby, check out Ch. 6.

GENERAL AND BAY AREA-WIDE RESOURCES

Adams Safety Training
925-454-0895
www.adamssafety.com
This local training company provides private pediatric first aid and CPR courses in offices and homes all over the Bay Area. They also will conduct classes in Spanish.

American Heart Association
www.americanheart.org
Log onto the website to search for local organizations providing AHA-approved CPR and first aid courses.

American Red Cross Bay Area
85 2nd St., 7th Fl.
San Francisco 94105
415-427-8000
www.bayarea-redcross.org
PARENT RATING: ☆ ☆ ☆ ☆
The Red Cross offers low-cost classes in CPR and first aid—including infant

and child CPR, safety for child care providers, and babysitter training—all over the Bay Area. Parents say these classes fill quickly and advise signing up well in advance.

Association of Labor Assistants and Childbirth Educators (ALACE)
P.O. Box 390436
Cambridge, MA 02139
888-22ALACE or 617-441-2500
www.alace.org
A nonprofit association certifying childbirth educators and doulas, ALACE focuses on natural childbirth and home birth, and provides educational materials and referrals to local childbirth educators and doulas.

Birthing From Within
www.birthingfromwithin.com
This style of childbirth classes, based on the eponymous book by Pam England, focuses on birth as a spiritual rite of passage and teaches

laboring women mindfulness-based labor pain reduction.

Bradley Method of Natural Childbirth

(American Academy of Husband-Coached Childbirth)
Box 5224
Sherman Oaks, CA 91413-5224
800-4-A-BIRTH (800-422-4784)
www.bradleybirth.com
PARENT RATING: ☆ ☆ ☆ ☆ ☆

The Bradley Method is a system of husband-coached natural childbirth and emphasizes breathing and relaxation. Classes are typically held in small groups over the course of 12 weeks, beginning in the sixth month. The website provides referrals to local instructors.

Childbirth and Postpartum Professionals Association (CAPPA)

P.O. Box 491448
Lawrenceville, GA 30043
888-MY-CAPPA
www.cappa.net

A membership and certification organization for childbirth professionals including educators and doulas, CAPPA encourages natural childbirth. The website lists members by state.

Fast Response

800-637-7387
www.fastresponse.org

This school teaches CPR and first aid for both health care providers and the general public, and provides American Heart Association certification. The classes cover infant, child, and adult CPR. Teachers include nurses, EMTs, and paramedics. They offer classes in Marin, Alameda, and Contra Costa counties, and in San Francisco. They will also provide private classes.

KidSafe CPR

800-375-4250
info@kidsafecpr.com
PARENT RATING: ☆ ☆ ☆ ☆ ☆

"CPR Gil" Guglielmi, a dad and certified Red Cross CPR and first aid instructor, teaches these straightforward, informative, and fun infant/child CPR, choke saving, and first aid classes for groups in private homes throughout the Bay Area. He has a very helpful "flow chart" approach and infant-sized dummies for each student. Comments: "I've taken quite a few of these classes, and it was the best one I've ever done. . . . It went really fast . . . he made everything so simple to remember! . . . Great service as he came to our house for a CPR party."

Hypnobirthing

www.hypnobirthing.com
You can find out more about hypnosis techniques for labor, as well as local certified educators, at this website.

International Childbirth Education Association (ICEA)

P.O. Box 20048
Minneapolis, MN 55420
952-854-8660
www.icea.org
PARENT RATING: ☆ ☆ ☆ ☆

This well-regarded group grants professional certification to childbirth educators (ICCE designation) and doulas. The website features a database of certified instructors and doulas.

Lamaze International

2025 M St., Ste. 800
Washington, DC 20036
800-368-4404
www.lamaze.org

Lamaze International's mission is to promote normal, natural, and healthy childbirth. The website provides referral to local Lamaze-certified instructors.

San Francisco

Bay Area Home Birth Collective

415-273-5185
www.bayareahomebirth.org
PARENT RATING: ☆ ☆ ☆ ☆

This organization offers a "Homebirth Education Series" and support groups for couples planning to give birth at home.

DayOne

3490 California St., Ste. 203
(entrance on Locust St.)
415-440-3291
www.DayOneCenter.com
PARENT RATING: ☆ ☆ ☆ ☆ ☆

An upscale, privately run center for new and expectant parents in Laurel Village, DayOne offers popular classes in healthy pregnancy, childbirth preparation, newborn parenting, breastfeeding, infant safety, and infant CPR, as well as prenatal and new parent workshops and support groups on myriad topics. Nurses and lactation consultants teach the classes. The "value package" of childbirth preparation, breastfeeding, and newborn parenting classes is the best deal. Classes are small (7 students) and the classroom is attractive and comfortable. Comments: "State-of-the-art facility and experienced teachers who are experts in their field! . . . Worth the extra cost. . . . Great community feel. . . . Very convenient. . . . We loved our breastfeeding class. . . . Great classes!" See also Chapters 2, 3, 5, and 6.

Esther Gallagher

415-821-4490
www.esthergallagher.com

A doula and former midwife, this childbirth educator teaches private and group childbirth preparation, postpartum preparation, breastfeeding and infant care classes (in her San Francisco home or yours). In addition, she offers a unique monthly support group for the childbearing year, beginning in the second trimester and ending when your baby is 6 months old.

Kari and Craig Marble

415-845-1073
Kari@welcomeom.com
PARENT RATING: ☆ ☆ ☆ ☆ ☆

Kari, a certified yoga teacher and massage therapist, and Craig, a licensed acupuncturist, offer a childbirth preparation class called "Yoga and Massage for Labor: A Prenatal Partner Workshop." The class is designed to complement, not replace, other birth preparation classes, and teaches couples to relieve labor pain and strengthen bodies through massage and yoga. Kari also teaches infant massage classes for postpartum parents and babies, including time for parent discussion. Classes are held at CPMC (3838 California St.), The Mindful Body (2876 California St.), and in private homes.

Comments: "Kari has great wisdom and insight into baby massage and motherhood in general . . . magical. . . . For dads wanting to be more a part of the process, I would highly recommend [the partner workshop]."

Sarah McMoyler's Birth University (formerly The Lamaze Intensive Course)

707-746-7783
www.birthu.com

PARENT RATING: ☆ ☆ ☆ ☆ ☆

Parents lauded these one- or 2-day intensive Lamaze courses, taught by an experienced local labor and delivery nurse. She also offers classes in newborn care, breastfeeding, and infant/child CPR safety. All classes are held in San Francisco's Pacific Heights neighborhood, and focus on the "realities" of childbirth and new parenthood. Comments: "She was put on earth to teach parents . . . amazing . . . invaluable class . . . fabulous and really packed all the information into one day."

Natural Resources

816 Diamond St.
415-550-2611
www.naturalresourcesonline.com

PARENT RATING: ☆ ☆ ☆ ☆ ☆

This pregnancy, childbirth, and parenting center in Noe Valley offers a lending library and "eclectic approach" classes in childbirth preparation, childbirth advocacy, pregnancy, infant care, breastfeeding, infant massage, pediatric first aid, and infant/child CPR, among others. See also Ch. 6.

Parents Place San Francisco

1710 Scott St.
415-359-2454
www.parentsplaceonline.org

PARENT RATING: ☆ ☆ ☆ ☆ ☆

They offer a newborn parenting class for expectant parents, and lots of terrific workshops for after you have the baby. See also Ch. 6.

Pillowtalk: Modern Childbirth Education

415-456-8188
www.pillowtalk.com

PARENT RATING: ☆ ☆ ☆ ☆ ☆

Labor and delivery nurse Tori Kropp teaches private classes in San Francisco, Marin, and the East Bay, including baby care, modern childbirth preparation or refresher, breastfeeding, and infant CPR and safety. Parents universally recommended them, citing the emphasis on "realistic and practical" childbirth preparation.

San Francisco Paramedic Association

657 Mission St., Ste. 302
415-543-1161
www.sfparamedics.org

This group offers basic CPR and first aid classes for the public, and it will customize classes for groups.

North Bay

A.P.P.L.E. Family Works

4 Joseph Ct.
San Rafael
415-492-0720
www.familyworks.org

PARENT RATING: ☆ ☆ ☆ ☆ ☆

This nonprofit organization offers classes in childbirth preparation, sibling preparation, and CPR/first aid/choke saving. Private home or hospital childbirth preparation classes are available for moms on pre-term bed rest. See also Ch. 6.

Birthsisters/Georgia Montgomery, CD, CCE, LE

415-608-8308

www.birthsisters.com (private classes)

www.marinbirthingandparenting.com (group classes)

This childbirth and lactation educator and doula teaches the Marin Birthing and Parenting group's in-depth newborn care classes (including breastfeeding and making your home baby-ready) at Heller's for Children in San Rafael. She focuses on "empowering parents with information so that they are confident when they first come home with baby." She also provides private in-home classes on childbirth preparation, newborn parenting, and breastfeeding. Her childbirth preparation classes emphasize what to expect in the hospital and making informed choices, "with no agenda other than healthy mom and healthy baby." See also Ch. 5.

Barefoot and Pregnant

1165 Magnolia Ave.
Larkspur
415-388-1777
www.barefootandpregnant.com
PARENT RATING: ☆ ☆ ☆ ☆ ☆

Finally, an upscale, thoroughly modern parent resource center in Marin! This center offers a full range of services, from exercise to childbirth edu-

cation (taught by Moms on the Move, see below). Classes include traditional childbirth preparation or refresher, hypnosis for birthing, "family" care, and infant CPR, and there are also pre- and postnatal support groups and parent workshops. One unique offering is a weekend "retreat": childbirth classes for couples at a local inn. See also Chapters 2, 5, and 6.

Susan Bradford, LVN, CBE

San Rafael
415-453-0251
www.marinbirthdoulas.com
A former nurse, Susan Bradford has been working as a doula and childbirth educator in Marin since 1990. She offers an 8-week holistic childbirth preparation course entitled "The Birth Journey," focusing on the spiritual aspects of childbirth.

Bug a Boo

14 Bolinas Rd.
Fairfax
415-457-2884
www.bug-a-boo.com
PARENT RATING: ☆ ☆ ☆ ☆ ☆

This children's store offers "great" infant massage, infant and child CPR, and positive parenting courses.

Circle of Life Midwifery Center

145 Bolinas Rd.
Fairfax
415-456-2961
www.circleoflifemidwifery.org
The community childbirth educator at this center offers childbirth preparation classes with an emphasis on natural home birth.

Luray Eshelman, MA, RPT, ACCE

Marin Orthopedic Rehabilitation
Center
650 E. Blithedale, Ste. C
Mill Valley
415-388-5690

PARENT RATING: ☆ ☆ ☆

This certified childbirth educator has taught childbirth preparation classes in Marin for the past 27 years. Her series includes newborn care and breastfeeding, and she also offers a childbirth refresher course.

Gheri Gallagher, RN

415-457-6865

PARENT RATING: ☆ ☆ ☆ ☆ ☆

Parents gave these in-home CPR and child safety classes rave reviews. Gallagher teaches 3-hour private classes scheduled at the client's convenience.

Marin Birthing and Parenting/Marin Doula Circle

www.marinbirthingandparenting.com

See above under Birthsisters/Georgia Montgomery for group classes held at Heller's for Children, 514 4th Street in San Rafael. Many of the childbirth professionals who are members of this group also teach private classes, some with a holistic focus. Details about their services and contact information can be found on the website. See also Ch. 5.

Moms on the Move

707-762-6667
www.momsonthemove.net

PARENT RATING: ☆ ☆ ☆ ☆ ☆

Susan Lawler, a local labor and delivery nurse and certified childbirth educator, offers a one-day intensive or a 5-week series of childbirth preparation classes, as well as classes on hypnosis for birth, newborn care, breastfeeding, and infant CPR and safety. Classes are held in 3 locations in Marin (including Barefoot and Pregnant, see listing above), plus Petaluma. Comment: "A basic unbiased introduction to childbirth." See also Ch. 2.

Pillowtalk

See listing under San Francisco, above.

Marsha Podd, RN, CLE

415-883-4442
www.gotosleepbaby.com

This local nurse and lactation consultant offers in-home classes in CPR and newborn care.

East Bay

Bananas, Inc.

5232 Claremont Ave.
Oakland
510-658-7353
www.bananasinc.org

PARENT RATING: ☆ ☆ ☆ ☆ ☆

This nonprofit agency provides classes in infant and child first aid/CPR/emergency care, as well as other parenting classes, publications, and a parent library. They offer classes in many different languages, including Spanish. See also Ch. 6.

The Birth Home

Pleasanton
925-837-5898

This alternative birth center offers classes in natural childbirth, pregnancy/birth/parenting options, newborn care, and infant massage.

Birthways

570 14th St.
Oakland
510-869-2797
www.birthways.org
PARENT RATING: ☆ ☆ ☆ ☆ ☆

This nonprofit organization offers its own childbirth preparation classes focusing on natural birth, and provides a referral list of educators offering private classes (accessible on its website). Other classes include infant CPR, first aid, newborn care, parenting options, mindfulness-based pain reduction, infant massage, and child-rearing.

Janaki Costello, ICCE, IBCLC

510-525-1155
PARENT RATING: ☆ ☆ ☆ ☆ ☆

This educator, lactation consultant, and doula offers private childbirth preparation classes in the East Bay with an "eclectic" approach.

Fremont Swim School

42400 Blacow Rd.
Fremont
510-657-SWIM
www.fremontswimschool.com

This swim school offers American Heart Association-based CPR and first aid classes, some with a focus on infants and children. They also have locations in Newark and Livermore.

Anna Griffin, EMT

CPR Griffin
Oakland
510-653-8573
PARENT RATING: ☆ ☆ ☆ ☆ ☆

This EMT teaches infant and child CPR and basic first aid classes, at Alta Bates Medical Center, at the

Habitot Museum in Berkeley (www.habitot.org), and in private homes. Comment: "Great, well-informed teacher . . . very useful class."

The Nurture Center

3399 Mt. Diablo Blvd.
Lafayette
925-283-1346
www.nurturecenter.com
PARENT RATING: ☆ ☆ ☆ ☆ ☆

This highly recommended, full-service parenting center offers classes in newborn care, breastfeeding, childbirth preparation, hypnosis for birthing, infant massage, infant/child/adult CPR, childproofing, and postpartum adjustment, as well as a pregnancy support group. These are just a few of its many offerings! See also Chapters 5 and 6.

Pillowtalk

See listing under San Francisco, above.

Waddle and Swaddle

1677 Shattuck Ave.
Berkeley
510-540-7210
www.waddleandswaddle.com

A childbirth educator teaches these "community-oriented" childbirth preparation classes (series or one-day intensive) with a "holistic" approach. Classes cover labor preparation, nutrition, breastfeeding, and newborn care. There are also separate classes in infant massage, newborn care, and photographing babies, as well as support groups. See also Ch. 6.

Bay Area Birth Information

www.bayareabirthinfo.org

The mission of this non-profit group is to promote spontaneous labor and vaginal delivery, and "reduce unnecessary birth interventions." It operates as a referral service, with an online resource directory of providers (mostly located in the South Bay) who agree with their mission statement, including childbirth educators and hypnobirthing instructors. See also Ch. 5.

Birth Network of Santa Cruz County

www.birthnet.org

This website advocates private, non-hospital childbirth classes, and features a directory of local childbirth educators in Santa Cruz County. See also Ch. 5.

Blossom Birth Services

1000 Elwell Ct.
Palo Alto
650-964-7380
www.blossombirth.com

This nonprofit education, resource, and training center offers small group classes in childbirth preparation (both eclectic and natural approaches), hypnosis for childbirth, newborn care, breastfeeding, sibling preparation, twin preparation, infant massage, and CPR. They also maintain lists of local childbirth educators providing private classes (visit the center or their website). See also Chapters 5 and 6.

CHANGE of the Peninsula

400 Ben Franklin Court
San Mateo
650-340-9642
www.changeofthepeninsula.org

The Center for Healing and Global Evolution, or CHANGE, has a "mission to provide an environment for healing, learning, and growth." They offer a "Birthing from Within" childbirth preparation class taught by a doula, and a couple's yoga class to prepare for labor.

Patty Dougherty

831-475-0451
pattyd@aawsom.com

PARENT RATING: ☆ ☆ ☆ ☆

This certified childbirth educator offers childbirth preparation classes either in a group setting in Redwood City or in a private class at the client's home.

Harmony Birth Resources

621 E. Campbell Ave., Ste. 14
Campbell
408-370-3702
www.harmonybirth.com

This combination yoga studio and childbirth education center offers classes with a holistic approach, including "Birthing from Within," breastfeeding, what to expect in childbirth, infant care, infant massage, "natural remedies" for pregnancy, and signing with babies.

Metropolitan Adult Education Program

1224 Del Mar Ave.
San Jose
408-947-2300
www.metroed.net

This organization offers classes throughout San Jose and Campbell in childbirth preparation and Lamaze, newborn care, infant massage, and CPR.

Los Olivos Women's Medical Group Childbirth Education Program

Mission Oaks Hospital
Wellness Center
15891 Almaden Rd., Ste. 100
Los Gatos
408-356-0431 ext. 209
www.losolivos-obgyn.com

This medical group offers childbirth preparation classes (series or one-day intensive) taught by RNs.

Palo Alto Medical Foundation, Education Division

795 El Camino Real
Palo Alto
650-853-2960
www.pamf.org

PARENT RATING: ☆ ☆ ☆ ☆

This medical group offers classes in breastfeeding, pregnancy and new-born care, and childbirth preparation. It also offers classes in its Fremont location.

Santa Clara Adult Education

1840 Benton St.
Santa Clara
408-423-3500
www.scae.org

This community group offers CPR and first aid for parents and day care providers, as well as many parenting programs for after your baby's birth. See also Ch. 6.

Labor Doulas

A labor doula, also called a labor assistant or labor coach, can help mothers before, during, and after birth with physical, emotional, and informational support. Before birth, a doula will meet with the family to decide on a birth plan. During labor, the doula generally comes to the home and then the hospital to help you relax and get through labor, using massage and relaxation techniques. In addition, the doula can serve as your advocate at the hospital, especially when hospital staff members change shifts. Most doulas focus on a natural, nonmedicated approach to labor. Some doulas also work with families in the postpartum period—doing everything from helping with breastfeeding, to cleaning, doing laundry, running errands, caring for older siblings, and cooking. Some also do pre- and postnatal massage. For more on postpartum doulas, see Ch. 5. In the Bay Area, fees ranged from $500 to $1500 for labor support in 2005.

Doulas are not licensed or regulated by the state. And unless they also have a nursing or midwifery background, they do not have medical training. They have learned by attending many births over the years, and that's why it's important to find one with a lot of experience. To avoid conflict, make sure the doula understands her role is for emotional support, not to take the place of your doctor or midwife. You also should ask your doctor or midwife whether he or she minds having a doula in the delivery room. Before hiring a doula, make sure you are very comfortable with her on a personal level. Obviously, it's a rather personal decision to have a doula in addition to your partner in the delivery room. If it's the right fit, however, many moms reported it was a nice treat to have someone taking care of them during the birth and postpartum.

To learn more about doulas, local moms recommend reading *The Doula Book: How a Trained Labor Companion Can Help You Have a Shorter, Easier, and Healthier Birth*, by Marshall Klaus, MD, John Kennell, MD, and Phyllis Klaus, MEd.

How do you find a doula? Again, word of mouth is probably the best method. Your doctor or midwife may also have a list of doulas with whom he or she is comfortable working. As in a child care provider search, be sure to check at least 3 references, particularly since no government agency regulates doula services. You may even want to do a full background check. Ask the prospective candidates about their backgrounds, experience, and philosophies, as well as provisions for backup. National organizations such as ALACE, CAPPA, and ICEA, listed above under prenatal education, can help you find local labor doulas who have gone through a particular organization's training program. You may also contact DONA, listed below, for local referrals to their certified doulas. In addition, several Bay Area resource centers regularly offer "doula nights" where parents may meet local doulas, as well as providing referrals. Contact DayOne or Natural Resources in San Francisco, Barefoot and Pregnant in Marin, Waddle and Swaddle in Berkeley, Birthways in Oakland, The Nurture Center in Lafayette, Change of the Peninsula in San Mateo, or Blossom Birth Services in Palo Alto. All are listed above under Prenatal Education.

For referral sources for birth doulas and postpartum doulas, listings of individual doulas, and more information about postpartum doulas, check out Ch. 5.

Doulas of North America (DONA)
P.O. Box 626
Jasper, IN 47547
801-756-7331 or 888-788-DONA
www.dona.com
PARENT RATING: ☆ ☆ ☆ ☆ ☆
This professional association includes doulas who have completed training and agreed to the DONA Code of Ethics and Standards of Practice. The website lists doulas by region.

Cord Blood Banking

Cord blood banking is a relatively new phenomenon. In this procedure, cells from a newborn's umbilical cord are collected immediately after the baby and placenta have been delivered. Then the blood is either donated to a blood bank for public use or stored at a private blood bank for future personal use. Because cord blood contains a high percentage of stem cells (the cells that create other cells and are found in bone marrow), it has been used instead of marrow for people needing transplants for diseases like cancer, leukemia, and sickle cell anemia. Cord blood cells also appear to pose fewer transplant barriers than bone marrow, allowing a greater number of potential recipients.

Particularly for those with a family history of such diseases (e.g., with an older child suffering from leukemia), banking a younger sibling's cord blood may make sense. However, the American Academy of Pediatrics has concluded that there is not enough evidence to warrant the *routine* collection and storage of cord blood. Cord blood banked for personal use is handled by private companies. Currently the industry is unregulated, though there have been calls for regulation as some private cord blood banks have gone bankrupt. The cost of private banking for one year ranged from $1,100 to $2,000 in 2005. The National Institute of Health (NIH) nonprofit cord blood banks are solely for public donation, and while the AAP encourages public donation over private banking, currently there are no public cord blood donation sites in the Bay Area. Either way, you need to plan early (at least 2 months before delivery for some banks) if you would like to have your baby's cord blood collected. The research on this topic is evolving, so talk to your doctor about the latest pros and cons in your particular circumstances and about the current transplant success rates. Also, if you are considering banking cord blood, check out a very useful website: www.parentsguide.cordblood.com.

PUBLIC CORD BLOOD DONATION

Children's Hospital Oakland Children's Research Institute Western Area Community Cord Blood Bank

510-450-7605
www.chori.org/siblingcordblood/index.html
Children's Hospital is home to a sibling cord blood donation program funded by the NIH.

National Marrow Donor Program

800-627-7692
www.marrow.org
Call or check the website to find out about the current locations and status of cord blood donation programs in the Bay Area, or to get a volunteer packet.

Stemcyte

400 Rolyn Place
Arcadia, CA 91007
866-783-6298
www.stemcyte.com
This private corporation aims to be the largest donor cord blood bank in the world, and collects cord blood at no charge at various hospitals.

PRIVATE CORD BLOOD BANKS

All of these private cord blood banks were accredited by the American Association of Blood Banks as of 2005:

California Cryobank, Inc.

3228 Nebraska Ave.
Santa Monica, CA 90404
800-400-3430
www.mycordblood.com

Cord Blood Registry (CBR)

1200 Bayhill Dr., Ste. 301
San Bruno, CA 94066
888-932-6568
www.cordblood.com
This company also offers free storage to families needing to store cord blood for a sick family member.

Cryo-Cell International

3165 McMullen Booth Rd., Bldg. B
Clearwater, FL 33761
800-786-7235
www.cryo-cell.com

Lifebank USA
45 Horsehill Rd.
Cedar Knolls, NJ 07927
877-543-3226
www.lifebankusa.com

Viacord
245 First St.
Cambridge, MA 02142-1292
866-668-4895
www.viacord.com

Infertility and Third-Party Reproduction

Over 6 million American women and their partners suffer from infertility—that's about 10% of the U.S. population of reproductive age. Fortunately, medical advances have made it possible for many of those couples to have children. Techniques range from surgically correcting problems with the male or female reproductive system, to prescribing drugs to stimulate ovulation, to employing assisted reproductive technologies (ART). The most well-known ART is in vitro fertilization (IVF). Techniques are evolving, so be sure to check with your doctor for the latest developments.

If you are experiencing fertility problems, first talk to your OB/GYN. He or she may give you some tests and/or prescribe medication, or may directly refer you to a reproductive endocrinologist. For more on how to find a specialist locally, see below. For male fertility issues, see a urologist with a sub-specialty in andrology. Be sure you see a genuine board-certified specialist and not merely a physician with an interest in fertility. To check a doctor's credentials, see the *Directory of Board-Certified Medical Specialists* (available in most public libraries), or the American Board of Medical Specialties (www.abms.org). Always check a physician's background with the California Medical Board (www.medbd.ca.gov).

You can also check the success rates of potential clinics. The Society for Assisted Reproductive Technology (SART) and the Center for Disease Control (CDC) report live birth data. Visit the CDC's website (www.cdc.gov/nccdphp/drh/art.htm) to see the report, or call the CDC (770-488-5372) to get a printed copy. SART's website (http://sart.org) also lists member clinics meeting its quality standards.

The costs for these procedures vary widely. The U.S. average cost of an IVF cycle in 2004 was $12,400. Locally, patients report spending $12,000-17,000 or more for a full cycle at a private clinic. A large part of that cost is the medication, and some local parents report purchasing the drugs outside the U.S. at substantially reduced prices. California law requires group health insurers covering hospital, medical, or surgical expenses to *offer* employers coverage for infertility diagnosis and treatment. But nothing requires employers to buy the coverage. And IVF is not a covered treatment under the law. Check your insurance plan carefully. In addition, some clinics offer package plans for a flat fee, in which some of the fee will be refunded if the treatment is not successful. These outcome-based plans have raised ethical questions in the medical community. For more information, contact RESOLVE, see resources below.

Third-party reproduction uses eggs, sperm, embryos, or a uterus donated by a third person (donor) to allow an infertile person or couple to have children. Donors may be known or anonymous. Either way, experts advise consulting an attorney familiar with the legal issues. Most of the time, contracts need to be signed before these procedures are done, and sometimes adoption needs to take place afterward. Experts also recommend seeing a professional counselor to help with the psychological issues of third-party reproduction. Many of the clinics listed below have counselors on staff or provide referrals. Costs of these procedures are generally higher than for traditional IVF because third-party donors must be compensated for their expenses and inconvenience. Many expenses will not be covered by your own health insurance since the procedures involve treatment of a third party. For example, local parents estimate spending as much as $75,000 in the surrogacy process on agency fees, legal work, and the surrogate's expenses and fees. Going solo eliminates the agency fee, but local parents report it's a long, difficult process to find a qualified surrogate on one's own. They found agencies provided more qualified surrogates and helped greatly with the administrative process, which otherwise can be a huge headache.

REGULATION OF FERTILITY PROGRAMS

Fertility clinics, laboratories, and donor programs are regulated by voluntary professional organization guidelines and some federal and state laws. Federal law requires ART clinics to report their success rates to the CDC, see above, and also requires andrology labs to register with the Health Care Finances Administration (HCFA) and to adhere to strict standards. Surrogacy agencies, however, are not regulated, so be sure to check references carefully given what is at stake—and the amount of money you will be entrusting to them! Here are some places to seek advice about clinical practices and ethics:

American Association of Tissue Banks (AATB)
1320 Old Chainbridge Rd., Ste. 450
McLean, VA 22101
703-827-9582
www.aatb.org
This nonprofit professional organization publishes a list of sperm banks meeting its guidelines for donor testing, screening, and specimen storage.

American Society for Reproductive Medicine (ASRM)
1209 Montgomery Hwy.
Birmingham, AL 35216
205-978-5000
www.asrm.com
This professional organization (along with SART) publishes minimum standards for ART programs as well as guidelines for laboratories and donation programs.

California Department of Health Services
Licensing and Certification
916-552-8700 or 800-236-9747
www.dhs.ca.gov
This department licenses fertility clinics in California.

College of American Pathologists
325 Waukegan Rd.
Northfield, IL 60093
800-323-4040
www.cap.org
About one-third of all clinics reporting statistics to SART are accredited voluntarily by this lab accreditation program.

QUESTIONS TO ASK ABOUT FERTILITY PROGRAMS

In selecting a fertility program, you'll want to consider not only the physicians' experience, but also the clinic's location (it's important for some procedures that the clinic be located close to your home), cost (since treatment may not be covered by insurance), the clinic's embryologist's experience, and success rates. In general, you will want to ask all of the questions you would ask a prospective obstetrician, as discussed earlier, plus the following:

◆ What are the physicians' credentials and experience?

- Is the doctor a member of the American Society for Reproductive Medicine? Is the clinic a member of the Society for Assisted Reproductive Technologies (SART)? Does the program meet the ASRM guidelines? Is the lab accredited?
- What is the fee structure? Are payment plans available? Does insurance cover the fees?
- Are the lab and ultrasound open on weekends and holidays? Can procedures be done on weekends? (This may be important to your treatment.)
- What procedures does the doctor perform?
- What are the clinics' success rates? Specifically, what are the clinics' live birth vs. pregnancy rates?
- Based on your own particular situation, what would be your likelihood of success?
- What tests will the doctor order before recommending ART?
- Does the clinic have counselors available?
- Does the clinic freeze extra embryos? If yes, what are the fees?
- If you are considering third-party reproduction, be sure to ask about affiliated donation banks, referrals to potential surrogates, donor and surrogate selection and screening, consent, compensation, and confidentiality.

GENERAL INFERTILITY RESOURCES

American Society for Reproductive Medicine
PARENT RATING: ☆ ☆ ☆ ☆ ☆

See the listing under Regulation of Fertility Programs, above. This professional organization has a comprehensive website featuring fact sheets, lists of member physicians by geographic area, and links to other resources (notably the affiliated Society of Reproductive Surgeons, www.reprodsurgery.org).

Organization of Parents Through Surrogacy (OPTS)
P.O. Box 8170
Gurnee, IL 60031
847-782-0224
www.opts.com

This national surrogacy support group provides information, networking, support, and referrals.

RESOLVE
7910 Woodmont Ave., Ste. 1350
Bethesda, MD 20814
888-623-0744 (help line)
www.resolve.org
PARENT RATING: ☆ ☆ ☆ ☆ ☆

Local parents highly recommend this national nonprofit infertility association and its local chapter. It provides advice, publications, and referrals to specialists. The website provides a wealth of information and links to other resources; it's a great place to start your research.

RESOLVE of Northern California

312 Sutter St., Ste. 405
San Francisco
415-788-6772
415-788-3002 (telephone assistance program)
www.resolvenc.org
PARENT RATING: ☆ ☆ ☆ ☆ ☆

This local chapter offers a telephone assistance program that allows you to speak confidentially with a peer counselor and obtain professional referrals. It also offers monthly workshops, support groups, infertility awareness meetings, pre-adoption meetings, symposia on infertility and adoption, a newsletter, and a library.

Society for Reproductive Endocrinology and Infertility

www.socrei.org
The website of this national professional organization of board-certified reproductive endocrinologists lists members by geographic area.

CLINICS AND DOCTORS

Advanced Fertility Associates Medical Group
Sae Sohn, MD

1100 S. Eliseo Dr., Ste. 107
Greenbrae
415-464-8688
www.marinfertility.com

Alta Bates Medical Center In Vitro Fertilization Program
Ryszard Chetkowski, MD

2999 Regent St., Ste. 101-A
Berkeley
510-649-0440
www.abivf.com
PARENT RATING: ☆ ☆ ☆ ☆ ☆

Fertility Physicians of Northern California
G. David Adamson and Valerie Baker, MDs

• Palo Alto
  540 University Ave., Ste. 200
• San Jose
  2581 Samaritan Dr., Ste. 302
800-597-2234
www.fpnc.com

Craig Marble, LAc

San Francisco
415-595-1073
cmarble@speakeasy.org
PARENT RATING: ☆ ☆ ☆ ☆ ☆

This alternative healer uses nutrition, Chinese herbal medicine, and acupuncture for fertility issues and prenatal and postpartum care. Comment: "I had an ultra high-risk pregnancy. Craig's skillful and compassionate care helped me overcome a history of miscarriage. . . . My family knows him as 'the miracle worker.'"

Pacific Fertility Center (PFC)
Philip Chenette, Carolyn Givens, Carl Herbert, Isabelle Ryan, and Eldon Schriock, MDs

55 Francisco St., Ste. 500
San Francisco
415-834-3095
www.infertilitydoctor.com
PARENT RATING: ☆ ☆ ☆ ☆ ☆

PFC also offers an egg donor agency to patients.

Reproductive Science Center
Susan Willman, MD

- Orinda
  89 Davis Rd., Ste. 280
  925-254-0444
- San Ramon
  3160 Crow Canyon Rd., Ste. 150
  925-867-1800
- Fremont
  1999 Mowry Ave., Ste. 1
  510-494-2000
www.rscbayarea.com

Stanford Medical Center
Reproductive Endocrinology and
Infertility (REI) Center

300 Pasteur Dr., Ste. A370
Stanford
650-498-7911
www.stanfordivf.com

The center also offers support groups for people experiencing infertility.

UCSF Center for Reproductive Health/
UCSF In Vitro Fertilization Program
Marcelle Cedars and
Victor Fujimoto, MDs

2356 Sutter St., 7th Fl.
San Francisco
415-353-7475
www.ucsfivf.org
PARENT RATING: ☆ ☆ ☆ ☆ ☆

Wu's Healing Center

1014 Clement St.
San Francisco
415-752-0170
www.wushealingcenter.com

This alternative medicine center provides infertility evaluations and pre- and postnatal treatments with acupuncture, acupressure, and Chinese herbs.

Zouves Fertility Center
Christo Zouves, MD

901 Campus Dr., Ste. 214
Daly City
800-800-1160
www.goivf.com

AGENCIES AND ATTORNEYS

California Cryobank, Inc.

700 Welch Rd., Ste. 103
Palo Alto
650-324-1900
www.cryobank.com

Mary Cedarblade, Esq.

P.O. Box 477
Fairfax
415-459-8994
E-mail: cedarblade@aol.com

Center for Surrogate Parenting

15821 Ventura Blvd., Ste. 675
Encino, CA 91436
818-788-8288
www.creatingfamilies.com

Family Fertility Center

2855 Mitchell Dr., Ste. 104
Walnut Creek
925-977-4850
www.surromother.com

Law Offices of Diane Michelsen

3190 Old Tunnel Rd.
Lafayette
800-877-1880
www.familyformation.com

Woman to Woman Fertility Center

3201 Danville Blvd., Ste. 160
Alamo
925-820-9495
www.womantowomanfertilitycenter.com

Adoption

Adoption is another option for those who cannot or choose not to have children. There are basically 4 different approaches to adoption in California: private agency adoption, public agency adoption, independent adoption, or international adoption.

In a *private agency* adoption, the agency helps you through the application process, does the home study, offers parent education, locates a child, places the child, does post-placement follow-up, and helps finalize the adoption. (In a home study, a social worker meets with and assesses the prospective parents. You'll need to provide income and medical histories, and undergo background checks.) You may also locate a birth mother on your own and have the agency do everything else. Either way, you will need an attorney to do the legal end of the work, and you should have your own attorney represent you even if the agency has its own. Make sure the agency is licensed by the State of California and has no consumer complaints filed against it. (Check with the Adoptions Branch of the California Department of Social Services.) Also, check to see that the agency is accredited by the Council on Accreditation for Children and Families Services. Your attorney should be in good standing with the State Bar of California and preferably a member of a specialized association of adoption attorneys. Local families say the process takes at least a year from home study to a child's placement. Costs range from $5,000-30,000, with local families reporting spending about $10,000-15,000. The main cost variable is how much of the birth mother's expenses you pay. (California law allows the adopting family to pay certain medical and living expenses, but not to pay placement fees.) The private agency's advantage is its experience and resources, but its disadvantage is that the wait may be longer than in independent adoption.

In a *public agency adoption,* the agency performs functions similar to those of a private agency. But public agencies, run by the California Department of Social Services, work to place children who are already in the system, meaning their parents' rights have been involuntarily terminated for one reason or another. Generally, this means older children rather than newborns, and may mean children with special needs. The chief advantage of working with a public agency is the cost—it is nominal (zero to $2,500), and financial assistance or subsidies may be available. The disadvantages are having to deal with bureaucracies (and if you wish to adopt a newborn, there are very few available).

In *independent* adoption, you hire a facilitator to do the search (or you conduct a search on your own), a social worker or agency to do the home study, and an attorney to finalize the adoption. You gain a greater degree of control over the process (and you may shorten the time to adopt), but a search on your own requires a lot of time, you may have no recourse if the birth parent takes off with your money, you won't have post-adoption follow-up, and it may be more expensive ($8,000-30,000+). In addition, facilitators (unless they are also attorneys) are not licensed, so there is no governmental oversight.

International adoption has become more and more popular recently. California ranked second in the nation in international adoptions in 2005, with more than 1,000 children coming here from foreign countries yearly. In international adoption, you will also work with an agency, but to adopt a child from overseas. This usually means the domestic agency (working with foreign agencies or facilitators) will help you go through home study, locate a child, get INS approval to bring the orphan back to the U.S., and finalize the adoption overseas. Costs range from $7,000 to $25,000, not including travel costs, but they depend on the country. In the Bay Area, the most popular countries from which to adopt children are China and Russia. Adopting internationally is generally a more predictable (and faster) process than domestic adoption. But the information you receive about the child's medical and social history may be limited, and some countries restrict certain people from adopting (such as single parents or same-sex couples).

No matter which approach you take, check with the IRS and your tax adviser regarding the current status of tax credits for adoption expenses (www.irs.ustreas.gov) and your employer for adoption benefits and leave policies. The Family and Medical Leave Act does cover adopting parents, and many employers are offering adoption benefits.

QUESTIONS TO ASK AN ADOPTION AGENCY OR ATTORNEY

Be sure to check references of anyone you hire, preferably by contacting parents who have already gone through the process. Most reputable agencies and attorneys will provide you a list of references.

◆ How many years have you been in business? How many adoptions do you do per year? What is your accreditation and licensure (agencies)? Are you a member of the bar (attorneys)?

◆ What types of services do you offer (domestic, international, birth mother search, open adoption, pre- and post-adoption support and education)?

◆ How long does an adoption take?

◆ How much does it cost (ask for it to be itemized in writing and in advance)?

◆ What do you need to do the home study and to approve parents?

◆ Are there age, religion, or race restrictions for prospective parents, or restrictions on single parents, working parents, parents with other children, or same-sex couples?

◆ What kind of information will I receive about the child and the birth parents?

GENERAL ADOPTION RESOURCES

www.Adopting.org

www.Adoption.com

www.Adoptionprofessionals.com

www.Adoptivefamilies.com

These websites offer searchable directories of adoption resources.

www.adoptachild.org

Access the Inter-Country Adoption Registry, a database and forum of information about agencies provided by parents who have been through the process.

Council on Accreditation for Children and Family Services, Inc.
120 Wall St., 11th Fl.
New York, NY 10005
212-797-3000
www.coanet.org
This national organization accredits adoption agencies.

International Adoption Clinic Children's Hospital Oakland
747 52nd St.
Oakland
510-428-3010
PARENT RATING: ☆ ☆ ☆ ☆ ☆

This clinic provides pre-adoption medical consults and record reviews of adoptees from foreign countries, plus post-adoption medical evaluation, developmental screening, and counseling.

National Adoption Information Clearinghouse

330 C St., SW
Washington, DC 20447
888-251-0075
http://naic.acf.hhs.gov
PARENT RATING: ☆ ☆ ☆ ☆ ☆

This congressionally established agency provides an invaluable website that should be your first step in researching adoption. They have information on every conceivable aspect of adoption and list local resources.

Natural Resources

816 Diamond St.
San Francisco
415-550-2611
www.naturalresourcesonline.com
PARENT RATING: ☆ ☆ ☆ ☆ ☆

This center periodically offers a workshop on adoption featuring local attorneys, social workers, and facilitators.

PACT, An Adoption Alliance

4179 Piedmont Ave.
Oakland
510-243-9490
888-448-8277 (Adoptive Parent Peer Support Line)
www.pactadopt.org

This nonprofit organization provides adoption-related services for children of color and their families. This is not a licensed adoption agency, but they facilitate adoptions and offer educational events, counseling, and post-adoption services. Their website is very useful.

RESOLVE

PARENT RATING: ☆ ☆ ☆ ☆ ☆

See the listing under General Infertility Resources, above. National and local chapters provide useful publications and highly recommended local workshops on adoption.

U.S. Citizenship and Immigration Services (USCIS)

800-375-5283
www.uscis.gov

This agency oversees inter-country adoptions. Get their publication M-249, "The Immigration of Adopted and Prospective Adoptive Children."

U.S. Department of State, Office of Children's Issues

202-736-9130
www.travel.state.gov

This agency provides information about international adoption (by country) and U.S. visa requirements.

AGENCIES

ACCEPT

339 S. San Antonio Rd., Ste. 1A
Los Altos
650-917-8090
www.acceptadoptions.org
Also offices in San Francisco and San Rafael
PARENT RATING: ☆ ☆ ☆ ☆ ☆

This licensed nonprofit agency for international adoption works throughout the Bay Area. They provide counseling, home study, country selection, child referral, and post-placement services. They will also do home study and post-placement services for independent domestic adoptions. Parents called ACCEPT "efficient,

70

supportive, and helpful . . . everyone I know has had a good experience with them."

Adopt International

1000 Brannan St., Ste. 301
San Francisco
415-934-0300
www.adopt-intl.org
Also offices in Oakland, Petaluma, and Menlo Park

This licensed nonprofit agency operates throughout the Bay Area. They offer international and domestic adoption, outreach services, counseling, birth parent screening services, education, home study, post-placement services, and social activities for adoptive families.

Adoption Connection (Jewish Family and Children's Services)

1710 Scott St.
San Francisco
415-359-2494
www.adoptionconnection.org
PARENT RATING: ☆ ☆ ☆ ☆ ☆

This licensed nonprofit, nonsectarian agency works throughout the Bay Area on domestic adoptions only. They are open to same-sex couples and offer many helpful workshops.

Bay Area Adoption Services, Inc. (BAAS)

465 Fairchild Dr., Ste. 215
Mountain View
650-964-3800
www.baas.org
PARENT RATING: ☆ ☆ ☆ ☆ ☆

Parents called this licensed nonprofit agency for international adoptions "experienced and ethical."

California Association of Adoption Agencies (CAAA)

www.california-adoption.org
This professional association of California adoption agencies lists its members on its helpful website.

California Department of Social Services, Adoptions Branch

744 P St.
Sacramento, CA 95814
800-KIDS-4-US
www.ChildsWorld.ca.gov
This bureau licenses adoption agencies, and its website has a directory of licensed private and public agencies.

The Family Network, Inc.

820 Bay Ave., Ste. 206
Capitola
831-462-8954
www.adopt-familynetwork.com
This licensed nonprofit agency for international adoption works throughout the Bay Area and will also do home study, counseling, and post-placement services for domestic adoption (no placement).

Future Families, Inc.

1671 The Alameda
San Jose
408-298-8789 or 888-922-KIDS
www.futurefamilies.org
This licensed nonprofit agency works with families in the 408, 415, 510, 650, and 831 area codes only. They provide domestic adoption and foster care services, focusing on fost-adopt (foster care leading to adoption), foster parent adoption, or concurrent (open) adoption. Their fees are minimal for fost-adopt services (and a

stipend may be available). They also provide home study, training, therapy, and support services.

Independent Adoption Center
391 Taylor Blvd.
Pleasant Hill
925-827-2229
www.adoptionhelp.org
This is the oldest and largest agency facilitating "open adoptions" (where birth parents and adoptive parents maintain contact).

Joint Council on International Children's Services
117 South Saint Asaph St.
Alexandria, VA 22314
703-535-8045
www.jcics.org
The oldest and largest affiliation of licensed, nonprofit international adoption organizations in the world, this group has a fabulous website.

Kinship Center
124 River Rd.
Salinas
831-649-3033
www.kinshipcenter.org
This licensed agency works statewide. They have a small infant adoption program but focus on fost-adopt for special needs children already in the system (fees may be waived or a subsidy available). They will also do home study for independent adoptions.

Partners for Adoption
800 S. Broadway, Ste. 210B
Walnut Creek
925-946-9658
www.partnersforadoption.org

This licensed nonprofit agency for international adoptions works with families statewide, and with agencies from countries all over the world. They also offer counseling, home study, and post-placement services.

ATTORNEYS

American Academy of Adoption Attorneys
Box 33053
Washington, DC 20033-0053
202-832-2222
www.adoptionattorneys.org
This is a professional organization of adoption attorneys providing referrals.

Academy of California Adoption Lawyers
818-501-8355
www.acal.org
The website of this specialized bar association for adoption and assisted reproduction attorneys lists members and has helpful answers to legal questions.

Gradstein and Gorman
Marc Gradstein, Attorney-at-Law
1204 Burlingame Ave., #7
Burlingame
650-347-7041

Law Offices of Adams and Romer
Susan Romer, Esq.
1191 Church St.
San Francisco
415-643-5423
www.adamsandromer.com

Law Offices of Diane Michelsen
See listing above under General Infertility Resources.

State Bar of California

180 Howard St.
San Francisco
415-538-2000
www.calbar.ca.gov

This organization licenses and disciplines attorneys. Check to make sure your attorney does not have a history of complaints or malpractice suits filed against him or her.

SUPPORT GROUPS FOR ADOPTIVE PARENTS

Cooperative Adoption Consulting Ellen Roseman

415-453-0902
www.adoption-facilitator.org
PARENT RATING: ☆ ☆ ☆ ☆ ☆

This well-regarded open adoption facilitator also runs support groups for adoptive and birth parents.

Families for Russian and Ukranian Adoptions (FRUA)

www.frua.org/norcal

This is a national organization with a Northern California regional chapter.

Families with Children from China

www.fwcc.org (national website)
www.fccncalif.org (local chapter)
E-mail: boardfccncalif@yahoo.com

This international network has a Northern California chapter and a helpful website. Prospective parents are welcome, and membership includes families with children from countries other than China.

Families Adopting in Response (FAIR)

650-856-3513 (warm line)
www.fairfamilies.org
PARENT RATING: ☆ ☆ ☆ ☆ ☆

This volunteer organization provides a magazine, local events, support groups, and educational workshops for adoptive families.

Las Madres

877-LAS-MADRES
www.lasmadres.org
adoptivemoms@lasmadres.org

This mothers' group has an Adoptive Moms support group for all types of adoptions, offering social events and a playgroup.

Neighborhood Parents Network

877-648-KIDS
www.npnonline.org

This East Bay parents' group has an extensive offering of volunteer support groups, including ones for adoptive families. See in Ch. 6 under Mothers' and Parents' Groups and Clubs—East Bay.

Parents Place

www.jfcs.org

Locations in San Francisco, San Rafael, Santa Rosa, and Palo Alto

This parenting center provides adoption and infertility counseling, and periodically offers workshops on issues relevant to adoptive families.

Stars of David

www.starsofdavid.org
PARENT RATING: ☆ ☆ ☆ ☆ ☆

This is a "great" nonprofit support and education group for Jewish families built through adoption. Find contact information for the 2 local chapters (East Bay and South Bay) on the website.

415-451-TAPS
TAPS provides a telephone advice line with referral, information, and support for parents raising adopted children.

Help for Kids With Special Needs

Parents of children with special needs will want to tap into the many local resources, from medical to educational programs, designed especially for children facing physical, psychological, or developmental challenges. We've listed some places to start, below. In addition, here are some tips from local parents of children with disabilities:

◆ Parent-run Family Resource Centers, see below for listing, are the best places to find out about local resources and parent support groups. This is where you should go to start your research and get help finding your way in the often confusing educational, governmental, and medical systems. Some of these centers also have very helpful mentor programs. For more information, go to www.frcnca.org (site for the coalition of California's 47 Family Resource Centers).

◆ State-funded Regional Centers, see below for listing, are also helpful resources for children with developmental disabilities. Since they implement all the Early Start (ages 0-3) programs, they should be your next stop.

◆ Learn about the federal and state laws regarding the rights of the disabled, so that you know your child's rights before, for example, you meet with a school district. An advocacy organization such as CASE, PAI, or DREDF, see below, can provide guidance and representation.

◆ Find a pediatrician specializing in developmental or behavioral pediatrics, or whichever specialty applies to your child's disability. Your local Family Resource Center or Regional Center is a great place to find referrals. You can also check out the pediatric departments of 3 leading hospitals: Children's Hospital Oakland, Lucile

Packard Children's Hospital at Stanford, and the University of California at San Francisco (see listings above under Hospitals).

◆ Contact your local school district for special education programs and testing (free and mandated by law).

◆ Check out your local library for books on tape and other resources for the disabled.

◆ Be proactive. You are your child's best advocate!

SPECIAL NEEDS RESOURCES

California Department of Developmental Services
P.O. Box 944202
Sacramento, CA 94244-2020
800-515-BABY (2229)
(Early Start Program)
www.dds.ca.gov

PARENT RATING: ☆ ☆ ☆ ☆ ☆ (for local regional centers)

This state agency provides services and support to children with developmental disabilities. The agency operates 7 Developmental Centers throughout California for inpatient treatment, and funds nonprofit, private Regional Centers to help families access local resources. Local Regional Centers are listed below. The agency also administers the "Early Start Program" of early intervention, information, and referrals for babies and toddlers with developmental disabilities, offered through a variety of public and private organizations.

Golden Gate Regional Center
• Corte Madera
5725 Paradise Dr., Ste. 100
(Building A), 415-945-1600
• San Francisco
120 Howard St., 415-546-9222

• San Mateo
3130 La Selva Dr., Ste. 202,
650-574-9232
www.ggrc.org

North Bay Regional Center
• Napa
10 Executive Ct., Ste. A, 707-256-1100
• Santa Rosa
2351 Mendocino Ave., 707-569-2000
www.nbrc.net

Regional Center of the East Bay
• Concord
2151 Salvio St., Ste. 365
925-798-3001
• Oakland
7677 Oakport St., Ste. 300
510-383-1200
www.rceb.org

San Andreas Regional Center
• Campbell
300 Orchard City Dr., Ste. 170
408-374-9960
• Gilroy
7855 Wren Ave., Ste. A
408-846-8805
www.sarc.org

Additional locations in Salinas and Watsonville

California Department of Health Services—California Children Services (CCS)

185 Barry St., Lobby 6, Ste. 255
San Francisco
415-904-9699 (Northern California regional office)
www.dhs.ca.gov

This state program provides medical services for physically disabled children in California. Services include diagnostic evaluation, treatment, referrals to specialists, and therapy. Families meeting certain income guidelines receive free or low-cost care; others pay based on a sliding scale. Every county has a CCS office through the county health department.

California Department of Health Services—Medically Vulnerable Infant Program

916-323-8010 (main office in Sacramento)
www.dhs.ca.gov

This state program provides home visits to families with "medically fragile" infants (graduates of NICUs) to minimize developmental delays. Services include case management, referrals, intervention, support, counseling and education, health and developmental assessments, and therapeutic consultation.

Center for Access to Resources and Education (CARE) Parent Network

1350 Arnold Dr., Ste. 115
Martinez
925-313-0999 or 800-281-3023
www.careparentnetwork.org

This Family Resource Center provides support groups, a warm line, education, referrals, and resources for Contra Costa County families of children with special needs. They offer an Early Start program from newborn to age 3.

Children's Council of San Francisco

445 Church St.
San Francisco
415-276-2900
www.childrenscouncil.org
PARENT RATING: ☆ ☆ ☆ ☆ ☆

This nonprofit resource and referral agency offers free information, training, and consultation to parents and caregivers of children with emotional and behavioral problems, and regularly publishes a list of local resources.

Children's Health Council

650 Clark Way
Palo Alto
650-326-5530
www.chconline.org
PARENT RATING: ☆ ☆ ☆ ☆ ☆

This organization provides programs and services for children with learning, behavioral, or developmental difficulties, including diagnosis, evaluation, therapy, research, parent education, and outreach.

Community Alliance for Special Education (CASE)

1500 Howard St.
San Francisco
415-431-2285

This nonprofit organization provides information and advocacy services for children needing special education.

Call for a handbook on special education rights and for a free consultation.

Disability Rights Education and Defense Fund (DREDF)

2212 Sixth St.
Berkeley
510-644-2555
www.dredf.org

PARENT RATING: ☆ ☆ ☆ ☆ ☆

This is the leading national law and policy center for disability civil rights, and they provide advocacy services for disabled persons and their families. Go to them to learn about your child's civil rights, particularly educational rights. Comment: "They put me in touch with everyone I needed. . . . They saved me!"

Family Resource Center at Community Gatepath

1764 Marco Polo Way
Burlingame
650-259-0189
www.communitygatepath.com

PARENT RATING: ☆ ☆ ☆ ☆ ☆

This Family Resource Center provides support and education to families of children with special needs in San Mateo County. They publish a useful special needs resource directory for San Mateo County.

Family Resource Network

5232 Claremont Ave.
Oakland
510-547-7322
www.frnoakland.org

PARENT RATING: ☆ ☆ ☆ ☆ ☆

This highly recommended Family Resource Center provides advocacy, support groups, training, and resources for families with children with disabilities in Alameda County.

Matrix

94 Galli Dr., Ste. C
Novato
415-884-3535
www.matrixparents.org
Also locations in Napa, Rohnert Park, and Vallejo

PARENT RATING: ☆ ☆ ☆ ☆ ☆

This nonprofit Family Resource Center provides support, information, training, and referrals for families of children with disabilities in Marin, Sonoma, Napa, and Solano counties.

Parents Helping Parents

3141 Olcott St.
Santa Clara
408-727-5775
www.php.com

PARENT RATING: ☆ ☆ ☆ ☆ ☆

This highly recommended nonprofit organization for parents of children with special needs in Santa Clara County offers an Early Intervention Program for infants and toddlers newborn to 3 years old, help with special education programs, support and information groups, a mentor parent program, an assistive technology center, a siblings program, parent training, and play groups.

Protection and Advocacy, Inc. (PAI)

100 Howe St., Ste. 185-N
Sacramento, CA 95825
800-776-5746
415-924-7416 (local advocacy office)
www.pai-ca.org

PARENT RATING: ☆ ☆ ☆ ☆ ☆

This "wonderful" advocacy group represents people with disabilities and their families, and works to advance the rights of the disabled.

Support for Families of Children with Disabilities/Open Gate Family Resource Center
2601 Mission St., 3rd Fl.
San Francisco
415-920-5040
www.supportforfamilies.org
PARENT RATING: ☆ ☆ ☆ ☆ ☆

This group and its "awesome" Family Resource Center (jointly run by Support for Families, CASE, and the SF Unified School District) offers support groups, peer counseling, and a warm line for families of children with disabilities in San Francisco. They publish a useful directory of local resources.

Through the Looking Glass
2198 Sixth St., Ste. 100
Berkeley
510-848-4445
www.lookingglass.org

This nonprofit group provides a national family resource center, support groups, and many evaluation, intervention, and support services for families of the disabled.

Your Rights in the Workplace

If you are a working parent-to-be, you should be aware of your rights in the workplace during pregnancy and after giving birth (or adopting a child). The following information incorporates only the minimum legal requirements; be sure to check your individual employment agreement or policies, which may be more generous.

◆ Federal and state laws prohibit employment *discrimination on the basis of pregnancy.* Thus, generally an employer can't fire or demote you, or refuse to hire you, because you are pregnant. A new state law requires employers to provide pregnant employees with "reasonable accommodations" related to pregnancy. For example, you may be able to transfer to a less strenuous position during pregnancy. If you can't do your job, you must be offered the same benefits as your employer offers other disabled workers (e.g., disability leave or easier duties).

◆ The federal Family and Medical Leave Act of 1993 (FMLA) and a similar state law (the California Family Rights Act) allow employees to take up to 12 weeks of *unpaid family and medical leave* when the employee is "unable to work because of a serious health condition" (including pregnancy or a family member's illness). Only public agencies and private employers with 50 or more employees are required to comply, and you must have worked for the employer for a year before you are eligible (and put in at least 1,250 hours during that year). Medical leave can be taken intermittently or on a reduced work schedule (e.g., for prenatal care, if you have periods of morning sickness rendering you unable to work, or if you are undergoing a series of fertility treatments requiring bed rest). Your employer must continue to maintain your group health insurance coverage and other benefits during your leave (on the same terms as if you had continued to work).

◆ Under the FMLA and state law, eligible employees may take up to 12 weeks of *unpaid leave* (in a 12-month period) *for the birth, adoption,* or *foster placement of a child.* This law applies to both men and women.

◆ In California, FMLA leave for the birth of a child can be added onto any *Pregnancy Disability Leave.* California law allows women to take up to 4 months of *unpaid,* doctor-certified, job-protected pregnancy disability leave before or after a child is born. In effect, then, you could take up to 7 months off for the birth of a child, provided you were actually "disabled" for 4 of those months. This disability law applies to employers with 5 or more employees and has no waiting time requirement or minimum hours of work requirement, significant benefits for California families.

◆ *California State Disability Insurance* (SDI) covers most non-government employees for pregnancy disability. SDI provides partial wage replacement during disability, up to a maximum of $840 per week in 2005. In most cases, the disability period for a normal pregnancy is up to 4 weeks before the due date and 6 weeks afterward. But your doctor may certify you for a longer period (e.g., for a Caesarean section).

◆ Recently, California became the first state in the nation to enact a *Paid Family Leave* (PFL) law. Recognizing that many people could not afford to take unpaid FMLA leave, the law allows employees to collect up to 6 weeks of compensation in a 12-month period when they are on leave to bond with their newborn (or adopted child), or to care for a seriously ill family member. Only employees who are covered by SDI or an employer's private plan can get partial pay through the state PFL insurance fund, up to a maximum of $840 per week in 2005. Paid leave must be taken during the FMLA leave, and not when the employee is already receiving SDI benefits for other reasons (e.g., pregnancy disability). Your employer may also require you to use up to 2 weeks of an earned but unused vacation leave. Go to www.paidfamilyleave.org for more information.

◆ Under the Family Medical Leave Act and state law, eligible employers must give employees taking FMLA leave their old job or an *"equivalent"* job with "equivalent" pay, benefits, and working conditions upon return from leave. Similarly, when you return from pregnancy disability leave, your employer must reinstate you to the same or a comparable position.

◆ If you intend to take leave, you should give your employer reasonable notice. Most experts advise telling your employer at the beginning of your second trimester. Be sure to review your leave and benefits plans with your human resources department (including getting your baby on your insurance plan), and make arrangements with your supervisor for someone to cover your responsibilities while you are gone.

Finally, bear in mind that studies have shown that taking longer maternity leave helps prevent or mitigate the symptoms of postpartum depression. So take as much as you can afford! Consider banking accrued vacation and sick days while you are pregnant to provide further compensation during postpartum leave. Go to www.workoptions.com to download a free guide for how to propose maternity leave to your employer.

WHERE TO GET HELP

If you feel your rights have been violated, or have questions about your individual situation, here are some organizations that can help:

Equal Employment Opportunity Commission (EEOC)

1801 L St., NW
Washington, DC 20507
800-669-EEOC
www.eeoc.gov

This federal agency enforces federal pregnancy discrimination laws.

Equal Rights Advocates

1663 Mission St., Ste. 250
San Francisco
415-621-0672
800-839-4ERA (advice and counseling hotline)
www.equalrights.org

PARENT RATING: ☆ ☆ ☆ ☆ ☆

This is a women's public interest law center engaged in litigation and public advocacy. The website has useful information about the FMLA and other pregnancy-related laws, and the hotline provides free assistance to women facing pregnancy discrimination and medical leave issues.

Legal Aid Society of San Francisco/Employment Law Center

600 Harrison St., Ste. 120
San Francisco
415-864-8848
800-880-8047 (Work and Family Project hotline)
www.las-elc.org

PARENT RATING: ☆ ☆ ☆ ☆ ☆

This public interest law center specializes in employment discrimination law, particularly family and medical leave issues. The center offers free advice and information through its hotline, limited representation, workshops to parents' groups, impact litigation, and lobbying and legislative work. The website has very helpful brochures on your workplace rights.

State of California, Department of Fair Employment and Housing

800-884-1684
www.dfeh.ca.gov

This department enforces state discrimination and medical leave laws, including the California Family Rights Act.

State of California, Employment Development Department SDI Program Offices

800-480-3287 (SDI program statewide)
877-238-4373 (PFL program statewide)
www.edd.ca.gov

The EDD administers the SDI and Paid Family Leave programs; get forms and apply for SDI and PFL benefits here.

U.S. Department of Labor– Wage and Hour Division

866-4-USWAGE
www.dol.gov/esa/whd

This federal agency enforces the FMLA and informs the public on working women's rights. Get a fact sheet on the FMLA.

CHAPTER 2

TAKING CARE OF YOURSELF: Pre- and Post- Natal Fitness

Regular, physician-approved exercise can be a great benefit to healthy women with low-risk pregnancies—it can increase energy levels, aid in sleeping and maintaining an appropriate weight gain, relieve many of the physical discomforts of pregnancy, minimize stress, and help the body prepare for labor and delivery. Exercise can also help speed up the postpartum recovery period. Many new moms, eager to shed those pregnancy pounds, reclaim their bodies through exercise. Reflecting the popularity in recent years of yoga and Pilates for pregnant and postpartum women, another benefit is the stretching and toning of muscles that have been used during labor. Yet another benefit to joining a pre- or postnatal exercise class is the bonding that occurs between women who are either getting ready to give birth or who are in the pospartum period of life with a new baby. Many enjoy sharing advice and the general camaraderie that occurs when they are able to work out and spend some time talking with women in similar situations. Of course, if you are pregnant, you should check with your physician before beginning any new exercise program. Many medical professionals say that pregnancy is not the best time to begin a new routine.

From pre- and postnatal aerobics, yoga, and swimming, to personal trainers with a special certification in working with pre- and postnatal women—there are plenty of exercise options for moms-to-be and new moms. In this chapter, we'll tell you about those that Bay Area parents have shared with us. We will help you answer the following questions:

- Where can I find a prenatal or postpartum exercise, yoga, or aqua-aerobics class?
- Where can I find a personal trainer who has experience working with prenatal and postpartum women?
- Where can I find a fitness center that offers child care?
- What are some good walks or hikes for me to take with my baby?
- Where can I get a prenatal or postpartum massage?

TIPS FOR PRE- AND POSTNATAL EXERCISE

- Always get your physician's approval before exercising during pregnancy or after delivery. Don't be surprised if many classes and fitness centers ask you for a note from your physician approving your exercise routine, especially if you are pregnant.
- Be sure to find out what credentials and experience your fitness instructor has in working with pregnant and postpartum women. There are several different certifications available, including Dancing Through Pregnancy, Moms in Motion, and Healthy Moms Fitness, which are recognized as industry leaders in providing training and certification to fitness instructors to teach pre- and postnatal exercise. The Aerobics and Fitness Association of America also offers a certification. For yoga certification, Whole Birth Yoga is a locally offered certification program for pre- and postnatal yoga instruction.
- Each trimester of your pregnancy brings its own demands, requiring you to modify your exercise. Be sure to check in with your instructor and physician and let them know where you are in your pregnancy and any special concerns you may have.

◆ Don't get overheated—drink lots of water and stop before the point of sweating profusely. Drink, drink, drink, and drink plenty of water before, during, and after exercising.

Pre- and Postnatal Aerobics, Yoga, Pilates, Fitness Classes, and Personal Trainers

Listed below are fitness centers, exercise and yoga studios, and hospitals that pregnant and postpartum women have recommended to us. Many of these centers offer drop-in classes, while some offer a series that requires advance registration, so be sure to call ahead first. Prices vary, but group exercise classes run from approximately $7 to $20 per class and personal trainers run from $50 to $120 per session. You can often buy a package of classes that reduces the individual price of each class or training session. Since class schedules, hours, and fees change frequently, please call ahead for up-to-the-minute information, or check the website (if available).

San Francisco

Baby Boot Camp
415-290-2764
www.babybootcamp.com
PARENT RATING: ☆ ☆ ☆ ☆ ☆

This 75-minute outdoor group strength-training workout that focuses on helping moms get back into shape has taken the Bay Area (as well as the country) by storm! Offering classes all over the Bay Area, Baby Boot Camp is ubiquitous! The classes are designed for mom and baby and focus on building strength, improving posture and core strength and flexibility, as well as functional exercises for motherhood. Moms bring their babies to class and use strollers as an integral part of the workout. Because no babysitter or day care is needed, Baby Boot Camp is the perfect solution for the woman who wants to maintain a healthy lifestyle while spending time with her child. Class times are flexible for working and stay-at-home moms. Kirsten Horler, a Certified Personal Trainer and mother of 2, launched Baby Boot Camp in the Bay Area in 2001 after she could not find a fitness program that addressed the physical and logistical challenges of being a mom. Since that time, the company has expanded the program through licensing. Now more than 125 cities in 17 states offer Baby Boot Camp classes. Bring water and either a yoga mat or blanket suitable for exercising on the grass. The class is compatible for babies either in a stroller, front carrier, or by the side of your mat. Participants are free to take care of their babies as needed. Visit their website or call for a class schedule for your area.

The Bar Method
3333 Fillmore St.
441-6333
www.barmethod.com
PARENT RATING: ☆ ☆ ☆ ☆ ☆

Opened in 2001 by Burr Leonard and Carl Diehl, the Bar Method™ has revolutionized how people are thinking about exercise. Dubbed "the new Pilates," the Bar Method is famous for creating long, firm thighs, lifted "seats" and pulled-in abs. The method combines yoga, isometrics, and orthopedic back exercises into a rigorous one-hour routine at a ballet bar and on floor mats. The workout, consisting of 8 or 9 strengthening exercises followed by stretches, maintains an intense pace and burns fat and increases stamina. They offer a pre- and postnatal class that follows the basic format of the regular class but with special modifications for expectant women. Pregnant clients are invited to take either class, with first-time pregnant clients being required to take the prenatal class for 5 sessions before joining a regular class. Pregnant clients can then take the regular class, and teachers gladly assist with modifications to the workout as needed. Pregnant clients are asked to bring in a note from their doctor stating that strengthening and stretching exercise classes are safe for them. The Bar Method offers child care for morning classes in its expanded child care room; reservations are recommended. Between the inviting aroma of freshly brewed coffee each morning and other amenities such as an immaculate locker room, massage services, and great child care, the Bar Method is a true haven for every new mother! Visit their webpage and look for the "new mom special" which is a best kept secret!

Bay Club
150 Greenwich St.
415-433-2200
www.sfbayclub.com
The Bay Club offers popular pre- and postnatal yoga classes with Kari Marble. See below under Individual Pre- and Postnatal Fitness Instructors.

Bernal Yoga
461 Cortland Ave.
415-643-9007
www.bernalyoga.com
This yoga studio offers prenatal, mom and baby yoga, and toddler yoga.

California Pacific Medical Center (CPMC)
3698 California St.
2nd Fl. Rehab Gym
415-600-0500
www.cpmc.org (Women's Health Resource Center)
CPMC offers In-Shape Prenatal Fitness, an ongoing prenatal exercise program that meets twice a week for a 60-minute workout. It includes low-impact aerobics and yoga stretches led by 2 physical therapists for expectant moms. CPMC also offers Kari Marble's popular Prenatal Yoga class one night a week. This 90-minute class teaches pregnant women meditations, visualizations, breath practice and yoga poses that are tailored to meet the needs and abilities of all participants.

The Dailey Method

3249 Scott St.

415-345-9992

www.thedaileymethod.com

PARENT RATING: ☆ ☆ ☆ ☆ ☆

The Dailey Method—the Bay Area's original barre class—promises to make you longer, leaner, stronger, and fit! This rigorous one-hour workout includes a combination of ballet barre work, core strengthening, yoga, and orthopedic exercises. The Dailey Method welcomes pregnant women with a written note of consent from their doctor. Since they opened in 2000, they have had many pre- and postnatal clients and teachers, including founder Jill Dailey McIntosh, take the class throughout their pregnancies with minor modifications to the workout. Teachers gladly assist expecting clients with such modifications. Child care is available Monday through Friday mornings.

Day One

3490 California St., 2nd Fl.

415-440-3291

www.dayonecenter.com

PARENT RATING: ☆ ☆ ☆ ☆ ☆

This inviting state-of-the-art center for new and expectant parents offers a "Smart Nutrition for Mom" workshop as well as one on "Getting Your Body Back." For full write-up, see Ch. 5.

Ellie Herman Studios

1452 Valencia St.

415-285-5808

www.ellie.net

This popular Pilates studio doesn't offer anything specifically for pre- or postnatal women, but rather offers many different levels of Pilates workouts (both mat work and equipment), which pregnant and postpartum women often attend.

Fitness for Mothers

415-215-2986

www.fitnessformothers.com

anna@fitnessformothers.com

A former Club One/Pinnacle Fitness trainer and mother, Anna Ostashevskaya offers several unique 60-minute programs to mothers that focus on postpartum fitness including aerobic exercise and resistance training with flexibility work. Her classes include Stonestown Strollers, which is a free weekly fitness stroll for new moms and their babies; the Ocean Beach Strollex, which meets seasonally, and a Creative Motion class for moms and toddlers, which is a serious 55-minute circuit workout and is held at Congregation Sherith Israel, 2266 California Street. Anna also offers one-on-one personal training and several other classes related to prenatal and postpartum fitness. Anna O., as she is known, is an ACE certified personal trainer and "maternal wellness" consultant.

Integral Yoga Institute

770 Dolores St.

415-821-1117

www.integralyoga.org

The institute offers a prenatal Hatha yoga class. They also offer a parent and baby yoga class for newborns and pre-crawling babies. This class includes gentle stretching, chanting, breathing, deep relaxation, and discussion.

International Orange

2044 Fillmore St.
888-894-8811
www.internationalorange.com
This clean-swept ultra-modern yoga studio is many mothers' favorite oasis. They offer primarily Hatha yoga classes, including a prenatal class, as well as spa services.

Iyengar Yoga Institute

2404 27th Ave.
415-753-0909
www.iyisf.org
Featured in the December 2000 issue of *American Baby* magazine, this studio offers a popular prenatal yoga class and a parent/baby class for postpartum women or dads and their pre-crawling infants. Classes are open to all levels; no previous experience is necessary.

Jewish Community Center of San Francisco

3200 California St.
415-292-1234
www.jccsf.org
PARENT RATING: ☆ ☆ ☆ ☆ ☆

This gleaming, state-of the-art fitness center opened its doors in early 2004 in the new JCC building and offers myriad excellent classes for expectant women and new mothers alike. Kim Becker, group exercise and Pilates manager, and Jennifer Morrice, yoga manager, are spearheading this effort. They offer a group prenatal and postnatal fitness classes, as well as prenatal yoga and a Mommy/Daddy and Me yoga class taught by Rachel Yellin, who is certified in prenatal yoga and is also a certified doula. In the aquatics department, they offer a popular prenatal aqua fitness class. They also offer a 75-minute outdoor stroller fitness class for moms and babies. The JCC is also staffed with several personal trainers who have pre- and postnatal training and certification, and child care is available with an advance reservation. Comment: "Excellent prenatal yoga and prenatal water aerobics."

Kaiser Permanente San Francisco Medical Center

2425 Geary Blvd., Mezzanine level
415-833-4120
This hospital offers pre- and postnatal yoga. Babies are welcome to the postnatal class. See Whole Birth Yoga below.

The Kundalini Yoga Center

1390 Waller St.
415-978-3932
415-863-0132 (frequently answered voice mail)
This center offers prenatal yoga classes.

The Mindful Body

2876 California St.
415-931-2639
www.themindfulbody.com
PARENT RATING: ☆ ☆ ☆ ☆ ☆

Consistently voted the "Best Yoga Studio" by *The San Francisco Chronicle*, The Mindful Body offers prenatal and postpartum yoga classes, specifically designed for pregnant and postpartum women to enhance the body's ability to move comfortably through the different stages of pregnancy and to recuperate from childbirth. Kari Marble's classes are very popular!

Natural Resources
816 Diamond St.
415-550-2611
www.naturalresourcesonline.com
This full-service parenting center offers, among many other classes, Nutrition for Healthy Pregnancy class, Is Your Body Ready? Prenatal Fitness Workshop, and Get Your Body Back! Postpartum Fitness Workshop.

Open Door Yoga
1500 Castro St.
415-824-5657
www.opendooryoga.com
This Noe Valley yoga studio offers a Mommy and Me yoga class where drop-ins are welcome or where you can buy a package. They also offer a prenatal/preparing-for-childbirth yoga class. Parents rave about many of the teachers, especially Jane Austin.

OutFit Fitness
1505 Northpoint St.
415-225-7795
www.outfitfitness.com
PARENT RATING: ☆ ☆ ☆ ☆ ☆

Get back into shape with this outdoor fitness training bootcamp. Owner and certified personal trainer Jennifer Jolly and her team of certified personal trainers lead a 75-90 minute rigorous outdoor fitness program in a variety of picturesque locations throughout the city. This Fitmom and Friends Boot Camp class, is specifically for pregnant women and new moms and their babies. The workout varies according to the fitness level of participants and includes cardio and strength training. They have an

inclement weather meeting spot in the neighborhood. Bring your baby and a jogger, stroller, or baby carrier and prepare for a challenging workout! Space is limited—early reservations recommended.

Comment: "The workouts are tough but great—I could never do a real push-up before or run 1½ miles, but now I feel much stronger and firm. I am totally addicted and cannot go back to working out in a club."

Presidio YMCA
Lincoln Way at Funston
(Building 63)
415-447-9622
www.ymcasf.org
PARENT RATING: ☆ ☆ ☆ ☆ ☆

This YMCA offers a popular prenatal and postpartum aerobics class consisting of an intense but suitable step aerobics class, hand weights, and floor work. The instructor is especially good at tailoring the exercise to your stage of pregnancy and your fitness level. Non-crawling or walking babies are welcome. If you want to try the class before joining the Y, you can purchase a "day pass." Comments: "This is an amazing workout—even for non-pregnant women. . . . I go for the exercise, but also to socialize and get caught up in the world of urban moms and babies!"

Purely Physical Fitness
1300 Church St.
415-282-1329
This friendly neighborhood gym permits strollers, so you can park your baby in front of your Stairmaster.

San Francisco Buddhist Center
37 Bartlett St.
415-282-2018
www.sfbuddhistcenter.org
This center offers a prenatal yoga class of gentle stretches for pregnant women to prepare for a relaxed labor and birth. They also offer mommy and baby yoga that includes gentle stretching to help replenish your body and focus on strengthening your pelvic floor and abdominal muscles.

San Francisco Kaiser Permanente
415-833-4120
Pre- and postnatal yoga classes are held at 2425 Geary Blvd., in the Mezzanine, Conference Rm. 4. Drop-ins welcome. See Whole Birth Yoga below.

Strong Heart Strong Body
3556 Sacramento St.
415-353-5616
PARENT RATING: ☆ ☆ ☆ ☆ ☆
This posh Pacific Heights studio is enjoying their larger space and offering more options than ever before. They offer one-on-one personal training, Pilates, and one-on-one yoga, and they have pre- and postnatal certified trainers, Elyse Hoffman and Tracy Hartway, as well as owner E.A. Morgan, available to help you maintain your fitness level throughout your pregnancy or get you back into shape afterwards. It is possible to bring infants to workout sessions, as long as they are in a stroller and not mobile.

Studio Valencia
See under "Individual Pre- and Postnatal Fitness Instructors"—Elizabeth Bessamir.

Sherith Israel
2266 California St.
415-346-1720
www.sherithisrael.org
kmarble@speakeasy.org
PARENT RATING: ☆ ☆ ☆ ☆ ☆
They offer a popular parent and baby/toddler yoga class (birth-3 years), led by Kari Marble. This is one of the few yoga classes in the city where crawling babies and walking toddlers are welcome! Moms get to practice yoga while their little ones play alongside with age-appropriate toys in this wonderfully large and aesthetically pleasing space. The last portion of the class incorporates babies and toddlers. Parent Comment: "Kari's classes are wonderful. . . . In addition to being a nurturing presence, she is a patient instructor who verbalizes instructions well."

St. Luke's Hospital
3555 Cesar Chavez St.
415-626-(BANY) (2229)
www.stlukes-sf.org
This hospital offers pre- and postnatal yoga.

University of California, San Francisco
Millberry Union
500 Parnassus Ave.
415-476-1115
www.cas.ucsf.edu/mps/
This group offers a prenatal and postpartum exercise class called Fit for Two. This class is designed to

condition your body during pregnancy and prepare for delivery by stimulating circulation, building strength and flexibility, and increasing stamina. This is also a great class for getting back into shape after childbirth. Babies are welcome.

Whole Birth Yoga

www.wholebirthresources.com
wholebirth@earthlink.net

Whole Birth Yoga offers unique prenatal yoga and support classes at several area hospitals and yoga studios including San Francisco Kaiser and South San Francisco Kaiser. For a schedule, fees, and registration, visit their web site. For full description, see under South Bay.

Yoga Garden (formerly Castro Yoga)

286 Divisadero St.
415-552-9644
www.yogagardensf.com

Formerly Castro Yoga, the Yoga Garden continues to offer pre- and postnatal yoga classes, including a parent/baby class for non-mobile babies and a parent/toddler class where mobile babies are welcome.

Yoga Loft

321 Divisadero St.
415-626-5638

This yoga studio offers prenatal yoga, yoga for moms and babies, and an afternoon yoga class with child care.

Yoga Tree

www.yogatreesf.com
- 1234 Valencia St., 415-647-9707
- 780 Stanyan St., 415-387-4707
- 519 Hayes St., 415-626-9707
- 97 Collingwood St., 415-701-9642

Yoga Tree offers prenatal and mom and baby postpartum yoga.

PARENT RATING: ☆ ☆ ☆ ☆ ☆

Moms especially recommend Elise Collins's class at the Stanyan St. location and Jane Austin and Britt Fohrman's classes at the Valencia St. location.

North Bay

Baby Boot Camp

See under San Francisco.

The Bar Method

208 Bon Air Shopping Ctr.
Greenbrae
415-461-4461
www.barmethod.com

One of the San Francisco studio's favorite teachers, Cindy Root, has proudly opened her own doors in Marin. For full description, see under San Francisco.

Barefoot and Pregnant

1165 Magnolia Ave.
Larkspur
415-388-1777
www.barefootandpregnant.com

Since the printing of the first edition of this book, a retreat for expectant and new parents has arrived on the scene—Barefoot and Pregnant. Among other services, they offer a wide variety of exercise, including prenatal yoga, and mom and baby yoga (see Moms on the Move below) all in their beautiful light-filled yoga studio. They also offer a prenatal yoga class with child care for second- or third-time-plus moms. Their classes are designed to help you safely improve, support, or maintain your current level of fitness, while focusing on the areas that require special attention. Their retail boutique features maternity fitness apparel, including lines by Mothers in Motion and Raising a Racquet. They are also well-known for an inviting menu of spa offerings, including prenatal and postnatal body treatments and massage. They also offer acupuncture that is popular with women in their first trimester who are experiencing the typical symptoms of nausea, fatigue, and headaches, as well as women who are uncomfortably past their due dates. Visit their website for details.

Bay Club Marin

220 Corte Madera Town Ctr.
Corte Madera
415-945-3000
www.bayclubmarin.com

PARENT RATING: ☆ ☆ ☆ ☆ ☆

This relatively new state-of-the art health club is very popular among Marin moms. Among myriad class offerings, they offer Bump Fitness, a prenatal and separate postnatal fitness program. The prenatal class combines weight training, cardiovascular fitness, aquatic exercise, yoga and Pilates, all under the American College of Obstetrics guidelines. The postnatal fitness class uses spinning, weight exercises, and stability ball work to train your whole body, especially the core muscles of your abs and back. One of the best things about this class is that you are welcome to bring your new baby. The Bay Club Marin also offers a prenatal yoga class. Club membership is required.

The Dailey Method

11 First St.
Corte Madera
415-927-1133
www.daileymethod.com

See under San Francisco. Child care is available Monday through Saturday mornings and during the afternoons Monday through Wednesday.

Elan Health and Fitness Center

- Petaluma
  1372 N. McDowell Blvd.
  707-765-1919
- San Anselmo
  230 Greenfield Ave.
  415-485-1945

www.elanfitness.com

This family-run health and fitness center, exclusively for women, offers the Moms on the Move exercise classes (see below). In addition they offer one-on-one certified trainers. Child care arrangements are available.

Fairfax Health Club and Aerobic Center

713 Center Blvd.
Fairfax
415-459-1030
www.fairfaxgym.com

This club offers personal trainers and certified fitness specialists who have extensive experience working with pregnant women.

Gold's Gym

10 Fifer Ave.
Corte Madera
415-924-4653

This gym offers certified personal trainers who are experienced in working with expecting mothers.

Kaiser Permanente Santa Rosa Medical Center

401 Bicentennial Way
Santa Rosa
707-571-4000
www.kaisersantarosa.org

This hospital offers a prenatal nutrition and exercise class. Call 707-571-4167 for details.

Marin YMCA

1500 Los Gamos Dr.
San Rafael
415-492-9622
www.ymca.net

While not specifically offering prenatal classes, this YMCA offers low-impact aerobics, stretching and toning, and yoga classes that many pregnant women attend. They also offer one-on-one fitness training and child care.

Mill Valley Community Center

180 Camino Alto Ave.
Mill Valley
415-383-1370
www.millvalleycenter.org

PARENT RATING: ☆ ☆ ☆ ☆ ☆

This state-of-the-art community center offers a popular combined pre- and postnatal exercise class 3 mornings a week, which includes strength training and flexibility exercises.

Moms on the Move

707-762-MOMS (6667)
www.momsonthemove.net

PARENT RATING: ☆ ☆ ☆ ☆ ☆

Moms on the Move is an innovative exercise program, offering pre- and postnatal exercise and yoga classes for the expectant and new mom. Moms on the Move is directed by Susan Bullen-Lawler, R.N. and mom. Susan has devoted her professional life to childbearing women since 1977. In addition to teaching fitness classes, Susan is a practicing Labor and Delivery nurse at Marin General and Petaluma Valley hospitals and is well known for her childbirth preparation classes (see Ch. 1). Classes include prenatal and postnatal yoga, mom and baby yoga, yoga for healthy backs, new mom's forum, mom's yoga, expecting mom's forum, and mom's sculpt and mat class. Segments of all classes may be modified to suit your fitness level. All instructors are trained and certified by the internationally recognized Moms on the Move certification teacher training. Marin classes are held at Barefoot and Pregnant in Larkspur (see above) and as this book goes to press they are planning to have classes at the Elan Fitness Center in San Anselmo. Sonoma classes are held at the Elan Fitness Center in Petaluma, (see above).

Mt. Tamalpais Racquet Club

1 Larkspur Dr.
Larkspur
415-924-6226
www.mttamrc.com

PARENT RATING: ☆ ☆ ☆ ☆ ☆

Enjoy this neighborhood fitness facility's group exercise classes from yoga to step aerobics to aqua aerobics and cycling. Child care is available for children 3 months and up at reasonable rates.

Osher Marin Jewish Community Center

200 N. San Pedro Rd.
San Rafael
415-444-8000
www.marinjcc.org

PARENT RATING: ☆ ☆ ☆ ☆ ☆

This center offers a water exercise class that is very popular with pregnant and postpartum women members. They also offer a one-on-one pre- and postnatal resistance training program. A personal trainer with experience in training pregnant and postpartum women provides a supportive and motivated environment to prepare your body for the physical demands of pregnancy and childbirth and to strengthen and tone your body afterwards. This fitness training includes using bands, floorwork stretching, resistance training, free weights, and machines. Infants are welcome to accompany moms in either a car seat or a stroller. Training is by appointment only.

Queen of the Valley Hospital

100 Trancas St.
Napa
707-252-4411
www.thequeen.org

This hospital offers postnatal fitness classes. Call 707-251-1850 for details.

Roco Dance and Fitness

237 Shoreline Hwy.
Mill Valley
415-388-6786
www.rocodance.com

PARENT RATING: ☆ ☆ ☆ ☆ ☆

This award-winning dance and fitness center offers Pilates, spinning, aero-

bics, and yoga. Child care is available.

Santa Rosa YMCA

1111 College Ave.
Santa Rosa
707-545-9622
www.ymca.net

This YMCA offers a pre- and postnatal aqua aerobic class.

Strawberry Recreation Center

118 E. Strawberry Dr.
Mill Valley
415-383-6494
http://strawberrymarin.org

This center offers a great water aerobics class in their wonderful outdoor pool. While it isn't a class specifically for pregnant women, many do attend.

Terra Linda Community Center

670 Del Ganado Rd.
San Rafael
415-485-3344
www.cityofsanrafael.org

The pool is open from March through October and offers an aquatic exercise program during that time.

Turtle Island Yoga

7A Mariposa Ave.
San Anselmo
415-453-8642
www.turtleislandyoga.com

See under Whole Birth Yoga, South Bay.

WholeBirth Yoga

See under South Bay.

X Gym

401B Tamal Plaza Dr.
Corte Madera
415-924-9496

PARENT RATING: ☆ ☆ ☆ ☆ ☆

Short on time? X Gym is the answer! This one-on-one personal training center has a unique program where you go twice a week for a 20-minute strength training workout. Comment: "It's very effective and great for people (with babies and young children) with a limited amount of time." Training sessions are by appointment only.

Yoga Center of Marin

142 Redwood Ave.
Corte Madera
415-927-1850
www.yogacenterofmarin.com

This center offers 2 prenatal yoga classes a week. Drop-ins welcome.

Yoga Garden

412 Red Hill Ave., Ste. 12
The Essex Center Building
San Anselmo
415-485-5800
www.yogagardenstudio.com

This popular yoga studio offers ongoing pre- and postnatal yoga classes that provide a supportive environment for both pregnant women and new mothers. The prenatal class includes postures and breath awareness that will help maintain your well-being throughout your pregnancy and will enhance your endurance, strength, and flexibility in preparation for birth. Both of these classes are ongoing, but registration is suggested.

The Yoga Source

1570 4th St.
San Rafael
415-460-1232
www.theyogasource.net
PARENT RATING: ☆ ☆ ☆ ☆ ☆

This small yoga studio offers yoga for moms and babies from time to time. Class size is limited to 10, so call in advance to reserve your spot. Drop-ins (if space is available) are welcome.

Yoga Studio

- Mill Valley
  650 E. Blithedale Ave.
  415-380-8800
- Larkspur
  2207 Larkspur Landing Circle
  415-380-8800
www.yogastudiomillvalley.com
PARENT RATING: ☆ ☆ ☆ ☆ ☆

This wonderful yoga studio (voted Best Yoga Classes in Marin County in the 2005 *Pacific Sun* Reader's Poll) offers a popular prenatal yoga class with Zoë Collier. Zoë is certified in prenatal yoga and Kripalu yoga. She is also a longtime doula and childbirth educator (see Ch. 5 under Marin Doula Circle). Working moms especially love her class since it meets three nights a week. The prenatal class helps cultivate health and prepare for birth through gentle yoga postures and breath awareness in a supportive environment. She also teaches expecting parents a prenatal partner yoga workshop in preparation for labor and delivery that parents rave about. Other moms report that instructors are happy to modify their regular class to accomodate pregnant women. Comments: "Zoë's prenatal yoga classes are a very special treat. They combine meditation, stretching, breathing and some real exertion yoga specifically designed for those of us with growing bellies and changing bodies. Zoë creates an atmosphere that is peaceful yet focused, and she includes special meditations for the baby. . . . I highly recommend her classes. Zoë knows how to challenge pregnant women—appropriately. We walked away from the prenatal partner workshop much more emotionally attached to one another and our future together as parents."

East Bay

Alta Bates Medical Center

2450 Ashby Ave.
Berkeley
510-204-1334
www.altabates.com
Alta Bates offers Whole Birth prenatal yoga. For description, see under South Bay.

Baby Boot Camp

See under San Francisco.

Berkeley YMCA

2001 Allston Way
510-848-9622
www.baymca.org
PARENT RATING: ☆ ☆ ☆ ☆ ☆
The Berkeley YMCA offers 3 classes for pre- and postnatal needs, including aerobics, yoga with Betsy Appell, and the very popular water aerobics class. Child care is available. Besides being a great workout, the prenatal water aerobics includes time to socialize with other moms-to-be. Buy a "community pass," good for just these classes without having to pay a monthly or annual fee. Comment: "The prenatal yoga class resulted in my being able to sleep better than I have in months."

Berkeley Yoga Center

1250 Addison St., Ste. 209
510-843-8784
www.BerkeleyYoga.com
PARENT RATING: ☆ ☆ ☆ ☆ ☆
This beautiful yoga center overlooks Strawberry Creek Park in a converted warehouse with brick walls and hardwood floors. The center offers both pre- and postnatal yoga classes. In the prenatal class, the instructor prepares pregnant women for labor and delivery through postures, breathing exercises, and relaxation. The postpartum class is oriented to the special needs of new mothers. Non-mobile babies (pre-crawling) are welcome; an assistant is available to help with all babies. Comment: "This class gave me not only the physical conditioning that I needed before going into labor, but also [taught me] meditation and conscious relaxation."

Karen Casino

1432 Derby St.
Berkeley
510-644-2066
kcasino@comcast.net
PARENT RATING: ☆ ☆ ☆ ☆ ☆
Karen offers The Pregnancy Workout and The New Mother's Workout in her home studio. Her pregnancy workout includes Pilates, pelvic tilts, and exercises for the entire body that aim to ease pregnancy and labor as well as postpartum recovery. The new mother's workout is a 10-session class designed to remodel the body after childbirth, focusing on the muscles affected during pregnancy and childbirth. Babies are welcome, and there is a babysitter on hand. The pregnancy class is ongoing, and pregnant

women may join at any time. A sliding fee schedule is available.
Comments: "Karen is supportive, and her sessions are fun and informative. . . . Much more personal than any exercise studio. . . . She's an excellent instructor and gives you the individual attention you need." Karen also offers private classes.

Club One
1200 Clay St.
Oakland
510-895-1010
www.clubone.com
This full-service fitness center offers group exercise classes as well as all the standard gym equipment. They also have a personal trainer on staff with experience in working with pre- and postnatal women. Child care is available.

Courthouse Athletic Club
2985 Telegraph Rd.
Oakland
510-834-5600
www.courthouseac.com
This full-service fitness center offers group exercise classes as well as a well-equipped gym for members. Child care is available.

The Dailey Method
4409 Piedmont Ave.
Oakland
510-206-7725
www.thedaileymethod.com
This is the Dailey Method's newest studio, opened in May 2005. For description, see under San Francisco.

Ellie Herman Studios
3929 Grand Ave.
Oakland
510-594-8507
www.ellie.net
See under San Francisco.

Flow Like a River Yoga
2718 Telegraph Ave.
Berkeley
510-841-0651
www.flowlikeariveryoga.com
Lynn Zamarra offers a myriad of classes for moms-to-be and new parents as well as babies, including a prenatal yoga class, a baby massage and yoga class followed by postpartum yoga, a mommy/baby/early toddler yoga dance class, mommy/toddler yoga, and children's yoga. Many of her classes are followed by an hour of "time out for parents," where babies and children go to child care and parents have a Kripalu Hatha yoga experience for strengthening, balancing, and calming.

Fourth Street Yoga
1809C 4th St.
Berkeley
510-845-YOGA (9642)
www.4thstreetyoga.com
PARENT RATING: ☆ ☆ ☆ ☆ ☆
Serving the Berkeley community for almost 10 years, Fourth Street Yoga offers both pre- and postnatal yoga classes. The prenatal class is a beginning class designed for pregnant women who want to increase awareness of their bodies. The postnatal class aims to bring the body back to its original strength and tone. Infants are welcome at this class. Many moms commented on how much they enjoyed the prenatal class: "It flowed well, and she had a great way of

working with us in our growing bodies. . . . The instructor is very clear in
her direction and is very knowledgeable about how pregnancy changes
your ability to move."

Healthy Human Yoga

37353 Fremont Blvd.
Fremont
510-796-9642
www.healthy-human.com
This yoga studio offers a pre- and
postnatal yoga class as well as a
"yoga stretch'" and "gentle yoga" that
many moms-to-be seem to like!

Helene Byrne's Post
Pregnancy Exercise

Montclair Women's Cultural
Arts Center
1650 Mountain Blvd.
Oakland
510-530-5710
www.exerciseafterpregnancy.com
Author of *Exercise after Pregnancy:
How to Look and Feel Your Best*, Helen
Byrne has become one of the Bay
Area's experts on postpartum exercise
and offers her Post-Pregnancy
Exercise Workshop. A mother herself
and ACE certified personal trainer
(with special certifications in pre- and
postnatal exercise), her 6-week, post-
pregnancy workshop uses the Pilates
method of body conditioning to restore
alignment and balance during the
postpartum period. Helen has a professional background in dance and
Pilates training. Babies are welcome at
the class and she has a child care
assistant to help with them. As this
book goes to press she is getting
ready to launch 2 postpartum exercise

videos. See www.befitmom.com for
more information on them.

John Muir/Mt. Diablo
Health System

Women's Health Center
1656 N. California Blvd.
Walnut Creek
925-947-3331
www.johnmuirmtdiablo.com
This center offers a Pregnancy Yoga
class and a Mommy and Me yoga
class. Prenatal yoga explores postures
for pregnancy, labor, and delivery,
including deep breathing, stretching,
strengthening, and relaxation. Mommy
and Me yoga is offered to moms and
their pre-crawling infants. Yoga postures and breathing techniques are
taught to help restore and rebuild the
body, mind, and spirit.

Kaiser Permanente

www.members.kaiserpermanente.org
• Fremont Medical Center
  39406 Paseo Padre Prkwy
  510-248-3455
This hospital offers a prenatal yoga
class.
• Oakland Medical Center
  280 W. MacArthur Blvd.
  510-752-1100
This hospital offers a prenatal exercise class.
• Pleasanton Medical Offices
  7601 Stoneridge Dr.
  925-847-5172
They offer a prenatal yoga class.

Kaiser Permanente Walnut Creek Medical Center

1425 S. Main St.
Walnut Creek
925-295-4190

This medical office offers prenatal yoga.

Mountain Yoga

2071 Antioch Ct.
Oakland
510-339-6421
www.mountainyoga.org

This friendly yoga studio offers both pre- and postnatal classes taught by Anja Borgstrom. Babies are included in the postnatal class. These classes are known for fostering a sense of community, resulting in friendships and informal mother's groups. Anja also teaches Hatha Blend classes, which are also popular with some pre- and postnatal moms.

Namaste Yoga

6416 College Ave.
Oakland
510-547-YOGA (9642)
www.namasterockridge.com

This friendly yoga studio offers pre- and postnatal yoga, as well as birthing yoga workshops for partners, and other family-oriented classes.

The Nurture Center

3399 Mount Diablo Blvd.
Lafayette
925-283-1346
www.nurturecenter.com

See under Whole Birth Yoga, South Bay.

Oakland YMCA

2350 Broadway
Oakland
510-451-9622
www.ymcaeastbay.org

The YMCA offers many group exercise classes appropriate for moms-to-be and new mothers, including low-impact water aerobics and water walking. Child care is available.

Orinda Parks and Recreation Community Center

26 Orinda Way
Orinda
925-254-2445
www.ci.orinda.ca.us

This community center offers a prenatal and postpartum yoga class, to which babies up to one year old are welcome.

Piedmont Yoga

3966 Piedmont Ave.
Oakland
510-652-3336
www.piedmontyoga.com

Piedmont Yoga offers a prenatal yoga class as well as a mom and baby yoga class taught by Vicky Roper.

Pleasanton Parks & Community Services StrollerJam

925-931-5340
www.ci.pleasanton.ca.us/parks.html

This is an aerobic class for mom and music and motion class for baby. Classes are held both indoors and outside depending on the weather. Classes meet at the Veteran's Memorial Building in Pleasanton, 301 Main Street. Advance registration required.

Seventh Heaven Body Awareness Center

2820 7th St.
Berkeley
510-665-4300
www.7thheavenyoga.com

This full-service yoga center offers a combined pre- and postnatal class to support women through the phases of pregnancy, birthing, and post-delivery. Emphasis is placed on gentle postures to create ease, build strength, and deepen the connection between the expectant mother and her baby. All levels are welcome.

Stroller Strides

1-866-FIT-4-MOM
www.strollerstrides.com

In 50 minutes you will get a total body workout, improving your cardio endurance, strength, and flexibility, all with your baby and stroller! The class includes lots of power walking and intervals of body toning using exercise tubing and the stroller. Babies are kept engaged by incorporating songs during the strength training part of class. All classes are taught by nationally certified instructors who are also moms. Stroller Strides is a national exercise program that is offered in many locations in the East Bay (including the Tri-Valley of Danville, San Ramon, Dublin/Pleasanton), mid and North Peninsula. Visit their website for specifics.

Synergy Fitness

1124 Solano Ave.
Albany
510-527-9005
www.synergyfitness.com

This center offers one-on-one personal fitness and Pilates training with trainers who are experienced in working with pre- and postnatal women.

ValleyCare Heath System

LifestyleRX Medical Fitness Center
119 East Stanley Blvd.
Livermore
925-454-6342
www.valleycare.com

This fitness center offers a prenatal Pilates class where no prior yoga experience is required. They also offer a Mommy & Me stretch and tone class for new moms and babies 5 months and younger. The Mommy & Me class is offered at the Lactation Center at ValleyCare Medical Center, 3160 Santa Rita Rd., Pleasanton. To register call 925-416-3598.

Vara Healing Arts

850 Talbot Ave.
Albany
510-526-YOGA (9642)
www.varahealing.com

This unique yoga studio offers prenatal yoga and a variety of postnatal classes and 35 styles of massage, including a pregnancy massage. They are located in a fresh and unique renovated former church and pride themselves on being one of the most beautiful yoga spaces in the East Bay.

Washington Hospital Healthcare System

2000 Mowry Ave.
Fremont
510-791-3423
www.whhs.com

This hospital offers a prenatal exercise class that includes cardio exercise and stretching. It's intended to help expectant women keep moving! Becky May, certified childbirth educator and certified prenatal fitness educator, teaches the class.

Whole Birth Yoga

See under South Bay.

Yogalayam

1723 Alcatraz Ave.
Berkeley
510-655-3664
www.yogalayam.org

PARENT RATING: ☆ ☆ ☆ ☆ ☆

Saraswathi Devi offers ongoing pre- and postnatal yoga classes that you can join at any time. Babies are welcome at the postnatal class. She offers a sliding fee schedule. She also offers a popular yoga course that complements childbirth preparation instruction, as well as couples yoga and massage for childbirth, pregnancy, and postpartum periods. Moms swear by her classes: "She knows a lot about how the body changes when pregnant, and her class really resulted in my aches and pains diminishing. . . . Her class is gentle, nurturing, and restorative."

The Yoga Room

The Julia Morgan Center
2540 College Ave.
Berkeley

www.yogaroomberkeley.com

PARENT RATING: ☆ ☆ ☆ ☆ ☆

The Yoga Room is a yoga co-op, with several teachers offering classes for varying fees. Barbara Papini (510-601-1883) offers an ongoing prenatal beginning yoga class to assist women in preparing for childbirth. Her class emphasizes the Iyengar style, which stresses a healthy alignment of the spine and increased self-awareness. No previous yoga experience is necessary. Everyone seems to love this class!

South Bay

Baby Boot Camp

See under San Francisco.

The Bar Method

128 De Anza Blvd.
Crystal Springs Village
San Mateo
650-573-3330
www.barmethod.com

Owners Noreen Dante and Laura Stein offer the same great classes as their San Francisco and Marin counterparts. See under San Francisco.

Betty Wright Swim Center

Community Association for Rehabilitation Inc.
3864 Middlefield Rd.
Palo Alto
650-494-1480

PARENT RATING: ☆ ☆ ☆ ☆ ☆

This center offers prenatal aquatic exercise classes in a warm indoor pool twice a week. Drop-ins are welcome.

Blossom Birth Services

1000 Elwell Ct.
Palo Alto
650-964-7380
www.blossombirth.com

PARENT RATING: ☆ ☆ ☆ ☆

This resource center offers prenatal yoga classes that aim to enhance awareness of the body and its dramatic changes during pregnancy. They also offer a mother-baby yoga class, where new moms bring their babies and join others in stretching, relaxing, and rejuvenating! In a Moving with Baby class, new moms learn exercises and stretches that incorporate interacting with their babies. No previous experience is necessary for the yoga classes.

California Yoga Center

570 Showers Dr., Ste. 5
Mountain View
650-947-9642
www.californiayoga.com

The center offers a prenatal Iyengar yoga class. Drop-ins are welcome. Pregnant and recently postpartum women are also welcome to attend several Level I classes.

CHANGE of the Peninsula

Center for Healing and Global Evolution
400 Ben Franklin St.
San Mateo
650-340-YOGA (9642)
www.changeofthepeninsula.org

PARENT RATING: ☆ ☆ ☆ ☆ ☆

CHANGE has a number of movement classes and workshops for the new and expectant mother, including a prenatal yoga class, a mom and baby yoga class, and an Integral Hatha Yoga class with babysitting. In this class, crawling babies, toddlers, and children up to 6 years old are welcome to either participate in class with their parent or have stories read to them by a babysitter.

Dolphin Yoga & Doula Center

650-867-1991
www.dolphinyogaanddoulacenter.com

This center offers prenatal yoga classes, both in their studio and at-home semiprivate classes.

Devine Design

3199 S. Bascom Ave.
Campbell
408-371-5313
www.devinedesignfitness.com

They offer personal fitness training with trainers who have prenatal and postpartum experience.

Downward Dog Yoga

94 Manor Dr.
Pacifica
650-355-YOGA (9642)
www.downwarddogyoga.com

Downward Dog Yoga offers a prenatal yoga class and a couple of other family-oriented classes.

El Camino YMCA

2400 Grant Rd.
Mountain View
650-969-9622
www.ymcamidpen.org

In addition to a full offering of group exercise classes and a state-of-the-art fitness center, this Y offers 3 specific classes for prenatal and postpartum women that are quite popular. They offer a pre- and postnatal exercise class, which consists of modified low-impact aerobics and strength training.

They also offer a pre- and postnatal aquatics exercise class as well as a prenatal yoga class.

Inner Reflection and Harmony Birth Resources

621 E. Campbell Ave., Ste. 14
Campbell
408-370-2134
www.inner-reflection.com

Among other offerings, this unique resource center offers prenatal yoga and postnatal mom and baby yoga, both taught in the style of Whole Birth Yoga (see below). They also offer a New Mom's Restorative Yoga class.

Peninsula Jewish Community Center

Byer Athletic Center
800 Foster City Blvd.
Foster City
650-212-PJCC (7522)
www.pjcc.org

The sparkling new Peninsula JCC offers a great 5-week postpartum fitness class where you can bring your baby. The 75-minute program is designed to help you get back in shape with your baby nearby. Working out at your own pace, the workout includes step aerobics, strength training, cardio kickboxing, spinning, and much more. Enjoy the camaraderie and support created by working out with other moms.

Kaiser Permanente

www.kaiserpermanente.org

These locations offer prenatal and/ or postnatal yoga classes.

- Kaiser Permanente Daly City Medical Offices
  395 Hickey Blvd.
  650-301-4445
- Kaiser Permanente Milpitas Medical Offices
  611 S. Milpitas Blvd.
  408-945-2732
- Kaiser Permanente Redwood City Medical Center
  Health Education Center,
  1150 Veterans Blvd.
  650-299-2433
- Santa Teresa Medical Center
  250 Hospital Prkwy.
  San Jose
  408-972-3340
- Santa Clara Medical Center
  900 Kiely Blvd.
  408-885-5000
- Kaiser Permanente South San Francisco Medical Center
  395 Hickey Blvd.
  650-301-4445

Lucile Packard Children's Hospital at Stanford Medical Center

Perinatal Education
650-723-4600

Stanford offers several options for maternity fitness. The Fit for Two Prenatal Program is designed for the healthy pregnant mother. This class includes yoga and Pilates that are especially designed for expectant and new mothers. They also offer Prenatal Yoga, which emphasizes body awareness and focused breathing for use in pregnancy, labor, and postpartum recovery. Also, they periodically offer a Stroller Fitness class.

Menlo Park Recreation Center

700 Alma St.
Menlo Park
650-858-3470
www.menlopark.org

PARENT RATING: ☆ ☆ ☆ ☆

This community center has myriad fitness options for pregnant and post-partum women. They offer a full aquatics exercise program as well as aerobics, including the Stretch and Firm class which is popular with pregnant women.

Mills-Peninsula Health Center

Community Education Garden Room
100 S. San Mateo Dr.
San Mateo
650-696-5600 (The Wellness Center)
www.mills-peninsula.org

PARENT RATING: ☆ ☆ ☆ ☆ ☆

Mills-Peninsula offers a prenatal and postnatal yoga class that aims to increase relaxation, flexibility, and strength. They also offer a very popular aquatic stretch and tone class, a low-intensity aquatic exercise program geared toward pregnant women and new mothers.

No Excuses, Your Fitness Partner

905 Middlefield Rd.
Palo Alto
650-325-1273
www.noexcusesfitness.com

This fitness center offers one-on-one personal training, with trainers and Pilates instructors who have experience in working with prenatal and postpartum women.

Pacific Athletic Club

200 Redwood Shores Prkwy.
Redwood City
650-593-4900
www.pacclub.com

The Pacific Athletic Club offers Bump Fitness, a carefully designed exercise program for expectant women and new moms. See under Bay Club Marin for further details.

Palo Alto YMCA

3412 Ross Rd.
Palo Alto
650-856-9622 (general numbers)
650-842-7162 (Director, group exercise)
www.ymcamidpen.org

Modified low-impact classes specifically intended for pregnant and post-partum women are held twice a week. Babies are welcome.

Reach Fitness Club

707 High St.
Palo Alto
650-327-3224
www.reachfitness.com

This club offers personal trainers who are experienced in working with pregnant and postpartum women.

San Mateo Parks and Recreation Department

330 W. 20th Ave.
San Mateo
650-522-7400
http://www.erecreg.com/

Their Power Stroll class in Central Park is great for new moms and babies who love the outdoors. The same instructor also teaches a Strollerobics class, which is a complete body workout that includes aerobic dance, kick-boxing, ballet, weight-lifting, toning and yoga stretches, all with your baby and stroller. Child care available for older siblings.

San Carlos Parks and Recreation Department

Burton Park, Kiwanis Community Center
1017 Cedar St.
San Carlos
650-802-4382

Certified prenatal fitness instructor Patty Dougherty teaches a prenatal fitness class that incorporates low-impact aerobics, muscle toning, light weight training, and supportive tips and advice for expectant mothers. Patty is also a well-known and respected childbirth educator and labor coach and has been working with expectant mothers for years!

Sequoia Hospital

Health & Wellness Services
702 Marshall St.
Redwood City
650-482-6065

PARENT RATING: ☆ ☆ ☆ ☆ ☆

They offer a prenatal yoga class that features postures to ease labor discomfort and strengthen the abdominal muscles.

Stretchworks

3636 Florence St., Ste. A
Redwood City
650-321-1500
www.meridianstretching.com

They do not offer a specific class for pregnant or postpartum women, but rather welcome and integrate them into regular classes with the instructor modifying their sequences.

World Yoga Healing Arts Center

1530 South Market St.
Walnut Creek
925-274-YOGA (9642)
www.world-yoga.com

This yoga studio offers a popular prenatal yoga class taught by Petronella Van Berry.

Whole Birth Yoga

831-425-7731 (Robin Sale, founder)
www.wholebirthresources.com
wholebirth@earthlink.net

Whole Birth Yoga trains instructors to offer unique prenatal, postpartum and couples yoga, and support classes. Since the first of edition of this book, Whole Birth Yoga has literally exploded, offering classes at yoga studios and hospitals throughout the Bay Area. You may find founder and owner Robin Sale teaching classes at Santa Cruz Dominican Hospital (831-462-7709) and at A Mother's Place in Santa Cruz (831-423-1325). Her trained instructors offer classes at several area hospitals, including Kaiser Permanente San Francisco (415-833-8611), Kaiser Permanente Freemont (510-248-3455), Alta Bates Hospital in Berkeley (510-204-1334), Sequoia Hospital in Redwood City (650-368-2229), Kaiser Permanente Pleasanton (925-847-5172), and Valley Health Plan in San Jose/Willow Glenn (408-885-5957). They also offer classes at Blossom Birth Services (650-964-7380), the Yoga Center of Los Gatos (408-356-2627), Full Lotus Studio in downtown Morgan Hill (408-892-2820), Inner Reflection and Harmony Birth Resources in Campbell (408-370-2134), the Nurture Center in

Lafayette (925-283-1346), and Turtle Island Yoga in San Anselmo (415-453-8642). A typical class is 2 hours and is divided into 3 parts: a topic relevant to pregnancy or motherhood; mindfulness meditation and deep relaxation; and prenatal or postpartum yoga. The postnatal class incorporates pre-crawling babies into postures and movement, and includes time for mothers to share stories and advice. Visit the above website, which features Whole Birth Yoga's offerings and instructors.

The Yoga Solution, Marti Foster

- Palo Alto
  435 Middlefield Rd.
  650-566-9953 (studio)
- Portola Valley
  3130 Alpine Rd.
  650-851-3500

408-323-8833 (Marti Foster)
www.yogasolution.com

In this prenatal yoga class for couples and pregnant women, you learn special yoga postures to practice during the changing phases of your pregnancy as well as calming breathing techniques. The couples class focuses on creating a nurturing bond between you and your baby and allows you to share this experience with your partner. Marti also offers private in-home instruction.

The Yoga Wellness Center

35 N. San Mateo Dr.
San Mateo
650-401-NICE (6423)
www.yogawellnesscenter.com

The Yoga Wellness Center offers a class for pregnant women called Yoga for Pregnancy. Drop-ins are welcome.

Individual Pre- and Postnatal Fitness Instructors

Listed below are some personal trainers and fitness instructors who work as free-lancers in several different locations and studios. Contact them directly or check their website (if available) for venues, schedules, and fees.

San Francisco and North Bay

Cynthia Bahmani

415-519-5926

Cynthia's Full Circle Fitness practice features pre- and postnatal Pilates classes at the San Francisco Jewish Community Center, Strong Heart Strong Body, as well as in-home private classes. A mom herself, Cynthia has a background in sports medicine.

Elizabeth Bessamir

415-931-7291

Bay area favorite, Elizabeth teaches mommy and baby yoga at Kaiser Hospital in Daly City for members and non-members and a prenatal class at Downward Dog Yoga in Pacifica.

Zoë Collier

415-847-8600
zoecollier@hotmail.com

Zoë offers popular prenatal yoga classes at the Yoga Studio in Mill Valley and Larkspur Landing (see above). She also offers private prenatal yoga classes and a private day-long childbirth preparation class in clients' homes. She is certified in prenatal yoga and is also a DONA certified doula (see Ch. 5) and childbirth educator, who came to yoga while traveling in Asia over a decade ago. She has also been a practicing doula for over 13 years and is certified by the Association of Labor Assistants & Childbirth Educators (ALACE) and Doulas of North America (DONA).

Leslie Ford, CPT

415-717-5020
lesliegford@hotmail.com

Leslie is an ACE Certified Personal Trainer and is certified in pre- and postnatal fitness through ISSA. She offers personalized workouts aimed to energize and strengthen the muscles needed for the demands of motherhood.

Tracy Hartway

650-557-1434

Offering personal training and yoga for moms and moms-to-be, Tracy combines nearly 10 years of experience in fitness, yoga, and childbirth education. She is a mom herself. A former pre- and postpartum yoga instructor at The Mindful Body in San Francisco and The Mill Valley Yoga Studio, Tracy currently offers her one-on-one personal training out of the Strong Heart, Strong Body studio.

See above under Strong Heart Strong Body in San Francisco. Comment: "Amazing teacher. . . . the best!"

Elyse Hoffman

415-395-0864

Many moms, both new and experienced, work out with Elyse and like their results. Elyse offers personal training at Strong Heart Strong Body in San Francisco. She is a certified personal trainer with certifications in pre- and postnatal fitness. Try to schedule your postpartum workout program several months in advance, as Elyse is popular!

Comments: "Elyse will motivate you and keep you in check while at the same time making sure that your workout is fun. . . . Elyse knows when to raise the bar and take you to the next level to achieve your goals."

Kristen Horler

415-290-2764
888-990-BABY (2229)
www.babybootcamp.com

In addition to her ever-popular Baby Bootcamp classes, Kristin offers pre- and postnatal personal training at her private home studio in Mill Valley. She also teaches spinning at the Bay Club Marin.

Infinity Personal Training

415-576-1050
www.infinitytraining.com

Infinity trainer and owner, Michelle Gagnon specializes in prenatal exercise and offers a great prenatal and postnatal personal training package.

Noël Li-Chassé

415-221-8525

Noël offers private pre- and postnatal yoga classes, specializing in sessions at clients' homes. Noël is a certified yoga instructor, massage therapist, and mom.

Kari Marble, MA, RYT

415-845-1073
kari@welcomeom.com

Kari is a certified yoga teacher, massage therapist, and infant massage instructor with a passionate specialization in the childbearing years and supporting healthy families. A mother of 2 young children, Kari teaches prenatal, postnatal, and parent-toddler yoga classes at locations including The Mindful Body, The San Francisco Bay Club, CPMC, and Temple Sherith Israel. Her classes are highly regarded for their revitalizing and centering practice, educational content, and warm, nurturing community. She also offers massage and bodywork. See under "Pregnancy and Postnatal Massages."

Julie Rappaport

510-273-2417
www.yogabliss.com

Julie is a certified yoga teacher with 20 years of training and experience. She teaches pre- and postnatal yoga in various studios in San Francisco, Berkeley, and Oakland. She also offers private or semiprivate classes. Visit her website for more information.

Union

395-0864
www.unionsf.com

Union is a partnership dedicated to helping women get fit and stay fit through pregnancy, motherhood, and beyond. With nearly 20 years combined experience, founders Tracy Hartway and Elyse Hoffman provide expertise in prenatal and postpartum personal training, yoga, and co-active life coaching. Tracy has been a mentor for many prenatal yoga teachers in the area and has worked as a doula/birth assistant and is certified in a childbirth education program. Elyse has worked with moms-to-be for many years and is certified in Dancing Through Pregnancy. Elyse and Tracy see clients at Strong Heart Strong Body and in homes, as well as offer an occasional workshop at DayOne.

East Bay

Betsy Appell

415-254-0706
betsy@berkeleydoula.com
www.berkelelydoula.com

Betsy is a certified pre- and postnatal yoga instructor (as well as a certified doula and hypnotherapist and hypnobirthing teacher). She teaches in her home as well as in the yoga classes at the Berkeley YMCA. She also offers private pre- and postnatal yoga sessions where she creates a customized home practice for her clients. Visit her website for class schedule.

Saraswathi Devi

510-986-9370
www.yogalaym.com

Saraswathi Devi is a certified Prana yoga instructor and has been teaching yoga for nearly 35 years. She has a strong commitment to teaching yoga to pre- and postnatal women and teaches classes out of Yogalayam in Berkeley. Her classes, which include The Inner Approach to Childbirth, provide a practice in preparing for labor and focus on poses, breath work, imagery, and vision. She also teaches a massage and bodywork class for expectant couples as well as postnatal mother/baby yoga classes, one for babies up to one year old and a parent/toddler class for toddlers up to 3 and a half years old. Saraswathi also teaches yoga in schools and all over the country.

Kim Frank

510-548-8066
learnmatwork@yahoo.com

Kim offers private, one-on-one, in-home training in Pilates mat work for new and expectant mothers. A mom and 2-time C-section veteran herself, she has considerable experience working with women recovering from C-sections. Her fee depends on the frequency of the training sessions.

Jnana Gowan

510-734-4122

Jnana is a certified Hatha yoga instructor, Reiki II Practitioner and Whole Birth yoga instructor at the Nurture Center in Lafayette and at Turtle Island Yoga in San Anselmo. She also offers spa services in the home (such as pedicures for when you can't reach your own toes) that are popular with pregnant women and new mothers. See www.heavenlyma-ma.com for more information.

Andrea Evadne Kennerley

510-508-1408
www.optimumpilates.com
kennerley@lmi.net

Andrea is a STOTT certified Pilates instructor and offers private classes for prenatal women and one-on-one mat Pilates for postnatal moms, but sans the little one! She works in the East Bay and San Francisco. Visit her website for details.

Dawn Loretz

510-531-9062
dawn@yahoo.com

Dawn Loretz offers an ongoing prenatal exercise class, in a small group setting, operated out of her studio in Oakland. Among her other credentials, she is a certified physical therapist and is also a mom.

Julie Rappaport

510-273-2417
www.yogabliss.com

See above under North Bay.

Deborah Saliby

510-527-9266
www.envisionings.com

Deborah teaches yoga at various studios, including Seventh Heaven in Berkeley and Vara Healing Arts Center in Albany. Visit her website for current venues. She also is a hypnotherapist and teaches hypno-birthing education classes and birthing workshops.

Marie Morel-Seytoux

510-245-7587
www.marieandron.com/prenatalfit-ness

At the time this book goes to press, Marie is taking a short break from teaching her popular pre-and postnatal exercise classes in West Contra Costa County. She plans to resume teaching shortly. Visit her website for details.

Petronella Van Berry

510-843-6566
petcabo@yahoo.com

Petronella offers pre- and postnatal yoga classes at World Yoga Healing Arts Center in Walnut Creek and the Berkeley Yoga Center. She also offers private lessons.

Susan Schreier Williams
510-482-2276
Susan is an Alexander Technique certified teacher who works with pre- and postnatal women who want to reduce tension and pain by learning a "relaxed state of attention." She offers small, ongoing classes. Babies are welcome in the postpartum class.

South Bay

Julia Roberts
408-746-2752
She offers Iyengar yoga classes in Sunnyvale and Mountain View where she welcomes pregnant and postpartum women.

A New Being
Fitness, Massage and Support for Birth and Motherhood
415-424-5588
www.anewbeing.com
PARENT RATING: ☆ ☆ ☆ ☆ ☆
Denise Hontiveros offers a birth fitness class, and a postnatal fitness and fertility fitness class in addition to pre- and postnatal massage. Denise is an ACE-certified personal trainer and ICEA perinatal fitness instructor and Pilates instructor. She teaches private and semiprivate sessions at clients' homes and at various fitness studios in San Francisco and the Peninsula. She also teaches Baby Boot Camp sessions (see above) in Pacifica, Moss Beach, and Half Moon Bay.

Favorite Fitness Facilities with Child Care

The facilities listed below are some of parents' favorite fitness centers that offer child care, in addition to those noted under Classes, above. Reservations are required in most clubs, and the services are usually for members only. Most facilities require babies to be at least 3 months old, but some take younger ones. Child care arrangements in fitness centers are typically available for a limited time, depending on the age of the child, usually for one-half hour up to 2 hours, at varying costs. Most are quite reasonable, and a few are free. Weekday mornings are usually the most popular times for moms to exercise, so it can be difficult to get a spot for an infant, since most facilities have a limited number of spots, with fewer available for infants than toddlers and older children. If you plan on using child care at a gym, your best bet is to talk to parents who use the service and spend some time observing the child care room before you join. Take note of child-to-staff ratios, safety, and caregivers.

San Francisco

Bakar Fitness Center at UCSF Mission Bay

1675 Owens St.
www.mbfitness.ucsf.edu

This new facility (opening as this book goes to press) located along China Basin, down the street from SBC Park, offers a child care facility while you work out. You don't have to be a UCSF affiliate to join.

Bar Method Exercise Studio

3333 Fillmore St.
415-441-6333
www.barmethod.com

PARENT RATING: ☆ ☆ ☆ ☆ ☆

See above under Classes. The Bar Method has an attractive (and recently enlarged) child care room with many age-appropriate toys and caring caregivers. Child care is available for morning classes, Monday through Saturday. Reservations are strongly encouraged. You can make reservations up to a week in advance. Cancellations must be made at least 4 hours in advance.

Bay Club

150 Greenwich St.
415-433-2200
www.sfbayclub.com

PARENT RATING: ☆ ☆ ☆ ☆ ☆

See above under Classes. According to many parents, the Bay Club, an upscale, full-service fitness club, has a great child care program where the child care providers really make an effort. You can book up to 2 weeks in advance, and they accept infants as young as 6 weeks old.

The Dailey Method

3249 Scott St.
415-345-9992
www.thedaileymethod.com

See above under Classes. Child care is offered in their cheery child care room for many morning classes, Monday through Friday. Moms love many of the caregivers. Reservations recommended. There is a 12-hour cancellation policy.

Jewish Community Center of San Francisco

3200 California St.
415-292-1200
www.jccsf.org

PARENT RATING: ☆ ☆ ☆ ☆ ☆

See above under Classes. Since the first edition of this book, the San Francisco JCC has re-opened. Its new and gleaming facility, which includes a state-of-the art gym and fitness center, is a big player in the exercise scene in the city, especially for parents. The child care room is large and bright, and is divided into two rooms during peak times, to accomodate more children and to keep infants out of the way of tumbling toddlers. "Drop in" child care is offered for children 2 through 10 years of age Mondays through Friday mornings. Advance reservations are recommended though, and you'll need to attend a 15-minute orientation before you can use the child care facility. Orientations are scheduled several times a week. Call to make an appointment.

Presidio YMCA

Lincoln Way at Funston
(Building 63)
415-447-9622
www.ymcasf.org

PARENT RATING: ☆ ☆ ☆ ☆

Since the Y remodeled their facilities a few years ago, their "childwatch" area is larger and improved with new age-appropriate toys. Overall, the child watch staff does a good job. It can be difficult to get reservations for infants, especially during the morning. Infants must be at least 3 months old. The Y starts taking reservations for any particular day 2 days in advance (and not sooner).

Richmond YMCA

360 18th Ave.
415-666-9622
www.ymcasf.org

This is a smaller facility than the Presidio Y, but it also offers group exercise classes and more. This Y offers "childwatch" during the day.

Stonestown Family Branch YMCA

333 Eucalyptus Dr.
415-759-9622
www.ymcasf.org

"Childwatch" here accepts infants as young as 6 weeks.

24 Hour Fitness Sport

www.24hourfitness.com
- 1645 Bryant St.
  415-437-4188
- 1850 Ocean Ave.
  415-334-1400

These locations offer child care for babies 6 months and up.

The Airport Health Club

432 Aviation Blvd.
Santa Rosa
707-528-2582

Kids Korner is available for babies who are at least 6 months old.

The Bar Method

208 Bon Air Shopping Ctr.
Greenbrae
415-461-4461
www.barmethod.com

See above under Classes. Child care is offered on a first-come, first-served basis for many weekday morning classes. Reservations may be made prior to your class time to secure your child's spot. The child care facility is equipped with snacks, toys, books, drawing materials, and DVDs.

Bay Club Marin

221 Corte Madera Town Ctr.
Corte Madera
415-945-3000
www.bayclubmarin.com

PARENT RATING: ☆ ☆ ☆ ☆ ☆

San Francisco's famed Bay Club opened their gleaming Marin club in August 2002 with all the same great amenities, including child care. Babies as young as 6 weeks are welcome. Reservations recommended. Comment: "It can be tough to get an infant into the Play Club during weekday mornings, as spaces for babies are limited, but this is true for most fitness centers."

111

The Dailey Method

11 First St.
Corte Madera
415-927-1133
www.thedaileymethod.com

PARENT RATING: ☆ ☆ ☆ ☆ ☆

See above under Classes. The Dailey Method offers child care for morning classes, Monday through Saturday, as well as some afternoon weekday classes. Parents and kids alike rave about the caregiver, Jacqui Cisne. Reservations are recommended, and there is a 12-hour cancellation policy.

Elan Health and Fitness Center

- San Anselmo
  230 Greenfield Ave., 415-485-1945
- Petaluma
  1372 N. McDowell Blvd., 707-765-1919

www.elan.com

See above under Classes. Elan takes babies as young as one month old.

Fitness Factory

19310 Sonoma Hwy.
Sonoma
707-939-7116
www.sonomafitnessfactory.com

Infants must be at least 6 months old.

Gold's Gym

515 5th St.
Santa Rosa
707-545-5100
www.goldsgymsantarosa.com

Infnants must be at least 4 months old.

Marin YMCA

1500 Los Gamos Dr.
San Rafael
415-492-9622
www.marinymca.org

"Childwatch" available for babies who are at least 7 weeks old.

Marin Fitness

2025 Novato Blvd.
Novato
415-892-5688

Marin Fitness offers child care for babies who are at least 6 months old.

Meridian Sports Club at Rolling Hills

351 San Andreas Dr.
Novato
415-897-2185
www.meridiansportsclub.org

"Kids club" is available for babies 6 months old and up.

Mill Valley Community Center

180 Camino Alto
Mill Valley
415-383-1370
www.millvalleycenter.org

Child care is available for babies 3 months old and up.

Mt. Tamalpais Racquet Club

1 Larkspur Dr.
Larkspur
415-924-6226
www.mttamrec.com

They offer child care for babies who are at least 6 months old.

Nautilus of Marin

- San Rafael
  100 4th St., 415-485-1001
- Novato
  1530 Novato Blvd., 415-898-2582
www.nautalisofmarin.com

This facility offers child care with no particular minimum age requirement.

Osher Marin Jewish Community Center

200 N. San Pedro Rd.
San Rafael
415-444-8038
www.marinjcc.org

"Kidcare" is available for babies who are at least 4 months old and for children up to 7 years old.

Petaluma Valley Athletic Club

85 Old Corona Rd.
707-789-9898
www.pvac.com

Child care is available for babies 4 months old and up.

Roco Dance and Fitness

237 Shoreline Hwy.
Mill Valley
415-388-6786
www.rocodance.com

There is no particular minimum age for infants using the child care facility here.

Santa Rosa YMCA

111 College Ave.
Santa Rosa
707-545-9622
www.scfymca.org

"Childwatch" is available for babies of all ages.

Stan Bennett's Health and Fitness

- Santa Rosa
  760 Montecito Center, 707-537-6796
- Santa Rosa
  3345 Santa Rosa Ave., 707-579-9500
- Rohnert Park
  6595 Commerce Blvd., 707-585-3232
Child care is available for babies 6 months old and up.

East Bay

Albany YMCA

921 Kaines St.
Albany
510-525-1130
www.baymca.org
PARENT RATING: ☆ ☆ ☆

This YMCA usually has one child care provider in a small room adjacent to the gym. Care is fine according to most, but the linoleum floors can be a bit rough for toddlers who aren't quite walking. Child care providers here are not licensed to change diapers, so they'll come get you from your workout to do this. Comment: "Very caring staff, mostly experienced moms."

Berkeley YMCA

2001 Allston Way
510-848-9622
www.bayca.org

Parents who are Y members staff the "childwatch" room. They take infants as young as 8 weeks. The room is reportedly busy, but there's a great kindergym that young children love with lots of toys and art, and even a computer!

Blackhawk Pinnacle Fitness

3464 Blackhawk Plaza Cir.
Danville
925-736-0898
www.ballyfitness.com
They take infants starting at 3
months old.

ClubSport

- San Ramon
  350 Bollinger Canyon Rd.
  925-735-8500
  www.clubsportsr.com
Comment: "Child care is super here!"
- Pleasanton
  7090 Johnson Dr.
  925-463-2822
  www.clubsports.com
These clubs take infants as young as
6 weeks old.

Courthouse Gym

2985 Telegraph Rd.
Oakland
510-834-5600
Child care is offered for babies who
are at least 12 weeks old. Child care
is staffed by members; reduced
membership rates are given in return.

The Dailey Method

4409 Piedmont Ave.
Oakland
510-206-7725
www.thedaileymethod.com
See above under Classes. The Dailey
Method's newest location (opened
summer 2005) offers child care for
many weekday morning classes.
Reservations recommended. There is
a 12-hour cancellation policy.

Harbor Bay Club Gym

200 Packet Landing Rd.
Alameda
510-521-5414
www.harborbayclub.com
Babies of all ages are welcome in
their child care.

Mariner Square Athletic Club

2227 Mariner Square Loop
Alameda
510-523-8011
www.marinersq.com

This is a nice, clean child care facility
with a play fort, play kitchen, and
more for babies and kids, 8 weeks
old and up. Best of all, it is free to
members!

Oakwood Athletic Club

4000 Mt. Diablo Blvd.
Lafayette
925-283-4000
www.oakwoodathleticclub.com
This club offers child care for babies
as young as 6 weeks old.

Schoeber's Athletic Club

3411 Capital Ave.
Fremont
510-791-6350
www.schoeberclubs.com
This club offers child care for babies
and children from 6 months old and
up.

Walnut Creek Sport and Fitness

1908 Olympic Blvd.
Walnut Creek
925-932-6400
www.wcsf.net
This club offers child care for babies
as young as 6 weeks.

The Bar Method

128 De Anza Blvd.
Crystal Springs Village
San Mateo
www.barmethod.com

See above under Classes. Child care
is available for many weekday morning classes. Reservations are strongly
encouraged.

Bayhill Gym and Fitness

Cherry Ave.
San Bruno
650-583-2582
www.bayhillgym.com

This club offers child care for children
2 years old and up.

Courtside Club

14675 Winchester Blvd.
Los Gatos
408-395-7111
www.courtsideclub.com

This club accepts infants as young as
6 weeks old.

El Camino YMCA

2400 Grant Rd.
Mountain View
650-969-9622

"Childwatch" here accepts infants as
young as 6 weeks.

Decathlon Club

3250 Central Expwy.
Santa Clara
408-738-2582
www.decathlon-club.com

This club offers child care for infants
as young as 5 weeks old.

Fitness 101

400 Scott Dr.
Menlo Park
650-321-7900
www.fitness101.com

This club offers "fitkids" child care for
infants as young as 6 weeks old.

Foster City Athletic Club

1159 Chess Dr.
Foster City
650-377-1991
www.fcathletic.com

This club offers child care for infants
who are at least 4 months old.

Peninsula Jewish Community Center

Byer Athletic Center
800 Foster City Blvd.
Foster City
650-212-7522
www.pjcc.org

This new fitness center features child
care for babies as young as 6 weeks
old. Advanced reservations are recommended.

Los Gatos Swim and Racquet Club

14700 Oka Rd.
Los Gatos
408-356-2136
www.lgsrc.com

This club offers child care for babies
beginning at no particular minimum
age.

Pacific Athletic Club

200 Redwood Shore Pkwy.
Redwood Shores
650-593-4900
www.pacclub.com

This club will take infants as young
as 6 weeks old.

115

Palo Alto YMCA

3412 Ross Rd.
Palo Alto
650-856-9622 (general number)
650-842-7162 (Director, group exercise)
www.ymcamidpen.com
The "childwatch" facility here takes babies as young as 7 weeks old.

Peninsula Covenant Community Center

3623 Jefferson Ave.
Redwood City
650-364-6272
www.peninsulacovenant.com
This facility's child care accepts babies who are at least 6 months old.

Comment: "All of their classes are great, especially the water aerobics, and they offer excellent child care!"

Peninsula Family YMCA

1877 S. Grant St.
San Mateo
650-286-9622
www.ymcasf.org/peninsula
Infants must be at least 2 months old for their "childwatch."

Prime Time Athletic Club

1730 Rollins Rd.
Burlingame
650-697-7311
www.primetimeathleticclub.com
Child care is available for infants as young as 6 weeks old.

Royal Athletic Club

1718 Rollins Rd.
Burlingame
650-692-3300
www.royalathleticclub.com
Child care is available for infants as young as 6 weeks old.

Sequoia Branch YMCA

1445 Hudson St.
Redwood City
650-368-4168
www.ymcamidpen.org
This facility offers "childwatch" for babies who are at least 3 months old.

24 Hour Fitness Sport

- Daly City
  373 Gellert Blvd., 650-756-3303
- San Mateo
  520 El Camino Real, 650-323-7922
www.24hourfitness.com
These clubs offer child care for babies who are at least 6 months old.

Favorite Walks and Hikes

There are many wonderful places to walk and hike with a baby or young child in the Bay Area. Here are a few favorites:

San Francisco

Baker Beach

Located off Lincoln Boulevard, between the Sea Cliff neighborhood and Golden Gate Bridge, a walk on Baker Beach is best on a warm day, with a front or back pack. If you are really up for exploring, there are a couple of dirt trails in the Presidio that lead down to the beach. See also in Ch. 8.

116

City Guides: Free Walking Tours

www.sfcityguides.org

Learn a little history about your city with baby by taking a San Francisco Public Library-sponsored City Guide walk. They offer 27 different walks each week. Just meet your badge-wearing guide at the designated venue. Walks are free and usually last between 1½ to 2 hours. Not all walks are stroller friendly, so either bring baby in a frontpack or other carrier or call in advance. Visit their website for a complete schedule of walks.

Crissy Field (Marina)

Enjoy a walk or jog all the way from Fort Mason to Fort Point. Choose between the paved path next to the road, or the loose gravel path that hugs the shoreline. Don't forget to bring a windbreaker and to stop off at the Warming Hut Café and Bookstore, located about three-quarters of the way to Fort Point, or Crissy Field Center Café, which is about a mile walking away from the bridge.

Fort Funston

Skyline Blvd. (about one mile south of Sloat Blvd.)

415-556-8371

There are great walking paths and hang glider viewing here.

Golden Gate Park

www.parks.sfgov.org

The nation's largest urban national park offers many hikes and walks appropriate for babies and strollers. A fun and easy one is around the Rodeo Lagoon. Or take a stroll around Stow Lake at John F. Kennedy Dr. and feed the ducks with your little one. Or watch model boat sailing at Spreckels Lake on the weekends. The Strybing Arboretum and Botanical Gardens both offer walking tours. See Ch. 8.

Lake Merced

Skyline Blvd. at Lake Merced Blvd.

415-831-2700

Great paved paths go around the perimeter of the reservoir. Perfect for strollers!

Mountain Lake Park Loop

Lake St. and 12th Ave.

Part of this under-a-mile loop is paved, and the other part is gravel. One of the nice things about this walk is that it ends up at Mountain Lake Park's playground which features a little lake where you can feed the ducks—if the pigeons let you!

Noe Valley Stroller Group

www.noestrolls.com

This play group on wheels meets at various locations in the city to take stroller walks with their little ones. It's a great way to exercise, meet new moms, and enjoy our wonderful city with your baby! They have regular strolls, a jogging group, and much more. The walks are geared for kids (newborn to age 3) who are in strollers. The group also has Fitness Fridays, which features a workout with a group member who is also a personal trainer. To join, all you have to do is e-mail your first name and your baby's name and age to their website, or visit their website for venues and show up at one of their strolls. Membership is free.

Additional Resources for Walks and Hikes in San Francisco

◆ *Skating Unrinked in the San Francisco Bay Area* by Richard Katz features paved trails which are not only great for skaters, but also for strollers!

◆ *Hidden Walks in the Bay Area* by Stephen Altschuler is a great guide to many walks in San Francisco.

◆ *Stairway Walks in San Francisco* by Adah Bakalinsky is a wonderful guide to getting to know your city while your baby is still in a front carrier!

Stonestown Strollers

415-759-2626
415-564-8848
www.shopstonestown.com
www.fitnessformothers.com

This is a great place for moms to exercise for free. This one-hour fitness program is designed by mothers for mothers. Certified fitness trainer Anna O. will help you achieve a stronger, leaner body by using your stroller for cardio resistance training with your baby. See above under Fitness for Mothers (classes).

Wednesday Stroller Walks in Golden Gate Park

415-750-5105 (Friends of Recreation and Parks)
415-750-5226 (Michelle Canning, volunteer manager of Friends of Recreation and Parks)
www.frp.org

Enjoy fresh air and exercise, meet other parents, and learn a little Golden Gate Park history. These walks are designed for parents with strollers, as guides stay on paved paths. They meet the first and third Wednesday of

every month, rain or shine. A free one-hour stroll begins at 10 a.m.

North Bay

Adventurers with Toddlers

418 Napa St.
Sausalito (office)
415-331-8882 (Lonnie Greenfield)

Lonnie Greenfield, a trained volunteer guide at the Terwilliger Nature Education Center, leads fun-filled hikes for parents and toddlers that are too big for a backpack and too small to hike very far. "Hike" toddler style, with lots of exploration and time for snacks, and learn about trees and flowers while enjoying the great outdoors. Different locations each outing, each month. Geared for children 18 months through 5 years old. Advance registration required at many Marin recreation departments, including Sausalito. (http://sausalito.recware.com).

Angel Island

www.angelisland.org

Kids will love taking the ferry to Angel Island from San Francisco, Tiburon, Oakland, or Vallejo. Once you are there, chose a 5-mile perimeter loop, which takes you past Camp Reynolds, a Civil War-era garrison with spectacular views. A shorter but steeper route is the 3.7-mile loop up to Mount Livermore, which also has great views.

Blackie's Pasture, Tiburon

www.tiburonpeninsulafoundation.org
Right off Tiburon Boulevard, at the intersection of Trestle Glenn, you will find Blackie's Pasture. This park offers plenty of parking in 2 lots, with paved flat trails, perfect for strollers, offering great bay views. The 1.5-mile path will take you all the way to downtown Tiburon. There is a nice playground that is scheduled to be renovated in late 2005 (as well as restrooms) on the way.

Blithedale Summit Open Space Preserve

Larkspur

This is a pleasant walk along Larkspur Creek, and the redwoods keep it nice and cool, even on hot days! Be aware that this path is not stroller friendly. Use a front carrier or backpack for your little one. Take Madrone Ave. (across from the Lark Creek Inn) to the end.

Creekside Path (from Corte Madera to Ross)

This is a nice hiking or biking trail that runs along a creek past Corte Madera Town Park, Piper Park in Larkspur, and Creekside Park in Greenbrae. It's great for strollers. Take it to the College of Marin or all the way to Ross.

Crown Road

Northridge/Baltimore Canyon
Open Space Preserve
Kentfield
This wide, 3-mile flat fire trail on Mt. Tam has many trails branching off of it. You can expect to be joined by lots of hikers and runners—some with dogs—and plenty of shade. Take College Ave. to Woodland Road, and take the second left on Evergreen Road. Go to the top of the hill, and turn left on Crown Rd.

Lagoon Trail, Sausalito

This mostly flat trail begins at the Marin Headlands Visitor Center Bunker (415-331-1540.)

Las Gallinas Ponds

(Near McInnis Park, off Smith Ranch Road in Terra Linda)
Miles of levee trails that surround ponds of the local sanitary district (yes, hard to believe!) offer sightings of great blue herons, egrets, geese, and pelicans. Hikes vary in distance depending on how many ponds you decide to circle. Be sure to take along binoculars and sunscreen, as shade is scarce.

Muir Woods (Mill Valley)

415-388-2595
www.visitmuirwoods.com/trails.htm
Muir Woods has a couple of easy to moderate trails that work well with a baby in either a jog stroller or a front carrier or backpack. The Main Trail Loop from the Visitor Center to Cathedral Drive is an easy one-hour, one-mile round trip unpaved trail. The Fern Creek Trail, a moderate 3-mile trail, takes about 2 hours.

Phoenix Lake Loop, Ross

This 2.8-mile scenic loop starts at Natalie Coffin Greene Park in Ross (at the end of Lagunitas Rd.) and goes through the watershed lands around Phoenix Lake. You will need a front carrier or backpack for this trail which is narrow and rough in parts (there are some stairs). If you have a jogger or bike trailer, stay on wider Shaver Grade, keeping Phoenix Lake to your left. You can take this all the way up to Five Corners and back, making for a nice long 4-mile walk.

Point Reyes National Seashore

415-464-5100
www.trails.com
www.nps.gov/pore

The park has over 140 miles of trails and 3 visitor centers. There are short, scenic hikes from the Bear Valley Visitor Center. The Earthquake Trail starts across the street from park headquarters; it is flat and paved. Call ahead for park maps.

Additional Resources for Walks and Hikes in the North Bay

◆ **www.marintrails.com/Kids/kidsintro.html**

Marin trails offers 3 types of hikes, with babies, toddlers, and children. The website provides a great deal of information, including how much shade each hike typically has, approximate mileage, and good directions.

◆ **www.plumsite.com/bayareamoms/outandabout/naturetrails/trails.htm**

This is a great mom-inspired website of favorite walks/hikes in Marin.

◆ **www.bahiker.com/kids.html**

This detailed website has all you need to know about hiking in the Bay Area. It includes photos, information on trail specifics, distances, restrooms, paved or gravel trails, shade, etc.

◆ *Best Hikes with Children: San Francisco's North Bay*, by Bill McMillon and Kevin McMillon.

◆ *Easy Hiking in Northern California*, by Ann Marie Brown, contains 14 hikes in Marin, 4 in the East Bay, and many in Yosemite and Tahoe, all of which are suitable for preschoolers.

◆ *Hiking in Marin, 133 Great Hikes in Marin County*, by Don and Kay Martin.

◆ *Skating Unrinked in the San Francisco Bay Area*, by Richard Katz features paved trails that are not only suitable for skaters, but also for strollers!

◆ *Backpacking with Babies and Small Children: A Guide to Taking the Kids on Day Hikes, Overnighters and Long Trail Trips*, by Goldie Silverman

Samuel P. Taylor State Park, Lagunitas

415-488-9897

www.parks.ca.gov

This park has several flat paved trails that go through stunning redwood groves. It is suitable for jog strollers or backpacks.

Tennessee Valley (Golden Gate National Recreation Area)

www.nps.gov/goga

This lovely 1.8-mile unpaved trail is fairly flat and leads out to the ocean and a protected cove. Bring your baby in a jog stroller or a front- or backpack and a picnic for the beach. The trail is located off Hwy 1. Take Tennessee Valley Road to the end to meet the trailhead where there is a parking lot.

Shoreline Trail

China Camp State Park, San Rafael

This mainly flat and picturesque 2-mile trail is perfect for contemplation with your little one! Moss-covered oaks, foot bridges across creeks, and plenty of meadows with an occasional deer or turkey are just some of the highlights of this tranquil trail.

Verna Dunshee Trail

Mount Tamalpais State Park (Mill Valley)

This trail, although less than a mile, is an all-time favorite, circling the very top of Mount Tam. It has been recently repaved and many families enjoy taking kids there for a quick jaunt and pointing out all the big landmarks—San Francisco, the Pacific, plus bridges and more. Take Panoramic Hwy. to a right on Pantoll

Rd. Then take a right on East Ridgecrest Blvd. to the East Peak parking area.

East Bay

Alameda Creek Regional Trail, Fremont

510-562-7275 (East Bay Regional Park District information phone line)

This trail goes right through the tri-cities of Fremont, Union City, and Hayward.

Briones Park, Lafayette, and Martinez

www.ebparks.org/parks/briones.htm

Two trails suitable for front- and backpacks or jog strollers are Old Bear Creek Rd. (which is nearly flat) and Alhambra Creek Valley.

Cesar Chavez Park, Berkeley

At the end of University Drive, this is a nice mile-and-a-half-paved flat loop next to San Francisco Bay. It is great for strollers, but not on windy days!

Coyote Hills Regional Park, Fremont

This parks features a paved trail that circles around the wildlife sanctuary.

East Bay Moms

6000 Contra Costa Rd.

510-653-7867

www.eastbaymoms.com

Among other events and outings, this popular mothers' group offers weekly hikes and stroller walks with other parents and their little ones. The group's $90 annual membership fee includes a newsletter and unlimited participation in scheduled events with an emphasis on outdoor exercise with other mothers and babies. See Ch. 6.

Huckleberry Regional Preserve, Oakland

www.ebparks.org/parks/huck.htm

There is a 1.9-mile loop suitable for front- or backpacks, with beautiful vegetation and plenty of shade for the little ones.

Kennedy Grove on San Pablo Dam Road in El Sobrante offers a nice loop.

Lafayette-Moraga Trail

www.ebparks.org/parks/lafmotr.htm

This fairly flat 3-mile paved trail is perfect for strollers. A picnic area and playground adjacent to the parking lot makes this walk popular among mothers' groups.

Lake Elizabeth (Fremont)

Take the less than 3-mile flat paved trail that loops around the lake.

Lake Merritt (Oakland)

This 3-mile paved loop is a favorite walk for moms and dads and little ones.

Miller Knox Regional Park in Point Richmond

This park has a flat paved path that circles a duck pond and offers great bay views.

Mount Diablo State Park (Danville)

925-837-2525 visitors center (closed Mon. and Tues.)

www.ebparks.org/parks/irontr.htm

Although much of Mt. Diablo is rugged terrain, the gentle .7-mile loop Fire Trail near the summit makes a nice family hike. Rock City is a beau-

tiful hiking area with lots of rocks for kids to climb. There is a moderate trail from here that takes about 90 minutes round-trip with a baby in a front- or backpack. Iron Horse Trail, connecting the cities of Concord and Dublin, is also a great all-day 12.7-mile hike for either a jog stroller or front- or backpack.

Point Pinole Regional Shoreline (Conta Costa County)

One mile off the Richmond Parkway, this 3.6-mile loop, overlooking San Pablo Bay, has slight hills, but there is a shuttle on most days that you can always catch if you run out of steam. Seee www.bahiker.com/eastbayhikes/pointpinole.html.

Point Isabel Regional Shoreline (El Cerito)

www.ebparks.org/parks

This is an East Bay favorite, with lots of paved paths along the bay. Be prepared to be joined by lots of dogs.

Redwood Regional Park

Off of Skyline Blvd., East Ridge trail, an easy 3.7-mile loop, begins at the Skyline Drive Staging Area. It promisess a wide scenic trail with a few gentle-grade hills—perfect for a jogger. See www.bahiker.com/eastbayhikes/redwood.html.

Tilden Park (Berkeley Hills)

510-525-2233

www.ebparks.org/parks/bot.htm

This is one of the best parks for children in the Bay Area! Pony rides, steam trains, and beach swimming are offered. The Nimitz Trail to Inspiration Point on Wildcat Canyon Rd. is a popular mile-long paved trail

Additional Resources for Walks and Hikes in the East Bay

◆ **www.ebparks.org/parks/htm**
This great website gives all the particulars on East Bay parks and trails.

◆ **www.bahiker.com/kids.html**
This site gives details for several East Bay hikes suitable for young children.

◆ *Best Hikes with Children: San Francisco's South Bay*, by Bill McMillon (includes the East Bay).

◆ *Easy Hiking in Northern California*, by Ann Marie Brown, contains 14 hikes in Marin, 4 in the East Bay, and many in Yosemite and Tahoe, all which are suitable for preschoolers.

◆ *Skating Unrinked in the San Francisco Bay Area*, by Richard Katz features paved trails that are not only suitable for skaters, but also for strollers!

that is suitable for strollers. For backpackers, the Lone Oak Trail is a 2.9-mile dirt trail with a fairly gentle climb. The Environmental Education Center offers Tilden Tots outings for children ages 3 and 4. Outings feature a nature hike with parents that focus on a theme, such as spiders or leaves. These walks are quite popular, so call to register in advance. The Tilden Park Botanical Garden is also a great place for walking; kids can either explore or look at plants from the stroller.

South Bay

Alum Rock Park, San Jose

408-259-5477
www.sanjoseca.gov/prns/
Alum Rock was a spa with mineral baths 100 years ago. Today it is a nature preserve with 13 miles of trail, many of which are suitable for young children. Take the mostly shaded 2-mile Creek Trail at the east end of Penitencia Creek Rd. It has a gradual incline and plenty of beautiful scenery.

Alviso Slough Trail (Alviso, outside of San Jose)

408-262-5513
Follow a portion of this flat 9-mile trail built around salt ponds at the tip of San Francisco Bay, with stunning views of the East Bay Hills and Santa Cruz Mountains on clear summer days. The trail is accessible from the Alviso Marina, located at the end of Hope Street.

Coyote Creek Parkway (Coyote Hellyer Park, near San Jose)

408-225-0225

http://www.geocities.com/
bayareaparks/CoyoteCreekTrail/
CoyoteCreekTrail.htm

This 15-mile-long, paved, mostly level, multi-use trail runs along Coyote Creek from South San Jose, through the Coyote Valley, and ends at Anderson Lake in Morgan Hill.

Henry Cowell Redwoods State Park (south of Felton, Santa Cruz County)

831-335-7077

http://www.bahiker.com/
southbayhikes/henrycowell.html

Take the easy paved 4.7-mile Redwood Grove loop trail that runs through the redwoods.

Hidden Villa Ranch (in Los Altos Hills near San Jose)

650-949-8650 (administration)
650-949-8641 (camping)
www.hiddenvilla.org
http://www.bahiker.com/
southbayhikes/hiddenvilla.html

There are more than 7 miles of trails to roam, including a moderate to easy 3.7-mile loop, in addition to an actual working farm with farm animals, oak-studded grasslands, organic gardens, and Adobe Creek's woodland watershed.

Huddart Park (Woodside)

www.bahiker.com/southbayhikes/
huddartdean.html

This park on Kings Mountain Road offers short loops that are great for little ones.

Loch Lomond Recreational Area (Felton/Santa Cruz)

831-335-7424

www.ci.santa-cruz.ca.us/wt/llra/
llra.html
http://www.bahiker.com/
southbayhikes/lochlomond.html

This lake area includes a moderate 4.9-mile loop.

Los Gatos Creek Trail, Los Gatos

408-356-2729 (park office)
www.parkhere.org/prkpages/lgcreek.
htm

This is a nicely paved trail—7.4 miles from Leigh Ave. to Main St. Perfect for a stroller!

Mid-Peninsula Regional Open Space District

650-691-1200
www.openspace.org

This organization oversees literally thousands of acres of open space from the mountains to the bay, many of which feature great trails. Visit their website for specifics on their "most accessible trails" that are perfect for strollers and young children.

Moms and Tots Hiking Club, El Camino YMCA

650-969-9622
www.ymcamidpen.org

This popular group of moms and babies ages 3 to 8 months meets each Wednesday in a 6-week series for progressive hikes through Rancho San Antonio State Park. Trails are suitable for a jog stroller or a front- or backpack.

Monterey Peninsula Recreational Trail

831-335-7424
http://www.mprpd.org
This easy flat path runs from Monterey to Pacific Grove, for bikers and strollers alike!

Rancho San Antonio State Park and Open Space Preserve, Los Altos

408-867-3654 (park office)
www.parkhere.org/prkpages/rancho.htm
One of the Bay Area's most popular hikes, this park includes 26 miles of trails, meadows, and an educational working farm that is open for observation year-round. Summer weekends get very crowded. The Rancho San Antonio Trail is a paved .75-mile trail.

Sawyer Camp Trail (San Mateo)

http://www.bahiker.com/southbayhikes/sawyercamp.html
This trail begins in Millbrae at Hwy. 280 and in San Mateo on Skyline Blvd. and runs along the Crystal Springs Reservoir. It is a 7-mile paved path along Crystal Springs Reservoir and is one of the most popular recreation trails in the Bay Area!

Shoreline Park (Mountain View)

http://www.bahiker.com/southbayhikes/shoreline.html
This park offers a smooth flat trail with interesting birds to see. Contact the Shoreline Acquatic Center at 650-965-7474 for details.

Additional Resources for Hikes and Walks in the South Bay

◆ **www.bahiker.com**
This great website contains information on 15 popular family hikes in the South Bay.

◆ **http://pages.prodigy.net/rhorii/sccparks.htm**
Includes specifics about parks and trails in Santa Clara County.

◆ *Best Hikes with Children: San Francisco's South Bay* by Bill McMillon.

◆ *Peninsula Tales and Trails*, by David Weintraub and produced by the Midpeninsula Regional Open Space District, offers information about the district's 25 open space preserves, encompassing nearly 50,000 acres in San Mateo, Santa Clara, and Santa Cruz counties. It includes trail route difficulty ratings, making it easy to see which ones are suitable for young families.

◆ *Skating Unrinked in the San Francisco Bay Area* by Richard Katz features paved trails that are not only suitable for skaters, but also for strollers!

Sierra Club's Loma Prieta Chapter (San Mateo and Santa Clara Counties)

This local chapter sponsors regular "Babies on Backs" hikes, 2-4 miles long at local parks, with little ones in front- or backpacks or jog strollers. Open to Sierra Club members and non-members. Contact Sonya Braadski at 650-856-9366.

Additional Fitness Resources

◆ *Strollercize,* by Elizabeth Trindade and Victoria Shaw offers stroller-based strength training, stretching and cardiovascular workouts, with an emphasis on safety for mom and baby. Comment: "A great way to bond with your baby and shed those pregnancy pounds!"

◆ *Kinergetics: Dancing with Your Baby for Bonding and Better Health for Both of You,* by Sue Doherty

◆ *Strong Women Stay Young,* by Miriam Nelson (www.strongwomen.com)

◆ *Real Fitness for Real Women: A Unique Work-Out Program for the Plus-size Woman,* by Rochelle Rice

◆ **www.workoutsforwomen.com** Can't afford a personal trainer? This website offers personal fitness training for women, including a pregnancy workout.

◆ **www.strollerfit.com** This is the official Strollerfit website. They promise to teach you how to "turn your stroller into a portable fitness machine!"

◆ **www.expectingfitness.com** This website describes itself as "your source on pre- and post-natal fitness."

◆ **www.fitmaternity.com** This website sells maternity fitness wear.

◆ **www.mothersinmotion.com** This website sells maternity fitness wear and has tons of useful information on fitness for new and expectant mothers, including links to local resources and classes.

◆ **www.titleninesports.com** This leader in women's fitness wear offers maternity workout wear and a few great nursing bras that make working out possible between feedings! Check out their retail stores in Berkeley and Palo Alto too.

Pregnancy and Postnatal Massages

Having a massage can help stave off those pregnancy aches and pains and also help restore and rejuvenate your body after delivery. Other benefits of pre-and postnatal massage therapy may include improving circulation, directing blood flow and nutrients to mother and baby, increasing metabolism rates, ensuring the production of vital hormones and the elimination of toxins, promoting relaxation, reducing stress and anxiety, and calming the mind and body.

When making an appointment for a pregnancy massage be sure to ask if a note with your physician's approval is required. You should also ask whether the masseuse is a licensed professional (a Certified Massage Therapist, CMT), and what kind of experience he or she has in working with pregnant or postpartum women. In addition, you may want to inquire about whether they use a special massage table for pregnant women to allow for a full body and back massage. On this table, you lie comfortably on your stomach—the table has a hole in it and a mesh basket to support the belly. Some practitioners do not use these tables because they believe that lying on the stomach in this manner places an unhealthy strain on abdominal muscles. Instead, they perform a prenatal massage in a side-lying position with many pillows and wedges for comfort.

The following are some spas and professionals specializing in pre- and postnatal massages in the Bay Area whom we have heard about from other parents—this list is by no means complete, as many more full-service spas, salons, and individual practitioners offer these types of massages. Prices are usually dependent on the length of the massage, but they still vary from one professional or organization to another, so be sure to inquire before making an appointment.

San Francisco

The Bar Method
3333 Fillmore St.
441-6333
www.barmethod.com

California Pacific Medical Center Women's Health Resource Center
3698 California St.
415-600-0500
PARENT RATING: ☆ ☆ ☆ ☆

They also give massages in hospital rooms! Comments: "CPMC is a true bargain—a great massage at an affordable price. . . . A real treat during my ninth month! . . . Just what I needed to get rid of my neck and shoulder muscle aches from nursing and carrying my baby. . . . Better than all the $100 massages I got!"

Heaven Day Spa
2209 Chestnut St.
415-749-6414
www.heavendayspa.com

Kari Marble, MA, CMT
415-845-1073
kari@welcomeom.com

PARENT RATING: ☆ ☆ ☆ ☆ ☆

Kari specialties include prenatal and postpartum bodywork and neuromuscular reprogramming.

Comments: "Kari is amazingly nurturing and knowledgeable. Her massages got me through pregnancy and completely rebalanced my postpartum body. . . . She is the tops! . . . Kari's massage work is intense—my body is renewed every time! . . . A massage with Kari is one of the best gifts anyone can give a new parent!"

LaBelle Day Spa
133 Kearny St.
415-433-7644
www.labelledayspas.com

The Mindful Body
2876 California St.
415-931-2639
www.themindfulbody.com

Novella Spa and Salon
2238 Union St.
415-673-1929

Elizabeth Obermeyer
415-752-7484

Renew Bodyworks
Ellin Pearlman, CMT
2295 Chestnut St., Ste. 3
415-577-6000
Ellin will do home visits to mothers on bed rest.

Spa Nordstrom
San Francisco Center, 5th Fl.
865 Market St.
415-977-5102
Comment: "Couldn't have made it through the third trimester without Nordstrom's pregnancy massage!"

Spa Radiance
3011 Fillmore St.
415-346-6281
www.sparadiance.com

PARENT RATING: ☆ ☆ ☆ ☆ ☆

Comments: "The best of the best massages ever! . . . A real postnatal treat!"

The Sports Club LA
747 Market St.
415-633-3900
www.thesportsclubla.com

Janet Stock, CMT
415-771-1125

PARENT RATING: ☆ ☆ ☆ ☆ ☆

Janet is a massage therapist specializing in massage and acupressure for women. She is certified in Swedish, acupressure, prenatal, labor and delivery, postpartum, and infant massage. Janet has a private practice in San Francisco, and she also works at the Women's Health Resource Center at California Pacific Medical center. Comments: "I thought the massage was great—great pressure and use of pressure points. . . . Janet is very informed and sensitive to women's needs."

128

Jewish Community Center of San Francisco

3200 California St.
415-292-1200
www.jccsf.org
The JCC offers a full range of "spa services," including pre- and postnatal massage.

North Bay

Asanté Day Spa

18 Mary St.
San Rafael
415-460-6506
www.asantespa.com

Barefoot and Pregnant

1165 Magnolia Ave.
Larkspur
415-388-1777
www.barefootandpregnant.com
Pre- and postnatal massages are only some of many spa offerings at this true sanctuary for new moms and expectant women. They also feature "babymoon" packages where one can indulge in spa treatments and exercise classes during the day and enjoy a peaceful night's sleep at the Mountain Home Inn in Mill Valley.

Espirit Skin Care

36 Tiburon Blvd.
Mill Valley
415-383-3534
A favorite in Southern Marin!

Birth Doulas Marin

203 Devon Dr.
San Rafael
415-451-7287
www.birthdoulas.net

Laurie Campion, CMT and Nutritionist

640 Mission St.
San Rafael
415-389-8434

Michelle Leifer/HellerWork

415-454-4325

Elizabeth Obermeyer

415-752-7484

Samantha Stormer

645 Tamalpais Dr.
Corte Madera
415-924-9096
PARENT RATING: ☆ ☆ ☆ ☆ ☆
Comment: "Samantha gives a very intense but relaxing postpartum massage, . . . teaches you about pressure points to relieve pain. . . . [and] since she is also a birth doula, she really understands prenatal and postpartum needs and issues."

Elaine Steinbrecher

415-459-2415

Stellar Spa

26 Tamalpais Dr.
Corte Madera
415-924-7300

Tea Garden Springs

38 Miller Ave.
Mill Valley
415-389-7123

Whole Health Associates Center for Integrative Medicine

Dolores Caruthers, CMT
1368 Lincoln, Ste. 109
San Rafael
415-454-4325

Bodywork Central
5519 College Ave.
Berkeley
510-547-4313

Bridget Scadeng
2421 4th St., #B
Berkeley
510-526-3493

Chanti Smith
510-432-8181

Claremont Resort and Spa
41 Tunnel Rd.
Berkeley
800-551-7266

Mama Massage
Christina Del Gallo, CMT
510-531-5963

Motherwit
Lisa Rasler, LM, CPM, CMT
510-530-1178

Moving Light Massage and Body Works
510-841-6263 or 510-525-8539

Vara Healing Arts
850 Talbot Ave.
Albany
510-526-YOGA (9642)
www.varahealing.com

South Bay

AvantGard Day Spa
1224 El Camino Real
San Carlos
650-591-1498
www.avantspa.com

Body Presence
904 Laurel St.
San Carlos
650-593-9652

Body Therapy Center
368 California Ave.
Palo Alto
650-328-9400
www.bodymindspirit.net

Blossom Birth Services
1000 Elwell Ct.
Palo Alto
650-964-7380
www.blossombirth.com

Center for Therapeutic Massage
1905 Palmetto Ave., Unit E
Pacifica
650-359-3921

Integrated Health Care Center for Wellness
2290 Birch St.
Palo Alto
650-321-7193

LaBelle DaySpa
- Palo Alto
  95 Town and Country Village
  650-327-6964
- Stanford
  36 Stanford Shopping Center
  650-326-8522
www.labelledayspas.com

**A New Being
Fitness, Massage and Support for Birth and Motherhood**
415-424-5588
www.anewbeing.com

Peninsula Jewish Community Center

Byer Athletic Center
800 Foster City Blvd.
Foster City
650-357-7733
www.pjcc.org

Sandra Caron European Spa

105 E. 3rd Ave.
San Mateo
650-347-9666
www.sandracaron.com

Bina Walker

Palo Alto
650-796-6645
Comment: "I consider her a great deep-tissue work person."

CHAPTER 3

OUTFITTING YOURSELF:
Finding Stylish
Maternity Clothes
without Breaking the Bank

Maybe it was the celebrity moms. Or maybe it was the arrival of the now-ubiquitous stretch fabrics. Whatever the reason, a revolution has occurred in maternity wear. Gone are the tent dresses adorned with bows. Enter: flattering, form-fitting designs straight from the runway. What we formerly dreaded buying has become so attractive that we would consider getting pregnant again just for the new clothes. (Well, almost.) Still, who wants to drive around the Bay Area sorting the hip from the matronly? To make your life easier, we've put together this chapter on the best and worst of Bay Area maternity clothes shopping. We'll tell you what (and what not) to buy and when to buy it, and give you the lowdown on where to find good values and clothes you'll actually want to wear (at least for a few months . . .). Check out our list of Bay Area moms' favorite online sources too. Happy shopping! This chapter answers the following questions and more:

- What kinds of maternity clothes should I buy, and when should I buy them?
- Where can I find the best deals on maternity clothes?

- What kinds of clothes are the best value, and which are a waste of money?
- Where can I find gently used maternity clothes?
- I'm overwhelmed by the choices online. What do parents recommend?

When to Buy

If you are like we were during our first pregnancies, you probably think you'll need maternity clothes from the first month on. Relax. Don't rush out and buy *anything* until you need it, or you may end up not wearing it at all when the seasons change. For first-time moms, this could be anywhere from the fourth to the sixth month. Second timers, unfortunately, will need things a bit sooner.

For the first few months, you'll want clothes that expand comfortably, but maternity clothes will look ridiculous. For this awkward in-between stage, when your normal size does not fit but you're too small for maternity clothes, local moms recommend dresses, pants, and skirts made of stretch fabric with elastic or drawstring waists. Anything without a true waist, like empire styles, hip huggers, wrap dresses, or sweater dresses, also worked for us. Use longer shirts or sweaters to cover your expanding waistline. Babystyle and Gap (see listings below) both sell great "transition wear"—pants and skirts with stretch that you can wear before and after baby. You can also try the old "leave the top button open" trick. A wonderful invention, the Bella Band, can help you do this without risking losing your pants. The Bella Band, www.bellaband.com, is a seamless fabric band that fits over your waistband and extends the life of your pre-pregnancy wardrobe (as well as holds up maternity clothes that are too big or, when you are further along, clothes that tend to fall down around the hips). See below for stores. Another trick: you can sometimes get by with buying clothing in slightly larger sizes that you can use again later while you are losing the pregnancy weight. In the meantime, start asking friends and relatives for hand-me-downs—our favorite source of maternity clothes!

Sometime in the second trimester, you'll probably need some maternity clothes, and that's when you should shop. Realistically, you may only wear these clothes for 4 to 6 months, and they can be expensive, so think carefully before you buy. One of the benefits of shopping locally is that you can buy one or 2 things at a time, as you need them. You may also want to consider quality over quantity. Also remember, it's best to borrow, borrow, borrow! And when you are finished, lend, lend, lend.

What to Buy and Where to Buy It

What should you buy? If you need to dress up for work, start with a couple of pants suits in neutral or black stretch fabric. Local moms recommend pants because it's a rare Bay Area workplace where you need to wear a skirted suit, and you can then wear the pants without the jacket on the weekends. Buy basic colors and save the truly trendy looks for shirts and other accessories—you may be able to wear the suit itself again in subsequent pregnancies with different accessories. You can also buy a fun skirt, or pants, to coordinate with the jacket for more work options. Keep in mind that slim skirts tend to look better than full ones on pregnant women, and a solid line of color from head to toe is slimming. A simple black dress that can be worn to work with a jacket or sweater, and then used for nights out with a wrap, is also a great bet.

Your basic shopping choices for work clothes are chain stores like Pea in the Pod (high-end), Mimi (middle-tier), or Motherhood (low-end), or boutiques. When shopping at a less-expensive store, be careful of low-quality clothing—you will be wearing and cleaning these clothes so much over the next few months that quality really does matter, especially for your key pieces. Moms highly recommended local boutiques like Mom's the Word, Glow Girl, and Japanese Weekend, as well as national chain babystyle, for knockout work and special occasion wear.

For casual clothes, Bay Area moms recommend a few staples: seasonless khaki and black stretch pants, a pair of comfortable jeans, a stretch cotton button-down shirt, a couple of T-shirts, some supportive camisoles, and a cotton cardigan (or preferably, a twin set) in a flattering color. You can expand on that repertoire as you see fit and according to the season. Remember, if you live in the city it will never be "summer" so don't worry about shorts or sundresses unless you plan weekends in Sonoma. Keep it simple: buy clothes in coordinating colors so you can mix and match. Now is not the time to take on an entirely new style or color scheme; you want to be able to blend in elements of your existing wardrobe (e.g., your existing accessories). Take the focus off your waistline with styles that emphasize other areas, such as your bust (which undoubtedly looks more full!) or neckline.

As for where to buy casual clothes, Bay Area moms universally recommended The Gap or Old Navy, where you can find fashionable items that won't break your budget. Or try Target, with the chic Liz Lange for Target line, for weekend basics. Then supplement with some splurges at the boutiques—e.g., fun tops or skirts—if you can afford it. Many moms were thrilled to find their designer jeans in maternity sizes at Pea in the Pod, Mom's the Word, Glow Girl, or babystyle.

Probably the most important thing to buy is a couple of good support bras to fit your expanding bust. Smaller women may not need maternity bras at all; just find a good supporting bra in a larger size (usually a cup size larger and one to 2 inches larger in diameter, measuring the chest just under the breast). Nordstrom's lingerie department is a great place to get fitted for regular bras; according to local moms, the salespeople seem to be more knowledgeable than those at your average department store. Most larger women will want real maternity bras, which you can find at maternity stores (high-end, but with great customer service and fitting) or Mervyn's/Target (low-end—know what size you are before you buy). Either way, you'll need at least 2 (one to wash and one to wear).

When you get to the ninth month, shop for some nursing bras, preferably at a lactation center where the salespeople know how to fit nursing moms. Believe it or not, you'll get even bigger while you nurse, so you'll need to buy a size or so larger than your pregnancy size! This is why buying nursing bras as maternity bras probably won't work for most people. The most comfortable nursing bra, by common consensus among local moms, is the Japanese Weekend Hug bra. There are no annoying hooks or buttons to deal with, and it's built like a comfortable jogging bra, albeit with narrow straps, so you can even wear it while you sleep. (Yes, you may need it then too.) Another great cotton nursing bra is the Bravado, which comes in several different colors. While it has hooks, it's also very comfortable and provides more support than the Japanese Weekend version.

Whether to buy maternity underwear is a personal decision. Some moms did without it altogether and just wore their normal bikini bottoms or thongs under the belly. Others found it more comfortable to go the "over the belly" maternity underwear route. The best options for underwear shopping, according to local moms, are Japanese Weekend (high-end) or Target or Mervyn's (low-end).

You may or may not need a maternity swimsuit, depending on your lifestyle or the season. The first time around, we wore regular swimsuits one size up and let them stretch. Obviously, you shouldn't try this with a suit you really care about wearing again post-pregnancy! The second time, we were just too big for regular suits and went straight to maternity. Our advice: wear a regular suit (J. Crew makes a good tank with underwire support) until you really need a maternity suit. Then, if you plan to swim a lot during pregnancy—a great prenatal workout!—buy a good one at a boutique or maternity fitness website. Quality is important because all that stretching may cause lower-end suits to run. Mothers-in-Motion (sold at boutiques and online, see below) offers high quality suits. Less expensive suits are fine if you don't plan to spend a lot of time in them; Gap, Old Navy, and Motherhood stores carry some great basic suits at very reasonable prices.

With all the time you will spend staying in shape (see Ch. 2), you will also need quality athletic apparel to keep up with you. Local boutiques Glow Girl and Mom's the Word, as well as online stores Fit Maternity, Raising a Racquet, Mothers-in-Motion, and Title 9, all offer great maternity and nursing fitness wear. You can find comfortable yoga pants at Gap Maternity.

Your feet will undoubtedly swell during pregnancy. Don't stretch and ruin expensive shoes if you anticipate wearing them again postpregnancy. We found we either had to buy bigger shoes or wear mules or tennis shoes during the last trimester. (Skip laces, though, because at the end you won't be able to bend down to tie them!) And you may want to switch from stiletto heels to something more substantial to keep your balance during those final months.

Opinions (even between us) are sharply divided on nursing shirts and dresses. Some of us found them a waste of money in the Bay Area, where we never faced any kind of hostility to nursing in public. Some thought it was more time consuming to find the special openings in nursing shirts than just to undo a few buttons on a normal button-down shirt, or put the baby under a big shirt or sweater, and still discreetly nurse. Others thought the nursing shirts were helpful, easier to nurse in since the baby's head wasn't hidden up a large shirt, and more discreet. And nursing clothes, previously so unfashionable, have made big improvements in recent years, with attractive nursing wear available through babystyle, Japanese Weekend, and Motherwear, see below. Our advice: try both and see what works for you, but don't buy a bunch of nursing shirts until you figure it out.

Overall, we recommend looking for clothes that will stand up to a lot of wear, including many washings, over a short period of time. Cotton and stretch fabrics are best for fit, durability, comfort, and breathability; pregnant women tend to get overheated. Skip anything that is uncomfortable or everyday clothes that must be dry cleaned; you'll spend enough just buying the clothes themselves! And make sure you have at least one or 2 fabulous outfits to boost your confidence during those hormonal low points.

What about used clothing? There are many good local resale stores selling maternity clothing; most are children's resale boutiques with small selections of maternity wear. Many parents also lauded the new kids on the block, Maternity XChange and Merry Go Round, for a large selection of new and gently used maternity clothing at deep discounts. In resale, selection varies a great deal, and sometimes you simply need to be in the right place at the right time. Sometimes you can find bargains on barely worn high-end clothing (usually priced at one-half to one-third of the new retail price). Suits and dresses often fall into this category. On the other hand, at some resale stores we have seen a lot of low-end casual wear priced the same as it would be new, in which case you are better off just buying it new! Our advice is to know the brand names and new clothes prices before you hit the resale stores. That way, you will know whether you are really buying a bargain. Don't forget to consign your maternity clothes when you are done with them!

Top Sources for Maternity Clothes

1. **Mom's the Word** (San Francisco and Walnut Creek boutique)

2. **Glow Girl** (Mill Valley boutique)

3. **babystyle** (several Bay Area stores, or online at www.babystyle.com)

4. **Gap or Old Navy** (in select stores, or online at www.gap.com or www.oldnavy.com)

5. **Japanese Weekend** (San Francisco boutique, online at www.japaneseweekend.com, or in other local boutiques)

6. **Target Stores** (especially the Liz Lange for Target line)

7. **Hand-Me-Downs!**

What Not to Buy

Here's what *not* to buy, unless money is not an issue:

- Special occasion dresses (borrow them instead). If you cannot borrow, or will attend a number of fancy events while pregnant, buy a simple black seasonless number that can be dressed up or down as necessary, or just one completely fabulous dress you'll wear again and again. Mom's the Word, Glow Girl, Pea in the Pod, and babystyle are good sources for special occasion wear.

- Outerwear (except perhaps the Japanese Weekend "mommy and baby" coat that can be zipped up postpartum around a baby in a front carrier). Most coats, especially double-breasted ones, will accommodate pregnancy, or try a wrap or poncho.

- Sleepwear, except maybe nursing pajamas. You can borrow your husband's pajamas or wear T-shirts or nightgowns during pregnancy. Some found it easier just to wear old T-shirts at night during nursing; when they got soiled they could throw them in the wash and get another. Others really appreciated the convenience of nursing pajamas. Some moms though found the nursing slits in the nursing pajamas were a little *too* revealing.

◆ Large numbers of really trendy outfits (you'll feel ridiculous wearing them again in subsequent pregnancies). Try a trendy piece here and there to accent your basics, or buy trendy accessories that you can use again after delivery.

◆ Anything in horizontal stripes (why do so many manufacturers make maternity clothes in stripes?) or loud patterns. Black or navy is most slimming.

◆ Anything that looks like it will not withstand a lot of washing or feel comfortable.

Best Ways to Save Money on Maternity Clothes

1. **Borrow clothes from friends and family who have just given birth.**

2. **Scour the resale stores for bargains on high-end merchandise.** Just beware of paying too much for low-end brands.

3. **Shop Target Stores or Old Navy for casual wear.** You'll be surprised at what you find for $20 and under.

4. **Hop in the car and go to the Motherhood outlets in Gilroy, Vacaville, or Petaluma for career and evening wear at drastically reduced prices.** Call first to check selection!

5. **Get a Bella Band to expand your regular clothes.**

6. **Wear non-maternity clothes as much as possible.** Clothes for larger women are sometimes less expensive than maternity clothes. Transitional clothes made of stretch fabric will help before and after baby.

DEPARTMENT AND CHAIN STORES

These stores all have more than one Bay Area location. If the address is not listed below the store name, check the website for local stores.

babystyle
www.babystyle.com
- Burlingame
  1319 Burlingame Ave.
  650-342-1534
- Santa Clara
  Valley Fair Mall
  2855 Stevens Creek Blvd.
  408-246-9703

PARENT RATING: ☆ ☆ ☆ ☆ ☆

Originally a web retailer, babystyle now has 2 upscale Bay Area specialty stores featuring a large selection of stylish maternity clothing. You'll find everything from casual to career to special occasion outfits, as well as "transition" wear and "hip" nursing wear, swimwear, diaper bags, and lingerie. Check out the online outlet page for discounts on high-end designer wear. The online store is a great option for those in outlying areas who can't make the drive to the boutiques but want the latest styles. Lines include: babystyle (house label), Blue Cult, Blue Dot, Notice, Velvet, Chiarakruza, Citizens of Humanity.

Burlington Coat Factory/ Baby Depot
www.burlingtoncoatfactory.com

PARENT RATING: ☆ ☆ ☆

This discount retailer carries a small selection of casual maternity clothes, mainly jeans and casual shirts. Prices are low (almost everything under $20), but as is often the case with discounters who buy stock from other retailers, selection will vary by store and season. You may want to call first before heading out to the store. Lines include: Oh Mama, On the Way, Angels, B Sports.

Gap
www.Gap.com

PARENT RATING: ☆ ☆ ☆ ☆ ☆

Gap Maternity—available in select stores and online—features well-priced, fashionable basics like stretch pants, jeans, camisoles, cotton shirts, and sweaters. We love these clothes for reasonable prices, style, and comfort! These were our most-worn casual outfits. Pants come in many different waist styles and lengths, from capris to boot cut. They also sell knit pants that can help you during those transitional months, and swimsuits. They have a great return policy—they'll take back anything, no questions asked, at any Gap store or via mail.

JC Penney Company
www.jcpenney.com

PARENT RATING: ☆ ☆

Penney's prices are very reasonable, and selection is fairly broad, particularly online. You can find mainly casual clothes, as well as a few career and dress items, swimsuits, and bras. Unfortunately, however, the clothes look much better in the catalog than they do in person. We were disappointed in what we saw: clothes tended to be oversized, fabrics cheap, and styles a bit out-dated. The 5-piece knit set at $80 is less expensive than the Belly Basics "pregnancy survival kit" it mimics, but the quality of the Penney version is much poorer. However, this is a good place to pick up inexpensive maternity hose and underwear. Lines include: Duo.

Maternity Xchange
www.maternityXchange.com
PARENT RATING: ☆ ☆ ☆ ☆ ☆

What a great idea! Maternity Xchange—a go-between for pregnant women looking for bargains and postpartum women looking to unload their maternity clothing—hosts monthly sales around the Bay Area. New and nearly new name brand clothing sells for up to 75% off retail prices (though 35-45% off is typical). Much of the new clothing comes from local designers (e.g., Maximum Mama Maternity, www.maximummama.com) and from overstock at local retail stores. Consignors receive 50% of the selling price after items sell. Comment: "They had a lot of quality brands, and the clothes were in very good condition or new."

Mervyn's California Stores
www.mervyns.com
PARENT RATING: ☆ ☆

Owned by Target Stores, Mervyn's is a department store with locations throughout California. (They do not offer online shopping.) Like Target, it has a selection of well-priced casual maternity clothes. Almost everything retailed for under $40 in 2005. Unlike Target, however, its styles are a bit out-dated, and clothes look cheap. Clothes were made of nonbreathable polyester blends, T-shirts featured horizontal stripes, and jeans and khakis sported huge panels, even on the rear. Selection was very limited and there were no career clothes when we visited. Stick to the inexpensive cotton maternity underwear and (if you've been fitted elsewhere and know your size) cotton nursing bras by Leading Lady. Lines include: Holly Robinson Peete, High Sierra.

Mimi Maternity
www.mimimaternity.com
PARENT RATING: ☆ ☆ ☆

Motherswork, the largest manufacturer and retailer of maternity clothing in the country, owns the Mimi Maternity, A Pea in the Pod, and Motherhood chain of stores and their online counterparts. Mimi is the middle-tier brand, with stand-alone mall stores and boutiques within Macy's Department Stores. They carry everything from career to casual to special occasion, as well as intimates, swimwear, and nursing wear. Like its sister store Pea in the Pod, Mimi is at the higher end of the price spectrum, according to local moms. But its prices are a bit lower than Pea in the Pod's, many times for the same items. The best value is the Mimi Essentials line of basic shirts and pants, with T-shirts at $20-25 and pants at $50. You'll also find a decent selection of stylish dresses and suits. Insider advice: hit the periodic sales. Designer lines that don't sell at Pea in the Pod are often sent here for markdown.

Motherhood Maternity
www.motherhood.com
PARENT RATING: ☆ ☆ ☆

Motherhood is the low-priced end of the Pea in the Pod/Mimi/Motherhood national chain stores. Don't expect high-quality stuff. But you can find "decent, cute, inexpensive" casual basics like cotton shirts, shorts, pants, and casual dresses for under $30. This is definitely the place to buy your weekend T-shirts, shorts, and jeans (unless you want designer), and well-priced maternity bathing suits. The store also offers a selection of cotton nursing pajamas and shirts. Word to the wise: petite women may find even the smallest sizes run very large, so be sure to try clothes on for fit. Comment: "Excellent product for the price. . . . A lifesaver."

Motherhood Maternity Outlets

- Petaluma
  Petaluma Village Factory Outlets
  707-763-3261
- Vacaville
  Factory Stores at Vacaville
  707-446-4792
- Milpitas
  Great Mall of the Bay Area
  408-262-0950
- Gilroy
  Gilroy Premium Outlets
  408-847-7560

PARENT RATING: ☆ ☆ ☆ ☆

Overstock and out-of-season Pea in the Pod/Mimi/Motherhood clothes are sent to these outlets for mark-down. Selection varies according to the season, but generally you can find everything from basics to career to special occasion outfits. A great place to find big-ticket items like suits, this outlet also carries the regularly priced Motherhood line. "Lifesavers . . . well worth the drive . . . the best for me," raved local moms. Insider advice: call first to check

selection, and beware of buying too much just because it's a bargain.

Nordstrom
www.nordstrom.com
PARENT RATING: ☆ ☆ ☆ ☆ ☆

Famous for its customer service, this department store's online catalog features a huge selection of high-fashion, designer maternity wear, such as Citizens of Humanity and Earl Jeans, Liz Lange, Olian, Japanese Weekend, Childish, and Juicy Couture. They also carry the full line of Belly Basics maternity wear, one of our favorites. This is a great source for Kate Spade and Nicole Miller diaper bags, as well as Mustela skin products for those inevitable stretch marks. Nordstrom's lingerie department is also a good place to find supportive bras during pregnancy, and they carry Bravado nursing bras online. We like Nordstrom for its generous no-questions-asked return policy and free exchanges. You can return online orders to stores. Insider advice: the maternity selection varies by store, and some stores do not carry it at all, so check with your local store before you go. The full selection is available online.

Old Navy
www.oldnavy.com
PARENT RATING: ☆ ☆ ☆ ☆ ☆

Local moms love Old Navy's Mom-to-Be collection, available in select stores and online. Prices are very reasonable (everything under $45 when we shopped recently), but styles are fashion-forward and fun, and feature natural fibers (thank you!). The collection consists mainly of casual clothes, with a few dresses and swimsuits. Returns are easy: mail it back or take it to your local store. Insider advice: the flagship store (4th and Market streets, downtown San Francisco) has the best selection. Comments: "Cute and fashionable. . . . Great styles, great prices."

A Pea in the Pod

- San Francisco
  345 Sutter St.
  415-391-1240
- Palo Alto
  608 Stanford Shopping Center
  650-321-0752
- Santa Clara
  Valley Fair Shopping Center
  2855 Stevens Creek Blvd.
  408-984-7100

www.apeaninthepod.com

PARENT RATING: ☆ ☆ ☆ ☆

This chain is at the high end of the Pea in the Pod/Mimi/Motherhood group, with stores in upscale locations all over the country. It's great if you want designer labels; Lilly Pulitzer, Diane von Furstenberg, Chaiken, Shoshanna, Anna Sui, Tocca, and Nicole Miller were all featured when we visited. The store provides a good selection of work clothes and special occasion outfits, and if you need to wear a nice suit to work, you'll find it here. You can also get designer jeans (Seven Jeans, Citizens of Humanity, Joe's Jeans) and T-shirts (Three Dots, Michael Stars) in maternity sizes. The very useful Bella Band is one of their best sellers. But almost everyone we surveyed had the same reaction: it's "expensive." You may find T-shirts and khakis elsewhere at lower prices,

but if you're in search of upscale labels, and good service, start here.

Ross Dress for Less Stores

www.rossstores.com

PARENT RATING: ☆ ☆

This national chain of discount stores features a sporadic stock of maternity clothes. Selection is limited to casual shirts, pants, and dresses. We noticed most of the "designer labels" were inexpensive brands also carried at JC Penney and Mervyn's. On the plus side, prices were very low; everything was priced under $20. But don't expect current styles or great customer service. Our salesperson was not very helpful, and we had to point to our enormous bellies to find the maternity clothes rack. Lines include: Oh Mamma, Duo, Baby's Nest, We're Together, Planet Motherhood.

Target

www.target.com

PARENT RATING: ☆ ☆ ☆ ☆ ☆

We were pleasantly surprised by Target's selection of attractive, reasonably priced maternity clothing made of stretch cotton. We were even happier when they began offering Target-priced pieces by high-end maternity designer Liz Lange. (Not the same designs as those you'll find at Liz Lange.com, but in one mom's words, "pretty darn good for the price.") We found great solid-color cotton twill shorts for $15 and khaki pants for $25 with updated waistbands. T-shirts and polo shirts were $15, and Target even offered some decent cotton skirts and blazers for under $30 and sweaters for $20. You won't see a huge selection of work clothes here, or any special occasion outfits, but this is a great place for weekend basics. We also appreciate the "no hassle" 90-day return policy. "Great and inexpensive . . . a surprising place to find knockabout maternity clothes . . . good deals on basics." say local moms. Lines include: Liz Lange for Target, In Due Time.

LOCAL BOUTIQUES AND RESALE STORES

San Francisco

Chloe's Closet
451A Cortland Ave.
415-642-3300
www.chloescloset.com
PARENT RATING: ☆ ☆ ☆ ☆

This Bernal Heights children's consignment shop carries a selection of maternity and nursing wear. They feature mainly good condition casual clothes from labels such as Japanese Weekend, Target, Gap, and Pea in the Pod, all at 60% or more off retail prices. Styles are current, as the owner buys only clothes that are not more than 5 years old. Consignors receive 40% of the item's selling price in cash or 60% in store credit, after the item is sold. They also carry breast pumps. Comment: "Awesome."

CPMC Newborn Connections
3698 California St.
415-600-BABY (2229)
PARENT RATING: ☆ ☆ ☆ ☆

This hospital lactation center doesn't carry maternity clothes, but it offers a small selection of nursing wear, mainly casual cotton shirts and dresses.

You will find an extensive array of nursing bras in all sizes, with "helpful and knowledgeable" salespeople (often lactation consultants) to assist with sizing. They also sell support hose and maternity skin care products. Lines include: bras by Bravado, Japanese Weekend, Anita, and Leading Lady. Moms in the postpartum unit at CPMC applauded the fact that they could shop from their bed; hospital staff brings around a cart of goodies for "in-room shopping"!

DayOne
3490 California St., Ste. 203
415-440-3291
www.dayonecenter.com
PARENT RATING: ☆ ☆ ☆ ☆ ☆

This attractive, well-organized, parent center features the largest and "best" selection of nursing bras in the city (with very helpful salespeople, often lactation consultants). They also sell the popular Glamourmom camisole top with built-in bra, support items such as the Bella Band, nursing nightclothes, maternity skin care products, nursing supplies (we loved their nursing pads), and vitamins. Lines include: bras by Japanese Weekend, Bravado, Anita, Medela, and Melinda G.

Due Maternity
3112 California St.
415-674-9850
www.duematernity.com
PARENT RATING: ☆ ☆ ☆ ☆ ☆

This upscale Santa Barbara boutique opened a San Francisco branch in fall 2005, with a maternity outlet (overstock or previous year merchandise) to follow. They offer high-quality, stylish

144

designer maternity wear, from casual to special occasion. They also sell nursing bras from Bravado, Melinda G, and Japanese Weekend, diaper bags, pre-and postnatal beauty products, nursing apparel, parenting books, and gifts. Lines include: Michael Stars, Earl Jeans, Chiarakruza, diaper bags by Kate Spade, 2 Chix, Meet Me in Miami, Naissance on Melrose, Juliet Dream, Homme Mummy, Ripe, Notice, Fragile, Momzee, Maternal America, Bella Dahl, Noppies, Fleurville.

Japanese Weekend

500 Sutter St.
415-989-6667
www.japaneseweekend.com
PARENT RATING: ☆ ☆ ☆ ☆ ☆

Consistently one of the most popular brands of maternity clothes in the Bay Area, JW offers great basic suits, pants, skirts, and shirts, many in a lightweight, luxurious stretch jersey. This local manufacturer has stores in San Francisco and San Jose, and you can also find the clothes at other local boutiques, at Nordstrom.com, and at the manufacturer's website. Casual and career clothes are "very convertible from day to evening to weekend." Some pants feature the underbelly "OK" waistband, which many found very comfortable. Others have the "during and after" expandable waistband, useful for those first few months after giving birth when you aren't quite back to your old size. The JW nursing bras (Hug or jog bra style) are the best we've found—they are comfortable enough to sleep in, and allow easy access with no snaps. They have some attractive nursing clothes (no

mean feat!) and even a line for women carrying multiples. Most found the clothes "expensive" but "durable," "comfortable," and a "good value." "I loved my maternity jeans," said one mom. Styles are usually very current. Check out the seasonal sales for great bargains. A city mom's favorite!

Minis

2278 Union St.
415-567-9537
PARENT RATING: ☆ ☆ ☆ ☆ ☆

This Union Street kids' clothier also offers stylish maternity wear for mom. Selection consists largely of basic cotton and cotton/Lycra casual wear, with a few very nice suits and dresses. Prices are comparable to other boutiques carrying the same brands. Moms found the staff "very helpful." Lines include: Belly Basics, Minis (house label), Duet, Olian, Japanese Weekend.

Miranda's Mama

3785 Balboa St.
415-221-5862
www.mirandasmama.com
PARENT RATING: ☆ ☆ ☆ ☆ ☆

A new addition to the Richmond district, this children's resale shop also carries gently used maternity and nursing wear, breast pumps, and breastfeeding supplies. Items are usually priced at half of the new retail price, and labels include everything from Target and Old Navy on up to Pea in the Pod, Japanese Weekend, and occasional European brands. Consignors receive 40% of the sale price or 50% in store credit. Comments: "We love going there. . . . Everything is clean and stylish."

Mom's the Word

3385 Sacramento St.
415-441-8261
www.shop2bmom.com

PARENT RATING: ☆ ☆ ☆ ☆ ☆

This Presidio Heights boutique, now with a Walnut Creek branch, is a favorite of city moms. If we could give it a 6-star rating, we would. The store features "nice choices" of upscale career and casual maternity clothing, as well as special occasion dresses, lingerie, sleepwear, swimsuits, and some nursing wear. We found nothing we wouldn't want to wear (which says a lot for a maternity store!). Prices are surprisingly reasonable, not as high as Pea in the Pod, and selection is more stylish. Moms report sales associates are "very helpful," especially when sizing for bras, and pay customers a great deal of "personal attention." Lines include: Michael Stars, Velvet, Cadeau, Susana Monaco, Chaiken, Diane von Furstenberg, Citizens of Humanity, Blue Cult, and Seven Jeans, and nursing bras by Bella Materna, Bravado, and Anita. They also sell the popular "Perfect Pant" (designed by the owner of the Marina boutique Dress) and the Bella Band.

North Bay

Barefoot and Pregnant

1165 Magnolia Ave.
Larkspur
415-388-1777
www.barefootandpregnant.com

The boutique in this parent resource center/exercise facility carries maternity fitness clothing (e.g., yoga pants, tops, swimsuits), nursing bras by Bravado, and Medela breast pumps and nursing supplies.

Glow Girl

7 Throckmorton Ave.
Mill Valley
415-383-4141
www.glowgirlmaternity.com

PARENT RATING: ☆ ☆ ☆ ☆ ☆

This hip, upscale boutique is the only of its kind in Marin. Now Marin moms-to-be need not journey to the city for urban chic maternity clothes! The store focuses on affordable casual wear and attractive accessories such as diaper bags, jewelry, hats, scarves, and shoes. They also specialize in designer jeans in maternity sizes, and sell special occasion, career, and fitness wear. Stay for a bottle of water in the store's big comfortable chairs. Appointment services and home delivery are available. Lines include: the Bella Band, Belly Basics, Bravado, Chaiken, Citizens of Humanity, Chantal Renee, Chiarakruza, Earl Jeans, Japanese Weekend, Juliet Dream, Michael Stars, Naissance on Melrose, and Olian. Comments: "Great selection . . . I bought most of my clothes there. . . . I felt somewhat like a hipster wearing those sassy Earl Jeans."

Merry-Go-Round

401 Miller Ave., #C
Mill Valley
415-381-2535

PARENT RATING: ☆ ☆ ☆ ☆ ☆

This is not your typical resale store! From the moment you walk in, you feel like you are in an upscale boutique. The owner only buys high-end brands, so you don't have to wade through low-quality stuff. A true delight! Glow Girl sends their over-stock here. Representative brands include Liz Lange, L'Attesa, Michael Stars, Juicy Couture. They also have a parent information center with everything from local activities to schools, and even a children's play area to entertain your youngsters while you shop. Sellers receive 30-50% of the item's selling price upfront (in cash or trade).

Outgrown

1417 4th St.
San Rafael
415-457-2219
PARENT RATING: ☆ ☆ ☆ ☆

This longtime kids' resale store also features a rack of consignment maternity wear. Moms say the store has "sporadic stock" but "good prices." While you won't find a lot of high-end brands, most shirts and pants are priced under $10. Negotiation is sometimes possible. Consignors receive 40% of the sales price when the items sell.

Play It Again Kids

508 4th St.
San Rafael
415-485-0304
PARENT RATING: ☆ ☆ ☆

This kids' resale shop offers a very small selection of maternity clothes. Prices are very reasonable—$5-10 for most items—but brands tend to be low-end and stock limited. The store offers a 40% split to consignors.

Baby World

Oakland
- 6000 College Ave.
  510-655-2828
- 3923 Piedmont Ave.
  510-547-7040
- 4400 Telegraph Ave.
  510-655-0726

PARENT RATING: ☆ ☆ ☆

Baby World is a general baby gear retailer (part of the Baby News chain), and it offers a small selection of nursing bras and accessories.

Bearly Worn

1619 N. Broadway
Walnut Creek
925-945-6535
PARENT RATING: ☆ ☆ ☆ ☆

This kids' resale store carries a small selection of used maternity clothes on consignment. When we visited, the selection was varied and included some high-end brands like Mimi (with higher prices to match) and some lower-end brands like Motherhood (in the $10 range). The store offers a 50% split to consignors on maternity wear.

Child's Play

5858 College Ave.
Oakland
510-653-3989
PARENT RATING: ☆ ☆ ☆ ☆

This resale store offers seasonal maternity and nursing wear, from casual to career to special occasion. The owner buys only mid- to high-end brands such as Pea in the Pod, Gap, and Japanese Weekend. Consignors receive 50% in cash or 60% in store credit after an item sells.

Maternity Clothes

147

Cotton & Company

www.cottonandcompany.com

- Oakland
  5901 College Ave.
  510-653-8058
- Lafayette
  3535 Mt. Diablo Blvd.
  925-299-9356

PARENT RATING: ☆ ☆ ☆ ☆

One of the few upscale boutiques in the East Bay, Cotton & Company offers a small selection of chic, mainly casual maternity clothes and nursing bras amid a general baby store. Prices are on par with those at other boutiques offering the same lines. Lines include: Belly Basics, Bella Materna, Bravado, Japanese Weekend, Leading Lady.

Crackerjacks

14 Glen Ave.
Oakland
510-654-8844

PARENT RATING: ☆ ☆ ☆ ☆ ☆

Crackerjacks offers new and used maternity clothes within a kids' consignment store. The selection of new clothes is limited (mainly nursing wear and bras), but the store offers a huge selection of well-priced, used maternity wear in good condition, including name brands like Belly Basics, Mimi, A Pea in the Pod, Gap, and Old Navy. Look carefully and you may find a high-quality used outfit at a reasonable price. The store purchases used clothes outright for 50% of the used price, and salespeople are very helpful.

Fashion After Passion

1521 Webster St.
Alameda
510-769-MOMS (6667)

PARENT RATING: ☆ ☆ ☆ ☆

A maternity and kids' store, this boutique offers new and used maternity and nursing wear, nursing bras, and breast pump rentals. They have a huge selection of nursing bras, and also sell the Glamourmom nursing tank. This is a good place to unload your gently used clothing; it is one of the few stores that will pay sellers outright for goods.

Finders Keepers

2222 2nd St.
Livermore
925-449-7793

PARENT RATING: ☆ ☆ ☆

This kids' resale store also features used maternity clothes in its well-organized layout. The owner accepts many different brands and everything from casual to career and evening wear. Consignors receive 50% of the sales price after the clothing sells.

Kids Again

6891 Village Pkwy.
Dublin
925-828-7334

PARENT RATING: ☆ ☆ ☆ ☆ ☆

This children's resale store also sells used maternity clothes on consignment. Many different brands are featured, and clothes are priced accordingly. Consignors receive 50% of the sales price. The store features a play area for kids.

Lora's Closet

- Berkeley
  2926 College Ave.
  510-845-3157
- Lafayette
  3618 Mt. Diablo Blvd.
  925-283-3963

PARENT RATING: ☆☆☆☆☆

Formerly a branch of Lauren's Closet, see below, this resale store features "great" used maternity clothes on consignment.

Lauren's Closet

1420 Park St.
Alameda
510-865-2219

PARENT RATING: ☆☆☆☆☆

This local kids' resale store offers used maternity clothes on consignment. The selection of maternity clothes is decent and well priced, and the owner is very selective about what she buys, so only name brands are represented. The store offers a 50% split to consignors. The store's play area will entertain the kids while you shop.

Mom's the Word Maternity

1628 N. Main St.
Walnut Creek
925-937-6818

PARENT RATING: ☆☆☆☆☆

This upscale boutique, see San Francisco listing, offers a large selection of fashionable casual, career, and special occasion maternity clothing, nursing clothing, sleepwear, and swimwear. There is even a small play area for the kids while you shop.

The Nurture Center

3399 Mt. Diablo Blvd.
Lafayette
925-283-1346
www.nurturecenter.com

PARENT RATING: ☆☆☆☆☆

This resource and lactation center carries a large selection of nursing clothing and nursing bras, including the Bravado bra, one of our favorites. Quality nursing supplies (such as Medela and Avent) are also available. They also offer "transition" wear that can be used during both early pregnancy and postpartum nursing.

Servin's Second Time Around

17279 Hesperian Blvd.
San Lorenzo
510-276-8705

PARENT RATING: ☆☆☆

This kids' resale store buys and sells used maternity clothing. Representative brands are mainly lower-end Mervyn's and Target labels, and prices are fairly low. The store pays cash for used maternity clothing, usually 30-40% of the used sales price.

Snickerdoodles

442 Hartz Ave.
Danville
925-820-4956

PARENT RATING: ☆☆☆☆☆

This popular kids' resale store also carries a selection of used maternity clothing on consignment. Brands range from Motherhood to Mimi to Pea in the Pod, and selection usually includes career as well as casual styles. Prices for brand-name suits in excellent condition can be high, but you can also find low-priced casual wear. Consignors receive 40% of the sales price after goods sell.

They Grow So Fast
3413 Mt. Diablo Blvd.
Lafayette
925-283-8976
www.theygrowsofast.com
PARENT RATING: ☆ ☆ ☆ ☆ ☆

An East Bay favorite! This constantly expanding kids' resale store also offers consignment used maternity clothes. The owner is selective about what she buys, and better brands are represented. You can find quality used clothing at about one-third of the new retail price, depending on condition. The store accepts clothing on consignment according to the season, and consignors receive 40% of the sales price.

South Bay

Bearly Worn
35 W. Manor Dr.
Pacifica
650-355-5089
PARENT RATING: ☆ ☆ ☆ ☆

This children's consignment store also offers used maternity clothes.

Representative brands include Gap Maternity, Pea in the Pod, and Mimi, and prices are about half of new retail prices. The store purchases clothing outright and accepts consignments.

Japanese Weekend
377 Santana Row, #1115
San Jose
408-260-7676
PARENT RATING: ☆ ☆ ☆ ☆ ☆

See listing under San Francisco, above.

Ricochet
1610 S. El Camino Real
San Mateo
650-345-8740
PARENT RATING: ☆ ☆ ☆ ☆

This resale store features high-end gently used (some never worn) maternity clothing at reasonable prices, usually one-third to one-fourth of retail prices. Representative brands include Mimi Maternity, Pea in the Pod, and Japanese Weekend, all in excellent condition. The store also offers special occasion wear, and has a $10-and-under sale rack.

Online and Catalog Shopping for Maternity Clothes

In this age of the internet, don't forget 24-hour shopping from home —a favorite choice for busy people. Parents we surveyed shared their favorite catalog and online maternity shopping sources. Here they are:

BabyCenter
www.babycenter.com
PARENT RATING: ☆ ☆ ☆ ☆

While you are chatting away or looking for information in Baby Center's popular online community, you can

shop for maternity clothing by Belly Basics, maternity active wear by Mothers-in-Motion, nursing bras and underwear by Bravado and Medela, the Glamourmom nursing tank, and support items like the Bella Band.

150

Belly Basics

www.bellybasics.com

PARENT RATING: ☆ ☆ ☆ ☆ ☆

Home of the 4-piece "pregnancy survival kit" created by 2 pregnant fashion executives (a dress, a shirt, pants, and a skirt in cotton/spandex solid colors), the Belly Basics website offers up-to-date and comfortable clothes, including cotton shirts, T-shirts, "Work Essentials" separates, jeans, dresses, and swimsuits. We like this line for its comfortable waistbands (the "best" according to local moms), durability, and style. You can't order at the website, but it lists local boutiques carrying Belly Basics' clothes. (See also Nordstrom.com, and babycenter.com, above).

Belly Dance Maternity

www.bellydancematernity.com

You can find hip maternity clothes from top designers such as Belly Basics, Bravado, Cadeau, Childish, Chiarakruza, Diane von Furstenberg, Olian, Japanese Weekend, Michael Stars, Earl Jean, and Citizens of Humanity.

ebay

www.ebay.com

PARENT RATING: ☆ ☆ ☆ ☆ ☆

The king of all garage sales, eBay has a huge variety of maternity clothes, from "new with tags" to used. Our recent search turned up nearly 19,000 maternity items. You never know what you'll find! Be sure to calculate the shipping charges into your bargain hunting.

Fit Maternity and Beyond

www.fitmaternity.com

PARENT RATING: ☆ ☆ ☆ ☆

This website and catalog offers a great collection of maternity and nursing fitness wear, and maternity and nursing sports bras. They even have maternity tennis clothes!

Euphoria Maternity

www.euphoriamaternity.com

Euphoria sells maternity clothes by many of the top designers (Japanese Weekend, Olian, Belly Basics, Chiarakruza), and nursing clothing and bras. This is a great place for hard-to-find sizes like petites and plus sizes.

Lands' End

www.landsend.com

PARENT RATING: ☆ ☆ ☆ ☆

A recent addition to this catalog is maternity and nursing wear. The collection consists of classic, hardy basics like polo shirts, T-shirts, and many different styles of pants, as well as sleepwear and swimwear. All are well-priced ($20-40 range). Styles are conservative and tend to be less form-fitting than you'll find in designer labels. We like their guarantee: if you are not satisfied for any reason, at any time during your use of a product, return it for a refund.

Liz Lange Maternity

www.lizlange.com

PARENT RATING: ☆ ☆ ☆ ☆ ☆

This may be the closest place to the Bay Area to get Liz Lange's full line of upscale, *très chic* maternity clothes; as of this writing her only retail stores are in New York and Los

Maternity Clothes

151

Angeles. A former fashion editor, Liz Lange designs very current clothes that "fit very well." Some say the prices are "obscenely high" (what do you expect?), but if you can afford it and want to wear the very latest, this is it.

Mommy Chic

www.mommychic.com

You can find great career and evening clothes at this online retailer. They also carry a line of basic, stylish knitwear. We loved their black Audrey Hepburn-channeling "Tiffany" dress for day or evening.

Mothers-in-Motion

www.mothers-in-motion.com

PARENT RATING: ☆ ☆ ☆ ☆ ☆

This site offers a good selection of hard-to-find upscale maternity athletic wear. Some local boutiques also carry this brand.

Motherwear

www.motherwear.com

PARENT RATING: ☆ ☆ ☆ ☆

Motherwear offers fashionable, non-matronly nursing wear for discreet nursing in public. They also carry plus sizes. Though we don't usually like nursing wear, this catalog made us reconsider.

Naissance on Melrose

www.naissanceonmelrose.com

PARENT RATING: ☆ ☆ ☆ ☆

This is the online version of ultra-hip Naissance on Melrose, a popular Los Angeles maternity emporium. Reportedly they provided much of Jennifer Aniston's maternity wardrobe on the TV series *Friends*. They are often featured in *In Style* magazine.

You must be very comfortable with your body to wear these belly-baring styles, but if you can pull it off, great. You'll look like a celebrity mom! Lines include: Naissance on Melrose (house label).

Raising a Racquet

www.raisingaracquet.com

These maternity "kits"—for pregnant tennis players, golfers, and yoga enthusiasts—come in adorable boxes and make great gifts.

Title Nine Sports

800-609-0092 (catalog)
www.title9sports.com

PARENT RATING: ☆ ☆ ☆ ☆ ☆

A favorite for workout-crazed moms-to-be, this East Bay sportswear company—catalog and online—offers a great cotton nursing bra, as well as under-the-belly maternity cotton/spandex workout pants and shorts.

Veronique Maternity

888-265-5848 (orders)
www.veroniquematernity.com

PARENT RATING: ☆ ☆ ☆ ☆ ☆

Shop with celebrities and fashion-savvy New Yorkers at this upscale Manhattan boutique. You can order your designer maternity wear by telephone. Lines include: Chaiken, Cadeau, Earl, Citizens, Diane von Furstenberg, Nicol Caramel.

CHAPTER 4

ALL THAT BABY "STUFF":
Shopping for Gear, Nursery, Clothes, Toys, Photography, and Childproofing

Few things are more life changing than having a baby. With your newfound responsibilities and role as a parent, your life isn't the only thing that feels a change; your pocketbook will too! In this chapter, we will introduce you to Bay Area parents' favorite baby gear retailers. This chapter will answer the following questions and more:

◆ What is some general shopping advice for preparing for the baby's arrival?
◆ Which items are essential and which ones are not?
◆ Where can I go to buy basic baby gear?
◆ Where can I find stores to furnish the baby's nursery?
◆ Where can I find the best baby clothes and shoes?
◆ Where are some good resale shops?
◆ Where can I go to buy great baby toys and books?
◆ Where can I find a great baby photographer?
◆ How can I get my home childproofed?

Baby Gear and Nursery Essentials

Baby gear, equipment, and furniture can be purchased at baby superstores, specialty stores, mail order catalogs, and online. Superstores offer unparalleled one-stop shopping for new parents. Some Bay Area parents'

153

favorites are a consortium of retailers that operate under the name Baby News. These stores are owned and operated individually, but they are associated in that they buy together from the same distributor. The collective buying results in better wholesale prices for them. There are also less expensive superstores, such as Toys "R" Us, which carry a vast collection of moderate and low-end brands of baby gear. Specialty stores are often locally owned and run, and tend to offer a smaller selection of higher-end products. Online sources and mail order catalogs offer the convenience of shopping from home. Some online sites offer great discounts on name-brand gear—we've listed some at the end of this section.

General Shopping Advice

◆ To help ensure your baby's safety and comfort, do your homework before shopping. We suggest reading the book *Baby Bargains* by Denise and Alan Fields, in which the authors review products by manufacturer and style, and share parents' opinions on the pros and cons of each. They have a great website too which features a message board where you can get loads of information about baby products (www.windsorpeak.com).

◆ Before your baby arrives, visit a few baby gear stores to get a sense of what you need to buy and which brands and models you like. Find a store that has a lot of equipment on the floor and is service-oriented so a salesperson can demonstrate how to use the equipment, and you can actually try everything out too. Take it from us, knowing how to set up the crib or fold a stroller is better learned *before* your baby arrives!

◆ Focus on one or 2 products per visit to avoid baby gear burnout.

◆ Baby gear retailers are great places to survey other parents as to what products they like or don't like and why.

◆ Keep receipts and instructions for each item in a safe place, such as a folder in a kitchen drawer.

CAR SEAT

If there is one thing that you should do before your baby's arrival, it is purchase and install your infant seat. By state law, hospitals may not permit you to drive home with your baby unless you have a properly installed infant car seat. Safety experts agree you should never buy or use a previously owned car seat, as you won't know whether the car seat has been in an accident or if it has been recalled. If it has, it could be unsafe. Also, technology is always improving, so skip the hand-me-down this time. Car seat specifications are always being improved, so a car seat purchased only a few years ago may not meet current safety standards. Infant car seats are generally around $50-75, and we strongly advise spending the money and buying a new one. Almost all new car seats have easy carry handles and snap into accompanying strollers for your convenience. Don't forget to fill out and mail the registration card that comes with your car seat so that you can be contacted if there is a recall.

ONLINE RESOURCES FOR CAR SEAT SAFETY

www.aap.org/family/carseatguide.htm

The American Academy of Pediatrics website offers a "family shopping guide" to car seats. They concisely explain the different types of car seats and their features, as well as height and weight requirements. They have detailed information about almost every car seat on the market—truly a great resource for parents!

www.chp.ca.gov/html/safetyseats.html

This Highway Patrol website offers detailed information on California's requirements for infant and child car seats.

www.seatcheck.org

1-866-SEAT-CHECK (7328-24325)

On this website, you can search by zip code the National Highway Traffic Safety Administration's listing of child passenger safety seat inspection locations nationwide. You may also get this information by calling their toll-free number.

www.safewithin.com/childsafe/child.seats.cgi

This website offers basic car seat safety information and advice.

www.nhtsa.dot.gov

800-424-9393 (Dept. of Transportation's Vehicle Safety Hotline)

This is the website for the U.S. Department of Transportation's National Highway Traffic Safety Administration. It features a car seat inspection station locator, information on car seat recalls, and a plethora of information about car seat safety. Or call the Vehicle Safety Hotline.

www.safekids.org

The National Safe Kids Campaign's website offers an excellent car seat locator feature to help you pick the best car seat for your child.

www.carseatdata.org

This website has an interactive compatibility database that allows you to search for which seats work best in which cars.

155

Car Seat Mystique

Many parents find it confusing to know when to change car seats, and with so many different models out there, it can be a little overwhelming. To help sort this all out, we've outlined the 3 basic types of car seats on the market for the different stages of your child's growth:

◆ Infant seats (for infants and babies up to 20 pounds) must be rear-facing, preferably in the middle of the back seat and never in the front seat of a car, especially a car with front seat passenger airbags. Be sure to have the base installed before the baby comes, and have someone bring the car seat to the hospital on the day that you both go home. And remember to dress your baby in clothing with legs (as opposed to a nightgown or sack), so that you can properly buckle him up.

◆ "Convertible" car seats are for when a baby has outgrown the weight or height limit on his infant seat—usually by 20 pounds. Convertible seats should have a 5-point harness, and safety experts say that babies should stay rear-facing in the "convertible" seat until he is both past his first birthday and over 20 pounds. Once a baby reaches 20 pounds he may ride forward facing in the convertible seat.

◆ A child who hits 40 pounds and has outgrown the "convertible" seat can graduate to a "booster seat," as most are still too small to use regular seat belts without risk of abdominal or spinal-cord injuries. Booster seats are designed to raise a child up so that the regular seat belt can rest properly across the lap and shoulders. When a booster seat is used properly, the lap belt rests below the child's hipbones, touches the thighs, and is snug. The shoulder belt should cross the center of the child's shoulder and not cut across the neck. A 2003 study by Partners for Child Passenger Safety found that the use of a booster seat, instead of a seat belt alone, reduced injuries 59% for children ages 4 through 7 involved in crashes.

◆ While the law in California requires children to remain in booster seats until they are either 6 years old or 60 pounds, the National Highway Traffic Safety Administration's recommendation, issued in 2002, specifies that children should be in booster seats "until they are at least 8 years old, unless they are 4' 9" tall."

Car Seat Safety

The world of car seats can be one of the most over-whelming and confusing safety issues for parents. With conflicting advice and recommendations, it's not easy to sift through all the information out there on car seat safety, never mind properly installing and using car seats. Because there are hundreds of child safety seats and seat belt configurations, there are also many ways to install car seats. Making sure you install them properly is essential.

The National Highway Traffic Safety Administration estimates that up to 85% of infant and child car seats are incorrectly installed, putting children at greater risk in a car accident. Safety experts can't stress enough the importance of following manufacturers' directions. Correctly installed car seats shouldn't budge more than an inch from side to side. When in doubt, it is a wise idea to have the installation and use of the seats checked.

Many baby superstores that sell car seats will help install or check your car seats, and often will do so for free. In addition, local police departments, such as the ones listed below, often sponsor such programs. For other areas, call your police department or the National Safe Kids Buckle Up Campaign (800-441-1888) and inquire, or visit www.seatcheck.org to locate your closest check site.

Child Passenger Safety Program—San Francisco Police Department
415-575-6363 (Information and Appointment Phone Line)

California Highway Patrol
Corte Madera
415-924-1100

Precious Cargo
415-898-1616
www.yourpreciouscargo.com
Precious Cargo offers hands-on child passenger safety workshops for groups or individuals, specializing in on-site installations and inspections.

NEW CALIFORNIA BOOSTER SEAT LAW

Effective January 1, 2005, California Law requires children to ride in the back seat in a properly secured child passenger safety restraint until they are at least 6 years old or weigh 60 pounds . (Prior regulations only applied to children up to age 4 or who weigh at least 40 pounds.) You may report unrestrained children in cars to the California Highway Patrol by calling 800-TELLCHP.

BASSINET, MOSES BASKET, AND SIDECAR

After a car seat, the next most important item is a comfortable place for the baby to sleep when you bring her home. Many newborns prefer the cozy confines of a bassinet, Moses basket, or sidecar (a 3-sided bassinet that attaches to your bed to accommodate co-sleeping). However, most babies outgrow a bassinet by 3-4 months, and a Moses basket even sooner, so it's a great idea to borrow one if you can, provided it is in good condition and safe (no loose pieces of wicker that the baby can pick off). If you decide to buy one, these items run from $90 to $300 for a Moses basket with linens (sheets, liners, decorative skirts, and hoods), and up to $500 for an heirloom-quality wicker bassinet. Alternatively, many babies sleep in a crib from day one and do just fine.

What You Really Need

- ◆ Infant car seat and head and neck support insert
- ◆ Crib or bassinet
- ◆ Changing table or dresser combination
- ◆ Bouncy seat
- ◆ Infant bathtub
- ◆ Diaper pail
- ◆ Diapers, either cloth with wraps or covers or disposable
- ◆ If bottle feeding: 4 bottles and slow-flow nipples, pediatrician-recommended formula, and bottle brush
- ◆ Two to 4 pacifiers for newborns
- ◆ Toiletries and health items (thermometer, baby Tylenol, baby shampoo and wash, nail clipper, nasal aspirator)
- ◆ Diaper bag
- ◆ Stroller
- ◆ Basic baby parenting book
- ◆ Highchair (not until 5-6 months)
- ◆ Baby spoons and feeding accessories
- ◆ Bibs

INFANT BATHTUB

An infant bathtub is a little plastic tub that is placed inside your tub. The smaller space offers security, comfort and convenience in bathing an infant. It allows the baby to recline and lets you have both hands free to wash her. When your baby can sit up well enough on her own (around 6–8 months) she can use a bath seat that is also placed inside your tub. Even with these helpful tools, however, never leave a baby or small child unattended in any amount of water for even a second! Infant bathtubs and seats run around $25-40.

STROLLER

When out and about, babies depend on either Mom's or Dad's bulging biceps or a sturdy stroller to get around. Even tired toddlers and preschoolers often favor a stroller over walking. What style you choose—whether it's a stroller that fastens an infant car seat to either a metal frame (most of the high-end brands offer this feature); a light-weight easily collapsible umbrella stroller; or a more rugged carriage or pram—depends on your lifestyle

EXPERT ADVICE FROM THE STROLLER QUEEN

Overwhelmed by your stroller options? You might benefit from the expert advice of Janet McLaughlin, the "stroller queen." Visit www.windsorpeak.com where she moderates a chat group about strollers with more than 3,500 members.

and needs. Options to consider are whether or not the stroller converts to a carriage, where the baby faces, ease of folding, weight, whether the seat reclines, and if there is a sunshade and ample-size storage basket. Given the variety of features and models available, the wide price range of strollers is similar to that of the car market—from $50 for your basic bare bones to more than $500 for a fancy imported pram, and more than $700 for either the trendy Bugaboo Frog Stroller imported from the Netherlands with award-winning ergonomic design or the innovative Stokke Xplory stroller which lifts baby higher off the ground than other strollers for more visual stimulation.

BOUNCY SEAT

A bouncy seat is undeniably a necessity. It's a great place to set your baby down when you need to shower, answer the phone, eat dinner, or just take a break from holding your baby. It also gives your baby a view of the world other than the one seen when lying on his back. If you don't receive one as a shower gift, go ahead and buy one—you won't regret spending the $40-75.

DIAPER BAG

Take your time in selecting a diaper bag, as it will be with you every day for the next couple of years! This is a personal item with many different styles to chose from—a backpack may appeal to one person, while a messenger bag is better for another, and a stylish shoulder tote works for yet another. The Skip Hop diaper bags (www.skiphop.com) are especially popular for new moms and dads alike—they are hip, stylish, functional, and unisex. Their best feature is that these bags are designed to easily fit over a stroller's handlebars. The fun Fleurville bags (www.fleurville.com) are another stylish option, with their great fabrics and designs, that seem to be popular. Be sure to try out several styles and think about how they will work with your lifestyle. Diaper bags come in all price ranges, and don't forget that you can always make your own out of your favorite bag or backpack.

BABY CARRIER

Carrying a baby either in a frontpack or a sling has become very popular. Babies love to be carried close to your body, and a baby carrier lets your hands be free. Your baby will love going on walks with you and taking in her surroundings. Bay Area parents' favorites include the Baby Bjorn Carrier Active that features ergonomically designed shoulder and waist straps that work together to provide lumbar support and allows one to breastfeed without taking the baby out, the popular lightweight and foldable New Native baby carrier, and the Nojo Baby Sling. Parents said that their babies either loved or loathed the sling, so try to borrow one first. Baby carriers are great, but they

What Would Be Nice to Have

- ◆ Breast pump (if breastfeeding)
- ◆ Baby carrier or sling
- ◆ Glider or rocker
- ◆ Baby monitor
- ◆ A few developmental toys and small baby board books
- ◆ Mobile
- ◆ Baby gym
- ◆ Cell phone for Mom! (to have your spouse or partner, caregiver, and pediatrician a dial away!)
- ◆ Exersaucer (not until 4-5 months)
- ◆ Portable crib or play yard
- ◆ Shelving or a closet organizer
- ◆ Tape or CD player and lullaby tapes and CDs

are useful for a limited time, as once baby is a certain weight and length, it won't be comfortable for you to carry him tied on to you. They range from $50 to $120. Once your child outgrows a front carrier, consider the Playtex Hip Hammock Child Carrier. It helps "hoist" a baby 5 months and older on to your hips. Some baby carriers, like the Premaxx Euro, are versatile enough to be used for both—it's a baby sling for the first 5 months and then converts to a hip hammock for a baby up to 18 months old. Two websites that parents find particularly helpful in comparing slings are: www.kangarookorner.com and www.thebabywearer.com.

BABY MONITOR

Baby monitors are a great way of hearing your baby without actually being in her room. They are especially useful if you live in a 2-story house or a large home. Many are battery operated and can be carried from room to room. One of the neatest ones we've seen is mobile—strap the Velcro band of the AnyWhere Compact Monitor around your wrist and hear your baby wherever you are! Monitors range from $25 to $65.

BABY SWING

Most parents say that their baby either loved or hated a swing. Don't rush out and buy one—borrow one from a friend first to see whether your baby likes it. Baby swings range from $75 to $170.

PORTABLE CRIB/PACK 'N PLAY

A portable crib is great to have for travel as well as when your baby becomes mobile and you need to step away from her for a minute. Choose carefully. Focus on the size and weight, rather than the color scheme, if you plan on traveling a lot with the baby. Portable cribs range from $60 to $150, depending on manufacturer and features.

CRIB

By 3-4 months of age, your baby will have outgrown his bassinet. Unless you are embracing the concept of co-sleeping in a family bed, your baby will likely be transitioning to a crib. Order a crib before your baby arrives, because many stores don't stock a lot of models, and an order may take 6 to 8 weeks to fill, and sometimes longer! Delivery and setup usually costs $50 extra, but is worth it when you discover in the process that you are missing a part or, worse, that the crib is defective.

Like car seats, safety experts agree that you should never buy or use an old crib, which may present safety hazards, including spindles not being spaced narrowly enough, lead paint, and turned posts. Cribs sold today are certified by the Juvenile Products Manufacturers Association (JPMA), which sets standards for most baby products, including cribs, strollers, high chairs, and portable cribs. (See box.) Cribs come in all different types of styles, finishes, and prices—from $100 for a metal one from a discount retailer like Target to designer imported models for close to $1,000! Happily, most hardwood cribs made by quality domestic manufacturers cost between $250 and $500.

CRIB MATTRESS AND BEDDING

The most important considerations for crib mattresses and bedding have to do with safety. You want a tight fit between the mattress and crib. Essential pieces of bedding include a crib sheet and a mattress pad. A dust ruffle is purely for decor, and a baby quilt and pillows are safety hazards. If you buy bumpers, they should by tied on by snaps or short ties. However, some babies may think about using bumpers in ways that they were not intended, such as climbing out of the crib. Also, some people think bumpers are a suffocation hazard since a mobile baby may be inclined to explore between the bumper and the crib. Basic mattresses start at $50 and go up to $150. Crib bedding (sheets, bumpers, and crib skirts) range from $100 to $800 depending on whether you opt for ready-made or custom-made pieces.

CHANGING TABLE

Changing tables, made at a comfortable height for your back when changing your baby, range from basic no-frills models to fancy ones that match cribs or are combined with a dresser and are priced between $90 and $500. These can take as long as cribs to order, so it's a good idea to order one when you are still pregnant and also to set it up with some of baby's clothes and diapers *before* you have the baby. The last thing you'll feel like doing when you come home from the hospital is setting up a changing table and stocking your diaper station.

HIGH CHAIR

Once you begin to feed your baby solids (4-6 months), you'll need a high chair. There are many wonderful styles on the market today—

Making Sense of All Those Safety Stickers

When you shop for baby gear, you will become familiar with several organizations that play an important role in making sure that only the safest baby products hit the stores for parents like you to buy. You will see certification stickers from the organizations described below. While these stickers and approvals are helpful, be aware that in no way do they ever guarantee safety.

U.S. Consumer Products Safety Commission

301-504-0580
www.cpsc.gov

The U.S. Consumer Product Safety Commission (CPSC) is an independent federal regulatory agency that develops voluntary standards for thousands of products. They also recall and ban unsafe baby products. You can register on this website to have current recall information e-mailed to you. To report defective or dangerous products, call 800-638-2772.

Juvenile Products Manufacturers Association

856-638-0420
www.jpma.org

The Juvenile Products Manufacturers Association (JPMA) is a national trade organization representing 250 manufacturers and/or importers of infant's products in the United States, Canada and Mexico. The JPMA has created an extensive certification program to help parents choose safe baby gear. Their website offers buying tips and product safety information.

National Highway Traffic Administration

800-424-9393
www.nhtsa.gov

The National Highway Traffic Administration (NHTA), part of the U.S. Department of Transportation, sets and enforces performance standards for motor vehicles and equipment, including issuing guidelines on buying, installing, and using child-safety seats. Call or check the website for a list of car seat inspection stations by zip code. You can also check this website for car seat recalls.

from black leather-look vinyl seats to classic wooden high chairs or sleek wooden ones such as the Svan High Chair. Select one with a wide base to prevent it from tipping over and with an easy tray release mechanism that can be managed with one hand. A 5-point harness is also a good safety idea. High chairs cost from $50 to $220. When your baby outgrows a high chair, many parents opt for booster seats or a toddler/preschooler chair, such as the popular Stokke KinderZeat.

ROCKER OR GLIDER

A rocker or glider is a luxurious gift if you are lucky enough to receive one! They are a wonderful place to feed your baby and to help put her to sleep as well as to read to her when she is a bit older. However, it may be difficult to use a glider with a breastfeeding pillow, as it's a tight fit. Gliders retail for $250-500.

CLOSET ORGANIZER

You can store the baby's first clothes in baskets under a changing table or in dresser drawers. If using a closet, small shelves and cubby-holes, or rods at varying heights, will maximize your baby's closet space. Instead of buying a separate dresser, build a set of drawers in the closet—either ready-made closet storage pieces or, if you want to spend the money, a custom-built storage unit.

NATIONAL CHAINS

Here is what Bay Area parents have to say about several national chains of baby gear retailers. Call the toll-free numbers listed, check the yellow pages, or visit their websites for a store location near you.

Baby Superstores

Babies "R" Us
888-BABYRUS (222-9787)
www.babiesrus.com
PARENT RATING: ☆ ☆ ☆ ☆
While this store is owned by Toys "R" Us, this baby superstore offers sur-prisingly better-quality merchandise, including moderate to some upscale baby gear. They now even carry a nursery line by Wendy Bellissimo. Service is only slightly better than at Toys "R" Us. They carry almost all the major brands of car seats, cribs, and strollers, and a nice selection of infant clothing as well as many other baby accessories. Now City and Marin parents don't have to drive as

far to frequent Babies "R" Us, with the recent opening of the Marin City/Sausalito location. They offer a convenient baby registry, and online shopping is also a breeze.

Baby Depot at Burlington Coat Factory

800-444-COAT (2628)
www.coat.com
PARENT RATING: ☆ ☆

This store is known for having a great selection of high-end brands of baby gear, including strollers, car seats, cribs, changing tables, and dressers, at discounted prices. However, most agree that the staff is neither helpful nor knowledgeable. Several parents reported mix-ups in ordering items and long and agonizing delays. Their return policy is also undesirable—they offer no cash refunds under any circumstances (even if a product breaks or is defective, they only offer store credit). Bottom line: Don't set up a gift registry here, and don't buy anything from them unless it is off the floor.

Specialty Chains

babystyle

- Burlingame
  1319 Burlingame Ave.
  650-342-1534
- Santa Clara
  Valley Fair Mall
  2855 Stevens Creek Blvd.
  408-246-9703
www.babystyle.com
See under clothing.

BEST BUYS FOR DIPES AND WIPES

Bay Area moms agree that Costco and Target have the best prices on disposable diapers and wipes. If you can stand trekking out to these mega-stores, the savings are worth the trip. Target is also great for basic baby equipment, which they often put on sale to get you there.

Bellini

1651 Botelho Dr.
Walnut Creek
925-274-0829
www.bellini.com
PARENT RATING: ☆ ☆ ☆ ☆ ☆

Bellini features beautiful cribs, beds, changing tables, and dressers of their own label, mostly all direct from Italy. They also carry a large selection of upscale bedding, strollers, car seats, portable cribs, high chairs, and many other baby accessories.

Ikea

- Emeryville
  4400 Shellmound St.
- East Palo Alto
  1700 E. Bayshore Rd.
1-800-434-IKEA (4532)
http://www.ikea.com/ms/enUS
PARENT RATING: ☆ ☆ ☆ ☆

Parents can't seem to get enough of this super-sized contemporary European-inspired furniture store and so much more! It's especially great for short-term needs such as toddler beds and storage options, and they offer great décor and accessories for little ones, including throw rugs, bookshelves, desks, easels, wooden toys, and more.

Jacadi Paris

1215 Burlingame Ave.
Burlingame
650-558-1122
www.jacadiusa.com

Since the first edition of this book, we are dismayed to discover that the Danville and Walnut Creek stores have closed. However, the Burlingame location is still standing strong. This small, upscale, French boutique offers exquisite coordinating fabrics, bedding, wallpaper, and nursery accessories. Most of the nursery furnishings and décor are not in the store (which primarily carries a high-end line of imported clothing from France) and can only be viewed and ordered from a catalog.

Pottery Barn Kids

800-430-7373
www.potterybarnkids.com

PARENT RATING: ☆ ☆ ☆ ☆ ☆

Pottery Barn Kids is the latest retailer to dive into the juvenile products market. Many moms wonder how mothers before them decorated their kids' rooms! They offer traditionally designed cribs, beds, and desks, and other furnishings and accessories for baby's room at prices that aren't cheap, but aren't ridiculous either. They have a wonderful selection of matching bedding and accessories for cribs and beds that changes several times a year. Products are also available via their website and mail order.

Order early, or you may have to wait for back-ordered items. Join Pottery Barn Kids at one of their sing-alongs, which feature local children's musicians. Visit their website for details.

The Right Start

800-548-8531
www.rightstart.com

PARENT RATING: ☆ ☆ ☆ ☆ ½

Since the first edition of this book, The Right Start has changed owners, but they still offer a choice selection of high-end baby gear from birth to age 3. They offer strollers and car seats; travel, feeding, health, and bath accessories; and specialize in carrying developmentally oriented toys and educational videos and books for infants and young toddlers. They carry an extensive array of smaller baby gear items and accessories such as booster seats, teethers, Mustela toiletries, and potty training accessories. They also have a large selection of nursing products, including pillows and pumps. You can order online as well.

Discounters

Target

www.target.com

PARENT RATING: ☆ ☆ ☆ ☆

This mega-store offers a decent selection of moderate-end baby gear, including bassinets, strollers, high chairs, décor for baby's nursery, and many baby accessories. Moms particularly like their bedding, as several designers design specifically for Target, including Rachel Aswell of Shabby Chic. Service is lacking, but good buys can be found. Many parents prefer ordering online.

Toys "R" Us

800-869-7787

www.toysrus.com

PARENT RATING: ☆ ☆

New and expectant parents can stock up on baby gear here, including strollers, cribs, car seats, and diapers at moderate prices. However, they don't carry any of the high-end brands. They are best for smaller items like feeding and travel accessories. Service is lacking, so if you have questions, go to a more service-oriented retailer.

JC Penney

www.jcpenney.com

JC Penney offers great deals on moderate-end brands of baby gear, nursery furnishings, bedding, and accessories. Goods are available online if there isn't a store nearby.

Sears

www.sears.com

Sears offers a mediocre selection of mid- to lower-end quality baby gear and equipment. You'll find brands such as Cosco, Graco, and Evenflo at moderate prices.

BAY AREA RETAILERS

Here is what Bay Area parents have to say about their favorite local stores for all of their baby gear:

San Francisco

Citikids

152 Clement St.

415-752-3837

www.citikids.com

PARENT RATING: ☆ ☆ ☆ ☆ ☆

Part of the consortium of Baby News retailers, Citikids is San Francisco's primary full-service baby gear retailer offering everything that new and expectant parents will need for the first couple of years of their baby's life. They are always receiving new products and have one of the largest displays of strollers in the Bay Area, including many high-end brands. They also have many top-quality car seats, gliders, swings, baby carriers, diaper bags, high chairs, portable cribs, nursing and bottle-feeding accessories, childproofing items, and more. They offer a wonderful selection of baby furniture, including high-end baby cribs, wicker bassinets, coordinating bedding, changing tables, dressers, and lamps, as well as upscale baby clothing and developmental toys. You might find better bargains elsewhere, but this friendly family-run business wins the prize for service. They will gladly demonstrate equipment and tell you the pros and cons of each type. They also will check on the proper installation of your car seat without asking whether you bought it from them. The friendly and helpful staff is unparalleled in the area and well worth it! Comment: "Richard, the owner, is a terrific help with everything. For example, he puts in car seats and is happy to show me again and again how to do it when I forget."

Country Living–Unique and Natural Furniture

1033 Clement St.

415-751-1276

PARENT RATING: ☆ ☆ ☆ ☆ ☆

Known to San Francisco parents as a great place to get bargains on unpainted furniture, Country Living carries changing tables, cribs, dressers, rockers, children's tables and chairs, bookshelves, desks, and bunk beds. All of their furniture is made of solid wood and can be bought either finished or unfinished if you want to save some money and do it yourself, or hire a decorative painter to custom paint the furniture to match your nursery theme. Service is friendly and helpful.

DayOne

3490 California St.

415-440-3291

www.dayonecenter.com

PARENT RATING: ☆ ☆ ☆ ☆ ☆

This state-of-the-art parenting center has a wonderful boutique that really makes it every new parent's one-stop shop! Since the first edition of this book, they have spent the last few years combing the country for the best baby products and apparel and feature these choice high-end finds in their welcoming store. They offer the best strollers, car seats, layette needs, Stokke furniture and Dutalier gliders, baby carriers, stylish diaper bags, smaller accessories such as bottles and feeding supplies, skin care products including those by

Kiehls, travel and safety products, as well as all the nursing supplies you could ever need, including pumps and of course the My Brest Friend breastfeeding pillow (the founder of DayOne is the same guy who also invented My Brest Friend!). They have the best nursing bra selection in all of San Francisco and maybe even in the entire Bay Area. They also specialize in carrying a nice selection of developmental toys for infants and the young toddler. See also in Ch. 5.

Giggle

2110 Chestnut St.

415-440-1884

www.egiggle.com

PARENT RATING: ☆ ☆ ☆ ☆ ☆

The idea behind owner Allison Wing's "happy, healthy baby store" is health and design, offering everything you need for a safe and healthy nursery. They offer organic crib bedding for baby that features vibrant saturated colors and is produced in accordance with strict ecological standards, such as not using formaldehyde and other harmful chemicals on fabrics. They also carry what they consider to be some of the safest and healthiest baby gear and products, including car seats, a bouncy chair, the Stokke crib and bassinet system, the Stokke KinderZeat, and the highly coveted Bugaboo Frog stroller. While you are there you can also pick up air purifiers, non-toxic cleaners, and crib mattress encasements for the allergy-prone baby. Giggle also has a nice selection of quality organic cotton apparel for infants, including the Speesees line which uses low-impact and environmentallly sound dyes.

Jonathan Kaye

3548 Sacramento St.

415-563-0773

PARENT RATING: ☆ ☆ ☆ ☆ ☆

The original store (they opened a baby store in 2000, see below) is exclusively devoted to young children's high-end bedroom furnishings and accessories. They feature hand-painted toy chests and tables, lamps, nightlights, and bookends, as well as unique wall hangings and handmade quilts. They also offer a wonderful selection of classic toys as well as educational and developmental toys.

Jonathan Kaye Baby

3615 Sacramento St.

415-922-3233

www.jonathankaye.com

PARENT RATING: ☆ ☆ ☆ ☆ ☆

Among San Francisco's most elegant baby boutiques, Jonathan Kaye Baby is a block away, and across the street, from the original store. This store is devoted exclusively to babies, offering customized nursery design services including furniture featuring whimsical designs, and painted wall murals. They carry beautiful wicker bassinets and Moses baskets, high-end cribs and chests, and an elegant selection of high-end custom or ready-made crib bedding, as well as unique accessories to complete your baby's nursery. We've heard from one Bay Area mom that this tony boutique will match prices for nursery furnishings at Lullaby Lane in San Bruno! They also carry a choice selection of upscale clothing and developmental toys.

Karikter

418 Sutter St.

415-434-1120

This fun European comic and design boutique is of interest to adults and children alike! The shop carries

Most Useful Baby Gear for City Life

◆ Baby Bjorn baby carrier

◆ A versatile stroller with a car seat attachment bar

◆ Lightweight reclinable stroller (many like the Maclaren, Combi Savvy Z, and Peg Perego Pliko strollers)

◆ Baby jogger

◆ Skip Hop diaper bag that fits perfectly over stroller handles

◆ Halo sleep sack—a great wearable blanket (that can't be kicked off) to ward off those chilly nights!

unique accessories including book-ends, lamps, clocks, posters, feeding accessories, towels, and occasionally bedding that feature characters including the Little Prince, Babar, Wallace and Gromit, Elmer and Noddy, and Tintin.

Maison de Belles Choses

3263 Sacramento St.

415-345-1797

PARENT RATING: ☆ ☆ ☆ ☆ ☆

Maison de Belles Choses carries an elegant selection of imported caned beds and custom-made iron beds from France for your toddler when she is ready to transition out of the crib. See a full description and rating under the Baby and Children's Clothing section of this chapter.

Mudpie

1694 Union St.

415-771-9262

PARENT RATING: ☆ ☆ ☆ ☆

Mudpie offers designer-quality and designer-priced baby furnishings, including antique reproduction cribs, beds, changing tables, and dressers, as well as crib sheets, customized bedding, matelasse bumpers, hand-made quilts, rugs, and lights. In-home designer services are also offered by appointment. This talented team will gladly assist you in creating a one-of-a-kind nursery or room for your baby or young child.

Pratesi at Wilkes Bashford

375 Sutter St.

415-291-9480

Pratesi baby has come to San Francisco and most fittingly can be found on the lower level of one of San Francisco's finest clothiers—Wilkes Bashford. If you want the finest and most luxurious bedding for your baby's bassinet or crib, look no further than Pratesi. Now the family-owned Italian luxury bed linens company is offering their same magnificent quality linens in sophisticated European patterns for your little one. Prints include jacquard white storks, blooming flowers, and elegant garlands all set against their crisp white elegant backgrounds of the finest quality cotton. You can even splurge and purchase the entire bassinet with matching linens and décor. They also offer the comfiest terry hooded towels and robes as well as one-of-a-kind christening gowns adorned with vintage European lace.

Scheuer Linens

340 Sutter St.

415-392-2813

www.scheuerlinens.com

PARENT RATING: ☆ ☆ ☆ ☆

A San Francisco institution, Scheuer Linens carries, among their elegant selection of linens, beautifully detailed crib bedding, including fitted sheets, comforters, quilts, and bumpers. They also offer custom-made imported bedding and accessories for the baby's room. Scheuer offers stellar service and a friendly attitude.

Baby News Outlet

1445 Santa Rosa Ave.
Santa Rosa
707-542-1006
www.babynewsonline.com
PARENT RATING: ☆ ☆ ☆ ☆ ☆

Baby News Outlet is part of the consortium of Baby News Bay Area baby gear retailers. Like its sister retailers, it carries high-end baby gear and clothing. However, unlike the other Baby News stores, Baby News Outlet is distributor owned, which means it carries discontinued models of many items at great prices. Their staff is helpful and knowledgeable.

Cribs and Bibs

1460 1st St.
Napa
707-226-5965
See under East Bay.

Goodnite Moon

117 Corte Madera Town Ctr.
Corte Madera
415-945-0677
www.goodnightmoon.com
PARENT RATING: ☆ ☆ ☆ ☆ ☆

One of Marin's best baby furniture and accessories boutiques, Goodnite Moon carries quality furnishings for your baby's nursery and child's room, including hand-painted dressers, lamps, toddler beds, custom-made bedding, and many wonderful accessories like kid's art, toys, diaper bags, books and bookends, blankets, and more. Furniture lines include Maine Cottage, Universal Interiors, Vermont Tubbs, Vermont Precision, Art for Kids, EG Furniture, Lexington, Little Castle, and many others. Prices for furniture and custom bedding compare favorably to other retailers. Watch for their 10% discount on furniture orders, usually in August. One of the most impressive features of this store is the great customer service. Store manager,

Most Useful Baby Gear for North Bay Life

- ◆ Baby backpack (with a sun canopy)
  - ◆ Jog stroller (great for off-road adventures)
  - ◆ Baby Bjorn (for walks and hikes before your baby is big enough for the jog stroller)
    - ◆ Sunscreen and safari-style sun hats with flaps to protect baby's ears and neck
    - ◆ Large blanket that is water resistant on one side and fleece on the other—these blankets are perfect to store in the car for that quick picnic at the park or beach!

Mary Ann, will sit down with you and thoughtfully help you select the right bed, dresser, or whatever you need for your baby or young child. Comment: "The service could not have been more helpful and friendly, including getting good advice on which beds to buy for our sons. . . . Our boys love their bunk beds, and we feel good about having bought a quality piece of furniture that we know is safe for them."

Heller's for Children

514 4th St.
San Rafael
415-456-5533
www.hellersforchildren.com

PARENT RATING: ☆ ☆ ☆ ☆ ☆

Part of the Baby News consortium of baby retailers and in business since 1958, Heller's is a Marin parent's staple. They have a large store filled with almost everything you'd ever need for your baby's first 2 years, including a large selection of high-end strollers, car seats, joggers, gliders, high chairs, diaper bags, baby carriers, toys, baby books, and baby clothing and sleepwear. The second floor has an extensive collection of furnishings for baby's room, including cribs, dressers, changing tables, and bassinets. They also have a nice selection of developmental toys for infants, including colorful, multisensory toys, mobiles, and activity gyms. The staff is knowledgeable and friendly.

Mill Valley Baby Company

12 Miller Ave.
Mill Valley
415-389-1312
www.millvalleybabyco.com

PARENT RATING: ☆ ☆ ☆ ☆ ☆

Owned by local mom Lily Kanter, this exquisite shop offers all you could ever want for your baby's or young child's room and more! The entryway of the store is marked by a 135-gallon tropical fish tank—little kids walking by can't resist pulling their moms inside, and once inside, moms can't help themselves from making a purchase or 2. The large light space is filled with beautiful bedroom vignettes of cribs and kids' beds, as they offer a large number of quality lines of kids' furniture that include Morigeau-Lepine, Art for Kids, Little Castle, EG Furniture, Paint Box, Vermont Precision Woods, Maine Cottage, Farmhouse Furniture, and Corsican. They also carry changing tables, desks, cute Adirondack chairs, picnic tables, art tables, toy chests—you name it. In the bedding department, they feature exquisite crib linens and sheets and duvet covers for kids by Catamini, Serena & Lilly, and the Gordonsbury Co. Favorite baby gift items include their line of personalized baby items, such as picture frames, burp cloths, pillows, baby blankets, and wooden letters. They also offer customized birth announcements and feature an impressive and unique collection of colorful wall art for children's rooms, largely done by local artists. A unique collection of baby and kids' accessories are displayed throughout the store, including Moses baskets, the Bugaboo stroller and accessories, European sleep sacks, European melamine dishware, and a great selection of Old World-inspired toys and top-drawer clothing for babies, including Ralph Lauren, Zutano, and Lilly Pulitzer. For Mom, they carry stylish diaper bags and colorful leather brag books.

Sanders Furniture

825 W. Francisco Blvd.
San Rafael
415-459-5757
www.sandersfurniture.com

PARENT RATING: ☆ ☆ ☆ ☆

This furniture store offers finished and unfinished wood beds for children, as well as a great selection of bookcases, dressers, children's table and chair sets, and nightstands.

East Bay

Baby News Outlet

3060 Pacific Ave.
Livermore
925-449-3020
www.stanforddistributing.com

This retailer, part of the Baby News consortium, features last year's baby gear styles and patterns at discounted prices.

Baby World—The Children's Place

• Berkeley
   6000 College Ave., 510-655-2828
• Oakland
   4400 Telegraph Ave., 510-655-0726
www.stanforddistributing.com

PARENT RATING: ☆ ☆ ☆

Also part of the Baby News consortium of baby retailers, Baby World is a true baby superstore, carrying an extensive selection of cribs, bassinets, strollers, car seats, gliders, dressers, and other baby gear. However, we've heard that the staff is not as knowledgeable about various models of baby gear, and the pros and cons of each, as they might be elsewhere.

They also have a nice selection of high-end baby clothing.

Berkeley Kids' Room

6022 College Ave.
Oakland
510-420-0811
www.berkeleykids.com

Berkeley Kids' specializes in bedroom furnishings for young children, including beds, dressers, bunk beds, rugs, lamps, and bedding. They also carry a small selection of cribs and changing tables for infants.

Cribs and Bibs

1281 Franquette Rd., Ste. C
Concord
925-682-5888

The new owners of what was Leonard's Tot shop for 50-plus years have carried on the tradition of specializing in baby and children's furniture. They feature more than 100 cribs to choose from, as well as dressers, changing tables, beds, bookshelves, rockers, toy boxes, and coordinating bedding. They also offer baby gear, including car seats, strollers, high chairs, and nursing and bottle-feeding supplies.

Earthsake

1772 4th St.
Berkeley
510-559-8440
www.earthsake.com

This store offers natural products for a baby's nursery, including maple cribs, organic cotton crib mattresses and bedding, receiving blankets and towels, and laundry flakes.

House

1848 4th St.
Berkeley
510-549-4558
www.houseinc.com

This new specialty shop features a vast selection of 100% cotton bedding and apparel, some of which is also carried by upscale boutiques throughout the Bay Area. They offer fine linens for baby with crib sheets and coordinating bumpers made out of elegant vintage-inspired prints. They also feature soft and easy playwear for infants and toddlers up to size 4T, including poplin pants and jumpers and an old-fashioned jersey dress with an apron that buttons onto the dress.

Kids N' Cribs

1820 A St.
Antioch
925-778-2229
800-320-3257
www.kids-n-cribs.com

Kids N' Cribs, a family-operated business, specializes in carrying furniture for your baby's nursery and child's room. They have more than 50 cribs and beds on display. They also offer bedding and accessories, reams of basic baby gear, including car seats, strollers, and breast pumps, developmental toys for infants and toddlers, and a nice line of baby clothing, including sizes for newborns and preemies.

Kids Room

40524 Albrae St.
Fremont
510-490-1313
www.Kids-Room.com

The Kids Room offers an extensive selection of 25 different children's furniture lines, including bunk beds, dressers, twin beds, toddler beds, mattresses, lamps, and beanbag chairs. The large showroom features furnishings in solid hardwoods,

Most Useful Baby Gear for East Bay Life

- ◆ Jog stroller
    - ◆ Quality car seat and good car toys (such as a Magna Doodle and books)
        - ◆ Large blanket that is water resistant on one side and fleece on the other—these blankets are perfect to store in the car for that quick picnic at the park or beach!
- ◆ Insulated lunch bag
- ◆ Pull wagon for neighborhood rides and to load up with stuff to take to cookouts

including oak and maple, as well as a variety of color laminates. Owner Lanny Witt will match any price in the Bay Area. Another added bonus is that unlike most other furniture stores, Lanny can get you many items within a week. They do not carry cribs or any baby furnishings.

Rockridge Kids
5511 College Ave.
Oakland
510-601-5437

PARENT RATING: ☆ ☆ ☆ ☆ ☆

Located on the same block in Rockridge on the Oakland/Berkeley border for almost 25 years, this classic children's department store is an East Bay institution. Nishan Shephard is the proud and helpful owner of this truly special store that offers the very best of basic baby gear. They also carry baby clothing up to size 3T, including preemies, unique bedding for babies and children, and a thoughtful selection of classic toys, featuring Radio Flyer wagons and Kettler trikes. Rockridge Kids also has one of the best car seat installers around town; the Highway Patrol sends people to him to have their car seats properly installed. The store is as service-oriented and as kid-friendly as you can find. Salespeople are eager to offer you useful information about specific products, and the owner encourages little shoppers to play with the train tables. The store is also very involved in the community of Rockridge; 10% of all profits is given to the schools in the community.

Baby Land Furniture
1990 W. San Carlos St.
San Jose
408-293-1515
www.babylandfurniture.com

Baby Land offers a large selection of moderately priced wooden furniture for babies and toddlers, including cribs, cradles, and dressers. They also offer moderately priced strollers, car seats, and other baby gear and accessories. Be forewarned, however, that their return policy is store credit only, and for unopened merchandise. One mom reported that she received 2 Pack 'n Play cribs from the store as shower gifts, and when she went to return one and exchange it for something else, they wouldn't take it back since it had been opened.

Baby Super Store and Rocker World and Furniture for Kids
1523 Parkmoor Ave.
San Jose
408-293-0358
www.babysuper.com

PARENT RATING: ☆ ☆ ☆ ☆ ☆

Baby Super is true to its name—a true baby superstore. It's actually 3 stores in one and offers everything from cribs, beds, and bedding, to strollers, car seats, high chairs, gliders, and rockers. Their best feature is the numerous displays of infant and kids' rooms, which help you visualize your baby's or child's room. Parents speak highly of their customer service and assistance.

Hoot Judkins

- Redwood City
  1269 Veterans Blvd., 650-367-8181
- San Bruno
  1400 El Camino Real, 650-952-5600
- Fremont
  5101 Mowry Ave., 510-795-4890

www.hootjudkins.com

While these stores are not exclusively devoted to children's furniture, they carry solid wood baby furniture, including beds, rockers, toy boxes, bunk beds, step stools, rocking horses, and dollhouses. Items come unfinished, but special orders may be placed to have items finished for you.

Kiddie World Center

1899 W. San Carlos
San Jose
408-275-6651

Kiddie World Center carries all of your child's furniture needs, from cribs to high chairs and changing tables, to twin and full beds, bunk and trundle beds, as well as desks and bookshelves. They also offer outdoor furnishings, including redwood modular play structures and sandboxes.

Lullaby Lane

556 San Mateo Ave.
San Bruno
650-588-7644
800-588-7644
www.lullabylane.com

PARENT RATING: ☆ ☆ ☆ ☆ ☆

Family-owned and operated for more than 50 years, Lullaby Lane offers one-stop shopping for all of your baby's needs. This store has a large floor space covered with an extensive selection of strollers, joggers, car seats, high chairs, baby carriers, baby furniture, and bedding at some of the Bay Area's most competitive prices. They also have a nice selection of baby clothing. Lullaby Lane has a small clearance center just down the street (570 San Mateo Ave., 650-588-4878) where real bargains can be found. The retail store has a semi-annual closeout sale, but you need to get there before the doors open. Lullaby Lane also offers a free seminar almost every month on selecting and using baby gear. It's a great way to learn about what to look for in

Most Useful Baby Gear for South Bay Life

- ◆ Car seat gallery and other toys for the car
  - ◆ A versatile stroller with a car seat attachment bar (great for mall shopping)
    - ◆ Baby sun block and safari-style sun hat with flaps to protect baby's ears and neck
      - ◆ Baby swimsuit that is made out of special SPF fabric that offers UV protection

quality and safety. They also demonstrate car seat installation, strollers, high chairs, and cribs. Bay Area moms say that "The Lane" "stands out for knowledgeable staff and excellent customer service. . . . You really get the sense that it's family run and owned. . . . I liked everyone I dealt with there."

Modernmini

2087 Avy Ave.
Menlo Park
650-233-9260
www.modernmini.com

"The best in modern design for your little one!" If cool contemporary lines appeal to you, then this is where you may want to look for furnishing your baby's nursery or child's room. Owned and run by Pazit Kagel, a mother and designer who designed much of the furniture she carries, Modernmini features unique contemporary styles for baby and beyond.

Planet Kids

1145 El Camino Real
Menlo Park
650-329-8488
www.planetkidsbabynews.com

A member of the Baby News consortium of baby superstores, Planet Kids offers high-end infant and children's furniture, a large selection of ready-made and customized bedding, high-end baby gear, including strollers, car seats, and high chairs, and child-proofing products. They also offer individual design services by appointment. They carry a nice selection of developmentally oriented toys for infants and toddlers. The staff is friendly and knowledgeable. Planet Kids features built-in entertainment for your little one in its Galaxy Playroom.

Talbots Toyland

445 South B St.
San Mateo
650-342-0126

PARENT RATING: ☆ ☆ ☆ ☆

In business for more than 50 years, Talbots "has it all" in baby gear. They carry an enormous selection at good prices, including medium- and high-end strollers, bassinets, car seats, and baby carriers, along with other baby accessories and a wonderful selection of toys.

INDIVIDUAL NURSERY DESIGNERS AND MURALISTS

We know this doesn't come under the heading of necessities, but the Bay Area offers many talented designers and muralists who specialize in making a one-of-a-kind nursery or child's room.

Tammy Artis

510-266-3799
Tammy specializes in murals for children's rooms.

Baby Barker Art

415-384-0184
www.babybarkerart.com
Lisa Barker offers custom murals for babies' and kids' rooms that feature

whimsical designs and non-toxic paints.

A Child's Eye View
510-653-3304

This talented team of interior designers specializes in creating nurseries and children's rooms.

Croworks Decorative Painting
415-454-6809

PARENT RATING: ☆ ☆ ☆ ☆ ☆

Victoria Bohlman does beautiful faux, painting, and glazing designs for babies' or children's rooms, especially girls' rooms.

Toni De Bella
415-453-9332
www.tonibarbara.com

PARENT RATING: ☆ ☆ ☆ ☆ ☆

Parents love the work of this talented muralist! She will also custom-paint furniture and has painted some of the adorable furniture featured at Jonathan Kaye Baby.

Serena Dugan
415-203-4746
www.serenadugan.com

The secret is out—Serena is the one behind the decorative walls of the Pottery Barn catalogs! She specializes in one-of-a-kind walls and will transform your child's room with her exquisite work.

The Flying Brush
415-285-0322

Teresa O'Connor offers unique painting for kids, including custom murals and furniture.

Jane Richardson Mack
415-485-5722
www.muralistjane.com

Specializing in painting murals and trompe l'oeil, Jane has more than 15 years' experience with decorative pinning, including being featured in the Marin Designer Showcase. Her work for children's rooms includes painting exquisite canvas murals that can be easily taken with you or moved to another room.

Magpie Decorative Painting
415-614-0191
www.magpiepainting.com

This enthusiastic and talented duo creates whimsical murals and hand-painted furniture with artistry and style.

Masterpiece Murals
800-242-2003

June Gomez will transform your baby's or child's room into an enchanted environment.

Novak Art Studio
916-294-0035

They specialize in creating walls, tiles, and furniture for kids' rooms.

Oliver's Collection
415-291-9035

Featured in the 2003 San Francisco Décorator Showcase House, Shirley Robinson von Karl and her talented team will work with you to paint one-of-a-kind decorative furniture for your child's room.

Claire Petitt
415-939-3338
www.clairepetitt.com

Claire is a designer and painter, specializing in children's rooms and custom-painted murals and furniture.

Vacationing or Visiting Baby

Are you wondering where your sister's 8-month-old baby is going to sleep when he visits you next month? Or, now that you have your vacation booked, are you wondering how you are going to lug all that baby gear with you? Leave it behind, and let a baby equipment rental agency be your answer. These companies rent a large inventory of strollers, car seats, portable cribs, swings, joggers, high chairs, cribs, and much more. You make your reservation either via phone or on their website. Within a couple of days, a representative will call you to confirm and make delivery or pickup arrangements.

Little Luggage
877-FLYBABY (359-2229)
www.littleluggage.com
This San Francisco-based company rents baby gear in the Bay Area for your visiting friends and relatives with babies. They will come to your house and set up a crib or drop off a stroller or high chair with friendly and reliable service. They also offer the option for guests to pick up baby equipment at San Francisco Airport.

Baby's Away
800-571-0077
www.babysaway.com
Baby's Away is the largest baby and child gear rental service in the country with 30 locations. At press time, they do not have a Bay Area location, but serve parts of Hawaii, Colorado ski resorts, and other popular vacation destinations. Call or visit their website for locations and details.

Lullaby Lane
650-588-7644
www.lullabylane.com
This full-scale baby superstore located in San Bruno also rents baby equipment.

Jane Resnick, Interior Design

415-641-4858

Jane Resnick specializes in designing babies' and children's rooms. She has clients all over the Bay Area.

Michael Stehr

510-506-2234

Michael is primarily a fine artist who does custom interior paint finishes, including murals and decorative painting.

Gabriella Tabak

415-331-1222

www.gabrielladesign.com

Gabriella specializes in murals and decorative painting.

BUYING BABY GEAR ONLINE AND THROUGH MAIL ORDER

Myriad websites sell baby gear and accessories, some at great prices. Here are several recommended to us by parents. However, remember that saving $50 on a stroller purchased online might not be worth it when it breaks or arrives defective. Your neighborhood retailer, by contrast, may offer repairs! Also, be sure to get all the details on delivery charges and arrangements before you place your order—some parents have reported high shipping costs and deliveries of nursery furniture that only went as far as their front door.

*These sites also carry baby clothing:

www.babybundle.com*
www.babycenter.com*
www.babyproductsonline.com
www.babysupercenter.com

www.babysupermall.com
www.babystyle.com*
www.poshtots.com
www.thebabyoutlet.com

The following are comprehensive online baby retailers that offer specialty items for baby as well.

Baby Catalog of America

800-PLAYPEN (752-9736) (catalog)
www.babycatalog.com

This comprehensive online and mail order baby boutique offers the "lowest advertised price" on all baby gear, many of which are high-end brands. Join the "Baby Club" for $25 the first year and receive an additional 10% discount.

eBay

www.ebay.com

Baby product makers and stores are quietly selling overstocked, new items on eBay at prices that are much lower than most major retailers. Just be aware of products that have been recalled or are soon likely to be recalled. Verify the safety of your purchase by obtaining the model number and checking with the Consumer Products Safety Commission (www.cpsc.gov).

Kids Club

800-363-0500 (catalog)
www.kidstuff.com

Kids Club offers deep hard-to-beat discounts on high-end baby equipment and accessories to club members. Membership is $18 a year and well worth it if you plan on buying a lot of baby gear. Non-club members may purchase items, but at slightly higher prices.

ONLINE BABY PRODUCT REVIEWS

The following websites offer reviews of baby gear and equipment:

- ◆ www.babycenter.com
- ◆ www.consumerreports.org
- ◆ www.epinions.com
- ◆ www.deja.com
- ◆ http://parents.berkeley.edu

Online and Mail Order Resources for Nursery Bedding and Accessories

Baby Bedding Online
www.babybeddingonline.com

Best for Babies
www.bestforbabies.com

babystyle
www.babystyle.com

Company Kids
800-323-8000 (catalog)
www.companykids.com

Garnet Hill
800-622-6216 (catalog)
www.garnethill.com

Graham Kracker
800-489-2820 (catalog)
www.grahamkracker.com

Linens for Us
www.linensforus.com

Land's End
800-345-3696 (catalog)
www.landsend.com

The Land of Nod
800-933-9904 (catalog)
www.landofnod.com

Pottery Barn Kids
800-430-7373 (catalog)
www.potterybarn.kids.com

Stephanie Anne
888-885-6700 (catalog)
www.stephanieanne.com

Warm Biscuit Bedding Co.
800-231-4231 (catalog)
www.warmbiscuit.com

You may also want to check out websites of individual designers and manufacturers of baby and children's bedding.

Unique Baby Accessories and Gifts Available Online

We've seen so many adorable and unique baby accessories and gifts that are available over the internet that it's hard to include them all. Here are a handful of businesses that offer them, many of which were started by Bay Area moms!

Baby Keyes
www.babykeyes.com
Ruth Keyes offers the "perfect personal baby gift," from personalized burp cloths, monogrammed fancy pants, bibs, onesies, Ts, and more.

Baby O Baby
www.babyobaby.com
This mom offers great monogrammed newborn caps, burp cloths, bibs, baby blankets, and more.

Darimi Kidz
www.darimikidz.com
Darimi Kidz offers the popular Sun Busters swimsuits and hats that offer an ultra-violet protection factor of 50-plus, wet or dry, that blocks out 98 percent of all UV rays.

Gotcha Covered Baby
www.gotchacoveredbaby.com
This clever mom got tired of looking at her baby's plain car seat cover and decided to replace it with a brighter, whimsical design. Your baby can also ride in style and have a one-of-a-kind stylish car seat cover.

Mimi the Sardine
www.mimithesardine.com
Mimi offers unique Swedish prints awash in brilliant color that have been laminated for bibs, art and cooking aprons, place mats, lunch bags, and more. Kids just love her whimsical patterns!

Modernseed
www.modernseed.com
Started by two Bay Area moms—a graphic designer and business woman—Modernseed is a unique children's goods website offering cutting edge and contemporary children's furniture, clothing, design, toys, and accessories—everything you need for the "modern mini!"

Posh Baban
www.poshbaban.com
Laura Russell-Jones offers a wide array of luxurious infant apparel and gifts. She features hand-knit sweaters and baby outfits, imported from Europe, as well as many personalized items for baby and the full line of Bed Head pajamas. She also offers stunning silver baby gifts, exquisite christening outfits, smock dresses, and tasteful children's jewelry.

THE EBAY BUZZ

Are you looking for something very specific such as that sailboat Pottery Barn sheet set that is already out of stock or a certain Peg Perego stroller that is back ordered for a couple of months? Before you give up your search, you might want to try looking for the item on eBay. Many Bay Area parents have success finding specific hard-to-find items—such as toys, clothing, and Halloween costumes—you name it. They say that eBay has great search capability, allowing you to search for specific items, and somehow there is almost always someone who has what you are looking for—often brand new and in its original packaging . . . a minor miracle of the free market! A word to the wise: Just be cautious of recalled or soon to be recalled items. Always verify the safety of your purchase by obtaining the model number and checking with the Consumer Product Safety Commission (www.cpsc.gov).

Modernseed

www.modernseed.com
See under "Unique Baby Accessories and Gifts Available Online."

Stroller Depot

www.strollerdepot.com
They offer great discounts on name-brand strollers, including many high-end brands.

One Step Ahead

800-274-8440 (catalog)
www.onestepahead.com
This store is similar to Right Start, offering select major baby gear items such as strollers, high chairs, and car seats, and specializing in smaller baby accessories for use around the house or when traveling, such as monitors, and bathing, feeding, and childproofing items.

Right Start

800-LITTLE-1 (548-8531) (catalog)
www.rightstart.com
See description under Baby Gear retailers. They often offer a 10-15% discount if you order online.

Toys "R" Us

www.toysrus.com

Babies "R" Us

www.babiesrus.com*
Two sane alternatives to these mega-stores!

Baby and Children's Clothing

Everyone loves baby clothing, and you'll love it even more when you have a baby! To make buying baby clothing even more irresistible, the Bay Area has some of the best baby clothing retailers in the country. We've done our best to peruse the Bay Area and ask moms and dads about their favorite baby and children's clothiers. Many baby superstores carry wonderful selections of clothing and shoes, so be sure not to miss those listed in the Baby Gear section above. We've also included some Bay Area parents' favorite places to shop for children's clothing online and through mail order catalogs.

NATIONAL CHAINS

Here is what Bay Area parents have to say about several national chains of clothier retailers. Check the yellow pages or each chain's website for a store location near you.

Specialty Chains

babystyle
- Burlingame
  1319 Burlingame Ave., 650-342-1534
- Santa Clara, Valley Fair Mall
  2855 Stevens Creek Blvd.,
  408-246-9703
www.babystyle.com

PARENT RATING: ☆ ☆ ☆ ☆ ☆

This stylish website and catalog, attributed with making pregnancy easier and parenthood more hip, now has 2 Bay Area retail stores—so you can shop their fabulous selection in person! Babystyle offers a carefully edited selection of products, including designer apparel for babies, kids, and moms-to-be. Babystyle also features their own brand of hip apparel, unique toys, charming nursery décor, top-rated baby gear, and a wonderful transition and nursing collection.

Baby Gap
www.babygap.com
PARENT RATING: ☆ ☆ ☆ ☆ ☆

This locally headquartered chain is a favorite among Bay Area parents and features irresistibly cute clothing. Even though you may see many other babies in the same outfit, this doesn't seem to stop most Bay Area parents from buying here. Lines change about every 8 weeks, after which whatever is left goes on sale at a deep discount. Their flagship store in downtown San Francisco has an entire floor for babies and kids. Most Gap Kids stores also carry a selection of the current baby line of clothing. Goods are also available online.

The Children's Place
www.childrensplace.com
PARENT RATING: ☆ ☆ ☆ ☆

This national chain offers moderately priced playwear and dressier wear, as

HELPFUL SHOPPING TIPS FOR CLOTHING

- Wait until after your baby shower to buy, as you may receive several gifts of clothing.

- Unless your doctor expects that you are having a small baby, don't buy too many things in the newborn size, 0-3 months. Most of these items won't fit a baby larger than 10 to 12 pounds.

- Keep track of how many gifts you receive in what sizes and save gift receipts. You may want to exchange some gifts for different sizes.

- Make exchanges as soon as you can. If you're like most new moms and put it off, you'll find the unworn outfit with tags still on it hanging in your baby's closet a year later!

- European-style boutiques often have strict return and exchange policies, often requiring that they be done within two weeks. Department stores offer the most liberal return and exchange policies.

- Buy cotton—it's the most comfortable fabric for babies. Their delicate skin knows the difference between natural and synthetic fibers. Cotton is also easier to wash than many synthetics.

- Buy only machine-washable clothing. If you didn't have time to do your own hand-washing before your baby was born, you definitely won't have time to do it after your baby's arrival!

- One-piece outfits such as stretchy suits and rompers are best for babies, since two-piece outfits tend to "ride up" each time you lift your baby.

well as outerwear and sleepwear for infants and young children.

Gymboree
www.gymboree.com
PARENT RATING: ☆ ☆ ☆ ☆

A Bay Area-based designer and company popular with many Bay Area moms, Gymboree offers colorful coordinating ensembles for infants and children. Styles are slightly more traditional than Gap's lines. Clothing lines change about every 8 weeks. What's left goes on sale at great savings.

Jacadi Paris
1215 Burlingame Ave.
Burlingame
650-558-1122
PARENT RATING: ☆ ☆ ☆ ☆

This boutique chain offers traditional European baby clothing, featuring hand-crafted and embroidered designs. See a complete description under the Baby Gear section.

Janie and Jack

www.janieandjack.com

PARENT RATING: ☆ ☆ ☆ ☆ ☆

Since our first edition, Janie and Jack is the most exciting addition to the category of national chain stores for baby clothing. The owners of Gymboree have put their designers on a plane to Paris and come back with some fabulous classic designs for baby and toddler ensembles! The stores have an anything but national chain-like feel to them though; with merchandise displayed in wooden armoires, you feel more like you are in a Parisian boutique. Clothing is very classic with old-fashioned European styling. Visit their website which showcases the entire collection each season. Bay Area moms report that they have great sales and many love to buy baby gifts here since they are attractively packaged, and are easy about returns and exchanges. At press time, there are stores in Pleasanton, Corte Madera, and San Jose.

Old Navy

www.oldnavy.com

PARENT RATING: ☆ ☆ ☆ ☆

If you and your baby can stand the blaring music and football-field size of the store, Old Navy offers moderately priced basics for babies, toddlers, and kids. Bay Area moms generally agree that Old Navy's styles aren't quite as cute or stylish as their sister company Baby Gap, and the selection isn't as large either; however, they certainly are less expensive. They offer affordable prices and hip styles of decent-quality clothing that don't have to last more than one season anyway! Items are also available online.

Bloomingdale's

www.bloomingdales.com

Bloomies has an extensive upscale infant and children's department, featuring designer labels including DKNY and Ralph Lauren—what else would one expect?

JC Penney

www.jcpenney.com

Penney's offers moderately priced playwear and dressy wear for infants and children, including labels such as Carter's and Health Tex.

Macy's

www.macys.com

PARENT RATING: ☆ ☆

While the service could use improvement, Macy's infant department in San Francisco offers one of the largest selections of moderately priced infant and toddler clothing through size 4T. For the Corte Madera store, the offerings are much slimmer, especially for toddler sizes. They also do not carry children's shoes at this location.

Nordstrom

www.nordstrom.com

PARENT RATING: ☆ ☆ ☆ ☆ ☆

Nordstrom has a great infant and children's department, with a variety of designer playwear clothing. Popular lines/products: Hartstrings, Little Me, Ralph Lauren, Tommy Hilfiger, Mulberribush, and their own moderately priced Baby N label. They also carry special-occasion wear from newborn on up. Popular lines/ products: Imps Original suits (boys),

Florence Eiseman dresses, and Posie hand-sewn christening gowns. The staff is very service-oriented.

Neiman Marcus

www.neimanmarcus.com

PARENT RATING: ☆ ☆ ☆ ☆

Neiman's has a small but unsurprisingly upscale baby and toddler's department, featuring designer playwear and elegant special-occasion wear. Popular lines/products: Florence Eiseman party dresses, Posie christening gowns.

Discounters and Baby Superstores

Babies "R" Us

www.babiesrus.com

PARENT RATING: ☆ ☆ ☆ ☆

This store has an impressive selection of moderate name-brand clothing such as Carter's and Little Me at discounted prices (30% or more off retail) for newborns, toddlers, and children. They carry all the baby basics, such as sleepers, rompers, and Ts, as well as more hip styles for your preschooler and beyond.

Carter's Childrenswear

Factory Stores of Vacaville
Vacaville
707-447-7440
(Other outlet locations: Petaluma, Folsom, Gilroy, and Milpitas.)
This outlet offers 30% off retail prices for first-quality Carter's playwear, sleepwear, and layettes, sizes newborn to 6X. Irregulars are also available at deeper discounts.

Marshalls

www.marshallsonline.com

PARENT RATING: ☆ ☆ ☆

This national discount department store is well known for its quality and name-brand labels at deep discounts. Inventory varies with store location, but their infant and children's department is usually worth checking out. Of course it takes a lot of energy to weed through all those racks, but Bay Area moms report finding some very cute dresses and shoes for their kids there at great prices. They also carry some great toys—sometimes the same items as the more expensive toy stores—yet all marked down of course.

Mervyn's California

www.mervyns.com

PARENT RATING: ☆ ☆ ☆

Mervyn's offers moderately priced baby and children's clothing at great savings, especially when on sale. Mervyn's is a great place to stock up on basics such as Ts, socks, and sleepers. You can also occasionally find great designer knockoffs.

The Oilily Store

186 Stanford Shopping Center
Palo Alto
650-323-1996
www.oililyusa.com
Oilily, a Dutch-owned company, offers fun and vibrant ensembles designed mostly in The Netherlands. Their clothing is made from their own one-of-a-kind printed fabrics for infants and children up to size 16, and for women. You either love their fabrics and styles or you don't—it's a

definite, funky, anything but Old World look!

OshKosh B'Gosh

Gilroy Premium Outlets
408-842-3280
Petaluma Outlet Mall
707-766-8113
http://corp.oshkoshbgosh.com/company/locator/storelocator.html

Oshkosh B'Gosh offers modest savings at this outlet, but is still a favorite among Bay Area moms. They have a small section where everything is discounted an additional 30-50%. For other locations (Napa, Pacific Grove, Vacaville), visit their website.

PARENT RATING: ☆ ☆ ☆ ☆

Comment: "Good selection of moderate- to low-priced clothes—mostly attractive, good basics . . . good prices."

Ross Dress for Less

www.rossstores.com

This discount department store offers a selection of infant and toddler clothing, and toys, at great values. Selections tend to vary by each store location, but it is worth checking out.

Target

www.target.com

PARENT RATING: ☆ ☆ ☆ ☆

You can get great buys on Target's own line of 100% cotton baby and toddler clothing, under the Cherokee label. Many Bay Area moms buy all of their kids' play clothes here at low prices.

BAY AREA RETAILERS

Here is what Bay Area parents have to say about their favorite local baby and children's clothiers:

San Francisco

Beleza

1947 Union St.
415-345-8900
www.beleza.com

PARENT RATING: ☆ ☆ ☆ ☆ ☆

Beleza is Portuguese for beautiful, and this sweet little boutique of children's clothing and accessories (sizes newborn through 8) truly lives up to its name. They offer a great combination of fashionable playwear and nicer outfits for your little ones, featuring 15 clothing lines, including classic European styles by Deux Par Deux, Floriane, Confetti and Coccoli to more modern fashions such as those by Wonderboy, Dogwood, and OneKid. The focal point of this shop though is on their own exclusive label, which is hand-embroidered, 100% cotton imports from Brazil. Their signature line includes Prima cotton layette pieces, pajamas, christening pieces and dresses, all with whimsical hand embroidery. They also exclusively carry a high-end smocking dress line from Brazil that is well priced because they import the line directly. They also carry a selection of crib shoes and shoes for toddlers, as well as blankets, bikinis, and shoes, all from Brazil and all with handmade touches. They have a great book selection, mostly classic titles, in the back, and some small European and unusual toys.

1887 Dance Shop
2206 Union St.
415-441-1887
The 1887 Dance Shop specializes in carrying dancewear for young children as well as many costumes and dress-up clothes year round. They also carry one of the best selections of Halloween costumes for little ones!

DayOne
3490 California St., Ste. 203
415-440-DAY1 (3291)
www.dayonecenter.com
PARENT RATING: ☆ ☆ ☆ ☆ ☆
This outstanding parents' resource center runs a fabulous boutique that carries a nice selection of quality baby clothing as well as developmental toys for babies. They feature beautiful chenille and fleece baby blankets, sleepers, and sacks, as well as a nice selection of comfy clothing and caps for preemies. Popular lines/products: Victoria's Kids sweaters, Zutano (100% cotton ensembles), Oink Baby, and Halo sleep sacks.

Dottie Doolittle
3680 Sacramento St.
415-563-3244
800-372-2062
www.dottiedoolittle.com
PARENT RATING: ☆ ☆ ☆ ☆ ☆
This one-of-a-kind store is a longtime favorite among San Francisco moms and grandmas alike, as owner Maggie Chafen has been in business for 30 years! The interior of the store has just undergone a full-scale face-lift—check out their bright and inviting redone space! Dottie carries exquisite

---

Favorite Local Baby and Children's Clothiers in San Francisco

Most Hip Baby Clothing
Baby Gap
Pumpkin

Best Sales
Baby Gap
Dottie Doolittle

Most Traditional Baby Clothing
Dottie Doolittle
Mudpie
Maison de Belles Choses

Special Occasions (Christenings, Weddings, and Parties)
Dottie Doolittle
Mudpie
Neiman Marcus
Nordstrom

Halloween Costumes
Baby Gap
1887 Dance Shop
The Disney Store
Mervyn's
Old Navy

clothing for both play and special occasions, featuring many traditional-style designers, for newborns through size 16 for girls and size 14 for boys. They offer beautiful baby sweaters and blankets and adorable ensembles for your toddler, preschooler, and young grade-school child too. Dottie is best known for its wonderful little girls' party and special-occasion dresses, and irresistible bows and hair accessories. The annual holiday party dress shopping trip is a requisite pilgrimage for city and suburban moms alike! They also have a full selection of boys' clothing from classic shirts and pants by Polo to hip playwear and Hawaiian shirts. And of course, they carry all the little Eton suits, shortalls, coveralls, and little navy blazers and ties that every mother dreams of dressing her son in! They also carry a thoughtful selection of toys—from initial charm bracelets, watches, and jewelry kits for girls to plastic sharks, miniature train sets, and robots for boys. It's a great place to pick up a quick birthday gift. Service is always friendly and helpful. Be sure to get on their mailing list to be notified of their semiannual sales that always draw crowds. Popular lines/products: Sophie Dess of France (smocked dresses), Imp Originals (boys' suits), Carriage House, Gordon & Co., Hartstrings, Kitestrings, Le Top, Petit Bateau, Hearthside Handworks (custom hand-knit sweaters), and Posie christening gowns.

D'Lynnes Dancewear

2253 Union St.
415-292-4028
See under North Bay.

Giggle

2110 Chestnut St.
415-440-1884
See under nursery.

Jean et Marie—La Boutique Pour Bébés

100 Clement St.
415-379-1111

PARENT RATING: ☆ ☆ ☆ ☆

Owner Monica Labbe offers an elegant collection of European imports and high-end domestic clothing for infants and young toddlers. She is friendly and helpful and occasionally has her own little ones in the store helping her! They also carry a small selection of unique imported toys, including those by the French company, Vilac. Popular lines/products: Sophie Dess ensembles for baby girls and boys, Absorba, Le Top, Catamini, Petit Bateau.

Kids Only

1608 Haight St.
415-552-5445
www.kidsonly-sf.com

Kids Only remains true to the Haight/Ashbury neighborhood's reputation by featuring some of the hippest babywear in town. They feature tie-dye and Batik outfits made by local artists for newborns and young children. They also have a small toy selection, including developmental and wooden toys and stuffed animals featuring Curious George, Madeline, and Pooh. Popular lines/products: Baby M (animal print blankets/ensembles), Baby Lula, and Cherry Pie outfits (reportedly bought by Madonna in bulk for her daughter).

Kidiniki

2 Embarcadero Center
415-986-5437
www.kidiniki.com

PARENT RATING: ☆ ☆ ☆ ☆ ☆

While the financial district isn't the most likely place for such an elegant baby boutique, Kidiniki offers upscale shopping for many mom execs. In infant and toddler playwear and in dressier wear up to size 4T, the owner proudly offers a variety of price points for shoppers. They have a wonderful selection of baby blankets, sweaters, and hats, as well as small toys (including Thomas the Tank Engine trains) and accessories that complete any gift. Popular lines/products: Le Top, Chicken Noodle, Victoria's Kids, Confetti, Absorba.

Kindersport

3566 Sacramento St.
415-563-7778
www.kindersport.com

PARENT RATING: ☆ ☆ ☆ ☆ ☆

Kindersport carries wonderful top-quality outdoor gear for infants to preteens, including swimsuits with built-in polyfloats for the new swimmer, and ski jackets and outfits for toddlers and children. They also carry a great assortment of coordinating gloves, hats, and boots. Watch for end-of-the-season sales for great savings. Popular lines/products: Spyder and Cacao ski suits, Mystic swimsuits with UV protection, JetPilot wet suits and life vests, Boeri ski helmets, Dale of Norway ski sweaters. Comment: "Stephanie is great in fitting the kids—so patient and knows just what to recommend for their age."

Maison de Belles Choses

3263 Sacramento St.
415-345-1797

PARENT RATING: ☆ ☆ ☆ ☆ ☆

We all know how the French love to dress their babies in the finest, and now San Francisco parents are doing the same. This shop is busting with exquisite children's clothing, including imported hand-smocked dresses and rompers, classic outfits for boys, cozy velour sleepers, French and English pajamas, lovely dress coats, and beautiful European knits. They also carry unique baby gifts such as handmade Italian cashmere blankets, hand-embroidered linens and pillows, and original paintings for your baby's nursery. They also offer a fine selection of French furniture, including caned beds and custom-made iron beds for when your *petit pois* is ready to transfer out of the crib. These pieces are for the parent who wants to give her child something to be passed down for generations.

Minis—Kids and Maternity Wear

2278 Union St.
415-567-9537
www.minis-sf.com

PARENT RATING: ☆ ☆ ☆ ☆ ☆

Mini's features its own line of stylish clothing for little ones, and even expecting moms. (See Ch. 3.) Known for their excellent quality, their merchandise features European styling and is all made in San Francisco. They carry sizes for newborns through 10 years. Mini's has a small selection of educational and classic toys and carries a nice selection of European shoes. They also carry Bugaboo strollers and Stokke baby furniture.

Mudpie

1694 Union St.

415-771-9262

PARENT RATING: ☆ ☆ ☆ ☆ ☆

Among San Francisco's choicest baby boutiques, Mudpie offers beautifully designed clothing for infants, much of which is imported from France and Italy. They also offer Burberry's line for baby as well as Lilly Pulitzer's. Mudpie is where you might shop for the dressy ensemble that a christening, wedding, or party calls for. They carry wonderful classic toys, including china tea sets, small metal carousels, and other Old World-inspired toys, as well as clever puzzles, books, imaginative costumes, and special accessories for your baby's or child's room. Popular lines/products: Petit Bateau, Magil, Bon Point, Bains-Plus, Posie handsewn christening gowns.

Murik Children's Store

73 Geary St.

415-395-9200

www.murikstore.com

PARENT RATING: ☆ ☆ ☆ ☆

Murik carries a great selection of beautiful clothing for babies and young children, including many unique lines from Belgium, Italy, and the Netherlands.

Newborn Connections

3698 California St.

415-600 -BABY (2229)

www.cpmc.org/newbornconnections

This one-stop resource for you and your baby is located in California Pacific Medical Center's Lactation Center. It is well stocked with quality apparel for infants and has a nice selection especially for preemies, as well as nursing bras, loungewear and nightwear, including nursing pajamas, parenting books, maternity and baby products, breast pumps and breast-feeding supplies. If you are delivering your baby at CPMC, you can request in-room shopping through their "traveling boutique service."

Pumpkin

3366 Sacramento St.

415-567-6780

www.pumpkinbabes.com

PARENT RATING: ☆ ☆ ☆ ☆

"Hip clothes for cool babes," is Pumpkin's mantra, and they are not joking! They specialize in carrying the most fashion-forward brands for babies and kids such as Tea Collection, Chipie, Lucky, Queen Bee, Juicy Couture, Quicksilver, and James Perse among others. They also have unique baby gifts and darling sibling gifts such as stylish big brother/sister Ts.

Small Frys

4066 24th St.

415-648-3954

www.smallfrys.com

PARENT RATING: ☆ ☆ ☆ ☆

This sweet Noe Valley boutique offers a wide selection of wonderful infant and children's clothing in sizes newborn to 7 years. They also have a wonderful collection of toys, blankets, and accessories. Popular lines/products: OshKosh, Absorba, Kushies, and Chicken Noodle.

Baby & Children's Clothing

Thursday's Child

1980 Union St.

415-346-1666

PARENT RATING: ☆ ☆ ☆

This children's store carries cute essentials, such as ladybug slickers and boots and colorful Ts. They also carry clothing for girls from newborn to age 14 and for boys from newborn to 7 years old.

Yountville Clothes for Children

2416 Fillmore St.

415-922-5050

PARENT RATING: ☆ ☆ ☆ ☆ ½

Pacific Heights' neighborhood baby boutique, Yountville carries largely upscale European-imported baby and toddler clothing. Watch for their occasional sales when real bargains can be found. It is a great place to shop for special-occasion outfits and gifts. While it offers a small selection of ensembles, they are unique and as one Pacific Heights mom said, "made to last—the kind you keep in storage for your next baby." Comment: "This is the kind of store where the salespeople will recognize you if you shop there once a month or so, which makes it even nicer!"

North Bay

Baby Nook Boutique

Marin General Hospital

250 Bon Air Rd.

4th Floor Central

415-925-7474

The Baby Nook offers babies and moms lots of accessories and necessities including breast pumps, feeding pillows, nursing nightgowns, nursing bras, baby outfits, Baby Bjorn carri-ers, big brother,/big sister items, books, and beautiful gift items. All proceeds benefit the women, infants, and children's services at the hospital.

Bella Bambino

823 Grant Ave.

Novato

415-898-6453

PARENT RATING: ☆ ☆ ☆ ☆ ☆

Bella Bambino offers a fun selection of upscale playwear for babies and toddlers, up to size 4T. Popular lines/products: Baby Lulu, Zutano, Pepper Toes, Baby Rhino, and Bella Note.

Bug a Boo

14 Bolinas Rd.

Fairfax

415-457-2884

www.bug-a-boo.com

PARENT RATING: ☆ ☆ ☆ ☆

This unique store carries infants' and children's clothing, specializing in offering brightly colored clothing for newborns up to size 6X. You won't find those traditional soft pastels for baby here! They also carry outerwear as well as developmental toys, whimsical rain boots, books, blankets, bibs, and cool diaper bags for moms and dads. They also offer a great selection of seasonal items such as swimwear, sun hats, and sunglasses for your little ones! In addition to children's clothing, Bug a Boo offers a new mothers' group and parenting classes such as CPR, first aid, and infant massage. (See Ch. 6.) Popular lines/products: Zutano playwear, Molehill outerwear (for little skiers), and Manhattan Toy Co. And while they are not connected in any way, you can expect to find the Bugaboo Frog Stroller here!

Favorite Local Baby and Children's Clothiers in the North Bay

Most Hip Baby Clothing
Ciao Ragazzi
Mill Valley Mercantile
Scout
Swing

Best Sales
Baby Gap
Mervyn's
Old Navy

Special Occasions (Christenings, Weddings, and Parties)
Nordstrom
Toni Tierney

Halloween Costumes
Baby Gap
Child's Delight
(see under toys)
D'Lynnes
Dancewear
Noodle Soup

Ciao Ragazzi
532 San Anselmo Ave.
San Anselmo
415-454-4844
PARENT RATING: ☆ ☆ ☆ ☆ ☆

This upscale baby boutique opened its doors in March 2001. They offer a variety of clothing for infants, toddlers, and young children (up to size 8 for boys and size 12 for girls). They also have an impressive selection of children's shoes to chose from, including many European imports. In addition, they have a nice selection of unique toys, games, and other accessories. Popular lines/products: Benedict Boys, Cotton Caboodle, One Kid for Boys, and Zyno for boys, Confetti, Three Palm, and Shortcakes for girls. Shoes include Aster, Buckle My Shoe, Naturino, and Primigi.

Citrus
13 Main St.
Tiburon
415-435-1321

Citrus is a charming little boutique in picturesque downtown Tiburon that features many items for Mom (such as tasteful faux designer purses and shoes) but also has a small and unique collection of baby apparel. They feature adorable whimsical sweaters by baby area local Christine Foley, as well as cute and colorful socks and crib shoes, and elegant baby blankets. This is a small store with many breakable items—so it isn't a great place to bring strollers or toddlers on the go!

D'Lynnes Dancewear
1835 4th St.
San Rafael
415-456-4747
www.dlynnesdance.com

D'Lynnes has every costume, either for dress-up or Halloween, that your little one could ever dream of. From Cinderella to pirates and Pokeman, they carry an extensive selection of costumes as well as dancewear for young children year round.

Half Pint

450 1st St. E.
Sonoma
707-938-1722

PARENT RATING: ☆ ☆ ☆ ☆ ☆

Half Pint carries a nice selection of upscale American and European playwear and dressy wear for babies and children from newborn to size 10 for boys and size 16 for girls. They carry some of the more trendy items for young children such as sparkly shoes and Doc Martins, and distinguish themselves from other children's clothiers with their large inventory for boys. They also carry a thoughtful selection of nursery accessories including Moses baskets, prints for the nursery, and classic toys. Popular lines/products: Catamini, Jean Borget, Miniman, Baby Lulu, Flapdoodles, Flowers by Zoe, Charlie Rocket.

Kidiniki

310 Strawberry Village
Mill Valley
415-383-3110
www.kidiniki.com
See under San Francisco.

Mill Valley Mercantile

167 Throckmorton Ave.
Mill Valley
415-388-9588

PARENT RATING: ☆ ☆ ☆ ☆ ☆

Family-owned and operated, Mill Valley Mercantile (formerly only a women's clothier, which is now next door) opened its doors for babies and young children in September 2000. Since then, it has quickly become a Marin and Bay Area favorite for outfitting babies and toddlers in upscale play clothes. The sisters who manage the store are both moms and offer lots of friendly advice about everything from parenting to kids' clothing. They also carry beautiful baby blankets, a wonderful collection of children's books, wooden toys, and developmental toys. Popular lines/products: Zutano, Cotton Caboodle, Petit Bateau, Shortcakes, Dogwood, Cherry Pie, Rico, Under the Nile, Little Chum, and Manhattan Toy Co.

Noodle Soup

- San Anselmo
  718 San Anselmo Ave
  415-455-0141
- Corte Madera
  117 Corte Madera Town Center
  415-945-9683

Noodle Soup's 2 locations offer an adorable selection of upscale infant and children's clothing. They also carry a great selection of unique toys, puppets, and Halloween costumes, including infant sizes. Popular lines/products: Flapdoodles, Baby Lulu, Sweet Potatoes.

Scout

125 Matheson St.
Healdsburg
707-431-0903

PARENT RATING: ☆ ☆ ☆ ☆ ☆

This beautiful baby boutique features high-end infant apparel, much of which is imported from France. Lines include Petit Collin, Deux Par Deux, Berchet, Zutano, Mulberribush, and Isabelle Garriton.

Sweet Potatoes Inc.
857 Grant Ave. #B
Novato
415-898-8234
www.sweetpotatoesinc.com
See under East Bay.

Swing
467 Magnolia Ave.
Larkspur
415-924-2500

PARENT RATING: ☆ ☆ ☆ ☆ ☆

This new fashion-forward boutique opened their pretty doors in spring 2005, and Marin moms just love it! They offer a great selection of stylish clothing for babies and kids, much of which is organized in their unique shelving that resembles giant doll-houses. (You can special order the shelving for your child's room too!) Featured items and lines include the popular rhinestone design "Lemon" T-shirts, Charlie Rocket, Petit Bateau, Lulu, Cotton Caboodle, Zutano, At Home, as well as some European- and Los Angeles-based labels such as Les Petits Chapelais, Kid Rascal, and Junk Food. They have a wonderful selection of accessories such as cute hair bows and clips, fun flip-flops, embroidered Chinese sandals, as well as a thoughtful selection of Old World toys, many of which are from Europe.

Toni Tierney
1406 4th St.
San Rafael
415-256-1272
www.tonitierney.com

A native of San Anselmo and graduate of the Fashion Institute of Design and Merchandising in San Francisco, Toni Tierney offers adorable children's clothes in boutiques all over the country. But you don't have to look any farther than her very own shop in downtown San Rafael to outfit your little ones in her truly memorable fashions! She is best known for including pieces of vintage lace, antique trims and buttons, and other pretty adornments on her children's clothing, and creating unique pieces such as apron front dresses which are fashioned out of pretty 1950s table-cloths and 1940s embroidered tea towels. Her line of 3-piece cotton knit infant and toddler outfits with leggings, T-shirts or onesies and knit caps are also very popular. All of the adorable fashions are made from 100% cotton and are designed with lots of playtime and durability in mind!

The White Rabbit
601 San Anselmo Ave.
San Anselmo
415-456-1938

PARENT RATING: ☆ ☆ ☆

In business for more than 25 years, The White Rabbit could use a little updating. They offer traditional baby and children's clothing, including some smocked dresses and English coats. They do better in the non-clothing area and carry beautiful baby blankets and silver cups and spoons. They also carry traditional christening gowns.

Chicken Noodle Outlet

954 60th St.
Oakland
510-658-5880

This line of adorable children's play-wear is known for their witty 100% cotton prints. This outlet offers 40-70% off previous season's overruns.

A Child's Place

1898 Solano Ave.
Berkeley
510-524-3651

A Child's Place offers a wonderful selection of fun, comfortable, and casual clothing for infants and children at moderate to high-moderate prices. They feature many 100% cotton items. They have a few dressier things for girls, but for boys the main style is casual. They also carry some thoughtful accessories and toys for babies and young children. Popular lines/products: Flapdoodles, Charlie Rocket.

Claude Vell

1506 Walnut St.
Berkeley
510-665-7783
www.claudevell.com

With the arrival of Claude Vell on the scene, Berkeley babies and kids have exquisite French frocks to wear with their Birkenstocks! Owner and native of France, Dorothee Mitrani-Bell (also owner of 2 neighborhood restaurants), carries this beautiful line of "very French" looking clothing for babies and children that reflects sophisticated but sensible styling. Claude Vell is best known for their unique fabrics—unusual knits and woven blends of cotton, acrylic, wool, linen, lycra, and rayon, over dyed to produce a myriad of irresistible muted tones. Claude Vell offers lines for both boys and girls, including dresses, skirts, jumpers, blouses, jackets, vests, turtlenecks, T-shirts, and accessories.

Cotton and Company

5901 College Ave.
Oakland (Rockridge)
510-653-8058
www.cottonandcompany.com
PARENT RATING: ☆ ☆ ☆ ☆ ☆

This adorable baby and children's clothier offers some of the most upscale ensembles for little ones in the East Bay. They also carry children's shoes, including European imports, and have wonderful accessories, as well as hats, mobiles, and layette items. They offer high-end bedding, and their staff is friendly and helpful. They also have a train table set up for children to play with while Mom shops. Popular lines/products: Clothing: Hartstrings, Sophie Dess, Florence Eiseman, Mulberribush, Flapdoodles, LeTop, as well as several French imports.

House

1848 4th St.
Berkeley
510-549-4558
www.houseinc.com

See description under Baby Gear Retailers.

Kids Are People Too

- Pleasanton
  537 Main St., 925-462-5974
- Castro Valley
  3356 Village Dr., 510-247-1258

This cute clothing store carries moderately priced quality clothing for preemies, infants, and toddlers, plus some young children's sizes up to size 6X. They carry a broad selection of sleepers, buntings, nightgowns, and other infant and toddler wear. They specialize in clothing for special occasions such as christening gowns and outfits and wedding attire, including dresses for flower girls and tuxedos for toddlers and little boys. They also carry an extensive selection of holiday dresses for girls, including the smocked variety, as well as a small selection of wooden toys, including blocks and carpenter's sets. Popular lines/products: Alexis, Buster Brown, Baby's Own, Baby Dove, Lito, Alexandra.

Lil' Ladies and Gents

168 Marketplace
San Ramon
925-901-0970

PARENT RATING: ☆ ☆ ☆ ☆

This special-occasion clothier for infants and young children offers a large selection of traditional clothing for dressy occasions, such as christenings, weddings, birthdays, and baby's "coming home from the hospital." They carry miniature tuxes; suits for boys with dress shirts, sweater vests, and ties; and special-occasion dresses for girls, including flower girl, holiday, and smocked dresses. The friendly and helpful shop owner describes her clothing as what "could have been worn 40 years ago and God willing can be worn 40 years from now!" They also have a nice selection of "casual dressy" ensembles, such as white linen and cotton outfits, which are popular for outdoor professional photographs. They try to carry a lot of things that you don't

---

Favorite Local Baby and Children's Clothiers in the East Bay

Most Hip Baby Clothing
This Little Piggy Wears Cotton
Sioban Van Winkel Functional Art

Best Sales
Baby Gap
Sara's Prints
Sweet Potatoes Outlet

Special Occasions (Christenings, Weddings, and Parties)
Cotton & Company
Lil' Ladies & Gents

Most Traditional Baby Clothing
Cotton & Company

Halloween Costumes
Sweet Potatoes

see in department stores. In fact, Nordstrom sends business here. Comment: "Excellent dress-up clothes at reasonable prices." Popular lines/products: Strasburg (smocked dresses).

The Nurture Center

3399 Mt. Diablo Blvd.
Lafayette
925-283-1346
www.nurturecenter.com

PARENT RATING: ☆ ☆ ☆ ☆ ☆

This resource center for new parents has a pleasant retail store that sells handmade quilts and lovely baby clothing. It's a good place to pick up an extra outfit or a gift, especially if you are already there for one of their many great new parents' support groups. (See Ch. 6.) Popular lines/products: Kushies, Sweet Potatoes, Le Top.

Sara's Prints (factory outlet)

3018A Alvarado St.
San Leandro
510-352-6060
www.sarasprints.com

Sara's Prints is best known for quality sleepwear and underwear for children, made from 100% flame-resistant long-staple cotton, imprinted with some of the cutest designs you have ever seen! They also carry a popular fleece jacket with Velcro closures and a hood—they call it "possibly the best infant/toddler jacket ever made," and we couldn't agree more! Four times a year, the outlet is open for one- to 2-week factory sale events where overstocks and last season's items are sold for at least 50% off retail. Comment: "My kids love the underwear—no itchy waistbands."

Siobhan Van Winkel Functional Art

6371 Telegraph Ave.
Oakland
510-652-1415

This unique children's clothing and gift shop offers some of the funkiest and most darling clothing for newborns to 6-year-olds in the East Bay! Siobhan's carries handmade items from more than 30 local artists, including one-of-a-kind fleece hats and sun hats, hand-knit sweaters, silk-screened onesies, reversible dresses (including one that is shaped like a spaceship!), ponchos, dolls, and puppets, as well as jewelry and bags for Mom.

Sweet Potatoes, Inc.

- Albany
  1224 Solano Ave.
  510-527-7975
  800-634-2584
- Danville
  806 Sycamore Valley Road West
  925-314-8437
www.sweetpotatoesinc.com

PARENT RATING: ☆ ☆ ☆ ☆ ☆

Start your shopping from the back of this outlet, where the modest bargains may be found, to the front, where full-priced new collections are predominantly displayed. A Bay Area mom's favorite, Sweet Potatoes offers a collection of comfortable cotton infant and children's coordinating outfits with its own label for newborns and toddlers, including S.P.U.D.Z. for boys (Sweet Potatoes' sportswear line for newborns to size 7) and Yams for girls (sizes 4-14). They also offer locally made party dresses in infants' and girls' sizes, as well as comfortable and good-quality Halloween costumes for babies and toddlers—a rare find! The store features a small enclosed play area, which makes shopping with a toddler manageable.

Talbots Kids
1188 Broadway Plaza
Walnut Creek
925-938-6555
www.talbotskids.com
PARENT RATING: ☆ ☆ ☆ ☆ ☆

This well-known women's clothier also houses Talbots Kids. They offer a traditional line of clothing for babies and boys and girls, ages 6 months to 7 years. They also carry a nice line of christening outfits. Comment: "These clothes really hold up to a lot of washings—cute and good quality."

Teddy's Little Closet
- Berkeley
  2903 College Ave., 510-549-9177
- Orinda
  2 Theater Sq., 925-254-6672

Independently owned and operated, this shop carries moderate- to high-priced quality clothing for infants and young children. They also carry unique accessories for babies, including nightlights, one-of-a-kind receiving blankets, quilts, and classic toys. They own Sweet Dreams, a children's toy store that is connected to the Orinda store, and offers all the classics. Popular lines/products: Clothing: Cotton Caboodle, Mulberribush, Sweet Potatoes, OshKosh, Flapdoodles, Kushies, Oink Pig. Toys: Lego, Playmobil, Barbie, Brio, Thomas the Tank Engine.

This Little Piggy Wears Cotton
1840 4th St.
Berkeley
510-981-1411
www.littlepiggy.com
PARENT RATING: ☆ ☆ ☆ ☆ ☆

With 5 stores in California (and one in Scottsdale, Arizona), this charming children's line has really taken off! The Berkeley boutique features their own select line of infant and children's clothing made from 100% high-grade yarn-dyed cotton in striking solids as well as playful and colorful prints, for which they are best known. They have a great variety of basic playwear such as leggings and matching Ts, rompers and bloomers, and the ever-popular long johns. They also carry "fashion" pieces such as dresses, velour and terry cloth sweat suits, ruffle capris, and boxer-style shorts/pajamas for boys. They now have adult pajamas in matching prints for the kiddies! In addition to the clothing, they carry a thoughtful selection of interesting toys and accessories for babies and toddlers too. Other popular lines/products: Baby Lulu, Charlie Rocket, Flowers by Zoe, Petit Bateau. This Little Piggy Wears Cotton plans to open a shop in the Stanford Shopping Center in Palo Alto in fall 2005.

Waddle and Swaddle
1677 Shattuck Ave.
Berkeley
510-540-7210
www.waddleandswaddle.com

This childbirth and new parent education and resource center offers a large selection of retail therapy as well! The front of the store carries a good selection of upscale outfits for babies, newborn to 24 months. Popular lines/products: Zutano, Kushies.

They also feature organic cotton baby blankets and accessories, pashmina blankets and booties, cotton shearling jackets for baby, cardigans, unique development infant toys and books, and more. They will even deliver gifts if you can't make it to the shower! (See also in Chapters 1, 5, and 6.)

South Bay

Calla
985 Santa Cruz Ave.
Menlo Park
650-322-5524
This lovely Lilly Pulitzer store carries Lilly for children!

The Children's Shoppe
325 Sharon Park Dr.
Menlo Park
650-854-8854
www.thechildrensshoppe.com
PARENT RATING: ☆ ☆ ☆ ☆ ☆

This elegant and upscale infant and children's boutique carries imported fashions for your little one's dressier occasions. These include a wonderful assortment of carefully selected clothing from France, Italy, Germany, and Denmark. They also carry hard-to-find European christening gowns and outfits. In The Children's Shoppe you'll also find beautiful baby blankets, as well as dressier European-made shoes, and a small but thoughtful selection of toys for infants and toddlers. This is definitely a special shop that caters to those who appreciate elegant Old World-inspired styles for their children. Popular lines/products: Clothing: Petit Bateau, Bon Point, Sonia Rykiel, Cacherel,

---

Favorite Local Baby and Children's Clothiers in the South Bay

Most Hip Baby Clothing
The Oilily Store

Best Sales
Baby Gap
Nordstrom

Halloween Costumes
Baby Gap
Old Navy
The Spirit Store (open in season on San Mateo County Fairgrounds)

Most Traditional Baby Clothing
The Children's Shoppe
The Kids Company

Special Occasions (Christenings, Weddings, and Parties)
Bloomingdales
Neiman Marcus
Nordstrom
P. Cottontail &
Company

Florian, Babar, Mini Man, Arctic Kids, Sophie Dess. Shoes: BabyBotte, Aster, Naturino, More 8. Accessories: Churchill Weavers, Pappa and Ciccia (baby blankets).

Howard's Children's Shop

115 E. 4th Ave.
San Mateo
650-343-1518

This elegant specialty shop has a beautiful collection of dresses, jackets, and rompers for babies, toddlers, and children.

The Kids Company/ Footsteps Shoe Store

1201 San Carlos Ave.
San Carlos
650-595-7745
www.thekidsbiz.com

PARENT RATING: ☆ ☆ ☆ ☆ ☆

This lovely clothier for children, in the words of the owner, is "very traditional" and "offers nothing hip-hop or trendy." They feature upscale quality infants and children's clothing up to sizes 12-14, including sweaters, shorts, sleepwear, and layette items. They also have a huge selection of special-occasion attire, including christening gowns and outfits, tuxes for little boys, and flower girls' dresses. At the back of the store is a large children's shoe store which is run by the clothing store owner's daughter—many say that the selection is better than Nordstrom's! Their thoughtful selection of toys for babies and toddlers includes cloth books and developmental toys. This may be among the best places for one-stop upscale clothing shopping for little ones in the South Bay! Popular lines/products: Clothing: Hartstrings, K. C. Parker, Impact, Sweet Potatoes, Chicken Noodle, Sara Louise (christening gowns), and Petit Bateau (christening gowns). Shoes: Elefanten, Stride Rite, Doc Martens, K-Swiss, Vans, Converse, Birkenstock. Toys: Manhattan Toy Co.

Los Gatos Baby & Tot Boutique

49 N. Santa Cruz Ave.
Los Gatos
408-354-5454
www.losgatosbaby.com

PARENT RATING: ☆ ☆ ☆ ☆ ☆

This stylish baby boutique is stocked with some of the chicest fashions for boys and girls ages newborn through 5 years old. The owners spent several years in Europe, and they take great delight in featuring many European designers, such as Luna Luna. They also carry American lines such as Hartstrings and Ralph Lauren. Beautiful layette items, colorful separates, snuggly fleece jackets, party dresses, and adorable sweaters for boys and girls abound. The staff takes extra care to help parents make their selections. They also carry a nice selection of girls' shoes as well as nursery décor, toys, and accessories.

P. Cottontail and Company

527 Main St.
Half Moon Bay
650-726-0200

This store offers attractive baby and preemie basics, as well as top-quality children's shoes, christening gowns and outfits, and accessories for your baby's nursery.

Rebecca Rags, Inc. Outlet

10200 Imperial Ave.
Cupertino
408-257-7884
www.rebeccarags.com

Rebecca Rags (the girl's line) and Ruff! Rags (the boy's line) offer unique children's clothing, both dressy and casual wear, in bright, cheery velours, knits, and linens. This outlet has a large selection of end-of-season overruns, seconds, and samples at great savings—20% off wholesale. They are well known for their fall and spring sales.

Tiny Tots Togs

138 Railway Ave.
Campbell
408-866-2925
www.tinytots.com

Tiny Tots Togs specializes in 100% cotton clothes for infants and children. They also carry a wide selection of developmental toys, diaper covers, and breastfeeding supplies, including pump rentals and sales.

Favorite Mail Order Catalogs and Online Resources for Baby and Children's Clothing

Baby Gap
www.babygap.com

Old Navy
www.oldnavy.com

The Wooden Soldier
800-375-6002 (catalog)

Children's Wear Digest
800-242-5437 (catalog)
www.cwdkids.com

Hanna Andersson
800-222-0544 (catalog)
www.hannaandersson.com

Land's End
800-963-4816 (catalog)
www.landsend.com

L.L. Kids (catalog)
800-552-5437
www.llbean.com

Talbot's Kids
800-543-7123 (catalog)
www.talbots.com

Patagonia Kids
800-638-6464 (catalog)
www.patagonia.com

www.redapple1.com

www.agingerhouse.com

www.precious-child.com

www.babyultimate.com

www.babystyle.com

www.oneofakindkid.com

www.basicbrilliance.com (cotton clothing for babies and kids)

www.littlefollies.com (hand-smocked fleeces and classic clothing)

www.orientexpressed.com (hand-smocked children's clothing)

Shoes

It may be hard to believe, but before your little bundle of joy reaches his first birthday he'll be on the verge of walking and will need a pair of shoes! When shopping for your child's first shoes, find a store that offers knowledgeable and helpful salespeople who know how to measure your child's foot properly. Your baby's first shoes should fit well, as he'll still be learning how to walk. It's also important that his first shoes have a soft and flexible sole. Remember not to go too crazy the first few times; children's feet grow fast. You'll be visiting the shoe store in another 3 or 4 months to buy the next size up.

We've listed stores that specialize in children's shoes, but be sure to check out the children's clothiers and baby superstores listed in the above sections, as many carry a good selection of children's shoes.

NATIONAL CHAINS

Here is what Bay Area parents have to say about several national chains. Check the yellow pages or their individual websites for a store location near you.

Department Stores

Nordstrom
www.nordstrom.com
PARENT RATING: ☆ ☆ ☆ ☆ ☆

Nordstrom has one of the best infant and toddler shoe departments in the Bay Area, carrying casual and dressy styles and most major brands, such as Stride Rite and Elefanten. In fact, as far as department stores go, it's the tops for baby and children's shoes. The staff is friendly and helpful, and they often offer a balloon to your child and take a Polaroid picture of her when you are buying her first pair of shoes.

Discount Stores

Mervyn's California
www.mervyns.com
PARENT RATING: ☆ ☆ ☆

Mervyn's carries a small selection of moderately priced and mostly casual children's shoes. Be sure to come with your child's current shoe size, as you won't receive department store or specialty shoe store service here.

Payless Shoes
www.payless.com
PARENT RATING: ☆ ☆ ☆

Payless offers great values on moderate–end sneakers and other casual shoes. They often carry a nice selection of character or theme shoes (such as Bob the Builder or fire trucks), as well as ballet shoes and sneakers with flashing lights that will delight your toddler or preschooler. Service can be spotty.

Target
www.target.com
PARENT RATING: ☆ ☆ ☆ ☆

Target has a limited selection of mostly casual, inexpensive shoes for children, including rain boots, snow boots, and sneakers. They have dress shoes for girls for every season. Be sure to know your child's current shoe size, as there is no one here offering to measure your child's foot! Comment: "It's a great place to save money on shoes your child won't wear every day—like dress shoes—or [to] find an inexpensive pair of sandals."

Specialty Chains

Baby Gap
www.babygap.com
PARENT RATING: ☆ ☆ ☆ ☆

This ubiquitous chain carries great inexpensive sneakers in a variety of colors for babies and toddlers and occasionally carries other styles of shoes, such as bucks for boys or Mary Janes for girls.

Kids Foot Locker
www.kidsfootlocker.com
PARENT RATING: ☆ ☆ ☆

This store carries a large selection of infant and toddler sneakers, sandals, and boots. Brands include Nike, K-Swiss, Adidas, Timberland, DKNY, Jordan, and Reebok.

Niketown
278 Post St.
415-392-6453
www.niketown.com

Parent rating: ☆ ☆ ☆ ☆

While it may be a hike to go downtown, find parking, and walk to Niketown, it's truly a unique shopping experience. The children's department is on the fourth floor and offers a zillion styles of booties and sneakers specially made for babies and toddlers that are not typically sold at department stores or other shoe stores. Nikes for tots offers more than a name brand; we know a mom whose toddler had a pair of Nikes from Niketown that lasted almost 6 months and wore beautifully.

Nike Factory Store
www.niketown.com
Gilroy Premium Outlets
Gilroy
408-847-4300
Visit their website for other locations, including Folsom and Vacaville.

This outlet store offers a number of styles of previous seasons' sneakers for children at about 30% off retail prices.

Reebok Factory Store
www.reebokoutlet.com/content/store-locators.asp
Factory Stores of Vacaville
707-452-0235
This outlet carries sneakers for toddlers and young children at modest savings. For other locations (Gilroy, Pacific Grove, and Petaluma), visit their website.

206

Stride Rite

www.strideritecorp.com/stores.asp

PARENT RATING: ☆ ☆ ☆ ☆ ☆

This is a great place to shop for baby's first shoes as well as shoes for the active toddler. Staff is knowledgeable and helpful. For store locations, visit their website.

Stride Rite (outlet)

Petaluma Outlet Mall

707-782-0545

PARENT RATING: ☆ ☆ ☆ ☆ ☆

This outlet is reportedly every Marin parents' best-kept secret when it comes time to buy kids new shoes. We are told that the store is rarely crowded, and service is stellar. Best of all, they offer the same shoes, with plenty of in-season styles and sizes to choose from, that department stores do but for half the price! Visit their website for other outlet store locations, including Gilroy and Milpitas.

What to Do with those Outgrown but Barely Worn Shoes?

Good Soles

www.goodsoles.org

If your toddler is like most, she will outgrow her shoes well before they wear out. This can be a little frustrating, especially if you've been taken in by the latest fashion craze or bought expensive shoes for her! But thanks to a thoughtful and clever Bay Area mom, now children in need can have those nearly new shoes that your little one has outgrown. Good Soles coordinates the collection of gently worn shoes and distributes them to local agencies that provide resources for needy children. All you have to do is take your child's gently worn shoes to one of several local children's shoe retailers or to a Bright Horizon Children's Center and deposit them in a collection container. Good Soles does the rest. They are especially interested in receiving donations of shoes for toddlers of walking age through age 5. For a list of their collection sites, visit their website, www.goodsoles.org.

BAY AREA RETAILERS

Here is what Bay Area parents have to say about their favorite local stores for baby and children's shoes:

Junior Boot Shop

Laurel Village Shopping Ctr.
3555 California St.
415-751-5444
PARENT RATING: ☆ ☆ ☆ ☆ ☆

A San Francisco parents' staple for years now, this down-to-earth shop carries much more than rain boots, including high-end traditional infant and children's shoes. You won't see too many trendy brands and styles here—just the classics. Name brands include K Swiss, Merrill, Stride Rite, Elefanten, Naturino, and Jumping Jacks. The store is quite child-friendly with a knowledgeable and helpful staff who keep a record of your children's shoe sizes.

Howard's Shoes for Children

Stonestown Galleria
3251 20th Ave. #149
415-681-3700
PARENT RATING: ☆ ☆ ☆ ☆ ☆

This local chain of 4 stores in the Bay Area is a great place to shop for baby's first pair of shoes. They also offer quality shoes for toddlers and young children, including brands such as Stride Rite, Elefanten, Ecco, Vans, Sketchers, Nike, and New Balance. Comment: "They have a good selection and friendly, helpful staff."

Brooks Shoes for Kids

3307 Sacramento St.
415-440-7599
PARENT RATING: ☆ ☆ ☆ ☆ ☆

Formerly Tuffy's Hopscotch, the hopscotch still greets playful shoppers upon their arrival, but under new ownership, which now only offers shoes. The store is quite kid-friendly, offering a large hopscotch pattern in the entryway for kids to jump around on while trying out their new shoes, as well as a foozball game in the second room and a play kitchen too. Most of the staff is knowledgeable and helpful. Popular lines/products: shoe brands including Elefanten, Brakkies, Aster, Mod 8, Shoe-be-Do, New Balance, Nike, and Stride Right.

Children's Boot Shop

826 Grant Ave.
Novato
415-897-1460

Offering much more than boots (although they really do carry cowboy and rain boots), this traditional children's shoe store carries a wide variety of casual and dressy shoes ranging from sneakers to patent leather Mary Janes. Brands include Stride Rite, Birkenstock, and Reebok.

East Bay

Howard's Shoes for Children

16 Broadway Ln.
Walnut Creek
925-280-8100
See a complete description under
San Francisco.

South Bay

The Children's Shoppe

325 Sharon Park Dr.
Menlo Park
650-854-8854

This store offers quality shoes for
infants through teens, carrying only
European brands such as BabyBotte,
Aster, and Naturino. See a complete
description under Baby and
Children's Clothing.

Footsteps Children Shoes

1201 San Carlos Ave.
San Carlos
650-595-7745
www.thekidsbiz.com

This wonderfully stocked children's
shoe store is located behind an affiliated and equally fabulous infant and
children's clothing store (The Kids
Company). They offer an extensive
selection of quality baby and children's shoes, including Stride Rite,
Elefanten, and Converse. The knowledgeable and helpful staff sends post-
cards to customers every 3 months
reminding them when they last
bought shoes for their children.

Howard's Shoes for Children

• Palo Alto
198 Stanford Shopping Center,
650-325-9300

• Cupertino
Vallco Fashion Park
10123 N. Wolfe Rd., 408-257-6200

See a complete description under
San Francisco.

Manny's Shoes

708 Santa Cruz Ave.
Menlo Park
650-325-5171

PARENT RATING: ☆ ☆ ☆ ☆ ☆

This no-frills store offers shoes for all
of your child's needs. They feature
American classics such as Stride Rite,
European styles such as Elefanten,
and sportier styles such as Nike,
Reebok, Vans, Keds, Tevas, and Doc
Martens. They also offer a broad
selection of sandals, boots, ballet
slippers, and tap shoes.

Naturino

29 University Ave.
Los Gatos
408-339-5131
www.naturinolosgatos.com

PARENT RATING: ☆ ☆ ☆ ☆ ☆

This wonderful children's footwear
store is located in Old Town Los
Gatos where they say "professional
fit, fashion, and fun come together."
They feature fine European shoes
(Naturino, Moscino, and Oilily) and
accessories for children of all ages
(such as socks and tights imported
from Denmark), as well as for moms.
From first walkers to sports shoes
and sandals, dress-up and casual,
they have an incredible selection for
both boys and girls—more than 140
styles to choose from!

Toys and Books

Since the first edition of this book, we have noticed a decline in the number of local children's toy stores. Sadly enough, for whatever reasons, it seems as though some have shut their doors. Still, the Bay Area abounds with many stores that carry a great variety of toys and children's books. Many baby superstores, specialty stores, baby and children's clothiers, and museums are alert to this trend and are stocking their shelves with more quality toys and books than ever before, so look for them in the previous sections. We have included some local favorites and some online resources for you to check out here.

At each stage of your child's development, new skills emerge, and how she plays and what she plays with substantially affect how she develops these skills. Whether it's simply playing a game of patty-cake or exploring with an elaborate play structure, as a parent, you are the one who determines your baby's environment, which in turn shapes her development. So buy wisely!

One book that we especially like and have found helpful in choosing toys is the *Oppenheim Toy Portfolio* by mother and daughter Joanne and Stephanie Oppenheim. They published a new edition each year, in which they review hundreds of toys for babies, toddlers, and preschoolers. They also suggest many fun games to play with your baby that don't require purchasing anything at all. It's a great resource for all new parents! Their website, www.toyportfolio.com, provides updates, reviews of toy award winners, and helpful parenting articles.

NATIONAL CHAINS

Check their individual websites or your yellow pages for the store nearest you:

The Disney Store
www.disney.com
PARENT RATING: ☆ ☆ ☆ ☆

The Disney Store offers toys, clothing, and accessories featuring everyone's favorite storybook characters, such as Winnie the Pooh, Pinocchio, Peter Pan, all the "princesses," and 101 Dalmatians. They carry great Halloween costumes too! Comment: "Just visiting the store is a great outing for your kids if your pocketbook can stand it!"

Imaginarium

www.imaginarium.com

This favorite chain has been bought by Toys "R" Us, and as result sadly closed most of their retail stores, yet their website, accessible via Amazon.com is a favorite of parents. It is more like a specialty toy store, featuring an impressive selection of educational and developmental toys for infants on up. They carry Lamaze, Wimmer Ferguson (well known for their black and white infant developmental toys), Sassy, Brio, Thomas the Tank Engine trains and accessories, Madeline dolls and toys, Clifford, Lego, Felt Kids; outdoor toys such as balls, sand toys, and a toddler's first set of golf clubs; as well as all the traditional items like Play Doh. They also stock a few Halloween costumes.

KB Toys

www.kbtoys.com

PARENT RATING: ☆ ☆ ☆

The few KB Toys that remain in the Bay Area (as most have closed) are packed with many tempting toys for toddlers and beyond. They carry a small number of toys for babies. While they don't carry the higher-end educational toys, there is still something there for almost everyone. Parent comment: "A smaller, more compact version of Toys "R' Us. . . . They have all the trucks, action heroes, and Barbie dolls you could want."

Lakeshore Learning

www.lakeshorelearning.com

PARENT RATING: ☆ ☆ ☆ ☆ ☆

This is where your child's preschool teacher stocks up on all those great educational materials and games that make kids think and have fun at the same time! Bay Area parents have

---

BIKE HELMETS—IT'S THE LAW!

When you buy your child's first trike or bike, you'll also want to buy an infant, toddler, or youth bike helmet. Kids under age 18 are required by law to wear a properly fitted and fastened bicycle helmet while riding a bicycle as either driver or passenger—**even when parents have the child in a passenger seat or trailer**. Take your child with you when buying the helmet to ensure the best and safest fit. Kids are also required by law to wear a helmet while skateboarding, rollerblading, or riding a scooter. It is estimated that approximately 75% of fatal bicycle crashes involving children could have been prevented with bicycle helmets. Unfortunately, national estimates indicate that bicycle helmet use among child bicyclists ranges from 15 to 25%.

their choice of 3 retail stores: Walnut Creek, San Leandro, and San Jose. Otherwise, peruse their website and order from there.

Learning Express
www.learningexpress.com
This national chain of franchises specializes in toys with an educational bent for children of all ages, including dress-up and pretend-play items, Legos, Thomas trains, and a small selection of developmental toys for infants by Lamaze and Early Years. They also carry personalized gifts that make great birthday gifts or favors such as sand buckets with the child's name painted on, and more.

Marshalls
www.marshallsonline.com
While better known for great bargains on clothing, many Marshalls stores have great toy departments. In fact, some Bay Area moms report that they see, deeply discounted at Marshalls, many of the same toys carried by more expensive stores.

Target
www.target.com
While lacking the charm of your neighborhood toy store, Target has an impressive selection of toys for all ages, including Legos, LeapFrogs, Parents Magazine toys, train tables, Fisher-Price, Care Bears, Barbies, Playmobil, K'nex building sets, sports equipment and bikes, a large selection of outdoor riding toys, and more!

Toys "R" Us
www.toysrus.com
PARENT RATING: ☆ ☆ ☆
If you don't mind the scale of this mega-store and its frequent lack of service, it carries all the major brands of toys and books, including a large selection of baby toys, organized according to children's stages of development.

BAY AREA RETAILERS
Here is what Bay Area parents have to say about their favorite local toy stores:

San Francisco

Ambassador Toys
• 186 West Portal Ave., 415-759-8697
• 201 Clay St. (2 Embarcadero Center, Lobby level), 415-677-4303
PARENT RATING: ☆ ☆ ☆ ☆ ☆
Ambassador Toys is a classic toy store, featuring an impressive selection of wooden toys, including Thomas the Tank Engine trains, wooden dollhouses, and all the desired baby dolls, including Corolle and Madame Alexander. They also offer strollers for dolls, kitchen and tea sets, and beautiful kites. Name brands include Bruder trucks, Playmobil toys, and Plan Toys. They carry a unique selection of books featuring many foreign language children's books. Toys are arranged according to theme, e.g., there is a fire truck section and a dinosaur section, which makes shopping quick and easy!

The Ark

3845 24th St.

415-821-1257

PARENT RATING: ☆ ☆ ☆ ☆ ☆

This Noe Valley neighborhood store is packed with classic toys that continue to delight every child. They feature wooden toys such as play kitchens and smaller items such as toy trains (including Brio and Thomas), beautiful stuffed animals, puzzles, games (including a soft indoor baseball and bat for an active toddler), unusual hand-painted puppets from Germany, and musical instruments for toddlers.

A Child's Delight

3251 20th Ave.

Stonestown Galleria

415-242-3334

www.achildsdelight.com

See under North Bay.

Favorite Websites and Catalogs for Infant and Children's Toys

Back to Basics Toys
800-356-5360 (catalog)
www.backtobasicstoys.com

Constructive Playthings
800-832-0572 (catalog)
www.constplay.com

Discovery Toys
www.discoverytoysinc.com

Earthwise Toys
www.naturaltoys.com

FAO Schwarz
800-426-8097 (catalog)
www.faoschwarz.com

Hearthsong
800-325-2502 (catalog)
www.hearthsong.com

Imagine the Challenge
800-777-1493 (catalog)
www.imaginetoys.com

Leaps & Bounds
800-477-2189 (catalog)
www.leapsandbounds.com

Lilly's Kids
800-545-5426 (catalog)
www.lillianvernon.com
Great Halloween costumes!

Sensational Beginnings
800-444-2147 (catalog)
www.sensationalbeginnings.com
Great Halloween costumes!

Smarter Kids
www.smarterkids.com

Totally Thomas' Toy Depot
800-30-THOMAS (catalog)
www.totallythomas.com

Thomas the Tank Engine
www.thomasthetankengine.com

Toys to Grow On
800-542-8338 (catalog)
www.toystogrowon.com

www.storeofknowledge.com

www.zebrahall.com
"Extraordinary toys for all ages from around the world"

Best Bets for Children's Books in San Francisco

Alexander Book Company
50 2nd St.
415-495-2992
www.alexanderbook.booksense.com

Book Passage
The Ferry Bldg.
415-835-1020
www.bookpassage.com

Borders Books and Music
400 Post St.
415-399-1633
www.borderstores.com
They have an extensive parenting book section.

Bernal Books
410 Cortland Ave.
415-550-0293

Barnes and Noble
2550 Taylor St.
415-292-6762
www.barnesandnoble.com

Books Inc.
• Laurel Village Shopping Center
3515 California St., 415-221-3666
They have a great parenting book section.

• *2251 Chestnut St., 415-931-3633
They have a large children's section, complete with child-sized chairs.
www.booksinc.com

The Booksmith
1644 Haight St.
415-863-8688
www.booksmith.com

*Borders Books and Music
Stonestown Galleria
233 Winston Dr.
415-731-0665

www.borders.com
This store has a huge children's section, with lots of room for them to roam!

Browser Books
2195 Fillmore St.
415-567-8027
They have a small children's section, with table and chairs in the back, and an impressive parenting section.

Christopher's Books
1400 18th St.
415-255-8802

City Lights Bookstore
261 Columbus Ave.
415-362-8193
www.citylights.com

A Clean Well-Lighted Place for Books
601 Van Ness Ave.
415-441-6670
www.bookstore.com
This one-of-a-kind bookstore offers friendly and knowledgeable service.

Cover to Cover Booksellers
3812 24th St.
415-282-8080
www.covertocover.booksense.com

Green Apple Books
506 Clement St.
415-387-2272
They have great used books!

Waldenbooks
255 West Portal Ave.
415-664-7596

*These stores host story hours, usually on weekends. Call each store for details.

DayOne

3490 California St., Ste. 203
415-440-3291
www.dayonecenter.com
See above under Baby Gear.

Growing Up

240 West Portal Ave.
415-661-6304
This neighborhood toy store offers all the classics and more, including wooden toys and puzzles, Brio trains, and Legos.

Jeffrey's Toys

685 Market St.
415-243-TOYS (8697)
Jeffrey's Toys is a traditional toy store, offering developmentally and educationally oriented toys as well as those that are just plain fun, including many stuffed animals and characters.

Just For Fun—Scribble Doodles

3924 24th St.
415-285-4068
This fun little store is jam-packed with all kinds of smaller toys, perfect for birthday parties, as well as stickers, cards, and stationery for little ones!

Kumquat

9 Clement St.
415-752-2140
This pleasant neighborhood shop, which features works of many local artists along with other craft items for the home, has recently expanded its unique toy section. Kumquat offers a great selection of hard-to-find European and Old World-inspired children's toys from puzzles to pull toys, to wooden trucks, and much more. They also carry a special line of Swedish baby blankets, silver baby gifts including baby cups, and beautiful one-of-a-kind photo albums.

San Francisco Museum of Modern Art

151 3rd St.
415-357-4035
This museum gift shop offers many unique toys and books for toddlers and children, focusing on the arts, learning, and development.
Comment: "Not your run-of-the-mill toys and books, truly special items."

Standard 5 & 10

3545 California St.
415-751-6767
This Laurel Village "five and dime" offers a full aisle of toys for almost every age, featuring Playmobil, Lego, Thomas the Tank Engine, and more. With fewer toy stores in the city these days, it's a great place to pick up that last-minute birthday gift. Service is friendly and helpful.

The Warming Hut Café and Bookstore

Crissy Field
415-561-3040
This wonderful café and bookstore has a nice little section of toys and books for children that reflect themes of nature, ecology, and marine life. Toys include paint your own birdhouse feeders, play camping sets, and more.

Toys & Books

A Child's Delight

- Corte Madera
  105 Corte Madera Town Center
  415-945-9221
- San Rafael
  3880 Northgate Mall
  415-499-0736

www.achildsdelight.com

PARENT RATING: ☆ ☆ ☆ ☆ ☆

This upscale toy store offers an inviting array of educational and imaginative toys for infants on up. They specialize in carrying toys that require children to use their minds, including dress-up and pretend clothing and play structures, Thomas and Brio wooden trains, and other wooden toys such as handmade dollhouses and rocking horses from France. They also feature all the classics, such as Radio Flyer wagons, Madame Alexander dolls, and other treasures from your own childhood! They have a broad selection of infant toys, including brands such as Papa Gepetto, Lamaze, Sassy, Chicco, Plan Toys, and several independent brands. They pride themselves on carrying many specialty items. They also carry many Halloween and dress-up costumes year round.

Bay Area Discovery Museum

E. Fort Baker
557 McReynolds Rd.
Sausalito
415-487-4398
www.badm.org

PARENT RATING: ☆ ☆ ☆ ☆ ☆

The large gift shop of this recently renovated children's museum is a wonderful toy store, featuring some of the best toys that have to do with nature and the outdoors, such as butterfly nets, ant houses, bird feeders, and more! See in Ch. 8.

Doll Houses, Trains and More

300 Entrada Dr.
Novato
415-883-0388
www.dollhouses-trains-more.com

PARENT RATING: ☆ ☆ ☆ ☆ ☆

This 9,000-square-foot store is full of wonderful train tables for preschoolers to adults, including the popular wooden Brio trains. They also have an extensive selection of dollhouses and furnishings. Salespeople are very helpful.

Hopscotch Kids

352 Miller Ave.
Mill Valley
415-381-9858

Hopscotch carries a thoughtful selection of toys, including Brio and Thomas wooden trains, Corolle dolls, and high-quality infant and toddler toys by Playmobil and Lego, among other brands.

Solaria's Toy World

Bon Air Shopping Center
Greenbrae
415-459-5160

PARENT RATING: ☆ ☆ ☆ ☆

Solaria is an independent store stocked with all the best toys. They carry all the classics and high-end toys for toddlers and young children, including Brio and Thomas wooden trains, Madame Alexander dolls, Muffy Bears, wooden dollhouses, and Playmobil. They have one of the best Brio selections around—so good that many customers come here from San Francisco. They also have an impressive doll and dollhouse selection.

Toy Chest
- San Rafael
  1000 5th Ave., 415-451-4942
- Healdsburg
  401 Center St., 707-433-4743

PARENT RATING: ☆ ☆ ☆ ☆ ☆

This upscale toy store carries a vast selection of high-quality toys, such as those by Playmobil and Plan Toys. They also offer many classic toys, featuring Curious George, Madeline, and Radio Flyer wagons, and educational toys, including Brio and Thomas trains, wooden kitchens, and play food. They also have a great selection of Halloween costumes in season.

Best Bets for Children's Books in the North Bay

*Barnes & Noble Booksellers
2020 Redwood Hwy.
Greenbrae
415-924-1016
www.barnesandnoble.com

*Book Passage
51 Tamal Vista Blvd.
Corte Madera
415-927-0960
www.bookpassage.com

More of a community center than a bookstore, Book Passage offers all the best for even the tiniest reader in the family, including special children's story hours, sing-alongs featuring the renowned Miss Kitty, and visits from renowned authors.

*Borders Book Store
588 W. Francisco Blvd.
San Rafael
415-454-1400
www.borderstores.com

Copperfield's
- Napa
  3900 Bel Air Plaza, Ste. A
  707-252-8002
- Sebastopol
  138 N. Main St., 707-823-2618
- Santa Rosa
  2316 Montgomery Dr.
  707-578-8938
- Petaluma
  140 Kentucky St., 707-762-0563

Comment: "Best in the area!"
www.copperfields.com

First Street Books
850 College Ave.
Kentfield
415-456-8770

Great Overland Book Company
215 Caledonia St.
Sausalito
415-332-1532
They have great used books!

Reader's Books
130 E. Napa St.
Sonoma
707-939-1779
www.readersbooks.com

Whyte's Booksmith
615 San Anselmo Ave.
San Anselmo
415-459-7323

*These stores often host story hours. Call the stores for details.

Toy Symphony

8920 Northgate Mall
San Rafael
415-491-0302
www.toysymphony.com

This toy store offers toys that use children's imaginations. Favorite toys include wooden and paper dolls and puzzles, Madame Alexander dolls, Vecta Blocks, Radio Flyer wagons, wooden dollhouses, and Brio trains.

The Toyworks

- Santa Rosa
  2759 4th St. #B, 707-526-2099
- Sebastopol
  6940 Sebastopol Ave., 707-829-2003

In business since 1977, this full-service toy store carries a large selection of developmental toys for babies and toddlers by brands such as Ambi and Playmobil. They also carry many handcrafted and imported toys from Europe for young children, including wooden trains and wagons.

East Bay

A Child's Delight

5607 Bay St.
Emeryville
510-653-1575
www.achildsdelight.com

See under North Bay.

Cynthia's Educational Toys and Games

City Center Sq.
501 14th St.
Oakland
510-452-4099
www.cynthiastoys.com

Cynthia's is a small boutique toy store that carries some unique items,

such as multicultural toys, as well as general toys, tapes, and books. The owner is very knowledgeable and helpful about age appropriateness of toys, and she offers very personalized service in selecting the right one.

Games Unlimited

- Danville
  Livery and Mercantile Shopping Center
  800 Sycamore Valley Rd. W.
  925-838-6358
- Concord
  1975 Diamond Blvd.
  Willow Shopping Ctr.
  925-798-1176

www.gamesunlimitedonline.com

The oldest toy store in Danville, this independently owned and operated toy store carries "specialty toys," including Lamaze infant toys, Playmobil, Brio, and Thomas trains, Corolle dolls, Bruder trucks, Breyer horses, and Creativity for Kids, along with many other smaller brands.

Golden Apple Learning Store

Gateway Square
Pleasanton
925-460-5163
www.goldenapplels.com

Golden Apple carries quality toys for newborns, toddlers, and young children, including Brio trains, Erector Sets, art supplies, developmental toys, books, puzzles, and blocks.

G.R. Doodlebug

- Danville
  700 Sycamore Rd. W.
  925-362-1560
- Pleasanton
  350A Main St.
  925-600-1360

Best Bets for Children's Books in the East Bay

*Barnes & Noble
- Berkeley
  2352 Shattuck Ave., 510-644-0861
- Oakland
  98 Broadway, Jack London Sq.,
  510-272-0120
- Walnut Creek
  1149 S. Main St., 925-947-0373
www.barnesandnoble.com

The Book Tree
6123 La Salle Ave.
Oakland
510-339-0513

Black Oak Books
1491 Shattuck Ave.
Berkeley
510-486-0698
www.blackoak.com

*Borders Books and Music
5903 Shellmound
Emeryville
510-654-1633
www.borders.com
Visit their website for other locations.

Cody's Bookstore
- *Berkeley
  1730 4th St., 510-559-9500
- Oakland
  2454 Telegraph Ave., 510-845-7852
www.codysbooks.com

Moe's Bookstore
2476 Telegraph Ave.
Berkeley
510-849-2087
www.moesbooks.com

Mr. Mopps' Children's Books and Toys
1405 Martin Luther King Jr. Way
Berkeley
510-525-9633
Kids just can't resist the Big Bird chair in the book room!

Pegasus Books
- Berkeley
  2349 Shattuck Ave., 510-649-1320
- Berkeley
  1855 Solano Ave., 510-525-6888
- Berkeley
  5560 College Ave. (Pendragon Books), 510-652-6259
www.peagsusbookstore.com
These stores have an impressive selection of new and used children's books.

The Storyteller
30 Lafayette Circle
Lafayette
925-284-3480

Walden Pond
3316 Grand Ave.
Oakland
510-832-4438
www.waldenpondbooks.com

*These stores offer story hours or other children's events. Call the stores for details.

www.grdoodlebug.com

Voted "best of the East Bay" by *Diablo Magazine* in 2005, toys such as Thomas trains, Corolle dolls, and plush teddy bears and infant toys abound at G.R. Doodlebug. They also specialize in personalized gifts such as piggy banks and have one of the largest kids' stickers departments in the area.

Handlebar Toys

3535 Plaza Way
Lafayette
925-284-4631

Handlebar is a traditional children's toy store, well stocked with all the high-end essentials, including Playmobil, Galt, Brio and Thomas trains, and Madame Alexander dolls.

Montclair Toy House

6115 La Salle Ave.
Oakland
510-339-9023

In business since 1946, the Toy House is an old-fashioned toy store. They offer a nice selection of toys for all ages by the best manufacturers, including Brio and Playmobil.

Mr. Mopps' Children's Books and Toys

1405 Martin Luther King Jr. Way
Berkeley
510-525-9633

PARENT RATING: ☆ ☆ ☆ ☆

In business for more than 40 years, Mr. Mopps' classic toy store has become a Berkeley tradition. Despite some complaints we heard about the lack of customer service, Mr. Mopps' is consistently rated "Best Toy Store" in the *East Bay Express*. Packed with creative toys for all ages in all price ranges, this small toy store has a good children's book section too. They feature infant toys by Lamaze and The First Years, Fisher-Price toys, Barbie dolls, and Legos, as well as high-end toys. Toys are organized according to theme, such as cars and trucks, dress-up, art supplies, and dolls. Mr. Mopps' also carries playhouse furniture, tea sets, pretend food, science and nature toys, games, models, marionettes, and more.

The Report Card

1595-B2 Holiday Lane
Fairfield
707-426-3711
www.reportcard.net

PARENT RATING: ☆ ☆ ☆ ☆ ☆

This is a unique educational resource store for teachers and parents, offering all the best activity books and more to give your child a head start in his academic career!

Sweet Dreams

- Berkeley
  2921 College Ave., 510-548-8697
- Orinda
  2 Theater Sq., 925-254-6672

PARENT RATING: ☆ ☆ ☆ ☆ ☆

Sweet Dreams is a distinctively eclectic toy store (under the same ownership as Teddy's Little Closet, the children's clothier. See under Baby and Children's Clothing). They offer a wide selection of toys, including high-quality developmental toys for infants by Ambi, and Brio trains, Lego, and Playmobil for toddlers and preschoolers. They also carry a variety of novelty and holiday items, including jewelry and barrettes, books, dolls, and sand toys. The Orinda store includes an old-fashioned candy counter with jars brimming with gummies and sour patch kids. The Berkeley location has a separate candy store down the street. Both stores offer friendly and helpful service.

The Learning Game
- Cupertino
  Crossroads Shopping Ctr.
  20540 Stevens Creek Blvd.
  408-996-8064
- Los Gatos
  301 N. Santa Cruz Ave.
  408-395-4064
www.learninggame.com

This "educational superstore for teachers, parents, and kids," is a real family favorite. They specialize in carrying high-quality and fun educational resources, including toys for infants on up. They carry almost every educationally oriented toy out there such as manipulatives, puzzles, charts, science and arts and crafts projects.

Morrison's
400 Industrial Rd.
San Carlos
650-592-3000
PARENT RATING: ☆ ☆ ☆ ☆ ☆
A great teacher supply store filled with all the neat things kids play with in preschool.

Palo Alto Sport Shop & Toy World
526 Waverly St.
Palo Alto
650-328-8555
PARENT RATING: ☆ ☆ ☆ ☆ ☆
In business since the 1930s, this is one of Palo Alto parents' favorite toy stores. They offer a wide variety of toys for all ages, including Brio and Thomas trains, dolls of all sorts, activity kits such as jewelry-making, mini baseball gloves for toddlers, small basketball hoops, Kettler trikes, and a thoughtful selection of developmental toys for infants. The store is noted for its knowledgeable and helpful staff.

The Play Store
508 University Ave.
Palo Alto
650-326-9070
www.playstoretoys.com
PARENT RATING: ☆ ☆ ☆ ☆ ☆
This unique store specializes in carrying high-end wooden toys such as rattles for infants and play kitchens and cradles for toddlers. There is absolutely nothing plastic in the store! The staff is helpful and knowledgeable. Goods are also available via mail order.

The Wooden Horse
Kings Court Center
796 Blossom Hill Rd.
Los Gatos
408-356-8821, 888-356-8821
www.woodenhorse.com
PARENT RATING: ☆ ☆ ☆ ☆ ☆
This specialty toy store offers a thoughtful selection of high-end toys for infants on up. They feature developmental toys for babies, wooden kitchens and play structures, Brio and Thomas trains, Madame Alexander dolls and many other dolls, a "do-it" and "make-it" area full of interactive toys and art projects, as well as an impressive selection of Kettler trikes and Radio Flyer wagons. The staff is helpful and friendly and has a special play area for kids while parents shop.

Toys & Books

Best Bets for Children's Books in the South Bay

Barnes and Noble
- Redwood City
  1091 El Camino Real,
  650-299-0117
- *San Mateo
  Hillsdale Mall, 650-341-5560
www.barnesandnoble.com
Visit their website or check the yellow pages for other locations.

Books Inc.
- *Burlingame
  1375 Burlingame Ave.,
  650-685-4911
- Palo Alto
  157 Stanford Shopping Center,
  650-321-0600
www.booksinc.com

Borders Books
322 W. El Camino Real
Sunnyvale
408-730-5050
www.borders.com
Visit their website for other locations.

B. Dalton Bookseller
408 Hillsdale Mall
San Mateo
650-994-1177
Barnes and Noble now owns B. Dalton, so for other locations either visit their website (below) or check the yellow pages.

Coastside Books
432 B Main St.
Half Moon Bay
650-726-5889

*Hicklebee's Children's Books
1378 Lincoln Ave.
San Jose (Willow Glen)
408-292-8880
www.hicklebees.com

Linden Tree Children's Records & Books
170 State St.
Los Altos
650-949-3390
www.lindentree.booksense.com
They have a great selection of children's foreign language books, too!

*These stores offer story hours or other children's events. Call the stores for details.

Resale Shops for Babies and Children (Equipment and Clothing)

If you've never shopped at resale shops before, you might start once you have a baby. Resale shops are great places to clothe your baby, pick up an extra Pack 'n Play or stroller, or find a fresh batch of toys or a book or 2 for your little one—all at great savings. Resale shops are also an excellent way to clean out your house or garage and make a little money too. You can sell your baby's outgrown baby equipment and toys as well as the outfits that no longer fit . . . when you're ready to let go of them. One thing to remember is that because the store and seller usually take a 60/40 split, don't expect to get that much money for your items at resale shops. If you have an expensive item, you might want to consider selling it yourself through craigslist.org or through your local mothers' group—many offer classified ads in their monthly newsletters. One mom reports that she sold all of her baby's outgrown furniture, strollers, and a Kettler trike on Craig's list. She sold the things very quickly and also got a nice check.

The Bay Area abounds with many wonderful resale shops. Many have helpful and friendly staffs with strong social consciences, donating their unsold items to local charities. We suggest that you call these stores ahead of time to confirm their hours, as many are owned and run by sole proprietors, resulting in store hours and policies that periodically change. If you are periodically looking for something in particular, you may want to call ahead to a few shops to check their inventories.

BAY AREA RESALE SHOPS

Here is what Bay Area parents have to say about their favorite local resale stores for all of their baby gear and clothes:

San Francisco

Chloe's Closet
451A Cortland Ave.
415-642-3300
www.chloescloset.com
PARENT RATING: ☆ ☆ ☆ ☆ ☆

Chloe's Closet is making a splash in Bernal Heights by offering exclusively gently worn baby, children's, and maternity clothing. They now consist of 2 stores—one for clothing and another next door devoted to baby gear (toys, strollers, baby carriers, etc.). They carry some new items as well, such as different baby carriers. They also have lots of toys, including dolls, Legos, and trains. Comment: "It is awesome . . . very impressed."

Clothes-Go-Round

391 Arguello Blvd.

415-752-0665

PARENT RATING: ☆ ☆ ☆ ☆ ☆

This small, charming resale shop around the corner from the Clement St. neighborhood is constantly chock-full of last season's or last month's baby and kids' fashions! They are known to have a great selection of snowsuits, in season, and offer many high-end labels. The service is helpful and accommodating.

Goodwill Boutique

61 West Portal Ave.

415-665-7291

This traditional secondhand store carries a small selection of children's clothes, but you can usually find a variety of infants' and children's Halloween costumes to chose from in season.

The Junior League's Next-to-New Shop

2226 Fillmore St.

415-567-1627

They only carry a small amount of children's clothing, but it's worth checking out, as the quality and labels are usually quite good.

Peek-A-Boutique

1306 Castro St.

415-641-6192

PARENT RATING: ☆ ☆ ☆ ☆ ☆

Owned and operated by a couple for more than 12 years, this children's

clothing and baby gear resale shop is *the* resale shop in San Francisco. They offer parents one of the best venues for finding bargains and getting rid of baby clothing and gear they no longer need. They offer used and some new clothes for infants and young children, as well as shoes, furniture, and basic baby gear, such as cribs, mattresses, bedding, strollers, car seats, baby carriers, swings, and gates. They also carry new smaller baby gear and accessories, such as bathtubs, potties, and childproofing equipment, and new and used toys. Most items are in very good condition and have great prices, and the store is very child-friendly with a small play area. They will also help you place and sell your items on eBay for a fee.

Miranda's Mama

3785 Balboa St.

415-221-5862

PARENT RATING: ☆ ☆ ☆ ☆ ☆

We've heard a lot of nice things about this resale shop and its enthusiastic owner, Carrie O'Brien—and yes, she really is Miranda's mama! She carries mainly gently worn baby and children's clothing as well as maternity apparel. She also carries baby gear, including cribs and linens, bassinets, changing tables, gliders, bouncy seats, and baby carriers. Her cribs come with manuals for correct setup, and she prides herself in offering only those items that meet current safety standards. When in doubt, the owner will research items before accepting them. She also carries a lot of breast-feeding equipment and supplies, including pumps, clothing, pads, and other feeding supplies, as well as a nice selection of children's books, parenting books, toys, and videos.

Seconds-To-Go

2252 Fillmore St.

415-563-7806

This pleasant resale shop offers baby and children's clothing, toys, books, and baby furniture from time to time. They also are great about taking previously used baby gear (such as infant bathtubs and exersaucers) that Salvation Army often will not accept. All proceeds directly support the scholarship fund for Schools of the Sacred Heart.

Town School Clothes Closet

3325 Sacramento St.

415-929-8019

This traditional resale shop offers used children's clothing for infants up to teens, as well as toys that are in very good condition. All proceeds benefit the Town School for Boys.

North Bay

Outgrown

1417 4th St.

San Rafael

415-457-2219

PARENT RATING: ☆ ☆ ☆ ☆

This consignment store has been in business for 25 years and offers a large selection of children's clothing from infants to teens. Despite its small physical space, it is well stocked and organized, making shopping quick and easy. They also carry some basic baby gear items, such as cribs, changing tables, car seats, joggers, and exersaucers. One mom found like-new Sorel snow boots for

$15 and a ballet tutu that her little girl won't stop wearing. Outgrown is a Marin mom's favorite!

Play It Again Kids

508 4th St.

San Rafael

415-485-0304

PARENT RATING: ☆ ☆ ☆ ☆

This popular and successful store has been in business now for more than 10 years and specializes in offering top-quality used clothing for infants and toddlers. One mom found some great (Obermeyer) ski clothing, and another bought a bike trailer there. They also have an extensive selection of used nursery furnishings, such as cribs, changing tables, gliders, and bassinets. They carry baby gear, including gently used swings and bouncy seats, as well as Baby Bjorns, car seats, strollers, high chairs, bedding, books, and toys. They offer new toys, featuring pretend-play and science themes. The staff is friendly and helpful and has a special inclination toward customer service—regulars keep wish lists on file and are called when their item comes in the store. Moms who have sold stuff there report that the staff are very fair and courteous and make the consigning process easy. If your item doesn't sell within a certain period, they will donate it for you. Otherwise, you come in to pick up your check. Play It Again Kids is located next to Heller's and down the street from the Salvation Army donation spot—you may be headed to both or all 3!

WHERE CAN I DONATE BABY CLOTHING AND BABY GEAR?

Another option to donating to a resale shop is to donate your items to a charity. In addition to the Salvation Army and Goodwill, here are a few other organizations:

San Francisco

Clothing and Furniture Program at St. Anthony's Foundation
101 8th St.
415-241-8300
www.stanthonysf.org
This longtime nonprofit gladly accepts previously worn children's clothing, shoes, strollers, and high chairs. They even pick up for free if you live in San Francisco!

La Casa de Las Madres
1850 Mission St.
415-503-0500
www.lacasa.org
La Casa de las Madres offers emergency residential shelter to battered women and their children while providing counseling, family-based services, and referrals. Among other items, they can always use unopened baby formula and disposable diapers if you have any sizes and brands that you no longer are using.

Raphael House
1065 Sutter St.
415-474-4621
www.raphaelhouse.org
Raphael House is a family shelter supported by non-governmental funding. They have a thrift shop to help support the shelter and each resident family receives some money to shop there for clothes, toys, and household items. Baby equipment in good condition is appreciated and new toys only (due to legal considerations).

San Francisco Homeless Prenatal Program
415-546-6756
www.homelessprenatal.org/donor_info.html
This organization accepts many infant items such as gently used bottles, car seats, and extra disposable diapers.

North Bay

Women Helping All People
79 Cole Dr., Ste. 5
Marin City
415-332-1703
www.mcwhap.org
Women Helping All People conducts various workshops and classes for parents and children. They accept baby gear and clothing that it is in good and useable condition. Call ahead of time to make arrangements.

Community Action Partnership of Sonoma County

707-544-6911

www.capsonoma.org

This nonprofit organization that runs several shelters for women and children accepts previously worn children's clothing and shoes. Call or visit their website for shelter locations and phone numbers.

Building Futures with Women and Children

1395 Bancroft Ave.
San Leandro

510-357-0205, ext. 107

www.zoaatc.com

This organization provides homeless and battered women and children shelter. Baby wipes are almost always welcome.

Bananas

5232 Claremont Ave.
Oakland

510-658-7353

www.bananasinc.org

This child care resource and referral center will accept used children's clothing and baby gear for low-income moms and kids in need.

Birthright International

2924 Clayton Rd., Ste. C
Concord

925-798-7227

www.birthright.org

This nonprofit crisis pregnancy center accepts clean and gently worn maternity and baby clothes and disposable diapers.

The Elsa Segovia Center

795 Willow Rd., Bldg. 323-E
Menlo Park

650-326-9898

www.clara-mateo.org

This nonprofit homeless shelter provides needed services to the growing homeless population in the Bay Area. They will accept children's clothing and shoes as well as some baby gear such as strollers and cribs.

Resale Shops

Merry Go Round

4o1C Miller Ave.
Mill Valley
415-381-2535
www.merrygoroundmv.org

PARENT RATING: ☆ ☆ ☆ ☆ ☆

A true departure from its predecessor, this mom-owned store offers a nice selection of quality used clothing for infants to preteens, higher-end maternity clothes, as well as toys, books, and basic baby gear, including car seats and strollers. The owner is very particular about what she buys and only sells top brands—(e.g., not the Target variety). Comment: "You won't believe you are in a resale store! . . . way better than the store that used to be here!"

Wee Threads

530 Miller Ave.
Mill Valley
415-381-1700

PARENT RATING: ☆ ☆ ☆ ☆ ☆

This popular children's resale shop carries children's attire and furnishings, featuring European, unique, and boutique labels in sizes preemie to 12. Classic toys, vintage furniture, wooden high chairs, practical backpacks, antique christening gowns, flower girl dresses, and brand-new baby gift items define the atmosphere of the shop, with a nice balance between play wear and dressier clothing. Resale items are next to new, being previously owned but not necessarily previously used! There is a play area for children while you shop, and parking is easy. Comment: "Wee Threads has changed the face of resale for me! . . . I was thrilled that I can find brand names, some never

even worn, for remarkable affordable prices . . . don't miss out! . . . When I step inside this light and cheerful store, I feel like I am on a treasure hunt. . . . Teresa is knowledgeable and friendly."

Yeah, Baby

42G Bolinas Rd.
Fairfax
415-459-4493

East Bay

Bearly Worn

1619 N. Broadway
Walnut Creek
925-945-6535

This children's resale shop is jam-packed with decent brands and prices for all kinds of children's clothing. They also carry some baby gear such as strollers and car seats.

Crackerjacks

14 Glen Ave.
Oakland
510-654-8844

PARENT RATING: ☆ ☆ ☆ ☆ ☆

Voted "Best Consignment Store" by the *Oakland Tribune,* Crackerjacks has been in business for more than 15 years. This boutique-like resale shop carries secondhand name-brand clothing for babies and children. They also have a lot of baby gear, including strollers, high chairs, and toddler beds. Maternity clothing and a few new items for babies are also available. (See Ch. 3.) Customers may ask to be notified when a particular item they are looking for arrives.

Darla's Baby Boutique

10400 San Pablo Ave.
El Cerrito
510-526-KIDS (5437)

In business for more than 13 years, Darla's occupies a huge space; she needs a lot of room to pack in her new and used clothing for infants and children as well as used baby gear, furniture, toys, and books. Her new clothing is discounted since she buys directly from manufacturers. She also maintains a wish book to keep track of customers' desired items.

Finders Keepers

2222 2nd St.
Livermore
925-449-7793

Finders Keepers offers quality infant and children's clothing and an entire room full of baby equipment and furniture (such as cribs and strollers) in a well-organized and kid-friendly environment. Prices are competitive, and the staff are all experienced moms, ready and willing to help you shop or lend a hand with your little one.

Hannah's

1871 Solano Ave.
Berkeley
510-525-3488

Hannah's offers quality used clothing for babies and children, as well as some used toys and accessories. They tend to have a nice selection of European and boutique labels.

Kids Again

6891 Village Pkwy.
Dublin
925-828-7334
PARENT RATING: ☆ ☆ ☆ ☆ ☆

Kids Again is part of a large shopping complex that includes a women's clothier and home furnishings store. They carry used clothing for infants and children, baby equipment, and furniture, as well as toys. They also carry a few new items, including cribs, at a discount. They have dressing rooms and a nice play area for little ones. There are many great bargains to be found here!

Lora's Closet

• Berkeley
  2926 College Ave.
  510-845-3157
• Lafayette
  3618 Mt. Diablo Blvd.
  925-283-3963

This resale shop is known for offering quality children's clothing in very good condition.

Lauren's Closet

1420 Park St.
510-865-2219
Alameda
PARENT RATING: ☆ ☆ ☆ ☆ ☆

In business for more than 10 years, this store is consistently voted "Best Local Resale Store" by the *Alameda Times Star* and is often featured on local news broadcasts. Known for its high-quality resale items, this well-organized store offers clothing for infants and children (including brands such as Hartstrings, Gap, and Gymboree) as well as maternity wear (see Ch. 3), baby gear (such as Maclaren and Peg Perego strollers, and exersaucers), furniture (including bassinets, cribs, and changing tables), toys (such as play structures), and books. Family owned and operated, the staff offer excellent customer service, although they are known to be particular when buying used goods.

Making Ends Meet

3544 Fruitvale Ave.
Oakland
510-531-1135

This secondhand store offers clothing for babies and children, as well as some baby equipment and toys. Customers may ask to be called when a particular item comes into the store.

Second Time Around

17279 Hesperian Blvd.
San Lorenzo
510-276-8705

They offer great prices on used clothing for infants and children as well as baby equipment and furniture such as cribs, car seats, changing tables, and strollers. They also have a good selection of toys and books.

Silver Moon

3221 Grand Ave.
Oakland
510-835-2229

This charming consignment shop, decorated like a moon with a navy ceiling and silver baskets filled with hats and accessories, carries a nice selection of children's and baby clothes. Everything is in excellent condition. They have baby gear (such as bouncy seats and Pack 'n Play cribs), furniture, and toys.

Snickerdoodles

442 Hartz Ave.
Danville
925-820-4956

PARENT RATING: ☆ ☆ ☆ ☆ ☆

Voted "Best East Bay Consignment Store" by *Diablo Magazine,* this inviting boutique-like resale shop offers children's clothing, brand-name baby equipment (many strollers and cribs), games, books, and quality wooden toys. Prices are very good—about a quarter of retail—and items are in excellent condition.

They Grow So Fast

3413 Mount Diablo Blvd.
Lafayette
925-283-8976

PARENT RATING: ☆ ☆ ☆ ☆ ☆

This local consignment shop cleverly shares a large space with Ponytails Children's Hair Salon. They are well-organized, offering clothing for infants and children, furniture, toys, and books. A very kid-friendly atmosphere makes shopping easier.

Toy Go Round

1361 Solano Ave.
Albany
510-527-1363

PARENT RATING: ☆ ☆ ☆ ☆

In business for more than 25 years, Toy Go Round calls itself the Bay Area's first resale toy store. This children's shop carries both new and resale items in excellent condition, featuring Little Tikes play houses and kitchens. They carry a nice selection of new toys such as Brio trains and other wooden toys and blocks. The shop owners keep tabs for regular customers who come in to recycle their children's toys. They offer a very kid-friendly environment, featuring a Brio train table for little shoppers to play with while parents shop. They also carry seasonal items such as rain and snow clothing and a variety of Halloween costumes.

South Bay

Bearly Worn Children's Resale Store
35 W. Manor Dr.
Pacifica
650-355-5089
Bearly Worn offers gently worn clothing for infants and children, as well as books, toys, baby furnishings (such as cribs and changing tables), strollers, and car seats at great prices. They have inventory arriving daily and have a special play area for your kids while you shop. A true Bay Area favorite!

Dimples
1375 Blossom Hill Rd.
San Jose
408-264-0500
This upscale resale shops carries a variety of brand-name clothing for infants and children, as well as toys.

Junior League of Palo Alto—Mid Peninsula Shop
785 Santa Cruz Ave.
Palo Alto
650-328-7467
This shop carries a small selection of name-brand clothing for infants and children. They also occasionally have some baby equipment.

The Kidz Shoppe
Cambrian Park Plaza
14454 Union Ave.
San Jose
408-879-0989
In business for more than 10 years, The Kidz Shoppe calls itself the oldest used baby and children's clothing store in Santa Clara County. They also carry previously owned toys, books, and baby furnishings and equipment, from cribs to car seats. The store is well stocked and caters to all budgets. An attractive feature of this store is that they rent snowsuits. They also have a nice selection of Halloween costumes, in season.

Little Cousins
138 W. 25th Ave.
San Mateo
650-341-8726
This upscale children's resale shop is known for carrying brand-name clothing for infants and young children. They also offer a large selection of baby equipment and toys in excellent condition. The "infant room" hosts a bulletin board advertising recycled items for sale in the neighborhood.

Ricochet Kids Clothing
1610 S. El Camino Real
San Mateo
650-345-8740
PARENT RATING: ☆ ☆ ☆ ☆ ☆
Ricochet sells good-quality traditional children's clothing from newborn to size 14, and offers items that are very casual to dressier classic ensembles such as smocked dresses and European labels. They also carry reasonably priced wooden toys, including

Resale Shops

wooden trains that are less costly than Brio but are compatible. They carry clothing for all seasons year round so you can shop for the Hawaii-bound vacationing toddler in January! The very child-friendly and customer service-oriented staff is headed by the owner, Jill, who keeps a running wish list for regulars and calls them when their desired item comes in. She also offers private appointments for families to make it an easy and fun shopping experience!

Simplee Kidz
Almaden Oaks Shopping Ctr.
6055 Meridian Ave., #160
San Jose
408-997-5439
www.simpleekidz.com
This children's resale shop offers previously "loved" clothes, toys, books, and some baby furniture and gear as well.

The Smiling Frog
1605 Hollenback Ave.
Sunnyvale
408-730-4100

www.thesmilingfrog.com
The Smiling Frog carries stylish pre-owned brand-name baby and children's clothing as well as toys, strollers, gear, and furniture. They also feature a play area for kids while you shop.

Too Cute
1375 Burlingame Ave.
Burlingame
650-348-CUTE (2883)
Too Cute offers a good selection of previously worn infant and children's clothing and accessories. There is a useful bulletin board for previously owned items for sale in the neighborhood in the "infant room."

Ubyan
540 Bascom Ave.
San Jose
408-998-1867
This shop offers a large selection of both new and used baby and kid's clothing, shoes, toys, strollers, furniture, and other baby equipment.

Baby and Child Photographers

The Bay Area abounds with many talented photographers who specialize in photographing babies and young children. Be sure to shop around and see their work. Photographers have a wide variety of styles—indoor and outdoor, formal and informal, black and white, color, and hand-tinted. Also, consider your child's age when you are taking professional photographs. Professionals say that the best age for baby pictures is when she can sit up and smile, but can't yet crawl. This is a small window of time, roughly from 6 to 8 months. Many babies begin crawling around 9 months, which makes it difficult to capture those classic poses. And once they begin to walk, it's best to wait another year or 2!

San Francisco

Martha Bruce
415-822-7581
www.marthabruce.com
Martha specializes in black and white photography of "kids being kids."

Leslie Corrado
415-431-3917
www.lesliecorrado.com
Leslie specializes in black and white photography in outdoor settings and produces spectacular work.

Tami DeSellier
415-668-5930
www.tamailand.com
PARENT RATING: ☆ ☆ ☆ ☆ ☆

One of our personal favorites, Tami specializes in black and white photography of babies and children under 3 years old. We had Tami photograph each of our own children, and were tremendously pleased with the results. Tami really knows how to get your baby to smile and bring out his little personality on film! She is credited with the photo on the back cover of this book.

Heather Glasgow
www.studioheather.com

Jennifer Loomis
415-420-3883
www.jenniferloomis.com
Best known for her trend-setting maternity photography, Jennifer also photographs children and families. She works in San Francisco, Seattle, and New York.

Laurel Photography
415-331-1057
Laurel Thornton specializes in black and white children's portraiture.

Kathi O'Leary
415-359-1900
www.kathioleary.com

Schumacher Photography
415-596-6695
www.schumacherphotography.com
Specializing in black and white relaxed and natural portraiture photography—on location and in studio.

North Bay

Rana Halprin
415-721-5374

Serena McCallum
415-407-3152
415-435-2788
Serena specializes in black and white candid portraits of young children.

Chere Pafford
Sonoma
707-996-8775
www.cherepafford.com
Chere specializes in photographing children outdoors on black and white film.

David Peters
San Rafael
415-453-2776

Linda Russell
San Rafael
415-459-3639

Mary Small
Sausalito
415-332-5605

Dana Davis
Berkeley
510-658-7617
www.danadavisphoto.com

Johannah Hetherington
Oakland
510-663-7408
www.johannahphoto.com
PARENT RATING: ☆ ☆ ☆ ☆ ☆
Johannah specializes in "simple, soulful, black and white hand-printed portraits of children and their kin-folk." Comments: "Johannah's work is real art. . . . She is easygoing and fun to work with—very accommodating and has a special way with babies and young children."

Almudena Ortiz
Berkeley
510-526-0692

Stephanie Tabachnikoff
Oakland
510-632-5886

Carmen Urquiza
Oakland
510-339-3236
Carmen specializes in hand-coloring.

Classic Kids
• San Mateo
   650-522-9705
• Los Gatos
   408-354-9116
www.classickids.net
Classic Kids is known for their "hip shots" of kids as well as their mantra, "Never try to make a kid sit still!"

Melissa Lynch
408-723-8944

Andrew Michaels
Palo Alto
650-323-6126

Phoenix Studios
Los Gatos
408-354-5667

Portraits by Rebecca
408-848-4555

Deborah Stern
408-997-9250

Childproofing and Home Safety

Just when you think you have this baby thing down to a science, your little bundle of joy starts moving . . . first creeping, then crawling and then teetering and tottering to full-fledged walking! Congratulations—you have moved into the next stage of parenthood! Now that your little one is free to move about, there's lots of trouble she can get into at home, from electrical outlets to poisons, to unsafe cribs and soft bedding that can suffocate, to dangling window blind cords that can strangle. There is also the potential drowning danger that an accessible toilet poses, furniture that may come crashing down on a toddler if he climbs or pulls hard enough on it, or that glass framed picture over the baby's crib that could fall in an earthquake.

More than 4.5 million children suffer injuries in the home each year, many of them serious. As a parent, you will certainly need to monitor your mobile child's moves. However, there is a lot that you can do to create a safe environment so that you may also relax a little. There are many retail stores and mail order catalogs where you can buy basic childproofing gear. Home Depot or your local hardware store will often carry many of the basics, like the child safety cabinet locks and other essentials. Almost all the major baby superstores listed earlier in this chapter, under the Baby Gear section, carry babyproofing equipment and products.

As an alternative to doing it yourself, an increasing number of Bay Area parents are turning to childproofing services. Rather than poring through those mail order catalogs and spending weekends installing locks and gates, many parents simply hire a professional. After an easy in-home consultation and estimate, the job is done more efficiently than you could imagine! Some will do the home assessment and installation on the same day. Some also will do earthquake and pool safety as well as babyproofing. The general fee for childproofing is about $60-75 an hour for installation plus the cost of the parts. While this may sound daunting, most experts are very efficient and can childproof an average home in a couple of hours or so. To follow are some resources for professional childproofers:

The Childproofer
Mark Altman
800-374-2525
www.childproofer.com
PARENT RATING: ☆ ☆ ☆ ☆ ☆

This company offers childproofing product sales and installation in San Francisco, Marin, and the East Bay. They also offer a home safety assessment where they'll assess the hazards in your home and advise you on how

to minimize them for your baby. They have a great website for safety tips and potential hazards at home for babies and young children. They now offer childproof pool fences. Comments: "Experts and very efficient. . . . Full of wonderful, hard-to-find, real–world advice on babyproofing. . . . Very knowledgeable about which childproofing products worked and which ones didn't. . . . You just can't beat the

Child Safety

235

efficiency in how quickly they install childproof cabinet latches!"

CradleRock Children's Center
415-497-2173
www.craddlerockmusic.com
PARENT RATING: ☆ ☆ ☆ ☆ ☆

Lars Bergholdt from CradleRock Children's Center works with parents throughout the entire San Francisco Bay Area to make their homes safer for babies and toddlers, while always keeping a certain aesthetic in mind. After completing an in-home consultation that takes between one and 2 hours, he discusses their specific recommendations with them and addresses their concerns. They can either have him do the installation right away or schedule another appointment. He is an accepted member of the International Association for Child Safety and also conducts child safety seminars in the Bay Area for mothers' groups and others. Comments: "Lars is amazing! He did a wonderful job childproofing our home—his solutions are carefully thought out as well as aesthetically pleasing. . . . He is patient, professional, and a pleasure to work with."

Larry's Baby Safety Services
Larry Mitchell
650-493-4908 or 800-690-7233

Larry provides all childproofing services including earthquake proofing, as well as car seat installations and checks, drawer and cabinet latches, stairway, fireplace and specialty gates, and kitchen and bathroom safety items. He serves the South Bay, San Francisco, and some parts of the East Bay.

Safe and Sound Child
Rachel Murray
510-338-0222

Owner, mother, and civil engineer by training, Rachel Murray of Safe and Sound will come to your home and provide an indoor, as well as outdoor, assessment of the potential hazards to your baby and how you can minimize them. She sells and installs the babyproofing products herself. Rachel primarily serves the East Bay, but will also service some parts of San Francisco and Marin. Comments: "Very knowledgeable, neat, and reasonably priced. . . . She gets an amazing amount accomplished in an hour!"

Home Safety Services
Martin Simenc
888-388-3811 or 650-652-9173
www.homesafety.net
PARENT RATING: ☆ ☆ ☆ ☆ ☆

Martin Simenc, "The Safety Guy," will come to your home for $50 to assess the potential hazards to your baby. You pick and choose which products you want to purchase and have him install. He'll often do the installation of products during the same visit. He also provides earthquake safety and removable pool fencing. Based in Redwood City, he serves almost the entire Bay Area. Comments: "Expert advice and workmanship. . . . Neat, flexible, and efficient."

Safety by Design
916-772-3389

These wonderful babyproofers are also firemen in Burlingame! As trained paramedics, they've seen it all, so safety is their first priority. Bay Area parents say that they do a great job!

Never leave children unattended in cars—not even for a minute.

Now that you're a parent, running errands and hopping in and out of the car can take a lot longer with a baby and car seat to contend with. But never leave your child in a car alone. In fact, a new law in California makes it illegal to leave a child in a car alone—even for a minute. Effective January 31, 2002, it is illegal in California to leave a child under 6 unattended in a car. Known as Kaitlyn's Law, more information about this law and the scary consequences of leaving kids in cars alone can be found at http://www.kidsincars.org.

Pool Covers Inc.

834 Ohio Ave.
Richmond
510-233-4141
800-662-7665
www.poolcoversinc.com

Very popular in Marin and across the Bay Area, Pool Covers, Inc. carries a large variety of pool covers and offers installation and lots of information about the use and the benefits of each product.

Protect a Child Pool Fence Company

800-992-2206
www.protectachild.com

This company provides a unique, transparent mesh fence that is strong and secure, climb resistant, and removable in minutes. Call them for a free estimate. They serve the Bay Area.

All-Safe Pool Covers

www.allsafepool.com

All Safe features a huge selection of their own brand of pool covers, including the innovative "web" pool cover. Visit their website to find a dealer near you.

Safe Solutions

925-735-0700

Safe Solutions sells and installs basic childproofing products.

Online Childproofing Resources

www.jpma.org
856-439-0500
This is the website for the Juvenile Products Manufacturing Association, which works with the Consumer Products Safety Commission to develop standards for baby gear.

www.safetystore.com
888-723-3897
This website offers convenient one-stop shopping for childproofing products and more.

www.kidsstuff.com
This company says it is the only mail order catalog dedicated to child safety. The catalog, called *Perfectly Safe,* is also available online.

www.mommyshelperinc.com
316-684-2229
This website offers shopping for childproofing products and advice.

www.dannyfoundation.org
800-833-2669
The Danny Foundation is a non-profit organization that seeks to prevent injuries from cribs and other baby equipment by conducting research and providing leadership in setting regulatory standards for safe nursery equipment. The foundation was created in memory of 23-month-old Danny, who tragically died because of an unsafe crib.

www.infanthouse.com
866-INFANT(463-268)-5
One of the largest childproofing companies with locations nation-wide. Call or visit their website for in-home consultations.

Other Safety Concerns

Aside from the basic childproofing of the home, parents should be aware of the other potential hazards from which to protect their babies and toddlers. There are many more resources on each of these areas, but we'd like to make you aware of some of them.

EARTHQUAKE PROOFING

As residents of the Bay Area, we all know we have chosen to live in earthquake country. Now that you are a parent, it's even more important than ever either to make an earthquake kit or purchase one. And don't forget to throw in all the essentials for your baby or young child, including extra formula, bottles, water and food, diapers and wipes, and a blanket for that extra person you now have in your life! Following are a few websites to help you either make or purchase a kit for your family:

www.earthshakes.com
650-548-9065
This Burlingame business (owned by a mother) sells several different ready-made earthquake kits.

www.earthquakestore.com

www.iprepare.com

www.kitsincase.com
These "2 chicks trying to survive" offer comprehensive kits that not only provide emergency and first-aid basics, but also include a step-by-step guide to creating your own family disaster plan.

FIRE SAFETY AND ESCAPE PLANS

Now that you are a parent and responsible for another life, there couldn't be a better time to prepare and practice your escape plan in case of a fire. Children under 5 are more than twice as likely to die in a fire as older children and adults are. Visit the National Fire Protection Association's website at www.nfpa.org for advice on how to put together your family's fire escape plan. Be sure to install smoke detectors inside, and outside, every bedroom and on each level of your home. Also, test your smoke detectors monthly and replace the batteries every 4 to 6 months. You may also want to consider installing an automatic sprinkler system in your home.

CARBON MONOXIDE DETECTORS

The *Journal of the American Medical Association* reports that carbon monoxide is the leading cause of accidental poisoning deaths in America. Carbon monoxide (CO), an invisible, colorless, and odorless gas, cannot be detected by the human senses. Exposure to excessive levels of carbon monoxide in the air may result in loss of consciousness, coma, and even death. The primary causes of accidental CO poisoning are largely linked to defective furnaces, fireplace flues and oil heaters, as well as motor vehicle exhaust fumes.

There are a number of steps you can take to reduce the risk of carbon monoxide poisoning in your home. Make sure that all home systems are working correctly—e.g., consider annual inspections for heating systems, chimneys, and flues and have them cleaned by a qualified technician, and never leave a car or lawn mower engine running in any enclosed space. A carbon monoxide detector or alarm should also be installed in areas where CO is most likely. Today many smoke detectors come with a CO detector. As with a smoke detector, be sure to check the batteries regularly. As of press time, there is a bill pending in California that would require the installation of carbon monoxide detectors in all homes and buildings in the state. The law would be similar to existing requirements for smoke detectors.

LEAD POISONING PREVENTION

About one in 22 children in the United States have high levels of lead in their blood, according to the Center for Disease Control and Prevention. Children are more susceptible to lead poisoning since their brains and nervous systems are more sensitive to the damaging effects of lead. The long-term health effects of lead for them can be devastating, including damage to the brain and nervous system, and behavioral and learning problems, such as hyperactivity and slowed growth. Lead also poses a significant health hazard to unborn babies, so if you are pregnant, you should pay careful attention to lead hazards.

Lead is often found in the paint of older homes (painted before 1978), as well as in the drinking water as a result of lead plumbing. People most often get lead in their bodies by breathing or swallowing lead dust, or by eating soil or paint chips containing lead. Babies and young children often put their hands and other objects in their mouths, which can have lead dust on them. Home sellers and landlords are required to disclose known information regarding lead-based paint hazards in or on the property, including copies of any inspection reports. They also are required to provide purchasers and renters with an EPA pamphlet titled *Protect Your Family from Lead in Your Home*.

Children are often tested for blood lead levels at one year of age, so be sure to ask your pediatrician about this test. A blood test is the only way to know if your child has lead poisoning. Also, never remove lead paint yourself—many families have been poisoned by the lead dust

Other Household Poisoning Prevention Tips

 Have the number of the San Francisco Bay Area Regional Poison Control Center posted near your phone (800-876-4766) along with the national number (800-222-1222). Calls get patched through to your local poison control center.

 Keep a bottle of syrup of Ipecac (it induces vomiting) for each child less than 5 years old. Never use it unless instructed to do so by the Poison Control Center or your doctor.

 If you suspect a child has been poisoned, call the Poison Control Center, but dial 911 immediately if the child is unconscious, having convulsions, or having difficulty breathing.

that is created from scraping or sanding lead paint. If you do hire a professional painter, be sure to hire someone who is lead certified. Finally, the only way to know if you have lead in your water is to have it tested. You can call your local health department or water supplier to find out how to test the water in your home. Be sure always to flush the tap for at least 30 seconds before using water, and use cold water when cooking—less lead will leak from any lead plumbing with cold water than with hot water. Boiling water does not reduce lead in water.

LEAD POISONING PREVENTION RESOURCES

There are a number of resources where you can learn about lead poisoning prevention. The following are a few such resources:

The U.S. Environmental Protection Agency, National Lead Information Clearinghouse
800-424-5323
www.epa.gov/lead
This agency offers several free lead prevention booklets about testing your home for lead and reducing lead hazards when remodeling your home. Call the toll-free number to obtain copies.

EPA's Safe Drinking Water Hotline
800-426-4791

California Childhood Lead Poisoning Prevention Website
www.dhs.ca.gov/childlead/

Childhood Lead Prevention Program
San Francisco Department of Public Health
415-554-8930
They offer free lead testing for women, infants, and children.

San Francisco Public Utility Commission
877-737-8297
This organization will test your water for lead for $25.

www.dhs.ca.gov/childlead/html/B40-sf.html
This website lists certified lead professionals in the Bay Area.

LEADING RISKS TO INFANTS AND CHILDREN

In a report published in 2004 in the journal *Pediatrics*, 2 pediatricians reviewed the leading risks to infants and children. Their main point is that most of the greatest dangers can largely be prevented without the need for further scientific inquiry or change in legislation—simply by vigilance on the part of the parent or primary caregiver. Here is what they said were the most important hazards:

Sudden Infant Death Syndrome
Car accidents
Burns
Poisoning
Drowning
Choking
Guns

Electrocution
Secondhand smoke
Sunburn
Sports injuries
Power tools
Obesity

CHAPTER 5

SURVIVING THE
FIRST FEW MONTHS:
Postpartum Help

While the first few weeks at home with a newborn are full of joy, this time is often turbulent as well. New parents are typically sleep deprived, having to attend to frequent feedings, diaper changes, and other needs of the baby. Additionally, while both parents may engage in child care, new mothers may most often feel that their lives are reduced to changing diapers, feedings, and rocking and soothing the baby. As a new mom, you may begin to believe you will never have a normal life again! In addition, giving birth is an emotionally charged experience, and a new mom's hormones fluctuate greatly in the early weeks, resulting in what many call the "baby blues." In some instances, this can escalate into postpartum depression.

Our advice is to anticipate these changes and make a postpartum plan *before* you give birth. This chapter answers the following questions to help you develop such a plan:

◆ What is a baby nurse and postpartum care doula, and where can I find them?
◆ What are lactation consultants, and what do their certifications mean?
◆ Where can I join a breastfeeding support group?

243

- How can I get groceries, meals, and other necessities such as baby supplies delivered to my home?
- How can I get professional advice concerning postpartum depression?
- Where can I get access to special "warm" lines and stress lines? (Warm lines are usually for those non-emergency situations when a parent needs special help in anything ranging from breastfeeding to babysitting.)
- What are the best places to nurse or change my baby in public?

Baby Nurses and Postpartum Doulas

Many of us live great distances from our families, and the option of having a family member help in the early weeks of new parenthood isn't available. Hiring a baby nurse has become a popular alternative for gaining an extra pair of hands during this happy but hectic time. Even if you do have family living nearby, you may not want to impose on them—or be imposed upon by them—and may prefer to hire a baby nurse or postpartum care doula, who provides short-term professional help.

In general, the baby nurse and postpartum doula field is unregulated. Practitioners range from having little training and experience to being highly skilled professionals with years of training and experience. It is important to interview candidates and ask about their background, training, and credentials, and you should always check references and work eligibility documentation (see Ch. 10). Also, don't forget to ask if they carry insurance should they have an accident in your home.

Since the first edition of this book, it seems as though the doula and baby nurse community has grown significantly. According to Doulas of North America (DONA), there are now close to 4,700 doulas registered in the United States—a 21% increase since 2003. Reflecting this doula boom in the Bay Area, many doulas have organized themselves into "doula circles" or "doula groups." Such groups exist for San Francisco, Marin, the East Bay, and the Peninsula. They are not run exactly the same (e.g., the San Francisco group has a website that lists members), but what they all seem to offer is a "one-stop shop" for

Tips for New Motherhood Survival

- Stock your freezer before your baby is born and/or order take-out for the first few weeks.

- Plan ahead of time for help, such as a friend, family member, postpartum doula, or lactation consultant.

- Enlist the support of a friend or relative to assist with laundry, meals, and light housekeeping . . . or simply plan on letting the house get messy. Or, if you already have a regular cleaning person, consider temporarily giving him or her more duties, such as laundry.

- Buy baby supplies (diapers and wipes) in bulk and/or order supplies online (see Ch. 4) and have them delivered.

- Put essential baby news (gender, name, date, weight) as well as the state of the parents (for example, we are either nursing or sleeping) on your voice mail to avoid energy- and time-consuming phone calls.

- Keep it simple: Focus on your baby and yourself—you both need nourishment and rest—everything else can wait (yes, even those thank-you notes and baby photos)!

- Nurture yourself physically—eat well, sleep, rest, and exercise (with your doctor's approval).

- Develop a support system—get out and meet other new moms by joining a new mothers' group (see Ch. 6).

- Get outside every day, even if it's only a walk around the block! Vitamin D helps stabilize mood swings.

- Take breaks when you can; a brisk walk, bubble bath, or hour to yourself can make a difference in your attitude and perspective.

- Keep realistic expectations; your job first and foremost is caring for your baby (as well as for yourself).

- Structure your day; list one small errand to do, one person to call, and do something fun for yourself.

referrals of trained and experienced birth and postpartum doula professionals. The groups meet monthly for education and peer support. Members are active in the local birth community, and they participate in continuing education and regular peer review to ensure professionalism and quality of service. One of the most helpful things that active members in these groups do is to participate in "Meet the Doula" nights at most of the major parenting resource centers and hospitals, as listed below. These workshops feature information on what a birth or postpartum doula does, the benefits of doula services, introductions to local doulas, and whether or not having one either for birth or afterward is right for you and your family—information not to be missed if you are considering hiring one!

BABY NURSES

While not always distinguishable, in general a postpartum care doula emphasizes caring for the parents (especially the mother) while they are learning to care for their baby, and a baby nurse focuses on caring for the baby. Baby nurses may or may not be registered nurses, but are professionals skilled in newborn care. A baby nurse typically holds either a Licensed Vocational Nurse (LVN) degree or a Registered Nurse (RN) degree from an accredited university. An LVN completes one or two years of nursing training and works in the field of obstetrics, including postpartum care and the newborn nursery. An RN completes a minimum of 2 to 4 years of nursing training and works in all areas of obstetrics, including postpartum care, high-risk antepartum care, the well-baby nursery and the neonatal intensive care unit. While it is always a good idea to take note of a care provider's credentials, many hospitals and well-respected professionals in the field stress that a baby nurse's experience is more important than her degree.

Baby nurses are usually scheduled to begin working the day you bring your baby home from the hospital. They usually work on a full-time schedule, from 8 to 12 hours, day or night, and their duties focus exclusively on caring for the baby during the post-delivery period. Many baby nurses do not offer 24-hour care. While some new parents do find 24-hour care best fits their needs, keep in mind that the post-birth period is a very intimate time for your family, and you may not want to have anyone from outside your family—no matter how helpful—living with you around the clock.

A baby nurse who works at night (sometimes referred to as a "night nurse") usually sleeps in the baby's room, or has a baby monitor in her room, and tends to the baby while parents rest. When the baby wakes up, the baby nurse either brings the baby to her mother to nurse or bottle feeds the baby. After the feeding, the baby nurse takes charge of the process of burping, changing, and settling the baby back to sleep. Of course, you decide what specific areas you would like assistance with. One of the great services that baby nurses often provide is documenting the baby's eating, sleeping, and diaper patterns to identify any problems. Most importantly, a good baby nurse should be able to teach and support a mother in bonding with her baby, make parents self-supportive, and identify what other kind of help they may need. Baby nurses are usually not responsible for household duties such as housekeeping or for care of other children in the family, although some do offer this service, and many will do the baby's laundry.

Of course, an extra pair of hands can be expensive. Fees typically start at $20-25 per hour in the Bay Area, and we are increasingly seeing rates in the $27-30 per hour range. The rates are higher for multiples, typically $25-35 per hour for twins. Registered Nurses are rarely under $30 an hour. Some mothers have been known to fly baby nurses in from other cities where fees are lower. Fees are based on the candidate's training and experience as well as her specific duties. According to Bay Area moms, the best way to find a baby nurse is a referral through a trusted friend. Another good resource is a Bay Area mothers' group newsletter (see Ch. 6), which often has baby nurse listings and referrals. The San Francisco Mothers of Twins Club newsletter is especially helpful, as many parents of multiples rely heavily on outside help for these first few months!

Personal referrals are generally the best resource in finding a suitable baby nurse, but agencies can also be a help here. While some agencies specialize in placing baby nurses, most nanny agencies also place them. An agency will send you several prescreened candidates to interview during your pregnancy. After you select one, the agency will reserve the baby nurse and not place her elsewhere within 2 weeks or so of your due date. Most (but not all) agencies charge a flat registration fee of up to $300 to conduct a search and present candidates to you. Upon hiring an agency's candidate, the agency charges a referral fee that is usually a percentage (20-35%) of the baby nurse's total gross income for the assignment.

Although most agencies try to fill immediate needs, baby nurses generally get booked long in advance, so plan early. From what we've learned, starting your search sometime in the first or second trimester is not too early.

Baby nurses and doulas come from a broad range of experiences and training. When screening and interviewing candidates, be sure to ask about their experience, training, and any specializations as well as your anticipated needs. Also, it's important to try to get a clear understanding of the candidate's philosophy with respect to newborn care, such as whether she advocates breast- or bottle feeding, scheduled feedings versus demand feeding, having the baby sleep on her back rather than her side or tummy, and so on. It is important to find someone who's compatible with your approach (and your pediatrician's) to newborn care and parenting.

POSTPARTUM DOULAS

A postpartum doula is someone who is trained or experienced in providing postpartum care for a new mother and some newborn care. The word *doula* has a Greek origin, and translates to "mothering the mother." Some postpartum care doulas are also labor and birth doulas (see Ch. 1), while others specialize in providing postpartum care, which can include everything from caring for the mother and baby, and breastfeeding assistance, to light housekeeping and meal preparation, and general reassurance to the new mother. A doula's experience may vary greatly; some doulas are better versed in breastfeeding assistance and other aspects of newborn care than others. It is best to discuss your needs thoroughly with an agency and/or with prospective candidates.

Doulas of North America (DONA) is the primary national certification organization for labor and birth doulas (see Ch. 1). Since the first edition of this book, DONA has begun a postpartum doula training and

"First Five" Newborn Home Visits

In 1998, California voters passed Proposition 10 (The California Children and Families Act), which added a 50-cents-per-pack tax on cigarettes. Not many realize it, but these taxes fund a statewide program in California known as First Five (named after the first 5 years of a child's life). First Five funds reach children and families in every neighborhood with programs and services to promote early childhood development, including newborn home visits. If you are interested in receiving a home visit by a nurse or child care provider after you come home from the hospital with your baby, be sure to ask your health care provider about this initiative.

certification program. Postpartum doulas certified by DONA have attended DONA-approved postpartum doula training workshops and have completed certain educational and experience requirements. The National Association of Postpartum Care Services (NAPCS) also certifies postpartum doulas. Although DONA and NAPCS may be among the most recognizable certification organizations, there are other reputable doula training and certification programs in the Bay Area (and elsewhere), such as Blossom Birth Services in Palo Alto and The Doula School in the East Bay. And while there are many different offerings of postpartum training and certification, some professionals note that there are also many good people without formal training who have significant experience with postpartum work. Even with training, there is no substitute for an experienced doula.

As with finding a baby nurse, your best bet in finding a postpartum doula is through a personal referral. You can also typically find a doula through organizations dealing with childbirth, birth educators, lactation centers and consultants, baby nurse agencies, the website for Doulas of North America (www.dona.com) and the website for the National Association of Postpartum Care Services (www.napcs.org/default.htm).

Postpartum doulas are usually hired on a part-time basis, for a minimum number of hours per day (such as 3 to 4 hours) and range from $20 to $90 an hour in the Bay Area, depending on their training and experience as well as responsibilities for a particular job. Fees for evening hours can be higher than for day hours. Most of the major nanny agencies in the Bay Area mentioned in Chapter 9 place baby nurses and doulas, so be sure to refer to them. The following are additional placement agencies that specialize in placing baby nurses and doulas, parent resource centers that offer referrals, and the names of individual doulas and baby nurses that Bay Area parents have shared with us. Since some of these same people and organizations offer labor support services and lactation consulting, we have included these resources here as well. (See also Ch. 1.)

AGENCIES FOR POSTPARTUM BABY NURSES AND DOULAS

Entire Bay Area

Bay Area Baby Nurses and Doulas
800-526-9996 or 415-899-1889
www.bayareababynurses.com
PARENT RATING: ☆ ☆ ☆ ☆ ☆

Serving San Francisco, Marin, the Peninsula, and the East Bay, Kay Baker, RN, places baby nurses and doulas that are matched to a family's needs. Services include guidance on newborn care, breastfeeding support, and help with errands, meals, and light housekeeping. Kay Baker is the owner and has a stellar reputation. Parents also rave about nurse Nancy Ducey: "She was really fabulous—we were totally comfortable having her in our home at night." Debra Grant, RN. is also another favorite among parents.

Doulas of North America (DONA)
www.dona.org/Areas/California.html
The above website includes a link to DONA certified doulas in California.

National Association of Postpartum Care Services
www.napcs.org/default.htm
The above website includes a link for referrals for postpartum doulas nationwide.

San Francisco and North Bay

Barefoot and Pregnant
1165 Magnolia Ave.
Larkspur
415-388-1777
www.barefootandpregnant
PARENT RATING: ☆ ☆ ☆ ☆ ☆

Dedicated to pregnant women and new moms, Barefoot and Pregnant has been nurturing new and expectant mothers since 2003 with fitness and spa offerings as well as new parenting workshops and many other wonderful resources, including a monthly "Meet the Doulas" night.

DayOne

3490 California St., 2nd Fl., Ste. 203
(Entrance on Locust)
San Francisco
415-440-Day1 (3291)
www.dayonecenter.com

PARENT RATING: ☆ ☆ ☆ ☆ ☆

This wonderful state-of-the-art parent
resource center hosts a "Meet the
Doulas" night from time to time. This
evening tends to focus on birth doulas,
but also addresses the role of the
doula during postpartum care. They
also keep binders with listings of childbirth and postpartum care doulas, as
well as night and day nannies. For full
description see under Breastfeeding.

Birth Doulas of Marin

415-451-7287
www.marinbirthdoulas.com

PARENT RATING: ☆ ☆ ☆ ☆ ☆

This "collective" of doulas is a group
of well-trained professional doulas
who have been practicing since 1984
exclusively at Marin General Hospital,
providing support during labor and
delivery. Many of these doulas offer a
variety of independent postpartum
services once you are home with
your baby. Parents may meet these
doulas at monthly "Meet the Doula
Nights" at Marin General, although
the focus of these meetings is typically labor support. All of these doulas
are mothers and have professional
training or certification credentials.

Marin Doula Circle

www.marinbirthandparenting.com
The Marin Doula Circle is a group of
about 25 birth and postpartum
doulas, with varying degrees of certification, including some having

DONA certification. Most have been
practicing doulas for more than 10
years. They meet monthly and offer
referrals to one another.

Moms on the Move Doula Group

707-762-MOMS (6667)
www.momsonthemove.net

Founded in 1977 by Susan Edwards-
Bullen, RN, CD, CPD, Moms on the
Move is an organization committed to
optimizing the health, education, and
support of childbearing women and
their families throughout the pregnancy and postpartum period. They consist of a dedicated staff of obstetrical
and fitness professionals and offer a
wide range of classes and services,
including certified postpartum doulas
who are also RNs and midwives.
They work in Marin and also occasionally in San Francisco.

Natural Resources

816 Diamond St.
San Francisco
415-550-2611
www.naturalresourcesonline.com

PARENT RATING: ☆ ☆ ☆ ☆ ☆

This helpful parent resource center
hosts a "Meet Local Doulas" evening
once a month and maintains a helpful
binder of information about doulas
(some containing client feedback)
and lactation consultants.

Parents Place

1710 Scott St.
San Francisco
415-359-2454

PARENT RATING: ☆ ☆ ☆ ☆

This full-service parenting center has
one of the city's largest bulletin

boards where nannies, babysitters, and baby nurses advertise.

San Francisco Doula Group

www.sfdoulagroup.com

PARENT RATING: ☆ ☆ ☆ ☆ ☆

A recent development since the first edition of this book, the San Francisco Doula Group has formed a "one-stop shop" for referrals of trained and experienced birth and postpartum doula professionals. The group meets monthly for education and peer support. Each doula listed on this site is active in the local birth community, participates in continuing education, "understands her role as a non-medical birth and/or postpartum professional," and has agreed to participate in regular peer review to ensure professionalism and quality of service. Active members participate in "Meet the Doula" nights at parenting resource centers such as DayOne and Natural Resources.

East Bay

Birth Professionals of the Bay Area

510-595-5534

www.birthprofessionals.milagros.org/

Samsarah Becknett, CHP, PD, heads this group of caregivers and educators which is dedicated to excellence in birth and postpartum services. They also offer doula training and certification.

Birthways

570 14th St.
Oakland
510-869-2797
www.birthways.org

PARENT RATING: ☆ ☆ ☆ ☆ ☆

This nonprofit, volunteer organization hosts a "Doula Information Night" and maintains a list of local baby nurses and doulas. They also offer lactation consultant referrals, as well as breastfeeding supplies. See their website for a listing of individual postpartum care providers and doulas.

Loving Arms Doula Service

510-525-1155, Janaki Costello
510-563-2831, Alice Elliott
510-527-7210, Carol Shattuck-Rice
www.openheartdoulatraining.com

This group of 3 certified doulas each maintains a separate clientele, but they share duties in cases of emergency. They serve the East Bay, and charge $900 for labor support, including meeting before the birth and a postpartum checkup after birth. Costello is also a lactation consultant providing breastfeeding help after birth, and Elliott and Shattuck-Rice both offer postpartum doula services. They get you off to a good start with your new baby by helping with breastfeeding and basic baby care. They also run errands, do food shopping, and handle meal preparation, kitchen cleanup, and laundry.

The Nurture Center

3399 Mt. Diablo Blvd.
Lafayette
925-283-1346
www.nurturecenter.com

PARENT RATING: ☆ ☆ ☆ ☆ ☆

This Contra Costa County parenting center run by 2 local moms maintains listings of professional doulas. They also host a free "Postpartum Information Night" from time to time which is always an insightful evening with a panel of postpartum experts.

UC Berkeley Parents Network

http://parents.berkeley.edu/
recommend/medical/
babynurse.html

PARENT RATING: ☆ ☆ ☆ ☆ ☆

At this website you can find parents' frank opinions on just about everything, including local doulas (East Bay focus).

Waddle and Swaddle

1677 Shattuck Ave.
Berkeley
510-540-7210
www.waddleandswaddle.com

This baby boutique and new and expectant parent resource center offers myriad classes and workshops, including a "Doula Information Night." They also have a great bulletin board where many East Bay moms find doulas.

South Bay

Bay Area Birth Information (BABI)

www.bayareabirthinfo.org

BABI is largely a resource and referral group of birth professionals in the South Bay. They host a "Meet the Doulas Night" where you can learn more about the role of a doula and whether a doula is right for you. This event is usually held at Tiny Tots Togs in Campbell. Please visit BABI's website for dates and registration.

Before Birth and Beyond

408-360-0714

This group offers certified postpartum doulas on the Peninsula from Redwood City to Santa Clara, including doulas experienced with twins.

Birth Doulas of Santa Cruz County

www.scdoulas.com

Birth Network of Santa Cruz County

www.birthnet.org

Both websites have referral lists of doulas in Santa Cruz County.

Blossom Birth Services

1000 Elwell Center
Palo Alto
650-964-7380
www.blossombirth.com

PARENT RATING: ☆ ☆ ☆ ☆ ☆

This childbirth education and resource center hosts a monthly "Meet the Doulas Night" and also offers doula and lactation consultant listings and referrals, as well as doula training classes. Visit their website for a list of providers.

CHANGE of the Peninsula

(based in the Center for Healing and Global Evolution)
400 Ben Franklin Ct.
San Mateo
650-340-YOGA (9642)
www.changeofthepeninsula.org

Among a plethora of other classes at the Center for Healing and Global Evolution, CHANGE offers a "Meet the Doulas" night. Visit their website for schedule information.

www.gentlebirth.org

This site lists doulas in the South Bay area.

INDIVIDUAL POSTPARTUM BABY NURSES AND DOULAS

San Francisco and North Bay

Marcia Armstrong

415-994-2581

According to *San Francisco* magazine, Marcia is known as the chosen baby nurse for "San Francisco movers and shakers." Marcia has more than 15 years of experience easing couples into parenthood—she does it all from teaching parents how to bathe baby to helping mom with breastfeeding and getting baby to sleep.

Susan Bradford, CPD

415-453-0251

Susan is a member of Birth Doulas of Marin (see above) and is among 4 women of that group who offer postpartum care.

Sara Duskin, RN, CLE, IBCLC

415-386-9250

PARENT RATING: ☆ ☆ ☆ ☆ ☆

A longtime favorite among city moms, Sara is a very supportive and informative British-trained nurse. She offers first-rate postpartum assistance, including newborn baby care and breastfeeding consulting. She'll meet you at your home when you leave the hospital and help you and your family embark upon the journey of parenthood in the most positive and nurturing way. Comments: "Sarah was my lifesaver! . . . I've gone back to Sarah with each of my 3 babies for the support and assistance that I needed to nurse."

Esther Gallagher, CPD

415-821-4490

www.esthergallagher.com

Esther offers postpartum care doula services within the city of San Francisco. With 20 years of experience including work as a childbirth educator and midwife, Esther's services are rated top-notch. A firm believer in providing nurture and support to new parents, Esther focuses on postpartum care, coming into your home for a limited number of hours each day and prioritizing your needs as a new parent. She provides lactation consultant services, housecleaning, and meal preparation among her postpartum care services. Esther is trained and certified by the National Association of Postpartum Care Services.

Melitta Hoder

415-586-8468

Melitta is a postpartum doula who also offers pre- and postpartum massage as well as infant massage. She trained at Natural Resources as well as the Nursing Mothers Counsel and DONA. She works in San Francisco and the northern Peninsula, and is a member of the San Francisco Doula Group. She does not work nights.

Karen Kresti, RN

415-626-4961

Karen has years of experience as an OB/GYN nurse, including time spent at Brigham and Women's Hospital in Boston and Stanford Medical Center, specializing in infant care and new parent education. She has experience working with twins and high-risk babies, and also works with singletons. She currently is putting her experience to work by offering a wide array of postpartum care services, including breastfeeding support and infant sleep consultations. Comment: "Karen is very caring and very supportive."

Georgia Montgomery, CPD

415-499-8308

Georgia is a member of Birth Doulas of Marin (see above) and is among 4 women of that group who offer post-partum care.

Bonnie Riopelle, CPD

415-381-1650

bonnieriopelle@go.com

Bonnie is a member of Birth Doulas of Marin (see above) and is among 4 women of that group who offer post-partum care. She received her train-ing and certification (before DONA started its program) through the Chapman Family Center in Los Angeles. Bonnie's services include mother and baby care, breastfeeding assistance, errand running, nursery set-up, and meal preparation.

Debbie Surkhe, CPD

415-472-5934

A member of Birth Doulas of Marin (see above), Debbie Surkhe offers full-service postpartum care, taking care of both mother and baby, and easing the transition into motherhood. She is certified by the National Association of Postpartum Care Services and has been a member of DONA since it started more than 12 years ago. Her services are available in San Francisco and Marin for full days and for overnights. Comment: "Debbie is very knowledgeable about babies and chil-dren and is a wonderful resource. She's a terrific listener and [was] always available for advice when I

needed it. But she never imposed her opinion or ideas on me. She's open-minded and progressive and could offer alternative suggestions to age-old baby problems. . . . She always made me feel like I was making the right decision regarding my baby."

Mary Nuckton, CPD
Rock a Bye Baby Postpartum Services

415-244-5666

Mary has 20 years of experience working with infants and families with young children in the Bay Area. She is certified by the National Association of Postpartum Care Services, and parents rave about her comfortable and helpful style!

Julie Overton, PD

707-762-6702

Julie offers a wide range of emotional and physical support to the new mother, including breastfeeding sup-port, new baby care, light housekeep-ing, and meal preparation. She also has experience with twins. She works mainly in San Francisco but also in Marin and Sonoma. Comment: "I can't say enough wonderful things about her. She's great at fitting in and doing what needs to get done!"

Katerina Wade, CPD

415-608-5304

Katerina trained as a pediatric nurse in the Czech Republic and has received doula training and certifica-tion from Blossom Birth Services. She offers postpartum support for new mothers, including breastfeeding sup-port, newborn care, household help such as meal preparation, errand run-ning, and household chores, sibling care, and much more. Katerina also has experience with twins. Comments: "Katerina has a wonderful ability to assess a situation and take charge in an unobtrusive way. . . . When I called other parents to get recommendation for Katerina, I was told over and over, to get her if I could!"

Angela Williams, RN, MA
415-457-7268
Mother of 5 and former hospice nurse, Angela is a Registered Nurse, baby nurse, and certified postpartum doula. She works primarily nights with newborns and arranges to be in your home when you first arrive home with baby. She specializes in all aspects of infant and maternal care, including baby's sleep and feeding schedule, lactation coaching, light housekeeping, baby laundry, and meal preparation. She usually works with a family for 2 weeks to 3 months and sometimes longer. Comments: "Angela truly cares for the whole family. . . . A rare gem."

East Bay

Judy Ballinger, RN, CMT, CD
www.doulaplusacupressure.com
Judy offers postpartum doula services for 4 hours per day (during daylight hours), one to 5 days a week. She addresses the major needs of the new mom such as sleep, fluids, and food. She answers new parents' questions, helps with breastfeeding positioning, changes bed linens, assists with that never-ending pile of laundry, runs errands, and provides newborn care. A little foot massage or shoulder release can be included.

Nancy Ducey, CPD
415-488-9316
PARENT RATING: ☆ ☆ ☆ ☆ ☆
Nancy has more than 20 years experience in providing postpartum care to new moms and babies. She received her training at Blossom Birth Services and settles moms and babies into a routine in no time! She works anywhere in Marin and in the East Bay locations as well as some parts of San Francisco.

Beth Hammond, CPD
925-330-0800
Beth makes the transition to parenthood easier by providing day and overnight care, breastfeeding education, newborn care, parent respite, strategies and parenting tips, and light housework including baby laundry, light cooking, and the general cleanup from caring for baby. The emphasis of her practice is overnight work, and she has experience with single babies, twins, and triplets. Her goal is to help educate and empower parents, give them the tools to help them cope and succeed at being new parents, and of course to give them a break while she is working in their home. She works in all of Contra Costa, Alameda, and parts of San Francisco with families of singles and multiples. She received her training from DONA, La Leche League for lactation support, and Newborn Connections at California Pacific Medical Center.

Ann Regan, CPD
510-847-9743
Ann is a certified postpartum doula serving the greater Berkeley area.

She helps ease the transition to parenthood by teaching baby care and infant massage, caring for mom and baby, and providing breastfeeding support. She works days and her services can include errands, light cleaning, sibling care, laundry, and preparation of healthy meals.

Treesa McLean, CD, CPD

510-728-8513
www.thedoulaschool.com
PARENT RATING: ☆ ☆ ☆ ☆ ☆

Treesa is an experienced and highly respected doula, offering birth and postpartum doula services. She is also the founder of The Doula School which offers doula training. Treesa works in the East Bay, Peninsula, and San Francisco. Comment: "Treesa far exceeded our expectations of keeping the house running. She helped me give the baby's first bath, and helped me to learn to nurse correctly, and she cooked up a week's worth of gourmet dishes . . . it was a lovely week and I had time to enjoy my baby, family, and all the friends who stopped by to visit."

Moon Mama's Childbirth and Family Services
Lisa Moon, CPPCP, CCE

510-644-3035
lisamoon@moonmamas.com
PARENT RATING: ☆ ☆ ☆ ☆ ☆

With more than 25 years of experience, Lisa will help you get a restful night's sleep and eat well with healthy home-cooking. She will also make your baby comfortable and happy. She offers postpartum care and support and "newborn and family resource consulting." Her baby care features a "moon mama baby spa," which she teaches to new parents. She is a certified childbirth educator and certified postpartum care provider by the Fourth Trimester and the National Association of Postpartum Care Providers. She is based in Berkeley and serves most of the Bay Area.

Constance Williams, CD

My Doula, Birth Assistant Services
510-558-7121

South Bay

Sandy Caldwell, CD, CPD

650-261-9171
PARENT RATING: ☆ ☆ ☆ ☆ ☆

Sandy is the mother of 3 grown daughters, a certified birth doula, and a postpartum doula. Many parents report her as a nurturing and experienced companion to expectant and new parents through pregnancy, labor, birth, and the "in arms" period following birth. In addition to being on the BABI board, she is a Blossom Birth Services board member and co-founder of the Peninsula Birth Circle.

Joanne Hass, CMT

650-726-7528
Joanne offers first-rate part-time postpartum doula services from South San Francisco to Mountain View. She is experienced with multiples.

Karen Pollack

925-330-5660
karen@doubletalkfortwins.com
www.doubletalkfortwins.com
PARENT RATING: ☆ ☆ ☆ ☆ ☆

Karen has been an educator at the Women's Health Center for John Muir/

Mt. Diablo Health Systems in Walnut Creek for 9 years and specializes in preparing couples who are expecting multiples. She also offers in-home consultations on scheduling and sleep issues for babies. She works throughout the Bay Area.

Postpartum Baby Nurses with Sleep Specialization

Dr. Noelle Cochrane
415-648-3243
Noelle is a child psychologist who also offers sleep training for babies and children of all ages.

Susie Collins-Romaine, RN
301-332-4518
susie@worldnet.att.net
www.properstartinc.com
Susie is a British-trained nurse with 30 years of experience helping babies sleep. She also specializes in multiples. While not currently based in the Bay Area, she has an established clientele here and makes many trips back, often to help families with a second or third baby. She also does telephone consultations.

Debra Grant, RN
1-800-526-9996
Debra is a night nurse and sleep consultant through Bay Area Baby Nurses and Doulas.

Elizabeth Green, CPD
650-269-9046
postpartumcare@aol.com
www.earlyparentingsupport.com
Elizabeth offers excellent postpartum care, as well as at-home breastfeeding support and sleep consultations among other early parenting topics. She is certified through the National Association of Postpartum Care Providers and is based in Sonoma.

Marsha Podd, RN, CLE
415-883-4442
www.gotosleepbaby.com
Marsha has over 20 years of experience as an OB/GYN nurse and Certified Lactation Educator, and she also has a degree in Child Development. In addition to lactation consultations, she also offers sleep consultations, either in person or by telephone.

Vivian Sonnenberg
415-383-0560
www.viviansonnenberg.com
Vivian is a very popular baby nurse and postpartum doula, with recent notoriety as a sleep consultant, or "sleep guru." She was trained as a pediatric nurse in Argentina and subsequently studied psychology and pediatrics. She has nearly 19 years of working with babies. While she does not do overnights, she promises to get your baby to sleep. Comment: "She is wonderful and changed our lives."

Breastfeeding Assistance and Support

As a new or expectant parent, you have probably been informed about the benefits of breastfeeding. The American Academy of Pediatrics recommends exclusively breastfeeding for the first 6 months with continuation of breastfeeding for the first year of life for optimal infant health and development. Breast milk helps strengthen a baby's immune system and is the perfect balance of water, fat, protein, vitamins, and minerals that your baby needs. In short, breast milk is designer baby food! Of course, bottle feeding your baby is perfectly fine—after all, you need to do what is best for you.

However, as many mothers can attest, learning to breastfeed can take unanticipated amounts of time and effort. While some mothers have no difficulty breastfeeding, others need help positioning and getting the baby to "latch-on" correctly, and consequently suffer from engorgement and sore nipples. If you are a new mother who has difficulty breastfeeding, you will likely benefit from a professional who specializes in providing breastfeeding support—a lactation consultant.

Many lactation consultants are nurses, although some are not. Some are certified by the International Board of Lactation Consultant Examiners, with the credential International Board Certified Lactation Consultant (IBCLC). This is the highest form of certification for a lactation consultant. An IBCLC has passed an independent examination and possesses the necessary skills, knowledge, and attitude to provide quality breastfeeding assistance to mothers and babies. An IBCLC candidate needs a minimum of 2,500 hours of clinical breastfeeding consulting before she can sit for the exam and is required to be engaged in continuing education. The IBCLC credential is the only official, international credential for those offering breastfeeding and lactation care and services.

Some lactation consultants are Certified Lactation Consultants (CLC), which means that they have received training and are certified to give one-on-one lactation support. Be aware, however, that there is another "CLC" credential that stands for "certificate as a lactation counselor." These people are not "certified" but rather are issued a certificate of attendance for completing a 5-day counselor course.

Breastfeeding

259

What You Need to Know About Breastfeeding in the Workplace

If you plan to return to work and wish to continue breastfeeding, since October 2001, all employers in the state of California are required to provide their employees who are nursing mothers with a private place, other than a restroom stall, in close proximity to their work station to pump breast milk. This place may be in the employee's work station. Employers are also required to provide unpaid breaks for these employees to pump milk. (Section 3.8, Section 1030, Part 3 of Division 2 of the Labor Code.) For more information, visit www.wicworks.ca.gov.

Make sure you ask a lactation consultant exactly which "CLC" credential they have. Other lactation consultants may be Certified Lactation Educators (CLEs). This means that they are qualified to teach breast-feeding classes and field questions over the phone. Certifications are helpful guides in knowing what kind of training a lactation consultant has had; however, no credential can ensure the best service. Be sure to interview or at least speak by phone with a lactation consultant before hiring one.

At many hospitals, a certified lactation consultant may visit a new mother in the maternity unit upon request or referral, or you can hire a lactation consultant privately to make a hospital visit. However, since a new mother's milk usually doesn't come in until 72 hours after delivery or later (well after discharge from the hospital, unless birth was by Caesarean section), assistance may not be needed until arriving at home. A lactation consultant will evaluate any initial breastfeeding challenges, and typically develops a plan for a new mother and baby with one or several follow-up consultations to track progress and the baby's weight.

Lactation consultants are either hospital-based or work in private practices, either individually or in a group. Some hospitals, such as Kaiser Permanente, offer lactation consultations either free or for a nominal fee, as they are part of the hospital's health plan and as such are available to members only. Fees for most hospital-based initial consultations, which include follow-up telephone advice, begin at $50 for the first session, which is typically at least an hour, and can go up to $100. Follow-up visits are usually less expensive. A private practice lactation consultant's rates range from $85 to $125 for an initial hour-long consultation. Similar to the hospitals, follow-up visits are less expensive, and telephone advice is usually free. At the more expensive end of this range are lactation consultants who do home visits, which they regard as the best way to help a breastfeeding mother. On a home visit, the lactation consultant gets a chance to see and assess the mother's environment, including the chair in which she is nursing. Some insurance companies cover the cost of these services, so be sure to request an insurance claim form, or a "super bill," at the end of a consultation. Also, some lactation consultants charge their fees on a "sliding scale," so be sure to ask whether or not they offer this service.

Breastfeeding mothers returning to work, or needing to leave their babies with someone else for a few hours, may want to pump breast milk for the baby to drink in their absence. A breast pump is helpful in relieving fullness as well. Many of the hospitals and lactation centers listed below rent or sell breast pumps, typically by the day, week, or month. Some private lactation consultants also rent them, or at least can help you rent one. The most efficient type of breast pump is a hospital-grade

The Mother's Milk Bank

Valley Medical Center, San Jose, 408-998-4550

One of 5 milk banks in the United States and the only one in California, the Mothers Milk Bank provides milk for special needs infants, including premature infants whose mothers cannot breastfeed. Donors are screened for HIV, HTLV, hepatitis B and C, rubella, TB, and syphilis. They pump their milk into provided freezer bags or sterilized glass bottles. Donors may deliver milk in a cooler to the bank or may arrange for pickup. If you have milk to spare and wish to be a donor, contact the bank at the above number.

electric pump, emptying the breast quickly and comfortably. Other types include a battery-operated pump and a manual pump. While these pumps are less expensive, they are also much less efficient, taking longer to empty the breast. If unsure of your need, we suggest renting a hospital-grade pump to decide whether or not you'd like to buy one.

Joining a group of breastfeeding mothers is a great way to enlist support and share your frustrations and successes. The following Bay Area hospitals and parent resource centers sponsor such groups and offer lactation support. Most hospitals' lactation centers are staffed with board-certified lactation consultants and/or certified lactation educators. In addition, some of the nanny agencies mentioned in Chapter 9 and postpartum care agencies and parenting resource centers, under the Baby Nurses and Postpartum Doulas section above, offer lactation consultant placements and referrals, so be sure not to miss them!

Entire Bay Area

Bay Area Lactation Associates (BALA)

510-524-5521

PARENT RATING: ☆ ☆ ☆ ☆ ☆

Serving the entire Bay Area, this non-profit organization is the Bay Area affiliate of the International Lactation Consultants Association. Their membership consists of nearly 100 breastfeeding professionals, including RNs, IBCLCs, and other licensed health care providers who provide breastfeeding consultations, information, and products, including the sale and rental of breast pumps. They include only those professionals who carry current professional liability insurance.

La Leche League of Northern California

28 W. Summit Dr.
Emeryville
650-363-1470 (referral line for local leaders)
800-LA-LECHE (525-3243) (national organization)
www.lalecheleague.org

Jury Service and Breastfeeding

Since 2002, the State of California exempts breastfeeding mothers from jury duty, and requires the State to take steps to eliminate the need for the mother to appear in court to make this request. For more information, visit www.wicworks.ca.gov. (Section 210.5 to the Code of Civil Procedure.)

This international nonprofit group is the mecca of breastfeeding support. Local chapters provide education, information, and support to women who want to breastfeed. La Leche offers free monthly meetings and support groups in various locations throughout the Bay Area, and a popular publication, *The Womanly Art of Breastfeeding*. Babies are always welcome at meetings. They also provide over-the-phone advice and online breastfeeding support, tips and information on breastfeeding, including where to rent an electric breast pump. Please be aware that the phone numbers listed for La Leche leaders in this section may be the home numbers of their volunteers.

San Francisco

Birthsisters

415-608-8308

www.birthsisters.com

See below under individual lactation consultants.

California Pacific Medical Center Newborn Connections

3698 California St., 1st Fl.

415-600-BABY (2229)

www.cpmc.org/newbornconnections

PARENT RATING: ☆ ☆ ☆ ☆ ☆

CPMC's Newborn Connections offers a breastfeeding assistance program, including free telephone advice, private one-on-one consultations with 10 internationally board-certified lactation consultants, and a breastfeeding mothers' support group that meets 3 times a week (visit their website for schedule and topics). New mothers benefit from the network of friends and discussion topics presented at the breastfeeding support groups, which are offered 3 times a week and are facilitated by a lactation expert. During the meetings, you can share experiences with other mothers and discuss specific topics of interest. They also offer breast pumps (rentals and sales) and a great selection of nursing bras and apparel in their boutique. Elaine Jewel, IBCLC, one of the consultants, was highly recommended by several mothers.

DayOne

For full description see under Baby Nurses and Postpartum Doulas—San Francisco and North Bay.

PARENT RATING: ☆ ☆ ☆ ☆ ☆

There is nothing like this state-of-the-art, privately run center for new and expectant parents, offering everything you need for successful breastfeeding and care for your newborn. DayOne offers an inviting and supportive environment in which to nurse your baby, internationally board-certified lactation consultants, certified lactation educators and registered nurses, breast pump rentals and sales, a current book and video library, and a beautiful boutique that features San Francisco's largest selection of nursing bras and other nursing and baby accessories and apparel. They offer one-on-one hour-long lactation consultations that can usually be scheduled the same day that you call. They offer telephone support from lactation consultants, breastfeeding classes and workshops, and feature a full-service Medela breast pump station including Symphony and Classic hospital-grade pumps for rent and sale. They also offer high-quality, effective herbal supplements designed to increase milk supply and a specially formulated multivitamin supplement for new mothers. Ask about their Breastfeeding Value Package, which includes an initial lactation consultation, 5 breastfeeding support group sessions, and baby weight tracking. DayOne's "new parent groups" meet throughout the week and often include discussions on breastfeeding. Join other nursing mothers to share tips and experiences pertinent to breastfeeding, including expressing and storing breast milk, breastfeeding in public, and taking care of the nursing mother. They also offer many workshops, including one about losing weight while breastfeeding, which is given by a registered dietician. Nancy Held, RN, MS, IBCLC, is the Executive Director of DayOne. She is joined by fellow DayOne owners and well-respected lactation consultants, Sara Duskin, CLE, IBCLC, and Bonnie Rosenstein, CLE. The retail staff members are all educated in using breastfeeding equipment, fitting nursing bras, and more! Comments: "First-rate care, service, and support. . . . A great place to go to meet other new moms who are going through all the joys and challenges that you are. . . . The people at DayOne couldn't be more supportive and encouraging!" See also Chapters 1, 2, 4, 6, and 9.

Kaiser Permanente Breastfeeding Center

2200 O'Farrell St.
415-833-3236 (breastfeeding center)
415-833-BABY (breastfeeding advice and appointments)

PARENT RATING: ☆ ☆ ☆ ☆

The center offers lactation consultations and breast pumps for rent and sale. They also sell breastfeeding supplies, including bras, bottles, and pads at a discount for Kaiser members. Comment: "Invaluable!"

La Leche League

San Francisco/Peninsula
650-363-1470
Call this number to locate a leader and meeting near you. See above under Entire Bay Area for full description.

Nursing Mothers Counsel (NMC)

650-327-6455 (referral line for the San Francisco and San Mateo chapter)
NMC is a nonprofit, nonaffiliated volunteer organization whose goal is to help mothers enjoy a positive breastfeeding experience. They have provided free information and support to nursing mothers since 1955. Counselors mainly offer over-the-phone assistance but also will make home visits for difficult situations. NMC also offers breast pump sales and rentals and often sponsors local talks on topics pertaining to breastfeeding.

San Francisco General Hospital Women's Health Center

1001 Potrero Ave.
415-206-3409
www.sfgh.org
The center offers private lactation consultations and breast pump rentals.

Seton Medical Center
The Breastfeeding Center
1900 Sullivan Ave.
Daly City
650-991-6435
www.setonmedicalcenter.org
The Breastfeeding Center is located on
the third floor of the hospital, across
from the nursery, and offers in-person
consultations by appointment, breast
pump rentals and sales, nursing bras,
and pillows. Join other new moms and
lactation educators at a free weekly
breastfeeding support group.

Silver Avenue Family
Health Center
1525 Silver Ave.
415-715-0300
This center offers breastfeeding assistance, including office consultations,
home visits, and telephone advice to
all clients, including women who are
eligible under the federally funded
Special Supplemental Nutrition
Program for Women, Infants, and
Children known as the WIC program.
(See under North Bay.)

Best Places to Nurse and Change  Baby when Out and About

When out with baby, it always helps to know where you might
change his diaper, or where you might stop to nurse her. Here are
some Bay Area parents' favorite spots:

◆ Nordstrom (Among mothers, Nordstrom is known for having a
  semiprivate room for nursing and clean changing facilities in its
  women's lounge as well as a "family room" in some locations.)

◆ Baby and children's stores (The Right Start, Gymboree, Baby
  Gap, as well as the larger baby gear retailers, have changing
  tables and have seen a nursing mother before!)

◆ Parent resource centers (DayOne, Natural Resources,
  Bananas, Blossom Birth, Barefoot and Pregnant, etc. are here
  to support new parents!)

◆ Coffee shops and bookstores (or any stores that have chairs
  scattered about and don't mind people lingering) offer a place
  to sit and nurse, albeit not a private one.

St. Luke's Hospital
The Breastfeeding Center
2555 Cesar Chavez St., 5th Fl.
415-641-6869
www.stlukes-sf.org

This hospital offers breastfeeding assistance, including office consultations and support groups, as well as breast pump sales and rentals. Ask for Mary Janowitz, RN, IBCLC (by appointment only).

University of California at San Francisco Medical Center
The Women's Health Resource Center
2356 Sutter St.
415-353-2667
www.ucsf.edu/whrc/lactation.html

The Women's Health Resource Center at UCSF offers lactation consultations as well as free telephone advice and breast pump rentals and sales. They feature state-of-the-art equipment and products to assist with breastfeeding, including pumps, nursing bras, nursing pads, and breastfeeding pillows. They are an official Medela and Hollister/Egnell Breastpump Rental station, as well as a WIC breast pump station for the San Francisco Department of Public Health. Women who have Medi-Cal may be eligible for rental benefits at no charge.

North Bay

La Leche League
North Bay/Sonoma County
707-523-8697
See under Entire Bay Area.

La Leche League of Marin
415-721-2842 (breastfeeding hotline)
See under Entire Bay Area.

Marin General Hospital, Lactation Center
250 Bon Air Rd., Rm. 4216
415-925-7522
www.maringeneral.com

PARENT RATING: ☆ ☆ ☆ ☆ ☆

The Lactation Center at Marin General provides counseling and support services for all Bay Area breastfeeding moms. The Lactation Center is located in the pediatric section of the hospital, next to the Family Birthing Center. Chris Costello, IBCLC, runs the center, and survey moms just love her! She and other certified lactation counselors and nurses are available for in-person breastfeeding consultations and education. Telephone advice is also available. The center offers a weekly drop-in breastfeeding support group open to all Bay Area nursing moms. The center works in cooperation with the BabyNook store, located next door, which offers breast pump sales and breastfeeding accessories, including nursing bras, nursing pillows, nursing apparel, and baby clothing and products.

Queen of the Valley Hospital
1000 Trancas St.
Napa
707-252-6541
www.thequeen.org

This hospital offers a breastfeeding support group through Napa's Healthy Moms and Babies Program.

Santa Rosa Memorial Hospital
The Family Birth Center
1165 Montgomery Dr.
Santa Rosa 707-525-5212 (infant nutrition/lactation services)

www.stjosephhealth.org/services/
lactation

This hospital offers lactation consultations and over-the-phone advice.

Sutter Medical Center of Santa Rosa
The Women's Health and Resource Center

625 Steele Ln.
Santa Rosa
707-576-4800
www.suttersantarosa.org

The Women's Health and Resource Center offers one-on-one lactation consultations and weekly breastfeeding workshops in English and Spanish. They also rent and sell pumps and breastfeeding supplies, including nursing apparel and bras at their retail store, The Source for Women, 707-523-8697.

Sutter Solano Medical Center

300 Hospital Dr.
Vallejo
707-554-4444
707-645-7316 (Great Beginnings Clinic)
www.suttersolano.org

This hospital offers one-on-one lactation consultations by appointment with Sandy Costa, RN. Call the above number for the Great Beginnings Clinic to make an appointment.

Women, Infants, and Children Program (WIC)

361 3rd St., Ste. C
San Rafael
415-499-6889
www.wicworks.ca.gov

WIC is a nutritional supplemental service that serves low-income families, providing nutritional counseling, education, and support for prenatal and postnatal women. They offer breastfeeding support groups and lactation consultants, as well as breast pumps, free of charge. They have an excellent website that features California breastfeeding laws and resolutions.

East Bay

Alta Bates Summit Medical Center

2450 Ashby Ave.
Berkeley
510-204-4444
510-204-6546 (The Breastfeeding Support Program)
www.altabates.com

This hospital offers a breastfeeding support group that meets twice a week at 2500 Ashby Ave. They also rent and sell breast pumps and breastfeeding supplies. While they offer telephone advice, they do not offer one-on-one lactation consultations at this time. They do, however, offer referrals for lactation consultations and as this book goes to press they are in the "design" phase of a full-fledged lactation center.

Birth Professionals of the Bay Area

Oakland
510-595-5534
www.birthprofessionals.milagros.org

See above under Baby Nurses and Portpartum Doulas.

Children's Hospital Oakland Breastfeeding Support Center

5400 Telegraph Ave.
Oakland
510-428-3000

www.childrenshospitaloakland.org
The center offers breastfeeding consultations by appointment. They offer breast pump rentals and a class on returning to work while breastfeeding.

Contra Costa Breastfeeding Advice Line
1-866-878-7767
This advice line is run by the Supplemental Nutrition Program for Women, Infants, and Children known as the WIC program. See under North Bay.

Eden Medical Center
The Women's Center
20103 Lake Chabot Rd.
Castro Valley
510-727-2715 or 510-537-1234
Eden offers postpartum lactation support at its on-site lactation center.

Highland Hospital (Alameda County Medical Center)
1411 E. 31st St.
Oakland
510-437-4800
510-437-4792
www.acmedctr.org
This hospital offers breastfeeding counseling to new mothers by appointment.

John Muir Medical Lactation Center
1656 N. California Blvd., Ste. 110
Walnut Creek
925-952-2777
PARENT RATING: ☆ ☆ ☆ ☆ ☆
Staffed by board-certified lactation educators, this center offers a full range of lactation support services, including one-on-one consultations, classes, breastfeeding supplies, and breast pump rentals and sales.

Kaiser Permanente
www.kaiserpermanente.org
• Antioch Medical Offices
3400 Delta Fair Blvd.
925-779-5192
This out-patient clinic offers breastfeeding assistance by appointment with Linda Draper, nurse practitioner and lactation consultant.
• Hayward Medical Center
27400 Hesperian Blvd.
510-784-2804 (lactation warm line)
510-784-4545 (breast pump rentals and sales)
510-784-6481 (appointments)
This hospital offers lactation support and consultations. Linda Harrell, RN, IBCLC, calls new mothers 4-5 days after they've returned home from the hospital to check to see if they have any breastfeeding questions. She offers one-on-one consultations by appointment. Call the warm line (above) at any time for over-the-phone advice, and a consultant will return your call within 24 hours. They also offer a breastfeeding support group in the Pediatric Clinic in the Sleepy Hollow Building on the second floor where they rent breast pumps and sell breastfeeding accessories.
• Oakland Medical Center
280 W. MacArthur Blvd.
Oakland
510-752-7557 (breastfeeding warm line advice and appointments)
510-752-2200 (pre-recorded breastfeeding information line)
www.kaiseroakland.org
Located in the pediatric clinic, this center offers breastfeeding consultations

through the After Care Center and Lactation Clinic which is open to Kaiser members only. Joanne Jasson, RN, IBCL, and her team of 3 other lactation consultants are available for one-on-one lactation consultations by appointment at the above number. They also rent breast pumps through the health education center at 3772 Howe Street and offer "Breastfeeding and the Working Mom," a class on breastfeeding while returning to work. One session is offered monthly.

- Pleasanton Medical Center
  7601 Stoneridge Dr., 925-847-5172 (health education)

This hospital offers one-on-one lactation consultations with Karin Gee, RN, CLC, by appointment.

- Walnut Creek Medical Center
  Walnut Creek
  1425 S. Main St.
  925-295-4368

They offer out-patient lactation consultations by appointment through Pat Ross, RN, IBCLC.

Other Resources for Breastfeeding

◆ www.breastfeeding.com
  This website contains helpful breastfeeding information, support, humor, and links.

◆ www.breastfeedingbasics.com
  This site offers answers to commonly asked questions about breastfeeding, as well as practical solutions to breastfeeding issues.

◆ www.aap.org
  This is the American Academy of Pediatrics website that includes many articles on breastfeeding.

◆ www.askdrsears.com
  This website includes all you would ever want to know about breastfeeding, including information about taking medications while nursing.

◆ www.babycenter.com
  This parenting site includes a lot of helpful tips and information about breastfeeding.

◆ *The Complete Book of Breastfeeding*, by Marvin S. Eiger, MD

◆ *The Nursing Mother's Companion*, by Kathleen Huggins, RNMS

◆ *Nursing Mother, Working Mother*, by Gale Pryor

◆ *The Nursing Mother's Problem Solver*, by Claire Martin (editor), et al.

◆ *The Breastfeeding Book*, by Martha Sears, RN, and William Sears, MD

◆ *The Ultimate Breastfeeding Book*, by Jack Newman and Teresa Pitman

La Leche League

East Bay referral line, 510-496-6009
Diablo/Contra Costa County, 925-274-3748
See under Entire Bay Area.

The Nurture Center

3399 Mount Diablo Blvd.
Lafayette
925-283-1346
www.nurturecenter.com
PARENT RATING: ☆ ☆ ☆ ☆ ☆

Among a plethora of extremely helpful offerings (including 26 classes), this impressive community resource center for new and expectant parents offers a Nursing Moms' Group. Topics discussed include sore nipples, engorgement, nursing in public, sex and breastfeeding, deciding when to wean, and other topics of interest to nursing moms. Deanna Jesus is the Program Director and Kay Goodyear, IBCLC, and her similarly well-qualified colleagues facilitate the discussion. They also offer breast pump rentals and sales and nursing apparel. (See Chapters 1, 4, and 6 for full description.)

San Ramon Regional Medical Center
The Breastfeeding Resource Center

6001 Norris Canyon Rd.
San Ramon
925-275-8459 (general information and appointments)
925-275-8447 (warm line)
www.sanramonmedctr.com
Certified lactation consultants offer education and support. The resource center also offers breastfeeding apparel and breast pumps for rental and sale.

Sutter Delta Medical Center

3901 Lonetree Way
Antioch
925-779-7200, ext. 4206
This center has a single lactation consultant who leads a breastfeeding support group. Babies and second- and third-time moms are welcome! Ask for Kimberly Chilcote, RN, IBCLC, and childbirth educator.

Valleycare Medical Center

5555 W. Las Positas Blvd.
Pleasanton
925-847-3000
925-416-3589 (lactation services)
www.valleycare.com
This hospital offers private lactation consultations and breast pump rentals and sales.

Washington Hospital

2000 Mowry Ave.
Fremont
510-797-1111
510-791-3423 (lactation services)
www.whhs.com
This hospital offers one-on-one lactation consultations, including free "latch clinics." They also rent breast pumps at their lactation center which is across the street from the hospital and open to the public.

South Bay

Blossom Birth Services

1000 Elwell Center
Palo Alto
650-964-7380
www.blossombirth.com
PARENT RATING: ☆ ☆ ☆ ☆ ☆

Among a plethora of other new parent needs, Blossom Birth Services offers breastfeeding support and referrals. See above under Baby Nurses and Postpartum Doulas for full description. Visit their website for their list of local providers.

Breastfeeding Care Center

32 W. 25th Ave.
San Mateo
800-205-0333 (WIC breastfeeding telephone help line)

Sponsored by a federally funded program, this center offers lactation consultation by appointment and lends breast pumps to women eligible under the Supplemental Nutrition Program for Women, Infants, and Children known as the WIC program. They also run a breastfeeding telephone help line and offer all services in English and Spanish. Based in San Mateo, they also have sites in Daly City, South San Francisco, Redwood City, Palo Alto, and Half Moon Bay.

Community Hospital of Los Gatos

815 Pollard Rd.
Los Gatos
408-871-7479 (parenting and breastfeeding services)
408-866-3905 (to schedule a lactation consultation)

PARENT RATING: ☆ ☆ ☆ ☆ ☆

This hospital offers one-on-one lactation consultations with International Board Certified Lactation Consultants, as well as breast pump rentals and sales, nursing bras and breastfeeding accessories, and a breastfeeding support group.

El Camino Hospital

Maternal Connections
Lactation Center
La Casa Real
2400 Hospital Dr., Ste. 1B
Mountain View
650-988-8287

PARENT RATING: ☆ ☆ ☆ ☆ ☆

Staffed by IBCLC registered nurses, Maternal Connections is a full-service lactation center offering lactation consultations, sales and rentals of breast pumps and supplies, videos, books, other educational materials on breastfeeding, and nursing apparel. You need not have delivered your baby there to use their services. A drop-in breastfeeding support group is also offered.

Good Samaritan of Santa Clara Valley

2425 Samaritan Dr., Rm. 410
San Jose
408-559-BABY (2229) (parenting and breastfeeding services)
www.goodsamsj.org

Good Samaritan's parenting and breastfeeding services offer over-the-phone advice and one-on-one consultations with International Board Certified Lactation Consultants. They also have a boutique that offers breast pump rentals and sales and accessories. Good Samaritan also offers a breastfeeding support group.

Healthy Horizons Breastfeeding Center

329 Primrose Rd., Ste. 103
Burlingame
650-579-2726 (appointments)
650-347-6455 (breastfeeding center)
www.babiesandmom.com

This full-service breastfeeding center offers private one-on-one lactation consultations as well as home visits. They also offer "latch checks," whereby a mother and her baby come in for a 15-minute mini-consultation to check for proper "latch-on." They rent and sell breast pumps and carry a large inventory of nursing supplies, including nursing bras for which they offer free fittings. They have hospital contracts with Seton Hospital and Mills Peninsula and staff the latter's breastfeeding question line and host free support groups for new breastfeeding mothers. In addition to serving the Peninsula, they serve the East Bay and San Francisco.

Kaiser Permanente

- Kaiser Redwood City
  Breastfeeding Center
  610 Walnut St. (in the pediatric clinic)
  650-299-2692
  www.kaiserpermanente.org

The center offers a full range of post-partum breastfeeding support.

- Kaiser Permanente Santa Clara
  Medical Center
  900 Kiely Blvd.
  408-236-6400
  408-236-5650 (newborn clinic)
  www.kaisersantaclara.org

This hospital offers one-on-one lactation consultations by appointment. You can also rent or buy a breast pump at their main pharmacy.

- Kaiser Permanente Santa Teresa
  Medical Center
  250 Hospital Pkwy.
  San Jose
  408-972-3000
  408-972-6715 (classes)
  www.kaiserpermanente.org

This hospital hosts an "after-delivery breastfeeding group appointment" which is led by a certified lactation educator in a small setting of no more than 4-6 new mothers.

La Leche League of the Peninsula
650-363-1470
See above under Entire Bay Area for full description.

- Menlo Park/Palo Alto chapter
  650-365-2070

They offer evening meetings, especially for mothers employed outside of the home.

- Santa Clara County chapter
  408-264-0994
- Sunnyvale chapter
  650-969-4713

Lucile Packard Children's Hospital Stanford University Medical Center-Lactation Center
725 Welch Rd.
Palo Alto
650-725-8767
650-723-9366 (breast pump rentals)

At the time this book goes to press, this lactation center is not offering out-patient lactation consultations or advice. We understand the hospital is reorganizing and that the center plans to re-open.

Peninsula Medical Center (Mills-Peninsula Health Services)
1783 El Camino Real
Burlingame
650-696-5600 (The Wellness Center and Community Education)
650-696-5151 (non-urgent breastfeeding question line)
www.mills-peninsula.org
PARENT RATING: ☆ ☆ ☆ ☆ ☆

The Wellness Center and Community Education department offers a class on breastfeeding and the working mom. Mills Health Center (1000 S. San Mateo Dr., San Mateo) hosts the Nursing Mothers Council. This drop-in breastfeeding support group meets weekly.

Nursing Mothers Counsel (NMC)

408-272-1448 (referral line for Santa Clara)
831-621-8412 (referral line for Santa Cruz)
650-327-6455 (referral line for San Mateo)

NMC is a nonprofit, nonaffiliated volunteer organization whose goal is to help mothers enjoy a positive breastfeeding experience. They have provided free information and support to nursing mothers since 1955. Counselors mainly offer over-the-phone assistance but also will make home visits for difficult situations. NMC also offers breast pump sales and rentals and often sponsors local talks on topics pertaining to breastfeeding.

O'Connor Hospital

2105 Forest Ave.
San Jose
408-947-2743

This hospital has a lactation consultant who offers private consultations. It also offers a weekly Nursing Mothers' Circle.

Palo Alto Medical Foundation

795 Camino Real
Palo Alto
650-853-2992
http://www.pamf.org

This group offers lactation consultations through Joanna Koch, IBCLC.

Regional Medical Center of San Jose

225 N. Jackson Ave.
San Jose
408-259-5000

This center offers a breastfeeding clinic for postpartum mothers.

Sutter Maternity and Surgery Center of Santa Cruz

2900 Chanticleer Ave.
Santa Cruz
831-477-2229
www.suttermatsurg.org

Lactation counseling and education is provided by Lili Wenzel Beggs, RN, IBCLC. Lili is a Sutter Perinatal Staff Nurse who has also worked with the Nursing Mothers Counsel, counseling breastfeeding mothers for the past 10 years. You can schedule a consultation appointment by calling the above number. The Lactation Center also rents Medela pumps.

St. Louise Regional Hospital

9400 No Name Uno
Gilroy
408-848-8663

Call Jana Tomasini for details regarding breast pump rentals and a weekly breastfeeding support group.

Sequoia Hospital

Maternity and Family Education Program
702 Marshall St.
Redwood City
650-367-5597 (calm line for telephone advice)
650-368-2229 (Health and Wellness Services for appointments)
www.sequoiahospital.org

Lactation consultants are available by appointment at Health and Wellness Services. The calm line, which is answered by lactation-trained Registered Nurses, is open on weekday afternoons. Sequoia Hospital also has a Family Room for parents who wish to weigh and feed their babies. They also have a new store that offers a variety of breast pumps, bras, and breastfeeding supplies for purchase. Medela pumps are available to rent.

INDIVIDUAL LACTATION CONSULTANTS

San Francisco

Sara Duskin, RN, CLE, IBCLC
415-386-9250
Sara is a lactation specialist and parent educator who works with many Bay Area families with newborns, twins, and preemies. She offers home visits for lactation support, sleep consultations, and general parenting support. See under Baby Nurses and Postpartum Doulas.

Michele Mason, CLE, IBCLC
415-550-9221
www.childfriendly.org
Michele Mason is a Lactation Specialist and Educator who has consulted new mothers and their babies since 1990, both independently and through groups and classes at San Francisco's Natural Resources. She offers personalized support services designed to kindle natural parenting instincts, giving parents a deeper sense of confidence with their babies. Founder of the Child Friendly Initiative, Inc., Michele is a nationally known advocate for children and their care-

givers. Michele serves on The Mother's Council in New York City and resides in San Francisco with her husband and 3 children. (See also under new moms support groups in Ch. 6.)

Georgia Montgomery, CD, CCE, LE (IBCL)
Birthsisters
415-608-8308
www.birthsisters.com
Georgia Montgomery, CD, CCE, LR, BLS, a member of the Birth Doulas of Marin, offers childbirth education and services as well as newborn care and education and lactation support. She will visit you at home and also in the hospital if requested.

Marsha Podd, RN, CLE
415-883-4442
www.gotosleepbaby.com
Marsha has over 20 years of experience as an OB/GYN nurse and Certified Lactation Educator, and she also has a degree in Child Development. In addition to lactation consultations, she also offers sleep consultations, either in person or by telephone.

East Bay

Joanne Bergeson, RN, IBCLC
510-881-8269

East Bay Breastfeeding Support Service
510-525-1155, Janaki Costello, IBCLC, ICCE
510-849-1271, Miriam Levitt, IBCLC
510-524-6917, Sue Wirth, IBCLC
This popular private practice group of certified lactation consultants is available for in-home consultations. This group also offers breast pumps for

sale and rental and serves Berkeley, El Cerrito, Oakland, and Richmond.

Meegan Ferrill, IBCLC, CLE
925-462-8786
Meegan works out of Healthy Horizons in Burlingame but will come to see you in the East Bay too!

Joan Gress, RN, IBCLC
510-204-4671

South Bay

Marcie Bertram, IBCLC
San Carlos
650-593-3659

Janice Curry, RN, IBCLC
San Jose
408-223-1134

Sheila Janaakos, MPH. IBCLC
650-579-2726
Sheila is one of the primary lactation consultants who staff Healthy Horizons in Burlingame (see above).

Joanna Koch, IBCLC
Los Altos
650-967-8715
650-853-2992

Laurie Schmiesing, RN, CLE, ICBLC
Mountain View
650-965-9219
Laurie teaches the breastfeeding class at Blossom Birth Services in Palo Alto. At this time, she is not offering at-home lactation consultation, but does rent and sell breast pumps and offers telephone advice and support.

Resources for Dealing with Postpartum Depression

Since the first edition of this book was published, much information has appeared in the media about postpartum depression. Celebrities such as Brooke Shields, who recently wrote of her own experience in her book *Down Came the Rain, My Journey through Postpartum Depression,* also have made postpartum depression more of a household word today. Postpartum depression (PPD) is a combination of symptoms that may occur any time during the first year following the birth of a baby. Symptoms in a new mother range from mild sadness or crying to a complete inability to care for herself or her baby. If you are a new mom and suspect that you are experiencing postpartum depression, contact your lactation consultant, obstetrician, pediatrician, or one of the many resources listed below. In addition, many medical centers in the Bay Area offer support groups for new parents, including groups that focus on helping mothers cope with postpartum depression. If you don't see your hospital listed here, call and ask whether they currently offer a support group. Also, for more information about postpartum depression, see *Beyond the Blues: Prenatal and*

Postpartum Depression—A Treatment Manual by Dr. Shoshanna Bennett and Dr. Peck Indeman, 2 of the Bay Area's best known professionals in the field, see below. Remember, you are not alone, and PPD is very treatable.

San Francisco and North Bay

California Pacific Medical Center Newborn Connections

3698 California St., 1st Fl.
San Francisco
415-600-BABY (2229)
www.cpmc.org/newbornconnections

This center offers a Postpartum Support Group for postpartum women experiencing emotional challenges after delivery—it is the only group of its kind in San Francisco. They offer help, understanding, and coping skills to reduce anxiety and develop realistic expectations. Join the drop-in weekly support group and get immediate help to alleviate overwhelming relationship difficulties, problems with sleeping, anxiety, depression, and intrusive thoughts. Meet other moms to lessen the isolation that often accompanies postpartum stress. Joanne Foote, MS, and Ceres Rutan, MA, co-facilitate this therapeutic support group. They are both mothers of small children and doctoral candidates in clinical psychology. Both have been treating postpartum depression for 5 years.

Jane Cunningham, MFT

415-459-8048

Nancy Gump, MFT

415-453-5333

Jane and Nancy are licensed marriage and family and child therapists with a focus on nurturing the mother.

They have been in Marin since 1985 and specialize in parenting, relationship issues (especially the issues surrounding couples after the birth of a child), creativity and work, and inner resources. They offer their services to individuals, couples, and mothers' groups.

Elizabeth Greason, LCSW

1036 Sir Francis Drake Blvd.
Kentfield
415-454-2636

Elizabeth runs PPD support groups and offers individual counseling. She specializes in working with women who are having difficulty adjusting to having a child.

Bethany Miller, PsyD

- San Francisco
  3020 Fillmore St.
- San Rafael
  711 D St., Ste. 207

415-518-7999
www.drbethnaymiller.com

Dr. Miller works with postpartum women in her private practice in her San Francisco and San Rafael offices. She has been working with postpartum women for the past 4 years and has specialized training and expertise in treating postpartum mood and anxiety disorders. She also provides support to new mothers (and fathers) who are finding the transition to parenthood stressful.

Postpartum Depression Resources

Bay Area Postpartum Stress line
1-888-773-7090
This stress line is available from 9 a.m. to 9 p.m. every day of the week.

Postpartum International
www.postpartum.net
This website hosts a worldwide referral network of local support groups and professionals dealing with PPD.

www.postpartumdepressionhelp.com

www.postpartum.net

Dr. Kathy Waller, MD
415-990-1579
Kathy is a UCSF-trained psychiatrist practicing in Marin County. She offers comprehensive mental health treatment for women in the postpartum period.

East Bay

Elizabeth Gayner, PsyD
- San Francisco
  1529 20th St.
  415-487-7402
- Oakland
  5835 College Ave., Ste. B3
  510-390-3060

Elizabeth is a licensed clinical psychologist, specializing in pre- and postpartum support groups for mothers, new mom adjustments, as well as individual counseling.

Alisa Genovese, MFT
510-286-7599
Alisa is a marriage and family therapist who among other services offers one-on-one counseling for mothers dealing with postpartum depression.

Birthways
See under Baby Nurses and Postpartum Doulas—East Bay.
A nonprofit, volunteer organization, Birthways offers a class entitled Prenatal and Postpartum Realities which addresses risk factors for pre- and postpartum depression and anxiety, warning signs, when to seek help, and steps to healing. Screening and resources are available.

John Muir Medical Center
1601 Ygnacio Valley Rd.
Walnut Creek
510-889-6017 (Dr. Shoshanna Bennett)
www.johnmuirmtdiablo.com
JMMC offers a free Perinatal and Postnatal Stress Support Group which is facilitated by Shoshanna Bennett, PhD. The group is open to the public.

Postpartum Depression

Lee Safran, MFT

1201 Solano Ave., Ste. #201
Albany
510-496-6096
www.leesafran.com

Lee is a certified marriage and family therapist offering psychotherapy for individuals, couples, and groups. In her private practice she focuses on prenatal, pregnancy, and postpartum issues. She offers individuals assessments and therapy, and also runs an ongoing Postpartum Stress Support Group that meets biweekly in North Berkeley. The benefit of the support group is to learn that you are not alone in your experience. Visit her website for details.

Dr. Shoshanna Bennett, Postpartum Assistance for Mothers (PAM)

Castro Valley
510-889-6017

One of the first Bay Area counselors to specialize in helping women with postpartum depression, psychotherapist Dr. Shoshanna Bennett is the president of Postpartum Support International. She also founded Postpartum Assistance for Mothers (PAM) in 1987. PAM offers support groups where women can share experiences, coping techniques, and parenting anxieties in a safe environment in the East Bay, South Bay, and South San Francisco areas. Dr. Bennett also counsels clients individually, providing a concrete strategy for recovery. She makes home visits when necessary and offers telephone support for women all over the country. Dr. Bennett is also the president of the Postpartum Health Alliance, a statewide organization.

South Bay

Dr. Peck Indman, EdD, MFT

San Jose
408-252-5552

She runs support groups for PPD and offers individual counseling.

The Stanford Treatment Research Center

701 Welch Rd.
Palo Alto
650-723-5886

This center conducts occasional studies of various treatments for depression during and after pregnancy, such as acupuncture and massage. Treatment is at no cost with most Bay Area providers. For more information call the above number or Dr. Rachel Manber at 650-724-2377, or e-mail STRC@med.stanford.edu.

Bay Area Postpartum Hot Line

888-773-7090

This hotline is staffed 7 days a week from 9 a.m. to 9 p.m. by volunteers from The Northern California Chapter of the Postpartum Health Alliance. All volunteers are survivors of PPD, and some speak Spanish. Leave a message, and your call will be promptly returned.

Hotlines, Warm Lines, and Stress Lines

Being a parent is an awesome responsibility—we all know that it comes with its share of challenges. When a new parent feels out of control, or needs a good listener and some reassurance, a hotline, warm line, or stress line can be of great assistance. It's nice to know that people are out there waiting to listen and wanting to help!

CRISIS LINES

Child Help Hotline
800-4-A-CHILD (422-4453)
The focus of this hotline is the prevention and treatment of child abuse.

Child Abuse Reporting Hotline
415-558-2650

PARENTING AND CHILD DEVELOPMENT ADVICE, WARM LINES, AND HOTLINES

San Francisco

Parents Place
415-931-WARM (9276) (8:30 a.m.-5 p.m.)
PARENT RATING: ☆ ☆ ☆ ☆ ☆
This is an advice line for parents with young children. Comment: "Great advice, great therapists."

TALK Line—Family Support Center
1757 Waller St.
415-441-KIDS (5437)
Located in the Haight, Telephone Aid in Living with Kids (TALK) is a non-profit organization that offers Bay Area parents a place to talk about parenting challenges and other issues. They are best known for their 24-hour hotline that provides parents with a trained volunteer to consult with in times of need. Drop-ins are welcome. Counseling is priced on a sliding scale.

East Bay

Alameda County Child Protective Services
510-259-1800
This agency investigates reports of child abuse.

Children's Hospital Oakland Child Health Resource Line
800-400-PEDS (7337)

Bananas
5232 Claremont Ave.
Oakland
510-658-6046
www.bananasinc.com
They provide advice for parents and child care providers.

Parental Stress Service
510-893-5444 (Alameda County)
1-800-829-3777 (24-hour family support hotline for Alameda County)
This group offers supportive services to parents, caregivers, and children such as counseling and crisis intervention. They also offer referrals to Alameda County resources.

Contact Care

408-279-8228

They provide 24-hour help and reassurance and provide crisis intervention to parents in Santa Clara County.

Family Stress Center

925-827-0212

Family Stress Service

650-368-6655 (Daly City to San Mateo)
650-692-6655 (Belmont to Menlo Park)
650-726-6655 (on the San Mateo coast)

Parent Information and Referral Center—Lucile Packard Children's Hospital at Stanford

650-498-KIDS (5437) or 800-690-2282

This center answers questions concerning your child's health, behavior, development, and safety. Hours are 7 a.m.-11 p.m.

Parent Support Sequoia Hospital

650-368-2229

Parents Helping Parents

408-727-5775

Meal Preparation and Delivery

Forget about cooking in those early weeks of parenthood and enlist a friend or family member to prepare some meals for you. One of the great benefits of joining a mothers' club is that they generally will provide new moms with at least one postpartum meal! Alternatively, the Bay Area has a tremendous number of reasonably priced restaurants and services that offer take-out and meal delivery, as well as personal in-home chefs. Here are a few favorite meal preparation and delivery services of Bay Area parents:

Jessie et Laurent

415-485-1122 or 800-MEAL-TO-YOU
www.jessieetlaurent.com

Jessie and Laurent delivers meals "lovingly prepared from the freshest, seasonal ingredients" in San Francisco, Marin, Sonoma, East Bay, San Jose, and the Peninsula.

Angelina's

California and 22nd Ave.
415-221-7801

In addition to their wonderful lunch time offerings, Angelina's also offers scrumptious week-day dinners to go (Mon.-Thurs.)—perfect for busy families!

Besos Foods

415-495-5490

www.besofoods.com

Besos delivers "farm-fresh meal kits" which include all the ingredients you need to cook a gourmet meal at home in about 20 minutes!

A Chef's Eye

510-339-0503

www.achefseye

A Chef's Eye offers personal chef services for San Francisco and most of the East Bay.

ChowBabies

415-751-0410

www.chowbabies.com

PARENT RATING: ☆ ☆ ☆ ☆ ☆

They offer home delivery of organic foods for babies and toddlers.

Citrus Kitchen

415-884-9688

www.citruskithchen.com

Organic homemade meals are prepared for fridge and freezer storage.

Girlfriend's Kitchen

510-681-3186 or 925-685-5341

www.girlfriendskitchen.com

PARENT RATING: ☆ ☆ ☆ ☆ ☆

Chef Vanessa Davisson will do all the grocery shopping and come into your home and quickly and quietly prepare a week's worth of healthy and delicious meals for you and your family!

Home on the Range

510-251-8030

They cook several meals daily and deliver to Oakland, Alameda, San Francisco, and Contra Costa counties.

Jane Peal Cuisine

415-826-2133

www.pealcuisine.com

PARENT RATING: ☆ ☆ ☆ ☆ ☆

Jane Peal offers gourmet vegetarian cuisine delivered to your home.

Mangia/Nosh

415-472-2894

www.mangianosh.com

PARENT RATING: ☆ ☆ ☆ ☆ ☆

Mangia/Nosh is a catering company that offers "meals to go."

Petit Appetit

415-601-4916

www.petitappetit.com

Many parents are turning to Petit Appetit to help them put healthy home-cooked meals on the table which kids are sure to love! They provide tasty, fresh, all-natural food made especially for your infant or toddler, packaged for your refrigerator and ready to be served. Petit Appetit also offers informational workshops to groups and parenting resources, provides in-home cooking demonstrations and classes, a wonderful cookbook, and a newsletter.

Room Service of Marin

415-389-887

www.roomservicemarin.com

They deliver meals from restaurants to your home.

Tiny Tummies

707-251-0550

www.TinyTummies.com

This newsletter can help you raise happy, healthy eaters by offering suggestions on how to cook healthy food for the whole family.

Waiters on Wheels
San Francisco
415-452-6600
www.waitersonwheels.com
Waiters on Wheels delivers meals from restaurants to your home.

Wally's Food Company
415-771-1395
www.wallysfoodco.com
Wally's offers freshly made gourmet meals delivered to your home.

East Bay

Girlfriend's Kitchen
See under San Francisco and North Bay.

Home on the Range
See under San Francisco and North Bay.

A Chef's Eye
See under San Francisco and North Bay.

South Bay

Adrienne's Gourmet Cuisine
650-593-4003
www.theladychef.com
Adrienne, a personal chef, offers grocery shopping and out-of or in-home meal preparation.

To Go!
650-692-4200
www.mealstogo.com
This service delivers meals from restaurants to your home for a fee.

Waiters on Wheels
See under San Francisco and North Bay.

Grocery Delivery

Safeway offers online grocery ordering and delivery at www.safeway.com. In addition, some grocery stores deliver for free, provided that you go to the store and do the shopping yourself. Other stores listed here will do your shopping as well as deliver for a fee.

San Francisco and North Bay

The BOX (Bay Area Organic Express)
415-ORGANIC (674-2642)
www.organicbox.com
PARENT RATING: ☆ ☆ ☆ ☆

Have a box of 14 to 16 different organic veggies and fruits delivered to your doorstep every week or every other week! Delivery is available throughout most of the Bay Area from Los Gatos to San Rafael.

Cal-Mart
3585 California St.
415-751-3516
415-751-2744 (fax)
PARENT RATING: ☆ ☆ ☆ ☆ ☆

They deliver faxed orders received before 12 p.m. on Monday, Tuesday, Thursday, and Friday to surrounding neighborhoods. The fee is $10. Otherwise, do your own shopping before 2 p.m., and they'll deliver for free!

Marin Milkman

888-USE-MILK (1-888-873-6455)

PARENT RATING: ☆ ☆ ☆ ☆ ☆

They offer home delivery of organic milk and other dairy products.

The Milkman

925-376-3385 or 800-464-6455

PARENT RATING: ☆ ☆ ☆ ☆ ☆

Serving most of the Bay Area, The Milkman offers home delivery of almost any dairy product (including yogurt, ice cream, and cheese) and a limited number of groceries. They also deliver fully cooked frozen meals such as lasagna, enchiladas, chili, macaroni and cheese, burritos, and chicken nuggets for kids. The Milkman's real specialty is a variety of gourmet soups that are made in small batches without preservatives, available in frozen 40-ounce pouches. Call for an order form and to arrange weekly delivery.

Real Foods

3060 Fillmore St.

415-567-6900

Shop here and spend over $100, and they will deliver your groceries for free. Otherwise, you can call in your order and pay $5 for delivery in surrounding neighborhoods.

Whole Foods

1765 California St.

415-674-0500

Whole Foods has an arrangement with a personal shopper and delivery service person (Chris, 415-933-9041) who, for $15.95, will do your legwork for you. He serves most of the San Francisco metro area and Walnut Creek. Another service, called From Store to Door, also delivers from Whole Foods. They offer same-day delivery if you call 800-529-5761 or fax your order to 972-774-0865. You may also e-mail your order at ISCOM@aol.com.

Planet Organics

800-956-5855

www.planetorganics.com

PARENT RATING: ☆ ☆ ☆ ☆ ☆

Serving Marin and San Francisco, this organic produce and grocery service will deliver to your home your pick of organic delicacies, including fruits and vegetables and other organic groceries such as cereal and peanut butter, weekly or bi-weekly. They offer a user-friendly custom-order form on their website.

Diaper Services

The jury is still out as to whether cloth or disposable diapers are more environmentally friendly. Cloth diapers use energy and water to launder, while disposable diapers often go to a landfill. The costs are about the same. If you decide on cloth diapers, you'll probably want to hire a diaper service that will pick up soiled diapers and deliver freshly laundered ones to your door. Here are the major diaper services that the Bay Area has to offer:

Tiny Tots

200 E. Campbell Ave.
Campbell
408-866-2900 or 800-794-5437
www.tinytots.com

PARENT RATING: ☆ ☆ ☆ ☆

For the most part, we've heard good things about Tiny Tots: "very convenient . . . helpful and knowledgeable staff . . . the newsletter is invaluable! . . . Their delivery is always on time, and diaper counts are accurate. . . . Staff is friendly, capable, and very service-oriented. . . . Their billing is efficient and a no-brainer. . . . Service is top-notch. . . . On the rare occasion of a mistake in the diaper count, they have overnight delivered the remaining diapers at no additional cost." Serving San Francisco, Alameda, Contra Costa, San Mateo, Santa Clara, and Santa Cruz counties Tiny Tots delivers and picks up diapers once a week. In addition to home delivery of diapers, they also have a store that sells diaper covers and accessories for the nursing mother. If you'd like a lesson in using cloth diapers, they'll send a representative to your home free of charge.

Tidee Diddee

800-892-8080

PARENT RATING: ☆ ☆ ☆ ☆

Serving San Rafael, Novato, Corte Madera, and Mill Valley, Tidee Diddee will deliver 80 diapers weekly and pick up dirty ones. They sell and rent diaper covers. There is a minimum 4-week commitment.

ABC Diaper Service

800-286-4222

PARENT RATING: ☆ ☆ ☆ ☆

We've heard mixed reviews about ABC: "ABC's prices compare favorably to other diaper services. . . . Not accommodating when we've called to change our order. . . . Problems with the diaper count and missing pickup days." Serving Alameda, Contra Costa, and Solano counties, ABC will deliver 80 diapers weekly and pick up soiled ones. They sell diaper covers. There is a minimum 4-week commitment.

Online Disposable Diaper Delivery

If you chose to go with disposable diapers, you may find it more convenient to order them online and have them sent to your door via the mail. Following are a few websites that offer this service:

www.diapersite.com

www.drugstore.com

www.target.com

www.walmart.com

www.walgreens.com

CHAPTER 6

KEEPING YOUR SANITY:
Join a Parents' Group

Joining a group of new mothers or parents is probably one of the most beneficial things that a new parent can do for herself or himself during the postpartum period. These groups are often the source of long-lasting bonds between parents, as well as playgroups and strong friendships for their children. For example, if you are a new mom and ready to venture out of the house—any time from when your baby is a few weeks to a couple of months old—you'll enjoy getting out to share baby stories with other new mothers and gain advice from experts on how to care for your infant.

Besides companionship and empathy, such groups also offer exposure to a variety of parenting styles (to help define your own style), provide emotional support with the transition to parenthood, and serve as a source of advice on all sorts of parenting issues. Mothers' and parents' groups offer socialization for babies too. In short, there is much to be gained by connecting with other new parents and learning from one another's experiences.

There are numerous types of parents' groups to choose from, and in this chapter we will answer the following questions:

◆ What is a new parents' group or a Mommy and Me class, and where can I go to join one?

- What are the benefits of joining a mothers' group, and how can I find out about joining one?
- What are parenting classes, and where do I go to take them?
- What kinds of special support groups exist for parents, and how do I join one?

New Parents' Classes (or New Mother/Father Support Groups)

Among the first type of group that new parents join with their babies, new parents' classes are most often offered by hospitals, parenting centers, or other professional facilitators. The atmosphere is casual—parents (mostly mothers) and babies sit in comfortable chairs or on mats on the floor, and a speaker or facilitator leads a discussion on a specific topic, such as sleeping through the night, breastfeeding, coping with depression, or adjusting to motherhood. It's a comfortable place to breastfeed or deal with a crying infant, as everyone there is in the same situation! These classes tend to focus on infants from newborns up to 8 or 9 months, when the crawling and discovering stage makes it more challenging to bring a baby.

The hospitals and parenting resource centers listed below offer new mothers' and/or new parents' classes and groups. If you don't see your hospital listed here, be sure to inquire there about a new parents' support group. Most of the hospital groups are free and open to all on a drop-in basis, except where indicated. Some hospitals charge a nominal fee if you didn't deliver there. The groups run by parenting resource centers typically charge a fee for a series or by individual session.

San Francisco

California Pacific Medical Center (CPMC)
Newborn Connections
3698 California St.
415-600-BABY (2229)
www.cpmc.org/newbornconnections
PARENT RATING: ☆ ☆ ☆ ☆ ☆

CPMC's pioneering perinatal center offers the New Family Forum, a free drop-in support group where new parents and babies ages newborn to 8 months interact with one another and share the joys and challenges of parenting. The group meets twice a week to discuss topics of interest, including childproofing your home, "ask the pediatrician," making your own baby food, exercise for new mothers, how to properly install a car seat, and the decision to return to work. Newborn Connections also offers monthly infant massage workshops, a baby signs workshop, breastfeeding support groups, and a postpartum depression support group (see Ch. 5).

Comments: "The CPMC groups were all great, very helpful, and a tremendous source of information for new and struggling parents. . . . CPMC was a significant influence in who I became as a mom. A great place for encouragement and friendship—I met my best friend there! . . . It is a great way to meet people and not feel like you are the only one out there going through all the things you're going through. . . . A great variety of topics. . . . A little on the crowded side at times, but still worth it."

Calvary Presbyterian Church

2515 Fillmore St.
415-346-3832
www.calvarypresbyterian.org

This church hosts a group of mothers, babies, and toddlers that meets one morning a week.

DayOne

3490 California St., 2nd Fl., Ste. 203
415-440-Day1 (3291)
www.dayonecenter.com

PARENT RATING: ☆ ☆ ☆ ☆ ☆

DayOne, a privately run center for new and expectant parents, is truly a unique resource in a very inviting atmosphere. They offer a full menu of new parenting classes and workshops, including several "new parents' groups." These weekly groups are organized around the infants' age group (birth to 3 months, 3-6 months, 6-8 months, and 8-12 months) and address issues that are relevant to the age group and the parents. The New Parents' Groups are designed to foster community and to provide new parents with a forum to share the joys and challenges of parenting and address specific issues. They also offer a Working Parents' Group which explores the challenges of continuing to work and parenting. The sessions are facilitated by DayOne professional staff members, all of whom are experienced nurses or psychologists in the maternal health field. Pre-registration is not necessary, as these groups meet on a drop-in basis. Babies are welcome to all groups! Parents are encouraged to stay after the group's meeting to enjoy each other's company.

Jewish Community Center of San Francisco

3200 California St.
415-292-1200
www.jccsf.org

The JCC offers Parallel Play, a side-by-side playgroup for babies and toddlers and their parents. Parents meet other parents and engage in various discussion topics on parenting. They offer 4 classes which are organized according to the age of the child, from newborn up to 2 years old. They also offer a weekend Shabbat playgroup for children ages newborn through 5 years old.

Kaiser Permanente San Francisco Medical Center

4131 Geary St., Ste. 435
415-833-4120
www.kaiserpermanante.org

The center offers several postpartum support groups, including one that focuses on baby care and development for parents with infants 0-7 months old. They feature and provide support on various parenting issues— growth, environment, feeding, crying, sleeping, safety, illness, return to work, and more.

Michele Mason's New Moms Support Group

406 Cortland Ave.
415-550-9221
www.childfriendly.org

Michele Mason is a lactation specialist and educator whom new mothers and expectant couples have consulted for more than 12 years, both independently and through groups and classes at San Francisco's Natural Resources. She now offers a new Moms' Support Group which meets weekly in her Bernal Heights office. This group discusses breastfeeding, sleep, postpartum care for moms, transitioning to motherhood issues, and more. Advance registration is recommended. Founder of the Child Friendly Initiative, Inc. Michele is a nationally known advocate for children and their caregivers. She serves on The Mother's Council in New York City and resides in San Francisco with her husband and 3 children.

Natural Resources

1307 Castro St.
415-550-2611
www.naturalresourcesonline.com
PARENT RATING: ☆ ☆ ☆ ☆ ☆

Many new mothers in the Noe Valley neighborhood couldn't imagine life without this community-based center that focuses on pregnancy, childbirth, and early parenting. This center is known to place some emphasis on natural and alternative methods of childbirth and childrearing, but offers a friendly welcome to all mothers, whether or not they opted for a natural childbirth! Natural Resources offers an ongoing drop-in group where mothers and babies up to 6 months old interact with other mothers and newborns and share their experiences of emotional and physical recovery after birth. This very popular mothers' group is known for spinning off playgroups. They also offer playgroups for parents and babies 7-12 months and another one for toddlers 13-24 months.

Parents Place

1700 Scott St.
415-359-2454
www.parentsplace.online.org
PARENT RATING: ☆ ☆ ☆ ☆

Parents Place began as a mother-infant support group in 1975 and has grown into a nationally recognized full-service family resource center for families with children of all ages. Among a large offering of parents' resources, including parenting classes and workshops, playgroups for parents and children to attend together, support groups, and child care resource and referral services, Parents Place offers a New Mother/New Baby Group. The group meets once a week for 8 sessions, focusing on issues pertinent to new parents with infants up to 6 months old. Pre-registration is required. Parents Place is a Jewish and Family Children's Services program and

welcomes parents of all faiths.
Comment: "May be the best parenting resource in town."

Temple Emanu-El Building Blocks

2 Lake St.
415-751-2541, ext. 118
www.emanuelsf.org/ed_ece.htm

This popular mommy and me group is for mothers and babies 3-18 months old and is open to temple members and non-members. They meet one morning a week for 12 weeks. They also have a program for toddlers, 18 months to 2.5 years old, called Stepping Up. Registration is required—these classes fill up fast!

North Bay

Barefoot and Pregnant

1165 Magnolia Ave.
Larkspur
415-388-1777
www.barefootandpregnant.com

This sanctuary for new and expectant mothers offers a number of inspiring support groups and workshops, including a New Moms Forum.

COPE Family Center

1340 Fourth St.
Napa
707-252-1123
www.copefamilycenter.org

Cope Family Center is dedicated to supporting parents and nurturing children through parent education, family support services, and child advocacy programs. They offer Baby Steps, an educational support group for parents of newborns through one year old. This group explores the topics of

---

Helpful Preemie Websites

www.preemieparents.com

This is a reading room for preemie parents

www.preemieparenting.com

www.emory.edu/PEDS/ NEONATOLOGY/DCP

An online resource center for developmental issues

feeding, sleeping, development, and health. Babies are welcome! Babies can graduate into the Terrific Toddlers group for parents of children ages 1 through 3 years old, They also have a mother's group in Spanish.

Bug a Boo

14 Bolinas Rd.
Fairfax
415-457-2884
www.bug-a-boo.com

PARENT RATING: ☆ ☆ ☆ ☆

This children's store offers a Mom and Baby Group facilitated by Mia Mitchell, which draws mothers of babies newborn to 8 months old from San Anselmo, Fairfax, Woodacre, San Rafael, and West Marin. Mothers bring their infants and discuss issues relating to infants and first-time parents. Advance registration is recommended.

Parents Place Marin

600 5th Ave.
San Rafael
415-491-7959
www.jfcs.org/index.html

Parents Place Marin offers comprehensive, nonsectarian services for Marin families with children of all ages, including support groups, parenting workshops, a drop-in play area, a resource library, counseling, expert consultation, and a child care bulletin board. Among their full menu of classes, they offer a New Mother/New Baby series for new mothers with babies up to 6 months old, providing information, discussion, and support. Call in advance to register. See under New Parents' Classes—San Francisco.

Pregnancy to Parenthood Family Center

555 N. Gate Dr.
San Rafael
415-491-5700

A program of Family Services Agency of Marin, this private nonprofit parenting center specializes in providing counseling to parents with children under 3 years old. They also offer a Baby's First Year, Mother Support, and Therapy Group that focuses on the care of babies up to one year old, infant development, postpartum depression, nurturing oneself, play between mothers and babies, developing a support system, and adjusting to parenthood. Fees are determined on a sliding scale. Drop-ins are welcome.

Sonoma Valley Hospital

347 Andrieux St.
Sonoma
707-938-2063 (Disty Thompson)
www.svh.com

Disty Thompson facilitates a popular new mother-infant support group for babies up to 12 weeks old.

Alta Bates Medical Center Perinatal Center

5730 Telegraph Ave.
Berkeley
510-440-0790
www.altabates.com

PARENT RATING: ☆ ☆ ☆

Alta Bates offers a weekly New Mother/New Baby support group for parents and babies. Groups are divided according to the ages of the babies, including birth to 6 months, 6 months to a year, and 18 months to age 2½.

Hayward Adult School Parent Education

22100 Princeton St.
Hayward
510-293-8599
www.adultedreg.com/hayward

This center offers a class for new parents called Parenting the Infant. Advance registration is required.

John Muir Women's Health Center

1601 Ygnacio Valley Rd.
Walnut Creek
925-941-7901
www.jmmdhs.com
cindy.tetzloff@jmmdhs.com.

PARENT RATING: ☆ ☆ ☆

The center offers a drop-in new mothers' group facilitated by Cindy Tetzloff.

Kaiser Permanente

www.kaiserpermanente.com
• Hayward Medical Center
  27400 Hesperian Blvd.
  510-784-4531

This hospital offers a drop-in Baby and Me group for new mothers.

- Oakland Medical Center
  280 W. MacArthur Blvd.
  510-752-7557

This hospital offers a new mother-and-baby support group for babies up to one year old through the health education center at 3772 Howe St.

- Richmond Medical Center
  901 Nevin Ave.
  Richmond
  510-307-2539

This hospital offers a support group for moms and babies up to one year old.

- Walnut Creek Medical Center
  1425 S. Main St.
  925-295-4484

Kaiser Walnut Creek's Mom/Baby Pump Station offers a New Mother/New Baby support group.

Krista Kell's Mothers' Groups

925-254-1844

PARENT RATING: ☆ ☆ ☆ ☆ ☆

Krista Kell, RN, facilitates groups of first-time mothers primarily from the Contra Costa area. She offers a 5-week class for $100 that focuses on issues pertaining to newborns and first-time mothers; the group itself largely selects the topics. She then helps the group continue to meet by forming playgroups and organizing other activities. She prides herself on enabling new mothers to bond and form lasting friendships. Krista is a registered nurse and Assistant Dean of Women at St. Mary's College.

Mothers Outreach & Support Team (MOST)
Virginia Duplessis, MSW, CD (DONA)

510-287-8789
www.MostForMoms.com
virginia@mostformoms.com

Mothers Outreach & Support Team (MOST) offers support and discussion groups for new moms (with babies 0-6 months old) in Berkeley, Lafayette, and El Cerrito. A $200 fee includes eight 20-hour sessions, quarterly reunions for the first year, and 300-page resource binder and refreshments. In addition to open discussion, each week features a specific topic such as infant massage, sleep, relationships, or identity and often includes a guest speaker or presentation. Many groups continue to meet on their own after the facilitated sessions have ended.

The Nurture Center

3399 Mt. Diablo Blvd.
Lafayette
925-283-1346
www.nurturecenter.com
nurturecenter@earthlink.net

PARENT RATING: ☆ ☆ ☆ ☆ ☆

Started by 2 local moms, this parent resource center and store offers great parent education and support groups, including an ongoing new parent/baby support group where parents of babies (ages 0-5 months in one group and 4 months and up in another) discuss topics of interest and network with other new parents. The focus is on making connections with other new parents, and sharing issues and insights about parenting a baby. The group is facilitated by Meri Levy, MA, CLE, mother of 3 and executive director of the Nurture Center. The first session is free. Advance registration is not required. They also offer an 8-week New Mom's Group facilitated by MOST founder Virginia Duplessis (see

291

above). The Nurture Center also offers other interesting classes, including infant massage, and classes on other parenting topics such as Childproofing; Using Baby Slings; Music Together; Photographing Your Family; Wills, Trusts, and Estate Planning; Rediscovering Yourself in the Midst of Motherhood; etc. Their quarterly newsletter is free for East Bay residents. Comments: "There is nothing else like this for new parents in Contra Costa! . . . A definite must!"

Sherry Reinhardt's Support Groups for Mothers

510-524-0821
www.supportgroupformothers.com
PARENT RATING: ☆ ☆ ☆ ☆ ☆

Coordinated and facilitated by Sherry Reinhardt, RN, MPH; she has been organizing and facilitating mothers' groups for over 20 years and has helped launch more than 500 First-Time Groups, primarily from the Berkeley/Alameda area. Most recently she has been offering her services in San Francisco. Her First-Time Moms' Groups are constantly forming and are organized by geography and age of baby. She also organizes groups for second- and third-time mothers and is available for individual consultations. Comments: "It was a huge relief to hear that other first-time moms were experiencing the same struggles that I was and that our babies and husbands had similar habits! . . . Sherry does a great job of creating a relaxed and inviting atmosphere that is conducive to deep bonding between the moms in her group."

Waddle and Swaddle

1677 Shattuck Ave.
Berkeley
510-540-7210
www.waddleandswaddle.com

Waddle and Swaddle offers a new moms' support group, with founder, Linda Jones-Mixon and often with Virginia Duplessis (see above). For full description of Waddle and Swaddle, see Ch. 5.

Washington Hospital Childbirth and Family Education Department

2000 Mowry Ave.
Fremont
510-791-3423
www.whhs.com

This hospital offers a weekly New Mother/New Baby support group.

South Bay

Blossom Birth Services

1000 Elwell Ct.
Palo Alto
650-964-7380
www.blossombirth.com

This popular parent's resource center offers a full menu of new parents' groups and classes. Among several facilitated groups is one for new parents and babies 0-6 months of age in which parents can network with other new parents, and learn tips on baby care, sleep, feeding and encouraging optimal infant development. Expecting moms are welcome too. They also offer a Blossom Babies group for parents of children ages 6-12 months, which addresses issues such as creating healthy meals, baby play and development, and balancing responsibilities inside and outside of the home. Other topics include adjustments in the couple relationship, changing sexuality, weaning, sleep, and parent burnout. There is also a Blossom Toddlers group for parents of babies aged 12-18 months. This group discusses feeding fussy toddlers, facilitating excitement for learning, setting limits, and whether and when to think about another baby. Other topics involve balancing parent care with baby care, choosing activities for toddlers, and nurturing old and new friendships. Your toddlers will enjoy playing in a safe environment, and you will be able to connect with other parents in an intimate and comfortable atmosphere. And finally, there is a group for parents of children 18-30 months. The intent of this group, Talking about Toddlers, is to discuss issues you are facing with your toddler but don't want to talk about in your child's presence—such as limit-setting, social interaction with other kids, eating issues, tantrums, sleep, and other topics that come from the parents who participate. Unlike the other groups, this one is without the kids.

The Children's Health Council Parenting Education
650 Clark Way
Palo Alto
650-688-3625
www.chconline.org
This center offers a 7-session class entitled Your Young Baby for parents of babies up to 6 months old, as well as Parenting Older Babies, aged 7-14 months. This series includes mini-lectures and group discussions on bonding, baby's crying, sleep, feeding, play and stimulation, and health issues. Babies welcome! Pre-registration is required.

Community Hospital of Los Gatos
815 Pollard Rd.
Los Gatos
408-378-6131
www.tenethealth.com/losgatos
PARENT RATING: ☆ ☆ ☆ ☆ ☆
This hospital offers a weekly New Mother/New Baby support group.

El Camino Hospital Maternal Connections Lactation Center
2500 Grant Rd.
Mountain View
650-988-8287
www.elcaminohospital.com
The center offers several new mothers' support groups, based on babies' ages.

Good Samaritan Hospital of Santa Clara Valley
2425 Samaritan Dr.
San Jose
408-559-BABY (2229)
www.goodsamsj.org
This hospital offers a New Mother/New Infant support group.

Kaiser Permanente Redwood City Medical Center Breastfeeding Center
1150 Veterans Blvd.
Redwood City
650-299-2433
This center offers an informal drop-in group for mothers and newborns up to 4 months old, and a group for mothers with infants 5-9 months old.

293

Peninsula Hospital (Mills Peninsula Health System)
1783 El Camino Real
Burlingame
650-696-5872
www.mills-peninsula.org
This hospital offers a new mother-infant support group.

Peninsula Parents Place
200 Channing Ave.
Palo Alto
650-688-3040
www.parentsplaceonline.com
Peninsula Parents Place offers several new parents' classes. See under New Parents' Classes—San Francisco.

Santa Clara Adult Education
1840 Benton St.
Santa Clara
408-423-3500
www.scae.org/infant.htm
In a class entitled Parenting the Infant 0-12 Months, parents share the joys and challenges of the first few months of parenthood and discuss health, nutrition, safety, sleep, and development. Babies included! Advance registration is required.

Sequoia Hospital Maternity and Family Education Program
170 Alameda de las Pulgas
Redwood City
650-368-BABY (2229)
www.sequoiahospital.org
They offer several new parents' groups, according to the babies' ages: birth to 5 months, 5-9 months, and 9-13 months.

Lucile Packard Children's Hospital at Stanford Medical Center New Family Program
211 Quarry Rd., Rm. NC
Hoover Pavilion
Palo Alto
650-723-4600
www.lpch.org

PARENT RATING: ☆ ☆ ☆ ☆ ☆

This center offers a popular New Family Program series of classes and support groups that includes Mother-Baby Mornings, Father-Baby Evenings, and a Working Mothers' Group. The Mother-Baby Mornings are designed for mothers and newborns and are led by an experienced postpartum facilitator. Intended to take you through the first 9 months of your baby's life, the group meets 2 mornings a week and is divided into 2 groups, depending on your baby's age, newborn to 5 months and 6-9 months. Activities include discussion and guest speakers, and the group is ongoing; you may join at any time. The Father-Baby group meets once a month to discuss issues unique to being a parent or father and includes guest speakers. The Working Mothers' Group is an evening meeting once a month for mothers who work outside the home. Costs for the series are $150 for families of Stanford-delivered babies and $175 for other families. Advance registration is required.

Mothers' and Parents' Groups and Clubs

Mothers' and parents' groups or clubs often are organized by volunteer parents and provide an opportunity to meet local parents with young children. These groups often offer monthly meetings for mothers, with speakers, playgroups, special-interest groups, family outings, moms' nights out, babysitting co-ops, monthly newsletters, and even meal deliveries to new mothers. Annual dues typically range from $25 to $50, with a few that are $75. Getting involved in one is also a nice way to participate in your community, as they often sponsor community service projects. Recently, many of the mothers' groups have taken advantage of the internet and created online group postings that include parenting questions and answers, suggestions for family vacations, preschools, etc. Here are the mothers' groups that we heard about—be sure not to miss any of their great websites! Also, if you don't see a club listed that you are looking for, visit the website for the San Francisco Bay Area Association of Mothers' Clubs at www.geocities.com/sfbamc/.

ENTIRE BAY AREA

MOMS Clubs

www.momsclub.org
momsclubscanw@aol.com
Mothers Offering Mothers Support (MOMS) is a national, nonprofit group supporting the choice of mothers to stay home and raise their children. Visit their website for links to local chapters, including San Francisco, Antioch, Antioch and Oakley (www.antiochoakleymoms.org), Oakland (www.momsclubofoakland.itgo.com), San Ramon/Dublin. (momsclubsanramon@yahoo.com), Danville, and San Jose.

MOPS (Mothers of Preschoolers)

www.mops.org
MOPS is a nonprofit Christian organization that works with local churches in bringing together mothers and children, from babies to preschoolers. The name is often misunderstood, as you don't need to have a preschool-age child to belong to this club! Visit their website for links to local chapters.

Mothers and More

www.mothersandmore.com
Formerly FEMALE (Formerly Employed Mothers at the Leading Edge), this international nonprofit organization has several active local chapters, including San Francisco and the South Bay. Geared specifically to women who have interrupted their careers to have children, Mothers and More has over 150 chapters and nearly 8,000 members worldwide. The group includes full-time mothers as well as those who

work outside the home. Mothers and More dubs itself "the network for sequencing women," borrowing a term coined by Arlene Rossen Cardozo in her 1986 book, *Sequencing: Having It All But Not All At Once—A New Solution for Women Who Want Marriage, Career, and Family*. The group offers myriad activities, including monthly meetings, playgroups, and moms' nights out. Locate local chapter leaders by visiting their website.

San Francisco

Golden Gate Mothers' Group
415-789-7219
www.ggmg.org
PARENT RATING: ☆ ☆ ☆ ☆ ☆
With literally hundreds of members, GGMG is the largest organized mothers' group in San Francisco, bringing together mothers from all parts of the city. Offering monthly newsletters, monthly meetings with featured speakers, moms' nights out, special events for toddlers and preschoolers, special family and holiday events, playgroups based on your baby's age, community outreach, and a meal delivery service for new mothers, GGMG has become a very popular group for mothers of children from infants through preschoolers. The yahoo group e-mail forum where members are free to ask parenting and related questions is very popular. Comment: "A true support system of committed mothers and interesting women!"

Noe Strolls
www.noestrolls@yahoo.com
San Francisco's playgroup on wheels, new moms and their babies and toddlers take stroller walks, jogs, trips to local museums, and much more. See Noe Valley Stroller Group in Ch. 2 under San Francisco Walks for more information.

San Francisco Mothers of Twins Club
www.sfmotc.org
See below under Other Groups.

North Bay

Corte Madera and Larkspur Mothers' Club
415-451-7234
www.cmlmc.org

Marin Parents of Multiples Club (MPOMC)
www.mpomc.org
See below under Other Groups.

Novato Mothers Club
415-458-3203
www.novatomothersclub.com
PARENT RATING: ☆ ☆ ☆ ☆ ☆
More than 200 members participate in this club's offerings, including weekly playgroups, children's outings, family events, guest speakers, and a monthly newsletter. Comments: "Excellent way to meet other mothers. . . . A great place to find a playgroup and get connected with other new moms. . . . I especially enjoy the hiking with moms and babies!"

Petaluma Mothers' Club
707-778-6494
www.petalumamothersclub.org

Ross Valley Mothers' Club

415-721-4576

PARENT RATING: ☆ ☆ ☆ ☆ ☆

With several hundred members, this very active club serves Greenbrae, Kentfield, Ross, San Anselmo, and surrounding areas. They offer age-specific playgroups, social events for kids and moms, guest speakers, a preschool night, community services opportunities, and a wonderful newsletter.

San Rafael Mothers' Club

415-451-7355

www.srmoms.org

PARENT RATING: ☆ ☆ ☆ ☆ ☆

The club serves San Rafael, San Anselmo, Fairfax, Sleepy Hollow, Terra Linda, Santa Venetia, and Marinwood. Comments: "San Rafael Mothers' Club was a real lifesaver and continues to be the best source of support that I have! . . . Very active and well organized."

Santa Rosa Mother's Club

707-525-5902

SRMothersClub@yahoo.com (membership information)

http://www.santarosamothersclub.org/

Sonoma Valley Mothers' Club

707-996-9890

svmc@vo.com

Includes mothers in Sonoma Valley, Sonoma to Kenwood.

Southern Marin Mothers' Club

415-273-5366

www.southernmarinmoms.com

PARENT RATING: ☆ ☆ ☆ ☆ ☆

Serves Sausalito, Marin City, Mill Valley, Tiburon, and Belvedere. Comment: "Excellent source of support! . . . Awesome newsletter!"

East Bay

Amador Mothers' Club

925-927-2444 (membership and referral line for the Tri-Valley Mothers' Clubs)

www.amadormothersclub.com/index-2.html

This club serves Dublin, Livermore, Pleasanton, and surrounding Tri-Valley areas. The focus is on infants and children up to age 5. They offer many playgroups, activities, outings, and parties that can provide a great social and support network.

Castro Valley Mothers' Club

510-475-6864 (membership and referral line for the East Bay Mothers' Clubs)

This group serves Castro Valley, Hayward, San Leandro, and surrounding areas.

Clayton Mothers Club

www.claytonmoms.com

Contra Costa Mothers' Club

925-988-3383

www.cccmc.us

Serving the Central Contra Costa County communities of Antioch, Bay Point, Clayton, Concord, Martinez, Pacheco, Pittsburg, Pleasant Hill, and Walnut Creek, the Contra Costa

Mothers' Club offers social and support opportunities for pregnant women and mothers of infants and children up to age 5, including moms-only meetings, playgroups, family activities, outings, a babysitting co-op, and newsletters. They welcome newcomers to general meetings.

East Bay Moms

510-653-7867

www.eastbaymoms.com

PARENT RATING: ☆ ☆ ☆ ☆ ☆

With members coming from Alameda and Contra Costa counties, and primarily from Oakland and Berkeley, this group's focus is on outdoor activities with infants, toddlers, and preschoolers. Activities include scheduled hikes, stroller walks, a monthly Mom's Night Out, and an informative monthly newsletter. Comment: "I don't know what I would do without this incredibly active and well-organized group of fun moms!"

East County Mothers' Club

925-473-2783

www.eastcountymothersclub.org

eastcountymoms@yahoo.com (membership information)

ECMC serves the East Contra Costa County communities of Bay Point, Pittsburg, Antioch, Oakley, Bethel Island, Knightsen, Brentwood, Byron, and Discovery Bay. ECMC is a non-profit organization of families with children up to age 5 offering play-groups, outings, and babysitting co-ops. ECMC welcomes mothers who work outside the home full time, those who work part time, those with home-based businesses, and those who stay at home full-time.

Fremont, Union City, Newark (FUN) Mothers' Club

510-475-6864

www.funmothersclub.org

This club serves mothers of children up to pre-kindergarten age in Fremont, Union City, and Newark. They organize activities for moms and kids, such as playgroups, nights out, children's outings, and other social events.

Hayward Mothers' Club

510-475-6864

This club is for expectant mothers and mothers of children up to age 6, and includes mothers from Hayward and San Lorenzo.

Iron Horse Mothers' Club

925-927-2444 (membership and referral line for the Tri-Valley Mothers' Clubs)

www.ironhorsemothersclub.com (general information)

ironhorsemothersclub@yahoo.com (membership information)

PARENT RATING: ☆ ☆ ☆ ☆ ☆

This club serves Dublin, Danville, and San Ramon, and includes the former San Ramon Mothers' Club.

Lamorinda Moms Club

925-941-4714

www.lamorindamomsclub.org

PARENT RATING: ☆ ☆ ☆ ☆

This club serves Lafayette, Moraga, and Orinda. Comment: "Has many different special-interest groups."

Mount Diablo Mothers' Club

925-927-2424 (membership information)

www.mdmcmoms.org

This is a social and support group for expectant mothers and mothers with children under 5 years of age. They serve Walnut Creek, Pleasant Hill, Concord, Clayton, and surrounding areas and welcome working mothers, at-home mothers, single mothers, and adoptive mothers.

Neighborhood Parents Network (NPN)

877-648-KIDS (5437)

www.npnonline.org

PARENT RATING: ☆ ☆ ☆ ☆ ☆

An energizing force, NPN is a broad-based information and support network for families of young children in the East Bay. NPN has a membership of more than 800 families. Members receive a monthly newsletter containing parenting articles, a calendar of events and activities, support group and playgroup listings, babysitting listings, and classified ads. They also offer events with featured speakers, panels and school directories on navigating the preschool and elementary school process, activities for kids, and many different types of support groups including groups for new moms, new dads, single parents, non-birth moms, attachment parenting, art moms, Asian moms, Swiss families, and Italian conversation. Their website is also a gold mine of East Bay parenting information. Not to be missed if you are in the trenches of early parenting in the East Bay! Definitely one of the best newsletters around! Comments: "An incredibly

comprehensive parents' group with offerings of every kind. . . . Great website!"

Parents, Resources, and More (PRAM)

www.pram.net

PRAM is a community-driven non-profit organization that supports families with young children living in the Greater Richmond area.

Pleasant Hill/Walnut Creek Mothers' Club

925-939-6466 (membership information)

www.mom4mom.org (general information)

4u2join@home.com (membership information)

This club is a network of parents and parents-to-be.

Pleasanton Mothers' Club

925-927-2444 (membership and referral line for the Tri-Valley Mothers' Clubs)

www.pleasantonmothersclub.com

PARENT RATING: ☆ ☆ ☆ ☆ ☆

This club offers many activities, outings, and events for mothers and their families in Pleasanton.

Tri-Valley Mothers' Club

925-927-2444 (membership and referral line for Tri-Valley Mothers' Clubs)

PARENT RATING: ☆ ☆ ☆ ☆ ☆

This is a social and support group for mothers with infants and children up to 5 years old in Alamo, Danville, San Ramon, and surrounding areas.

Burlingame Mothers' Club

650-635-6777 (membership information)

www.burlingamemothers.org
(general information)

PARENT RATING: ☆ ☆ ☆ ☆ ☆

This club of 300 members is for mothers with infants and children up to 5 years old. They offer speakers, playgroups, a babysitting co-op, a newsletter, and outings.

Coastside Mothers' Club

P.O. Box 331
El Granada, CA 94018
www.coastsidemothersclub.org

Serving Half Moon Bay, El Granada, Moss Beach, and Montara, this 150-member club supports mothers of children not yet in school. Visit their website for membership forms.

Foster City Mothers' Club

650-634-9767 (membership and general information)
www.fostercitymothersclub.org

Las Madres Neighborhood Playgroups (LMNP)

877-LAS-MADRES (527-6237)
www.lasmadres.org

Serving Santa Clara County, Las Madres is a large network of neighborhood playgroups organized by age, with special-interest groups for adoptive, single, and older mothers, and those with 3 or more children. Started more than 50 years ago, it's one of the Bay Area's oldest mothers' groups. Through LMNP, members find friendship, support, and new things to do, as well as an opportunity for their children to learn socialization skills.

Millbrae Mothers Club

www.millbraemothersclub.
homestead.com/
millbraemothersclub1~ns4.html
millbraemothers@yahoo.com

Pacifica Mothers Club

650-737-8230
www.pacificamothersclub.com/
index.html

The Mothers Club of Palo Alto/Menlo Park

650-306-8182
www.pampmothersclub.org

PARENT RATING: ☆ ☆ ☆ ☆ ☆

This club describes itself as the largest mothers' club on the peninsula, serving Palo Alto, Menlo Park, Los Altos, Mountain View, and Atherton. It provides a supportive community for mothers (and dads) and their young children. Most activities take place in the Palo Alto/Menlo Park area, but anyone on the Peninsula with a child under 5 is welcome to join. Playgroups and special-interest groups include adoptive, over-40, single and working moms, and stay-at-home and working dads. They also offer a babysitting co-op, opportunities for community service, and an active e-mail exchange.

Redwood City Mothers' Club

www.rwcmc.org (general information that includes a membership form)

This club is for mothers of infants and children under the age of 5 years in Redwood City and surrounding areas.

San Bruno Mothers' Club
650-871-8096
www.geocities.com/sanbrunomoms
This club serves San Bruno, South
San Francisco, Daly City, Millbrae,
San Mateo, Pacifica, and
Hillsborough.

San Carlos/Belmont Mothers' Club
www.scbmc.org

San Mateo Mothers' Club
www.sanmateomothersclub.org

**South San Francisco Mothers'
Club**
650-989-6782
www.southsfmothersclub.
homestead.com

How to Find or Start a Playgroup

For babies and toddlers who aren't in day care or preschool yet, a
playgroup is a great way for them to learn socialization skills and have
fun. It's also a great way for new parents to network, share parenting
stories, and form great friendships! Almost all of the mothers' clubs
listed above offer playgroups for many different ages of children.
However, you can also start your own playgroup with the following
tips:

- Decide who you'd like to invite to join the playgroup. You can meet
  new moms at parks and playgrounds, new parenting classes, and
  other activities for moms and babies or toddlers. You can also dis-
  tribute flyers at your pediatrician's office, the library, your church or
  synagogue, or other places frequented by parents of young children.

- Decide the age of the children you want in the playgroup. Children
  should be roughly the same age—especially when they are babies—
  we suggest within a 3-4-month span of each other.

- Decide whether you want a children's playgroup, a mothers' group,
  or a combination. Some groups work as a babysitting co-op, where
  a few moms leave their children with other moms and have some
  time off, and then swap duties. Other groups gather with both parents and children so moms have a regular meeting time to socialize with their babies and one another.

- Consider the size of your playgroup—anything over 10 can be over-
  whelming, especially if you meet inside one another's homes when

Parents' Groups

the weather isn't nice. For toddlers, a smaller group is even better; once they start walking, it's a different kind of a playgroup!

♦ Choose a day and time that works best for everyone in the playgroup. Keep in mind that young children are most active in the morning, before they need a nap. Most playgroups meet once a week, but sometimes meet more frequently.

♦ Have an initial organizational meeting, where you decide on scheduling and share names, addresses, phone numbers, and e-mails.

♦ Select a coordinator or leader for your playgroup. This person will coordinate requests, such as the need to change the time based on nap schedules or preschool.

♦ We suggest rotating your meeting venues, giving each mom a chance to organize or host the playgroup. The parent who is responsible for that week decides where to meet and makes reminder calls or e-mails.

♦ Keep things interesting by planning outings appropriate for the season, such as a trip to a pumpkin patch, a visit to Santa at the mall, a Valentine's Day party where older toddlers can help make valentines with their moms, and other holiday events and crafts.

Playgroup-Related Websites

For more information on how to form a successful playgroup, establish its rules, and develop ideas for playgroup hosts, try these websites:

www.onlineplaygroup.com

This site includes a playgroup starter kit and advice for how to revitalize a seasoned playgroup.

www.slowlane.com

This site offers advice for stay-at-home dads wanting to start a playgroup.

www.familyfun.com

This site offers all kinds of crafts ideas and outings for playgroups.

Other Groups

In addition to mothers' groups, there are many other groups for parents with babies and young children. These groups focus on a particular aspect or way of parenting:

ATTACHMENT PARENTING

Attachment Parenting International
- San Francisco
  415-820-9666
  www.attachmentparenting.org
  (general information)
- Concord/Walnut Creek
  www.babyknowsbest.com
- Peninsula
  easearles@prodigy.net

This group provides emotional, educational, and practical support to parents who practice or wish to learn about attachment parenting, which includes "wearing" your baby, breastfeeding, and co-sleeping.

SECOND- AND THIRD-TIME MOMS' GROUPS

East Bay

The Parenting Center Berkeley-Richmond Jewish Community Center
1414 Walnut St.
Berkeley
510-704-7475
The JCC offers a Mothers with Older Children and New Baby support group.

PARENTS OF MULTIPLES' GROUPS

San Francisco

San Francisco Mothers of Twins Club
415-440-TWIN (8946)
www.sfmotc.org
PARENT RATING: ☆ ☆ ☆ ☆ ☆

This group offers support and encouragement to mothers of multiples through monthly meetings, a monthly newsletter, semimonthly new moms' group support meetings, play dates, garage sales, social events, and membership in the National Mothers of Twins Club. Comment: "This group is great for meeting people who are coping with similar issues, particularly during those trying early months." For other areas, visit the National Organization of Mothers of Twins Clubs (www.nomotc.org) and download the forms for membership application, or call 800-243-2276.

North Bay

Marin Parents of Multiples Club
415-460-9049
www.mpomc.org
Providing educational and emotional support, this club is for all expecting parents and parents of multiples. Monthly meetings include support groups for each stage of multiples' development as well as speakers on

Parents' Groups

303

pertinent issues. Membership also includes a monthly newsletter, a big sister program that teams new moms with experienced ones, moms' nights out, community outreach, and annual holiday parties. They also host a popular annual garage sale.

Redwood Empire Parents of Multiples (Santa Rosa)
twins2tnt@aol.com

Sonoma County Mothers of Multiples
P.O. Box 9459
Santa Rosa, CA 95405
alp@sonic.net (membership inquiries)

This group meets monthly for a new mom discussion and general meeting.

East Bay

Contra Costa Parents of Multiples
925-431-8355
www.ccpom.homestead.com

DoubleTalk
A Resource for New Parents of Twins
925-330-5660
www.doubletalkfortwins.com
info@doubletalkfortwins.com

Karen Pollack, a longtime educator at the Women's Health Center for John Muir Medical Center (first presenting a portion of the Preparing for Multiples program and now facilitating the Adjustments to Life; Tips From the Experts component of the Marvelous Multiples program), facilitates a series of 8-week workshops for new mothers and their twins, newborn through 6 months. She also provides one-on-one consultations on

topics relevant to parents of twins. She offers workshops in Walnut Creek and one-on-one consultation services (DoubleTalk to Go) Bay Area-wide.

East Bay Mothers of Twins' Club
510-886-4930

Tri-City Mothers of Multiples
510-888-4444
This group serves Fremont, Union City, and Newark.

Triplet Connection
P.O. Box 429
Spring City, UT 84662
435-851-1105
www.tripletconnection.org

This is the headquarters of this international group that offers support and information, including a medical database, a newsletter, and referrals for expectant parents and parents of triplets, quadruplets, and quintuplets. They do not officially sponsor local support groups.

Twins by the Bay
www.twinsbythebay.homestead.com
Twins by the Bay, a member of the National Organization of Mothers of Twins Clubs, offers a daytime support group for new and expectant parents of multiples at Alta Bates Hospital in Berkeley and other locations. Visit their website for membership information.

South Bay

Coastside Mothers of Twins Club
www.cmotc.homestead.com/
CMOTC.html
Jmcca54324@aol.com,
Julie McCarron (membership
information)

This club serves Pacifica, Millbrae,
San Mateo, Foster City, and
Burlingame.

Gemini Crickets Parents of Multiples of the Silicon Valley
408-536-0811
www.geminicrickets.org
webmaster@geminicrickets.org
(membership inquiries)

This group serves San Jose and the
Silicon Valley.

Mid-Peninsula Parents of Multiples
650-599-2022
www.mppm.org

Santa Clara County Mothers of Twins
408-333-9062
www.sccmotc.com (general information and membership)

GAY PARENTS' GROUPS

Non-birth Moms' Group
510-528-3481

This group is for non-birth moms of
lesbian couples.

Our Family Coalition, The Bay Area Gay & Lesbian Family Group
870 Market St., Ste. 872
San Francisco
415-981-1960
www.ourfamily.org

This group includes more than 200
families throughout the Bay Area.
They plan social and educational
events each month where families
can enjoy potlucks at the beach, and
visit museums, parks, and the zoo.
Every 2 months, members who want
to help plan events meet and schedule upcoming events. Offering a
bimonthly newsletter, a weekly e-mail
update, and a website listing many
family resources, this group's goal is
to create a positive and nurturing
world for gay and lesbian families.

DADS' GROUPS

San Francisco

California Pacific Medical Center
See under New Parents' Classes–
San Francisco.
CPMC offers an "expecting fathers"
class.

DayOne
See under New Parents' Classes–
San Francisco.
This top-notch center for new and
expectant parents offers a popular
daddy and baby massage workshop.

Parents Place
1700 Scott St.
San Francisco
415-359-2454
www.jfcs.org

Among other programs and services
for parents, Parents Place offers support, coaching, and counseling for
fathers.

The California Parenting Institute

3650 Standish Ave.
Santa Rosa
707-585-6108, Bill Haigwood

The Dads' Connection is a free forum where low-income fathers of all ages can meet to discuss their role as parents. Recent topics included the legal rights and responsibilities of fathers under California family law, the rewards of raising a child with a partner or ex-partner, and finding where work fits in family life. Dads' Connection sessions are scheduled about every 4 to 6 weeks on a weeknight.

East Bay

At-Home Dads' Group

510-268-8950, Evan Weissman

This group of at-home dads meets Monday mornings with their kids either in Berkeley or Oakland. Depending on the weather, they hike, have a playgroup, or go on some other kind of outing.

East Bay Dads

www.eastbaydads.org

Active since 1998, East Bay Dads is a group of fathers with babies, toddlers, and preschoolers in the Oakland/Berkeley area. They meet Monday mornings at a local park, museum, or other venue. Their outings include hikes, A's games, train rides, and more! They have a very well organized and informative website, so Dad, check it out!

Fathers' Forum

drlinton@123yahoo.com
www.fathersforum.com

Dr. Bruce Linton, MFT, runs the Fathers' Forum program which offers men's groups for fathers (with babies or preschoolers), classes on becoming a father, walks for dads and children, as well as individual and couple counseling in the East Bay. The Fathers Forum Online is a virtual community for expectant and new fathers.

Silicon Valley Dads Groups

www.slowlane.com/groups/svd/
index.htm

The goal of this group is to provide support and camaraderie to fellow stay-at-home-dads. Stay-at-home-dads from several Silicon Valley communities get together at local parks with their children weekly and have dads' nights out and other activities.

YWCA of Silicon Valley

375 South Third St.
San Jose
408-295-4011
www.ywca-scv.org/
classes_counseling.html

This YWCA Counseling Center offers a variety of groups and workshops, including a Just for Dads group. This group focuses on infant development; learning through play; bonding between baby and dad; limit-setting and discipline; maintaining a healthy relationship within a family; and balancing work, home, and play.

www.bamin.org

The Bay Area Male Involvement Network (BAMIN) is a partnership of several Bay Area child service agencies who are working to increase the involvement of fathers and other significant men in the lives of children here in the Bay Area.

Lucile Packard Children's Hospital at Stanford Medical Center

They offer a father-baby group.
See under New Parents' Classes—South Bay.

STAYING-AT-HOME OR WORK ISSUES

Career Transitions Group

510-547-3704, Janet Keller (general information)
atcallbackcom@earthlink.net

If you are contemplating a return to work or considering a career transition, you may want to join this group for support, brainstorming, and encouragement.

Lucile Packard Children's Hospital at Stanford Medical Center

They offer a working mothers' group.
See under New Parents' Classes—South Bay.

WorksForMe

WorksForMe@yahoogroups.com

Works For Me is a network of mothers in the Bay Area who are in career transition. Members are stay-at-home moms, working moms, and entrepreneur moms. Their shared goal is to help each mom discover how to coordinate her career goals with her goals as a parent. The group sponsors seminars and networking events, in addition to an active online community.

ETHNIC AND INTERNATIONAL GROUPS

Our Colors

510-655-8264, Nadine
whatareyou2000@ivillage.com

This group is an interracial family forum for parents who are raising biracial, multicultural, transracial, or intercultural children.

Parliamo Italiano!

www.parentsnet.org

This Italian conversation group is part of the Neighborhood Parents Network. They meet once a week at a private home. Children are welcome.

GerMOMs

Kirstinpaydo@sbcglobal.net

This group of German/American mothers who are raising bilingual children meets in San Francisco weekly.

Parents' Groups

SPECIAL NEEDS SUPPORT GROUPS

The Bay Area offers several discussion and support groups for parents with special needs, including those related to issues of adoption, premature infants, and babies with disabilities. See Ch. 1 for more references.

Alta Bates Parent Share Group
Redwood City
925-935-9240, Linda Cole
This free support group is for parents of premature or sick babies.

Autism Society Support Group
Livermore
Louise Glueck, 925-373-6468
louiseglueck@yahoo.com

Down Syndrome Connection
117A Town and Country Dr.
Danville
925-362-8660, Martha Hogan (general information)
This organization offers support groups, workshops, and more for families with Down Syndrome children.

Early Start Program at the Golden Gate Resource Center
415-546-9222
Early Start is a nationally and state-supported program for families of young children (newborn to age 3) with, or at risk of, developmental delay. Among other services, they offer a multitude of support groups through their Family Resource Centers located in each county (of which the Golden Gate Resource Center is one).

The Family Resource Network
5232 Claremont Ave.
Oakland
510-547-7322
Staffed by parents of children with disabilities, this group provides support and resources to families of children with special needs. Services include a resource library, a quarterly newsletter, and support groups including A Father's Perspective: Part of the Team, a group for dads of kids with special needs.

Non-verbal Learning Disorders Support Group
831-624-3542 (hotline)
www.NLDline.com
This nonprofit volunteer organization provides support to parents of children with nonverbal learning disorders and other neurocognitive and neurobiological disorders. It offers monthly support groups, newsletters, a resource library, and parenting classes.

Open Gate
2601 Mission St., Ste. 300
415-920-5040
www.supportforfamilies.org
This center offers information, education, parent-to-parent support, resources, and referrals for families, including families of children with disabilities.

Parents Helping Parents

www.sfphp.com

- Hayward
  677 Paradise Blvd., 510-276-9479
- San Francisco
  594 Monterey Blvd., 415-841-8820

A parent-directed family resource center for children with special needs, this group sponsors workshops, parent support groups, a quarterly newsletter, and does referrals.

Support for Families of Children with Disabilities

415-469-4518 (resource line)
www.supportforfamilies.org

- San Francisco
  2601 Mission St., Ste. 804 (headquarters)
  415-282-7494, (general information)
- San Francisco
  300 Seneca Ave. (family resource center)

This parent-run organization provides support groups and emotional support to families of children with disabilities.

Through the Looking Glass

2198 6th St., #100
Berkeley
510-848-1112, ext. 107
www.lookingglass.org

This national organization provides services for parents with disabilities, including free, in-home occupational therapy and adaptive baby care equipment.

Helping After Neonatal Death (HAND)

888-908-HAND (4263)
www.handsupport.org (general information)
www.handonline.org (resources and support groups)

HAND is a volunteer group of parents founded to help other parents who have experienced the loss of a baby before, during, or after birth. They offer support groups for grieving parents and family members and 24-hour telephone crisis support. Their website includes a lot of helpful information, including several books and links on pregnancy and infant loss.

HAND of the Peninsula

- San Mateo and Santa Cruz counties
  650-367-6993
- Santa Clara County
  408-995-6102
  24-Hour Telephone Crisis Line (staffed by the Family Stress Service of San Mateo)
  650-692-6655 (Daly City to San Mateo)
  650-368-6655 (Belmont to Menlo Park)
  650-726-6655 (San Mateo Coast)

John Muir Women's Health Center

See under New Parents' Classes—East Bay.

The center offers a miscarriage support group and a postpartum stress support group. Contact Deborah Kight at 925-941-7908 for further information.

Parents' Groups

309

www.penparents.org

This is a network of grieving parents who have experienced pregnancy loss or the death of a child. It provides an opportunity for bereaved parents to connect with one another and discuss their loss.

Support After Neonatal Death (SAND)

- San Francisco
  415-282-7330
- East Bay
  510-204-1571 (Alta Bates Hospital)

SAND is a support group for parents who have lost a baby through miscarriage, stillbirth, or during or after birth.

ADOPTION SUPPORT RESOURCES

See Ch. 1.

SINGLE PARENTS' GROUPS

San Francisco and North Bay

A.P.P.L.E. FamilyWorks (Advancing Principles & Practices for Life Enrichment)

4 Joseph Ct.
San Rafael
415-492-0720
www.familyworks.org/parent.html

This organization offers a Single Parents' Support Group from time to time.

Bay Area Children First

- San Francisco
  999 Sutter Street
  415-922-2344

- Berkeley
  1400 Shattuck Street
  510-883-9312
  www.baychild.org/ContactOffice.html

This nonprofit organization offers counseling services to parents, including focusing on issues pertinent to the single parent.

Parents Without Partners of San Francisco and San Mateo County

415-905-4145

All single parents are invited to attend general meetings on the first and third Sunday of each month; child care is available.

Parents Place San Francisco Single Mothers' Support Group

See under New Parents' Classes— San Francisco.

Parents Place San Francisco periodically offers a support group for pregnant single women and single mothers of young children.

Parents Place Marin Single Mothers' Group

See under New Parents' Classes— North Bay.

Parents Place Marin periodically sponsors a support group for single mothers, pregnant single women, single mothers by choice, single adoptive mothers, or mothers ending a relationship.

East Bay

Bay Area Children First

See under San Francisco.

Berkeley YMCA Program

510-665-3238, Edna O'Brien-Brenner
eobrienbrenner@baymca.org

This YMCA offers a support group for single parents.

East Bay Single Parents Network (SPN)

EastBaySPN@yahoogroups.com

Parents Without Partners

www.parentswithoutpartners.org

This national organization for single parents of any age offers orientations in the Alameda/Oakland area twice a month.

Single Mothers by Choice

www.singlemothers.org
bayareasmc@hotmail.com

This is the Bay Area chapter of the national organization.

Support Group for Single Parents

925-855-1745, ext. 2, Liz Hannigan (general information)
925-258-9759, Milton Kalish (general information)

Drop-ins are welcome. Free child care is provided. They also offer a children's support group for ages 3-7.

South Bay

Peninsula Parents Place

200 Channing Ave.
Palo Alto
650-688-3040
www.parentsplaceonline.com

This parenting center periodically offers a support group for single parents.

Bananas
East Bay Stepfamilies

5232 Claremont Ave.
Oakland
510-653-6344
www.bananas.org

This stepfamily drop-in support group meets once a month to share experiences and helpful information.

Alliance of Collaborative Professionals

www.collaborativedivorceeastbay.com

This group offers legal, emotional, and financial support to divorcing parents.

A.P.P.L.E. FamilyWorks

See under Single Parents' Groups— San Francisco and North Bay.

This organization offers Parenting Apart classes that include a free workshop on Divorce Realities, a Single Parents' Support Group, Consider the Children seminar, and a Just for Kids group that focuses on support for children whose parents are divorcing.

Bay Area Children First

See under Single Parents' Groups.

They offer support groups for divorcing parents who are interested in creating a healthy coparenting plan and relationship.

Parents' Groups

**Kaiser Permanente Oakland
Psychiatric Department
Kids Divorce Support Group**
3900 Broadway
Oakland
510-752-1000
Dr. Mary Haake leads this group, which provides a safe place for young children to discuss with their peers the weighty issues of divorce. Groups are divided by age.

Kids Turn
1242 Market St., 2nd Fl.
San Francisco
415-437-0700 or 510-835-8445
www.kidsturn.org
PARENT RATING: ☆ ☆ ☆ ☆ ☆
Kids Turn is a nonprofit organization that helps children and parents

through divorce. Parents find their 6-week workshops (meeting once each week) very helpful. Kids and parents attend different workshops that meet simultaneously, with the kids' groups divided by age, the youngest group being age 4. There is also a special workshop for parents of children under 3. Fees are based on a sliding scale.

Touchstone Counseling Services
140 Mayahew Dr.
Pleasant Hill
925-932-0150
This service offers support groups for divorced parents and children of divorced parents.

PARENTING EDUCATION

As your baby grows (and you both outgrow new parents' groups), you may want to take a few parenting classes. We are fortunate in the Bay Area to have a great abundance of resources in this regard. They cover everything from parenting the toddler to dealing with discipline, managing anger, toilet training, and preparing your child for a new sibling. Here is a sampling of parenting education programs offered locally:

San Francisco

**California Pacific Medical Center
The Community Health Resource
Center**
2100 Webster St.
415-923-3155
www.cpmc.org/services/chrc/education
CPMC's Newborn Connections teams up with the Community

Health Resource Center to present occasional educational lectures for new and expectant parents. Topics include helping baby sleep, finding parenting advice on the internet, stimulating your infant, common illnesses in infancy, and nutrition while breastfeeding. CPMC also offers occasional lectures on toddler topics. Lectures are often held at CPMC's California Campus (3700 California St.).

City College of San Francisco Parent Education Program

1860 Hayes St., Rm. 139
415-561-1920
www.ccsf.edu

This program offers infant development classes relating to children up to 5 years old.

DayOne

See under New Parents' Classes—San Francisco.

This full-service, privately run center for new and expectant parents offers a unique selection of parenting classes and workshops, focusing on topics such as food and nutrition, first aid and CPR, potty training, body mechanics for new moms, finding child care, finding a preschool, umbilical cord banking, dad and baby massage, pumping breastmilk, musical play, and a "mini-photo session" for your child with Tami DeSellier (see Ch. 4)!

Jewish Community Center of San Francisco

3200 California St.
415-292-1200
www.jccsf.org

The JCC offers parent education seminars on topics such as separation, understanding children's behavior, understanding your child's temperament, and positive discipline strategies. For more information, call 415-292-1255.

Parents Place

See under New Parents' Classes—San Francisco.

This center offers a large range of parenting classes and workshops, including How to Take Care of Your Newborn, Raising Boys, Your One-Year-Old, Toilet Training, and Discipline Issues. Most are held in the evening with a nominal fee.

San Francisco Waldorf School

2938 Washington St.
415-931-2750
www.sfwaldorf.org/gradeschool/earlychildhood/parentingtoddler.asp

PARENT RATING: ☆ ☆ ☆ ☆ ☆

This school offers The First Three Years for parents and children up to 3 years old to explore the healthy physical and emotional unfolding of the very young child. Held in the new San Francisco Waldorf Family Center at 3105 Sacramento Street, these classes give children a meaningful social experience, while giving their parents a much-needed and well-deserved break.

Wu Yee Children's Services

Joy Lok Family Resource Center
888 Clay St.
415-391-4890
www.wuyee.org/programs/joylok.php

This new family resource center, located in the heart of Chinatown, provides a host of services for parents and caregivers of young children, from newborns to 5 years old. Among other things, they offer parenting education and workshops in Cantonese and Mandarin.

Childhood Matters with Rona Renner, RN

Sunday mornings, 9-10 a.m. on 98.1 KISS FM.

Childhood Matters is a call-in radio talk show for parents of young children, where parents join in for real conversations about the joys and challenges of parenting. The show features guest experts with information about important parenting topics such as how babies learn, single parenting, reading and school readiness, dealing with your 2-year-old, when should you call your pediatrician, and more! Call in with your parenting questions, toll free, at 1-877-372-KIDS. Host Rona Renner is an expert in child development, learning differences, temperament, and family communication. A mother of 4, she is a nationally recognized parent educator and has been a nurse for more than 35 years. A similar show, *Nuestros Niños*, is offered in Spanish and airs Sunday mornings from 8 to 9 a.m. on 1170 KLOK AM and 89.1 FM KBBF.

North Bay

A.P.P.L.E. Family Works
See under Single Parents' Groups—San Francisco and North Bay.

They offer workshops and services that focus on confident parenting, parenting a spirited child, and dealing with other temperament issues.

California Parenting Institute
3650 Standish Ave.
Santa Rosa
707-585-6108
www.calparents.org
The California Parenting Institute (CPI) is a nonprofit educational family resource agency founded in 1978 which serves families in Sonoma County. CPI offers a variety of programs for parents with children of all ages, including parenting classes for babies and toddlers, discipline classes for toddlers and preschoolers, infant

massage, yoga for moms, twos together, infant gym, kindergym, and classes on handling anger, positive parenting, single parenting, raising siblings, and much more. They also have an extensive lending library of parenting books and videos with multiple copies of the most popular books.

COPE Family Center
See under New Parents' Classes—North Bay.
COPE offers a full menu of parent education classes, including classes on parenting toddlers, positive discipline, cooperative coparenting, and more. Child care is available.

Parents Place Marin
See under New Parents' Classes—North Bay.

Parents Place Sonoma
1360 N. Dutton Ave.
Santa Rosa
707-571-8131
www.jfcs.org
This parenting center that "has everything to do with parenting" offers a full range of parenting classes and workshops on topics such as Nurturing Your Child's Self-Esteem, as well as drop-in play times and support groups. See under New Parents' Classes—San Francisco.

East Bay

Bananas
5232 Claremont Ave.
Oakland
510-658-7353
www.bananasinc.org
BANANAS is a nonprofit child care referral and support agency serving

families in northern Alameda County. They provide free parenting information, workshops, and child care referrals. They also offer training, workshops, classes, and technical support to caregivers. They are well known for their free handouts that offer all sorts of parenting advice on many topics. Either stop by or download them from their website. See also in Ch. 9.

Family Stress Center

2086 Commerce Ave.
Concord
925-827-0212
www.familystresscenter.org
This center offers parenting education and counseling.

Habitot Children's Museum

2065 Kittredge St.
Berkeley
510-647-1112
The museum offers parenting classes and workshops taught by professionals. Topics include sleeping and eating, choosing a preschool, positive parenting, terrific twos, discipline, fostering artistic development, and child safety. Class fees are determined on a sliding scale. Free child care is available for parents attending classes, if registered in advance.

Hayward Adult School

See above under New Parents' Classes—East Bay.
Hayward Adult School offers parent education classes.

The Nurture Center

See above under New Parents' Classes—East Bay.

Tri-City Health Center

39500 Liberty St.
Fremont
510-770-8133, ext. 129
This center offers free parenting classes that focus on children under age 6.

South Bay

Palo Alto Medical Clinic, Education Department

795 El Camino Real
Palo Alto
650-853-2960
www.pamf.org
This foundation offers parenting classes and support groups.

Parents Leadership Institute

555 Waverly St.
Palo Alto
650-322-5323
www.parentleaders.org
This parenting institute offers a host of parenting classes that build on a "parenting by connection" approach which emphasizes the "interplay of connection and communication." Classes include Connecting with Your Child Through Play, Tantrum Training, Remedies for Whining, Setting Limits with Children, Helping Our Children with Emotional Moments, and more. They also offer classes with children including Special Time and Special Playlistening classes (often called PlayMornings) and parent support groups.

Peninsula Parents Place

See under Single Parents' Groups. This parenting center offers a vast array of parenting classes on topics ranging from helping children with aggression to toilet training. See under New Parents' Classes—San Francisco.

Peninsula YMCA

1670 S. Amphlett Rd.
San Mateo
650-349-7696
www.ymcasf.org/Peninsula/
community.html

As part of the Project FOCYS, this YMCA offers parent education and workshops on topics such as positive discipline.

San Mateo Child Care Coordinating Council Mary's Room — Family Resource Center & Library

2121 S. El Camino Real, Ste. A-100
San Mateo
650-655-6770
www.thecouncil.net/parents.html

This new family resource center offers parent resources, workshops and classes, a lending library, and community resource information. Computers with internet access are available. Toys and books occupy children while parents use the library materials!

Santa Clara Unified School District Adult Education

1840 Benton St.
Santa Clara
408-423-3500
www.scae.org/infant.htm

This organization offers classes on parenting babies and toddlers.

Sequoia District Adult School

3247 Middlefield Rd.
Menlo Park
650-306-8866
www.adultschool.seq.org

Sunnyvale Cupertino Adult Education

591 W. Fremont Ave
Sunnyvale
408-522-2707
www.ace.fuhsd.org

Serving Sunnyvale and Cupertino, this school district offers adult community education, including a "support for parents" class and a host of classes for young children.

The Children's Health Council

See under New Parents' Classes—South Bay.

Serving the developmental needs of families and children for more than 50 years, the CHC was founded in 1953 by Dr. Esther Clark, Palo Alto's first pediatrician. They offer a wide variety of parenting classes and services.

YWCA

375 S. 3rd St.
San Jose
408-295-4011
www.ywca-svc.org/classes_
counseling.html

The YWCA offers a 3-evening class series on parenting the young child, ages one to 5 years. They focus on encouraging cooperation and good parent-child relationships, including reducing tantrums, stress, and conflicts. They also offer classes on developing parenting skills for single and divorced parents, parenting the child with challenging behavior, and more.

PARENTING E-MAIL DISCUSSION GROUPS

With so many parenting websites today, it seems as though the internet has quickly become a new parent's best friend—but not just for convenient shopping. Many parenting websites serve as a quick reference for everything from choosing baby gear to picking a pediatrician and child care. They can also be open forums for parents to share the joys and challenges of modern parenting. The websites listed below offer round-the-clock online conversations about topics that only parents would stay up into the wee hours of the night to talk about! Also, many local mothers and parents groups with their own websites host online parenting discussions.

The Virtual Village

www.npnonline.org

This e-mail discussion group is for Neighborhood Parents Network (NPN) members (an East Bay-based parents' group), with hundreds of members participating in this valuable information exchange. Members receive mail once a week, including requests for information or advice, babysitting, and announcements.

UCB Parents Network Mailing

http://parents.berkeley.edu/mlist.html (for membership information)

PARENT RATING: ☆ ☆ ☆ ☆ ☆

This is a parent-run e-mail exchange for parents in the Berkeley area. With immediate access to local parents' experience and advice, this is the best of its kind! ～

www.UrbanBaby.com

UrbanBaby offers an active online community for new parents. Go to the UrbanBaby Message Boards under the Community icon for advice and support from other parents. Share your stories in Parents Talk Back.

Parent Education

ADDITIONAL PARENTING ORGANIZATIONS AND WEBSITES

www.bayareaparent.com

You can now access *Bay Area Parent* online as an "e-book," including direct links to their articles and advertisers.

www.babycenter.com

Gather reams of parenting advice and electronic postings on everything from preconception and pregnancy to infants and toddlers. If you sign up and give your child's birth date, you will receive regular updates on what to expect at the various stages of your child's development.

www.babyzone.com

Offers different "zones" of information for new parents from preconception to newborns, toddlers, preschoolers, and more.

www.village.com

The pregnancy and parenting part of this website features an "ages and stages" section of your baby and toddler as well as advice from experts in the parenting field.

www.pediatrics.about.com/cs/ parentguides

A collection of websites with parenting information and advice.

www.parenthub.com/ parenting/parenting.htm

A collection of various parenting websites.

www.parentsunite.org

This is the National Parenting Association's website. It offers information and support for parent advocacy on local, state, and national issues.

www.parenting.com

This is *Parenting* magazine's website where you can view key articles from the current issue of the magazine and much more!

www.parenthood.com

Parents seem to love this website, especially as their family grows. Features include pregnancy tools such as a due date calculator, information on baby names, answers to common parenting questions, and an active online community

www.parentspress.com

This site provides a complete listing of Bay Area mothers' clubs and other groups.

www.plumsite.com/ bayareamoms

This site provides resources from local moms in Marin, including events for families and kids, hikes, and more.

www.preemieparenting.com

This helpful website focuses on parenting and caring for preemies.

www.slowlane.com

This is a searchable online resource and network for Stay At Home Dads (SAHD) featuring articles, media clips, and many links to sites on fathering issues.

www.zerotothree.com

This site offers reams of information from professionals for parents and caregivers about the first 3 years of a child's life.

CHAPTER 7

GETTING OUT:
Classes for Kids

No one wants to pressure a child to become a super kid. On the other hand, too many days at home watching Barney on television can get very old. On the theory that exposing your offspring to sports or the arts can be fun for both you and your children, we offer the following selection of Bay Area classes for kids.

In this chapter, we present classes appropriate for infants, toddlers, and preschoolers (through age 5) and tell you which classes are best for which ages. Typically, parents accompany children to classes if they are under 3 years old. Beginning around 3, children often go by themselves to short "drop-off" programs. We've divided the classes by subject matter, so you can easily jump to a topic—whether it's gym, swimming, music, art, dance, foreign language, or other sports—that interests you. If an organization offers multiple classes in different subject areas, we've included a complete listing the first time it is mentioned, and just the name under subsequent listings, so refer to the first listing for complete details.

Be sure to check current class offerings, schedules, and prices. And keep in mind, as parents reiterated to us, that the value of these classes is highly dependent on individual teachers. It's best to preview a class before you commit time and money to weeks and weeks of it, particularly since fees range from $10 to $25 per class for most classes. Most good programs offer free preview classes. You may also want to check the make-up class policy, as kids often get sick. Select a class that is not so large as to overwhelm your young child, who may be happier in a smaller group. Keep in mind that many of these locations, particularly gyms and art studios, offer wonderful children's birthday parties. Finally, check the museums section of the next chapter for more fun classes and workshops.

This chapter will answer the following questions and more:

◆ Where are the local classes, and which are parents' favorites?
◆ If we have only time for one class, which type should it be?
◆ What types of swimming lessons are offered, and which facilities are appropriate for my child?
◆ What approaches do different types of music classes teach?
◆ Which classes are appropriate for which ages?

Recreation Departments

Many municipal parks and recreation departments are a general resource for activities and offer great, low-cost classes for kids, running the gamut from swimming to gymnastics to music. If you don't find what you need in the listings below, be sure to check with your own city. Here are some parent favorites (**PARENT RATING:** ☆ ☆ ☆ ☆ ☆):

San Francisco

San Francisco Recreation and Park Department Tiny Tots and Kids Gym Programs
415-666-7079
http://parks.sfgov.org
The city's recreation department sponsors low-cost, weekly child development and play classes at recreation centers and playgrounds all over the city. The program is fairly free-form and includes creative arts and crafts, nature and science, games, books, large motor skills activities (running, driving tot vehicles, climbing, and so on), and music. Ages vary by location and start as young as 9 months. The new Richmond Recreation Center (415-666-7020) is a parent favorite for its large gym with lots of equipment. Parents especially recommended the programs at the Cow Hollow Playground (415-292-2003), Upper Noe Valley Recreation Center (415-695-5011), and Moscone Recreation Center (415-292-2006). About the last one, a parent commented: "A bit chaotic at times but has all the toys I can't fit in my house. . . . Good for kids older than 18 months."

San Francisco Recreation and Park Department Aquatics Programs

http://parks.sfgov.org

Some of the city's many public pools offer inexpensive swim lessons for preschool-age children with parent participation, as well as children's lessons for older kids. The following pools offer classes indoors and are heated to 80 degrees: Balboa (415-337-4701, 51 Havelock St.), Coffman (415-337-4702, 1700 Visitacion St.), Garfield (415-695-5001, 26th St. at Harrison St.), Hamilton (292-2001, Geary and Steiner Streets), Rossi (415-666-7014, 600 Arguello Blvd.), Sava (415-753-7000, 19th Ave. at Wawona St.). Comment: "Bear in mind these are public pools in a large city . . . if it doesn't look clean enough for your taste, go elsewhere."

North Bay

Belvedere-Tiburon Recreation Department

1505 Tiburon Blvd.
Tiburon
415-435-4355
www.btrecreation.org

Camp Miwok for preschoolers in the summer is not to be missed! They also provide many preschool enrichment classes during the school year.

Corte Madera Parks and Recreation

498 Tamalpais Dr.
Corte Madera
415-927-5072
www.ci.corte-madera.ca.us

Parents recommended the "Bouncing Babies" drop-in class (low cost, free play in an open gym) and the dance classes.

Larkspur Recreation Department

240 Doherty Dr.
Larkspur
415-927-6746
www.ci.larkspur.ca.us

Marinwood Community Center

775 Miller Creek Rd.
San Rafael
415-479-0775
www.marinwood.org

The "parent and toddler" class for pre-preschoolers is a favorite.

Mill Valley Parks and Recreation Community Center

180 Camino Alto
Mill Valley
415-383-1370
www.millvalleycenter.org

This is a beautiful new facility with indoor pool, fitness center, and gym. Swim classes fill quickly!

Novato Parks, Recreation and Community Services Department

917 Sherman Ave.
Novato
415-897-4323
www.ci.novato.ca.us

Ross Recreation

P.O. Box 117
Ross
415-453-6020
www.rossrecreation.org

We love the soccer and pee-wee sports programs. Comment: "Great summer camps for preschoolers!"

Classes for Kids

321

San Anselmo Recreation

1000 Sir Francis Drake Blvd.
San Anselmo
415-258-4640
www.townofsananselmo.org/
recreation/

Don't miss the gymnastics classes for ages one year and up—a parent favorite! Comment: "Real equipment but perfectly done for wee folks."

San Rafael Community Services

618 B St.
San Rafael
415-485-3333
www.cityofsanrafael.org/cs

Comment: "Camp Lemonade is great for ages 3-5 years."

Sausalito Parks and Recreation Department

420 Litho St.
Sausalito
415-289-4152
www.ci.sausalito.ca.us

The "Tot Club" for children under age 3 is a fun parent-child play time, and they also have many classes for preschoolers.

Strawberry Recreation District

118 E. Strawberry Dr.
Mill Valley
415-383-6494
http://strawberry.marin.org

They do inexpensive swim lessons in an outdoor pool.

East Bay

City of Berkeley Recreation Division

1947 Center St., 1st Fl.
Berkeley
510-981-5151
www.ci.berkeley.ca.us/recreation/

Parents recommended the inexpensive aquatics classes held at several different public pools, including Berkeley High School's "warm pool."

Lafayette-Moraga Recreation

Community Center
500 St. Mary's Road
Lafayette
925-284-2232
www.lafmor-recreation.org

Livermore Area Recreation and Park District

Robert Livermore Community Center
4444 East Ave.
Livermore
925-373-5700
www.larpd.dst.ca.us

This is a huge new community center with a gym and 2 outdoor pools.

Montclair Recreation Center

6300 Moraga Ave.
Oakland
510-482-7812
www.oaklandnet.com/parks/
facilities/

Parents raved about the low-cost tumbling, ballet, and sports classes (ages 2 and up).

Orinda Parks and Recreation Department

Orinda Community Center
26 Orinda Way
Orinda
925-254-2445
www.ci.orinda.ca.us/parksandrec/

Piedmont Recreation

358 Hillside Ave.
Piedmont
510-420-3070
www.ci.piedmont.ca.us

Pleasanton Parks and Community Services

- 200 Old Bernal Ave., 925-931-5340
- Dolores Bengston Aquatic Center
  4455 Black Ave., 925-931-3420
  Pleasanton
www.ci.pleasanton.ca.us/parks.html

San Ramon Community Center

12501 Alcosta Blvd.
San Ramon
925-973-3200
www.ci.san-ramon.ca.us

San Ramon Olympic Pool and Aquatic Park

99007 Broadmoor Dr.
San Ramon
925-973-3240
Don't miss this beautiful new facility with a wonderful indoor pool. Swimming lessons and gymnastic classes fill quickly.

Belmont Parks and Recreation Department

30 Twin Pines Lane
Belmont
650-595-7441
www.belmont.gov

Burlingame Parks and Recreation Department

850 Burlingame Ave.
Burlingame
650-558-7300
www.burlingame.org

Menlo Parks and Community Services

701 Laurel St.
Menlo Park
650-330-2200
www.menlopark.org
The gymnastics program at Burgess Center attracts 1,500 students per week (!), and the swim classes at Burgess Pool are also very popular.

Palo Alto "Enjoy" Program

Department of Community Services
Lucie Stern Community Center
1305 Middlefield Rd.
Palo Alto
650-463-4900
www.paEnjoy.org or www.city.palo-alto.ca.us
Art, music, gymnastics, soccer—they have it all for toddlers and preschoolers.

Classes for Kids

Gyms and Play Programs

These programs are the staples of kids' classes. If you do nothing else, try a play-based program, which often includes music and movement as well as development of large motor skills. We found that the drop-in programs offer flexibility and convenience, as you are not committed to one particular time slot in case you need to miss a class. If you want to meet other parents on a consistent basis, however, a regular class is probably best. Some facilities express age eligibility for their classes and programs in a decimal form: For instance, age 2.9 years means 2 years, 9 months old. When checking out a class, consider whether the equipment is appropriate for the age of the children in the class. Large gymnastics equipment should be scaled down to toddler size. For example, a balance beam should be inches, rather than feet, off the ground. Also examine the school's philosophy of teaching classes for babies and preschoolers; it's way too soon for competitive gymnastics! Rather, the class should build self-esteem and confidence along with developing skills.

San Francisco

Acrosports

639 Frederick St.
415-665-ACRO (2276)
www.acrosports.org
PARENT RATING: ☆ ☆ ☆ ☆

A consistent parent favorite, these popular movement and gymnastics classes include parent participation programs for ages 18-36 months, and drop off classes for older children. Run by a nonprofit organization, classes are held in a 4,700-square-foot facility in a landmark gym across from Kezar Stadium. They also provide great Kinder Camps during school breaks. Comments: "Not the cleanest facility around, but great if you have a good instructor. . . . Amazing teachers. . . . Very fun. . . . Especially great for boys, with lots of bouncing! . . . Facility can be difficult to manage with younger siblings as it is on several levels."

American Gymnastics Club

2520 Judah St.
415-731-1400
www.americangymnasticsclub.com
PARENT RATING: ☆ ☆ ☆ ☆

Designed for children of all ages, this gymnastics program bills itself as "more than just gymnastics," and aims to teach motor development, listening skills, teamwork, self-esteem, and discipline. Classes are small (8:1 student-teacher ratio). The club offers classes at all levels, beginning with the programs for walkers to 18 months, preschool gymnastics for ages 2-5, and progressing to competitive gymnastics. The youngest children (ages 18 mo.-2.6 years) attend parent participation classes. Comment: "Best for girls and children with longer attention spans, as there is a lot of following directions and stretching."

City College of San Francisco Child Observation Classes

1860 Hayes St., Rm. 139 (office)
415-561-1921
www.ccsf.cc.ca.us

PARENT RATING: ☆ ☆ ☆ ☆ ☆

City College child development students run free parents' and infants' groups (newborn to 14 months) and child observation classes (15 months to 5 years) at local churches and playgrounds throughout the city. College students learn by observing and teaching the parents and children. Classes include free play, circle time, snacks, and cleanup. Comments: "Basic socialization. . . . Good program that offers play, art, water projects, Play Doh, and sorting."

Congregation Sherith Israel

2266 California St.
415-346-1720, ext. 32
www.sherithisrael.org

PARENT RATING: ☆ ☆ ☆ ☆ ☆

In a large, clean, carpeted room with lots of well-maintained equipment and toys, the Temple offers weekday drop-in play programs for children (with their parents) from newborn to age 3 years. The classes include free play, circle and music time, puppets, parachute time, and snacks. Friday and Saturday groups celebrate Shabbat. Comments: "Lots of great indoor toys in a big open space but can get crowded. . . . Drop-in pass is a good feature, huge play area, less

frantic than Gymboree. . . . Great rainy day activity! . . . Teacher Mimi is effervescent and fun!" They also offer enrichment classes for pre-school-aged children (ages 2-6) on weekday afternoons, ranging from movement to art to karate. The newest addition to their lineup is a "great" mom and baby (birth to age 3) yoga class with instructor Kari Marble. Comments: "Excellent . . . lots of fun. . . . Room has more toys than I ever dreamed of. . . . Our children run around the room playing with toys and with each other, coming into our circle to climb on us, sing, and explore yoga poses."

DayOne Center

3490 California St. (enter on Locust St.)
415-440-3291
www.dayonecenter.com

PARENT RATING: ☆ ☆ ☆ ☆ ☆

DayOne offers weekly parent-baby play groups, organized by age (from birth to age 12 months) and facilitated by experienced nurses. Discussion centers on parenting topics of interest to the group. Moms can relax and breastfeed, and babies can interact and play in the center's lovely carpeted playroom/classroom. Drop-ins are welcome! Comment: "The parent/baby play groups were fantastic. The women I met in that group became my 'working moms group' and we still meet monthly."

Gymboree

www.gymboree.com (for Bay Area locations)

PARENT RATING: ☆ ☆ ☆ ☆

These developmental play, music, (and now) art classes (franchised all over the country) are divided by age, from newborn to 4 years. Classes received mixed reviews, from "very good program" and "good for younger kids" and "if you've got a climber, it's a great place to burn some energy," to "teachers are not great" and "we got sick every time we went" to "well organized but often too campy." The consensus was that "the value is completely dependent on the teacher." (Personally, we had a wonderful teacher for our Gymbabies class and loved it, mainly because it enabled us to meet other moms with new babies.) With that in mind, take advantage of the free preview class to check out the teacher. Others said that the classes are more worthwhile "once babies are really moving and can try out different movements." The padded equipment and mats are great for crawlers and toddlers learning mobility, and Gymboree is one of the few programs for very young babies in the city. The make-up policy is fairly flexible, which is nice when kids inevitably get sick! Some locations are also offering Baby Signs classes, teaching parent-baby communication via sign language.

Jewish Community Center of San Francisco

3200 California St.
415-292-1200
www.jccsf.org

PARENT RATING: ☆ ☆ ☆ ☆ ☆

A great resource for families in the city, the remodeled JCC is a "fabulous" and "wonderful" new facility, say parents. They have a plethora of different classes for young children. "Parallel Play" provides facilitated playgroups for parents with their babies and toddlers (up to about age 2). The Kindergym weekday drop-in play program for ages 1-3 is held in a large gym and is always crowded, but it features slides, tunnels, climbing apparatus, vehicles, songs, and parachute time. Gym Buddies, for ages 2-3 with a parent, introduces tumbling and equipment and includes play with tricycles, cars, and balls. Gymnastics skills begin in preschool gymnastics (ages 3-5). Music and dance classes begin at age 3 with ballet, tap, creative movement, and instruction in Jewish music and dance. There are Music Together group classes, or individual instruction in violin and piano. Children can also explore art classes in many media for ages 2 and up, with or without parents. Some of the more unique classes for toddlers and preschoolers combine gymnastics with dance, art, or swimming! The list goes on and on: Aikido, Capoeira, yoga, preschool sports, Family Fun days on weekends with special events. They also do birthday parties. Perhaps best of all, the 42,000-square-foot fitness center, with 2 pools and a hot tub, offers swim classes for children, both mommy-and-me (ages 6 months to 4 years) and learn-to-swim (ages 3 and up) types. Parents say these classes are the "best" in the city, but "depend highly on the instructor," and advise parents to "check out the instructor first" and "sign up early as the classes get booked quickly." The teaching pool is warm (90 degrees) and shallow (4 feet at the deep end), and instructors are Red Cross certified. Classes are open to the public. Comments: "Wow! . . . The locker rooms are very nice, and they provide towels and all the amenities."

My Gym

www.my-gym.com (for Bay Area locations)

This franchised gymnastics program has locations throughout the Bay Area. Parents participate in the developmentally appropriate classes for babies and toddlers (up to about age 3.6 years), which are divided by age and incorporate movement, music, and games. The independent classes for ages 3 and up focus on more advanced gymnastics skills, games, and relays. They say they have a 5:1 student to teacher ratio.

Parents Place

1710 Scott St.
415-359-2454
www.parentsplaceonline.org
PARENT RATING: ☆ ☆ ☆ ☆ ☆

This offshoot of Jewish Family and Children's Services provides a variety of great play and parenting classes for children and their parents. Selections include age-appropriate play classes or music classes from 6 months and up, art for ages 2-3 years old, cooking for ages 2-4, and many other parenting workshops and support groups. The drop-in play center (for children up to age 4) is open on some days if you just need to get out of the house. Classes are open to the public. Comment: "An incredible resource . . . my kids loved it."

Presidio YMCA

Lincoln Way at Funston (Building 63, Main Post Gym)
415-447-9622
www.ymcasf.org/presidio
PARENT RATING: ☆ ☆ ☆ ☆

Formerly a military base gym, this renovated facility offers an assortment of programs for preschoolers, including Biddy Sports for ages 3-5. Soccer, tee-ball, basketball, and tumbling are some of the options in the Biddy program. In addition, junior tennis classes start for children as young as 4. Membership is inexpensive and recommended, as "you can get your own workout while your children are in classes or [in] the 'child-watch' facility!"

San Francisco Gymnastics

920 Mason St. (in the Presidio)
San Francisco
415-561-6260
www.sanfranciscogymnastics.com
PARENT RATING: ☆ ☆ ☆ ☆ ☆

This gymnastics facility specializes in teaching gymnastics to preschoolers. Its Kinderbugs program provides age-specific classes beginning with walkers to age 6. The parent-child classes for toddlers are open and unstructured, progressing to more structured classes teaching gymnastics skills (without parents) beginning at age 4. They also do "great birthday parties" and "Parents' Night Out!" Comments: "A great gymnastics program for beginners, even toddlers. . . . The space is airy and clean. . . . Parking is easy. . . . Teachers are excellent. . . . They have a real method of teaching. . . . They're great with kids!"

Temple Emanu-El Early Childhood Programs

2 Lake St.
415-751-2541, ext. 118
www.emanuelsf.org

The Temple has 2 parent participation play programs for babies and toddlers: "Building Blocks" for newborns to age 18 months, and "Stepping Up" for ages 18 months to 2.6 years. Both feature a professional facilitator, opportunity for parent discussion, and age-appropriate activities, including celebrating Jewish holidays. These popular classes fill quickly.

UCSF Bakar Fitness and Recreation Center

1675 Owens St.
415-476-5646
http://mbfitness.ucsf.edu

Opened in September 2005 at UCSF's Mission Bay campus, this beautiful, 63,000-square-foot facility offers Kindergym classes for toddlers. Children can take parent-child or learn-to-swim lessons in the new indoor, warm water pool (while parents can enjoy a workout!). Unlike Millberry Center (see below), memberships are open to the public. Though you do not need to be a member to take classes, members receive discounted rates and priority in registration, as well as access to the Kids Club child care facility.

UCSF Millberry Recreation and Fitness Center

500 Parnassus Ave.
415-476-0334 (aquatics)
415-476-1115 (class registration)
www.cas.ucsf.edu/MPS/

PARENT RATING: ☆ ☆ ☆ ☆ ☆

Millberry Union offers Kindergymusic classes (movement, gymnastics, and music) for parents and children ages 18 months to 3 years, as well as private, semiprivate, and group swim lessons for children ages 6 months to 3 years. The group swim lessons for ages 6-36 months are of the parent-child water play variety, and those for ages 3 and up teach swimming. These popular classes fill quickly. They are open to non-members but members often fill the spaces first.

North Bay

California Parenting Institute

3650 Standish Ave.
Santa Rosa
707-585-6108
http://calparents.org

The mission of this nonprofit parenting organization is to support families and prevent child abuse. Their classes are open to all. Infantgym (crawlers to age 18 months), and Kindergym (ages 15-36 months), are parent-child classes where babies and toddlers can play on equipment and parachutes. "Two's Together" provides a pre-preschool environment for children (with their parents), including arts and crafts and music. The Institute also offers these classes in Spanish, and many wonderful parenting classes and support groups on various topics.

The Dance Palace Community Center

5th and "B" Streets
Point Reyes Station
415-663-1075
www.dancepalace.org

This nonprofit center offers a Baby Gym parent-child play class (birth through age 5), and several classes for preschoolers, including tae kwon do and tumbling, creative dance, and a clay workshop.

Gymboree

See listing under San Francisco.

Gymworld

555 E. Francisco Blvd., Ste. 19
San Rafael
415-482-8580

PARENT RATING: ☆ ☆ ☆ ☆ ☆

These gymnastics classes begin with parent participation classes for ages 18 months to 2 years. The facility is not huge, but clean and bright. Mom or Dad can drop off children ages 3 and up. Private and semiprivate instruction is also available. Comment: "Great for birthday parties . . . friendly instructors."

Jumping Jacks

• Mill Valley
Strawberry Recreation District Center, 118 E. Strawberry Dr.
415-383-6494

• San Rafael
San Rafael Community Center, 618 B St.
415-485-3333

PARENT RATING: ☆ ☆ ☆ ☆

Jumping Jacks offers an indoor gym with mats, obstacle courses, play structures, slides, songs, parachutes, games, bubbles, and more—all designed to build social and motor skills. Classes are divided by age, with one class for crawlers to 22 months, and another for ages 23 months to 3 years. You can drop in on a class or buy a series and create your own schedule. Comments: "Excellent. . . . Very fun on a rainy day. . . . Kind of like taking your kid to a dog park—chaos but they love it. . . . Unstructured play with parachute time at the end."

Marin Elite Gymnastics Academy (MEGA)

72 Woodland Ave.
San Rafael
415-257-6342
www.megagymnastics.com

PARENT RATING: ☆ ☆ ☆ ☆ ☆

This fully-equipped gym offers gymnastics classes for ages 2 and up, grouped by age and ability level. Preschool programs with age-appropriate equipment aim to build basic strength and coordination, as well as gymnastics skills. Parents attend classes with children under age 3. Comments: "Great for boys and girls. . . . Program is structured, so kids learn gymnastics skills as well as how to wait their turn and follow directions. . . . Well-organized classes, with routines."

Novato Parents Nursery School Toddler Time Program

1473 S. Novato Blvd.
Novato
415-897-4498
www.ccppns.org/npns/

PARENT RATING: ☆ ☆ ☆ ☆ ☆

These parent-child participation classes for ages 18 months-2.6 years received rave reviews. Designed to get younger children ready for pre-school, they are a 90-minute, twice-weekly, "less structured version of the preschool program." They teach social skills, taking directions, and motor skills.

Osher Marin Jewish Community Center

200 N. San Pedro Rd.
San Rafael
415-444-8000
www.marinjcc.org
PARENT RATING: ☆ ☆ ☆ ☆ ☆

The JCC's extensive children's pro-gramming, open to the public, includes the ever-popular Side-by-Side (Yad B'Yad) class. Side-by-Side, an introduction to a nursery school setting, provides art, music, and play—with parent participation—for pre-preschoolers ages 18 months to 3 years. The JCC also offers Music Together classes (ages 3 months to 4 years), movement and dance classes (ages 3 and up), and enrichment classes for preschoolers (theater, sports, cooking, yoga, art, science, and nature, among others). There are also parent-tot swimming (ages 9-36 months) and group learn-to-swim classes (ages 3 and up) in indoor and outdoor pools, as well as private and semiprivate swim lessons. Insider advice: Sign up early; Side-by-Side classes, in particular, fill very quickly! Side-by-Side classes are also held at Congregation Kol Shofar in Tiburon, in a more spacious classroom with an outdoor area (register through the JCC). Comment: "Great for swim-ming, great facilities."

Parenting From the Heart

30 Cowbarn Ln., #16
Novato
415-897-8994
E-mail:
heartfulparenting@yahoo.com
Taught by Bonnie Romanow, an experienced Waldorf educator, these parent-child classes offer children a "stimulating and nurturing environ-ment" to play creatively with toys made of natural materials. The class teaches parents appropriate ways to interact and respond to children's needs. The 2-hour morning class includes creative play, singing and movement, snack and story time, and simple crafts and toy making. There are 2 classes: one for walkers to age 21 months, and one for ages 21 months to 3.6 years.

Parents Place Marin

600 5th Ave.
San Rafael
415-491-7959
www.parentsplaceonline.org
PARENT RATING: ☆ ☆ ☆ ☆ ☆

Parents Place has a "beautiful" drop-in play center for families, as well as many wonderful age-appropriate play groups and parenting classes. You can learn baby sign language (birth through 14 months) to communicate with your baby. Classes for toddlers and preschoolers include cooking (ages 2-4 years), song and dance (ages 2-4 years), and yoga (ages 4-6 years). There is also a playgroup for parents and their special needs chil-dren. See the San Francisco listing for more details. Comments: "We love it there. . . . It's also air-conditioned in summer!"

Parents Place Sonoma

1360 N. Dutton Ave., Ste. C
Santa Rosa
707-571-8131
www.parentsplaceonline.org

PARENT RATING: ☆ ☆ ☆ ☆ ☆

This wonderful resource center has drop-in play times for babies and toddlers (through age 4) with their parents. You can enjoy stories, songs, and movement in the center's new playroom.

San Rafael Gymnastics

139-B Carlos Dr.
San Rafael
415-491-1290
www.srgym.com

PARENT RATING: ☆ ☆ ☆ ☆ ☆

Equipment at this Terra Linda gym includes all the Olympic events, a foam pit for jumping, a belt for children to learn to flip, trampolines, and a "tumble tramp." They offer parent-child classes for ages 18 months to 3 years, with an emphasis on free play. Four- and 5-year-olds take a more teacher-directed class and go through circuits such as ladders, tunnels, and tumbling. They also have a summer camp for ages 4 and up, and do birthday parties.

YMCA—Marin

1500 Los Gamos Dr.
San Rafael
415-492-9622
www.ymcasf.org/marin/

PARENT RATING: ☆ ☆ ☆ ☆

The Y's "Magic Moments" play programs (ages 14 months-4 years) teach music, art, games, and stories, and parents are free to participate.

For preschoolers, try the mini-sports program (ages 3-5 years), art classes (ages 3-6 years), or creative movement and ballet classes (ages 3-5 years). The Y also offers swim lessons in an indoor pool, beginning with parent-child water adjustment lessons for children 6-36 months, and progressing to learn-to-swim lessons for preschoolers ages 3-5 years. Comment: "Good swim classes for kids."

East Bay

Bay Island Gymnastics

3775 Alameda Ave.
Alameda
510-533-3939
www.bayislandgymnastics.com

Housed in a new 12,500-square-foot facility, this gymnastics program for children ages 2 and up begins with parent-child classes and progresses to drop-off classes. The classes include listening skills, obstacle courses, a trampoline, a zip line, a rock wall, and a foam pit. Preschool classes use equipment scaled to their size! Parents also can drop off children for "stay-n-play" mornings—3 hours of supervised fun. Comment: "Great birthday parties!"

ClubSport

- Pleasanton
  7090 Johnson Dr.
  925-463-2822
- Walnut Creek
  2805 Jones Rd.
  925-938-8700

www.clubsports.com

PARENT RATING: ☆ ☆ ☆ ☆

Gym Classes

331

These private health clubs offer a variety of children's programs, including gymnastics, dance, soccer, fitness, and yoga. Most are open to ages 2-3 and up. They also provide learn-to-swim private and group lessons for children ages 3 and up, all year round. The pools are outdoors and heated to 82-86 degrees. Classes are open to the public. Comment about the swim lessons: "A very good ratio for group lessons (4 children to one instructor)."

Diablo Gymnastics School

2411 Old Crow Canyon Rd.
San Ramon
925-820-6885
www.diablogym.com
PARENT RATING: ☆ ☆ ☆

This longstanding program (it has been around since the late 1960s) offers Kindergym classes for children ages 1-5 years in a large, newly renovated facility containing 2 gymnasiums. Kids can attend classes on their own beginning at age 3. Classes involve slides, climbing equipment, parachutes, and songs. Comment: "It draws from the local community— less equipment than Gymboree but fun."

Encore Gymnastics

- Brentwood
  2490 Sand Creek Rd.
  925-240-1133
- Walnut Creek
  999 Bancroft Rd.
  925-932-1033
www.encoregym.com

They offer gymnastics and dance classes with an emphasis on positive reinforcement. Gymnastics starts at age 14 months, and tap or ballet starts at 18 months; parents participate until children are 3 years old.

Golden Bear Gymnastics

UC Berkeley Department of Intercollegiate Athletics and Recreational Sports
Golden Bear Recreation Center
25 Sports Ln.
Berkeley
510-642-9821 (registration)
510-643-1133 (program information)
www.oski.org
PARENT RATING: ☆ ☆ ☆ ☆

These popular gymnastics classes for children ages 18 months and up are taught by professionals and college students and are divided by age. Parent participation is required for the youngest Bear Cubs classes (under age 3), which focus on play and movement. At age 3, kids start learning fundamental gymnastics skills without their parents. Parents say it's best for kids who are not easily distracted: class size is small (6 students) but held in a large gym with lots of simultaneous activity. Serious students can move into the competitive gymnastics program.

Gymboree

See listing under San Francisco.

Gymtastic!

1901 Camino Ramon, Ste. D
Danville
925-277-1881
www.gymtastic.com
PARENT RATING: ☆ ☆ ☆ ☆

This noncompetitive, recreational program offers classes in gymnastics, tumbling, and sports skills development.

The program encourages children to learn at their own pace. Children may start at age one (walking) and attend classes with parents until age 3.

Head over Heels Gymnastics

1250 45th St., Ste. E
Emeryville
510-655-1265
www.hohgymnastics.com
PARENT RATING: ☆ ☆ ☆ ☆ ☆

This nonprofit gymnastics school is housed in a 20,000-square-foot facility and claims to be the largest of its kind in Northern California. It's a large gym with a competitive team for older students, but they have a noncompetitive philosophy for toddler and recreational gymnastics classes. Classes include a generous dose of free play, plus circle time and instructional time for skill-building. Children begin at age 18 months in parent-participation classes, and they may attend classes solo beginning at age 3. They also offer "excellent" circus arts classes taught by a circus troupe for ages 4 and up, and they put on great shows. Comments: "Great facility, fun classes . . . giant facility. . . . We like the month-to-month no obligation policy."

Kids in Motion Gymnastics

4137 Piedmont Ave.
Oakland
510-601-8424
www.kimgymnastics.com
PARENT RATING: ☆ ☆ ☆ ☆ ☆

This program's focus is "noncompetitive" gymnastics classes with an emphasis on play. Children may begin at age 20 months, with classes including circle time and emphasizing

following directions. Parent participation is required in classes for children under age 3. They also offer a "parents' night out" several times per month. Comments: "They focus on young children and don't have a competitive team so it's just right for toddlers and preschoolers. . . . Great teachers and safe program."

The Little Gym

www.thelittlegym.com (for Bay Area locations)

This franchised gym, with locations in the East Bay, Peninsula, and South Bay as of 2005, provides a developmental gymnastics program for children ages 4 months to 12 years. There are parent-child classes for infants and toddlers, and preschool gymnastics classes for children ages 3 to kindergarten using gymnastics equipment and tumbling. They also have karate classes (ages 4 and up), sports skills development classes (ages 3-6), summer and holiday camps for ages 3-8, and even a Parents' Survival Night on weekend evenings.

Montclair Community Play Center's Toddler Program

5815 Thornhill Dr.
Oakland
510-810-0510
www.mcpckids.org
PARENT RATING: ☆ ☆ ☆ ☆ ☆

Parents rave about the toddler program run by this parent cooperative preschool. Held on weekday afternoons and Saturday mornings, the classes provide a pre-preschool environment for toddlers ages 15 months to 3 years. Parents participate in the

333

classes, and activities include indoor and outdoor play, art projects, music, and snack time. Preregistration is required for a 9-to-15-week session, and these classes are very popular. Comments: "A great introduction to 'school' with lots of time for free play and socializing. . . . It also gives you priority in admissions to the preschool program."

Temple Beth Abraham

327 MacArthur Blvd.
Oakland
510-547-7726
www.tbaoakland.org

PARENT RATING: ☆ ☆ ☆ ☆ ☆

Parents could not say enough good things about the temple's 2 programs for young children: Kindergym and Yad B'Yad (aka Side-by-Side). Both are held in a large matted room with abundant equipment and toys, such as blocks, books, ride-on vehicles, climbing structures, slides, a ball pit, art easels, and Play Doh tables. There is even a trampoline! Kindergym, for ages 9 months to 3 years, is available on a drop-in basis, and allows ample time for free play, followed by circle time with parachute and bubbles. Yad B'Yad is a series of classes for ages 15 months to 3 years, with free play followed by teacher-led snack, stories, songs, and bubbles. Friday sessions include Shabbat, but the other days do not contain any religious instruction. The reason for all this praise has a lot to do with the "welcoming" and "energetic" teacher, Dawn Margolin, who "constantly interacts with the children" and "knows everyone's name." Comment: "Loved it . . . highly recommended."

Tot Drop

925-284-3999 or 888-868-3767
www.totdrop.com

With locations throughout the East Bay, these drop-in classes for walking babies to preschoolers (ages 1-5 years) feature art, music, play, and socialization. They offer great flexibility; you design your own schedule to a maximum of 12 hours per week; you pay by the hour and may drop off your children.

Tri-Valley Gymnastics

180 Wright Brothers Ave.
Livermore
925-606-0936
www.tvgymnastics.com

This gym has a separate area for its "Mini Stars" program for children ages 18 months to 5 years, with appropriately sized equipment. Students also use obstacle courses, trampolines, a Tumble-Trak, and a foam pit. Classes for children up to age 3 include parent participation.

University Village Recreation Program

1125 Jackson St.
Albany
510-524-4926
http://villagerecreation.housing.berkeley.edu

PARENT RATING: ☆ ☆ ☆ ☆ ☆

This ever-popular UC-Berkeley program offers gymnastics (for ages 18 months and up), creative movement and dance (ages 3-5), and art (ages 2 and up) classes to the public and university communities. Gymnastics classes require parent participation with children up to age 3, and feature a lot of free time followed by circle

334

time. Parents rave about these classes as "fun and inexpensive . . . a great way to meet friends." Insider advice: sign up promptly after registration opens, as classes fill quickly.

Wee Play

1228 Solano Ave.
Albany
510-524-1318
www.wee-play.com

PARENT RATING: ☆ ☆ ☆ ☆ ☆

Just what parents ordered: an indoor play facility where you can drop in, no reservations required! Children ages 0-6 years are welcome in the well-stocked play area during open play hours. You can also drop off children for the afternoon mini-camp (ages 18 months to 3 years), where they can play for 3 hours (pre-registration required, monthly sessions)! Mini-camp is structured like preschool, with movement, art, drama, storytelling, and snacks. They also offer Music Together classes (newborn through age 4 years, see description under Music Classes, below). Comment: "We loved it!"

Windmill Gymnastics

5221 Central Ave., #2
Richmond
510-527-0570
www.windmillgymnastics.com

PARENT RATING: ☆ ☆ ☆ ☆

This 12,000-square-foot gym is packed with equipment and offers gymnastics and dance classes for ages 2 and up. Parents participate with children under age 4. Parents can watch children from the lobby through the windows, and there is a play area for younger siblings. Older students can join the competitive team.

YMCA-Downtown Berkeley

2001 Allston Way
Berkeley
510-848-9622
www.baymca.org

PARENT RATING: ☆ ☆ ☆ ☆

The largest YMCA in the East Bay offers inexpensive, low-key, open-gym, drop-in classes (ages 9 months and up), kindergym gymnastics, little sportsters soccer classes (ages 3-6), parent-child sports (ages 3-4 years), swimming (ages 6 months and up), art, and dance classes. The popular swimming lessons are held in a small, shallow, very warm indoor pool for the youngest children, and progress to a larger pool for older children.

YMCA of the East Bay

Branches in Oakland, Hayward, Fremont, Livermore, and Richmond
510-451-8039
www.ymcaeastbay.org

With 9 East Bay branches, this full-service YMCA offers many different programs for young children. Choose from kindergym, preschool sports, parent-tot (6-36 months) swim classes, or learn-to-swim classes for ages 3-5 using flotation devices. Comment about the Oakland branch: "Nice indoor pool . . . water can be chilly but the price is right for swim classes."

YMCA-Mt. Diablo Region

Branches in Oakley, Walnut Creek, Pleasant Hill, and Danville
925-609-9622
www.mdrymca.org

PARENT RATING: ☆ ☆ ☆ ☆

This YMCA has 4 large branches in Contra Costa and eastern Alameda counties, each offering preschool sports and swim classes.

South Bay

Aerial Tumbling and Acrobatics, Inc.
422 Blossom Hill Rd.
San Jose
408-224-5437
www.atagymnastics.com

This 7,000-square-foot gym offers recreational gymnastics classes for children ages 18 months and up. Classes for children under age 3 require parent participation. The gym features a Tumble Trak with a springy surface to introduce tumbling skills.

Airborne Gymnastics
2250 Martin Ave.
Santa Clara
408-986-8226
www.airborne-gymnastics.com

This 18,000-square foot facility offers gymnastics classes for walkers and up. The beginning classes (for children under age 3) require parent participation.

California Sports Center
www.calsportscenter.com
Three locations in San Jose:
- 336 Race St., 408-280-KIDS (5437)
- 832 Malone Rd., 408-269-KIDS (5437)
- 3001 Ross Ave., 408-264-5439

A Junior Olympic sports training facility, CSC offers gymnastics, swimming, and dance classes in 3 San Jose locations. The GymKids program (ages 18 months to 6 years)

requires parent participation up to age 3 and focuses on basic motor skills, gymnastics, and hand-eye coordination. Dancing Tots classes for preschoolers emphasize dance as a method to improve grace in gymnastics, and there are also tap, ballet, Irish dance, and Scottish dance classes. The swimming program offers parent-child classes for kids under age 3, and Red Cross learn-to-swim lessons for children ages 3 and up.

Gymboree
See listing under San Francisco.

Gymtowne Gymnastics
- San Bruno
  300 Piedmont Ave., Ste. 604
  650-589-3733
- Moss Beach
  850 Airport St.
  650-563-9426
www.gymtowne.com

A competitive gymnastics facility, Gymtowne also offers a Gym Mini program for children ages 1-6 years. Parents participate in the "free play" class for ages 1-2, and beginning at ages 3 to 3.6 years, children attend without parents in more structured classes with teacher direction. Classes are small (6 students per teacher), and they do birthday parties.

The Junior Gym
101 South B St.
San Mateo
650-548-9901
www.juniorgym.com

PARENT RATING: ☆ ☆ ☆ ☆ ☆

This popular program is designed to boost self-confidence in children through motor development, music, and movement. Terrific Tots is a motor development program for preschoolers (ages 2.9-5), incorporating arts and crafts, stories, circle, songs, motor development, and snacks in a preschool morning format. Parent-child gym classes for ages 6-36 months focus on developmental skills and include circle, parachute, obstacle courses. Gymnastics classes (ages 3 years and up, without parents) are divided by age. They also have "sports skills" classes for ages 4 and up, and a "parents' night out" program for ages 3-10 years.

MiniGym Explorations

4115 Jacksol Dr.
San Jose
408-559-4616
www.minigymexplorations.com
This preschool also offers a developmentally appropriate parent-child play program for children ages 8 months to 6 years, divided by age. The program combines play, art, songs, puzzles, circle time, gymnastics, and exercises, and it helps children get ready for preschool and kindergarten.

Palo Alto Jewish Community Center

4000 Middlefield Rd.
Palo Alto
650-493-9400
650-213-9316 (children's programs)
www.paloaltojcc.org
PARENT RATING: ☆ ☆ ☆ ☆ ☆
The JCC offers many different classes for children, including pre-gymnastics, sing and play, music, science, and art. Some of the most popular are the Yad B'Yad parent-child classes for ages birth through 24 months, giving toddlers a 90-minute preview of the preschool morning. Children ages 3 years and up may also take private and semi-private swim lessons during summer camps at the pool in the old JCC facility at 4000 Middlefield Road. Classes are open to the public. Note that sometime in the next few years when construction is complete, the JCC will move to the new Campus for Jewish Life, at 901 San Antonio Rd. in Palo Alto.

Peninsula Gymnastics

1740 Leslie St.
San Mateo
650-571-7555
www.peninsulagym.com
PARENT RATING: ☆ ☆ ☆ ☆ ☆
This 15,000-square-foot facility offers popular preschool gymnastics classes for children ages 2.6 and up (parent participation required until age 3).

Peninsula Jewish Community Center

800 Foster City Blvd.
Foster City
650-212-7522
www.pjcc.org
The PJCC has a new facility with a 50,000-square-foot Athletic Center, a new learning center, and an aquatics complex with indoor and outdoor pools and a kiddie pool. Their age-appropriate "Hugs and Blessings" play programs for children ages 12-26 months and up offer basic socialization, music, art, and physical activity for the pre-preschool crowd. Music Together classes (for newborns

until age 2 years) are also taught here. Enrichment classes for pre-school-aged children include cooking, basketball, soccer, music, art, gymnastics, drama, science, and Spanish. Classes are open to the public.

Peninsula Parents Place

200 Channing Ave.
Palo Alto
650-688-3040
www.parentsplaceonline.org
PARENT RATING: ☆ ☆ ☆ ☆ ☆

This center offers a multitude of classes and resources for parents and children, and all are open to the public. Classes for kids include age-appropriate play groups, baby music and movement for ages 4-14 months, toddler music and movement for ages 15-36 months, music for children ages 1-5, and art for ages 18 months and up. A great drop-in play center (ages 5 years and under) is open many weekdays, and there are parenting classes on almost every topic imaginable.

San Mateo Gymnastics

1306 Elmer St.
Belmont
650-591-8734
www.sanmateogymnastics.com
PARENT RATING: ☆ ☆ ☆ ☆ ☆

Billed as "the largest gymnastic facility in the Bay Area," this gym has been around since 1977. They have a "Baby and Me" program for walkers to age 2 years, and a Munchkins program for children ages 2-6. Parents participate until children reach age 3. Teachers include former Olympians, and though this is a serious training facility, the emphasis is on self-esteem in classes for younger students.

Santa Clara Unified School District Adult Education

1840 Benton St.
Santa Clara
408-984-6220 or 408-423-3500
www.scae.org

SCAE offers parenting and play classes for parents and children, new-born to 30 months, divided by age. Parents discuss developmental issues, and babies experience play, socialization, songs, games, and art.

Twisters Gym

2639 Terminal Blvd.
Mountain View
650-967-5581
www.twistersgym.com

This climbing gym's classes feature gymnastics, movement, and music for children, ages 18 months and up. Parent participation is required in classes for children under age 3.

West Valley Gymnastics

1190 Dell Ave., Unit I
Campbell
408-374-8692
www.wvgs.com

This competitive gym offers pre-school and recreational classes (ages one year and up) in addition to its team program. Parents participate in classes until children reach age 3. The classes are small, with a 6:1 ratio between students and teachers.

Whole Child Fitness

1514 Stafford St.
Redwood City
650-261-1693
www.wholechildfitness.com

This fitness center for kids offers a parent-child free play class for ages 12-36 months, infant massage classes, and physical fitness classes for children ages 4 and up.

YMCA of the Mid-Peninsula

(Branches in Palo Alto, E. Palo Alto, Mountain View, and Redwood City)
3412 Ross Rd.
Palo Alto
650-856-9622
www.ymcamidpen.org

PARENT RATING: ☆ ☆ ☆ ☆ ☆

With 5 Peninsula locations, this YMCA offers a multitude of classes for young children, including gymnastics, sports (hockey, soccer, and basketball), parent-tot swim classes for ages 6 months to 3 years, and learn-to-swim classes for ages 3-5. A parent comments that gym classes are "short . . . but inexpensive and well run." Some complain that the pool temperature is not warm enough for babies under age 2.

Swimming

Swimming lessons for children generally come in 2 flavors: parent-child classes, which focus on getting young babies and toddlers accustomed to the water, and formal swimming lessons, which actually teach older children to swim. Most swimming classes instructors require an adult to accompany each child under age 3 in the pool. The American Academy of Pediatrics recommends delaying formal swimming lessons until after the child reaches age 4, when he or she is developmentally ready. The Mommy and Me types of classes can be fun but won't teach survival skills in the water. Some places do offer more formal survival classes for younger children, but pediatricians say that they will not ensure a child's safety in the water. Experienced swim instructors also say toddlers who learn to "doggy paddle" may pick up bad habits that might be difficult to change when it comes time for them to learn correct strokes.

A swim tip: Make sure that the pool you choose for baby and toddler classes is kept very warm—90 degrees is optimal. Parents responding to our surveys complained that some of the adult pools offering children's classes weren't warm enough for babies and young children. If so, try one of the swim schools specializing in instructing children.

More insider advice: As long as the pool is warm, you don't need to spend a lot of money on lessons for children under age 3. Inexpensive classes through your local park and recreation department or YMCA are fine when they are of the parent-child variety, since you (the parent) will be the primary instructor, the main goal is having fun in the water, and children generally won't learn to swim until they are at least 3.

When a child is ready to begin the "learn-to-swim" type of lessons, we have found that it is usually worth the extra cost to pay for a private instructor in a high-quality program. Many times children will progress so much more quickly in private lessons that you will save money in the long run by not having to pay for as many sessions. Look for American Red Cross-certified swim instructors, and make sure your instructor is mature enough to handle a child in the water. High school age instructors, in our experience, often do not know what to do with a child who balks at getting in the water.

Many local recreation departments, community centers, and private clubs offer low-cost swim lessons. See above under the Recreation Departments section. The following pools stood out as parent favorites:

San Francisco

Golden Gateway Tennis and Swim Club
370 Drumm St.
415-616-8800
www.ggtsc.com
PARENT RATING: ☆ ☆ ☆ ☆ ☆

This private club offers private swim lessons to the public for all ages, as well as a parent-tot class for babies. The pools are beautiful, and if there is anywhere warm in San Francisco, this is it! Comments: "The water is always really warm which makes even an outdoor swim lesson on a cool day enjoyable, especially when mom or dad get to take a dip in the steaming hot tub. . . . They have a nice way of working with children . . . they are serious about skills yet fun. . . . Kirsten is the best teacher . . . she knows what it takes to get those little sharks and mermaids swimming."

The Janet Pomeroy Center (formerly Recreation Center for the Handicapped)

Herbst Pool
207 Skyline Blvd.
415-665-4241 or 415-665-4109 x. 5204
www.janetpomeroy.org
PARENT RATING: ☆ ☆ ☆ ☆

This private, nonprofit organization has long been offering Mommy and Me-type swim lessons to the public for ages 6 months to 5 years in its warm, therapeutic indoor pool. The pool's depth (2 to 6 feet) and temperature (90-93 degrees) are perfect for babies, and the classes are relatively inexpensive. Some complain that the changing room is not terribly fancy and that the pool closes occasionally for maintenance, but this is the only game in town if you want a truly warm indoor pool. Comment: "We sing songs and teach swim skills like kicking, blowing bubbles, and floating." Insider advice: Enrollment is by lottery, with preference to returning students, so you may want to make back-up plans if you don't get in.

Jewish Community Center of San Francisco

See listing under Gyms and Play Programs—San Francisco.

La Petite Baleen

See listing under Swimming—South Bay. Many San Francisco parents make the short commute to this San Bruno school.

Presidio Community YMCA

Letterman Pool
1151 Gorgas
415-447-9676
www.ymcasf.org/presidio
PARENT RATING: ☆ ☆ ☆ ☆

Skippers Program swim classes for children ages 6 months to 5 years begin with parents working with children on water adjustment (up to age 3) and progress to children learning swimming skills. The classes themselves received positive reviews, but many complained of the "variable" or "chilly" pool temperatures, even in the smaller pool heated to 86 degrees. Even so, these classes fill up fast. Comments: "Classes are inexpensive. . . . We love it."

UCSF Bakar Fitness and Recreation Center

See listing under Gyms and Play Programs—San Francisco.

UCSF Millberry Recreation and Fitness Center

See listing under Gyms and Play Programs—San Francisco.

USF Koret Health and Recreation Center

Parker and Turk Sts.
415-422-6697
www.usfca.edu/koret/
PARENT RATING: ☆ ☆ ☆ ☆

The University of San Francisco's fitness center is a sparkling, newer facility with an Olympic-size indoor pool. Parent-child group swim lessons for ages 9 months to 5 years are open to non-members and focus on water adjustment and beginning swimming skills. Private and semiprivate lessons

341

are also available. However, the water is kept at adult temperatures, so it may be too cool for young children, particularly babies.

Ann Curtis School of Swimming, Inc.

25 Golden Hinde Blvd.
San Rafael
415-479-9131
www.anncurtis.com

PARENT RATING: ☆ ☆ ☆ ☆ ☆

Founder Ann Curtis was an Olympic swim star during the 1940s, and this school has a stellar reputation. Group swim lessons (4 students per teacher) are held May through August in an outdoor, heated pool (85-87 degrees) for children ages 4 and up. The school is open to non-members, but members receive much-needed preference in scheduling lessons.

Marinwood Community Center Pool

775 Miller Creek Rd.
San Rafael
415-479-0775
www.marinwood.org

PARENT RATING: ☆ ☆ ☆ ☆

Open only during the spring and summer season, this public pool offers a parent-tot class for children ages 18-36 months, as well as private or group lessons for ages 3 and up. The pool is outdoors and heated to 82 degrees.

Meridian Sports Club at Rolling Hills

351 San Andreas Dr.
Novato
415-897-2185
www.rollinghillsclub.com

PARENT RATING: ☆ ☆ ☆ ☆ ☆

Parent-tot classes, for children ages 6 months to 3 years, and group lessons for ages 3 and up, are held during the summer in an outdoor pool heated to 82 degrees. Additionally, children may take private lessons year-round, as one of the club's 2 outdoor pools is covered in winter. Classes are open to non-members. Comment: "Very professional and effective."

Mt. Tam Racquet Club

Magnolia Ave. and Doherty Dr.
Larkspur
415-924-6226
www.mttamrc.com

PARENT RATING: ☆ ☆ ☆ ☆

This club features both indoor and outdoor heated pools, so classes are held year-round. American Red Cross-based parent-child swim classes for children ages 6 months to 3 years, as well as learn-to-swim group lessons for ages 4-8, are open to non-members. Private and semiprivate lessons are also available. Comments: "Small classes with only 3 students per instructor. . . . Tish [the director] is great!"

Nancy's Mommy and Me Swim School

San Rafael
415-459-5145

PARENT RATING: ☆ ☆ ☆

These classes received mixed reviews. Nancy's approach is to teach babies and toddlers lifesaving water techniques (e.g., holding their breath underwater, getting their heads above water, and swimming to the side of the pool). All classes are held at Nancy's home in San Rafael. Parent participation classes begin in a hot tub and progress to a small round covered pool heated to 92 degrees. She teaches babies as young as 3 months old, and mixes ages and abilities in classes.

Osher Marin Jewish Community Center

See listing under Gyms and Play Programs—North Bay.

Rafael Racquet and Swim Club

95 Racquet Club Dr.
San Rafael
415-456-1153

PARENT RATING: ☆ ☆ ☆ ☆ ☆

This club offers group learn-to-swim lessons for children ages 4 and up, and private lessons for ages 3 and up, during the summer season. The pool is well maintained, outdoors, and heated to 81-83 degrees. Classes are open to non-members. Comments: "Great, mature, well-trained teachers, from the director Marc Detraz on down the line. . . . Beautiful facility with views of the hills . . . wonderful place to watch your children learn to swim."

Ross Valley Swim and Tennis Club

235 Bon Air Rd.
Kentfield
415-461-5431

PARENT RATING: ☆ ☆ ☆ ☆

This private club offers group lessons for children ages 4 and up, and private lessons for all ages, in an outdoor, heated pool (81-83 degrees) during the summer season. Classes are open to non-members. Comment: "The private lessons are worth it, though groups are small with only 3 students per teacher."

Scott Valley Swim and Tennis Club

50 Underhill Rd.
Mill Valley
415-383-3483 (Paul Stasiowski, ext. 101)

PARENT RATING: ☆ ☆ ☆ ☆ ☆

Swim team coaches at this private club offer group and private learn-to-swim lessons for ages 4 and up. Classes are open to the public. Comment: "My daughter is just finishing her first week and is already floating on her back and swimming underwater to the instructor."

Sleepy Hollow Pool/Mark Anderson Aquatics

1317 Butterfield Rd.
San Anselmo
415-455-5952
www.shha.org

PARENT RATING: ☆ ☆ ☆ ☆ ☆

Mark Anderson Aquatics offers private and group learn-to-swim lessons to the public at this private pool, owned by the Sleepy Hollow Homes Association. Classes are held in a newly remodeled outdoor pool heated to 83 degrees during the summer season. Children must be 3 years old to participate, and there are no parent-tot classes. Comments: "Small class sizes . . . 3 students to one teacher . . . nice community feel. . . .

Swim Classes

343

They have a powerhouse swim team when your kids get older!"

Tiburon Peninsula Club

1600 Mar West
Tiburon
415-435-2169
www.tiburonpc.org

PARENT RATING: ☆ ☆ ☆ ☆

This private club offers private lessons to the public for children ages 3 and up in an outdoor heated pool during the summer season.
Comments: "They have lots of experienced teachers . . . convenient private lessons in 30-minute intervals . . . willing to work with beginning swimmers. . . . I have seen many 3-year-olds able to hold their breath and move around comfortably in the water."

YMCA

See listing under Gyms and Play Programs—North Bay.

East Bay

Albany Community Pool

1311 Portland Ave.
Albany
510-559-6640
www.albany.k12.ca.us

PARENT RATING: ☆ ☆ ☆ ☆

This heated (up to 84 degrees) indoor public swimming pool offers popular parent-tot classes for children ages 6 months to 4 years, and learn-to-swim classes for children ages 4 and up.
Comment: "Best for the 'mommy-and-me' class."

Bear Swim School

Berkeley
510-287-9010
www.bearswimming.com

Bear Swimming, a nonprofit competitive swim team, offers learn-to-swim lessons for children through its swim school. Lessons run April through October in the outdoor West Campus Pool (2100 Browning Street, Berkeley), and classes are small (3 students per instructor). The instructor does not get in the water or teach water survival per se, but does focus on teaching how to swim correctly according to methods developed by the school.

Canyon Pool Swim School

21 Campbell Ln.
El Sobrante
510-223-4600

PARENT RATING: ☆ ☆ ☆ ☆ ☆

This popular school specializes in teaching children to swim. They offer both a parent-baby class (8-42 months) and learn-to-swim classes (beginning at age 3.6 years) during the spring and summer season. Groups are kept at 5 students maximum per teacher, and private and semiprivate lessons are also available. Comments: "A very warm outdoor pool (90 degrees), lots of personal attention, and great teachers. . . . The teachers are all adults. . . . My kids have had great success in learning to swim there. . . . We love it."

ClubSport

See listing under Gyms and Play Programs—East Bay.

Contra Costa Jewish Community Center

2071 Tice Valley Blvd.
Walnut Creek
925-938-7800
www.ccjcc.org

This community center offers both private (for all ages) and group (for ages 2 and up) swim lessons to the public in an outdoor pool heated to 78-81 degrees during the summer season. They also have a "tiny tots" class for babies and toddlers with their parents. JCC membership is required for classes, but guest passes are available.

Fremont Swim School

- Fremont
  42400 Blacow Rd., 510-657-SWIM (7946)
- Newark
  37400 Cedar Blvd., 510-794-SWIM (7946)
- Livermore
  2821 Old First St., 925-373-SWIM (7946)

www.fremontswimschool.com

PARENT RATING: ☆ ☆ ☆ ☆ ☆

Classes are held year-round in indoor pools heated to 92 degrees. Tiny tot classes (for ages 6 months to 3 years) require parent participation and teach water adaptation and safety skills such as getting to the side of the pool. Preschool classes for ages 3-5 focus on water safety, front float, and beginning strokes, and children attend on their own.

Harriet Plummer Aquatic School

1150 Nogales St.
Lafayette
925-943-7331
www.harrietplummeraquatics.com

PARENT RATING: ☆ ☆ ☆ ☆ ☆

This swim school offers private learn-to-swim lessons year round in a residential setting. In the winter, the outdoor pool (heated to 94 degrees) is enclosed with a dome. They begin with children as young as 3 years old and specialize in teaching children. Parents say Harriet is a wonderful teacher with great success in getting even fearful children to swim.

Haufler Aquatics Swim School

3500 Mountain Blvd. (class location)
4100 Redwood Rd., Ste. 189 (office)
Oakland
510-446-7946
www.haufleraquatics.com

PARENT RATING: ☆ ☆ ☆ ☆ ☆

In operation since 1981, this school offers swim lessons during the summer season at Holy Names University in Oakland, in a recently refurbished pool heated to 82-85 degrees. They start kids at age 3 and specialize in teaching children to swim. The classes are small, with a 3:1 student-teacher ratio maximum (often 2:1) in groups, and they also offer private lessons. Comments: "Worth the price . . . warm pool . . . great teachers from college swim teams. . . . They use their own method of teaching. . . . My kids love it."

Swim Classes

Little Dipper Swim School

553 Boyd Rd.
Pleasant Hill
925-932-5861
www.littledipperswimschool.com
PARENT RATING: ☆ ☆ ☆ ☆ ☆

Since 1981, this home-based swim school has specialized in teaching babies, toddlers, and preschoolers to swim. The outdoor pool is heated to 94 degrees, and during the winter months, it is covered with a dome for warmth. The parent-child classes for children under age 3 are small (5 students), and unlike most tot classes, teach children to swim independently. Children ages 3 and up can choose private or semiprivate classes. "It's not fancy, but they are very successful in teaching children to swim at a very young age. . . . The teachers provide a lot of positive reinforcement and personal attention."

Mills College Pool

510-430-2170
www.mills.edu
PARENT RATING: ☆ ☆ ☆ ☆ ☆

Parents highly recommended the swim lessons at this outdoor pool (heated to 80 degrees) on the Mills College campus. They offer parent-child (ages 6 months to 4 years) and preschooler (ages 3-5) group lessons during the summer, and private lessons all year. Classes are open to the public. Comments: "Clean, beautiful pool. . . . They have a large shallow end for teaching and a lovely grassy area."

Piedmont Swim Club

777 Magnolia Ave.
Piedmont
510-655-5163
PARENT RATING: ☆ ☆ ☆ ☆

This private club opens its swim lessons to the public during the summer. Kids as young as 3 years old may begin lessons in the club's 90-degree outdoor pool. Comment: "Worth the extra cost . . . good teachers."

Roberts Regional Recreation Area and Pool

10570 Skyline Blvd. (at Joaquin Miller Rd.)
Oakland
510-482-0971 (pool)
510-636-1684 (registration)
www.ebparks.org
PARENT RATING: ☆ ☆ ☆ ☆

The park district offers Red Cross-method group and private swim lessons during the summer in the outdoor, heated Roberts Pool. Group classes for children under age 5 require parent participation.

Sherman Swim School

1075 Carol Ln.
Lafayette
925-283-2100
PARENT RATING: ☆ ☆ ☆ ☆ ☆

This longtime favorite (they've been teaching kids to swim since 1961!) offers private and semiprivate learn-to-swim lessons in outdoor pools heated to 90-92 degrees during the spring, summer, and fall. Their 3 pools range in depth from 6 inches to 12 feet, so even infants as young as 9 months old may take lessons. Parent participation is recommended for infants and toddlers. Parents highly recommend their approach and say they are very successful in teaching children to swim. Comments: "Worth the price. . . . Our kids learned more there in 2 lessons than in all the other previous group lessons combined. . . . Sign up early because they fill quickly."

Strawberry Canyon Recreation Area Pool

1 Centennial Dr.
Berkeley
510-643-6720
www.oski.org
PARENT RATING: ☆ ☆ ☆ ☆ ☆

This university outdoor pool, open to the public, offers private, semiprivate, and group lessons for children ages 6 months and up during the summer season, following American Red Cross methods. Classes for children up to age 3 require parent participation. Tiny Tots group lessons for ages 3-5 maintain a 4:1 ratio between students and teachers. Parents rave about the quality of the instruction, as many of the teachers come from the university's swim team. The pool water is kept warm, but it can be cool on the deck.

YMCA

See listing under Gyms and Play Programs—East Bay.

South Bay

Aitken's Peninsula Swim School

1602 Stafford St.
Redwood City
650-366-9211
www.peninsulaswim.com
PARENT RATING: ☆ ☆ ☆ ☆

For 38 years this swim school has been teaching children ages 6 weeks and up, in an indoor/outdoor pool heated to 91 degrees. They offer baby-parent, private, semiprivate, and group lessons. Classes incorporate songs and games.

Almaden Valley Athletic Club (AVAC) Swim School

5400 Camden Ave.
San Jose
408-267-4032
www.avac.us
PARENT RATING: ☆ ☆ ☆ ☆ ☆

This popular and well-regarded club specializes in teaching children to swim, and they designed their pool specifically for teaching swimming lessons. They offer group classes for children ages 6 months and up in a shallow indoor pool (2.5-4.5 feet) heated to 90 degrees. In the parent-child water adaptation classes for children under age 3, the ratio is small (5-6 students to 1 teacher). Children age 3 and up are grouped by age and ability, with a student-teacher ratio of 4 to 1. Parents can watch from a covered viewing area.

Betty Wright Swim Center at the Community Association for Rehabilitation (C.A.R.)

3864 Middlefield Rd.
Palo Alto
650-494-1480
www.c-a-r.org
PARENT RATING: ☆ ☆ ☆ ☆ ☆

This rehabilitation center offers year-round swim classes to the public in its warm indoor pool. Choose from parent-child group classes for children ages 4 months to 3 years, group learn-to-swim classes for ages 3-5, or private lessons. Comments: "The water is 90-91 degrees—perfect. . . . Warm water—great teacher."

California Sports Center

See listing under Gyms and Play Programs—South Bay.

DACA (DeAnza Cupertino Aquatics) Swim School

21111 Stevens Creek Blvd.
Cupertino
408-446-5600
www.daca.org

PARENT RATING: ☆ ☆ ☆ ☆ ☆

Though they also have a well-regarded competitive team, this popular school specializes in teaching preschoolers. They offer weekly private, semiprivate, and group classes in a 90-degree indoor pool. Parent-tot classes begin at 3 months, and learn-to-swim classes begin at 3 years.

La Petite Baleen Swim Schools

- San Bruno
  434 San Mateo Ave., 650-588-7665
- Half Moon Bay
  775 Main St., 650-726-3676
www.swimlpb.com

PARENT RATING: ☆ ☆ ☆ ☆ ☆

The indoor pools at this children's swim school—a favorite of both city and Peninsula parents—are very warm (90 degrees) and great even for young babies. Parent-tot classes, from ages 2 to 36 months, focus on water adjustment and play. Once a child reaches 30 months and demonstrates certain skills, he or she may enter a learn-to-swim class without a parent. Comments: "The classes are small and focus on technique. . . .

Hands down the best program around for teaching young children to swim. . . . Love it. . . . Great teachers. . . . My kids love getting ribbons at each level. . . . The only program I've seen where 2-year-olds actually learn to swim! . . . They are looking to open a branch in the city, which would be so wonderful! . . . If you really want your child to learn to swim, there's just no place like LPB. . . . It's been unbelievable to see my 3-year-old son's progress, how proud he is of his accomplishments and how much he loves to swim now."

Los Gatos Swim and Racquet Club

14700 Oka Rd.
Los Gatos
408-356-2136
www.lgsrc.com

PARENT RATING: ☆ ☆ ☆ ☆ ☆

Lessons are open to the public and are taught in an outdoor pool heated to 82 degrees. Parent-tot classes for children ages 6-36 months teach water adjustment, and learn-to-swim group and private lessons begin at age 3.

Palo Alto Jewish Community Center

See listing under Gyms and Play Programs—South Bay.

Peninsula Covenant Community Center Swim School

3623 Jefferson Ave.
Redwood City
650-364-6272
www.peninsulacovenant.com or
www.pcaswimteam.com

PARENT RATING: ☆ ☆ ☆ ☆

Private and semiprivate learn-to-swim classes are held year round in an outdoor pool heated to 82 degrees for children ages 3 and up. In the summer the center also hosts parent-tot classes for ages 6 months and up. You do not need to be a member to take swim lessons.

Peninsula Jewish Community Center Aquatics Program

800 Foster City Blvd.
Foster City
650-212-7522
www.pjcc.org

The PJCC has a beautiful, huge new Athletic Center with indoor and outdoor pools, a kiddie pool, and a whirlpool. Both large pools have designated "teaching areas" with depths of only 2.5 feet—perfect for the little ones. They offer parent-child group classes for ages 6 months to 3 years, learn-to-swim classes beginning at age 3, and private and semiprivate lessons for all ages. Classes are open to the public.

Taft Swim School

57 E. 40th Ave.
San Mateo
650-349-SWIM

PARENT RATING: ☆ ☆ ☆ ☆ ☆

Founded by a nationally renowned swimmer, this family-owned school has been teaching children to swim since 1955 in its indoor pool heated to 88 degrees. Parent-tot classes teach water safety habits. Small group lessons for children ages 4 and up teach children to swim.

YMCA of the Mid-Peninsula

See listing under Gyms and Play Programs—South Bay.

Music

With so many studies documenting the benefits of early music education to brain development, you won't want to miss out on exposing your children to music . . . even beginning in infancy! While there are a few programs (e.g., Suzuki) that provide formal musical instrument instruction to children as young as 3, most others recommend delaying those types of lessons until ages 6-7, when the hands are developmentally ready and the child has begun to read (and has expressed interest in learning an instrument). Developmentally appropriate programs for young children instead focus on singing, dancing, developing pitch and rhythm, and playing simple instruments such as drums and xylophones. There are several major methods of teaching music to young children, and out of those methods have arisen several major schools or music instruction franchises. You may want to familiarize yourself with each of their approaches before deciding on a class for your child.

Here are the 5 major methods of teaching music to young children:

◆ **Dalcroze-Eurhythmics** (www.dal-crozeusa.org), based on the teachings of Swiss composer and educator Emile Jaques-Dalcroze, emphasizes 3 basic elements of music: rhythm, dynamics, and tone and form. Students do activities designed to get them to listen, respond through rhythmic movement, and invent in classes. They learn music through movement. Contact the Dalcroze Society of America, via the website listed above, for certified educators in your area.

◆ **Kodály Method** (http://kodaly.hnu.edu or www.oake.org), based on the work of Hungarian composer and educator Zoltan Kodály, focuses on singing and is used worldwide. (Kodály was a composer of children's choruses.) In the Kodály philosophy, everyone has innate musical ability, music should be introduced as early as possible to everyone's education, and we should teach music so that it is "not a torture but a joy for the pupil . . . [and will] instill a thirst for finer music." The Kodály method primarily uses singing games, folk music, props, hand signs, and solfege names (e.g., do-re-mi) to teach music, and later incorporates instruments. This method is not franchised, but many classes incorporate elements of this method.

◆ **Orff-Schulwerk** (www.aosa.org), based on the philosophy of American composer Carl Orff, is a method of teaching music emphasizing singing, chanting rhymes, clapping, and keeping a beat with instruments like drums, xylophones, and glockenspiels. Log onto the website for more details. Certain of the classes listed below incorporate this teaching method, but the method is not franchised.

◆ **Suzuki Method** (www.suzuki-music.com), originating in Japan, introduces instruments (primarily violin, cello, and piano), to children as young as 2-3 years old. Students do not learn to read music until they have mastered technique, meaning they can actually play music. They listen to the music repeatedly and watch their peers playing music before they attempt to play, and they are taught in groups rather than individually. Parents play a huge role, attending all lessons and working with children at home. The website has listings of local Suzuki Method instructors.

◆ **Yamaha Music Education System** (www.yamaha.com or www.yamaha-mf.or.jp/english/) also began in Japan, when in the 1950s the Yamaha Corporation established a system of classes to teach customers how to use its keyboards. Now an international system of sequential group classes, they begin at age 4, require parent participation, and emphasize listening, actually playing music, and singing. The goal is to develop rhythm, melody, harmony, and musical creativity.

And here are the major schools or franchises teaching music to young children:

◆ **Kindermusik International**
(www.kindermusik.com or 800-628-5687) is a series of classes designed for children ages newborn to 7 years. Classes are divided by age, and within each age range there are 4 to 6 different semesters of classes, each with a different theme. Generally class tuition includes a CD of the semester's music and home materials incorporating the theme. In the Kindermusik philosophy, "Every child is musical, and every parent is the child's most important teacher." Kindermusik is a national program; classes are taught by individual licensed instructors at various locations locally. Log onto the website to find a licensed educator near you.

PARENT RATING: ☆ ☆ ☆ ☆ ☆

Comments: "Excellent, but depends highly on the teacher. . . . The teacher encouraged my child to actively sing, move, and play instruments rather than sitting passively. Helped my child develop 'pitch.' . . . Slightly more structured than other programs. . . . Best for babies under age 2." We took these classes when our children were babies, and loved them. (Unfortunately, our teacher has retired!) Here are some local Kindermusik educators recommended by parents we surveyed:

◇ Dianne "DeeDee" Lawton, San Francisco, 415-561-9754, www.kindermusikwithdeedee.com

◇ Charlotte Nytzen, Baby Birds Music, Marin locations, 415-383-3322, www.babybirdsmusic.com

◇ Melissa Ayotte, Marin locations, 415-721-1929, www.singandsign.net (She also teaches sign language for babies.)

◇ Fran Oglesby, Sonoma County Children's Music, Santa Rosa, 707-527-7900, www.childrenlovemusic.com

◆ **Music Together** (www.musictogether.com or 800-728-2692) is a research-based, developmentally appropriate national program of musical instruction for infants, toddlers, preschoolers, and kindergarteners. The group that put together this music program did much of the pioneering research about music and young children. The program focuses on "encouraging the actual experiencing of music rather than the learning of concepts or information about music." Classes are mixed age so siblings may attend together, and classes emphasize parental participation. The program is taught internationally by independent certified teachers. Each semester has a different musical instrument theme, such as drums, tambourines, and so on. Tuition includes a CD, a cassette, a songbook, and a book for parents about music education. Log onto the website to find a licensed educator near you and discover more about the program.

PARENT RATING: ☆ ☆ ☆ ☆ ☆

Again, your experience will depend on your instructor, but we took these classes with our toddlers and loved them. Comments: "What a great variety of music from all over the world. . . . We loved exploring the different meters, rhythms, and sounds. . . . The best recorded music of any of these children's programs, so it's a lot of fun for the parents too. . . . They allow each child to be creative, and there are no 'right ways' to do things.

. . . Beth Crespan in Marin is great . . . she has a wonderful way with children. . . . We love teacher Bettina Latman in Marin. . . . The CDs are lifesavers in the car." Here are some local Music Together educators recommended by parents we surveyed:

✧ Paul Godwin, Music Together of San Francisco, 415-596-0229, www.musictogethersf.com

✧ Kelly Wiley, Golden Gate Music Together (San Francisco/Marin), www.goldengatemusictogether.com

✧ Beth Crespan, Music Together of Marin, 415-388-2464, www.music4families.com

✧ Stacy Walden, Music Together with Stacy (Bay Area Discovery Museum), 415-595-7298

✧ Julie Tanenbaum, East Bay Music Together, 510-843-8641, www.eastbaymusictogether.com

◆ **Harmony Road Music Courses** (www.harmonyroadmusic.com), developed by a Yamaha instructor, is a franchised program for young children, beginning at age 18 months. Not surprisingly, students use a digital keyboard. The classes require parent participation and incorporate solfege (do, re, mi) singing, movement, rhythm, and ear training. We have not personally experienced these courses or received feedback on them, but some of the local schools offering them include:

✧ San Francisco School of Music, 1383A 9th Ave., 415-294-5050

✧ Santa Rosa Conservatory of Music, 1615 Cleveland Ave., Santa Rosa, 707-535-0800, www.santarosacm.com (affiliated with the SF School of Music, above)

✧ Harmony Road Music School at Piedmont Piano Company, 4382 Piedmont Ave., Oakland, 510-652-1222, www.piedmontpiano.com

✧ New Mozart School of Music, Palo Alto, 650-324-2373, www.newmozartschool.com

In addition to the Kindermusik and Music Together classes listed above, the following music classes stood out as parent favorites:

San Francisco

Avi Downes' Piano Studio for Children

415-606-3100

In her private studio in the Richmond/Seacliff neighborhood, San Francisco native and European-trained concert artist Avi Downes specializes in teaching piano to young children. Children ages 3 and up receive private lessons in piano technique and music theory, taught in a fun, upbeat style.

Jon's School of Music

- San Francisco
  4150 Balboa St. (class location)
- Berkeley
  Shepherd of the Hills Lutheran Church, 401 Grizzly Peak (class location)

415-971-5435 (office)
www.jsom.com

PARENT RATING: ☆ ☆ ☆ ☆ ☆

Musician Jon Merker, formerly of the Music Time program, teaches classes for young children in San Francisco and Berkeley. He developed the curriculum himself, children are grouped by age (from 12 months to 6 years) in small classes (no more than 8 students), and parents accompany the children. Classes include singing songs, learning musical notes and pitch, and playing actual instruments (keyboards, guitars, drums, violins, bass, cello, xylophones, brass, and woodwinds). Comment: "It's a fantastic class and space. Jon's 'hands-on real instruments' way of teaching class is pretty cool—real drum sets, guitars, and more for kids as young as one year old. . . . A definite must."

Jewish Community Center

See listing under Gyms and Play Programs—San Francisco.

Jump Up Music

St. John's Church, 25 Lake St. (class location)
San Francisco
415-672-3553 (Chris Molla, instructor)
www.jumpupmusic.com

PARENT RATING: ☆ ☆ ☆ ☆ ☆

The former director of Playsongs' music program (see below) and a beloved teacher among San Francisco parents, Chris Molla has created his own Orff-based music and movement classes, Jump Up Music. There are parent-child group classes for newborns to 18 months, and also mixed-age classes for infants through age 5. All classes include singing, dancing, games, rhymes, age-appropriate instruments, and group drumming, and almost all the music is played live or sung unaccompanied. Chris often accompanies students on guitar, accordion, and piano. Tuition includes a CD and songbook, and the repertoire includes folk songs from around the world, a smattering of his own compositions, and nursery rhymes. Comments: "Chris has amazing music classes! . . . Awesome. . . . Wonderful."

Mary Ann Hall's Music for Children

415-861-1121 (Jill and Steve Pierce, instructors)
www.musicforchildrenca.com (for class locations)

PARENT RATING: ☆ ☆ ☆ ☆ ☆

These sequential music classes for toddlers through age 6, with hands-on instruments, are held in several locations in San Francisco, Marin, and the Peninsula. The curriculum is 28 weeks in duration and extends throughout the school year. Beginning at age 4, children attend class on their own and receive piano lessons each week, and also do written activities in their music books. Music for Children is a national program involving live and recorded music, singing, movement, hands-on instrument play, rhythm training, and a different theme every week. We took these classes with our children and loved them! Comments: "I particularly liked how the teacher explained musical concepts by doing. For example, a quarter note was a walking beat, an eighth note was a running beat . . . the children really understood the notes because they were running around the room! . . . My children asked every morning if this was a 'music' day. . . . I loved the ear training activities where each child had to listen for his own particular music so he knew when to come out to perform his own dance. . . . Fun *and* educational classes!"

Natural Resources' Music Classes

816 Diamond St.
415-550-2611
www.naturalresourcesonline.com
PARENT RATING: ☆ ☆ ☆ ☆

Parents highly recommended these music classes with a professional cellist. Try a series, Rhythm Kids, for ages 18 months to 3 years, or a Mother/Baby Music Workshop for infants to 14 months.

Parents Place

See listing under Gyms and Play Programs—San Francisco.

Playsongs

49 Moraga Ave.
415-931-0149
www.sfplaysongs.com
PARENT RATING: ☆ ☆ ☆ ☆ ☆

This popular program now offers music classes, French playgroups, art classes, and nature walks—all under one roof! Under the direction of a new Venezuelan instructor, Jackeline Rago, their approach to music class-

es has changed in recent years. They now incorporate folk, popular, and contemporary music from around the world, using live music and recordings. They take children from newborns to age 5, and some classes are taught in Spanish. They also offer parent-child (18 months to 3 years) and preschooler (ages 3-5) French playgroups, with small class sizes (no more than 4 children). "Nature Walks and Nurture Talks" combines outdoor hikes with enhancing age-appropriate communication. Comments: "Very talented teachers . . . great art, music, and nature walk classes . . . nice space and easy parking in the Presidio. . . . World music classes offer the most variety of instruments and songs."

San Francisco Conservatory of Music, Preparatory Division

1201 Ortega St.
415-759-3429
www.sfcm.edu
PARENT RATING: ☆ ☆ ☆ ☆ ☆

The Conservatory's early childhood education department offers classes in several different musical theories, including Dalcroze-Eurhythmics and Orff-Schulwerk, for children ages 4 to 9. Students are asked to commit to classes for an entire academic year. Comments: "For serious music students . . . not a community music center [but] rather a Conservatory. . . . They pride themselves on the quality of players . . . high-quality performance-based lessons throughout the school year. . . . Pre-instrument classes get children used to the environment. . . . For older levels and private lessons one must audition with a prepared piece. . . . We are big fans. . . . My child's teacher is really wonderful with piece selection and assisting with the interpretation/phrasing of music." Note that the Conservatory will move in 2006 to "the heart of the San Francisco cultural scene on Oak Street behind Symphony Hall . . . a new state-of-the-art facility close to other artistic venues."

North Bay

Cradlerock Children's Center
642 Tiburon Blvd.
Tiburon
415-789-KIDS (5437)
www.cradlerockmusic.com
PARENT RATING: ☆ ☆ ☆ ☆ ☆

Owned by a husband and wife team, this center offers music classes (ages newborn through 5 years, divided into younger and older groups) that combine singing, dancing, and storytelling, using classical music, Americana music, and music from around the world. Students receive a "wonderful" CD of recordings sung and played by the teacher (a former opera singer with a master's degree in music), a handmade wooden instrument, and a booklet of songs. Children learn basic musical concepts by doing. Art classes include both weekly projects and free play, and are divided by age (one class for babies through 18 months, and another for 18 months to 3 years). Comments: "Lots of classical music. . . . Kids are always occupied and never sitting around. . . . Lara [the owner and teacher] has a beautiful voice. . . . Lara has an amazing voice, mesmer-

izing my son every time. . . . I cannot recommend them enough!" They also do childproofing (see Ch. 4).

Mary Ann Hall's Music for Children
See listing under Music—San Francisco.

The Music Hatchery
620 Petaluma Blvd. North, Ste. C2
Tiburon
707-775-3655
www.music-hatchery.com
This studio offers their own MusiKids age-appropriate group music classes for kids from newborn to age 6. Classes are small (8 students per class), and parents attend class with their children. The Kodály-based classes emphasize rhythm, singing, and hands-on experience with instruments.

Music Makers
240 Tiburon Blvd. (class location)
Tiburon
415-461-1066 (Cindy Cohen-Levy, instructor)
www.music-makers.org
PARENT RATING: ☆ ☆ ☆ ☆ ☆

These age-appropriate music classes for ages 18 months to 6 years include songs, finger plays, instruments, rhythm and movement, ear training, live music, music theory, and cassette tapes to take home. Each week focuses on a different instrument and theme, and children are taught about note values, beats, and so on. The classes incorporate Orff, Dalcroze, and Kodály methods. One of the unique features of this program is the visiting adult musicians, who show the children all about various instruments (strings, percussion, brass, woodwinds, and instruments from other cultures) and play live music. Also, all music in this class is played live by a pianist who accompanies the instructor and children; unlike other programs, there is no recorded music. Children actually play instruments in a group setting, and learn to play along to the beat. Parents accompany the children to class, and say the format is more "structured" and "instructive" than other more free-form music classes. The benefits are that children seem to "pay close attention" and even 2-year-olds can "recognize clefs and notes." As a result, the classes are popular among both city and Marin parents. Comments: "My child really loves the class. . . . Cindy does more than just sing songs—she teaches kids about the different types of notes and how many beats they get. . . . There is plenty of time allowed for the kids to play instruments. . . . She has high-quality instruments and guests." We took these classes with our children and loved them!

Osher Marin Jewish Community Center

See listing under Gyms and Play Programs—North Bay.

Parents Place Marin

See listing under Gyms and Play Programs—San Francisco.

Sebastopol Center for the Arts

6780 Depot St.
Sebastopol
707-829-4797
www.sebarts.org

This grassroots nonprofit arts center provides art, music, dance, and drama classes for young children, including ceramics for children as young as 2, a parent-child music and movement class for children under age 3.6 years, yoga and dance classes for ages 3-5, and creative dramatics for ages 4-6. There is even a community "junior chorus" for ages 4-6!

East Bay

The Crowden Center for Music in the Community

1475 Rose St.
Berkeley
510-559-6910
www.thecrowdenschool.org

This classical music school offers Orff-based preinstrument training for children ages 4-7, as well as Music Together classes for newborns to age 4.

Jingle Jamboree Music

1607 Solano Ave.
Berkeley
510-334-8851
www.jinglejamboree.com

PARENT RATING: ☆ ☆ ☆ ☆ ☆

Taught by a very popular music educator and preschool teacher, Jeff Luna-Sparks, these sequential classes incorporate the Kodály method. They start with babies, ages 6 months and up, and continue to age 9. Each year is a new level incorporating new skills, beginning with singing, then musical games, then percussion and melodic instruments, then beginning music reading, and so on. Comments: "We love Jingle Jeff! . . .

He uses puppets and props to teach musical concepts. . . . The songs are fun and my child is learning rhythm."

Jon's School of Music

See listing under San Francisco, above.

Kids in Tune

St. John's Episcopal Church
1707 Gouldin Rd. (class location)
Oakland
510-537-4206 or 800-720-0887

They teach purely Kodály-based classes (with an emphasis on singing, rhythm, and movement, and less emphasis on instruments) at preschools and recreation centers all over the East and South Bays, and in their own center in Montclair. They will also organize classes upon request from parents groups. They start with children as young as 18 months to age 7, grouped by age. Parents say the classes are "focused and structured . . . lots of use of puppets, musical games, and stories."

Nanci's Musiktime

Piedmont Recreation Center
358 Hillside Ave. (class location)
Piedmont
510-531-3190 (Nanci Schneidinger)
510-420-3070 (registration)
www.nanmusik.com

In addition to Kindermusik programs, Nanci Schneidinger teaches "Dance, Sing, and Play" classes, a curriculum she developed for children ages 3-6. She also offers a "Family Music Program" for toddlers ages 17 months to 3.6 years with their caregivers.

Wee Play

See listing under Gyms and Play Programs—East Bay.

South Bay

Almaden School of Music, Art and Dance

5353 Almaden Expwy., Ste. 12
San Jose
408-267-3651
www.almadenschool.com

This school recently merged with another studio and now has over 50 instructors. They offer private instrumental lessons, group music and movement classes (for children ages 18 months to 5 years), preballet and tap classes for ages 3-5, and art lessons for ages 4 and up.

Community School of Music and Arts

230 San Antonio Circle
Mountain View
650-917-6800
www.arts4all.org

This nonprofit community organization offers an early childhood music program (for ages 18 months to 6 years), with singing, dancing, and instruments. They also offer Suzuki recorder classes, and you can enroll children in private voice or instrumental music lessons. Plus, they offer art classes for children as young as age 2.

Lessons on "B"

25 North B St.
San Mateo
650-343-1579
www.lessonsonb.com

PARENT RATING: ☆ ☆ ☆ ☆ ☆

This popular studio offers early childhood music classes for infants and up, starting with an infant-family music class and progressing to the Harmony Road Music Course. They also do private piano and voice lessons. Comment: "My children both take music lessons there and really like the teacher, Miss Cynthia."

Mary Ann Hall's Music for Children

See listing under Music—San Francisco.

Mo Music

650-365-5355
www.momusic.org

In addition to Music Together classes (ages 0-4 years), this studio offers the Kids Sing classes, a Kodály-based, developmentally appropriate music program for ages 3-7 years, developed by Director Mona Dena. They hold classes in Redwood City, San Carlos, Foster City, Millbrae, and Woodside.

The Music Place, Fine Arts for Children!

1617 Willowhurst Ave.
San Jose
408-445-ARTS (2787)
www.musicplace.com

This private school offers music and fine arts classes for young children. Choose from family music classes (ages 0-5 with parent), early music awareness classes (for ages 2 and up), instrument readiness or performance classes (for ages 4 and up), or private music lessons. They also have locations in Sunnyvale, Santana Row, Los Gatos, Campbell, and Gilroy.

The Music School

728 W. Fremont Ave.
Sunnyvale
408-739-9248
www.themusicschool.org

A program of the Sunnyvale Presbyterian Church, this nonprofit school has long offered inexpensive music classes to the public. They begin with children as young as 12 months old and include singing, movement, playing xylophones and rhythm instruments, and gradual introduction to music reading. They also have a Broadway Babies theater class for ages 4-7.

The Music School of the Congregational Church of San Mateo

225 Tilton Ave.
San Mateo
650-344-4263
www.ccsm-ucc.org/ccsm/music.htm

Founded in 1983, this church school provides Orff-based, secular music education to children beginning at age 18 months. Parent participation is required until children reach age 3. Classes incorporate singing, movement, rhythm, stories, musical games, percussion instruments, xylophones and glockenspiels, and 4- to 5-year-olds also learn beginning keyboarding and reading music. The classes are open to the public.

Palo Alto Jewish Community Center

See listing under Gyms and Play Programs—South Bay.

Peninsula Jewish Community Center

See listing under Gyms and Play Programs—South Bay.

Peninsula Parents Place

See listing under Gyms and Play Programs—South Bay.

School of Music and Fine Arts

- Daly City
  200 Northgate Blvd.
  650-992-6481
- Pacifica
  86 Eureka Square Shopping Center
  650-738-1523
www.dcartmusic.com

This school has a system of progressive levels, awarding medals for completion of each level. Classes begin as young as preschoolers, with music, singing, or art. They also offer a class that combines music, art, and tumbling.

Tunes for Tots

Washington Elementary School
801 Howard Ave., Rm. 15 (class location)
Burlingame
650-576-8576 (office)
www.tunestots.com

These Orff-based classes with instructor Gina Baldridge involve singing, rhythm, movement, dancing, and playing instruments. Group classes are divided by age from one to 5 years. Parents participate in the classes for children under age 3.

Art

We found it best to delay formal art classes until our children were almost 2 years old, when they had sufficient hand-eye control and coordination to draw, paint, and learn to use scissors. Before that time, we introduced them to art by coloring and finger painting at home and attending drop-in classes at the Bay Area Discovery and Habitot museums (see Ch. 8). Visit the Kinderart website for fun arts and craft projects to do at home, many submitted by preschool teachers (www.kinderart.com). Some of the benefits of art for young children include developing small-motor ability, increasing attention span and concentration, promoting problem solving, and, of course, encouraging creativity and expression. Yes, there is a reason for all those preschool art projects! Among art classes for children, you will see 2 main approaches: "process-oriented" classes, and "product-oriented" classes. While we prefer the former, the decision is yours!

Art Classes

Art with Kimberly

Elevation Studio, 3423 Balboa St.
(class location)
650-738-2583 (Kimberly de Caires, instructor)
www.artwithkimberly.com

Led by an instructor with experience at many high-quality local arts organizations, these process-oriented classes begin with children as young as 18 months. Three-year-olds and up may stay without parents. Age-specific and mixed-age classes include drawing, painting, sculpture, and collage. The projects are open-ended and encourage experimentation and creativity, not "assembly line" crafts.

Jewish Community Center

See listing under Gyms and Play Programs—San Francisco.

KidsArt

360A&D West Portal Ave.
415-759-5757

This studio offers drop-off art classes for ages 4 and up. Each student works individually at his or her own pace, progressing from basic drawing to 3-dimensional drawing to forms and shapes to painting in different media.

Language in Action/Hola Kids/Arte Kids

See listing below under Foreign Language Instruction.

Parents Place

See listing under Gyms and Play Programs—San Francisco.

Playsongs

See listing under Music—San Francisco.

Precita Eyes Mural Arts Center

348 Precita Ave.
415-285-2311
www.precitaeyes.org

PARENT RATING: ☆ ☆ ☆ ☆

This community mural organization offers wonderful drop-in workshops using mixed media for children ages 18 months to 5 years. Comment: "It can be chaotic, but the materials and ideas are usually great fun." (Some parents complain that the neighborhood can be a bit dangerous at times, so be aware of your surroundings.)

Purple Crayon Art Studio

301 Cornwall St.
San Francisco
415-831-0693
www.purplecrayon.com

PARENT RATING: ☆ ☆ ☆ ☆ ☆

For the 2- and 3-year-olds, the format of these art classes is a set process-oriented project designed to encourage hand-eye coordination, followed by free time for open-ended drawing and painting. Older children can progress to sculpture, mobiles, masks, and dioramas. There is even a drop-in program for children from 20 months to 4 years! Comments: "Worth it. . . . Good supplies, and the teacher is very prepared. . . . Great birthday parties. . . . Nice, bright, open studio in corner location." Our 2-year-olds enjoyed these classes very much!

San Francisco Children's Art Center

692 Fort Mason Center (Building C)
415-771-0292
www.childrensartcenter.org
PARENT RATING: ☆ ☆ ☆ ☆ ☆

Parents say a "great" feature of this nonprofit center is that you can drop off your child, age 27 months and up, for a series of "quality" art classes. Classes are divided by age and feature painting, drawing, sculpture, printmaking, and collage. Comments: "We love the 'open studio' format. . . . Kids get to choose their own materials and create what they want (as opposed to a fixed project)."

Stretch the Imagination

2250 Union St.
415-922-0104
www.stretchtheimagination.com
PARENT RATING: ☆ ☆ ☆ ☆ ☆

Owned by a former elementary school teacher turned yoga professional, this studio offers a unique combination of art, yoga, and cooking classes for children as young as age 2, in a clean, sunny new facility. They are very popular! Since they are "drop-off" classes, be sure your child is ready for you to leave. They also do birthday parties!

North Bay

Art Is Happening

San Anselmo
415-456-4602 (Judy Dornbush)
PARENT RATING: ☆ ☆ ☆ ☆ ☆

Artist and beloved teacher Judy Dornbush teaches mixed-media classes for children ages 3.6 and up

in her home studio. Classes include, among many other things, ceramics, drawing, painting (watercolor and acrylic), 3-dimensional paper sculpture, silk painting, paper marbling, printmaking, tie-dye, and lots of imaginative play. Our preschooler took these classes and loved them! Comments: "Hands down the best classes my kids have taken anywhere. . . . A hidden gem! . . . What wonderful ceramic creations my child brought home, and great stories to go along with them."

Art Start

1407 4th St.
San Rafael
415-454-8332
PARENT RATING: ☆ ☆ ☆ ☆ ☆

This popular studio offers 6-week sessions or drop-in classes for children ages 2 and up. Younger children focus on painting and drawing, while older children engage in mixed media (including ceramics and sculpture) and make crowns and masks. Parents rave about the excellent materials, involved teachers, and "great drop-off policy" so kids can explore art on their own. We took these classes and can't say enough good things about them! Our 3-year-olds came home with bags full of their wonderful creations! Comments: "Both my children LOVE Art Start. . . . Wonderful variety of activities. . . . Lisa the owner is really fun, and the kids enjoy her. . . . Nice staff, great projects. . . . Great place for a play group gathering in the rainy season."

Art Classes

The Dance Palace Community Center

See listing under Gyms and Play Programs—North Bay.

Doodlebug

641 San Anselmo Ave.
San Anselmo
415-456-5989
www.doodlebugmarin.com
PARENT RATING: ☆ ☆ ☆ ☆

What began as a ceramics studio now offers much more—art workshops for preschoolers (ages 2 and up) in mixed media, clay, and mosaics. They also have occasional "pajama parties" where parents can drop kids for a night out! Comment: "They do great birthday parties!"

Falkirk Cultural Center

1408 Mission Ave.
San Rafael
415-485-3328 or 415-453-8518
www.falkirkculturalcenter.org
PARENT RATING: ☆ ☆ ☆ ☆ ☆

This center offers art classes with mixed media, painting, and clay to children ages 3 and up. Comments: "Great class with a really neat instructor, Patti McKay. . . . The price is right. . . . She even brings a snack and reads a story to the kids!"

Michelle's Art Camp

61 Black Log Rd.
Kentfield
415-461-8502
E-mail: sixtyone@pacbell.net
Artist and mom Michelle Montgomery offers process-oriented art classes for children ages 4 and up in several media, including clay, paint, wax, cloth, and wood. She references

nature and art history in an age-appropriate manner.

Osher Marin Jewish Community Center

See listing under Gyms and Play Programs—North Bay.

Sebastopol Center for the Arts

See listing under Music—North Bay.

Studio 4 Art

777 Grand Ave., Ste. 203
San Rafael
415-258-9926
www.studio4art.net
This studio offers classes for 2-year-olds on up to adults. Classes are open-format and include clay exploration, potting wheel, mosaics, painting and drawing, and printmaking. They also have many "open-studio" drop-in times!

YMCA—Marin

See listing under Gyms and Play Programs—North Bay.

East Bay

Art 'n Play

21001 San Ramon Valley Blvd.
San Ramon
925-479-0222
www.artnplay.com
This ceramics studio offers process-oriented art classes for children ages 18 months and up, including painting, glazing, and gluing. They also have "read, paint, and play" times in their "imagination center" play room stocked with all the tools for pretending to be a fireman, pirate, or grocer.

Kids 'n Clay Pottery Studio

1824 5th St.
Berkeley
510-845-0982
www.kidsnclay.com

Located in a landmark Victorian, this studio offers pottery-making classes for ages 3 and up. This is not the "paint ready-made pottery" type of class; rather, students actually "throw" their creations on the wheel.

Richmond Art Center

2540 Barrett Ave.
Richmond
510-620-6772
www.therichmondartcenter.org

PARENT RATING: ☆ ☆ ☆ ☆ ☆

This nonprofit visual arts center offers group classes for ages 3 and up in painting, drawing, and sculpture. Parents say the teachers are trained artists and the classes are "excellent."

University Village Recreation Program

See listing under Gyms and Play Programs—East Bay.

YMCA

See listing under Gyms and Play Programs—East Bay.

South Bay

Almaden School of Music, Art and Dance

See listing under Music—South Bay.

Art Forms

551 Foster City Blvd., Unit F
Foster City
650-345-2600
www.artformsschool.com

Founded by art school graduates, this school specializes in teaching children. They offer classes for ages 2 and up, including painting and 3-dimensional forms.

Community School of Music and Arts

See listing under Music—South Bay.

Kollage (Community School for the Arts)

801 Granada St.
Belmont
650-592-8842

PARENT RATING: ☆ ☆ ☆ ☆ ☆

With a mission to provide art education for everyone in San Mateo County, this nonprofit school offers classes in visual arts, ceramics, drawing, and mixed media for children ages 2 and up. The school also offers music and movement classes for preschoolers.

Palo Alto Art Center

1313 Newell Rd.
Palo Alto
650-329-2366
www.paenjoy.org (registration)
or www.city.palo-alto.ca.us/ artcenter/ (general information)

The children's art program at this center offers classes for children ages 18 months and up, in ceramics, drawing, painting and sculpture. Classes are also held at the Junior Museum and Zoo and Mitchell Park Community Center, and you register

Art Classes

for all classes through the Palo Alto "Enjoy!" program.

Palo Alto Jewish Community Center

See listing under Gyms and Play Programs—South Bay.

Peninsula Jewish Community Center

See listing under Gyms and Play Programs—South Bay.

Peninsula Parents Place

See listing under Gyms and Play Programs—South Bay.

Young at Art
- Cupertino
  19701 Stevens Creek Blvd.
  408-255-1414
- San Jose
  801 Hibiscus Ln.
  408-247-4325

This year-round school offers mixed-media classes for children as young as age 4.

Dance and Drama

Maybe it's the lovely costumes that lead even 2-year-olds to dream of being prima ballerinas. All that ambition is inspirational (and what mother doesn't adore dressing her daughter in a pink tutu!). But what you really want in a dance program for children under age 6, say experienced dancers, is a safe environment where teachers focus on moving to the music, rhythm, and creative expression, not formal ballet training, which is too demanding for young bodies. Most experts say the teacher should be showing students how to move more than teaching technique. And it goes without saying that pointe shoes are a no-no until children are much older and more developed. What's more, toddlers and preschoolers will vastly prefer actual dancing to standing at the bar learning positions! Parents also say to watch out for schools placing a heavy emphasis on performances—beyond your typical end-of-year recitals—or competitions at this age. If you visit and notice the students bear an eerie resemblance to JonBenet Ramsey, well, you know what to do. For a fairly comprehensive list of Bay Area dance schools and resources, go to www.baydance.com.

Ballet with Miss Tilly and The Abbe Studio

3119 California St. (office)
5499 California St. (ballet school)
5495 California St. (Abbe Studio)
415-923-9965 (unlisted number)

PARENT RATING: ☆ ☆ ☆ ☆ ☆

Owing to "Miss Tilly's" stellar reputation among well-heeled city parents as the "best," this very popular Richmond neighborhood program has a long wait list, so sign your child up early to ensure enrollment. Children must be 3 years old to begin ballet. The affiliated Abbe Studio next door now offers theater arts classes for preschoolers and up. Their recitals are held at Herbst Theatre!

The Ballet Studio of San Francisco

128 10th St.
415-861-5520
www.balletstudiosf.com

A new kid on the block! Run by well-known former San Francisco Ballet instructor and dancer Henry Berg, this nonprofit classical ballet school offers preballet classes for young children.

Glitter and Razz "Itty Bitty" Theater Workshops

The Marsh Youth Theater
1062 Valencia St. (class location)
415-759-5765
www.glitterandrazz.com

Students ages 4-6 work together in these classes to create original plays through dance, visual art, and drama. This group has also done summer arts camps at local preschools.

Jewish Community Center

See listing under Gyms and Play Programs—San Francisco.

Luna Kids Dance

510-644-3629
www.lunakidsdance.com
Locations in San Francisco, Marin, and East Bay

PARENT RATING: ☆ ☆ ☆ ☆ ☆

With a mission to "bring dance to all children," these developmentally appropriate "creative dance" classes got rave reviews. They emphasize creativity, improvisation, and games to teach dance fundamentals. Classes are open to toilet-trained children ages 3 and up, and parents participate in the some of the classes for 3-4 year olds. Comments: "We love that they encourage creativity and self-expression rather than specific techniques. . . . These are not ballet classes but [they do] teach movement."

Metronome Dance Center

1830 17th St.
415-252-9000
www.metronomedancecenter.com

This Potrero Hill ballroom dance center is now offering preballet classes for 3-4 year olds, progressing to ballet beginning at age 5.

San Francisco Youth Ballet Academy

3149 Vicente St.
415-731-2237
www.sanfranciscoyouthballet.org

Directed by a professional dancer, this classical ballet school offers preballet classes for ages 3-5. They are affiliated with the San Francisco

365

Youth Ballet Theatre, a nonprofit organization performing in local libraries and schools.

Shan-Yee Poon Ballet School

403 Arguello Blvd.
415-387-2695
www.poonballet.com

PARENT RATING: ☆ ☆ ☆ ☆ ☆

Founded by a European-trained professional dancer, this school has "spectacular" studio space. They offer a toddler program focusing on motor development for ages 2-4, with parent participation in the youngest classes. Creative ballet movement classes begin at age 4, and preballet at age 5. Comment: "Miss Byrne is a great teacher for 3-year-olds . . . very creative."

Sunset Movement Arts

1647 Taraval St.
415-665-6444

This Sunset neighborhood school offers preballet classes for preschoolers ages 3-5.

Westlake School for the Performing Arts

200 Northgate Ave., #4
Daly City
650-757-1244
www.wspadance.com

Children ages 3-6 begin with a ballet and tap combination class in this large, well-established program.

Young Performers Theatre, Theatre Arts Academy

Fort Mason Center (Building C), Fl. 3
415-346-5550
www.ypt.org

This "fabulous" youth drama organization offers classes for children ages 3 and up, including Let's Pretend for ages 3-5, with puppetry, storytelling, music, and dramatization (including the use of costumes and props!).

North Bay

The Dance Palace Community Center

See listing under Gyms and Play Programs—North Bay.

Happy Feet Dance Studio

15 Montford Ave.
Mill Valley
415-381-0811
E-mail: happyfeet_mv@yahoo.com

PARENT RATING: ☆ ☆ ☆ ☆ ☆

Instruction at this popular Marin studio begins with Tiny Toes, a parent-participation dance and movement class for children ages 2-3. Children ages 3 and up may take tap and jazz classes. Get on the waiting list early as these classes fill very quickly.

Luna Kids Dance

See listing under San Francisco.

Marin Ballet

100 Elm St.
San Rafael
415-453-6705
www.marinballet.org

PARENT RATING: ☆ ☆ ☆ ☆ ☆

This highly regarded classical ballet school and regional company offers classes for ages 3 and up, beginning with movement exploration for 3- and 4-year-olds and preballet for 5- and 6-year-olds.

Marin Dance Theatre

One St. Vincent Dr.
San Rafael
415-499-8891
www.mdt.org

Located on the campus of a beautiful Spanish-style mission, this nonprofit classical ballet school offers introduction to dance classes for ages 3-4, and preballet beginning at age 5.

Marin YMCA

See listing under Gyms and Play Programs—North Bay.

Osher Marin Jewish Community Center

See listing under Gyms and Play Programs—North Bay.

Petaluma School of Ballet

110 Howard St.
Petaluma
707-762-3972

This school, a training ground for the Petaluma City Ballet, offers classes at its own studio and through the Petaluma recreation department. They begin with creative movement and music classes for ages 2 (with parents) through 4, and preballet starts at age 5.

Roco Dance and Fitness

237 Shoreline Hwy.
Mill Valley
415-388-6786
www.rocodance.com

PARENT RATING: ☆ ☆ ☆ ☆ ☆

This contemporary dance program and gym offers preballet and creative movement classes for children ages 3-6. Older children may move into hip-hop, modern, "breaking," and jazz.

Sebastopol Center for the Arts

See listing under Music—North Bay.

Stapleton School of the Performing Arts

118 Greenfield Ave.
San Anselmo
415-454-5759
www.stapletonschool.org

PARENT RATING: ☆ ☆ ☆ ☆ ☆

Age-appropriate classes at this long-time Ross Valley favorite (and non-profit organization) include Movement and Music for toddlers and their parents, Rhythm and Dance for 3-year-olds, Intro to Dance for 4-year-olds, and preballet for 5-year-olds. Insider advice: sign up early as classes fill quickly. Comments: "Teacher Sara is wonderful. . . . The classes are magical. . . . The kids learn to follow the teacher, move to the music, and enjoy themselves. . . . A fabulous *Nutcracker* production for older children. . . . End-of-year recitals are not to be missed."

Susan Lopez School of Ballet

985 Airway Ct., Ste. D
Santa Rosa
707-575-5088
www.susanlopezballet.com

Classes at this studio begin with preballet for ages 3-4. They emphasize the foundations for developing correct technique.

Ashkenaz

1317 San Pablo Ave.
Berkeley
510-525-5054
www.ashkenaz.com

This "child-friendly" multicultural community center for music and dance rents studio space to several teachers offering classes for children, including Indian dance (ages 4-6) and creative movement and ballet (ages 3.6 to 9). Check the website for current offerings.

Berkeley Ballet Theater School

2640 College Ave.
Berkeley
510-843-4687
www.berkeleyballet.org

PARENT RATING: ☆ ☆ ☆ ☆ ☆

Located in the landmark Julia Morgan Center for the Arts, this classical ballet school and youth company offers yearlong classes, including a preballet program for children ages 3.6-6 years.

Berkeley City Ballet

1800 Dwight Way
Berkeley
510-841-8913
www.berkeleycityballet.org

PARENT RATING: ☆ ☆ ☆ ☆ ☆

This well-regarded classical ballet school and company offers preballet classes for children beginning at age 4. The classes focus on creative movement and some beginning technique.

ClubSport

See listing under Gyms and Play Programs—East Bay.

Conservatory of Classical Ballet

1035 MacArthur Blvd.
San Leandro
510-568-7728
www.conservatoryofballet.com

Founded by a professional ballet dancer, this school teaches "pure classical style" ballet. Their preballet division begins at age 3.6, with both creative free dance and technical instruction.

Contra Costa Ballet School

2040 N. Broadway
Walnut Creek
925-935-7984
www.contracostaballet.org

The school of this pre-professional company offers a pre-ballet program for ages 3.6-4, emphasizing creative movement to music. Ballet classes begin at age 5.

Danspace

473 Hudson St.
Oakland
510-420-0920
www.danspace.com

PARENT RATING: ☆ ☆ ☆ ☆ ☆

This studio's highly recommended dance program for children begins at age 3.6 with creative movement classes. These classes focus on basic motor skills, coordination, and self-expression rather than technical positions, and parents say the teachers are all excellent.

Danville Ballet School—Ballet and Theatre Arts of Danville

190F Alamo Plaza
Alamo
925-831-9256
www.danvilleballet.org

This nonprofit pre-professional ballet company offers classes for ages 3.6 and up through the affiliated Ballet and Theatre Arts program.

Ann Davlin Dance School

2311 Stuart St.
Berkeley
510-843-9740

Classes for the youngest students begin at age 2, with an introduction to dance, floor exercises, balls, tambourines, and nursery rhymes. Classes for older students progressively introduce more formal dance elements.

East Bay Dance Center

1318 Glenfield
Oakland
510-336-3262

PARENT RATING: ☆ ☆ ☆ ☆

The official school of the nonprofit Move Dance Theatre, this center features an introductory dance class for children ages 3-5. Comment: "Upbeat, informal, positive environment."

Encore Gymnastics

See listing under Gyms and Play Programs—East Bay.

Ha Ha This A-Way

2525 8th St.
Berkeley
510-644-1788
www.hahathisaway.com

PARENT RATING: ☆ ☆ ☆ ☆ ☆

These popular Creative Movement/Theatre Arts classes for children beginning at age 3 are divided by age and include a blend of dance, drama, clowning, yoga, puppetry, music, tumbling, and storytelling, with improvisation encouraged. They also offer "yoga stories" classes for ages 4-8.

Julia Morgan Center for the Arts

2640 College Ave.
Berkeley
510-845-8542
www.juliamorgan.org

PARENT RATING: ☆ ☆ ☆ ☆ ☆

The Kaleidoscope program for children ages 4 and up provides creative dance and drama classes and camps. The emphasis is on creativity; children get to use props and costumes to invent their own characters and stories.

Kids 'N Dance

3369 Mt. Diablo Blvd.
Lafayette
925-284-7388
www.kidsndance.com

PARENT RATING: ☆ ☆ ☆ ☆ ☆

Taught at preschools and community centers as well as in their Lafayette Dance Center, these very popular classes incorporate weekly themes or stories, with music, costumes, and props to encourage creative expression. They begin with creative movement classes for children as young as 14 months (with parent participation until age 3). Some classes add gymnastics or tap elements, and preballet/modern classes begin at age 4. They also have "great" musical theater classes for ages 4-6.

Dance & Drama Classes

Lareen Fender's The Ballet School

1357 N. Main St.
Walnut Creek
925-934-2133
www.theballetschool.org

In the same location since 1978, this traditional ballet school offers preballet classes for ages 3.6 to 5 years. They are affiliated with a performing company, The Ballet Joyeux.

Little Feet Creative Dance and Movement

Kathleen Hogan
Berkeley
E-mail: artpour@hotmail.com

Popular instructor Kathleen Hogan offers dance classes for ages 3-7 in Berkeley, as well as through a number of East Bay preschools. The semi-structured, developmentally appropriate classes promote self-esteem, cooperation, body awareness, coordination and flexibility, improvisation and drama, and self-expression. She uses a lot of ethnic music and fun instruments. Parents say she is wonderful and the program is a "hidden gem, not to be overlooked!"

Luna Kids Dance

See listing under San Francisco.

Rhythm Room Dance and Movement Center

3330 Mt. Diablo Blvd., Ste. 101
Lafayette
925-283-4801
www.rhythmroomdance.com

This studio offers several classes for preschoolers, including ballet/jazz/tap and hip-hop.

University Village Recreation Program

See listing under Gyms and Play Programs—East Bay.

Valley Dance Theatre School

20 S. "L" St.
Livermore
925-243-0925
www.valleydancetheatre.com

A training ground for the nonprofit Valley Dance Theatre, this school offers creative movement classes for ages 3.6 to 5 years. Ballet begins at age 5. Their mission is to provide professional-quality theatrical productions, not recitals or competitions, and their focus is classical ballet.

YMCA

See listing under Gyms and Play Programs—East Bay.

South Bay

Academy of American Ballet

275A Linden St.
Redwood City
650-366-1222
www.geocities.com/julia_ball_us/aab.html

Stanford-trained director Julia Ball-Dugan emphasizes anatomically informed and injury-free dance in her ballet school. Preballet classes begin at age 3.6 years.

Almaden School of Music, Art and Dance

See listing under Music—South Bay.

Ballet San Jose Silicon Valley

40 N. 1st St.
San Jose
408-288-2820, ext. 223
www.balletsanjose.org

This well-regarded professional ballet company's school has an "open" division of classical ballet classes for children ages 4 and up.

California Sports Center

See listing under Gyms and Play Programs—South Bay.

Conservatory of Performing Arts

1401 Parkmoor Ave.
San Jose
408-288-5437, ext. 22
www.cmtsj.org

This offshoot of the San Jose Children's Musical Theater offers classes in acting, dance, voice, and production for ages 4 and up.

The Dance Affair

2905 Park Ave.
Santa Clara
408-243-4834
www.thedanceaffair.com

This established school offers mommy-and-me classes for children ages 18 months-2.6 years, and "kiddie combo" classes for preschoolers combining tap, ballet, and tumbling. Preballet starts at age 5.

L'Ecole de Danse

4000 Middlefield Rd.
Palo Alto
650-365-4596
www.lecolededanse.com

This classical ballet school offers creative dance classes for ages 4-6.

Kirkpatricks School of Dance

1701 Leslie St.
San Mateo
650-525-1900
www.kirkpatricksdance.com

Preschoolers' classes (for ages 3-5) consist of ballet, tap, and tumbling.

Kollage

See listing under Art—South Bay.

Menlo Park Academy of Dance

1163 El Camino Real
Menlo Park
650-323-5292
www.mpaod.com

Established in 1947, this multidisciplinary program begins with "mommy-and-me" classes for 2-year-olds, pre-dance classes for 3- and 4-year olds, and preballet for 4- and 5-year olds.

Miss Teri Dance Studio

- San Mateo
  38 South B St., Ste. 205
- Foster City
  1463 Beach Park Blvd.

650-342-3514
www.missteridancestudio.com

This studio offers ballet and tap combination lessons for children ages 3 and up. This is one of the studios with a competitive dance troupe.

Professional Ballet School

425 Harbor Blvd., #3
Belmont
650-598-0796
www.yabt.org

An offshoot of a semiprofessional ballet theater, this ballet and jazz school offers preballet classes for children ages 4-6.

Santa Clara Ballet School
3086 El Camino Real
Santa Clara
408-247-9178
www.geocities.com/Vienna/Strasse/
7530/SCBallet.html
This longstanding classical ballet
school (and professional company)
offers creative movement classes for
children ages 3-5.

Foreign Language Instruction

It's the new extracurricular activity for the under-5 crowd! We all know that the earlier children are exposed to a foreign language, the easier it becomes for them to learn it. Experts say children have the greatest potential to absorb language between about 7 months and age 12 or 13. With all the research showing the benefits to children who study foreign languages, it's no wonder that foreign language classes for babies, toddlers, and preschoolers have become so popular. The best programs use play, songs, and other "immersion" techniques to appeal to young children. Here are a few of them:

Centro Latino
2530 San Pablo Ave.
Berkeley
510-849-4504
www.centro-latino.net
They offer Spanish and Portuguese classes for children ages 3 and up, using games, music, and songs to teach everyday vocabulary.

Chinese American International School Summer Camp
150 Oak St.
San Francisco
415-865-6000
www.cais.org
This school offers a Chinese (Mandarin) immersion summer camp for children ages 3 and up, open to the public. The camps are structured like preschool and use activities like singing, crafts, stories, and dance to teach Mandarin.

Espanol for Kids
San Francisco
415-841-1681
www.espanolforkids.com
They offer Spanish classes for children as young as age 3. They do group classes and summer camps at the Noe Valley Ministry (1021 Sanchez St.), as well as classes for private groups and individuals.

French for Fun
3470 Mt. Diablo Blvd., Ste. A115
Lafayette
925-283-9822
www.frenchforfun.com

PARENT RATING: ☆ ☆ ☆ ☆ ☆

Parents rave about the mom-and-tot French playgroup for infants to age 2, and total immersion preschool-like programs (2-5 mornings a week) for ages 2-5.

German International School of Silicon Valley
310 Easy St.
Mountain View
650-254-0748
www.gissv.org

This German academic school (a branch of the German government, preschool through high school grades) also offers Saturday German language classes, and a summer immersion camp, for ages 3 and up. You need not be a student at the school to take classes.

German School of Fremont
510-247-8701
www.ugas-eb.org/fremontschool/

This Saturday language school offers classes for children ages 3.9 years and up.

German School of Marin
415-897-9771
www.germanschoolmarin.com

This Saturday language school offers classes for preschoolers and up, and also has a parent-toddler group (ages 18 months to 3 years). They meet in Novato.

German School of San Francisco
415-586-9060
www.germanschool.com

They offer German language classes for ages 2 and up on Saturday mornings in the Sunset neighborhood. Classes for younger children teach German via games, songs, and crafts, and parents accompany children under age 4.

Language in Action/Hola Kids/Arte Kids
• San Francisco
  2830 Baker St.
• Mill Valley
  363 Miller Ave.
415-440-4652
www.languageinaction.com

PARENT RATING: ☆ ☆ ☆ ☆ ☆

This popular school offers Spanish language instruction for children ages 2-12 years in their Cow Hollow and Mill Valley locations, and at schools and private homes around the Bay Area. Hola Kids classes include songs, movement, arts and crafts, stories, and games; they also offer Arte Kids classes that develop language through art projects. There are also 3-hour immersion playgroups. Insider advice: classes fill quickly in Cow Hollow, so sign up promptly. Comments: "Great Spanish-speaking instructors. . . . Enchanting programs. . . . I think of it as my child's Spanish language preschool. . . . They take the kids to the Cow Hollow playground. . . . It's been amazing for my daughter's brain to get the exposure to a second language, and coupled with some songs and activities, she's really got a comprehension of the language . . . we love it." East Bay and Peninsula parents can look for branches in their neighborhoods soon.

Les Petits Bouts

San Francisco (class locations)
510-521-0297 (Ingrid Rombaut, instructor)
E-mail: Lespetitsbouts1@yahoo.com

A native French speaker and former preschool teacher leads these French immersion playgroups, designed to teach French to children ages 3 and up. Groups are divided by age. Classes are held in the Cow Hollow (2830 Baker St.) and Bernal Heights (231 Cortland Ave.) neighborhoods.

Worldly Wise Language and Culture

Lafayette and Piedmont class locations
800-424-5522 or 925-285-3000
www.1worldlc.org

This group offers French and Spanish language and culture classes at several locations, beginning with parent-child music and movement classes for children as young as 12 months.

La Piccola Scuola Italiana di San Francisco

2616 Sutter St.
San Francisco
415-567-2663
www.lpsisf.org

Primarily an Italian immersion pre-school (ages 2-5), this school also offers an afternoon Italian playgroup for babies and toddlers (ages 6-24 months), with play, snack, stories, songs, and nursery rhymes. They also have a summer morning program for toddlers.

Playsongs (French Playgroups)

See listing above under Music—San Francisco.

South Bay German School

408-266-5100
www.sbds.org

They offer Saturday morning German language classes for preschoolers and up, in the Willow Glen neighborhood of San Jose.

More Sports Classes . . . and Yoga!

Your local recreation department, YMCA, or JCC should be your first stop in investigating "pee-wee" sports classes (ages 3 to 5 years, generally). We like these programs because they usually emphasize developing motor skills and confidence rather than competitive play—the best approach for children under age 6. Soccer is one of the mainstays for pee-wees because it doesn't involve as much hand-eye coordination as say, tennis. Yoga for children has also become increasingly popular in recent years, enhancing coordination, posture, and muscle development. Look for a teacher who specializes in teaching children, using easy-to-remember descriptive names for poses (and not holding the poses as long as adults do). Our children love yoga because many of the poses have animal names!

Some of the most popular programs are listed above under Recreation Departments and Gym and Play Programs. In addition, the following schools specialize in sports instruction:

Dave Fromer's Soccer Program

147 Elm Ave.
Mill Valley
415-383-0320
www.davefromersoccer.com

PARENT RATING: ☆ ☆ ☆

A veritable Marin institution, Dave Fromer runs a very popular, inexpensive, parent-child pee-wee soccer program on Saturdays in Mill Valley and Novato through the local recreation departments. For children ages 3-5, these classes focus on fun and basic skills, like dribbling the ball around cones, and there is no competitive play. Dave has been doing this for 30 years, and he also plays guitar and sings! Parents say it "can be fairly chaotic with scores of parents and preschoolers. . . . Some kids love it and some are a little intimidated. . . . Best if you want to learn to teach your child yourself." The camps for older kids (ages 4-5 and up) during school breaks and summers are very popular, much more structured, and some say much better than the pee-wee classes, with many more instructors, though they too can be very crowded. They also run a popular Winter Indoor Soccer League at gyms all over Marin, for boys and girls ages 4 and up, that offers competitive play.

Ha Ha This A-Way

For yoga, see listing above under Dance—East Bay.

Holly Go Lightly Yoga

Personal Fitness Institute of Marin
2240 4th St.
San Rafael
415-456-1610 (classes)
415-721-7307 (birthday parties)
E-mail: hollysalamun@yahoo.com

PARENT RATING: ☆ ☆ ☆ ☆ ☆

Preschool teacher and yoga instructor Holly Salamun teaches a great kids' yoga class at Personal Fitness of Marin, and also offers yoga birthday parties. She integrates stories, music, and games with the poses. Our kids love her!

Soccer Kids

176 Prince Royal Dr.
Corte Madera (office)
415-608-2608
www.soccerkids.com

PARENT RATING: ☆ ☆ ☆ ☆ ☆

Coach Jaime's "non-competitive, age-appropriate" soccer program for ages 3 through 8 is one of the most popular in San Francisco and Marin. It's a year-round program with small classes (15 children maximum) and personal instruction, held at various San Francisco and Marin parks. They also do birthday parties! Comments: "The best program for young children who aren't ready for/don't want to be on a competitive team. . . . Coach Jaime is great with the kids. . . . He focuses on skills in a fun way . . . no actual games against other teams. . . . Soccer Kids rules! . . . My child adores it."

Sports City Indoor Soccer Centers
* Cotati
  6700 Stony Point Rd.
  707-285-GOAL (4625)
* Santa Rosa
  921 Piner Rd.
  707-526-1320
707-526-2884 (registration for Little Kickers)
www.nbsportscity.com

The "Little Kickers" program introduces soccer skills to children ages 2-9 years. The non-competitive series of classes emphasizes fun and building self-confidence.

More Classes

Adventures with Toddlers
418 Napa St.
Sausalito (office)
415-331-8882, Loni Greenfield
PARENT RATING: ☆ ☆ ☆ ☆ ☆

Is your child too old for a backpack but too young for strenuous hiking? Try these nature walks for children ages 18 months to 5 years. Classes are offered through various Marin recreation departments, and hikes take place all over the county. Parents call them "a good speed" for toddlers and say they "learned about new, off-the-beaten-track places to go with kids." We took these classes and loved the fact that we could bring 2

Stretch the Imagination
For yoga, see listing above under Art—San Francisco.

The Yoga Garden
Jennifer Durand
415-753-1334
www.theyogagarden.com

An experienced yoga instructor, Jennifer Durand specializes in teaching yoga to children. In fact, she invented a board game, "The Yoga Garden," for just that purpose, and she uses music and storytelling to introduce the basic ideas of Hatha yoga. Children as young as 18 months may enroll in her classes, which combine music, dance, and yoga. She teaches classes at the JCC of San Francisco (see listing under Gyms and Play Programs—San Francisco).

children of different ages to the same class—a rarity! Plus, even the adults learned a lot about the native plants, insects, and animals in beautiful Marin County. Loni also does birthday parties. Comments: "Best in good weather. . . . Loni is extremely knowledgeable. . . . Kids love her."

Alphabet Soup
Marin Art and Garden Center
Ross
415-460-0614
PARENT RATING: ☆ ☆ ☆ ☆

Cooking, art, and gardening are among the activities offered in this multifaceted class, with weekly themes centering around local or

And Don't Forget . . . Best Museums for Kids' Classes:

- **Bay Area Discovery Museum,** Sausalito
- **Children's Discovery Museum of San Jose**
- **Habitot Children's Museum,** Berkeley
- **Lawrence Hall of Science,** Berkeley
- **Lindsay Wildlife Museum,** Walnut Creek
- **Museum of Children's Art (MOCHA),** Oakland
- **Palo Alto Junior Museum and Zoo,** Palo Alto
- **Randall Museum,** San Francisco
- **Tiburon Audubon Center,** Tiburon (summer camps)
- **Wildcare Terwilliger Nature Education and Wildlife Rehabilitation Center,** San Rafael

See Ch. 8 for more details about all these museums!

world cultures, current events, or holidays. Classes are divided by age and begin at age 18 months, but parents recommended waiting until children are over age 3 to fully appreciate the cooking projects.

East Bay Regional Park District Youth Programs

- Berkeley
Tilden Regional Park, Nature Area
510-525-2233
- Alameda
Crab Cove at Crown Beach
510-521-6887
- Fremont
Coyote Hills Regional Park
510-795-9385
510-636-1684 (central reservations)
www.ebparks.org

The park district offers inexpensive nature studies classes for children ages 3 and up at several East Bay parks. Tilden Tots, for 3-4 year olds, accompanied by their parents, is especially popular.

Kids Can Cook!
Montclair
510-428-2433
www.kidscancook.us

A former professional chef, Ellen Doren offers cooking classes for children ages 4-7 (divided into 2 groups by age). Classes are small (6 students maximum), and private cooking lessons are available.

Tiny Treks

P.O. Box 358
Menlo Park, CA 94026
650-322-5650
www.tinytreks.com

A mother of 4, Pamela Worth started these parent-child hiking classes in 1997 as an alternative to indoor activity. Classes meet in northern Peninsula, mid-Peninsula, southern Peninsula, South Bay, and Pleasanton areas (you choose the one most convenient to your home). You sign up for one class per week for the entire school year.

Tree Frog Treks

2112 Hayes St. (office)
San Francisco
415-876-3764
www.treefrogtreks.com

PARENT RATING: ☆ ☆ ☆ ☆ ☆

This group offers the popular Discovery Day Schools, weekly 2-hour science and nature exploration programs in San Francisco and Piedmont parks for ages 4-8. Classes feature live amphibians, snakes, lizards, turtles, and insects, as well as science experiments. They also run nature-themed summer camps in Golden Gate and Piedmont parks, starting with ages 4-6. Birthday parties and school programs are some of their specialties. The well-regarded director, Chris Giorni, is a natural history professor and former professional biologist. Comments: "Great hands-on interactive classes, camps, and birthday parties. The director, Chris, is fantastic. . . . I can't recommend them highly enough. The instructors are energetic and enthusiastic, and classes are fun."

What's Cooking

www.whatscooking.info

PARENT RATING: ☆ ☆ ☆ ☆ ☆

This mom-owned business offers creative cooking classes for kids ages 4 and above in a San Rafael home. Instructor and owner Michelle Stern, a former high school biology teacher, also teaches cooking classes at the Marin JCC, and will do private classes and birthday parties in Marin, Sonoma, Alameda, or San Francisco counties. Comments: "Fun, interactive, and educational . . . a new and creative activity for kids. . . . Michelle does a great job with the kids. . . . Thursday mornings my child would jump with excitement that 'today is cooking class day.' . . . She makes food fun for the kids . . . a broccoli casserole was a 'forest in the oven.' . . . My daughter gained tremendous confidence in the kitchen. . . . Great birthday parties too."

CHAPTER 8

GETTING OUT:
Parks, Museums,
Animals, Stories, and
Other Adventures

You are going to need to get out of the house sometime after you have your baby—and the sooner the better, in our opinion. Fortunately, the Bay Area is home to many great kid-friendly places to visit—indoor and outdoor, natural and man-made. Not all of these locales are appropriate for children under age 5, however. Hence, this chapter. We've selected age-appropriate activities, and divided them topically. From parks and playgrounds, to beaches and pools, museums, zoos and farms, libraries, transportation of all sorts, amusement parks, and special events—check them all out. We'll also tell you the best parent-tested family restaurants and vacation spots. Have fun!

Wherever you go with kids in tow, we recommend packing a few essentials: snacks, drinks, diapers, sun screen, an extra outfit for each kid, and sweatshirts and hats for everyone. You may find it helpful, as we do, to keep a bag in the car at all times with all of these items and replenish as necessary.

Always call ahead, as programs, hours, and admission prices may change. We've found that going online beforehand can be very useful; each organization's website, listed below, usually features helpful directions, maps, and parking or public transit information. Money saving tip: AAA or KQED membership often will get you discounted admission to museums, amusement parks, and other attractions; check before you go.

This chapter will answer the following questions and more:
- ◆ Which are the best parks and beaches in my neighborhood for kids?
- ◆ Which are the best places to see animals and wildlife?
- ◆ Which museums are worth visiting?
- ◆ What else can I do with my kids on a rainy day?
- ◆ Where can I find a free storytelling hour?
- ◆ What are the best outings for a train- or boat-obsessed youngster?
- ◆ Are there kid-friendly restaurants in my neighborhood?
- ◆ Where do Bay Area families recommend going for easy vacations, and what tips do they suggest for surviving travel with kids?
- ◆ Where can I find great entertainment or help for my child's birthday?

Parks and Playgrounds

As a new parent, you may find yourself spending more time at your local park than at home. In that spirit, we've put this topic first. We'd love to cover every park and playground in the Bay Area, but space limitations have forced us to confine ourselves to those rated as "favorites" by local parents who completed our surveys. For more comprehensive directories of parks and recreation areas, check out the regional park websites listed below or your local Parks and Recreation Department's website (many of which are also listed below). The Bay Area Kid Fun website also has links to many national, state, county, and local parks (www.bayareakidfun.com). The San Francisco Mothers of Twins Club has put out a book about Bay Area playgrounds, *Play Around the Bay* (www.sfmotc.org). In addition, you can find all sorts of information about California's many wonderful state parks on www.parks.ca.gov. On a related topic, see Ch. 2 under the Favorite Walks and Hikes section for fun, family exercise.

San Francisco

San Francisco Parks and Recreation Department

www.parks.sfgov.org

This website features a directory of facilities and tells you which facilities are being renovated. It's not a terribly user-friendly website, but it's a start.

Golden Gate Mothers' Group Parks and Playgrounds Directory

www.ggmg.org

PARENT RATING: ☆ ☆ ☆ ☆ ☆

A much better tool with easier navigation and more information than the recreation department site, this website has a wonderful interactive map of all San Francisco playgrounds, with descriptions and pictures of each location.

Alta Plaza Park

Jackson St. between Steiner and Scott Sts.

www.sfpt.org (for renovations update)

PARENT RATING: ☆ ☆ ☆ ☆ ☆

You get great views of the city from this Pacific Heights hilltop park and enclosed playground, where you can "bask in the sunshine" (but watch for the high winds!). The self-propelled miniature merry-go-round is always a hit. It's scheduled to be renovated by the end of 2006.

Bernal Heights Playground and Recreation Center

Cortland and Moultrie Sts.

The upper level of this 2-level park has a nice, sandy playground, and the lower level contains a recreation center and library. One of the play structures on the upper level is sized for toddlers.

Cow Hollow Playground

Off Miley St. (an alley off Baker St. between Greenwich and Filbert Sts.)

PARENT RATING: ☆ ☆ ☆ ☆ ☆

A perennial favorite, this playground is completely enclosed, very sheltered, and has all sorts of fun equipment, including a miniature cable car for climbing. Parents love it because the park is limited to ages 5 and under. It's quite the social scene on weekday mornings! Its small recreation center also has a popular tots program run by the Recreation Department; see Ch. 7 under Gym and Play Programs.

Douglass Playground

Douglass St. between Clipper and 27th Sts.

PARENT RATING: ☆ ☆ ☆ ☆ ☆

This enclosed playground and recreation center is a huge favorite among Noe Valley parents and is within walking distance of the 24th Street shopping and dining corridor.

Duboce Park

Duboce Ave. at Noe St.

This newly renovated and gated playground in Hayes Valley is great for toddlers and preschoolers, as the surface is rubber and the playground has equipment designed for children under age 5.

Glen Park Recreation Center and Playground

Bosworth St. and O'Shaughnessy Blvd.

This park features an enclosed playground, a recreation center, a canyon with a stream, and hiking.

Parks & Playgrounds

381

Golden Gate Park

Between Stanyan St. and the Great Hwy.

415-831-2745

www.parks.sfgov.org

PARENT RATING: ☆ ☆ ☆ ☆ ☆

The city's largest park, it has over 1,000 acres of meadows, forest, and gardens built on a former sand dune. Parents especially lauded the children's playground and carousel, but recommended that parents "supervise children closely" and "go during the week to avoid crowds." Kid-friendly activities include:

◆ **Carousel.** This is an antique 1912 Hirschel-Spillman merry-go-round on Kezar Dr. It was renovated in 2002 and is open only during the summer and on weekends during other months.

◆ **Children's Playground.** This is located at Kezar Dr. next to the Carousel, and was renovated in 2004. Other popular playgrounds are located at 45th Ave. (at Lincoln Way, featuring a large boat structure), and at 10th Ave. (at Fulton St., with a nice play structure but no fence).

◆ **Conservatory of Flowers** (Kennedy Dr., 415-666-7001, www.conservatoryofflowers.org). Remodeled and reopened in 2003, this famed tropical haven features beautiful and unusual flowers. You can picnic amid the flower gardens.

◆ **Japanese Tea Garden** (415-752-4227). This is best for walks with babies in carriers.

◆ **Model Yacht Sailing.** Most weekends you can watch people sailing model boats on Spreckels Lake opposite 36th Ave.

◆ **Picnic** in the park (415-831-5500 for group reservations) or visit the **Beach Chalet** at the Great Hwy. for brew pub food, ocean views, and a look at the restored WPA murals (415-386-8439 or www.beachchalet.com).

◆ **Stow Lake.** (Opposite 17th Ave. 415-752-0347). Rent a paddleboat or picnic along the banks.

◆ **Stroller Walks.** San Francisco Parks Trust offers free stroller walks every other week. Go to www.frp.org/stroller_tours.asp or call 415-750-5105 for a schedule. See also Ch. 2 under Favorite Walks and Hikes—San Francisco.

◆ **Strybing Arboretum and Botanical Gardens.** (9th Ave. at Lincoln Way. 415-661-1316, www.strybing.org). The beautiful botanical gardens are a great place for a stroller walk, and parents say it's "fun for exploring in a contained area." See also under Libraries and Storytelling.

◆ **Walking Tours.** Golden Gate Park Guides offer free historical walking tours of the park. Call 415-263-0991 for a reservation.

Grattan Playground

Stanyan St. at Alma St.

PARENT RATING: ☆ ☆ ☆ ☆

This Cole Valley neighborhood playground covers an entire city block, with an adjacent recreation center. A nice feature is the fenced grassy area.

Julius Kahn Playground

The Presidio, W. Pacific Ave. and Spruce St.

PARENT RATING: ☆ ☆ ☆ ☆ ☆

Many parents felt this beautiful, newly renovated park was a great place to meet other moms, but complained that it can be "overrun" with older children from nearby schools. Even so, a nice feature of this park is that it is fenced in and parking is usually easy. The equipment is new, modern, and innovative (including a water area), and the ground is covered with a springy material making for soft landings. The small recreation center is a nice place for a child's birthday party, and the scent of the eucalyptus grove is wonderful.

Lafayette Park

Laguna St. at Clay St.

PARENT RATING: ☆ ☆ ☆ ☆ ☆

This Pacific Heights park features an enclosed playground and a separate enclosed grassy area for playing ball or spreading a blanket. Comment: "Nice because little ones can't run away."

McKinley Square Playground

20th and Vermont Sts.

PARENT RATING: ☆ ☆ ☆ ☆

This Potrero Hill neighborhood park has a nice fenced playground and wonderful views. Unfortunately, it lacks a bathroom. Comment: "Plenty of parking, a great play structure, pretty views of Noe Valley, and it's always sunny in Potrero Hill."

Michelangelo Playground

Greenwich St. between Leavenworth and Jones Sts.

PARENT RATING: ☆ ☆ ☆ ☆

This great multi-level playground was recently renovated.

Moscone Playground and Recreation Center

Chestnut St. at Buchanan

PARENT RATING: ☆ ☆ ☆ ☆ ☆

This new, fenced playground opened to much fanfare several years ago and draws moms and caregivers from far and wide to enjoy its great structures, including nautically themed equipment. It has no shade, so bring your hats and sun screen. It also features a recreation center with popular programs for children under age 5. (See Ch. 7.) You can easily walk down Chestnut St. for lunch.

Mountain Lake Park

Lake St. at Funston Ave.

PARENT RATING: ☆ ☆ ☆ ☆

Feed the ducks and play in the bi-level playground of this popular park. You can also take a short stroller walk down the lakeside path. Caution: the playground is not enclosed, so watch kids carefully, especially on the lower level near the lake. Also, the long slide connecting the 2 levels of the park is too dangerous for toddlers.

Noe Valley Courts and Playground

24th and Douglass Sts.
Noe Valley

PARENT RATING: ☆ ☆ ☆ ☆ ☆

This small playground appeals to parents with babies and toddlers, and they often use the adjacent tennis and basketball courts for riding tricycles. Comment: "My favorite baby park."

Parkside Square Playground

28th Ave. at Vicente

This lovely Sunset neighborhood playground sits in a grove of trees. It was renovated in 2004 and features a preschool play area, a water feature, and sand play.

Richmond Playground

18th Ave. between Lake and California Streets

It's not fancy, but a nice neighborhood gathering place for outer Lake Street families.

Rochambeau Playground

25th Ave. between Lake and California Streets

This newly renovated playground, close to Sea Cliff, has a separate area for toddlers.

West Portal Playground

Lenox St. between Taraval and Ulloa Sts.

There is a large enclosed playground with a train structure, a recreation center, and a field. Pick up a sandwich or coffee down the street on West Portal Ave. and eat at the picnic tables near the playground.

North Bay

Marin Playgrounds

www.justplaygrounds.com

This excellent website and accompanying book (by Marianne Shine and Richard Shiro) feature a comprehensive directory of Marin County playgrounds by city and facilities. This is a great way to find a new playground near you! If you are overwhelmed, try some of our favorite North Bay parks and playgrounds, listed below.

Marin County Parks

http://maps.openspacecouncil.org/ Orgs/County_of_Marin.html

This website describes many Marin County parks.

Sonoma County Parks and Recreation

www.parks.sonoma.net

This website describes many Sonoma County parks.

Sonoma County Regional Parks

www.sonoma-county.org/parks

Angel Island State Park

www.angelisland.com or www. angelisland.org

PARENT RATING: ☆ ☆ ☆ ☆ ☆

Thirteen miles of hiking and biking trails, as well as spectacular views of the Bay, await you at Angel Island, the former Ellis Island of the West. To get there, take Blue and Gold Fleet ferries from San Francisco's Pier 41 (415-705-5555, www.blueandgoldfleet.com), the Angel Island ferry from Tiburon (415-435-2131, www.angelislandferry. com), the Alameda-Oakland ferry from Alameda or Oakland (510-522-3300, www.eastbayferry.com), or the Blue & Gold Fleet from Vallejo (707-643-3779, www.baylinkferry.com). There are 2 beaches, the main one at Ayala Cove near the ferry, and one at Quarry Point. Be sure to bring warm clothes. You can eat at the Cove Café (415-897-0715) on the island (open only seasonally) or bring a picnic lunch. See also Ch. 2 for family-friendly hikes.

Belvedere Community Park (Henry B. Allen Park)

San Rafael Ave. and Community Rd. (next to the Police Dept. and Town Hall)
Belvedere

PARENT RATING: ☆ ☆ ☆ ☆ ☆

This park features a totally renovated, not-too-crowded fenced playground for even very young children, with picnic tables nearby. Equipment includes new baby swings and climbing structures, and the weather is usually sunny. Toddlers like to ride their tricycles on the adjacent basketball court. You can pick up a decent sandwich at the Tiburon Deli on Ark Row.

Boyle Park

E. Blithedale Ave. between East and Carmelita Aves.
Mill Valley

PARENT RATING: ☆ ☆ ☆ ☆

This popular playground has been completely rebuilt, has a separate area for younger children, and has shaded picnic tables and a grassy play area nearby. Caveat: it can be quite crowded in the mornings.

Civic Center Park

Civic Center Dr. (off N. San Pedro Rd. across from the Civic Center)
San Rafael

PARENT RATING: ☆ ☆ ☆ ☆

The fenced toddler playground and duck pond will entertain kids. Model sailboat enthusiasts often hold races on weekends.

Corte Madera Town Park

Pixley and Tamalpais Drs.
Corte Madera

PARENT RATING: ☆ ☆ ☆ ☆ ☆

This park was renovated in 2001 and features a fabulous playground with swings, slides, a water and sand play area, a tricycle track, and a special climbing structure for the very young who usually can't navigate larger play structures. The park also offers many seating areas for parents. An insider's tip: the park is so popular that it can be virtually overrun with children and caregivers during mornings, and its large size makes it difficult to keep track of wandering children. Try the early afternoon hours if you want to avoid the crowds. Also, it is sometimes tough to navigate this park with children of different ages, since the big kids' area is separate from the toddlers' area. Corte Madera Town Center, a short drive down Tamalpais near Highway 101, is a good place to eat lunch and enjoy the popular fountain graced by an elephant statue.

Creekside Park

Bon Air Rd. (across from Marin General Hospital)
Kentfield

PARENT RATING: ☆ ☆ ☆ ☆

This park features a nice sunny playground with an adjacent shady picnic area (perfect for parking infants while the older kids play). It's not enclosed, but it is surrounded by playing fields so it's easy to keep track of wandering kids. Parking can be difficult on crowded Bon Air Road.

Parks & Playgrounds

Freitas Park

Montecillo Rd. next to Kaiser
Permanente Medical Center
Terra Linda

PARENT RATING: ☆ ☆ ☆ ☆ ☆

Known locally as the "water park,"
this park features a 3-ringed water
structure through which kids can run
and douse themselves in the summer.
Our toddlers had a ball! Bring a
beach umbrella as there is only one
small pergola structure and no shade.

Gerstle Park

D St. and San Rafael Ave.
San Rafael

PARENT RATING: ☆ ☆ ☆ ☆

There are several playgrounds and
shaded benches in this tree-filled
neighborhood park.

Hamilton Airport/Palmisano Park

At the end of Hangar Ave.
Novato

PARENT RATING: ☆ ☆ ☆ ☆

You will pass several other parks on
the way out to this one, but don't stop
at them. This is the best of the bunch,
with newer airport-themed structures
and sand and water play.

Hoog Park

Off Marin Oaks Dr. in the hills
of Ignacio
Novato

PARENT RATING: ☆ ☆ ☆ ☆

Parents say this park has "lots of
grassy hills and a contained playground" and is perfect for younger
kids.

Howarth Park

650 Summerfield Rd.
Santa Rosa
707-543-3282

PARENT RATING: ☆ ☆ ☆ ☆ ☆

This 152-acre park offers much more
than a great playground. (The playground features digging for dinosaur
bones, a Native American village, a
climbing net, an Old West town, and
a volcano!) It also has a lake for fishing and boating, many nice picnic
areas, an antique carousel, a miniature train ride (a simulated 1863
steam train), a jumpy house, an animal farm, and pony rides. The rides
and boat rentals are open only in
summer and on weekends during
other months, and the farm is open
only in summer.

Kay Park

Ross Dr. and Linda Way
(off Hwy. 1 in Tam Valley)
Mill Valley

PARENT RATING: ☆ ☆ ☆ ☆

If this park had bathrooms, it would
get our top rating. It's a neighborhood
park tucked away behind homes (in
fact, it's not visible from the street;
look for a gated path between the
houses on Ross Drive). We like its
privacy and security (it's fenced),
large lawn areas for games, and picnic tables. It's a nice place for a playgroup gathering, as you will likely
have it to yourselves!

Mount Tamalpais State Park

Panoramic Hwy.
Mill Valley
415-388-2070
www.parks.ca.gov

PARENT RATING: ☆ ☆ ☆ ☆ ☆

Miles of hiking trails and the 2,571-foot peak of Mount Tamalpais, where you can catch wonderful views of the ocean, bay, and city, are some of the attractions in this wonderful park. Bring a jog stroller or backpack, as trails are rocky and sometimes steep. See also family-friendly hikes listed in Ch. 2.

Muir Woods National Monument

Off Panoramic Hwy.
Mill Valley
415-388-2595
www.visitmuirwoods.com

PARENT RATING: ☆ ☆ ☆ ☆ ☆

This giant old-growth redwood forest features lots of hiking trails and picnic areas. The valley floor is stroller accessible and fairly cool in the summer. A caution: It can be very wet in the rainy season! Weekends can also be crowded with tourists. Lunch in the café; picnics are not allowed. See also family-friendly hikes listed in Ch. 2.

Peacock Gap Park

Peacock Dr. off San Pedro Rd.
San Rafael

PARENT RATING: ☆ ☆ ☆ ☆ ☆

Two adjacent playground areas make up this park; one is for the toddler crowd, and the other is for older children. Shaded benches and lots of sand for playing are great amenities. The park itself is not enclosed, but it is surrounded by fields and is very quiet, and the toddler lot is fenced. It can be cool, as it is near the Bay, but it is a great place for a playgroup outing.

Peri Park

Bolinas Ave. and Park St.
Fairfax

PARENT RATING: ☆ ☆ ☆ ☆

Recently renovated, this small, fenced park sits in a redwood grove and offers sand play, a water pump, and a log cabin. Downtown Fairfax eateries are within walking distance.

Pioneer Park

Off Novato Blvd. at Simmons Ln.
Novato

PARENT RATING: ☆ ☆ ☆ ☆ ☆

This is a very popular park, rebuilt in 2002. There is no fencing or shade, but kids will love the sand and water play.

Piper Park

Doherty Dr. next to the Police Dept.
Larkspur

PARENT RATING: ☆ ☆ ☆ ☆

An open playground and adjacent picnic tables make this a nice choice for groups. A caution: there is no shade from summer sun in the playground itself. It's not fenced, but is located well off the street.

Pixie Park

Marin Art and Garden Center, Sir Francis Drake Blvd. at Lagunitas Rd.
Ross
www.pixiepark.org

PARENT RATING: ☆ ☆ ☆ ☆ ☆

Pixie is a veritable Marin institution—a members-only cooperative park and a "must join" for Marin families with young children. Parents must contribute a number of hours in park maintenance and fundraising events. Parents appreciate the locked gate, the relative quiet, and the fact that everything is geared toward younger children. Only children ages 6 and under are allowed into the park. While you're there, check out the Butterfly Habitat Garden (outside the park, in the Marin Art and Garden Center).

Richardson Bay Lineal Park (aka Blackie's Pasture)

Begins at Blackie's Pasture Rd. at Tiburon and Trestle Glen Blvds. and continues into downtown Tiburon along the Bay

PARENT RATING: ☆ ☆ ☆ ☆ ☆

This park features a great walking path for stroller walks or bicycle rides, as well as a fenced playground about halfway down the path to Tiburon. Be sure to bring your stroller as it is a hike from the parking lot to the playground. The playground is slated for a renovation. A caution: there is little protection from the sun and wind, so be sure to bring hats and jackets.

San Anselmo Memorial Park

Off San Francisco Blvd. near Sir Francis Drake Blvd.
San Anselmo

PARENT RATING: ☆ ☆ ☆ ☆ ☆

A group of volunteer parents rebuilt the Millennium playground at this park in 2000, creating 2 great play areas for kids. One area is for toddlers and preschoolers, and one is for ages 6 and up. Innovative structures include castles, a train, a lighthouse, and a water play area. Caution: it is difficult to keep track of children of different ages, as the 2 areas are quite separate, and all the towers and

tubes make visibility limited. Also, there is no shade, so it can be hot in summer.

East Bay

East Bay Regional Park District

www.ebparks.org

PARENT RATING: ☆ ☆ ☆ ☆ ☆

This website features a useful directory of Alameda and Contra Costa counties regional parks and recreation facilities. The regional parks are a fabulous resource for hiking, swimming, and camping. Check out the "Regional in Nature" Activity Guide for wonderful activities for children, including nature hikes, free "family fun nights," and "family camporees" in the parks.

Websites for some popular municipal parks departments include:

- Berkeley
  www.ci.berkeley.ca.us/parks
- Concord
  www.ci.concord.ca.us/recreation/parksguide.pdf
- Orinda
  www.ci.orinda.ca.us/parkrec.htm
- Pleasanton
  www.pleasanton.com/community/parks.php
- San Ramon
  www.ci.san-ramon.ca.us/parks/
- Walnut Creek
  www.ci.walnut-creek.ca.us/parks/parksmain.htm

Adventure Playground

Berkeley Marina
160 University Ave.
Berkeley
510-981-6721
www.ci.berkeley.ca.us/marina/marinaexp/adventplgd.html

Older children (ages 7 and up) may hammer, saw, and paint to "build" parts of the playground; younger children will enjoy just playing on what is already built.

Aquatic Park

Bolivar Dr. at the west end of Bancroft Way
Berkeley

PARENT RATING: ☆ ☆ ☆ ☆ ☆

Parents rebuilt this fabulous enclosed playground, aka "Dreamland," in 2000, and it offers separate areas for kids under age 5 and for older kids, as well as turrets, mazes, and a very popular dragon slide. Bring a hat as it is very sunny. It also offers a great vantage point for watching trains go by if (like us) you have train-obsessed boys.

Central Park

12501 Alcosta Blvd.
San Ramon

PARENT RATING: ☆ ☆ ☆ ☆ ☆

Home of the San Ramon Community Center and pool, this park features a rose garden, a spectacular playground, water play, and picnic areas. It can be difficult to keep an eye on multiples here, and can be very warm in summer.

Civic Park

1375 Civic Dr. at N. Broadway
Walnut Creek
925-943-5852

PARENT RATING: ☆ ☆ ☆ ☆ ☆

This 10-acre park offers a fenced children's play area, a picnic area, a community center, a garden with a butterfly habitat, a gazebo, and arts studios.

Codornices Park

1201 Euclid Ave. at Eunice St.
Berkeley

PARENT RATING: ☆ ☆ ☆ ☆

This park features 2 separate play areas—the tot lot for younger kids (with a fence and a sandbox) and the older kids' area (with bigger swings, play structures, and a mammoth slide). Combine the outing with a walk through the Berkeley Rose Garden across the street.

Diablo Vista Park

1000 Tassajara Ranch Dr.
Danville

PARENT RATING: ☆ ☆ ☆ ☆ ☆

Famous for its mosaic water snake winding down the hillside, this 20-acre park has great play and picnic areas.

Emerald Glen Park

Tassajara Rd. and Gleason Dr.
Dublin

Soon to include an aquatic center, this park has a playground with water play and a rose garden.

FROG Park Playgrounds (Rockridge-Temescal Greenbelt)

Hudson and Claremont Sts. (Hardy Playground)
Redondo and Clark Sts. (Redondo Playground)
Rockridge
www.frogpark.org

PARENT RATING: ☆ ☆ ☆ ☆ ☆

After Friends of the Rockridge-Temescal Greenbelt (or FROG) organized construction of 2 wonderful new playgrounds on the Greenbelt in 2001, this area became known as Frog Park and draws parents and children from all over Berkeley and Oakland. Hardy is primarily for older children, but it does have a tot lot and sandbox. Redondo, the smaller of the 2, is for tots ages 2-5. Watch out for the adjacent creek.

Heather Farm Park

301 N. San Carlos Dr.
Walnut Creek
925-943-5858

This 102-acre park features a duck pond, gardens, an equestrian center, swimming, a playground, and picnic areas.

Kennedy Park

19501 Hesperian Blvd.
Hayward
510-670-7275
www.haywardrec.org

A petting zoo, pony ride, train ride, merry-go-round, and bouncy house add to the attraction of this playground.

Lafayette Reservoir

3849 Mt. Diablo Blvd.
Lafayette
925-284-9669
www.ebmud.com/services/
recreation/east_bay/lafayette/

This reservoir, operated by the East Bay Municipal Utility District, offers 925 acres of hiking trails, boating, fishing, and picnicking. There are 2 children's play areas near the picnic areas, as well as a popular paved trail. Rowboats and pedal boats may be rented.

Lakeside Park

Lakeside Dr. on Lake Merritt
Oakland

PARENT RATING: ☆ ☆ ☆ ☆

This is a great place for a stroll along the lake, with many spots to stop and feed the ducks. Don't miss the Kids' Kingdom Playground (Bellevue Ave. between Elita and Perkins Sts.).

Live Oak Park

Berryman St. between Shattuck Ave. and Walnut St.
Berkeley

PARENT RATING: ☆ ☆ ☆ ☆

Parents appreciate the fenced playground; kids like the swings, toddler-sized climbing area, and ride-on animals.

Mission Hills Park

Independence Dr. and Junipero St.
Pleasanton

PARENT RATING: ☆ ☆ ☆ ☆ ☆

This is a popular park because of the creek (with frog-filled lagoon and island) and the 50-foot slide built into the hill.

Montclair Park

6300 Moraga Blvd. at Thornhill
Montclair

PARENT RATING: ☆ ☆ ☆ ☆ ☆

This neighborhood park has 2 playgrounds, one for big kids and a
fenced one for toddlers. Feeding the
ducks is a favorite activity here,
though keep a careful eye on toddlers
around the unfenced pond.

Moraga Commons

St. Mary's Rd. off Moraga Rd.
Moraga

PARENT RATING: ☆ ☆ ☆ ☆ ☆

This ever-popular park "for younger
kids" features the Moraga Cooler
water structure through which kids
can run and spray themselves.

Mt. Diablo State Park

Danville

See listing in Ch. 2 under Favorite
Walks and Hikes.

Oak Hill Park

3005 Stone Valley Rd.
Danville

PARENT RATING: ☆ ☆ ☆ ☆ ☆

Kids love feeding the ducks and
geese, and you can stroll or bike
around the lake on level paths. There
is also a playground and more adven-
turous hiking terrain.

Old Ranch Park

1000 Vista Monte Dr.
San Ramon

PARENT RATING: ☆ ☆ ☆ ☆ ☆

This park offers a revamped playground with new equipment and picnic areas.

Orinda Park and Community Center

26 Orinda Way
Orinda

PARENT RATING: ☆ ☆ ☆ ☆ ☆

Remodeled several years ago, this
park in the center of Orinda is hugely
popular. There are separate big kids'
and little kids' areas, a gazebo, a
community center, and a paved bike
path.

Osage Station Park

816 Brookside Dr.
Danville

PARENT RATING: ☆ ☆ ☆ ☆ ☆

Stroll through the lovely rose garden
or visit the playground, which features a train station, "great" water
play, and picnic areas.

Piedmont Park

Highland Ave.
Piedmont

PARENT RATING: ☆ ☆ ☆ ☆ ☆

This 15-acre park is the hub of activity for Piedmont residents. It has a
nice tot lot at the Highland Avenue
entrance, or enter at Wildwood
Avenue for a scenic view of the Bay.

Pleasanton Sports Park

5800 Parkside Dr.
Pleasanton
925-484-8160

PARENT RATING: ☆ ☆ ☆ ☆ ☆

This park has over 100 acres of
sports facilities, including several
children's play areas.

Shannon Park

11600 Shannon Ave.
Dublin
925-833-6645

The water play area makes this an extremely popular park for kids.

Terrace Park

Terrace Dr. and Tevlin St.
Albany

PARENT RATING: ☆ ☆ ☆ ☆

This park features shaded picnic tables, wide fields, "good equipment" (swings, slides, climbing equipment), and "separate sides for older and younger kids."

Tilden Park

Entrances off Wildcat Canyon Rd. and Grizzly Peak Blvd.
Berkeley
510-562-PARK (7275)
www.ebparks.org

PARENT RATING: ☆ ☆ ☆ ☆ ☆

There are over 2,000 acres in this East Bay treasure, with spectacular hiking and views of the bay, including the following fun attractions for kids:

- **Reservable picnic areas** (510-636-1684).
- **Swimming at Lake Anza** (510-848-3028 or 510-848-3385). Visit the sandy beach during the season. Comment: "Best non-pool swimming!"
- **Little Train** (510-548-6100, www.redwoodvalleyrailway.com). A miniature steam passenger railway, a huge hit with kids, travels through stunning eucalyptus groves and offers views of the Bay. An even smaller train runs on Sunday afternoons on a track below the Little Train (510-486-0623, www.ggls.org).

- ◆ **Botanic Garden** (510-841-8732). This garden features beautiful native California plants from 12 geographic ranges; it's a good place for a leisurely walk.
- ◆ **Merry-Go-Round** (510-524-6773). This antique carousel has an organ and adjacent snack bar with "amusement park" fare.
- ◆ **Little Farm and Environmental Education Center** in Tilden Nature Study Area (510-525-2233). The EEC features interactive displays where kids can use microscopes to see pond life. Feed the animals at the farm! Naturalists lead nature walks by the ponds and through the hills and meadows, including the popular "Tilden Tots" program for ages 3-4. The adjacent picnic area and playground will also entertain kids.

Totland Playground

McGee Ave. and Virginia St.
Berkeley

PARENT RATING: ☆ ☆ ☆ ☆ ☆

This fenced playground was renovated recently and is very popular for families with young children. The sand and water play area is a huge hit, as are the communal toys.

Village Green Park

9540 Village Pky.
San Ramon

PARENT RATING: ☆ ☆ ☆ ☆ ☆

This is a popular playground and picnic area.

Midpeninsula Regional Open Space District
www.openspace.org

Santa Clara County Parks and Recreation Department
www.parkhere.org

San Mateo County Parks and Recreation Division
www.eparks.net

San Jose Regional Parks
www.sanjoseca.gov/prns/regionalparks/

Websites for some popular municipal parks departments include:

◆ Burlingame
www.burlingame.org/p_r/
◆ Campbell
www.ci.campbell.ca.us/communityandarts/parks.htm
◆ Los Gatos
www.los-gatos.org/main/parks.html
◆ Menlo Park
www.menlopark.org/departments/com/parks.html
◆ Mountain View
www.ci.mtnview.ca.us/citydepts/cs/parks.htm
◆ Palo Alto
www.city.palo-alto.ca.us/parks/
◆ Redwood City
www.redwoodcity.org/parks/
◆ San Jose
www.sjparks.org
◆ San Mateo
www.ci.sanmateo.ca.us/dept/parks/
◆ Sunnyvale
www.sunnyvale.ca.gov/departments/parks+and+recreation/

Bowden Park
Alma and N. California Sts.
Palo Alto
PARENT RATING: ☆ ☆ ☆ ☆ ☆

Great for the youngest children, this park offers a large children's play area full of equipment, such as a climbing gym and a brick wall maze. There are also attractive gardens, a small picnic area, and a redwood grove.

Briones Park
Arastradero Rd. between Foothill Expwy. and El Camino Real
Palo Alto
PARENT RATING: ☆ ☆ ☆ ☆

This park has a playground, a picnic area, and a tot area with a stationary locomotive.

Burgess Park
701 Laurel St. (park)
501 Laurel St. (pools)
Menlo Park
PARENT RATING: ☆ ☆ ☆ ☆ ☆

This is Menlo Park's main and newly renovated recreation area, with playing fields, a playground, and a gymnasium. New pools are being built, including a children's pool to replace the popular wading pool.

Burton Park
Cedar St.
San Carlos
PARENT RATING: ☆ ☆ ☆ ☆ ☆

The central park of San Carlos, it features 2 playgrounds, a fenced one for toddlers and one for older children.

Campbell (Central) Park

Gilman and Campbell Aves.
Campbell

PARENT RATING: ☆ ☆ ☆ ☆ ☆

This park features 2 water play areas: one in the fenced toddler area, and one for all ages.

Central Park

5th Ave. and El Camino Real
San Mateo
650-340-1520 (for train hours)

A miniature train for kids, play structures, and a Japanese Tea Garden grace this park.

La Colina Park

Los Pinos Way and Ansdell Dr.
San Jose

PARENT RATING: ☆ ☆ ☆ ☆ ☆

This park was renovated recently and has nice toddler and water play areas.

DeAnza Park

1150 Lime Dr.
Sunnyvale

You can find a playground, horseshoe pits, picnic areas, a skating rink, and more at this park.

Jack Fischer Park

Abbott Ave. and Pollard Rd.
Campbell

PARENT RATING: ☆ ☆ ☆ ☆ ☆

This park features play equipment for both toddlers and older children, including a stream that kids can activate on demand, and picnic areas.

Frontierland Park

Oddstad Blvd. at Yosemite Dr.
Pacifica

PARENT RATING: ☆ ☆ ☆ ☆ ☆

Completely renovated in 2002, this hilltop playground features nice views and is usually above the fogbank. There are 2 playgrounds, one for toddlers and preschoolers and one for children ages 5 and up. There are huge climbing structures and a water play feature.

Greer Park

1098 Amarillo Ave.
Palo Alto

PARENT RATING: ☆ ☆ ☆ ☆

This park offers a tiny tot area with a nautical theme, as well as traditional play structures and picnic areas.

Guadalupe River Park & Gardens

San Jose
408-277-5904 (Visitor Center)
408-298-7657 (Friends of Guadalupe River Park)
www.grpg.org

PARENT RATING: ☆ ☆ ☆ ☆ ☆

A 3-mile ribbon of park along the Guadalupe River in downtown San Jose, this park is still in development but already features several great areas for families:

- ◆ **Discovery Meadow**, at the southern end of the park, features the **Children's Discovery Museum** (see listing under Museums—South Bay), and **Monopoly in the Park**, a 930-square-foot outdoor monopoly board (see www.monopolyinthepark.com).
- ◆ **McEnery Park** (on the south side of San Fernando St., just east of the river) offers a great children's

play area, including climbing nets and ropes for older children, and spring toys and a model boat for younger children. A recreated model of the Guadalupe River flows through the park and provides ample water play.

- **Children's Carousel at Arena Green** (Autumn St. at Santa Clara St., across from the Arena) includes sharks representing San Jose's ice hockey team (408-999-6817).
- **Tot Lot.** Next to the carousel, these 2 state-of-the-art playgrounds include climbing structures made of nets and rope, in addition to traditional equipment.
- **Ranger Station and Visitor Center at Arena Green** (north side of Santa Clara St. at the river, 408-277-5904) provides exhibits on the birds, snakes, fish, and plants native to the river, as well as some educational programs.
- **Gardens** (at the northern end of the park, south of the San Jose Airport) include a rose garden and historic fruit tree orchard.

Gull Park
Gull Ave. between Kildeer Ct. & Swan St.
Foster City
PARENT RATING: ☆ ☆ ☆ ☆ ☆

With an adjacent sandy beach on a quiet inlet, this is the perfect spot for toddlers. There are 2 playground areas and a large lawn for throwing balls.

Hoover Park
2901 Cowper St.
Palo Alto
PARENT RATING: ☆ ☆ ☆ ☆

This park features a nice tiny tot area with a merry-go-round, crawling and climbing structures, swings, slides, and sand. A play area for bigger kids has a geodesic climbing dome to ascend, swings, and a roller-coaster slide.

Johnson Park
Waverly and Everett Sts.
Palo Alto
PARENT RATING: ☆ ☆ ☆ ☆ ☆

The big concrete slide here is a huge hit with kids.

Las Palmas Park
850 Russet Dr.
Sunnyvale

This park has a newer play structure, a spray pool, and a picnic area on an "island" in the lake.

Mitchell Park
East Meadow and Middlefield Rds.
Palo Alto

The tiny tot area has 6 gopher holes, slides and swings, bears in the sandpit to climb on, a shady wading pool with 2 green frogs, and a birthday party area.

John Morgan Park
540 W. Rincon Ave.
Campbell
PARENT RATING: ☆ ☆ ☆ ☆ ☆

There are 2 playgrounds (one with a water spiral play area), picnic areas, and sports fields.

Nealon Park
800 Middle Ave.
Menlo Park
PARENT RATING: ☆ ☆ ☆ ☆ ☆

Parents call this newly renovated playground "great."

Oak Meadow Park
University Ave. and Blossom Hill Rd.
Los Gatos

There are separate areas for toddlers and older children, with a stationary toy train and model airplane to entertain. It is also the home of the Billy Jones Wildcat Railroad and carousel (See listing under Trains, Planes, Boats, and Automobiles—South Bay).

Eleanor Pardee Park
851 Center Dr.
Palo Alto
PARENT RATING: ☆ ☆ ☆ ☆

This park features a tiny tot area, an apparatus play area, sheltered picnic tables and benches, and a stage.

Peers Park
1899 Park Blvd.
Palo Alto
PARENT RATING: ☆ ☆ ☆ ☆

There are grassy picnic areas, a wooden play structure, and a tiny tot area in this park.

Ramos Park
800 E. Meadow
Palo Alto
PARENT RATING: ☆ ☆ ☆ ☆ ☆

Parents say this park, with lots of open space, is a "great place to fly kites." The toddler play area has a sculpture in the sandpit and a climbing structure in the shape of a train.

Rinconada Park
777 Embarcadero Rd.
Palo Alto
415-329-2351 (pool)
PARENT RATING: ☆ ☆ ☆ ☆ ☆

Palo Alto's central park features 2 playgrounds and several pools, including a popular 5-leaf-clover toddler wading pool with a slide and giant plastic duck statues.

Seminary Oaks Park
Seminary Dr. and Santa Monica Ave.
Menlo Park
PARENT RATING: ☆ ☆ ☆ ☆ ☆

This sunny new playground offers 3 age-specific play areas, as well as a "relaxation garden" for adults.

Serra Park
730 The Dalles
Sunnyvale

There are picnic areas, a playground, and a spray pool in this park.

Shoreline at Mountain View Park
2600 N. Shoreline Blvd.
Mountain View
650-903-6392
PARENT RATING: ☆ ☆ ☆ ☆ ☆

There is a large lake for boating, and the paths are great for strollers or bikes. Comment: "Great place to fly a kite and to see ducklings in the spring."

Shoup Park
400 University Ave.
Los Altos
PARENT RATING: ☆ ☆ ☆ ☆

This park has a lovely creek.

Could Your Local Playground Use a Renovation?

Sadly, many of today's playgrounds still use yesterday's equipment. Many new legal requirements for playground safety have gone into effect in recent years, including compliance with the Americans with Disabilities Act. Check your playground's safety against the Public Playground Safety Checklist issued by the U.S. Consumer Product Safety Commission (Document #327, available at www.cpsc.gov/cpscpub/pubs/327.html). Some things to look for include: soft surfacing such as rubber or mulch, rather than concrete or asphalt; bucket swings designed for toddlers and located where they won't hit other children; mats at the bottoms of slides; guardrails on tall equipment; and no rusty equipment.

If you think your local playground could stand an update, you may not be alone. In San Francisco, the Neighborhood Parks Council, a coalition of community park groups, works to improve neighborhood parks (www.sfneighborhoodparks.com). Check their website for updates on park renovations or to get involved in improving a park. San Francisco Parks Trust also supports renovations to many San Francisco parks (www.sfpt.org). In other Bay Area communities, groups of parents have successfully spearheaded major renovations to favorite playgrounds by raising public and private funds and donating "sweat equity." With state and local budgets in crisis, these parent-led campaigns may be the only way to save outdated playgrounds from closure.

Stafford Park

Hopkins Ave. and King St.
Redwood City
PARENT RATING: ☆ ☆ ☆ ☆ ☆

The water play area is "the best," say parents. This newly renovated park features 2 adjacent play areas, one for big kids and one for toddlers.

Stulsaft Park

3700 Farm Hill Blvd.
Redwood City
PARENT RATING: ☆ ☆ ☆ ☆ ☆

"Great" fenced water play area, plus mammoth slides, make this a good outing, say parents.

Sunnyvale Baylands Park

999 E. Caribbean Dr.
Sunnyvale
408-730-7709 (information center)
408-730-7751 (reservations)

Set in open space and baylands, this park has a great Discovery Play Area with climbing structures, a seesaw snake, spring toys, sand terraces, talk tubes, and fossil imprints. There are also miles of trails for stroller walking.

Vasona Lake County Park

333 Blossom Hill Rd.
Los Gatos
408-356-2729

PARENT RATING: ☆ ☆ ☆ ☆ ☆

Wide lawns for play, picnic areas, and a new waterfront theme playground make this a very popular facility for families. There is also a lake for paddleboating, rowboating, or fishing.

Washington Park

850 Burlingame Ave.
Burlingame

Located in the heart of Burlingame, this is a popular park with a large playground and a recreation center.

Washington Park

840 W. Washington Ave.
Sunnyvale

PARENT RATING: ☆ ☆ ☆ ☆ ☆

This park offers innovative play structures, picnic areas, a pool, tennis courts, and horseshoe pits.

Willow Street Frank Bramhall Park

Willow St. and Camino Ramon
San Jose

PARENT RATING: ☆ ☆ ☆ ☆ ☆

This Willow Glen neighborhood park offers an enclosed, sandy area for toddlers, and another unenclosed play area with sand. The shade trees are a big plus in the summer months!

Favorite Beaches and Public Pools

We are fortunate to live in an area with great beaches and many pools. While Pacific beaches can be cool and foggy during the summer, and many are not safe for swimming (at least for children), kids will still enjoy a day at the beach making sand castles, hunting for shells, and splashing in tide pools. For serious swimming, check out the family-oriented pools and lakes listed below. You'll also find more pools listed under the Swimming section in Ch. 7. Don't forget the many area parks featuring "water play" via sprinklers during the summer months, which can sometimes be easier to navigate with babies and toddlers.

Baker Beach

Off Lincoln Blvd. near 25th Ave.

PARENT RATING: ☆ ☆ ☆ ☆ ☆

This sandy beach in the Seacliff neighborhood is probably about as sheltered as you will get in San Francisco, but the winds still blow. When the fog lifts, it offers views of the Golden Gate Bridge and has picnic tables in a grove of cypress trees. Note: The north end of the beach is sometimes used by nude sunbathers, and parking is very limited on warm weekends.

Crissy Field and Marina Green

Parking off Marina Blvd. west of Marina Green

www.crissyfield.org

PARENT RATING: ☆ ☆ ☆ ☆ ☆

Restored 100-acre Crissy Field is a wonderful place to spend a sunny morning, with its sandy beach, walking trails (great for strollers), and beautiful "can't beat it" Golden Gate Bridge views. It is almost always windy, so be sure to bring a sweatshirt and hat. On warm days, kids will enjoy wading in the shallow waters off East Beach. Don't miss the Warming Hut for lunch or snack located at the far west end of Crissy Field, toward the bridge. Comment: "They have great organic hot chocolate!" There are also a café and art and nature activities for kids at the Crissy Field Center, 603 Mason St., a bit closer to East Beach.

Fort Funston and Ocean Beach

Off Skyline Blvd. just south of John Muir Dr.

415-561-4323 (program information)

PARENT RATING: ☆ ☆ ☆ ☆

This beach features the stroller-friendly Sunset Trail along the cliff. You will have to carry the stroller down the stairs to the beach, however, and watch for fog.

China Camp State Park and Beach

N. San Pedro Road, east of Hwy. 101 San Rafael

415-456-0766

www.parks.ca.gov

PARENT RATING: ☆ ☆ ☆ ☆

Parents call this state park a "good day trip." This bay-front beach is rocky but warmer than Pacific beaches. The park features a museum depicting life in the Chinese shrimp-fishing village that thrived on the site in the 1880s. You can also hike one of the many trails (relatively easy walking but not stroller friendly) or picnic overlooking San Pablo Bay.

Drake's Beach

Point Reyes National Seashore, near Olema

415-464-5100

www.nps.gov/pore/

PARENT RATING: ☆ ☆ ☆ ☆

The 4-mile beach along Drake's Bay in Point Reyes includes a small café and a visitor's center. The national park has beautiful trails, and the visitor's center offers guided walks.

Beaches & Pools

399

McNear's Beach County Park

San Pedro Rd. at Cantera Way, east of Hwy. 101
San Rafael
415-499-6387
www.co.marin.ca.us/depts/pk/main/pos/pdmnbch.cfm
PARENT RATING: ☆ ☆ ☆ ☆

At this popular, family-friendly county park on San Pablo Bay, you can hang out at the sandy beach, picnic, play Frisbee on the lawn, fish off the 500-foot pier, swim in the public swimming pool, play tennis, or eat at the snack bar.

Muir Beach

Off Hwy. 1, west of Mill Valley
PARENT RATING: ☆ ☆ ☆ ☆

It's windy, but you'll enjoy the rugged scenery along the Pacific. Leave your stroller at home.

Rodeo Beach

Marin Headlands
Fort Cronkhite, at end of Bunker Rd.
Sausalito
PARENT RATING: ☆ ☆ ☆ ☆

This is a beautiful black sand beach at the far western end of the Marin Headlands. Comment: "The hike on the cliffs to the right of the beach is easy for kids and gives you a 180-degree view of the Pacific . . . . good walking and picnicking spot." Caution: Parking can be tight, this is not a swimming beach, and watch out for nude sunbathers. See also the nearby Marine Mammal Center listed below under Animals! Zoos, Farms, and Wildlife—North Bay.

Stinson Beach

Stinson Beach off Hwy. 1
415-868-1922
www.stinsonbeachonline.com
PARENT RATING: ☆ ☆ ☆ ☆

There are shaded picnic tables and a small playground in the nearby park. Note: No lifeguard is on duty during the winter, and surf can be dangerous. Get an early start on summer weekends, as traffic can be backed up 15 miles to Hwy. 101. Parkside Café (415-868-1272) or the Sand Dollar Restaurant (415-868-0434) are nice places for lunch or dinner. If you rent a house, try to get one in the private Seadrift development; they have the best beaches on both the ocean and the lagoon.

Strawberry Recreation District Pool

118 E. Strawberry Dr.
Mill Valley
415-383-1610
http://strawberry.marin.org
PARENT RATING: ☆ ☆ ☆ ☆

It can be a bit crowded on sunny days, but there is a nice wading pool for toddlers and a big pool for older children.

Tennessee Valley Beach

Off Tennessee Valley Rd.
Mill Valley
PARENT RATING: ☆ ☆ ☆ ☆

It's a 2-mile walk to this small Pacific beach; be sure to bring a jog stroller or backpack carrier, as regular strollers won't cut it on the rocky trail. There are fun tide pools in which young children can play. It can be foggy in the summer, so bring warm clothes.

Tomales Bay Beaches (including Heart's Desire Beach and Shell Beach)

Pierce Point Rd.
Inverness
www.parks.ca.gov

PARENT RATING: ☆ ☆ ☆ ☆ ☆

This state park's beaches feature "calm water . . . perfect for young ones."

East Bay

Clarke Swim Center

Heather Farm Park
1750 Heather Dr.
Walnut Creek
925-943-5856
www.ci.walnut-creek.ca.us

There is a large heated public pool and a children's wading pool at this center.

Contra Loma Regional Recreation Area

1200 Frederickson Ln.
Antioch
925-757-0404 (swim lagoon)
www.ebparks.org

PARENT RATING: ☆ ☆ ☆ ☆ ☆

This park features a great swimming lagoon with a sandy beach, as well as a large reservoir for boating and fishing.

Cull Canyon Regional Recreation Area

18627 Cull Canyon Rd.
Castro Valley
510-537-2240 (swim lagoon)
www.ebparks.org

PARENT RATING: ☆ ☆ ☆ ☆ ☆

This beautiful, clean (it's filtered) swim lagoon is surrounded by sandy

beaches and lawns for picnicking. Toddlers love frolicking in the sand and water, and parents don't have to worry about ocean waves. It's open in summer, staffed by lifeguards, and has a bathhouse and snack bar.

Del Valle Regional Park

7000 Del Valle Rd.
Livermore
www.ebparks.org

This park's 5-mile-long lake, set in a valley, has 2 swimming beaches with lifeguards on duty during the season. You can also rent boats in the marina, fish in the lake, or camp on its shores.

Don Castro Regional Recreation Area

22400 Woodroe Ave.
Hayward
510-538-1148
www.ebparks.org

PARENT RATING: ☆ ☆ ☆ ☆ ☆

The swim lagoon in this park is very popular in summer. The shallow waters of the lagoon, with a separate roped-off section for youngsters, are "great for toddlers." Like Cull Canyon, this park has a bathhouse, sandy beach, and lawns for picnicking. The adjacent lake is closed to swimming and boating, but open to fishing.

Lake Anza

See Tilden Park listing under Parks—East Bay.

Lake Temescal

6500 Broadway
Oakland
510-652-1155
www.ebparks.org

PARENT RATING: ☆ ☆ ☆ ☆

401

Enjoy swimming (lifeguards are on duty in summer), a snack bar, fishing, and picnic areas.

Prewett Family Park (Antioch Water Park)

4701 Lone Tree Way
Antioch
925-776-3070
www.ci.antioch.ca.us/citysvcs/prewett

PARENT RATING: ☆ ☆ ☆ ☆ ☆

This huge multi-pool public facility has many water slides, including one specifically for children under 4 feet tall.

Roberts Regional Recreation Area and Pool

Skyline Blvd. at Joaquin Miller Rd.
Oakland
510-482-0971
www.ebparks.org

PARENT RATING: ☆ ☆ ☆ ☆ ☆

This 100-acre recreation area set in a lush redwood grove features a popular heated pool that is open in summer. This park also has a great, newly renovated playground that is handicapped accessible.

San Ramon Olympic Pool and Aquatic Park

9900 Broadmoor Dr.
San Ramon
925-973-3240

PARENT RATING: ☆ ☆ ☆ ☆

This state-of-the-art facility offers 3 pools, including a water play pool for small children. Comment: "A great kids' area."

Shadow Cliffs Regional Recreation Area

2500 Stanley Blvd.
Pleasanton
925-846-3000
www.ebparks.org

This huge 250-acre park contains an 80-acre lake for swimming and trout fishing, a 4-flume waterslide, and picnic areas.

Strawberry Canyon Recreation Area

Centennial Dr., east of main UC Berkeley campus
Berkeley
510-643-6720
www.strawberry.org/swim

Though on the UC Berkeley campus, the West Pool and adjacent kiddie pool are open to the public.

South Bay

Almaden Lake Park

Almaden Expwy. and Coleman Ave.
San Jose
408-277-5130

This foothill park features a lake for boating or seasonal swimming, surrounded by a biking and strolling trail. There are also picnic areas and a playground, with separate areas for toddlers and older children.

Burgess Pool

Menlo Park
See listing under Parks—South Bay.

Burlingame Aquatics Center

1 Mangini Way (entrance on Oak Grove)
Burlingame
650-558-7322
www.burlingame.org/p_r/

This center is located at Burlingame High School but run by the Recreation Department and open year round to the public. It includes a 50-meter outdoor pool, heated to 79-82 degrees, and a shallow, warm water pool for children.

Gull Park

Foster City
See listing under Parks—South Bay.

Half Moon Bay State Beach (aka Francis Beach)

Hwy. 1 at Kelley Rd.
Half Moon Bay
650-726-8820

PARENT RATING: ☆ ☆ ☆ ☆ ☆

We've hit some spectacular days at this beach in the early fall when the fog recedes. It offers a long, open sandy beach and picnic areas. Parents also recommended the cliff-side walk and paved golf course trail near the Ritz-Carlton Resort, just south of the state beach.

Montara State Beach

Hwy. 1
Montara

PARENT RATING: ☆ ☆ ☆ ☆ ☆

This beach is popular with surfers.

Natural Bridges State Beach

Swift Ave. off Hwy. 1
Santa Cruz
831-423-4609

PARENT RATING: ☆ ☆ ☆ ☆ ☆

This beach offers spectacular scenery, including a natural bridge affording visitors views of the sea life below. It is also home to a monarch butterfly colony from mid-October until the end of February. You can combine it with a trip to the Seymour Marine Discovery Center; see listing under Animals! Zoos, Farms, and Wildlife—South Bay.

Rinconada Pool

See listing under Parks—South Bay.

Santa Cruz Beach and Boardwalk

Beach St.
Santa Cruz
831-426-7433
www.beachboardwalk.com

PARENT RATING: ☆ ☆ ☆ ☆ ☆

The boardwalk features rides, arcades, and lots of food stands. Comment: "Toddlers love the board-walk and beach."

Animals! Zoos, Farms, and Wildlife

We've found that doing anything involving animals—fish, fowl, or mammal—is a surefire way to please a toddler or preschooler. Did you ever think you would spend so many days at the zoo?

Aquarium of the Bay

Pier 39, Embarcadero at Beach St.
888-SEA-DIVE
www.aquariumofthebay.com
PARENT RATING: ☆ ☆ ☆ ☆

Focusing on the San Francisco Bay's marine environment, this aquarium features a moving walkway surrounded by huge tanks full of 23,000 aquatic animals, including rays, eels, octopuses, and sharks. The touch pools, giving kids the opportunity to touch bat rays, are also a hit. Comment: "Fun moving walkway but parking is pricey." Insider tip: AAA membership provides discounted parking at Pier 39.

San Francisco Zoo

1 Zoo Rd. (main entrance at Sloat Blvd. and 47th Ave.)
415-753-7080
www.sfzoo.org
PARENT RATING: ☆ ☆ ☆ ☆

The largest in Northern California, this zoo's ratings improved considerably after its recent renovation. Whereas some thought it "shabby" in our previous edition, now the majority find it a "fun place . . . amazing . . . very child friendly . . . great for kids . . . with something for everyone . . . a nice focus on conservation . . . the animals' living spaces are now modern, more natural environments rather than concrete cages." The new African Savanna area near the park's entrance is particularly inviting. Though it's not the size and scope of zoos in San Diego or Chicago, for kids it's still a great outing because of the fun children's areas. Favorites of children at the zoo include the newly remodeled Children's Zoo (where children can pet and feed domestic animals), the Little Puffer Steam Train, the carousel, the koalas, and the gorillas. The new Family Lemur Forest allows kids to see these endangered creatures up close. Best times to view animals are when they are being fed—the big cats are particularly entertaining. Cafés are available for lunch, including the new Leaping Lemur Café with improved fare, but we recommend bringing your own picnic. The playground near the old entrance to the zoo is older, but sure to please children who tire of walking around to all the exhibits. Be sure to bring a jacket and a stroller; the zoo is located near the ocean in one of the foggiest neighborhoods in the city, and exhibits are spread far and wide! Strollers and wagons are also available to rent. Insider tip: members of mothers' clubs, such as the Mothers of Twins Club, receive a discount on zoo membership, and AAA or KQED memberships also provide discounts on daily tickets.

Audubon Canyon Ranch

4900 Hwy. 1
Stinson Beach
415-868-9244
www.egret.org
PARENT RATING: ☆ ☆ ☆ ☆ ☆

Hike and view great blue herons and great egrets in miles of the Bolinas Lagoon Preserve, with beautiful views of Bolinas Lagoon and Stinson Beach. Nesting season is in March.

Environmental Discovery Center of Sonoma County

Spring Lake Regional Park
Santa Rosa
707-539-2865
www.sonoma-county.org/parks

This nature center features an indoor tidal pool with live, touchable sea creatures.

Five Brooks Ranch Pony Rides

Hwy. 1
Olema
415-663-1570
www.fivebrooks.com

Take your child on a hand-led pony ride around the Five Brooks pond to view turtles, great blue heron, and quail (ages 3 and up). They also offer trail rides (for older children), and riding lessons.

Madrone Audubon Society

707-546-7492 (general information)
707-527-6118 (Pee Wee Audubon programs)
www.audubon.sonoma.net

This Audubon Society chapter offers a Pee Wee Audubon program monthly on weekends, featuring guided, hands-on nature activities for children in Sonoma and Marin counties.

Marine Mammal Center

Marin Headlands
1065 Fort Cronkhite
Sausalito
415-289-SEAL (7325)
www.tmmc.org

PARENT RATING: ☆ ☆ ☆ ☆

TMMC is a nonprofit rescue and rehabilitation center for injured and stranded marine mammals (e.g., seals, sea lions, whales, dolphins, and sea otters). Patients vary by season, but kids will enjoy visiting them in the "hospital." The center also offers a variety of educational programs and beach walks. Comment: "The center is small, but a great place to see marine mammals up close. Spring is the best time to visit. We like to spend the rest of the morning at Rodeo Beach across the street."

Safari West Wildlife Preserve and Tent Camp

3115 Porter Creek Rd.
Santa Rosa
707-579-2551
www.safariwest.com

PARENT RATING: ☆ ☆ ☆ ☆ ☆

This 400-acre private wildlife preserve focuses on the propagation of endangered species. Home to over 400 mammals and birds, Safari West's inhabitants include zebras, giraffes, and lemurs, among others. Safari-vehicle tours led by naturalists last for 2½–3 hours, include a walk around the grounds, and are by appointment only. Overnight stays may be arranged in tent cabins, though these are best for kids over age 3. Comments: "A fun family outing . . . interesting . . . best for children old enough to understand the guides' commentary . . . good for a day trip."

Slide Ranch

2025 Shoreline Hwy.
Muir Beach
415-381-6155
www.slideranch.org

PARENT RATING: ☆ ☆ ☆ ☆ ☆

A partner of the Golden Gate National Recreation Area, Slide Ranch is "a

nonprofit agricultural and environmental education center in a small-
farm, coastal wilderness setting" on
134 acres. Slide Ranch focuses on
organic food production, resource
conservation and recycling, animal
husbandry, and open space conservation. Check out the Family Farm
Days and Parent-Child Workshops on
weekends, and seasonal events in the
spring and fall. Children can learn
about where food comes from in the
organic garden, feed the farm animals, explore the beach and tide
pools, do crafts, and enjoy picnic
lunches in the garden.

Sonoma County Farm Trails

800-207-9464
www.farmtrails.org (for locations)
This sustainable-farming organization
provides a map to Sonoma County
farms that are open to the public,
many of which offer opportunities to
pick your own produce and visit farm
animals.

Tiburon Audubon Center

376 Greenwood Beach Rd.
Tiburon
415-388-2524
www.tiburonaudubon.org
PARENT RATING: ☆ ☆ ☆ ☆ ☆

This 11-acre wildlife habitat and environmental education center on
Richardson Bay offers "fabulous"
summer day camps for children as
young as age 3, and family events
throughout the year, such as nature
walks. They also do nature birthday
parties and field trips. Insider tip: Be
sure to note on your calendar the first
day of summer camp sign-ups (usually in early February). Many camps

fill on the first day! Our children loved
their camps!

Victoria's Fashion Stables

430 Sprauer Rd.
Petaluma
707-481-3579
Pony rides, pony wagon rides, hay
rides, and a petting zoo are available.
Prices can be steep for individuals so
it's best to go with a group.

WildCare (Terwilliger Nature Education and Wildlife Rehabilitation)

76 Albert Park Ln.
San Rafael
415-453-1000
www.wildcaremarin.org
PARENT RATING: ☆ ☆ ☆ ☆

This rehabilitation center for injured,
ill, or orphaned wild animals offers
popular nature programs, including
tot walks, family walks, and camps.
Comments: "Not huge, but a great
place to stop in. Best times to visit
are during feedings at 12:30 and 4:30
p.m."

East Bay

Ardenwood Historic Farm

34600 Ardenwood Blvd.
Fremont
510-796-0199
www.ebparks.org
PARENT RATING: ☆ ☆ ☆ ☆

This 205-acre working farm run by
the East Bay Regional Park District
re-creates 19th-century agricultural
practices. The farm features live animals, a horse-drawn train and wagon
rides, a blacksmith shop, a Native
American village, a Victorian house, a

milk house, a picnic area, and gardens. Costumed docents give demonstrations of 19th-century farming and craft-making. The café has the basics, or bring your own picnic lunch. It's best for ages 3 and up. Avoid the winter months, when the grounds are open but there are no special events. "It's a great place to see farm animals," say parents.

Crab Cove Visitor Center

Crown Memorial Beach
1252 McKay Ave.
Alameda
510-521-6887
www.ebparks.org

Kids can learn about shoreline wildlife, visit the aquarium or the bay model, learn about Alameda's history, or explore the tide pools at this estuarine marine reserve. (Check the website for health advisories before you go; there have been instances of "swimmer's itch" at this beach.) The amusement park is long gone that—until World War II—made the area known as the "Coney Island of the West," but the beach has been restored. The Sea Squirts program for ages 3-5 provides nature activities, stories, and crafts. (See Ch. 7 under More Classes.) The visitor center is closed in winter.

Don Edwards San Francisco Bay National Wildlife Refuge

1 Marshlands Rd.
Newark
510-792-0222
http://desfbay.fws.gov/

Hike and fish in the miles of bay marshland or enjoy the many family programs such as bird walks and marsh exploration.

East Bay Vivarium

1827 Fifth St.
Berkeley
510-841-1400
www.eastbayvivarium
PARENT RATING: ☆☆☆☆

This is actually a reptile store, not a zoo, but kids will love seeing all the snakes, lizards, turtles, frogs, and tarantulas. Comment: "A good free outing for a rainy day."

Hayward Shoreline Interpretive Center

4901 Breakwater Ave.
Hayward
510-670-7270
www.haywardrec.org

This center features saltwater aquariums with bay wildlife and rotating exhibits of wildlife, plants, and history. Hike or bike on the Shoreline Trail amid wetlands, salt marsh, and ponds. Be sure to check the tide before you wander too far.

Lindsay Wildlife Museum

1931 1st Ave.
Walnut Creek
925-935-1978
www.wildlife-museum.org
PARENT RATING: ☆☆☆☆☆

This wildlife education and rehabilitation center features 50 kinds of live, non-releasable native wild animals and a discovery room with hands-on activities for kids under age 12. It's best to visit when they are feeding the animals, so call ahead for feeding times. Preschoolers can take wonderful science and nature classes.

Oakland Zoo

Knowland Park
9777 Golf Links Rd.
Oakland
510-632-9525
www.oaklandzoo.org

PARENT RATING: ☆ ☆ ☆ ☆ ☆

Favorite features of this African-themed zoo include the newly remod-eled Valley Children's Zoo where kids can pet and feed domestic animals, view an alligator or otters underwater, stroll through the Butterfly Garden, or take in a wildlife show in the amphitheater. Kids also love the miniature train (a scaled-down replica of a Civil War-era locomotive), the Sky Ride over the bison and elk range (with views of the bay), and the children's ride area with its antique carousel. Concession stands are available in the zoo, or picnic in Knowland Park. "Great for kids, and the weather is better than at the San Francisco Zoo . . . nice and compact . . . good rides . . . great scale for young kids . . . small but in a very nice park setting . . . worth the drive," rave parents.

Old Borges Ranch

1035 Castle Rock Rd.
Walnut Creek
925-943-5860

One of the first ranches in Contra Costa County, this is now a working and demonstration cattle ranch maintained by the park service. Children ages 2 and up will enjoy seeing farm animals, a working blacksmith shop, a windmill, antique farm equipment, and assorted farm buildings including the original ranch house. From the ranch you can access many hiking trails in the surrounding hills.

Rotary Nature Center

600 Bellevue Ave.
Oakland
510-238-3739
www.oaklandnet.com/parks/
facilities/rnc.asp

PARENT RATING: ☆ ☆ ☆ ☆

Run by the Oakland Parks and Recreation Department, this interpretive nature center offers many waterfowl to feed. You can watch the resident naturalists feed the birds daily or purchase feed at the center and do it yourself.

Shorebird Nature Center

160 University Ave.
Berkeley
510-981-6740
www.ci.berkeley.ca.us/marina/

PARENT RATING: ☆ ☆ ☆

The City of Berkeley's center features a 100-gallon saltwater aquarium displaying creatures from San Francisco Bay, a touch table, and other wildlife exhibits. Insider tip: the saltwater aquarium doesn't have many fish, and it's no more than a 5-minute trip around the center when the touch table is not up, so you may want to make this a stop on your way to other outings such as the Adventure Playground (see listing under Parks—East Bay).

Sulphur Creek Nature Center

1801 D St.
Hayward
510-881-6747
www.haywardrec.org

At this wildlife education and rehabilitation facility you can see reptiles, amphibians, fish, and arthropods, as well as birds and mammals. Best times to visit are for the docent talks where they introduce the animals; call ahead for times. The center also offers lots of nature classes and programs for children and families through the Hayward Area Recreation and Park District. Toddler Times, held once a month for ages one to 3, introduce animals and the natural world and usually involve an art project. Comment: "They do great birthday parties and even have a pet lending library!"

Año Nuevo State Reserve

Hwy. 1
Pescadero
800-444-4445 (reservations)
650-879-2025 (information)
www.parks.ca.gov
PARENT RATING: ☆ ☆ ☆ ☆ ☆

Año Nuevo features an elephant seal-breeding colony—the largest mainland colony in the world—from December to March, although seals generally can be seen year round. Take a guided 3-mile hike down the beach during breeding season; be sure to reserve early as tours fill quickly. Our kids thought this was a great outing. While in Pescadero, you can also visit the grounds of the Pigeon Point Light Station (650-879-2120), one of the tallest lighthouses in the U.S. and now a state historic park. See also Phipps Ranch, below.

Coyote Point Museum and Park

1651 Coyote Point Dr.
San Mateo
650-342-7755
www.coyoteptmuseum.org
PARENT RATING: ☆ ☆ ☆ ☆

Located in a lovely waterfront park on the bay, Coyote Point focuses on Bay Area habitats and is fun for all ages. The museum features live animals in habitats, an aviary, gardens, hands-on activities, and educational dioramas. The adjacent park offers playgrounds, picnic areas, a beach, airplane viewing, and walking and biking trails. Toddler Tuesday programs teach nature appreciation, sizes, shapes, and textures.

Deer Hollow Farm

Rancho San Antonio Open Space Preserve
Mountain View
650-903-6430
PARENT RATING: ☆ ☆ ☆ ☆

Run by the City of Mountain View Recreation Department, this working farm features pigs, goats, sheep, chickens, and other farm animals. Children can look at the animals but not feed or pet them. The farm is also an educational center where kids can learn about animal care and explore the surrounding wilderness preserve.

Fitzgerald Marine Reserve

California and N. Lake Sts.
Moss Beach
650-728-3584
www.fitzgeraldreserve.org
PARENT RATING: ☆ ☆ ☆ ☆

This inter-tidal marine reserve on San Mateo's coast is home to many

Zoos, Farms, & Wildlife

species of marine life and will fascinate all ages. You can picnic at the beach or take a tide pool walk. It's best to visit at low tide when marine life is exposed in the tide pools, and be sure to bring a sweatshirt as summer days can be foggy and cool.

Happy Hollow Park and Zoo
Kelley Park
1300 Senter Rd.
San Jose
408-277-3000
www.happyhollowparkandzoo.org
PARENT RATING: ☆ ☆ ☆ ☆

This park is for children ages 2-10, with a petting zoo (wild and domestic animals), children's rides (such as a carousel and a train), puppet shows, a Kids' Café, and reservable picnic areas. Parents say the park is "older" but "kids like it."

Hidden Villa Farm
26870 Moody Rd.
Los Altos
650-949-8650
www.hiddenvilla.org
PARENT RATING: ☆ ☆ ☆ ☆ ☆

This 1600-acre organic farm and wilderness preserve offers domestic animals, many children's programs in environmental education (most for ages 6 and up), and miles of hiking trails for everyone. A parent favorite is the Page Mill Road trail with educational markers. Call ahead as the farm is sometimes closed to the public during summer camp season.

Lintt Trout Farm
11751 San Mateo Rd.
Half Moon Bay
650-726-0845
Rent a pole and take your child trout fishing at this farm, where the staff will clean and bag your catch.

Palo Alto Baylands Nature Preserve
Embarcadero Rd. east to the bay
Palo Alto
650-329-2506
www.city.palo-alto.ca.us/parks/
baylands.html
PARENT RATING: ☆ ☆ ☆ ☆ ☆

Walk around the duck pond and feed the ducks, watch airplanes take off and land at the airport, hike through miles of trails along salt marshes and sloughs, walk on the boardwalk, and watch birds. The interpretive center offers nature walks and other educational programs.

Palo Alto Junior Museum and Zoo
See listing below under Museums—South Bay.

Phipps Ranch
2700 Pescadero Rd.
Pescadero
650-879-0787
www.phippscountry.com
PARENT RATING: ☆ ☆ ☆ ☆

Pick all the olallieberries, raspberries, and strawberries you want (in season from early summer to early fall), feed the barnyard animals, picnic, and watch the birds in the aviary. While in Pescadero don't miss lunch at Duarte's Tavern—they have a kids' menu (202 Stage Rd., 650-879-0464). See also Año Nuevo, above.

Prusch Farm Park

647 S. King Rd.
San Jose
408-926-5555
www.sjparks.org/Parks/
emmaprusch.htm

Originally a dairy farm, this park features a huge barn with sheep, pigs, cattle, ducks, chickens, geese, and rabbits, surrounded by a fruit orchard, gardens, and open grass for picnicking.

Seymour Marine Discovery Center

100 Shaffer Rd.
Santa Cruz
831-459-3800
www2.ucsc.edu/seymourcenter

Atop the cliffs overlooking Monterey Bay National Marine Sanctuary, this center is part of a working marine laboratory affiliated with the University of California at Santa Cruz. One of the most awe-inspiring exhibits is the huge skeleton of a blue whale outside the center. The interactive exhibits provide videotaped explanations by scientists (a bonus for children not yet reading), and there are touch tables to explore. They also provide tours of the working laboratory. Combine this trip with a visit to the Santa Cruz Beach Boardwalk; see Favorite Beaches and Public Pools—South Bay, above.

Indoor Playgrounds

A common lament of local parents is the lack of indoor play areas for kids. The price of Bay Area real estate being what it is, we may not all have dedicated play rooms at home. Try these indoor playgrounds, and don't forget the drop-in play programs listed in Ch. 7 (e.g., Recreation Centers, the Jewish Community Center, Parents Place, and Temple Sherith Israel in San Francisco; Corte Madera Recreation's "Bouncing Babies," Sausalito Recreation's "Tot Club," Jumping Jacks, and Parents Place in Marin; the Berkeley YMCA, Temple Beth Abraham, Tot Drop, and Wee Play in the East Bay; and Peninsula Parents Place). Also, check with your local shopping mall; many malls now have small play areas for children. Don't forget to wash your children's hands after they play; indoor playgrounds can be disease factories!

Bamboola

5401 Camden Ave.
San Jose
408-448-4386
www.whitehutchinson.com/leisure/
bamboola.shtml
PARENT RATING: ☆ ☆ ☆ ☆

This 30,000-square-foot indoor play area has an outdoor garden and sandbox, art projects, live performances, water play, a separate toddler area (for kids under age 3), and a café. Some parents felt it was "not the cleanest place in town."

Chuck E. Cheese's

www.chuckecheese.com

PARENT RATING: ☆ ☆ ☆

Games, rides, and pizza for kids center around "Chuck-E-Cheese," a giant rat! Kids love it; parents don't. Check the website for locations throughout the Bay Area.

The Jungle Fun and Adventure

www.junglefunandadventure.com

PARENT RATING: ☆ ☆ ☆

This indoor playground has climbing structures for older kids, an enclosed toddler area, and an adjacent pizza parlor. The Jungle received mixed reviews; as one parent put it, "Every kid I know likes the Jungle, but parents don't." Most parents felt the facilities were "too big and crowded" and appeared "not that clean." Others point out that it is best for kids ages 3 and up or under 18 months, as 2-year-olds are too old for the toddler area and too young for the big kids' area. Check the website for Bay Area locations.

Merlin's Magic Kingdom

Round Table Pizza
1565 Novato Blvd.
Novato
415-897-2512

PARENT RATING: ☆ ☆ ☆ ☆

This pizza parlor and indoor play area offers tubes, slides, and crawling structures for kids ages 10 and under.

Toob Town

6591 Commerce Blvd.
Rohnert Park
707-588-8100

PARENT RATING: ☆ ☆ ☆ ☆

This indoor playground for kids ages 2 and up features tube play structures, bumper boats, a dinosaur bounce, a toddler play area, and ball pits. Stay for a pizza lunch at the adjoining restaurant. Comment: "Loved it . . . moms can actually talk while kids play here."

Museums

Before you say, "my kid will never enjoy a museum," check out some of the museums listed below. Many are geared to young children, and some "adult" museums offer special children's programming. Keep in mind that many museums offer wonderful children's birthday parties. Be sure to check the Trains, Planes, Boats, and Automobiles section for more museums.

San Francisco

Most San Francisco museums offer free admission on the first Wednesday of the month. While that sounds like a good deal in principle, we recommend steering clear of the free days because the crowds can be overwhelming for younger children (and enough to give even the most patient of parents a migraine!). A money-saving hint: Many museums provide discounts to members of affiliated museums and to KQED or AAA members. Check with individual museums for policies.

Asian Art Museum

200 Larkin St.
415-581-3500
www.asianart.org
PARENT RATING: ☆ ☆ ☆ ☆ ☆

The "new" Asian, opened in 2003, features a plethora of interactive family programs. Storytelling for families takes place on weekends, when a storyteller weaves Asian myths and legends with objects on display in the museum's galleries. AsiaAlive is an interactive, drop-in program with live artist demonstrations (e.g., visiting Tibetan painters) and hands-on activities related to a monthly theme. There are also drop-in family art classes on the first Saturday of the month and in conjunction with special exhibits, and quarterly author readings and book-related activities for children. A wonderful Family Festival, celebrating Asian culture and art, is held biannually. The first Tuesday of the month features free performances and demonstrations.

California Academy of Sciences

875 Howard St. (temporary location)
415-321-8000
www.calacademy.org
PARENT RATING: ☆ ☆ ☆ ☆

In its full incarnation, the Academy includes the Natural History Museum, Steinhart Aquarium, and Morrison Planetarium. But until 2008 when the rebuilding of its home in Golden Gate Park is complete, the Planetarium is closed and the Aquarium and Natural History Museum are temporarily located in a much smaller facility downtown. Not all of the exhibits made the move, unfortunately. The Aquarium still offers hands-on exploration of starfish and coral in the Touch Tide Pool, and most of its fish, turtles, penguins, and reptiles are on display. Nature Nest in the Natural History Museum is a special place for kids ages 5 and under to play, with live animals and a water table. There are regular story hours. The Naturalist Center also provides additional hands-on activities for kids, like dissections and excavations. There is a decent, but busy, café for lunch. Comments: "This is a great membership to have, especially for a rainy or foggy day. . . . My kids love it." Some liked the temporary location for its small size; others thought it was "cramped . . . not great."

California Palace of the Legion of Honor

Lincoln Park
100 34th Ave.
415-863-3330
www.thinker.org
PARENT RATING: ☆ ☆ ☆ ☆ ☆

Although the European art and beautiful building may not interest children under age 5, squire them to the free gallery tour and art workshop on Saturday mornings for ages 3 and up. While visiting, take advantage of the spectacular views of the Bay from Lincoln Park. Dine in the museum's café or picnic in the park. There is also a children's theater on site, providing performances of children's stories (415-750-3640 for schedule).

Museums

deYoung Museum

Golden Gate Park
50 Hagiwara Tea Garden Dr.
www.thinker.org

The deYoung is scheduled to reopen in October 2005 in an all-new building. They plan to offer the children's art workshops currently being offered at the deYoung Art Center on Saturday afternoons for ages 3 and up (2501 Irving St., 415-682-2481), together with gallery tours for families.

Exploratorium

3601 Lyon St.
415-EXP-LORE (397-5673)
www.exploratorium.edu

PARENT RATING: ☆ ☆ ☆ ☆ ☆

This highly rated science and discovery museum features hands-on exhibits like the Tactile Dome, where you crawl around in the dark using your sense of touch to guide you. The Tactile Dome is "better for older kids," since it may be too scary for children under age 3. Kids ages 4 and up will get more out of the interactive exhibits, but younger kids will still love to push all the buttons even if they don't understand what it all means. Be sure to hit the Play Lab, a special play area for infants, toddlers, and preschoolers. Eat at the café or head to one of the many Chestnut St. eateries nearby. Comments: "Crazy fun. . . . Don't go on the free Wednesdays, it's a madhouse!"

Randall Museum

199 Museum Way
415-554-9600
www.randallmuseum.org
PARENT RATING: ☆ ☆ ☆ ☆

Run by the San Francisco Recreation and Park Department, this art and science museum sits atop Corona Heights, commanding spectacular views of the city. Though the museum's collection is small, kids will enjoy seeing the live animals (e.g., snakes and turtles) and the model train exhibit (the latter open Saturdays only, see www.ggmrc.org). The museum also offers many wonderful family classes and special performances, including drop-in art and science programs on Saturdays and camps during school holidays. The outdoor area was completely renovated in 2003, and now features thematic learning gardens, an outdoor art studio, a small amphitheater, and a beautiful lawn for picnics (there are no café facilities). You can also picnic and play in the adjacent Corona Heights playground. A Toddler Discovery Area was scheduled to open in fall 2005, featuring drop-in play and special toddler programming. Comments: "Good for a short visit on a rainy day . . . good theater programs . . . great for little kids . . . wonderful train room on Saturdays."

San Francisco Fire Department Museum

655 Presidio Ave.
415-563-4630 (during museum hours) or 415-558-3546 (voice mail)
www.sffiremuseum.org

PARENT RATING: ☆ ☆ ☆ ☆ ☆

Admission is free, and kids will enjoy the model fire engines (showing the development from hand pumpers to mechanized fire trucks), the collection of cast iron toys, and the antique fire engines and wagons on display.

San Francisco Museum of Modern Art

151 3rd St.
415-357-4000
415-538-2693 (Koret Education Center)
www.sfmoma.org

PARENT RATING: ☆ ☆ ☆ ☆ ☆

Much of this highly rated modern art museum will be beyond the comprehension of children under age 6, but there are several wonderful family events worth checking out. Family Day, twice a year, features hands-on art projects, docent-led gallery activities, music, and performances. Monthly hands-on Family Studios, directed by guest artists, include drawing, painting, collage, printmaking, and assemblage, and take place the third Sunday of every month. Children can enjoy drop-in art activities in the education center. There is a café and a great museum store on site.

North Bay

Bay Area Discovery Museum

E. Fort Baker
557 McReynolds Rd.
Sausalito
415-339-3900
www.baykidsmuseum.org

PARENT RATING: ☆ ☆ ☆ ☆ ☆

Along with many other Bay Area parents, we can't say enough good things about this hands-on museum for children ages 10 and under and their families. Kids as young as one year old will love it. Easily the most popular family destination in the Bay Area, this indoor/outdoor museum recently underwent a huge renovation and expansion. At the top of our children's list of favorites is Lookout Cove, the outdoor play area featuring a shipwreck, a crow's nest, a moored boat, a sea cave with tide pools, animal homes to build, and more. Permanent exhibits include Tot Spot (a newly renovated indoor/outdoor play area for kids under age 3), the San Francisco Bay Hall (with a great fishing boat to operate), Art Studios (drop-in art and ceramics projects and classes, in 2 different rooms separated by age), Media Clubhouse (for ages 6 and up), and the latest addition, the Wave Workshop science lab (with hands-on marine life experiments). The Discovery Theatre offers Miss Kitty's musical performances weekly, and a full schedule of low-cost, family-oriented performances. There is also a changing exhibit every quarter. The café has recently improved its menu to emphasize organic food, or you may want to bring your own picnic for the tables outside. The Discovery Store offers a range of stimulating toys for young children. Special family events occur throughout the year, and there are great camps during school holidays. We recommend joining the museum if you intend to make several visits per year; membership is inexpensive and provides free admission, special members-only programs, and discounts in the store. Our kids would visit every week if they could! Comments: "It can't be overrated. . . . A great place to go on rainy days . . . lots of activities . . . a beautiful location . . . good for a wide age range . . . excellent organic café with healthy food choices. . . . Go early, late, or midweek to beat crowds. By far the best deal for weekly outings," say parents.

Chabot Space and Science Center

10000 Skyline Blvd.
Oakland
510-336-7300
www.chabotspace.org

PARENT RATING: ☆ ☆ ☆ ☆ ☆

This science museum features a wonderful planetarium, a Mega-Dome Theater with a 70-foot dome screen for viewing science movies, telescopes for public viewing in the evenings, simulated space missions in the Challenger Learning Center (for older children), and a Discovery Lab with hands-on learning for children ages 2 and up. The museum offers a café for lunch and is located on 13 acres of East Bay parkland with great views of San Francisco and Oakland.

Hall of Health

2230 Shattuck Ave.
Berkeley
510-549-1564
www.hallofhealth.org

Sponsored by Children's Hospital Oakland, this is a free health-education museum and science center. Interactive exhibits teach older kids how the body works. Younger kids will enjoy the Kids on the Block puppet shows.

Habitot Children's Museum

2065 Kittredge St.
Berkeley
510-647-1111
www.habitot.org

PARENT RATING: ☆ ☆ ☆ ☆ ☆

This wonderfully hands-on, indoor art and discovery museum for children under age 7 is particularly appropriate for toddlers and preschoolers. Favorites include the water play exhibit (be sure to bring extra clothes), dress-up area and stage, wind tunnel, art projects, grocery store, infant-toddler garden for crawlers, and ride-on cars and trucks. There are great multidisciplinary classes for kids, and special family events occur often. Some found it "too crowded and hectic," especially on rainy days, but most appreciated the convenient downtown Berkeley location.

Junior Center of Art and Science

558 Bellevue Ave.
Oakland
510-839-5777

This museum features live animals, aquariums, a pottery studio, and a bird sanctuary. Fun, drop-in art activities (e.g., pottery) are offered for children ages 2 and up and their families.

Lawrence Hall of Science

1 Centennial Dr.
Berkeley
510-642-5132
www.lawrencehallofscience.org

PARENT RATING: ☆ ☆ ☆ ☆ ☆

A favorite of young children in this hilltop science museum is the Young Explorers Area, with puppets, blocks, books, and an insect zoo. Other fun areas are the interactive science exhibits, a biology lab with crabs, clams, snails, and even a boa constrictor to hold, the Gravity Wall, the outdoor science park, and the Idea

Lab (including Lego play!). There are many science and nature classes for kids ages 2 and up. The café offers decent fare and spectacular views of San Francisco and the Bay.

Museum of Children's Art (MOCHA)

538 9th St.
Oakland
510-465-8770
www.mocha.org
PARENT RATING: ☆ ☆ ☆ ☆

Younger children may not be interested in looking at the art, but they can *do* art projects in myriad classes and workshops. The Little Studio offers a great drop-in art space for children under age 6.

Oakland Museum of California

1000 Oak St.
Oakland
888-625-6873 or 510-238-2200
www.museumca.org
PARENT RATING: ☆ ☆ ☆ ☆

Most kids under age 5 won't be able to fully appreciate this extensive museum of the art, history, and natural sciences of California. Try taking them to see the dioramas of California wildlife in the Natural Sciences Gallery and the historic fire trucks. If you have older children, the Family Explorations Program offers fun hands-on activities for kids ages 5-12.

Valley Children's Museum

P.O. Box 305
San Ramon
www.valleychildrensmuseum.org
An interactive, hands-on, nonprofit children's museum in the Tri-Valley area was in the planning stages as of

summer 2005. Check the website for updates.

South Bay

Cantor Center for Visual Arts

328 Lomita Dr.
Stanford
650-723-4177
www.ccva.stanford.edu
PARENT RATING: ☆ ☆ ☆ ☆

This large and beautiful art museum and sculpture garden provides Family Tours every second Saturday afternoon, plus art classes for kindergarteners and up. Museum admission is free.

Children's Discovery Museum of San Jose

180 Woz Way
San Jose
408-298-5437
www.cdm.org
PARENT RATING: ☆ ☆ ☆ ☆ ☆

A fabulous, huge, interactive museum for children ages 13 and under, CDM offers exhibits and programs in science, technology, the arts, and the humanities. Older kids will enjoy climbing the multilevel tower and exploring the exhibits on transportation, communications, electricity, banking, the postal service, and so on, but stick to the early childhood center and bubbles exhibit for young children (ages 4 and under). Often you can participate in free parent-child workshops and drop-in art, science, and music classes. Parents particularly like the Circle Time for toddlers. Eat lunch in the Kids' Café or picnic in nearby Guadalupe River Park.

Palo Alto Junior Museum and Zoo

1451 Middlefield Rd.
Palo Alto
650-329-2111
www.city.palo-alto.ca.us/ross/
museum/index.html

PARENT RATING: ☆ ☆ ☆ ☆ ☆

This ever-popular nature, science, art, and history museum for children features hands-on exhibits, a small zoo, and a playground with a picnic area in the park next to the museum. A favorite is the Play Spot, an inter-active play area for kids under age 5. There are art and science classes for kids ages 2 and up. The museum is best for ages one to 5. Comments: "Small but great exhibits and classes. . . . Admission is free."

Rosicrucian Egyptian Museum

Rosicrucian Park
1342 Naglee Ave.
San Jose
408-947-3600
www.rosicrucian.org

With the largest collection of Egyptian artifacts in the western U.S., this museum features some unusual objects, including mummies, jewelry, a pyramid, and a full-scale replica of an Egyptian tomb. It's best for ages 3 and up.

San Jose Museum of Art

110 S. Market St.
San Jose
408-271-6840
www.sjmusart.org

Parents recommend the Kids Art Sundays, with free hands-on art activities and special performances for children. Museum members and their children can do even more structured art projects during the "Side by Side" time preceding the Kids Art program.

Tech Museum of Innovation

201 S. Market St.
San Jose
408-294-TECH (8324)
www.thetech.org

PARENT RATING: ☆ ☆ ☆ ☆ ☆

Who can live in the Bay Area without visiting a museum devoted to Silicon Valley's technology and innovation? Visit a "clean room," take a picture of yourself with a laser scanner, experi-ment with teleconferencing or movie animation technology, try being weightless like an astronaut, and experience a simulated earthquake. This museum is full of unique hands-on exhibits sure to intrigue parents as much as children, as well as an IMAX dome-screen theater. It's best for ages 3 and up. There is a nice café for lunch, and the on-site TechStore is guaranteed to empty your wallet.

Best Things to Do on a Rainy Day

We've found the best cure for cabin fever can be simple activities you can do at home, like renting movies, baking cookies, building forts and obstacle courses, pitching a tent in the living room, creating Play Doh works, jumping on bubble wrap, and doing art projects. If you are itching to get out, try one of the museums or indoor playgrounds listed above, a library or story hour listed below, or some of the following ideas to entertain your kids on rainy days:

Artopia Studios

Locations throughout the East and South Bays
www.artopiastudios.com (for locations)

This franchised chain of studios offers drop-in, do-it-yourself arts and crafts for all ages. Projects range from ceramics to mosaics to candle making. In addition to open studio, there are special times and projects for preschoolers and their parents.

Bowling

Bowling is perfect for the 3-and-up crowd; younger kids won't be able to hold the balls. Ask for lighter balls and have them put bumpers in the lanes so the kids' balls don't end up in the gutter zone. Kids don't usually need special shoes.

◆ Country Club Bowl

88 Vivian Way
San Rafael
415-456-4661
PARENT RATING: ☆ ☆ ☆ ☆ ☆
Pizza restaurant is on site.

◆ Boulevard Bowl

1100 Petaluma Blvd. S.
Petaluma
707-762-4581
PARENT RATING: ☆ ☆ ☆ ☆ ☆

◆ Presidio Bowling Alley

Building 93, Corner of Moraga and Montgomery Sts.
The Presidio
415-561-BOWL
PARENT RATING: ☆ ☆ ☆ ☆ ☆

The grill serves burgers and similar fare.

◆ Yerba Buena Gardens Bowling Center

See below under Other Amusements—San Francisco.

Ceramic Painting

Pick and paint your own pottery, and the studio will fire and glaze it for you to pick up a week later. Anything with kids' handprints or footprints make great gifts for relatives! Here are some places to try:

◆ Color Me Mine

Locations throughout the Bay Area
www.colormemine.com

◆ Terra Mia

1314 Castro St.
San Francisco
415-642-9911

◆ Doodlebug

641 San Anselmo Ave.
San Anselmo
415-456-5989

◆ Mimi's Pottery Place

237 Shoreline Hwy.
Mill Valley
415-388-8668

◆ Brushstrokes

745 Page St.
Berkeley
510-528-1360

Create It!
299 S. California Ave., #100
Palo Alto
650-323-1515
www.createitstudio.com

Fire Stations
Arrange a visit to your local fire station. They won't be as busy fighting fires in the rainy season, and kids will love to climb aboard the trucks and try on the equipment.

Grocery Stores and Farmer's Markets
Kids love to wander the produce section and point out different items. The outing is even more fun if the store has those miniature kiddie carts, so the little ones can push their own. Farmer's markets are wonderful if the weather is not too inclement.

Home Depot Stores
www.homedepot.com

Many Home Depot stores offer free Kids' Workshops on the first Saturday of every month. Theoretically kids must be 5 years old to attend, but we took our 2-year-olds and they loved it. An adult must supervise kids. Kids can make cool projects like mobiles or bird feeders (all out of prefabricated kits) and learn how to use tools.

Lakeshore Learning Stores
- San Jose
  1099 S. Bascom Ave.
  408-998-0794
- San Leandro
  144 Montague Ave.
  510-483-9750

- Walnut Creek
  1929 Mt. Diablo Blvd.
  925-944-1495

www.lakeshorelearning.com

The retail homes of the Lakeshore Learning Materials catalog adored by preschool teachers, these stores offer free crafts for kids ages 3 and up every Saturday. No reservations necessary.

Miss Kitty
- Sausalito
  Bay Area Discovery Museum
  (weekday mornings)
  415-339-3900
  www.baykidsmuseum.org
- Fairfax
  Bug-a-Boo
  14 Bolinas Rd., 415-457-2884
- Corte Madera
  Book Passage
  51 Tamal Vista, 415-927-0960

415-457-2576
www.misskittysings.com

PARENT RATING: ☆ ☆ ☆ ☆ ☆

At these locations regularly, the ever-popular Miss Kitty entertains children with her lively guitar playing, dancing, and singing. Kids adore her! For all ages, but the 2- to 4-year-olds are especially enamored.

Movies
- If you have a baby, try Sony Metreon's Reel Moms (in San Francisco, www.metreon.com), Lark Theater's Cinemamas (in Larkspur, www.larktheater.net), Century Theatres' Moms' Matinees (in San Jose and Daly City, www.cinemamas.com), or Parkway Theater's Baby Brigade (in Oakland,

www.picturepubpizza.com) programs. All welcome parents with babies during special screening times. (For more information see Special Events for Kids, below).

♦ Parents of children old enough to sit through movies should consider checking out the reviews at www.commonsensemedia.org before they decide to see a film. This site also features family-friendly reviews of television programming, videos/DVDs, music, and books.

PARENT RATING: ☆ ☆ ☆ ☆ ☆
Comment: "Great resource for being an informed and educated parent."

♦ Other groups who review media for child-appropriate content include the Coalition for Quality Children's Media (www.kidsfirst.org) and the National Institute on Media and Family (www.mediafamily.org).

Mrs. Grossman's Sticker Mania
3810 Cypress Dr.
Petaluma
800-429-4549
www.MrsGrossmans.com
PARENT RATING: ☆ ☆ ☆ ☆
Kids are obsessed with these stickers! Call the Consumer Relations Department to arrange a free tour of the plant where the stickers are made. Tours last for 45 minutes, including watching a video about the company, and kids get free samples at the end. There is a lunchroom for brown baggers.

Pet Stores
Pretend it's a zoo or you'll go home with a menagerie. One of the best is the East Bay Vivarium; see above under Animals! Zoos, Farms, and Wildlife.

Shopping Malls
Pretend the toy stores are museums or you'll come away with an empty wallet. One of the best for kids is the Sony Metreon. See below under Other Amusements—San Francisco.

Libraries and Storytelling

Many libraries and bookstores host free children's story times and special events, involving stories, finger play, songs, children's performers, or a combination of them all. These are great time fillers on rainy days, and besides, they are free! It may help to tell your youngster that a bookstore is a "library" so that you don't ruin your surprise book purchases. The following libraries and bookstores host parents' favorite storytelling hours and special events for children:

Asian Art Museum of San Francisco

See listing under Museums—
San Francisco.

Book Passage

Ferry Building, 1 Ferry Plaza
415-835-1020
www.bookpassage.com

PARENT RATING: ☆ ☆ ☆ ☆ ☆

This branch of the renowned Corte
Madera bookstore hosts children's
vocalist James K on Sunday mornings.

Borders Books and Music

Stonestown Galleria
415-731-0665

Helen Crocker Russell Library, Strybing Arboretum and Botanical Gardens

Golden Gate Park
9th Ave. at Lincoln Way
415-661-1316
www.strybing.org/library

San Francisco Public Libraries

415-557-4400
www.sfpl.org

PARENT RATING: ☆ ☆ ☆ ☆ ☆

Free family storytelling hours, as well
as films and special events, take
place at the Main Library Children's
Center and neighborhood branches.
The Children's Center is a wonderful
place to hang out on a rainy day.
Parents say the Richmond branch
library "has a great kids' section and
Saturday singing and reading." They
also rated the story times at West
Portal, Noe Valley, Potrero Hill, and
Presidio branch libraries very highly;

they felt the story times were "well
structured" and "very inviting." The
library also offers a "Dial-A-Story"
telephone line (415-437-4880).

Barnes & Noble Bookstore

2020 Redwood Hwy.
Greenbrae
415-924-1016
They provide storytelling monthly.

Borders Books & Music

588 W. Francisco Blvd.
San Rafael
415-454-1400
In addition to story hours, this store
often hosts vocalist Miss Kitty.

Book Passage

52 Tamal Vista Blvd.
Corte Madera
415-927-0960
www.bookpassage.com

PARENT RATING: ☆ ☆ ☆ ☆ ☆

Children's story time features the
ever-popular Christopher Smith, and
Miss Kitty also performs here.

Marin County Free Libraries

www.co.marin.ca.us/library
The following libraries belong to this
consortium:
- Bolinas
  415-868-1171
- San Rafael Civic Center
  415-507-4048
- Corte Madera
  415-924-4844
- Fairfax
  415-453-8092
- Inverness
  415-669-1288

- Marin City
  415-332-6159
- Novato
  415-897-1143
- Point Reyes Station
  415-663-8375
- San Geronimo Valley
  415-488-0430
- South Novato
  415-506-3165
- Stinson Beach
  415-868-0252

All of these libraries have story times for young children. Parental favorites Corte Madera and Novato received the highest parent ratings (☆ ☆ ☆ ☆ ☆).

Marinet Consortium of Public Libraries

www.marinet.info

The following libraries belong to this online card catalog consortium:
- Belvedere-Tiburon
  415-789-2662
  http://bel-tib-lib.org
- Larkspur
  415-927-5134
  www.ci.larkspur.ca.us
- Mill Valley
  415-389-4292, ext. 106
  www.millvalleylibrary.org
- San Anselmo
  415-258-4656
  www.townofsananselmo.org/library
- San Rafael
  415-485-3323
  www.srpubliclibrary.org
- Sausalito
  415-289-4121
  www.ci.sausalito.ca.us/library

All of these libraries host story times for young children and other special

family events. Belvedere-Tiburon's, San Anselmo's, and San Rafael's programs are parent favorites.
(PARENT RATING: ☆ ☆ ☆ ☆ ☆).

East Bay

Alameda County Library

510-745-1421

www.aclibrary.org

Branches throughout the county offer preschool story times and toddler times, as well as special events like magicians and puppet shows.

Barnes and Noble Book Stores
- Berkeley
  2352 Shattuck Ave., 510-644-0861
- Oakland
  98 Broadway, 510-272-0120
- Walnut Creek
  1149 S. Main St., 925-947-0373

Berkeley Public Library

510-981-6100

www.infopeople.org/bpl/

The main and branch locations of this library offer baby, toddler, and preschool story times, as well as other family programs.

Borders Books and Music

www.bordersstores.com

Popular children's story hours occur at many branches.

Cody's Books
- Berkeley
  1730 4th St., 510-559-9500
- Oakland
  2454 Telegraph Ave., 510-845-7852
  www.codysbooks.com

Contra Costa County Library

1750 Oak Park Blvd.
Pleasant Hill
925-646-6434
www.contra-costa.lib.ca.us
PARENT RATING: ☆ ☆ ☆ ☆ ☆

Branches throughout the county offer toddler and preschool story times and special children's events. The Danville, Lafayette, and San Ramon libraries are favorites

Livermore Public Library

Civic Center Library
1000 S. Livermore Ave.
Livermore
925-373-5500
www.ci.livermore.ca.us/lpl.html
The main library and branches offer lap sits and preschool story times.

Oakland Public Library

510-238-7241 (Children's Services)
www.oaklandlibrary.org
Call Dial-a-Story, 510-597-5054, to enjoy a free 3- to 4-minute story for children of all ages. The Main Library and many branches offer story hours.

Pleasanton Public Library

400 Old Bernal Ave.
Pleasanton
925-931-3400
www.ci.pleasanton.ca.us/library.html
PARENT RATING: ☆ ☆ ☆ ☆ ☆

The library offers toddler and pre-school story times and special children's events. "Great children's area," rave parents.

Atherton Library

2 Dinkelspiel Station Ln.
Atherton
650-328-2422
www.athertonlibrary.org
PARENT RATING: ☆ ☆ ☆ ☆ ☆

Parents rave about the toddler, pre-school, and pajama story times.

babystyle Story Hours

- Burlingame
  1319 Burlingame Ave.
  650-342-1534
- Santa Clara
  Valley Fair Mall, 2855 Stevens Creek Blvd.
  408-246-9703

www.babystyle.com
This baby store offers weekly story times with free refreshments.

Barnes and Noble Book Store

Hillsdale Mall
San Mateo
650-341-5560

Books Inc.

1375 Burlingame Ave.
Burlingame
650-685-4911
www.booksinc.net

Borders Books and Music

www.bordersstores.com
Popular children's story hours occur at many branches.

Burlingame Public Library

480 Primrose Rd.
Burlingame
650-558-7400
www.burlingame.org/library/

Both the main and branch library offer story times.

Hicklebee's Children's Books

1378 Lincoln Ave.
San Jose
408-292-8880
www.hicklebees.com

Kepler's Books and Magazines

1010 El Camino Real
Menlo Park
650-324-4321
www.keplers.com

Menlo Park Library

800 Alma St.
Menlo Park
650-330-2500
www.plsinfo.org
PARENT RATING: ☆ ☆ ☆ ☆

Palo Alto Children's Library

1276 Harriet St.
Palo Alto
650-329-2134
www.city.palo-alto.ca.us/library
PARENT RATING: ☆ ☆ ☆ ☆ ☆

The first free-standing public children's library in the U.S. features a Secret Garden behind the building. The library and its branches offer a plethora of children's events, plus ongoing story times.

Peninsula Library System

www.plsinfo.org

This system is a consortium of 32 San Mateo County libraries. Check out the website to get information on, and link to, the following libraries:

- Atherton
  650-328-2422
- Belmont
  650-591-8286
- Brisbane
  415-467-2060
- Burlingame
  650-558-7400
- Daly City
  650-991-8074
- East Palo Alto
  650-321-7712
- Foster City
  650-574-4842
- Half Moon Bay
  650-726-2316
- Menlo Park
  650-330-2500
- Millbrae
  650-697-7607
- Pacifica
  650-355-5196
- Portola Valley
  650-851-0560
- Redwood City
  650-780-7061
- San Bruno
  650-616-7078
- San Carlos
  650-591-0341
- San Mateo
  650-522-7800
- South San Francisco
  650-829-3860
- Woodside
  650-851-0147

Each of the branches offers children's programs. Parent favorites are the San Carlos Library's and San Mateo Library's storytelling hours
(PARENT RATING: ☆ ☆ ☆ ☆ ☆).

San Jose Public Library

180 W. San Carlos St.
San Jose
408-808-2039 (children's library)
www.sjlibrary.org

Story times for children of all ages happen regularly at the main library and branches.

Sunnyvale Public Library
665 W. Olive Ave.
Sunnyvale
408-730-7300
www.sunnyvalelibrary.org
They offer story times, special family performances, and a Dial-A-Story line (408-730-7333).

Trains, Planes, Boats, and Automobiles

In honor of our sons, we present a special section devoted to their favorite hobby: anything that moves! As one parent told us, "Toddler boys love all types of street car, BART, and cable car rides." Believe it or not, even public transportation can be a glorious adventure to a toddler or preschooler who has never ridden a bus or train, not to mention taken a ferry ride on the Bay. If you have a baby, be sure to use a baby carrier (e.g., front carrier or sling) rather than a stroller, as navigating some methods of public transit with a stroller can be a nightmare. (Ferries, fortunately, are an exception, since ferry operators are used to accommodating bikers.)

San Francisco

BART
www.bart.gov
Bay Area Rapid Transit serves a large portion of the Bay Area with fast, usually clean trains. Kids under 4 ride free.

Caltrain
800-660-4287
www.caltrain.com
PARENT RATING: ☆ ☆ ☆ ☆
It may be only a commuter rail to adults, but to kids it's an adventure on a "real" train. One of our favorite trips is San Francisco to Burlingame—short enough that boredom never sets in. A caution: getting on and off the train with a stroller can be a complicated proposition, so bring a lightweight, compact stroller or leave it at home. One child is free with paying adult.

Golden Gate Ferries
San Francisco Ferry Building
415-921-5858
www.goldengateferry.org
PARENT RATING: ☆ ☆ ☆ ☆ ☆
A much cheaper alternative to the Blue and Gold Fleet, these commuter

ferries ply the waters between San Francisco and Sausalito or Larkspur. Children 5 and under ride free. The boats are very comfortable and offer refreshments on board. Always dress warmly for a bay cruise if you want to go on deck for a view (which your children will certainly want to do!). The Ferry Building is also a great vantage point to see the boats come in and out, even if you never go aboard!

Golden Gate Model Railroad Club
Randall Museum
www.ggmrc.org
See listing above under Museums— San Francisco.

Golden Gate Railroad Museum
Hunter's Point Shipyard, end of Innes St.
415-822-8728
www.ggrm.org
This nonprofit organization restores steam engines and passenger trains. In addition to allowing the public to tour them on the weekends, they offer several of their restored engines for rental. With a little professional help, you can actually drive the locomotive! We wonder who will have more fun, the dads or the kids! Call ahead for reservations.

Little Puffer Steam Train
San Francisco Zoo
See listing above under Animals! Zoos, Farms, and Wildlife—San Francisco.

San Francisco Cable Car Museum
1201 Mason St.
415-474-1887
www.cablecarmuseum.com
PARENT RATING: ☆ ☆ ☆ ☆

This cable car barn and powerhouse museum features several antique cable cars, a film explaining how cable cars work, and lots of historical memorabilia about the cable car system. You can ride the Powell-Mason or Powell-Hyde lines to the museum; parking is very difficult in this Nob Hill neighborhood. It's best for ages 3 and up.

San Francisco Maritime National Historical Park
415-561-6662
www.maritime.org
PARENT RATING: ☆ ☆ ☆ ☆ ☆
This park includes:
- **USS** *Pampanito,* a WWII submarine. Pier 45.
- **Maritime Museum**. Beach St. at the foot of Polk St. This museum features maritime artifacts.
- **Hyde Street Pier**. Foot of Hyde St. on Jefferson St. This pier is home to many historic maritime ships, including some from the turn of the 19th century. The centerpiece is the 300-foot 1886 sailing ship *Balclutha*. This is one of our favorite adventures. Our boys think the ships belonged to pirates! Even though they were never pirate ships, they are great for pirate-obsessed kids!
- **Aquatic Park**. Picnic next to the museum (at the foot of Polk St.).

SS *Jeremiah O'Brien* Liberty Ship
Pier 45
415-441-3101
PARENT RATING: ☆ ☆ ☆ ☆
Kids ages 2 and up will enjoy touring this restored WWII Liberty Ship, which is berthed at Pier 45 but still cruises the Bay on special occasions.

Trains, Boats, etc.

427

Howarth Park Train

Santa Rosa

See listing above under Parks—North Bay.

Pacific Coast Air Museum

2330 Becker Blvd.
Santa Rosa
707-575-7900
www.pacificcoastairmuseum.org

This museum has a great collection of historic airplanes and memorabilia of the history of aviation, including a "Top Gun" F-14A Tomcat fighter. It's best to visit during one of their "open cockpit weekends." But the real highlight of the year is the annual Air Show, held each August at the Sonoma County Airport. At the show, antique and contemporary military and civilian aircraft do flybys and are available for viewing.

Traintown

20264 Broadway
Sonoma
707-938-3912
www.traintown.com

PARENT RATING: ☆ ☆ ☆ ☆ ☆

Even the very young will love riding the scaled-down steam train through 10 acres of park, including a stop at the animal petting area. Other rides (except the carousel) are best for ages 3 and up. Parents may find the whole thing a bit cheesy, but kids seem to adore it. There is a snack bar on site, but we recommend trying one of the many lovely wineries nearby for lunch, or picnicking on Sonoma Square.

Alameda-Oakland Ferry

• Alameda
  2990 Main St.
• Oakland
  Jack London Sq.
510-749-5837
www.eastbayferry.com

PARENT RATING: ☆ ☆ ☆ ☆ ☆

Ride the ferry from Alameda or Jack London Square to San Francisco's Ferry Building, Pier 39/Fisherman's Wharf, Pacific Bell Park, or Angel Island.

Blackhawk Museum

3700 Blackhawk Plaza Cir.
Danville
925-736-2280
www.blackhawkauto.org

Children (ages 6 and under admitted free) will like the Auto Galleries with over 100 historically significant cars. The Discovery Room with interactive exhibits is also a sure hit.

California State Railroad Museum

111 "I" St.
Sacramento
916-445-6645
www.csrmf.org

PARENT RATING: ☆ ☆ ☆ ☆ ☆

Okay, this museum is actually in Old Sacramento, not the Bay Area, but we've included it for parents of children who just can't get enough of trains. This is the queen bee of California railway museums, spanning 6 buildings of restored railroad cars and locomotives, with lots of interesting information about the history of railroads in California. From April to September you can ride behind a steam engine on the museum's Sacramento Southern Railroad (departing from the Central Pacific Railroad Freight Depot, 2 blocks south of the museum). There are special holiday-themed train rides in October, November, and December. They regularly host the popular "Day Out with Thomas the Tank Engine" event, where you and your kids can ride a passenger train driven by none other than the Really Useful Engine #1. (If you don't understand this reference, you probably don't need to go.)

Children's Fairyland Train
Oakland
See listing under Other Amusements—East Bay.

Diablo Valley Lines (Walnut Creek Model Railroad Society)
2751 Buena Vista Ave.
Walnut Creek
925-937-1888
www.wcmrs.org
This HO-scale model railroad club has an extensive layout and is open to the public on some weekends.

Golden State Model Railroad Museum
Miller/Knox Regional Shoreline
900 Dornan Dr.
Richmond
510-234-4884 or 510-758-6288
www.gsmrm.org
PARENT RATING: ☆ ☆ ☆ ☆ ☆
Home to a model railway club, this little-known gem boasts 10,000 square feet of working N-, HO-, and O-scale model railroads. Our train-obsessed 2-year-old was completely fascinated

by the extensive layouts, with realistic landscaping, buildings, and vehicles. It's best for ages 2 and up.

Kennedy Park Train
Hayward
See listing above under Parks—East Bay.

Little Train, Tilden Park
Berkeley
See listing above under Parks—East Bay.

Jack London Water Taxi Service
510-839-7572
www.jacklondonwatertaxi.com
Inner harbor estuary tours, a water taxi service, and private charters are available on this small boat, which picks up and drops off passengers at several points in Oakland and Alameda.

Niles Canyon Railway
6 Kilkare Rd.
Sunol
925-862-9063
www.ncry.org
PARENT RATING: ☆ ☆ ☆ ☆ ☆
Part of the original transcontinental railway, this historic railroad has been preserved and reconstructed. Visitors may take a 13-mile train journey through the Niles Canyon, which takes about an hour. Comment: "It's a haul to get out there, but worth it for a fun day trip."

Oakland Zoo Train
See listing above under Animals! Zoos, Farms, and Wildlife—East Bay.

Presidential Yacht *Potomac*

FDR Pier, 540 Water Street
Oakland
510-627-1215
www.usspotomac.org

President Franklin D. Roosevelt's Floating White House now rests at Jack London Square, where visitors may climb aboard and explore, or even take a cruise.

USS *Hornet* Museum

Pier 3, Alameda Point
Alameda
510-521-8448
www.uss-hornet.org

This WWII aircraft carrier has been transformed into a museum where you can tour the ship and see the footprints marking Neil Armstrong's first steps on land after his trip to the moon. Bring a baby carrier, not a stroller, as there are many stairs to navigate. Children 4 and younger are free with a paying adult.

Western Aerospace Museum

Oakland Airport, North Field
8260 Boeing St. (Building 621)
Oakland
510-638-7100
www.westernaerospacemuseum.org

Located in an authentic hangar, highlights of this indoor/outdoor aviation history museum include the Short Solent 4-engine Flying Boat formerly owned by Howard Hughes, an instrument trainer, and the sister plane to Amelia Earhart's craft. There are also some more modern Naval aircraft such as an F-14 Tomcat. If you have a group, arrange a "climb-aboard" guided tour for the kids.

Western Railway Museum

5848 Highway 12
Suisun (Solano County)
707-374-2978
www.wrm.org

Ride historic streetcars and electric trains from all over the west on this museum's restored track, maintained by the Bay Area Electric Railroad Association. There are a shaded picnic area and café for provisions. A special train will transport you to a pumpkin patch in October.

South Bay

Central Park Train

San Mateo

See listing under Parks—South Bay.

Happy Hollow Park & Zoo Train

San Jose

See listing under Animals! Zoos, Farms, and Wildlife—South Bay.

Hiller Aviation Museum

601 Skyway Rd.
San Carlos
650-654-0200
www.hiller.org

This aviation museum features vintage and futuristic aircraft, prototypes, photographic displays, and models. It's best for older kids, though even 2-year-olds will like seeing and climbing in the planes and helicopters and watching the takeoffs and landings at the San Carlos Airport. The preschool reading program, held monthly, provides a tour, aviation book reading, and art project for children ages 3-5.

Billy Jones Wildcat Railroad

Oak Meadow Park
Los Gatos
408-395-7433
www.bjwrr.org

Take a one-mile-long railroad ride around Los Gatos Creek, Oak Meadow Park, and Vasona Park on a scale train powered by turn-of-the-century locomotives. Ride the 1910 carousel across from the depot, accompanied by music from a repro-duction Wurlitzer organ.

NASA Ames Exploration Center

Moffett Field
Mountain View
650-604-6274
www1.nasa.gov/centers/ames

Visitors to NASA Ames Research Center can now enjoy the Exploration Center, with many interesting exhibits about space exploration. Highlights of the interactive exhibits include maneuvering a robot "rover," manag-ing air traffic at a fictional airport, and "flying" a Harrier jet in a mock-up cockpit. Displays include a Mercury capsule and numerous spacesuits. There is an immersion theater, with a 40-foot-wide curved screen, for viewing scenes from the Mars mission. Admission is free!

Roaring Camp Railroads

Graham Hill Rd.
Felton
831-335-4484
www.roaringcamp.com

They offer 2 scenic railroad tours, one on a steam train up a narrow-gauge track through the redwoods to Bear Mountain (1 hour round-trip), and the other through a state park along the San Lorenzo River to the beach at Santa Cruz (3 hours round-trip). They also host many special events, such as Thomas the Tank Engine and a holiday train.

Other Amusements

You probably know of major attractions like Great America and Six Flags, but there are some great hidden gems for younger children at other local establishments. Many of these places offer wonderful children's birthday parties as well:

San Francisco

Basic Brown Bear Factory

2801 Leavenworth St.
1-866-5BB-BEAR (522-2327)
www.basicbrownbear.com

PARENT RATING: ☆ ☆ ☆ ☆

Tours (designed, of course, to encourage you to buy) include the tale of how the teddy bear got his name, a walk through the factory and demonstration of how bears are made, and a time for each child to stuff, sew, groom, and bathe his own bear (with a little help from the facto-ry staff). It's entertaining for kids ages 2 and up. Bears are fairly inex-pensive, but be sure to bring extra money for all those cute clothes. Our kids enjoyed a wonderful birthday party here.

Build-A-Bear Workshop

www.buildabear.com

In this nationally franchised retail store, your child can build his or her own bear. Children may stuff their bears, give them hearts, and then dress them in myriad different outfits and accessories. Children ages 3 and up are welcome. See the website for Bay Area locations.

Ferry Building Marketplace and Farmer's Market

1 Ferry Plaza (Foot of Market St.)
www.ferrybuildingmarketplace.com
www.ferryplazafarmersmarket.com
PARENT RATING: ☆ ☆ ☆ ☆ ☆

The restored Ferry Building is now an ode to San Francisco's food culture, with great local restaurants and specialty markets. Don't miss Cowgirl Creamery's artisan cheeses and Hog Island's oysters. Taylor's Refresher is a family-friendly burger joint on the premises. Tuesday and Saturday mornings feature the famous San Francisco Farmer's Market, a wonderful place to stroll and sample wares. A branch of the acclaimed Corte Madera bookstore, Book Passage, often hosts Sunday morning sing-alongs and other activities for kids. See under Libraries and Storytelling—San Francisco, above.

Fisherman's Wharf and Pier 39

www.fishermanswharf.org or
www.pier39.com
PARENT RATING: ☆ ☆ ☆

Yes, it's touristy, but the wharf can be fun if you hold onto your wallet and go in the less-crowded early morning. Stick to the free sights, stroll the mercifully flat Embarcadero from the Ferry Building to Aquatic Park, and ride the ferries, cable cars, and trolley cars. In addition to the Aquarium of the Bay (see listing under Animals! Zoos, Farms, and Wildlife—San Francisco), parents recommend:

- ◆ **Blue and Gold Fleet Ferries** Pier 41. (415-705-5555, www.blueandgoldfleet.com).
  PARENT RATING: ☆ ☆ ☆ ☆
  Tourist ferries go to Alcatraz Island, Sausalito, Tiburon, Alameda/Oakland, Vallejo, and Angel Island; see Parks, above.

- ◆ **Alcatraz** (www.nps.gov/alcatraz).
  PARENT RATING: ☆ ☆ ☆ ☆ ☆
  Be sure to bring warm clothes and wear comfortable shoes. There is no food service on the island. Best for ages 3 and up.

- ◆ **Cable Cars.**
  PARENT RATING: ☆ ☆ ☆ ☆
  Two scenic lines (Powell-Hyde and Powell-Mason) terminate at Fisherman's Wharf, but you can also avoid the crowds of tourists and pick up the California St. line.

- ◆ **Carousel.** Pier 39.

- ◆ **Fire Engine Tours** (415-333-7077, www.fireenginetours.com).
  PARENT RATING: ☆ ☆ ☆ ☆ ☆
  Expensive, but kids love this narrated 75-minute ride from the Cannery on Beach St. through the Presidio, Fort Point, Golden Gate Bridge, Sausalito, and Union St. on a classic 1955 Mack Fire Engine. They do great birthday parties!

- **The Embarcadero.** Three miles of paved walkways along the waterfront make this a great stroller walk from Fisherman's Wharf to China Basin.
- **Musée Mechanique.** (Pier 45, 415-345-2000, www.museemechanique.org). This privately-owned collection of mechanical musical instruments (e.g., player pianos) and antique arcade machines is "quirky" but fun.
- **Restored Vintage Trolley Cars.** (www.streetcar.org).

PARENT RATING: ☆ ☆ ☆ ☆ ☆

Twenty-five different antique trolleys imported from all over the world grace the F Line. Market St. to Embarcadero (Ferry Building) to Fisherman's Wharf.

- **Sea Lions** (415-705-5500). Droves of sea lions can be found on Pier 39. Weather permitting, Marine Mammal Center volunteers lead free educational talks on weekends.
- **Street Performers.** Magicians, jugglers, comedians, and mimes hang out at Pier 39's "stage."

SBC Park (home of the San Francisco Giants)

24 Willie Mays Plaza
415-972-2000
www.sfgiants.com

PARENT RATING: ☆ ☆ ☆ ☆ ☆

What could be more fun than an afternoon at the ballpark eating hot dogs and watching the splash landing special effects when the Giants score a home run? The Giants' new "intimate" stadium makes it much easier for kids to follow the action. Admission for kids under age 2 is free, but kids over 2 will enjoy it much more. You may find yourself spending more time at the Coca-Cola Fan Lot behind the stadium (free and open to the public) than watching the game! The miniature, scaled-down copy of the park past the left field wall is a hit with older kids (ages 3 to 7) when it's not too crowded; kids can hit whiffle balls and run the bases. There are also a pitching game and giant slides; one set of slides is for children 20" tall and up, and the other is for children 42" tall and up. Or go on a day when they let kids run the real bases after the game. Make it an adventure and take Caltrain from the south or a ferry from Marin or the East Bay.

Sony Metreon

101 Fourth St.
1-800-METREON
www.metreon.com

PARENT RATING: ☆ ☆ ☆ ☆

Unfortunately, some of its child-related venues have closed, so we've had to downgrade our rating. Some parents found it "expensive" and "loud and overstimulating for very young children," but in Sony's huge indoor entertainment mecca you will find:

- **Sony Theaters.** There are 15 movie screens, including the largest IMAX screen in North America. "Reel Moms" movies for parents with babies screen every Tuesday at 11 a.m. Comment: "Great when they are little ones!"
- **Portal One.** This high-tech arcade includes a fun "bowl the streets of

San Francisco" virtual reality game. Games can be pricey.

◆ **Restaurants and shops**, including the Discovery Channel Store, are a sure hit.

Yerba Buena Gardens

221 Fourth St.
415-777-2800
www.zeum.org

PARENT RATING: ☆ ☆ ☆ ☆ ☆

A project of the San Francisco Redevelopment Agency to develop an entire city block as an urban destination for youth, the Rooftop at Yerba Buena Gardens now offers the following fun for kids:

◆ **Zeum.** This high-tech multimedia creative center is geared to older kids (ages 8 and up), but even parents of younger kids say it is "good for rainy days."

◆ **Carousel.** Kids of all ages love this restored 1906 carousel from San Francisco's former amusement park Playland-at-the-Beach.

◆ **Ice Skating and Bowling Center** (415-777-3727, www.skatebowl.com).

◆ **Playground.** The slides are quite steep for little children, but the 3-and-up crowd will love them. There is a large area for running, and our kids adore playing with the little fountains throughout the rooftop.

North Bay

Redwood Empire Ice Arena and Charles Schulz Museum

1667 W. Steele Ln.
Santa Rosa
707-546-7147
www.snoopyshomeice.com

PARENT RATING: ☆ ☆ ☆ ☆

Known as "Snoopy's Home Ice" in Charles Schulz's home town, this arena offers special Puppy Practice sessions for children ages 12 and under and their parents. Beginners can use chairs on the ice. The Schulz Museum next door, featuring many of the cartoonist's famous drawings, is a fun outing before or after skating. See www.charlesmschulzmuseum.org or call 707-579-4452 for details.

East Bay

Iceland Skating Rink and Skating School

• Berkeley Iceland
2727 Milvia St.
510-647-1620
www.berkeleyiceland.com
• Dublin Iceland
7212 San Ramon Rd.
925-829-4445
www.dubliniceland.com

PARENT RATING: ☆ ☆ ☆ ☆

These indoor skating rinks offer great tiny tots sessions for parents with preschoolers ages 3-5.

Children's Fairyland

Lakeside Park
699 Bellevue Ave.
Oakland
510-452-2259
www.fairyland.org

PARENT RATING: ☆ ☆ ☆ ☆ ☆

Fairy tales come alive in this 10-acre outdoor theme park, a Bay Area tradition since 1950 that was recently renovated. Children may play in storybook exhibits incorporating fairy tales and nursery rhymes, watch daily puppet shows, and ride the train, the boats, the miniature Ferris wheel, and the carousels. Be sure to buy a "magic key" to "unlock" the stories and nursery rhymes. All ages will enjoy the park, but it's especially fabulous for 2- and 3-year-olds. While there, take a walk through Lakeside Park to Lake Merritt and picnic around the lake. In the peak warm weather season, parents recommend going during the week as weekends are very crowded. Parents say this "offbeat" park "delights children."

Dunsmuir Historic Estate and Gardens
2960 Peralta Oaks Ct.
Oakland
510-615-5555
www.dunsmuir.org

Stroll around the grounds of this 50-acre historic estate with its 37-room, 19th-century neoclassical revival mansion and farm area. Enjoy Family Sundays with puppet shows, music, and magicians. Look for special Christmas holiday events.

Jelly Belly Factory
One Jelly Belly Lane
Fairfield
800-953-5592
www.jellybelly.com
PARENT RATING: ☆ ☆ ☆ ☆

This working candy factory is a good place to stop on your way to or from Lake Tahoe, as it is about an hour or so from San Francisco. You take an elevated walkway through the plant during the 40-minute tour, then return to the Visitor Center to sample the goods! There is an indoor/outdoor café. No reservations required for tours, but it's best to call ahead to verify they are in full operation.

Pixieland Amusement Park
2740 E. Olivera Rd.
Concord
925-689-8841
www.pixieland.com
PARENT RATING: ☆ ☆ ☆ ☆

Pixieland (in one form or another) has been entertaining families since 1950. Kid-oriented rides are best for ages 3 and up. The train, antique cars, and carousel are favorites for younger children.

South Bay

Bonfante Gardens Theme Park
3050 Hecker Pass Hwy.
Gilroy
408-840-7100
www.bonfantegardens.com
PARENT RATING: ☆ ☆ ☆ ☆ ☆

This unique and surprisingly picturesque theme park combines gardens, rides, and local history. The 75-acre park includes a huge greenhouse garden, a steam train, a mine coaster, a rock maze, a boat ride through gardens, an antique car ride, and a restored 1927 carousel. Comments: "Best for children 10 and under, as the rides are tame . . . very family-oriented . . . beautiful landscaping."

Adventures

Filoli Center

86 Canada Rd.
Woodside
650-364-8300
www.filoli.org

PARENT RATING: ☆ ☆ ☆ ☆ ☆

This grand 654-acre estate with a historic Georgian mansion is part of the National Trust for Historic Preservation. The stunning 16-acre formal gardens are a nice place for a stroller walk as most of the paths are made of bricks, and the house is wheelchair, thus stroller, accessible. You will need a front carrier or back-pack if you want to take a 3-mile guided nature hike, offered on Saturdays. There is a peaceful café on the grounds; no outside food or drink is allowed. Thus, it's best for parents with babies and not screaming or wandering toddlers!

Planetarium at DeAnza College

21250 Stevens Creek Blvd.
Cupertino
408-864-8814
www.planetarium.deanza.edu

This planetarium offers family astronomy evenings with shows and telescope viewing.

Family-Friendly Restaurants

Many families report that you need not entirely change your lifestyle after your baby arrives. While you won't likely be visiting Chez Panisse or the French Laundry with the baby, you don't need to stick to fast food. In addition to the well-known chains like Armadillo Willy's, California Pizza Kitchen, Chevy's, Fresh Choice, Hobee's, Johnny Rocket's, Left at Albuquerque, Mimi's Café, Pasta Pomodoro, Red Robin, and Taxi's, most restaurants in the Bay Area do their best to accommodate children. Parents advise bringing the little ones to brunch or lunch, rather than dinner, whenever possible; babies are less fussy during the day, and daytime meals are less formal. Dim sum is a particularly popular family outing. Several parents commented that big San Francisco hotel restaurants can be "very accommodating" since they are used to serving families. Ask your waiter to bring you a glass of hot water to heat bottles (safer than microwaving them), and order side dishes for kids if there is no children's menu. We also recommend bringing along small toys, crayons and coloring books, or sticker books to entertain toddlers during meals.

Local parents recommended the following restaurants for family-friendly dining:

Barney's Gourmet Hamburgers

- 4138 24th St., 415-282-7770
- 3344 Steiner St., 415-563-0307

Also locations in Berkeley, Oakland, and San Rafael

www.barneyshamburgers.com

They offer hamburgers, great curly fries, and shakes. Kids' menus come with crayons and paper.

Bill's Place

2315 Clement St.

415-221-5262

Hamburgers are a specialty, and there is a patio in back. They provide kids' menus and crayons.

Café Muse

75 8th Ave. at Fulton

415-668-6873

This is a great place for a sandwich or coffee while enjoying Golden Gate Park.

Chenery Park Restaurant

683 Chenery St.

415-337-8537

www.chenerypark.com

Tuesdays are kids' nights at this upscale Glen Park restaurant.

Curbside Café

2417 California St.

415-929-9030.

This café is wonderful for brunch. They don't provide a kids' menu, but they serve kid-appropriate food.

Ella's

500 Presidio Ave.

415-441-5669

This is a great place for weekend brunch or weekday breakfast or lunch. Unfortunately, it seems the rest of the city also has the same idea, so it's best to send someone ahead to get a table (no reservations accepted for breakfast or brunch). They have toys, colored pencils, and a kids' menu.

Giorgio's Pizza

151 Clement St.

415-668-1266

www.giorgiospizza.com

This neighborhood pizzeria is very tolerant of children! Kids love the pizza and the juke box. They offer a popular "kids' happy hour and make your own pizza" on Wednesday evenings.

Goat Hill Pizza

- 300 Connecticut Ave.
  415-641-1440
- 715 Harrison St.
  415-974-1303

www.goathill.com

They serve great sourdough crust pizza in a "large area where it's ok to be loud." They have "fast service, welcome kids, and provide coloring place mats, and pens."

Louis' Restaurant

902 Point Lobos Ave.

415-387-6330

Located just above the Cliff House overlooking Sutro Baths, this restaurant serves hamburgers and similar casual fare and is "very kid friendly."

Mel's Drive-In

- 2165 Lombard St., 415-921-2867
- 3355 Geary Blvd., 415-387-2255
- 1050 Van Ness Ave., 415-292-6357
- 801 Mission St., 415-227-4477

www.melsdrive-in.com

Restaurants

437

This chain of 50s flashback diners is open all night and has a kids' menu. Parents say it's "great for families" and "always a hit" with the kids, plus the kids' meals come in cardboard cars.

Park Chow
1240 9th Ave.
415-665-9912

This is a great place for a casual bite after visiting Golden Gate Park or its museums. The menu has "virtually everything," and they provide crayons.

Rainforest Café
145 Jefferson (Fisherman's Wharf)
415-440-5610
www.rainforestcafe.com

It's touristy, but you can sit in this restaurant and pretend you are in the rain forest, with animals on display and periodic tropical storms. They have a kids' menu; portions are very generous.

North Bay

Barney's Gourmet Hamburgers
See San Francisco listing.

Bubba's Diner
566 San Anselmo Ave.
San Anselmo
415-459-6862

This diner has "great comfort food" and a kids' menu.

The Cantina
• Mill Valley
  651 E. Blithedale
  415-381-1070
• Santa Rosa
  500 4th St.
  707-523-3663

• Walnut Creek
  1470 N. Broadway
  925-946-1010
www.greatmex.com

At this Mexican eatery, "they cater to kids while Mom and Dad can enjoy a beer." All locations have patio seating, they provide a kids' menu and balloons, and the Mill Valley location has several rooms for large parties (with tolerant staff!).

Casa Manana
• San Rafael
  711 D St.
  415-456-7345
• Fairfax
  85 Bolinas Rd.
  415-454-2384
• Terra Linda
  641 Del Ganado Rd.
  415-479-3032

At this Mexican-Salvadoran restaurant, "the waitresses love children and bring them a small plate of chicken, rice, beans, and cheese. You can eat outside on nice days and not stress over kids getting food on the floor."

Dipsea Café
• Mill Valley
  200 Shoreline Hwy., 415-381-0298
• San Rafael
  2200 4th St., 415-459-0700

This popular spot for breakfast and lunch (and now dinner in San Rafael) tends to be crowded on the weekends but offers crayons and a kids' menu.

Easy Street Café

- Larkspur
  574 Magnolia Ave.
  415-924-9334
- San Anselmo
  882 Sir Francis Drake Blvd.
  415-453-1984

This Creole brunch spot caters to children. The San Anselmo location has a play area for kids.

Half Day Café

848 College Ave.
Kentfield
415-459-0291

This is a great place for breakfast or lunch with the kids.

Hamburger Ranch and Pasta Farm

31195 No. Redwood Hwy.
Cloverdale
707-894-5616

Housed in a former gas station, this burger joint offers patio seating, summer barbecues, and a freezer full of ice cream.

Iron Springs Pub and Brewery

765 Center Blvd.
Fairfax
415-485-1005

Formerly the Ross Valley Brewing Company (not your typical brew pub), this casual and friendly restaurant serves delicious meals for parents, along with classic kids' entrées.

LoCoco's Italian Pizzeria

638 San Anselmo Ave.
San Anselmo
415-453-1238

Pizza and traditional Italian fare are served here, and kids get crayons. They don't provide a kids' menu, but will split portions.

Piatti

- Mill Valley
  625 Redwood Hwy., 415-380-2525
- Danville
  100 Sycamore Valley Rd.,
  925-838-2082
- Santa Clara
  3905 Rivermark Plaza, 408-330-9212

Parents recommend staking out a table outside for an early dinner at this upscale Italian eatery. They have a kids' menu.

Rafters

812 4th St.
San Rafael
415-453-4200

You can enjoy a micro-brew while the kids entertain themselves with crayons and feast on great pizza.

Star Restaurant

1700 Novato Blvd.
Novato
415-897-1970

This family-friendly place serves classic American fare and has a kids' menu.

The Station House

Main St.
Point Reyes Station
415-663-1515

This is a family-friendly place to stop on your way to the Tomales Bay beaches or Point Reyes National Park.

Restaurants

Sushi Boat

100 Smith Ranch Rd.
San Rafael
415-446-7200

A fleet of sushi-carrying boats parades in a circle around the sushi bar, fascinating our children. Comment: "Great service, and they will make special kid-friendly items." This is good place to stop for an early dinner before hitting the multiplex movie theater across the parking lot.

Taco Jane's

21 Tamalpais Ave.
San Anselmo
415-454-6562

This casual place has great Caribbean/Mexican food, outdoor seating, a kids' menu (with free cookies), and a friendly, kid-loving staff.

Waypoint Pizza

15 Main St.
Tiburon
415-435-3440

They have excellent pizza, and children can sit at their own kid-sized picnic table and color with crayons. The large party room at the rear of the restaurant is a good spot for a playgroup meal.

Yankee Pier

286 Magnolia Ave.
Larkspur
415-924-7676

Pretend you are at an upscale clam shack on the East Coast and you will get a sense of the ambience. Families enjoy fried clams, lobster, and chowder at picnic tables outside (with heat lamps for cold weather) while children play in the sandbox. They have a kids' menu and crayons.

Barney's Gourmet Hamburgers

See San Francisco listing.

The Cantina

See North Bay listing.

Doug's Place

20871 Redwood Rd.
Castro Valley
510-538-9155

This is a great place for breakfast, with almost every kind of omelet imaginable.

Emeryville Public Market Food Court

5959 Shellmound St.
Emeryville
510-652-9300

You can sample food from around the world, entertain the kids in the ride area or ball pit, then pop over to the children's section at Borders Books. Insider tip: it can be very crowded at lunch—try breakfast or snack time instead.

Filippos Pastaria

1499 Solano Ave.
Albany
510-524-4300

They have wonderful pasta and are kid-tolerant.

Pete's Brass Rail and Car Wash

201 Hartz Ave.
Danville
925-820-8281
www.petesbrassrail.com

This pub-style restaurant offers micro-brews for the parents, and burgers, hot dogs, and PB&Js for the kids.

Piatti

See North Bay listing.

Picante Cocina

1328 6th St.
Berkeley
510-525-3121

This casual, inexpensive Mexican restaurant offers a kids' menu and crayons.

Red Tractor Café

4920 Dublin Blvd.
Dublin

Formerly in Rockridge, they have moved east, serve American comfort food, such as macaroni and cheese, and supply crayons for kids.

Rick and Ann's

2922 Domingo Ave.
Berkeley
510-649-8538

This American cuisine spot has a great brunch, a kids' menu, and crayons.

Sweet Tomatoes

4501 Hopyard Rd.
Pleasanton
925-463-9285

They offer an all-you-can-eat, buffet-style lunch and dinner and special prices for kids during off hours. Ages 2 and under eat free.

Zachary's Chicago Pizza

* Rockridge
  5801 College Ave.
  510-655-6385
* Berkeley
  1853 Solano Ave.
  510-525-5950
www.zacharys.com

Move over, Pizzeria Uno. Zachary's thick-crust pizza is delicious. Unfortunately, the wait for a table can be long. Fortunately, they provide coloring books and crayons to pass the time.

South Bay

Applewood Pizza

227 1st St.
Los Altos
650-941-9222

Kids will love the pizza.

Austin's

1616 W. El Camino Real
Mountain View
650-969-9191

This Texas barbecue restaurant features cowboy decor.

Christie's

245 California Dr.
Burlingame
650-347-9440

This is a great place for breakfast.

Kuleto's Trattoria

1095 Rollins Rd.
Burlingame
650-342-4922
www.kuletostrattoria.com

This upscale Italian restaurant has a kids' menu and welcomes families, particularly in the early evening.

Max's

1001 El Camino Real
Redwood City
650-365-6297

This New York-style deli café has a kid's menu featuring hot dogs and macaroni and cheese.

Peninsula Fountain & Grill

566 Emerson St.
Palo Alto
650-323-3131

This American diner, known as the "Creamery," serves comfort food and great shakes. Get there early on weekend mornings to get a spot in a booth.

Piatti

See North Bay listing.

Santana Row

Santana Row at Olsen Dr.
San Jose
408-551-4611
www.santanarow.com

You can select from open-air stalls (associated with full-service restaurants) in this upscale outdoor shopping center, then proceed to an outdoor table to dine. Kids will enjoy playing amid the huge chess pieces and fountains. During the summer they have a jazz music series on some nights.

Stacks

361 California Dr.
Burlingame
650-579-1384

This Burlingame institution serves breakfast and lunch, and provides crayons for kids. It's good if you're not in a hurry.

Yankee Pier

378 Santana Row
San Jose
408-244-1244

See North Bay listing.

Special Events for Kids

The Bay Area is home to many special events for kids, from concerts and theatrical productions to seasonal holiday extravaganzas. How do you find out what is happening around town? Try your local newspaper first. The *San Francisco Chronicle*'s weekend pink pages usually carry a good selection of family outings. The local family periodicals, *Bay Area Parent* and *Parents Press,* contain local calendars of events, and you can pick them up at any baby store and many grocery stores for free. Or try the City Search website for your area (e.g., www.sanfranciscocitysearch.com or www.siliconvalley. citysearch.com or www.eastbay.citysearch.com) for listings of current events. San Francisco Arts Online (www.sfarts.org) offers a useful search tool; you can specify the date and genre for which you are searching. If you live in the South Bay, check out Palo Alto Online at www.paloaltoonline.com/calendar. The site features a good listing of current local events and things to do for families. The best source for current events is usually your local mothers' club newsletter or website!

Below are some of our favorite ongoing and annual events for families:

CONCERTS AND THEATER

San Francisco and Bay Area

The Buddy Club
510-236-SHOW (7469)
www.thebuddyclub.com
This troupe offers children's shows in San Francisco, Marin, and the East Bay from October through April. You can also hire the performers for birthday parties and special events. The shows are geared to children ages 2-12 and their parents, and include magicians, jugglers, singers, clowns, ventriloquists, acrobats, puppeteers, and lots of audience participation.

Concerts and Film Nights in the Park
Many park and recreation departments, as well as civic groups, sponsor concerts and film nights in local parks throughout the Bay Area in the summer season, some with movies appropriate for children. Check with your local park and recreation department, or in Marin go to www.filmnight.org.

Miss Kitty
See listing under Best Things to Do on a Rainy Day.

San Francisco Performances' Family Matinees
Herbst Theatre and Yerba Buena Center
415-398-6449
www.performances.org
PARENT RATING: ☆ ☆ ☆ ☆ ☆

This series of weekend afternoon performances—ranging from chamber music to jazz, vocal and instrumental performers, and modern dance—is perfect for children. They are relatively inexpensive, short enough for a child's attention span, and the performers share their instruments and answer questions.

San Francisco Symphony's Music for Families Series
Davies Symphony Hall
415-864-6000
www.sfsymphony.org
PARENT RATING: ☆ ☆ ☆ ☆ ☆

The Symphony offers a 4-concert family series on Saturday afternoons, combining great music with kid-friendly explanations of the instruments and show-and-tell. Kids ages 12 and under attend at half-price, plus subscribers get an activity guide to prepare kids for the shows. Comment: "A wonderful, inexpensive way to expose your children to great classical music."

The Sippy Cups
www.thesippycups.com
PARENT RATING: ☆ ☆ ☆ ☆ ☆

Made up of local parents, this band performs 60s- and 70s-era rock for children. See the website for gigs. Comments: "A great way to indulge your own taste and entertain your child at the same time. . . . Sure beats Raffi or the Wiggles!"

Young Performers Theatre

Fort Mason Center (Building C), Fl. 3
San Francisco
415-346-5550
www.ypt.org

PARENT RATING: ☆ ☆ ☆ ☆ ☆

This troupe offers a year-round program of 7 terrific children's theatrical productions. Child actors perform alongside adults.

North Bay

Actors' Theater for Children

Dohn Theater, Steele Lane Community Center
415 Steele Lane
Santa Rosa
707-543-3282
www.atfc.pon.net

This community group has been performing popular children's tales since 1971.

Bay Area Discovery Museum's Discovery Theatre

See listing under Museums—North Bay.

Tim Cain

www.timcain.com

PARENT RATING: ☆ ☆ ☆ ☆ ☆

This children's performer and recording artist is a favorite of parents and kids alike. Go to his website for local gigs. Comment: "My kids love Tim . . . he consistently engages them and gets them up and dancing." See also under Birthday Party—San Francisco and North Bay, below.

Lark Theater's "Cinemama" Series

549 Magnolia Ave.
Larkspur
415-924-5111
www.larktheater.net

You can bring your baby to these morning film screenings, with coffee and croissants available for purchase.

Luther Burbank Center for the Arts

50 Mark West Springs Rd.
Santa Rosa
707-546-3600
www.lbc.net

Family Shows target a range of age groups; some are for ages one and up, and others are for older children.

Masque Unit Junior Theatre of Marin

Showcase Theater, Marin Civic Center
San Rafael
415-499-6800
www.masqueunit.org

Founded in 1961, this troupe of women presents musical adaptations of classic children's stories. They perform one production a year, in March, for the Marin Youth in Arts program.

Rafael Film Center

1118 4th St.
San Rafael
415-454-1222
www.rafaelfilmcenter.org

This 3-screen movie house features family film classic matinees one weekend of every month.

Youth in Arts Performing Arts Series

Marin Civic Center
San Rafael
415-457-4878
www.youthinarts.org
PARENT RATING: ☆ ☆ ☆ ☆ ☆

This nonprofit organization stages live performances of music, drama, dance, storytelling, and so on, all geared to children.

East Bay

Ashkenaz

1317 San Pablo Ave.
Berkeley
510-525-5054
www.ashkenaz.com

This "world music and dance" community center hosts special shows for children on Sunday afternoons, with children encouraged to get up and dance to the music.

Julia Morgan Center for the Arts

2640 College Ave.
Berkeley
510-845-8542
925-798-1300 (tickets)
www.juliamorgan.org

The Kaleidoscope Sunday Matinee series is perfect for families. It features multicultural music, theater, and dance events, some with local performers, and children's tickets are half price.

Parkway Theater's Baby Brigade

1834 Park Blvd.
Oakland
510-814-2400
www.picturepubpizza.com

On Monday nights, parents may bring their babies (under age one) to this movie house and brew pub without fearing recrimination from fellow audience members. Babies are free. Pizza, sandwiches, pasta, beer, and wine are served.

South Bay

California Youth Symphony

650-325-6666
www.cys.org

This group of 500 Bay Area youth (ages 8-17) performs throughout the South Bay, and may inspire some future musicians.

Century Theatre's Moms' Matinees

• Century 20 Oakridge (San Jose)
• Century 20 Daly City
www.cinemamas.com

Certain Century Theatres offer special screenings for parents "in a baby-friendly environment." Check the website for current locations and times.

Children's Festival Theatre

Saratoga
http://childrens-festival-theatre.com

They put on children's performances in which all members of the cast are children. Every child who auditions receives a speaking role.

Children's Theater of Palo Alto

1305 Middlefield Rd.
Palo Alto
650-463-4970 (tickets)

Kids must be 8 years old to participate in the performances, but younger children will enjoy attending the shows, which tend to be classic musicals.

Adventures

445

Hillbarn Theatre
1285 E. Hillsdale Blvd.
Foster City
650-349-6411
www.hillbarntheatre.org

This is not specifically a children's theater, but this longtime company (since 1941) often performs family-oriented plays, such as *The Sound of Music*.

Peninsula Youth Theatre/ Children's Theatre in the Park
Mountain View Center for the Performing Arts
500 Castro St.
Mountain View
650-903-6000
www.mvcpa.com

The City of Mountain View hosts a variety of free family events, from performances by the Peninsula Youth Theatre to music from around the world.

San Jose Children's Musical Theater
1401 Parkmoor Ave.
San Jose
408-288-5437
www.cmtsj.org

This theater offers musical theater training and performances by and for kids.

Some of Our Favorite Seasonal Events

Check with your local Parks and Recreation Department for seasonal events. Many parks host Easter egg hunts, Earth Day celebrations, and Fourth of July extravaganzas. Your local shopping center is a good place to get a photo with Santa or the Easter Bunny. The 2-and-under crowd will likely run screaming from either of them, but you can always try! Local churches, synagogues, and Jewish Community Centers also host religious holiday events. Another fun fall or winter outing is a visit to a pumpkin patch or a tree farm, many of which have animals, hay rides, and candy for the kids. The best are located well outside the city, in Petaluma, Sebastopol, and Half Moon Bay. Below are some of our favorite events:

Spring

Easter Parade on Union Street
San Francisco
415-885-1335
PARENT RATING: ☆ ☆ ☆ ☆

The merchants hand out candy and sponsor entertainment and music.

Falkirk Cultural Center
1408 Mission Ave.
San Rafael
415-485-3328
www.falkirkculturalcenter.org

This historic mansion hosts several popular seasonal events, including a spring Alice in Wonderland Egg Hunt, summer concerts on the lawn, a haunted mansion in October, and a Victorian Holiday celebration.

Filoli Gardens Spring Fling
Woodside

This 654-acre estate, with gorgeous historic mansion and gardens, hosts a Spring Fling event with an egg hunt. See full listing under Other Amusements—South Bay.

May Fête Parade
Palo Alto
650-463-4921 (Palo Alto Recreation Special Events)
www.city.palo-alto.ca.us/entertainment/

The oldest children's parade in the Bay Area, this is an annual ritual for Palo Alto-area residents. Children march down University Avenue on the first weekend in May. A new addition to the festivities is the Town Fair at Addison Elementary School, following the parade.

Pixie Park Spring Fair
Marin Art and Garden Center
Ross
www.pixiepark.org
PARENT RATING: ☆ ☆ ☆ ☆ ☆

The Fair, held annually in May, features rides, games, and performances designed specifically for children under age 6. It's a must-do for Marin families, and kids love it!

Summer

County Fairs

These are often less expensive, more interesting, and less crowded than large amusement parks. We particularly like the Marin County Fair, held on the Fourth of July weekend at the Civic Center Fairgrounds (415-499-6400), for its farm animal exhibits and horse shows.

Gravenstein Apple Fair
Eagle Ranch Park
Sebastopol
800-207-9464
www.farmtrails.org

This August harvest festival includes music, crafts, contests, apple juice pressing, tastings, a corn maze, a petting zoo, hayrides, and blacksmith demonstrations. The children's area offers puppet and magic shows, sing-alongs, and art projects.

Italian Street Painting Festival
"A" St. between 4th and 5th Streets
San Rafael
415-457-4878 (Youth in Arts)
www.youthinarts.org

On the second weekend in June, professional artists and children alike create works of art with chalk on the pavement.

Mountain Play
Mt. Tamalpais
Mill Valley
415-383-1100
www.mountainplay.org
PARENT RATING: ☆ ☆ ☆ ☆ ☆

May and June weekends bring a classic musical performed in an outdoor amphitheater on Mt. Tam. This is an all-day event. Bring a picnic, stake your seats early, let the kids run wild, and enjoy the spectacular views of San Francisco and the Bay. After the show you can hike down the mountain if you bring a backpack carrier, or take the bus back to Mill Valley.

Arata Pumpkin Farm

185 Verde Rd. (off Hwy 1, 6 miles S. of Hwy. 92)
Half Moon Bay
650-726-7548
www.aratapumpkinfarm.com

PARENT RATING: ☆ ☆ ☆ ☆ ☆

One of the oldest farms around, they have miles of pumpkins, a petting zoo, pony rides, and hayrides during the fall season.

Cardoza Ranch

5869 Lakeville Hwy.
Petaluma
707-762-2065

PARENT RATING: ☆ ☆ ☆ ☆ ☆

This working ranch opens its doors to pumpkin pickers come October (and only in October), with hayrides and pony rides, a playground, a train, a haunted house, a bouncy house, and animal feedings. Weekends are more crowded, but all the rides are running.

Goblin Jamboree, Bay Area Discovery Museum

Sausalito
415-339-3900
www.baykidsmuseum.org

PARENT RATING: ☆ ☆ ☆ ☆ ☆

Each October the BADM offers a wonderful Halloween event for families, featuring games, candy, train rides, entertainment, a haunted house, etc. Kids love to dress up! See above under Museums—North Bay for full listing.

Lemo's Farm

12320 San Mateo Rd. (Hwy. 92)
Half Moon Bay
650-726-2342

PARENT RATING: ☆ ☆ ☆ ☆

This is a pumpkin patch extravaganza with a pony ride, a wagon train ride, a hayride, a petting farm, an air jumper, a haunted house, and, of course, you can buy pumpkins in autumn. They are open year round on every weekend. In winter, they sell Christmas trees.

Moraga Junior Women's Club Halloween Carnival

Campolindo High School
300 Moraga Rd.
Moraga

This annual carnival has long provided Lamorinda families an October day of games, crafts, pumpkins, and costume display, all to benefit charity.

Nicasio Valley Farms

5300 Nicasio Valley Rd.
Nicasio
415-662-9100

PARENT RATING: ☆ ☆ ☆ ☆ ☆

Visiting this organic pumpkin patch is one of our favorite October activities. Hayrides, a corn maze, and a jumpy house are some of the seasonal attractions. They also offer berry picking in summer.

Spring Hill Jersey Cheese's Great Peter Pumpkin Patch

4235 Spring Hill Rd.
Petaluma
707-762-3446
www.springhillcheese.com

You can pick your own pumpkin, taste fresh, hormone-free cheese and ice cream, dig for potatoes, or milk a cow at this dairy farm during October. Call for reservations for groups of 10 or more.

Winter

Christmas Fantasy in the Woods
Tilden Park Merry-Go-Round
Central Park and Lake Anza Drives
Berkeley
510-524-6773
On December evenings, families trek to Tilden Park to ride the carousel, visit Santa, see the decorated trees and lights, and enjoy holiday treats.

Christmas Tree Farms
www.farmtrails.org for Sonoma County farms

Deck the Hall
415-552-8000 (San Francisco Symphony)
www.sfsymphony.org
PARENT RATING: ★ ☆ ☆ ☆ ☆
Sponsored by the Junior League Committee of the San Francisco Symphony, this popular annual holiday concert is especially designed for toddlers and preschoolers with plenty of singing for the whole family. It can be very crowded, but it's a little social butterfly's favorite.

Embarcadero Center Ice Rink
Justin Herman Plaza
4 Embarcadero Center
San Francisco
415-956-2688
PARENT RATING: ★ ☆ ☆ ☆
This rink, open seasonally, is a beautiful spot to view the downtown holiday lights.

The Nutcracker
301 Van Ness Ave.
San Francisco
415-865-2000
PARENT RATING: ★ ☆ ☆ ☆ ☆
This annual holiday production of the renowned San Francisco Ballet takes place each December. It's best for ages 3 and up; younger kids probably won't sit through the whole perform-ance! If you are worried about the cost vs. attention span, try a less expensive *Nutcracker* put on by one of the many smaller ballet companies throughout the Bay Area. (See Ch. 7 under Dance for listings of many regional companies.)

Teddy Bear Tea, Ritz-Carlton Hotel
600 Stockton St.
San Francisco
415-296-7465
PARENT RATING: ★ ☆ ☆ ☆
Our preschoolers loved sipping hot chocolate, singing carols, and sitting on the bear's lap during the holiday season. It's expensive, but a great excuse to dress the kids up in their holiday finery and snap some great pictures in front of the elaborately decorated tree.

Winter Lodge Ice Rink
3009 Middlefield Rd.
Palo Alto
650-493-4566
www.winterlodge.com
Strollers are allowed on the ice at this seasonal rink.

More Resources for Family Outings

◆ *Bay Area Backroads* with Doug McConnell, www. bayareabackroads.com. The website for this popular television show on KRON-TV Channel 4 includes a searchable database of past stories.

◆ Bay Area Kid Fun, www.bayareakidfun.com, is a compilation of everything from amusement parks to museums to parks to restaurants.

◆ Go City Kids, www.gocitykids.com, is a national website with listings for outings and activities for children in many different cities, including San Francisco. To get their weekly e-mail newsletter of current family events, you need to subscribe.

◆ www.marin.org is a good place to find community organizations and a community calendar for Marin County.

◆ Tricia Brown, *The City by the Bay: A Magical Journey Around San Francisco.* This is the Junior League's illustrated children's guide to San Francisco.

◆ Dierdre Honnold, *San Jose with Kids: A Family Guide to the Greater San Jose and Santa Clara Valley Area.*

◆ Karen Misuraca, *Fun with the Family in Northern California: Hundreds of Ideas for Day Trips with the Kids.*

◆ Clark Norton, Fodor's *Around San Francisco With Kids: 68 Great Things to Do Together.* This book has ideas for older children.

◆ *Play Around the Bay.* This guide was put out by the San Francisco Mothers of Twins Club and includes helpful information about many area parks and playgrounds, as well as other outings. It's available at www.sfmotc.org.

◆ Elizabeth Pomada, *Fun Places to Go with Children in Northern California.*

◆ Marianne Shine and Richard Shiro, *Marin Playgrounds.*

Traveling with Your Kids

If you are like us, you are probably dreading that first airline or long car trip with your baby. Here are some tips to make life easier, and be sure to check out the following websites for more travel ideas:

◆ www.tinytravelers.net (travel advice)

◆ www.momsminivan.com (fun ideas to entertain your kids on trips)

◆ www.bayareafamilytravel.com (reviews of local and not-so-local destinations for family travel)

WHAT TO BRING

◆ If traveling by air, pack only as much as you can handle on your own. You will have the baby, a diaper bag, a stroller, and perhaps a car seat, so keep extra gear and clothing to a minimum, and plan to do laundry instead.

◆ Before you go, arrange for a portable crib at your destination. If you need to rent baby gear at your destination, try one of the rental companies listed in Ch. 4. If you travel by car frequently, a portable crib or playpen is a good investment.

◆ Take lots of diapers in your carry-on for transit (as many as one per hour of travel time). Don't waste space in your suitcase for a week's supply of diapers, however, as you can probably pick up some upon arrival. Or try shipping baby essentials to your destination. A great service, www.babiestravellite.com, will do this for you. Order several weeks in advance for free shipping.

◆ Invest in a roomy, easy-to-use diaper bag. We liked the backpack version for traveling, since it freed our arms for the baby and other gear. Fill the diaper bag with a changing pad, diapers, wipes, diaper cream, disinfectant, emergency medications for baby (e.g., Tylenol), toys, a fold-up potty seat for older kids, a change of clothing for each child, a cell phone, and snacks. We use disposable changing pads because who knows what you will find on airline seats and bathroom changing tables. Carry little plastic bags for dirty diapers and wet clothes.

◆ Toddlers love to carry their own backpacks or small, wheeled suitcases. Give your child a small pack filled with our favorite travel

451

aids: a small white board for drawing, a Magna Doodle, Leap Pads, crayons and a coloring book, sticker books, scotch tape and note paper, and board books. We like to wrap small, inexpensive toys and have each child open one during the flight. Some good websites for travel toys include Travel Tots (www.traveltots.com) and Kids Travel Toys (www.kidstraveltoys.com).

◆ Carry a laptop computer or a portable DVD player with headphones for a movie festival right in your airline seat. DVDs and players are often available for rent in the airport, or buy an inexpensive one at Costco. Ours has paid for itself many times over in parent sanity.

◆ Books on tape or CD are also great for family car trips. We get ours from our local library.

◆ When traveling with an infant by air, take an FAA-approved infant car seat. (Most car seats manufactured after 1981 are approved, and most are labeled as such; check your manual to be sure.) Get a stroller/car seat combination or a Snap-n-Go brand or similar lightweight frame on wheels for the car seat and roll it and the baby right up to the gate, where you can check the frame (and the car seat as well if you don't have a seat for the baby). Car seats are not required for air travel, but they do make life easier with infants, who tend to be lulled to sleep as if they are in a car. If you don't have a seat for your baby on the plane, use a front carrier to keep the baby safely up against you (and to free your arms). You will still need to hold your baby during takeoff and landing, however, as front carriers are not approved for such times.

◆ When traveling with a toddler by air, there are 2 schools of thought: Some like to take the toddler car seat (heavy as it is) on the plane because it restrains the child from moving around. Toddlers are notoriously adept at extricating themselves from regular seat belts. Others find the toddler seats terribly heavy and awkward to lug through the airport and maneuver onto the plane with all of the other stuff they are carrying. Don't expect any help from flight attendants in this regard. One solution if you travel frequently is the Sit 'n Stroll brand car seat that converts to a stroller with a collapsible handle (retails for about $200); this is also a great solution for travel to cities like New York where you are going to be taking taxis everywhere. Or if you are going to be traveling by car at your destination, leave the car seat at home and rent a car seat on the other end. Most major rental car agencies rent car seats for a minimal fee. Of course, if you are being met and picked up by someone upon arrival, you'll need a car seat in that person's car.

◆ An inexpensive umbrella stroller can be a lifesaver with a toddler in a busy airport. You can wheel it up and check it just as you get on the plane. (Don't check it with your luggage or it will likely be smashed on arrival.)

BOOKING TRAVEL

◆ Children under age 2 may ride free on most airlines as "lap babies," but we found that once our kids reached the age of mobility, it was worth buying them a separate seat. (Trust us; we've tried flying with 18-month-olds on our laps. You don't want to go there unless it is a very, very short flight!)

◆ When booking airline tickets, ask for an infant discount. Most carriers offer half-price fares for children under age 2.

◆ Some airlines offer infant bassinets in the bulkhead seats and business/first classes on long flights (particularly overseas flights on Virgin Atlantic Airlines and Lufthansa). These can be lifesavers.

◆ If you can't afford a seat for your baby, try to book flights during off-peak hours of the day. Reserve the window and aisle seats for yourself and your spouse or partner, and ask the gate agent not to seat anyone between you. Chances are, no one will want to sit in your row with a screaming baby anyway!

◆ Avoid red-eye flights. You will be exhausted enough after a daytime flight, and the only thing worse than a normal red-eye flight is one with a screaming baby. We've found that naptime flights make more sense.

◆ Stick to nonstop flights. Getting everyone and your gear from one flight to another, particularly with the risk of getting stuck in busy airports like O'Hare, is not worth the cost savings of changing planes.

◆ If you are using a car seat, be forewarned that most airlines will make you put your baby in the window seat to avoid blocking egress to the aisle. If you are traveling alone, you will then be stuck in the middle seat. Try booking a window seat and an aisle seat, and hope no one will want to sit in your row! Or stick to planes with a 2-5-2 configuration, giving you an aisle and the baby the window.

◆ Most airlines offer infant and child meals. Call ahead to reserve one for your child.

◆ Book seats as far forward as possible. The rear of the plane tends to be louder, and sitting near the exit means you have less distance to travel with all your gear and kids.

◆ Several parents recommended Amtrak trains for short trips, citing benefits such as "large aisles, plenty of leg room, the dining car, and the motion lulling baby to sleep."

◆ If you can afford it, Four Seasons resorts have wonderful amenities for children, including licensed babysitting services, kids' menus, welcome gifts and toys, milk and cookies, video libraries, and supervised kids' activities (www.fourseasons.com).

EN ROUTE

◆ Many airlines have stopped pre-boarding families with young children, even pregnant women with kids! You can try pleading with a gate agent (good luck), but we've found it's more effective if you have a premier-type frequent flyer card for the airline or fly family-friendly airlines (e.g., Southwest).

◆ Only the most modern and roomy of planes contains a fold-down changing table in the bathroom, so you may be relegated to changing the baby in your seat (much to your neighbors' chagrin). Be sure to change baby's diaper right before you board.

Family-Friendly Travel Agents:

Are We There Yet?
5725 Paradise Dr., Ste. 230
Corte Madera
415-945-6215
www.andavotravel.com

Ciao Bambino! Inc.
927 Sunnyhills Rd.
Oakland
510-763-8484
www.ciaobambino.com
Amy O'Shaughnessy specializes in family-friendly accommodations in Italy and France.

- During takeoff and landing, help your baby's ears clear by nursing or feeding him a bottle or juice box.
- The backpack of goodies should keep toddlers entertained during a flight, but in desperation we've found the airline's earphones (tuned to Disney Radio) to be a lifesaver. Jet Blue and Virgin Atlantic offer individual screens on the back of each seat, with children's programming available. Otherwise, you've hopefully brought your DVD player.
- Some parents have used Benadryl or other over-the-counter medications as sleep aids for their children. Others tell us those medications just made their children hyper. Be sure to check with your pediatrician and do a test run before you go.

AT YOUR DESTINATION
- Childproof your destination. Bring a few outlet plugs and make sure Grandma buys a baby gate for the stairs and puts away her medications.

FAVORITE EASY VACATION SPOTS FOR BAY AREA FAMILIES

CALISTOGA

Try **Calistoga Spa Hot Springs** (1006 Washington St., 707-942-6269, www.calistogaspa.com), with 4 outdoor pools, or **Indian Springs Resort** (1712 Lincoln Ave., 707-942-4913, www.indianspringscalistoga.com), with a "big, warm pool (heated by thermal geysers) and a large grassy area for play." Parents can take turns getting treatments while kids play in the pool.

CAMPING

800-444-PARK (state park campground reservations) www.parks.ca.gov

A hint: wherever you camp with kids, make sure the car is not too far away in case you need to make a fast exit. Parents recommended the following parks:

- **Big Basin Redwoods State Park**, near Boulder Creek in the Santa Cruz Mountains, 800-874-8368 (reservations), 831-338-8861 (information). They rent wooden platform tents complete with all the necessary gear and even breakfast fixings, making it easy on families.
- **Bodega Dunes Campground**, Sonoma Coast State Beach, Hwy. 1, Bodega Bay, 800-444-7275. Comment: "A beautiful setting but close to home . . . a long beach to walk on."

- **Butano State Park**, off Highway One on the San Mateo Coast south of Pescadero, 650-879-2040. Comment: "A beautiful redwood canyon with both drive-in and walk-in campsites and hiking trails make this an easy family weekend."
- **Costanoa Coastal Lodge and Camp**, north of Santa Cruz, 650-879-1100, www.costanoa.com. **PARENT RATING:** ☆ ☆ ☆ ☆ ☆ "Good for pseudo-campers," they have tent cabins, some with fireplaces and views, and there is a large campfire at the center of camp. There are miles of hiking trails in the area, and it is close to Año Nuevo State Reserve. (See under Animals! Zoos, Farms, and Wildlife—South Bay.)
- **Mt. Diablo State Park**, 96 Mitchell Canyon Rd., Clayton, 925-837-2525. Comment: "Views, views, views, and lots of rocks to scramble over." Try the Live Oak Campground near Rock City.
- **Samuel P. Taylor State Park**, West Marin, 415-488-9897. There are redwood groves and hiking, and it's a short drive to the Point Reyes area. Kids love scrambling over the hollowed-out ancient redwood trunks in the day-use area.

LAKE TAHOE

Lake Tahoe Resort Association, 530-583-3494 or 888-434-1262, www.tahoefun.org

- Some parents recommend "skiing weekends at smaller resorts like Sugar Bowl (530-426-9000, www.sugarbowl.com), Bear Valley (209-753-2301, www.bearvalley.com), or Homewood (530-525-2992, www.skihomewood.com) and avoiding bigger, more crowded resorts like Squaw Valley, Northstar, and Alpine Meadows." Sugar Bowl has a wonderful "Sugar Bears" kids' program, combining skiing and day care, for ages 3-5.
- On the other hand, Northstar is one of the few places where you can find day care for children as young as 2 years old! 530-562-1010 or 1-800-GO-NORTH (466-6784), www.skinorthstar.com.
- Squaw Valley (1-800-403-0206, www.squaw.com), the only true destination resort in Tahoe, offers amenities for non-skiers like shopping, restaurants, and a large skating rink at the top of the tram.
- Parents say that in addition to Northstar and Sugar Bowl, Diamond Peak (775-832-1177, www.diamondpeak.com) has an especially good kids' program.
- Kids ages 5 and under ski free at most of the resorts, but keep in mind that you'll probably be shelling out money for child care, rental equipment, and ski lessons.
- When booking accommodations, book as near to the chair-lift line as possible. Weigh the time and difficulty of getting yourself, your kids, and all the gear from your house or hotel room to the slopes, versus the cost savings of renting something farther away. Comment: "You will not believe how much gear you will have to carry around when you take kids skiing." A popular solution to the "schlep" is to rent a ski locker at the base lodge, and leave everything there all season.

- Speaking of gear, buying used equipment or renting for the season is a great alternative to shelling out hundreds of dollars for new ski equipment each year when your children change sizes. Try the Marin Ski Swap (October at the Marin Civic Center) or the San Ramon High School Ski Swap (November) for used gear. Most full-service ski shops have affordable seasonal rental programs allowing you to exchange outgrown equipment throughout the season.
- As an alternative with very young children, "Try cross-country skiing. . . . Mom and Dad can exercise with baby in tow." Royal Gorge Cross-Country Ski Resort (800-666-3871, www.royalgorge.com) features a Family Center where families can relax and change diapers, and starting at age 4 kids can enroll in the PeeWee Snow School.
- Don't forget summer in Tahoe, where you can enjoy sunny, warm beaches!

LAS VEGAS

www.golasvegas.cc (Tourist Bureau of Las Vegas)

www.lasvegaskids.net (kid-oriented activities in Vegas)

Comment: "Amazingly great fun for kids for 2 to 3 days maximum. . . . dolphins, shows, and sights." **The Four Seasons Mandalay Bay Resort** (www.fourseasons.com/lasvegas) is particularly family friendly and smoke free, as it lacks a casino, provides a licensed babysitting service, and has access to fabulous pools. Fun family activities in Las Vegas include:

- The lions at the MGM Grand Hotel (free).
- The white tigers at the Mirage Hotel (free).
- Circus acts at Circus-Circus Hotel (free).
- The dolphins at the Mirage Hotel.
- Shark Reef at Mandalay Bay Hotel (pricey aquarium, but fun, especially the hammerhead shark).
- The "mock" Eiffel Tower at the Paris Hotel. A great vantage point to see the Bellagio's musical Fountain Show. The Fountain Show is free, the Eiffel Tower is not.
- The amusement park inside the MGM Grand Hotel.

MENDOCINO COAST

www.mendocinocoast.com (Mendocino Coast Chamber of Commerce)

Take the Skunk Train through the redwoods (California Western Railroad, 800-77-SKUNK, 777-5865), spend a day at the beach watching whales, or hike through one of the nearby state parks.

MONTEREY/CARMEL

www.monterey.com (Monterey Peninsula Visitors and Conventions Bureau)

Comment: "A great weekend getaway." About Carmel, parents say: "Easy weekend trip . . . short drive with lots of kid- and dog-friendly hotels and restaurants. You can walk everywhere once you get there."

- **Dennis the Menace Playground.** Camino del Estero and Fremont (off Del Monte Ave.), Monterey

Traveling

Though its structures are a bit old (circa 1950), this playground is a perennial favorite because of its cartoon theme, steam engine, and lake with paddleboats.

◆ **Monterey Bay Aquarium.** 886 Cannery Row, Monterey 831-648-4800 831-648-4937 (advance ticket sales), www.mbayaq.org

PARENT RATING: ☆ ☆ ☆ ☆ ☆

This enormous aquarium is a sure hit with kids. Don't miss the Splash Zone, a special rock and reef exhibit for families, and the Touch Pools to feel the rays. The feeding shows, where microphoned divers and museum docents explain the wildlife, are fascinating for parents and children. Full- or self-service dining is available in the café. Insider tip: Buy your tickets through your hotel and skip the ticket lines.

◆ **Carmel Valley Ranch** (831-625-9500, www.wyndham.com/hotels/MRYCV), in the warmer Carmel Valley southeast of the Monterey Peninsula, is a popular choice for family lodging.

PARENT RATING: ☆ ☆ ☆ ☆ ☆

Comment: "All rooms are suites with separate living rooms and bedrooms, they provide high chairs for the rooms, and they have a pool."

◆ **The Inn at Spanish Bay** (831-647-7500, www.pebblebeach.com), though very upscale, is the most family friendly of the Pebble Beach resorts.

PARENT RATING: ☆ ☆ ☆ ☆ ☆

Comment: "They provide a welcome package for children with coloring books and crayons, a kids' menu in the dining room, licensed babysitting service, pool, tennis, and lovely walks along the beach. The concierge is very accommodating of children. Don't miss the bagpiper at cocktail hour!"

◆ If you must stay right in Monterey near the Aquarium (which we don't recommend as it is overpriced and you can find nicer options in nearby areas), parents gave the thumbs up to the **Monterey Plaza Hotel** (on Cannery Row, 831-646-1700, www.montereyplazahotel. com) and the **Hotel Pacific** (800-554-5542, www.hotelpacific.com).

◆ A little farther north, between Monterey and Santa Cruz, is the **Seascape Resort** (www.seascaperesort.com, 831-688-6800).

PARENT RATING: ☆ ☆ ☆ ☆ ☆

Comment: "Great family vacation on a beautiful beach. . . . They'll set you up for a sunset barbecue and bonfire on the beach." While there you can take in the Seymour Marine Discovery Center and the Roaring Camp Railroad as well. (See listings above under Animals! Zoos, Farms, and Wildlife and Trains, Planes, Boats, and Automobiles respectively.)

SAN DIEGO

The area is home to many kid-friendly destinations

PARENT RATING: ☆ ☆ ☆ ☆ ☆

◆ **Legoland**, Carlsbad, 760-918-5346, www.legoland.com. We particularly enjoyed Legoland—a beautifully landscaped park with rides suited to the 10-and-under crowd.

- **Sea World**, 800-25-SHAMU, www.seaworld.com.
- The world famous **San Diego Zoo**, 619-234-3153, www.sandiegozoo.com, a place that makes other zoos pale by comparison. Their primate exhibits are fascinating, and the lush gardens are not to be believed.
- If you can afford it, stay at the full-service **Hotel del Coronado** (www.hoteldel.com or 800-HOTELDEL) to appreciate it fully. Or try the **LaJolla Beach and Tennis Club** (800-640-7702, www.ljbtc.com), a family-friendly place with suites, a pool, and barbecues on the beach.

SEA RANCH

www.searanchrentals.com

Comment: "Renting a house is easy, you will get great R&R, and there are miles of beaches."

FAMILY CAMPS

If you are from the East Coast, you may think this is nuts, but family camps are all the rage in the Bay Area. Some of the most popular include:
- **Shady Creek Family Camp** (Nevada City, 800-826-7310, www.shadycreekcamp.com). This camp in the Sierra foothills has cabins and offers supervised activities for children from infants to age 12 each morning.
- **Stanford Sierra Camp** (Fallen Lake, South Lake Tahoe, 530-541-1244, www.stanfordalumni.org). This camp offers educational opportunities for parents and supervised activities for ages 3 and up.

HAWAII

- **Four Seasons Hualalai**, Kona, Hawaii (808-325-8000 or www.fourseasons.com).
  PARENT RATING: ☆ ☆ ☆ ☆ ☆
  It's expensive, but this Big Island resort has fabulous amenities for kids, including staff who will set up your poolside cabana with a Pack 'n Play crib, a wonderful man-made lagoon where you and the kids can snorkel among tropical fish without the wave factor, and a wading pool with a sandy bottom.
- **Hyatt Regency, Kauai** (808-742-1234, www.kauai.hyatt.com). They have a great kids' club program for children ages 3 and up, offer adjoining rooms for half price, and feature a swimming lagoon and miles of water slides.
- **Kona Village**, Kona, Hawaii (800-367-5290, www.konavillage.com).
  PARENT RATING: ☆ ☆ ☆ ☆ ☆

Next door to the Four Seasons, but a world away, is this longtime favorite American Plan resort where families come back year after year to stay in their own "hale" (luxury hut) on the beach or the pond. Sea turtles come to rest on the beach, babysitters are plentiful, and they have a great kids' program and kids' dinners, which children ages 6 and up can attend without a caregiver.
- **Kiahuna Plantation**, Poipu Beach, Kauai.
  PARENT RATING: ☆ ☆ ☆ ☆ ☆

These beachfront condominiums are individually owned, but some of the best are available through the Kiahuna Beachside website (www.kiahuna.com).

◆ **Kea Lani Hotel**, Wailea, Maui (808-875-4100, www.kealani.com).

PARENT RATING: ☆ ☆ ☆ ☆ ☆

Book a ground-floor room with an outdoor patio at this all-suites hotel.

MEXICO

◆ **Club Med Ixtapa** "is fabulous . . . great family vacation, plus parents really get a break." They offer kids' camps for infants and up, and prices are very reasonable at this all-inclusive resort. (888-WEB-CLUB or www.clubmediterranee.com).

◆ **Sheraton Hacienda del Mar in Los Cabos** "offers a kids' club, kids' menus, kiddie pool, and cribs." (www.sheratonhaciendadelmar.com).

◆ **Four Seasons Punta Mita** (near Puerto Vallarta) "has babysitting and wonderful kids' camps (ages 5 and up)." (www.fourseasons.com/puntamita).

NAPA/SONOMA

◆ **Country Sojourns** (800-495-9961 or www.countrysojourns.com) offers family-friendly vacation home rentals in Napa and Sonoma. They are a division of Beautiful Places, which offers more spacious and upscale rentals (www.beautiful-places.com). Renting a house is a great alternative to staying at bed-and-breakfast inns, which generally do not welcome families.

◆ **The Napa Valley Wine Train** features Family Fun Nights—kids are entertained with games, movies, and a meal in their own car while parents enjoy a 3-hour uninterrupted gourmet dinner! And while the parents' tab can be steep, kids are free! (Napa to St. Helena, 707-253-2111, www.winetrain.com).

Birthday Parties

Before you know it, the baby you swaddled only yesterday is on the verge of taking his first steps as well as celebrating his first birthday! What a milestone! There is something special about the first birthday, which often makes parents want to celebrate—after all, you've made it through the first year of parenthood. Many child development experts recommend a small gathering for the first birthday—following the old school rule of limiting the number of guests to the child's age. However, we know plenty of Bay Area parents (including ourselves) who pulled out all the stops for a big first birthday party for their little ones. They were great—but most of all, they were parties for the parents, as babies even at the big one-year mark are far too young to realize what a birthday is all about.

There are many great locales and entertainers for children's birthdays in the Bay Area—a true testament to the Bay Area as a young family's metropolis! We have listed the entertainers according to where they are based or where they do most of their business (except San Francisco and the North Bay which we have combined). Many entertainers serve the entire Bay Area. Also, most of the venues already mentioned in this chapter and in Ch. 7 also host birthday parties. Here are some more ideas for children's birthday parties:

- **Celebrate at a kid-friendly restaurant.** Kid-friendly restaurants, such as pizzerias and ice cream parlors, make great venues for children's birthday parties for kids ages 2 and up.

- **Hire a storyteller.** A storyteller can be a real hit at kids' parties! Try calling your local bookstore or library for a recommendation.

- **Reserve space at a local park or playground.** If you want a simple party but don't want to host it (or simply can't!) at your home, reserving a park space is a great and economical alternative. Many parks also have recreation rooms, which can come in handy in case of rain. Call your local Parks and Recreation Department for reservations and details. This is a popular option, so be sure to book as early as 2 to 3 months in advance!

- **Visit your local fire station.** This is always a great party theme for little boys and a great venue for parents—as it is free! Most fire departments will be glad to give kids a tour of their station, and may let them climb on the trucks, try on the jackets and boots, and demonstrate how the hoses and ladders work.

- **Create a mini-preschool setting.** Children aged 5 and under get a big kick out of a miniature preschool setting, with different activities occurring simultaneously in a yard or playroom. Outside, it might be painting, a sand or water table, or bean bag toss; inside it might be Play Doh, a sticker table, a puzzle table, or a bookmaking table (where the hosts have pre-stapled folded sheets of paper, stapled at the fold, ready to be filled with stickers or pictures).

- For slightly older children, at least 3 years old, **set up a scavenger hunt,** or **have children make their own goodie bags and let them "buy" their choice of little inexpensive favors** with pennies from a penny hunt (www.oreintaltrading.com is your best source for favors!).

Bay Area-Wide

All Star Showgrams

800-427-SHOW (7469)

www.allstarshowgrams.com

PARENT RATING: ☆ ☆ ☆ ☆ ☆

Serving the entire Bay Area, All Star's performers will come to your house as almost any popular children's character and entertain your child and his or her guests with dances, games, balloons, face painting, magic, and party favors. Parents rave about the success and reliability of this company.

Cold Stone Creamery

www.coldstonecreamery.com

PARENT RATING: ☆ ☆ ☆ ☆ ☆

With locations throughout the Bay Area, your nearest Creamery will bring an ice cream sundae bar, complete with servers, to your event. Comment: "Delicious and so easy on the parents!"

Fun Factory Parties

888-501-4FUN (4386)

www.funfactoryparties.com

This is a complete one-stop party store, from entertainment to equipment rental to party supplies.

Jump For Fun

800-281-6792

www.jumpforfun.com

PARENT RATING: ☆ ☆ ☆

This national company is the world's largest maker of inflatable vinyl air jumpers. They rent 15x15-foot jumpers in various themes that hold up to 10 children at a time. The company delivers and sets up the jumper. They leave the rest up to you, including supervising the kids.

Spectacular Productions

415-467-4467

www.spevents.net

This full-service event planning company has some very good entertainers for children's birthday parties, especially the pirate who performs magic tricks.

San Francisco and North Bay

Nick Barone Puppets

See South Bay listing.

Benny and Bebe's European Clowning, Magic, Mime & Puppetry

415-457-4386

www.magiccircus.com

They offer costumed characters, comedy magic shows, balloon sculpting, face painting, and more.

Birthday Fun with Princess Polka Dot

Marilyn Lorusso

415-382-1221

www.princesspolkadot.com

This popular children's entertainer sings, does magic tricks, has puppets, makes balloons, does face painting, tells stories, and more. Comment: "My daughter didn't stop talking about Princess Polka Dot. She loved her!"

TIPS FOR BABY'S FIRST BIRTHDAY

♦ Limit the number of guests so that excessive noise, stimulation, and confusion don't rouse the children too much.

♦ If the weather is nice, find an enclosed playground, keep the party very short (an hour and a half is enough), and don't plan any organized activity, other than having the kids play and eat some cake.

♦ Have 2 cakes—one that you serve your guests and another small one that you put in front of baby. This always makes very memorable moments and great photo opportunities! Both Safeway and Lucky stores will give you a free small cake for a baby's first birthday. Just bring in your baby's birth certificate a day or so ahead of time.

♦ If you are in a playgroup with many kids' birthdays during the same month, have one group birthday party and then have your own family's celebration on the actual birthday. (You can get away with this for the first couple of years!).

♦ If your child receives gifts, open them after guests leave.

Binky the Elf

415-296-0412
www.binkytheelf.com

Binky is best known as the elf at the Ritz Carlton Hotel's annual holiday Teddy Bear Tea. But Binky's repertoire extends well beyond the holidays. He offers birthday party entertainment that features almost any favorite children's character as well as theme parties such as children's theater, tea parties, laser tag, magic shows, puppet shows, face painting, treasure hunts, and more.

Bitzy the Clown

707-557-9779
www.bitzytheclown.com

Boswick the Clown

415-665-1909
www.boswick.net

PARENT RATING: ☆ ☆ ☆ ☆ ☆

Parents and kids both love Boswick for being a real clown! He has an impressive clown resume, including having toured with the Ringling Brothers and Barnum & Bailey Circus. He specializes in juggling, magic, and making balloon animals.

Birthday Parties

Tim Cain
415-488-9204
www.timcain.com
PARENT RATING: ☆ ☆ ☆ ☆ ☆

You are sure to love this nationally renowned recording artist for children who will enliven your child's birthday party. Tim arrives at your home with his guitar in hand, ready to sing favorites or his original songs.

The Clown Co.
415-621-2188
www.theclownco.com

Daly City Party Playhouse
56 Hill St.
Daly City
650-756-PLAY (7529)
www.mypartyhouse.com

This "full-service playhouse hosts kids' parties of all kinds, offering pizza and drinks and all kinds of fun for your kids featuring slides, mazes, bouncy houses, climbing tunnels, a rock-climbing wall, slides, and more."

Filly Folly the Clown
415-479-3249

Filly Folly is a Raggedy Ann clown who charms your little ones with balloons and lollipops and lots of one-on-one interaction.

James K
707-781-9838
888-303-4600
www.jamesk.com
PARENT RATING: ☆ ☆ ☆ ☆ ☆

James K is a nationally acclaimed children's songwriter and guitarist whom we are lucky enough to have living in the Bay Area! He will be sure to get your little ones hopping with his lively tunes. He also teaches music in elementary schools.

Jewish Community Center San Francisco
3200 California St.
415-292-1221
www.jccsf.org

Choose one of 4 themes (including Sunday swim party, art party, ceramics party, dance party) for a 2-hour party, complete with specialized activities and a room for your celebration. You only need to supply invitations, guests, and food, and the JCC staff will do the rest.

Kozy Klown
415-893-9542

A real clown about whom parents rave—"fun family entertainment, including face painting, balloons, and tattoos."

Little Women's Tea Parties
415-566-9422
www.littlewomensteaparties.com
www.teapartyinabox.com

This company offers dress-up tea parties that feature pictures, games, crafts, and afternoon tea. Alternatively, they'll package and ship everything for the perfect tea party!

Magic Dan
415-337-8500
www.magicdan.com
PARENT RATING: ☆ ☆ ☆ ☆ ☆

Dan Sneider puts on a great show for even the youngest audiences!

Missi Twist
415-225-6436
E-mail: missitwist@hotmail.com
PARENT RATING: ☆ ☆ ☆ ☆ ☆

This spectacular balloon artist is sure to impress and entertain your little ones. A big favorite among city moms!

Miss Kitty (Judy Nee)
www.misskittysings.com
PARENT RATING: ☆ ☆ ☆ ☆ ☆

An award-winning vocalist, entertainer, and recording artist, Miss Kitty is guaranteed to present a fabulous show at your child's party. She features all the classic children's songs plus original compositions, encourages singing and dancing along with the music, and allows time for each child to take the mike. Book well in advance, as Miss Kitty is a very popular choice. See also under Discovery Museum and Best Things to Do on a Rainy Day.

Penney the Clown
510-832-5696
www.penneytheclown.com
Penney can be a clown, fairy princess, or other fun character. She promises to add excitement to your child's party with magic, balloons, face painting, and dress-up.

Pepi the Clown
415-351-2085

Pranks for Memories
415-754-1786
E-mail: Brian@pranks4u.com
www.pranks4u.com
They offer great clown entertainment.

The Puppet Company
510-569-3144
www.puppetcompany.com
This professional puppeteer with over 30 years experience creates unique

puppet shows that include classics and fables.

Red Panda Acrobats
415-731-5037
www.redpanda2000.com
PARENT RATING: ☆ ☆ ☆ ☆ ☆

These Chinese acrobats will wow your little ones many times over with their performance. Ask for Wayne Huey—he was professionally trained in China with the Shanghai Circus Academy.

The Train Singer
Greg Schindel
707-459-3739
www.trainsinger.com
PARENT RATING: ☆ ☆ ☆ ☆ ☆

The train singer belts out popular and traditional train tunes, reflecting the sights, sounds, and history of the California Western's Skunk Train. Kids remember him most for his strong grasp of classic train lore tunes and the accompanying train sounds that he's a pro at making! The Train Singer also performs at the Bay Area Discovery Museum several times annually.

Tree Frog Treks
2112 Hayes St.
415-876-3764
www.treefrogtreks.com
PARENT RATING: ☆ ☆ ☆ ☆ ☆

If you have a reptile or nature fan in your family, then Tree Frog Treks is for you! Their naturalists host a Rock n' Reptile birthday party at your venue of choice and introduce your little one and guests to live rescued reptiles and amphibians, offering fun, hands-on science programming, and nature exploration. See also Ch. 7 under More Classes.

The Birthday Magician
925-778-3757
This award-winning magician offers birthday party fun for the entire family that includes live doves, a cute bunny, and audience participation.

California Kids Jump
P.O. Box 15583
Fremont
800-543-7675
They rent large inflatable vinyl air jumpers.

Fire Pixie Entertainment
39647 Embarcadero Terrace
Fremont
510-367-4517
www.firepixie.com
Since its inception, the company has grown to include more than 10 amazing performers, including character actors such as princesses and pirates and more, balloon twisters, face painters, and fire performers. Children's birthday parties are their specialty.

Ryan Majestic
510-981-1219
Ryan is a balloon artist. He does birthday parties in addition to his regular gig at Chevy's Restaurant.

Precious the Clown
510-594-1834
Precious will arrive at the party without her face painted, and with the children's help she'll paint her face and transform herself into a clown.

The Puppet Company
See listing under San Francisco.

Twinkles
925-937-5457
Carla Winter offers birthday party entertainment for children ages one and up that includes music, song and dance, magic, face painting, animal balloons, juggling, and caricature drawing.

Linda Zittel and the Magic Window Puppets
510-234-6266
This artist offers wonderful birthday party performances that feature storytelling with puppets, instruments, and finger puppet making for ages 2-7.

Aunt Willa's Pizza on Wheels
650-348-8865
www.pizzaonwheels.com
Aunt Willa makes and delivers delicious pizzas, drinks, green salad, and dessert to your door.

Babaloon & Tunes
888-339-7925 or 415-824-6725
www.babaloons.com
This company offers clowns or Teletubbies for all ages that perform balloon art, juggling, magic tricks, games, bubbles, singing, and face painting.

Nick Barone Puppets
1017 El Camino Real #460
Redwood City
650-365-8070
www.nbpuppets.com
PARENT RATING: ☆ ☆ ☆ ☆ ☆

Nick Barone is a special entertainer, offering original and traditional tales, told in classic style and featuring superbly crafted puppets. He brings to your home or event location a full puppet stage, lights and sound system, complete with a professionally recorded soundtrack featuring music, songs, and sound effects. After the show, Nick takes down the curtains and gives a behind-the-scenes look at the show. Nick also does puppet shows for libraries and recreation centers around the Bay Area.

Cosmo Jump

800-829-5867 or 650-570-5867
www.cosmojump.com

Cosmo Jump rents interactive inflatables, cotton candy machines, snow cone makers, and popcorn poppers.

Daffy Dave

650-326-3711
www.daffydave.com

Daffy Dave is goofy and wacky, but kids love him! Winner of the *Bay Area Parent*'s 2000 Reader's Choice Award, he is one of the area's most sought-after party entertainers.

D.W. Wilson's Ultimate Magic Show

650-369-9395

This magician has lots of experience in entertaining children, as he was part of the original Romper Room show.

Flying Teapot Puppets

650-595-8545
www.flyingteapot.com
E-mail: margaret@flyingteapot.com

Margaret Bloom, owner of this precious company, presents unique puppet shows in your home for birthdays for children ages 2-6. Her shows feature a full-size puppet stage, beautiful puppets, and live music and singing.

Frankie & Her Live Animal Friends

650-592-7987

Frankie entertains and educates young birthday guests with live animals such as rabbits, snakes, tortoises, and more.

Friendly Pony Parties and Barnyard Pals

650-738-0248

These pony rides and/or a barnyard zoo will come to your home for a unique and memorable party.

Happy Birds

408-268-0778
www.happybirds.com

Happy Birds offers unusual entertainment—they will bring a talented team of parrots to your home that play basketball, ride bikes, talk, sing, and roller skate.

Lizard Lady

650-355-4105
www.lizardladyreptiles.com

Lizard Lady offers unforgettable parties with her congenial reptiles from San Francisco to San Jose.

Magic and Puppets

415-731-3898

Puppeteer Joe Hoffman has 25 years of experience and offers wonderful entertainment for children's birthday parties.

Magic Mike's Funhouse

408-244-7469

www.magictimeproductions.com

Mike offers a musical magic show that features juggling, ventriloquism, and surprises for party guests. He is a winner of a Parent's Choice Award for best show for parties in the Bay Area.

Miss Carol's Magical Puppetime

650-620-9280

www.magicalpuppetime.com

Miss Carol features her handcrafted marionettes in a cabaret show of your choice. She has an impressive puppet collection of many familiar fairy tale, nursery rhyme, and circus characters. Sing-alongs, magic, and face painting are also part of the party.

Most Unique Parties & Ponies

831-338-9130

www.mostunique.com

This entertainer offers favorite costumed characters that feature magic, animals, puppets, games, music, face painting, and balloons. For extra-special birthdays, a barnyard petting zoo and pony cart rides are also available.

Pal Productions

650-355-0290

Pal Productions offers costumed characters that will entertain your party guests with dancing, games, and face painting. They serve most of the Bay Area.

Skates The Clown

650-365-1514

www.skatestheclown.com

www.qwickandeasy.com/balloons

Skates features magic, puppets, songs, games, balloon art, and face painting.

Celebrations by Jetta Jacobson

415-221-7199

An experienced early childhood educator and event planner, Jetta will organize and carry out your child's birthday party. She meets with you to learn about your child's interests and how to transform them into a memorable birthday celebration.

Goldfield Events

415-747-2297

www.goldfieldevents.com

Party planner Leslie Goldstein does children's birthday and holiday parties, including cupcake and cookie decorating and gingerbread house making.

It's a Piece of Cake

409 Lyon St.
San Francisco
415-929-1946

www.itsapieceofcake.net

This is a full-scale event and entertainment service for children, specializing in birthday parties. They offer stress-free party packages where every detail is handled from planning to cleanup.

Sophie's Stress Free Soirees— Unique Parties Planned and Created by Your Children

377 Shaw Rd.
South San Francisco
650-952-5502

www.sophieparty.com

PARENT RATING: ☆ ☆ ☆ ☆ ☆

Sophie Maletsky offers a full-scale party-planning service where she takes children's ideas and transforms them into birthday fantasies.

We know there many favorite bakeries out there, but here are just a few cake resources for that special birthday! Want to do it yourself? Try a practice round well before the party, and keep the cake cool until the last minute, lest your pirate ship become a shipwreck!

Baby Kakes

www.babykakes.com

This is a great website for cupcake pictures and toppers.

Cake Art Supplies

1512 5th Ave.
San Rafael
415-456-7773

You will find everything you need to make your own cake at this mecca of confectionary supplies.

Cake Gallery

290 9th St.
San Francisco
415-861-2253
thecakegallery.com

PARENT RATING: ★ ☆ ☆ ☆ ☆

This bakery scores for customer service and will draw almost any theme you want on your child's cake. Their cakes are delicious, and a big plus is that they deliver to your party venue.

Cake Works

613 York St.
San Francisco
415-821-1333

For that one-of-a-kind creation, Cecile is the one to call! She specializes in unique and artful cakes.

The Cupcake Fairy

415-642-3522
www.thecupcakefairy.com

PARENT RATING: ★ ☆ ☆ ☆ ☆

The Cupcake Fairy will work with you to come up with the perfect creation for your little one's special day. She works her magic which promises to be one of the most memorable outstanding birthday treats!

Debbie Does Dessert

556 San Anselmo Ave.
San Anselmo
415-457-7518
www.debbiedoesdessert.com

PARENT RATING: ★ ☆ ☆ ☆ ☆

Debbie can custom-make your cake to fit your party theme and can even scan and reproduce images on your cake. Her cakes are delicious!

Sibby's Cupcakery

415-613-4373
www.sibbyscupcakery.com

Sibby designs beautiful and scrumptious cupcakes for parties and other events. Her mini-cupcake is popular for first birthdays.

Online Resources for Birthday Parties

www.birthdayexpress.com
PARENT RATING: ☆ ☆ ☆ ☆ ☆

Shop for themed party supplies, favors, activities, and more on this extensive website.

www.birthdayinabox.com
PARENT RATING: ☆ ☆ ☆ ☆ ☆

This website offers the convenience of ordering pre-printed or blank invitations, coordinating paper goods, games, party favors, and personalized thank-you notes in dozens of popular children's party themes.

www.kids-party.com/games.shtml

This website features 100 kids' party games—both new and old!

www.amazingmoms.com/htm/KidsBirthdayParties.htm

This website is perfect for creativity-challenged parents, as it offers complete party plans for more than 30 themed parties.

www.billybear4kids.com/holidays/birthday/party/themes.html

This website features novel but inexpensive party favors, invitations, and more.

www.kidsparties.com/traditions.htm

Interested in knowing about birthday traditions around the world? Then check out this website.

www.partygamecentral.com

This website claims to be the largest party game website.

CHAPTER 9

IN SEARCH OF
MARY POPPINS:
Finding Competent
Child Care

Sometime toward the end of your pregnancy, you will begin thinking about child care. Given the high demand for good quality child care in the Bay Area, it is never too early to address this issue. Do a little legwork before baby arrives, such as asking friends about their child care arrangements, interviewing individual child care providers, and visiting day care centers—and if you like one, registering for a space (yes, even before baby arrives)!

Of course, your child care needs will depend on your postpartum life. If you are returning to work full-time after a maternity leave, you will probably require full-time help. If you work at home, work part-time, or are involved in activities that require you to leave the house part of the day, you will likely need part-time child care assistance. Even if you aren't sure about your plans for returning to work, you will certainly want some help, ranging from regular support to occasional babysitting.

In this chapter we will share what we know about finding competent child care in the Bay Area. We will help you answer these questions and more:

- What are my child care options?
- What are the pros and cons of each type of child care?
- Where can I go to obtain good child care, and what can I expect to pay for it?
- Who regulates the child care industry?
- How do I go about hiring a child care provider on my own?
- What are the legal issues involved in having someone work in my home?
- What are the best resources for finding babysitters?

California Child Care Licensing

In California, the Community Care Facilities Licensing Division of the Department of Social Services (DSS) (650-266-8843) licenses both day care centers and family day care homes. There are no state licensing requirements for in-home child care providers such as nannies and babysitters. Keep in mind that requirements for licensing a child care facility are minimal and basic, so the quality of licensed child care covers a wide spectrum.

However, license requirements do set some standards for the health and safe care of children by limiting the number and ages of children in the center or home. Additionally, a criminal record clearance through the Department of Justice and a "clean" Child Abuse Index Check, which indicates whether reports of suspected child abuse have ever been made against an individual, are required of all applicants and directors before a license is issued. All caregivers must also receive a tuberculosis clearance, and at least one person in the center or home must have 15 hours of health care training, CPR, and first aid. By law, parents also have the right to drop in unannounced at any time at their child's center.

Day Care Centers

Day care centers, whether privately or publicly run, provide child care in a setting other than a home for large groups of young children (usually anywhere from 12 to 150 children). Most are open long hours (typically 10 to 12 hours a day), year round, and tend to follow local school year calendars in terms of holidays and breaks. Licensed day care centers are required to offer physical, activity-oriented, and educational programs, often in age-defined "classrooms," under adult supervision. Many day care centers do not offer care for infants (especially those under one year old), and those that do usually have a limited number of spaces (typically 10 to 12 at most) due to state licensing requirements. Competition for these spaces can be keen. If you plan to have your child attend a day care center before his or her first birthday, we urge you to contact and tour centers early in your pregnancy, as some centers have waiting lists as long as one to 2 years!

PROS AND CONS

One of the main advantages of day care centers (compared to in-home care) is reliability, since you are not dealing with one individual but an organization of care providers. Many parents also appreciate that caregivers at day care centers are subject to a certain degree of accountability, since they are with others throughout the day, unlike an in-home caregiver. In addition, day care centers are usually open long hours and may be conveniently located in or near your workplace or neighborhood. Also, many parents appreciate the socialization with other children that day care centers offer, as well as their structured nature, including scheduled program activities.

The disadvantages of day care include the necessity of transporting your child to and from the center. (If you think it is difficult getting yourself out the door early in the morning to make it to work on time, plan on at least doubling that time in order to get you and your baby dressed, fed, and out the door!) Also, many day care centers charge a fee when a parent is late picking up a child. Some parents dislike the fact that most centers follow established schedules (for feeding and napping, for example) which may or may not be compatible with the baby's natural rhythms. (On the other hand, many parents appreciate this routine and attribute the fact that their baby takes a bottle or naps at a certain time to the schedule of their child's day care center.) In addition, day care centers can sometimes seem "institutional" in atmosphere, although it should be noted that many parents prefer such a setting to the quirks and unpredictability of family home care.

473

Since most day care centers are large and offer care for many children, your baby or child will have increased exposure to other children's germs. If your child becomes sick, you'll have to make arrangements for backup care since most sick children are asked to stay at home. Also, in some day care centers, staff turnover can be high, and care from various caregivers may affect your child's ability to adjust to the center. Finally, a day care center day can be a long stretch for a baby or young child to be in a non-home environment.

COSTS

Day care centers are either private, receiving little or no public funding, or are subsidized in varying degrees by public resources, including federal, state, and local funds. For many privately run centers, there are no subsidized spaces set aside for low-income families. For subsidized centers, however, the majority of spaces are generally set aside for lower-income families, and fees are determined on a sliding scale. Requirements for these spaces vary according to the source of the funding. For instance, in some cases one parent is required to be working or in training. Competition for the subsidized spaces can be fierce.

Many day care center directors advise planning interim child care arrangements well before the baby is born, in order to cover child care needs while on a waiting list. Interim arrangements might include planning and budgeting for a longer maternity leave, having a relative or nanny take care of the child, or taking a full payment space while waiting for a subsidized one, if eligible.

CARE PROVIDER TRAINING, EDUCATION, AND QUALIFICATIONS

California state regulations require that all teachers (caregivers) working in day care centers have at least 12 units of Early Childhood Education (ECE), and teacher's assistants must have at least 6 units of ECE. Directors and site directors must have 12 units of ECE as well as 3 additional ECE units in administration. Teachers in subsidized centers

HOW TO FIND OUT ABOUT OR FILE A COMPLAINT
AGAINST A CHILD CARE CENTER OR A FAMILY DAY
CARE HOME

To find out if a child care center or family day care home you are considering has a complaint against them, you can call Community Care Licensing (650-266-8843) or your local California Childcare Resource and Referral Network agency (415-882-0234, main office), who will forward the inquiry to Community Care Licensing. Complaints and inquiries may be made anonymously.

are required to have a Children's Center Permit (24 ECE units). Fingerprint and tuberculosis test clearance are required for all teachers.

LICENSING

In California, the Community Care Licensing Division of the Department of Social Services is the state authority that regulates child care. Regulations state that there must be 35 square feet of indoor space per child and 75 square feet of outdoor space per child. Centers in urban areas, such as San Francisco's financial district, often petition for a waiver of the outdoor space requirement since outdoor space is limited. Regulations also require one toilet and sink for every 15 children.

Regulations require all equipment to be age appropriate, and daily planned activities must include quiet and active play, rest and relaxation, and support for toilet training.

Regulations for child-to-caregiver ratios vary according to whether the facility is subsidized or not and per the age of the children. In non-subsidized centers, the maximum permitted child-to-caregiver ratios are as follows:

Infants (newborn-2 years): 4:1

Preschool (2-6 years): 12:1, or if the classroom has a caregiver and an aide, the ratio is 18:1

Child Care

475

In subsidized centers, the maximum caregiver-to-child ratios are as follows:

Infants (newborn-2 years): 3:1 with a maximum of 18 in one room
Preschool (2-6 years): 8:1 with a maximum of 24 in one room

Please note that regulations for non-subsidized centers do not include maximum numbers of children per classroom. For more information about day care licensing see www.ccld.ca.gov.

Under state law, licensed day care centers must make licensing reports that document a facility visit or substantiated complaint available to the public. A more thorough file for each licensed center is also available at an office of the State Department of Social Services Community Care Licensing Division. (For office addresses and telephone numbers, see under Day Care Licensing Offices.) You have the right to access any public information in these files.

Family Child Care

Family child care refers to child care provided in a person's private home for a fee. The state of California considers care for 2 or more children from 2 or more families a family child care home and requires a license to operate as such. The license confirms that the caregiver and her home have met standards for childproofing, cleanliness, and child-to-caregiver ratios. While all family child care homes are required to be licensed, there are many that are not. In these cases, it may be that unlicensed homes don't meet the standards, or that the caregiver has decided not to apply for the license due to the expense. Just remember that while licensing can be a helpful indicator of quality child care, it is certainly not a guarantee.

In selecting a day care center or family child care home, try to visit at least a couple of times and observe how the children are cared for, and what their day is like (for instance, are they indoors all day, how much time is spent with the television on, are they read to, how are they fed—on demand or at set times—and so on). Also, talk to other parents whose children are cared for there, as well as those who no longer have their children there, if you can get access to these people.

PROS AND CONS

Many parents prefer the homey environment of family child care, which offers consistency with caregivers since there are usually only one or 2. Because care is provided in a home, and space is more limited, there are usually fewer children than in day care centers. There is also a lower child-to-caregiver ratio than day care centers (see below), and many caregivers in family day care homes are experienced mothers with children of their own. Also, family child care is usually the least expensive form of child care (see below).

One of the most significant drawbacks to family child care for many parents is that the caregiver is not required to have any education or background in child development. And, as is generally the case with a day care center, the granting of a license is based on the physical environment rather than on how the children actually spend their day. Family child care also requires transporting your baby or child to the caregiver's home. Also, as with day care centers, backup care is needed if your child becomes sick, since family child care homes do not want ill children putting others at risk of infection.

COSTS

Family day care is usually the least expensive child care alternative (ranging from $7 to $15 per hour.)

CARE PROVIDER TRAINING, EDUCATION, AND QUALIFICATIONS

California state law requires all family day care home providers to complete 15 hours of CPR, first aid, health, and safety training. A current tuberculosis clearance and fingerprint records are required for all adults residing in the home and for all adults who are present in the home during the time children are in care. Unlike day care center teachers, they are not required to complete any ECE courses, although many providers voluntarily take ECE courses and/or have other qualifications gained through previous experience as teachers, nurses, or parents, for example.

Child Care

LICENSING

In California, the Community Care Licensing Division of the Department of Social Services is the state authority that regulates family child care homes. A licensed home must meet health and safety standards, and cleared caregivers must undergo a child abuse and criminal records check. Family child care homes can be licensed as either a small (6 to 8 children) or large (12 to 14 children) facility. A license limits the number and ages of children being cared for. See below for a summary of these restrictions. Also, when the caregiver has children of her own at home (which often is the case), they must be included in the overall number of children that she is licensed to care for.

Requirements for small family day care homes (which typically have one caregiver) include the following:

♦ If a family day care home is for infants only (newborn to 24 months), the caregiver's license restricts her to 4 infants and no other children.

♦ If licensed for 6 children, no more than 3 children may be under the age of 24 months.

♦ If licensed for 8 children, no more than 2 may be infants (newborn to 24 months), and 2 must be at least 6 years old.

Large family day care homes are required to have a primary caregiver and a full-time assistant so that the ratio of children to caregiver is 6:1. In order to be licensed as a large family day care home, the caregiver needs to have either been licensed for a small family day care center for at least one year, or have experience with a day care center. The following restrictions apply to large family day care homes.

♦ If licensed for 12 children, no more than 4 may be infants (newborn to 24 months).

♦ If licensed for 14 children, no more than 3 may be infants, and 2 must be at least 6 years old.

In-Home Care

In-home care is exactly that—care provided in the family home by a nanny, an au pair, or a regular babysitter. In some cases, the caregiver may live with the family.

PROS AND CONS

Parents who choose this option often point to the one-to-one ratio and individual attention a child gets from a single caregiver. Recent research has shown that these considerations can be especially important for infants. In-home care also provides parents with the most flexibility with respect to their schedules, including the great convenience of not having to pack a child up for the day each morning and make it out the door on time with both parent and child dressed and fed! Also, if your child becomes ill, unlike a family care home or day care center, you typically can rely on your in-home caregiver to care for your child at home, unless, of course, the caregiver becomes sick. Unlike a day care center that typically has a set schedule for feeding, napping, and playing for all of the children, with a single caregiver in your home, you set the schedule as well as rules for your baby's care. Also, having care provided in your home generally means that you decide who is going to care for your baby, unlike a day care center or family care home.

A drawback to in-home care is being dependent on a single person's reliability and health, unlike a larger organization such as a day care center. Loss of privacy, attachment issues (e.g., the "other mother" syndrome), possible language limitations (especially with au pairs), and less socialization with other children are also issues that should be carefully considered.

Other disadvantages include the higher cost compared to day care centers and family child care homes. Care in your home also means that you become an employer and are required to withhold taxes and possibly provide benefits such as health insurance and vacation time to your caregiver. Benefits typically include 2 weeks of paid vacation, 7 paid holidays, and 5 sick days a year. In-home care providers are also unlicensed and unregulated, and therefore each applicant's background, credentials, and references must be thoroughly checked. Your provider will be unsupervised (at least part of the time) while providing child care, so thorough reference checks are crucial.

COSTS

The number one disadvantage of this form of child care (excluding au pairs) is that it is expensive ($12-25 per hour for live-outs, the average being $15-20 per hour, and $1,600-3,000 or more per month for a live-in, depending on the level of candidates' experience, education, and skills). Annual 40-hour week child care in the San Francisco Bay Area can range from $17,000 to $32,000 and up. Of course, child care at home can be much more cost effective if more than one child is being cared for, and for this reason some parents opt to share a nanny with another family. This is known as a share care arrangement. For the costs of au pairs, see under Au Pair Agencies.

CARE PROVIDER TRAINING, EDUCATION, AND QUALIFICATIONS

One of the biggest drawbacks in relation to individual in-home care providers is that they are not legally required to have any particular training, education, or health and safety certification, such as CPR or first aid. Of course, if you are doing the hiring, you set the qualifications yourself. Also, many nanny agencies require their candidates to have various qualifications, including prior experience in working with babies and young children, specialized education and training in early childhood development, and CPR and first aid certification. Nannies placed through agencies are required by the state to undergo a background check through the TrustLine registry, which includes fingerprinting and checking court records. If you hire a caregiver yourself, you may also ask her to register with TrustLine. (See under Interviewing Candidates and Conducting Background Checks.) In short, however, the onus of setting the standards for an appropriate caregiver and checking and verifying references and background falls on you or an agency.

LICENSING

Privately hired in-home child care providers are legally exempt from licensing requirements.

HOW TO FIND COMPETENT CHILD CARE

Choosing child care is a laborious and emotionally intense task for any parent. We will give you an overview of the process here. Remember to give yourself plenty of time (at least 4 to 8 weeks to hire a caregiver to come to your home and even longer to find a day care center or family day care home). We also suggest setting up a filing system for all the information you gather as you explore your child care options. There are lots of resources and experts out there to help you, but ultimately, your budget and values, and your child's personality and well-being, are the most important factors in selecting the best possible arrangement.

WORKSHOPS AND SEMINARS ON CHOOSING CHILD CARE

The Bay Area has several parenting centers that offer workshops and seminars that aim to guide parents through the child care decision-making process. Here are the ones that parents shared with us. Because schedules and fees change, please call for current information.

Bananas

5232 Claremont Ave.
Oakland
510-658-0381
www.bananasinc.org

Bananas is a nonprofit child care referral and support agency serving families in Northern Alameda County. They provide free parenting information, workshops, and child care referrals. They also offer training, workshops, classes, and technical support to caregivers. They are well known for their free handouts that offer all sorts of parenting advice on many topics. Either stop by or download information from their website. They also offer a Choosing Infant Care workshop on a regular basis. This workshop helps parents understand their options and provides support in selecting appropriate care. Babies are welcome.

Alyce Desrosiers, LCSW

San Francisco
415-331-NANI
www.alycedes.com
alyce@alycedes.com

PARENT RATING: ☆ ☆ ☆ ☆ ☆

Alyce Desrosiers, licensed child psychotherapist and author of *How to Find a Nanny in the Bay Area*, offers personalized and individualized nanny placement services. She also conducts seminars on choosing in-home child care at several parent resource centers. Parents really value her personal service.

Child Care

481

Parents Place
1710 Scott St.
San Francisco
415-359-2454
www.jfcs.org

Parents Place regularly offers a workshop entitled How to Find a Nanny in the San Francisco Bay Area. This seminar is led by Alyce Desrosiers, LCSW, who consults with parents in helping them choose reliable caregivers for their children.

Children's Council of San Francisco
445 Church St., 2nd Fl.
San Francisco
415-276-2900
www.childrencouncil.org

The council offers a Choosing Child Care workshop on an ongoing basis.

It is also considered an excellent source for home day care referrals.

Child Care Coordinating Council
2121 S. El Camino Real, Ste. A-100
San Mateo
650-286-1157
www.thecouncil.net

The council offers a workshop several times a year entitled Good Beginnings . . . Choosing Child Care.

Marin Child Care Council
555 Northgate Ave.
San Rafael
415-472-1092 (administration)
415-479-2273 (referrals)
www.mc3.org

The council offers a seminar on choosing child care which parents call "very informative."

SELECTING A DAY CARE CENTER OR FAMILY DAY CARE HOME

The Bay Area has hundreds of day care centers and family day care providers. If you are considering using a day care center, begin to explore your options while you are pregnant. It is not unusual to be placed on several waiting lists well before your baby arrives. Call child care resources and agencies in your area for referrals to licensed child care centers and family day care homes and set up appointments to visit them. This is your opportunity to educate yourself and to begin evaluating your options. It will be much more difficult driving around town, visiting centers, and meeting with directors when you have a newborn with you.

California Department of Social Services—Community Care Licensing Division

www.ccld.ca.gov

The Community Care Licensing Division of the California Department of Social Services oversees the licensing of all child care facilities in California. Below is a list of local Community Care Licensing Offices in the Bay Area. Contact them for a listing of private and subsidized day care centers and family day care providers in your neighborhood or near your place of work.

San Francisco and San Mateo

Peninsula District
801 Traeger Ave., Ste. 100
San Bruno
650-266-8843

This office licenses child care centers and family day care homes in San Francisco and San Mateo counties.

FACTORS TO CONSIDER IN FINDING QUALITY CHILD CARE

Below are some factors to consider in finding quality child care. Of course the best assessment is your own feeling about a place. The more comfortable you feel, the easier it will be to leave your child in someone else's care.

◆ *Fewer children to each adult.* Research suggests that quality child care depends on a low child-to-adult ratio so each child can receive individual attention. This is especially important for infants.

◆ *Consistency with caregivers and a low turnover rate.*

◆ *Caring individuals.* The caregivers should be warm, caring people who sincerely enjoy and understand children.

◆ *An environment that appeals to children.* The environment should be inviting to children and appropriate for the ages of the children in care.

◆ *Involvement of children.* Quality child care facilities engage and involve the children with age-appropriate activities, toys, and schedules. Caregivers interact with the children.

◆ *Parental involvement.* Parents should feel that they are partners with their caregiver.

Child Care

North Bay

Redwood Empire District
101 Golf Course Dr., Ste. A230
Rohnert Park
707-588-5026
This office licenses child care centers and family day care homes in Marin, Sonoma, and Napa counties.

Department of Health and Human Services

Marin County—Licensing Department
10 N. San Pedro Rd., Ste. 1002
San Rafael
415-499-7118
This office licenses child care centers and family day care homes in Marin County.

East Bay

Bay Area District
1515 Clay St., Ste. 1102
Oakland
510-622-2602
This office also licenses child care centers and family day care homes in Alameda and Contra Costa counties.

South Bay

San Jose District
111 N. Market St., Ste. 300
San Jose
408-277-1289 (family day care homes)
408 277-1286 (child care centers)
This office licenses child care centers and family day care homes in Monterey, San Benito, Santa Clara, and Santa Cruz counties.

CALIFORNIA CHILDCARE RESOURCE AND REFERRAL NETWORK

The California Childcare Resource and Referral Network is a coalition of largely state-funded agencies that are located in every county in California. Several of these agencies are known as the 4Cs—Community Childcare Coordinating Council. They assist parents in finding child care by maintaining databases of local caregivers (licensed family day care homes and day care centers). They make referrals only, and never recommend a provider. They track providers' licensing status, the languages they speak, the age groups they serve, their schedules, and the number of spaces available. They also provide child care subsidy assistance to low-income families either in training or in the work force; license preparation, training, and professional support to child care providers; child care resources and options for children with special needs; and advocacy, public education, and support to the child care community. Their services are free and are available to all parents and child care providers. Referrals are offered in English and Spanish either on the phone or during drop-in times. The following is a list of state-funded child care resource and referral agencies in the Bay Area:

California Childcare Resource and Referral Network

Main Office
111 New Montgomery St.
San Francisco
415-882-0234
www.rrnetwork.org

PARENT RATING: ☆ ☆ ☆

Reviews ranged from "slightly better than the phone book" to "very helpful in directing me to family day care centers in my neighborhood." One frustration was that the network does not keep a current listing of which centers have openings and which do not. The useful website contains a variety of information, such as tips on finding child care that suits your family, as well as recent legislation and policies affecting child care.

San Francisco

Children's Council of San Francisco

445 Church St.
415-343-3300 (referrals)
415-276-2900 (administration)
www.childrencouncil.org

PARENT RATING: ☆ ☆ ☆ ½

The Council's Childcare Switchboard provides parents with free referrals for day care centers and family day care homes. The Referral Line database has more than 800 providers so referrals can be made to actual child care providers. Referrals are licensed but not screened. They also offer a child care resource room with child care referral listings, free workshops on choosing child care, a free newsletter, *The San Francisco Children's News,* and fingerprinting for child care

providers. Counselors are polite and helpful.

A common complaint was that they do not do your homework for you. They stress that they offer referrals rather than recommendations (e.g., listing a day care source does not ensure its quality). However, many agreed that it is a good place to start a child care search. Where else can you get a list of all the licensed facilities in your work area or neighborhood? They also have a Bayview/Hunter's Point office (1329 Evans St., 415-920-7280).

Wu Yee Children's Services

888 Clay St., Lower Level (family resource center)
706 Mission St., 6th Fl. (family center)
415-391-4956 (referrals)
415-391-8993 (administration)
www.wuyee.org

North Bay

Marin Child Care Council

555 Northgate Ave.
San Rafael
415-472-1092 (administration)
415-479-2273 (referrals)
www.mc3.org

Community Childcare Coordinating Council (4Cs of Sonoma County)

396 Tesconi Ct.
Santa Rosa
707-544-3084 (referrals)
707-522-1410 (general information)
707-544-3077 (administration)
www.sonoma4cs.org
info@sonoma4cs.com

Child Care

River Child Care Services

P.O. Box 16
Guerneville
707-887-1809 (referrals)
rcc@sonic.net

This office covers the Western
Sonoma County/Russian River area.

East Bay

Please note: Listings for Alameda
County and Contra Costa County are
separate.

ALAMEDA COUNTY

Community Childcare
Coordinating Council (4Cs of
Alameda County)

22351 City Center Dr., Ste. 200
Hayward
510-582-2182 (referrals for Hayward,
Castro Valley, San Leandro, and
San Lorenzo)
510-790-0655 (referrals for Union
City, Fremont, and Newark)
510-582-2182 (administration)
http://4c-alameda.org

Child Development Center for
Subsidized Childcare

756 21st St.
Oakland
510-272-0669
http://4c-alameda.org

This center provides subsidized child
care for children ages 18 months to 5
years old.

Bananas

5232 Claremont Ave.
Oakland
510-658-7101 (child care
resources center)
510-658-0381 (child care referral)
www.bananasinc.org

PARENT RATING: ☆ ☆ ☆ ☆ ☆

A central clearinghouse for child care
information and referrals for Alameda
County, this office offers referrals for
all types of child care, including day
care centers, family day care homes,
in-home care, shared care, and
babysitters. They have lots of names
of people looking for work, and will
provide you with sample interview
questions and contracts. They issue a
quarterly newsletter that contains free
listings mainly for shared in-home
care in Alameda County. You can
pick up a copy of this newsletter at
Bananas' office, or subscribe by mail
for a nominal fee. They offer a workshop on how to find infant child care,
including a discussion of the various
options. They also have a great parents' resource library, sponsor parent-
ing/caregiver workshops, and
produce a series of very popular and
useful one-page handouts on specific
topics related to parenting and child
development.

Child Care Links

1020 Serpentine Ln., Ste. 102
Pleasanton
925-417-8733 (referrals)
925-417-8740 (fax)
www.childcarelinks.org

This office provides child care referrals for southern and eastern
Alameda County.

CONTRA COSTA COUNTY

Contra Costa Child Care Council

www.cocokids.org
• Concord
  1035 Detroit Ave., Ste. 200
  925-676-5442 (administration)

- Concord
  2280 Diamond Blvd., Ste. 500
  925-676-5437 (referrals for central Contra Costa County)
- Antioch
  3104 Delta Fair Blvd.
  925-778-5437 (referrals for eastern Contra Costa County)
- Richmond
  3065 Richmond Pkwy., Ste. 112
  510-758-2099 or 510-233-KIDS (5437) (referrals for western Contra Costa County)

Oakland Licensed Day Care Association
6201 Doyle
Emeryville
510-658-2449
www.oldcoa.org

South Bay

Please note: Listings for San Mateo County and Santa Clara County are separate.

SAN MATEO COUNTY

Child Care Coordinating Council of San Mateo County (4Cs of San Mateo County)
2121 South El Camino Real, Ste. A-100
San Mateo
650-655-6770
www.thecouncil.net

Choices for Children
111 N. Market St.
San Jose
408-297-3295
www.choicesforchildren.org

This private nonprofit agency largely manages subsidized funding for child care for low-income families.

SANTA CLARA COUNTY

Community Child Care Council of Santa Clara County (4Cs of Santa Clara County)
111 E. Gish Rd.
San Jose
408-487-0749 (referrals)
408-487-0747 (administration)
www.4c.org

City of Palo Alto Child Care and Family Resources
Office of Human Services
4000 Middlefield Rd.
Palo Alto
650-329-2221
www.city.palo-alto.ca.us/familyresources/about_fr.html

This office provides a reference list of licensed infant and toddler care centers in Palo Alto.

Palo Alto Community Child Care
3990 Ventura Ct.
Palo Alto
650-493-2361
www.paccc.com

This private nonprofit organization is not part of the Resource and Referral Network, but does offer a brochure on child care choices and accredited programs available in Palo Alto. They also manage subsidized funding for child care services for low-income families.

Child Care

487

CHILD CARE CENTERS

The cost of child care centers is determined by several factors, including the age of the child (infants demand more care, and therefore are the most expensive), the quality and location of care, and whether corporate rates apply to the parents (some employers may subsidize their employees' child care costs or negotiate a better rate on their behalf). Expect to pay $900-1,400 per month for full-time infant care (this generally means infants up to 12 months old), around $700-1,000 for toddlers (usually ages 2–3), and $700-950 for preschoolers (usually ages 3–4). These rates are lower when corporate sponsorship fees apply, or when a day care center offers subsidized spaces. Subsidized spaces are determined on a sliding scale, depending on a family's income and eligibility. Fees are also less for part-time schedules (2 or 3 days a week), but these schedules are often difficult to obtain. Finally, to apply and get on the waiting list of many child care centers, you need first to complete a registration form and submit it with a registration fee that is usually between $10 and $50.

There are hundreds of day care centers and family day care providers in the Bay Area. Keep in mind that some employers contract with corporate day care providers and offer use of a day care center exclusively to their employees. Often the day care center will be in the company's building. Check with your employer to see what arrangements they may offer. Competition for spaces in these programs is often keen, so apply early. If that is not an available option, however, here are a few day care centers, open to the community at large, that we have found. Most day care centers have fixed hours of operation, usually from 7 a.m. to 6 p.m. and are open only on weekdays. Please call for specific hours. Because there are so many family care homes offering child care services, and because they may not necessarily be licensed, we have not listed any here. Please contact your local Resource and Referral Agency for a listing of licensed family day care providers near your home or workplace.

Children's Village
A Child Development Center
of Catholic Charities

250 10th St.

415-865-2610

Ages: 3 months to 6 years

Child/caregiver ratios: 3:1 for infants, 4:1 for toddlers, 8:1 for preschoolers

Total number of children: 100

Children's Village opened in October 2000 and is one of the largest downtown child care centers. Funded by Catholic Charities, Children's Village is nondenominational. It is housed in a former elementary school and has an extraordinary natural setting, including pleasant gardens and a large outdoor playground—rarities for an urban day care center. They have 2 infant rooms, accommodating 9 infants; 2 toddler rooms for 12; and several preschool rooms of 24 each. Parents of newborns are urged to apply for a space on the waiting list even before delivery. They have a limited number of subsidized spaces.

Civic Center Child Care
Corporation (C-5)

505 Van Ness Ave.

415-626-4880 (infant site)

www.c5children.org

Ages: 3-18 months

Child/caregiver ratios: 3:1 for infants, 3.5:1 for ages 19-24 months, and 4:1 for 25-36 months

Total number of children: 21

Located in the State of California Public Utilities Building, and close to the Civic Center, this day care center is open to the general public as well as state employees. C-5 prides itself on encouraging parental visits throughout the day. They also have a site for preschoolers (18 months to 5 years old) in the California State Building, 455 Golden Gate, 415-703-1277, where they have the capacity to take 16 toddlers and 25 to 30 preschoolers.

Easter Seals Healthy
Environments Child Development
Center

75 Hawthorne St.

415-744-8754

www.bayarea.easterseals.com

PARENT RATING: ☆ ☆ ☆ ☆

Ages: 6 weeks to 5 years

Child/caregiver ratios: 3:1 for infants (under 12 months), 4:1 (12-24 months), 6:1 for toddlers (25-36 months), 10:1 for preschoolers (3-5 years)

Total number of children: 80-90

This popular day care center is located one block from Moscone Center. The center is at full enrollment most of the time, resulting in a substantial waiting list. Many expecting parents apply and pay the $50 registration fee to get their names on the waiting list as soon as they know their due date. Part-time and full-time spaces are also offered for infants 2 to 3 days a week. Since the Government Services Administration provides space and supplies, priority is given to families employed by the federal government.

Katherine Michiels School

See in Ch. 10.

489

Marin Day Schools
www.marindayschools.org
PARENT RATING: ☆ ☆ ☆ ☆

Ages: Varies depending on campus

Child/caregiver ratios: Generally, 3:1 for infants (under 12 months), 4:1 for one-year-olds, 11:1 for 2-year-olds, and 10:1 for ages 3-5 (Sherith Israel Campus has some variations, see below.)

Total number of children: Varies depending on campus

Owned and operated by a national parent company, Bright Horizons, this is one of the largest private day care centers and preschools in the area, with more than 20 locations in the Bay Area. Some campuses take children as young as 3 months through 5 years, while others operate more as a preschool, taking children beginning at 2 years old. (See under Favorite Local Preschools in Ch. 10.) They offer year-round full-time and/or part-time care. They are notorious for being difficult to get into, especially for the infant day care programs at the downtown locations, and some of the preschool programs. Your best bet is to get on the waiting list before your baby is born! Some of these centers contract with local companies that give employees and their children preference. Marin Day School offers a limited number of "scholarships" to eligible families.

◆ Spear Street Campus
220 Spear St.
415-777-2081
Ages: 3 months to 4½ years old
Total number of children: 48
This campus offers an infant pro-gram for 12 and spaces for 36 older children. Corporate fees are available to PC World, Industry Standards, and Gap employees. Part-time spaces are available on a limited basis. Their facility includes a play yard, which is a rarity downtown.

◆ Hills Plaza Campus
2 Harrison St.
415-777-9696
Ages: 3 months to 5 years
Total number of children: 52
This campus has an infant program for 9 with a total of 52 children. Corporate fees are available to families employed by Gap, PC World, and Telespree. Part-time spaces are available on a limited basis.

◆ 221 Main St. Campus
415-495-1709
Ages: Infant through pre-k
Total number of children: 79-99
As this book goes to press, this facility is scheduled to open (fall 2005). While primarily intended for Gap, Inc. employees, it may offer some spaces to the community.

◆ San Francisco City Hall Campus
1 Dr. Carlton B. Goodlett Pl.
415-554-7560
Ages: 2 months to 5 years
Total number of children: 52
Located in City Hall, this campus largely serves families employed by the city. The infant program has a capacity of 9. Corporate rates are not available.

◆ Fox Plaza Campus
1390 Market St.
415-554-3979
Ages: 2-18 months
Total number of children: 12
This unique facility takes only 6 infants and shows preference for families working in the Fox Plaza building, mainly attorneys who work for the city.

◆ The Letterman Digital Arts Child Care Center (LDACC)
1 Letterman Dr., Bldg. B (The Presidio)
415-746-5444
Ages: infants through pre-k
Total number of children: 110
Primarily serving employees of Lucas Studios, this recently opened child care center (Summer 2005) is planning on a limited number of openings for the community for children ages 2 to 5.5 years old.

◆ Sherith Israel Campus (formerly California Street Campus)
2266 California St.
415-775-2211
Ages: 2-5 years
Child/caregiver ratios: 6:1 for 2-year-olds, 8:1 for 3-year-olds, and 9:1 for 4-year-olds and pre-kindergarten age
Total number of children: 175
The first of the 6 San Francisco locations of Marin Day Schools, this campus primarily operates as a preschool, taking children who are at least 2 years old by September of that school year. The 2's program is for 18 children. The overall facility serves 160 children, but since many of the preschoolers are on part-time schedules, typically there are no more than 90 to 95 children on-site at one time. See under Favorite Local Preschools in Ch. 10.

◆ Laurel Heights Campus
3333 California St.
415-775-2111
Ages: 3 months to 5 years
Total number of children: 130
This attractive facility was opened in 1999 and offers an infant program for 12 infants. Sixty percent of the spaces go to UCSF and USF families for whom corporate rates apply. Part-time spaces and fees are available.

South of Market Childcare at Yerba Buena Gardens
790 Folsom St.
415-820-3500
www.somacc.org
Ages: 3 months to 5/6 years
Child/caregiver ratios: 3:1 for infants, 4:1 for toddlers, and 8:1 for ages 4 to pre-kindergarten
Total number of children: 82

Opened in 1998, Yerba Buena is a large, attractive day care center. There is an infant program for 6 infants (3-18 months), a toddler program for 12 (18-36 months), and a preschooler program for 64 (3-5 years old). Competition for spaces in the small infant program is stiff. There also are a limited number of part-time spaces available. A subsidized program is located across the street at 366 Clementina St. (415-391-0389). Families must financially

491

qualify as low-income families to participate in this subsidized program.

St. Nicholas Child Care Center

5200 Diamond Heights Blvd.
415-550-1536
www.stnicholas-sf.com
Ages: 3 months to 5 years
Child/caregiver ratios: 4:1 for infants and 12:1 for toddlers and preschoolers
Total number of children: 90

St. Nicholas is a large child care center that has a full-time staff of 14. They offer care for an unusually large number of infants, serving 36 infants 3-24 months old. They also serve 16 toddlers ages 2-3; 21 preschoolers ages 3-4; and 16 preschoolers ages 4-5.

Tiny Giants Preschool and Child Care Center

See Ch. 10.

North Bay

Iniece Bailey Infant Toddler Center

100 Ebbtide Ave.
Sausalito
415-332-5698
Ages: 3-36 months
Child/caregiver ratios: 4:1
Total number of children: 60

This center offers full-time care with an infant program for 8, ages 3-15 months. Fees are determined on a sliding scale.

Belvedere Tiburon Childcare Center

1185 Tiburon Blvd.
Tiburon
415-435-4366
www.btccc.org
Ages: 2-8 years
Child/caregiver ratios: 6:1 for 2-3 years old, 12:1 for ages 4-5 years old, 12:1 for kindergarten age, and 14:1 for school age
Total number of children: 94

The Belvedere Tiburon Childcare Center (BTCC) is a private, nonprofit organization offering full- and part-time child care for up to 36 children, 2 years and up, as well as a pre-school program for children ages 3-5. The center also offers a drop-in program on a space-available basis. Parents need to have visited the center and filled out the necessary paperwork to be eligible for the drop-in program. All drop-in arrangements are to be made at least a day in advance. BTCC has a large outdoor area that features a play ship!

The Kid's Place

50 El Camino Dr.
Corte Madera
415-927-0498
www.kidsplaceofmarin.com
Ages: 6 weeks to 5 years old
Child/caregiver ratios: 4:1 infants (under 24 months) and 6:1 for ages 2-5
Total number of children: 50

This center offers full- and part-time infant, toddler, and preschool care, to age 5. The infant room has capacity for 16 infants (from 6 weeks to 2 years old).

Canal Childcare Center
215 Mission Ave.
San Rafael
415-457-1444
Ages: 3-8 years
Child/caregiver ratios: 8:1
Total number of children: 51

Part of Community Action Marin (an umbrella organization providing support to low-income families), this popular child care center caters mainly to working, low-income families. The center also offers after school care for school-age children. Fees are determined on a sliding scale.

Cradlerock Children's Center
642 Tiburon Blvd.
415-789-KIDS (5437)
www.cradlerockmusic.com/childcare

Cradlerock is really an in-home day care center, but given its uniqueness and the general shortage of quality day care in Southern Marin, we decided to include it here. They take newborns and are licensed to have up to 8 children. They offer art and music classes several times throughout the week, and plan on offering web cams, so you can check on your child throughout the day. See also in Ch. 7 under Music.

Creekside Village School
1787 Grant Ave.
Novato
415-898-7007
www.creeksidevillageschool.com
Ages: 6 weeks to 4 years, and kindergarten to first grade
Child/caregiver ratios: 4:1 (infants up to 18 months), 6:1 (18-24 months), 8:1 (2-year-olds), 10:1 (3-year-olds), 12:1 (4-year-olds), 14:1 (after school care)
Total number of children: 135

Located on a serene 2-acre property, Creekside offers care for 8 infants ages 6 weeks to 12 months. This center is also licensed for 18 one-year-olds, and the rest of the children are toddlers and preschoolers, up to age 4. Breakfast and a hot lunch are included in their fees, as well as special programs including Spanish instruction twice a week and music once a week. They offer flexible schedules, including part-time care for as few as 2 days, or 5-hour days. The summer program offers more organized outside activities and special entertainment.

Golden Poppy Preschool and Infant Center
50 El Camino Dr.
Corte Madera
415-924-2828
www.goldenpoppyschool.com
Ages: 6 weeks to 6 years
Child/caregiver ratios: 3:1 for infants under 12 months, 4:1 for ages 1-3, 6:1 for preschoolers (ages 3-6)
Total number of children: 130
PARENT RATING: ☆ ☆ ☆ ☆ ☆

This private day care center is licensed for 60 children in the infant and toddler center and 101 children in the preschool; however, they keep their numbers considerably lower, with caregiver to children ratios roughly twice what the state requires. They offer an infant and toddler program for 28 children up to 2 years old that includes 12 infants less than one year old and 16 children between one and 2 years old. When children reach age 2, they go to the pre-school. The preschool has eighteen 2-year-olds, twenty-four 3-year-olds, and twenty-four children ages 4 to 5 (pre-kindergarten). Golden Poppy offers full- and part-time spaces, including 2, 3, and 4 days of care a week, as well as a morning program and an extended care program. (These various schedules account for the overall total number of children.)

Marin Day School

For full description, see above under San Francisco. For other campuses, see Ch. 10.

◆ St. Vincent's Campus

#1 St. Vincent's Dr.
San Rafael
415-479-0531
Ages: 2 months to 5.5 years

◆ Downtown San Rafael

1123 Court St.
415-453-9822
Ages: 12 months to 5 years

Marin Jewish Community Center

200 N. San Pedro Rd.
San Rafael
415-479-2000
www.marinjcc.org
Ages: 3 months to 4 years
Child/caregiver ratios: 4:1 for infants and young toddlers, 6:1 for toddlers, and 7:1 for preschoolers
Total number of children: 140

Marin's JCC offers a popular infant and toddler full-day care program, known as kidcare. They offer care for 12 infants from 3 to 24 months and 18 toddlers ages 2-3. For children who are 3 years old by the early fall,

there is a preschool program and extended care. Applications for day care are taken throughout the year, and parents are advised to apply early.

Marin Lutheran Children's Center

649 Meadowsweet Dr.
Corte Madera
415-924-3792
Ages: 6 weeks to 3 years
Child/caregiver ratios: 4:1 for infants and 6:1 for toddlers
Total number of children: 38

This center offers care for up to 22 infants, although they prefer to keep it to 16, from ages 6 weeks to 2 years. They also offer care for 16 toddlers ages 18 months to 3 years. Part-time spaces are available on a limited basis, with a minimum of 2 full days a week.

Old Firehouse School

Mill Valley

This program accepts children as young as 13 months. For more information, see Ch. 10.

Robin's Nest Pre-School

www.robinsnestpre-schools.com/info.html

A popular and privately owned program, Robin's Nest was founded in 1985 in San Anselmo and now has 5 campuses in Marin and Sonoma counties. Admission is available year round as class openings permit, offering a morning, midday, and full-day program at most locations. Each is licensed to serve a different number of children. The Windsor location is the only campus offering child care for 8 infants, ages 14-24 months.

Robin's Nest locations also offer 3 or 4 days of care per week as well as flexible hours, including a morning program.

◆ **Mill Valley**
70 Lomita Dr.
415-388-5999
Ages: 2-6 years
Child/caregiver ratios: 7:1 for 2-year-olds, 7.5:1 for 3-year-olds, and 9:1 for 4-year-olds
Total number of children: 40

◆ **San Anselmo**
100 Shaw Dr.
415-459-4355
Ages: 2-5 years
Child/caregiver ratios: 6:1 for 2-year-olds, 8:1 for 3-5 years
Total number of children: 60

◆ **Windsor**
9451 Brooks Rd.
707-838-0549
Ages: 18 months to 8 years
Child/caregiver ratios: 4:1 for newborns (up to 12 months), 6:1 for 13-36 months, 12:1 for 30 months to 8 years
Total number of children: 120

East Bay

Association of Children's Services
3021 Brookdale Ave.
Oakland
510-261-1077
www.aocsweb.org
Ages: 2 weeks to 5 years
Child/caregiver ratios: 3:1 for newborns to 2 years, 4:1 for 2-3 years, 8:1 for 3-5 years
Total number of children: 85

The *Oakland Tribune* recently voted the Association of Children's Services (AOCS) (which sounds like more than one but is actually a single center) the best day care center in Oakland. Parents say that on average, the staff is better educated than at most other centers, with each program directed by an experienced teacher with a BA or an MA degree in early childhood development. Children over 30 months of age are expected to be part of the nursery school program. Depending on available space, you will either be notified of an opening or placed on the waiting list. If placed on the waiting list, it is recommended that you phone monthly to reconfirm your interest.

Bright Horizons Family Solutions
www.brighthorizons.com
One of the largest providers of employer-sponsored child care, Bright Horizons operates more than 325 child care centers worldwide. Many of their child care centers only accept families from the employers with whom they contract. However, some of their centers are open to the community, but they give preference to families employed by the corporate sponsor of these sites.

◆ **Garner Preschool**
2275 N. Loop Rd.
Alameda
510-769-5437
Ages: 2-5 years
Child/caregiver ratios: 8:1 for 2-4½ years and 10:1 for kindergarten age
Total number of children: 200

Child Care

The Child Day Schools

See Ch. 10. Call each campus for information on care for infants.

Child Educational Center

2100 Browning St.
Berkeley
510-548-1414

Ages: 3 months to 5 years

Child/caregiver ratios: 3:1 for infants (3-13 months), 4:1 for toddlers (13 months to 2 years), 5:1 for 2-year-olds, 7:1 for preschoolers (3½-4½ years), and 8:1 for pre-kindergarten (4½-5 years)

Total number of children: Not available.

CEC is a nonprofit day care center with attractive grounds and light and airy classrooms. The center is located 2 blocks from the North Berkeley BART station. Founded in 1981 by a group of parents, the center's board of directors is made up entirely of parents. CEC offers many scheduling options, and full- and part-time space and fees vary accordingly. See also Ch. 10.

Clark Kerr Infant Center

2900 Dwight Way (Building 5A)
Berkeley
510-642-9795
www.housingberkeley.edu/child/facstaff

Ages: 3 months to 31 months

Child/caregiver ratios: 3:1 for 3-24 months and 4:1 for 24-31 months

Total number of children: 24

UC Berkeley's child care facility opened in 1999 and primarily serves Berkeley faculty and staff families. They are licensed for 24 infants.

Cornerstone Children's Center

First Presbyterian Church
2407 Dana St.
Berkeley
510-848-6252
www.fpcberkeley.org/overview.asp

Ages: 6 weeks to 5 years

Child/caregiver ratios: 3:1 for infants up to 12 months, 4:1 for 1-2 years, 6:1 for 2-2½ years, and 8:1 for 2½-5 years

Total number of children: 88

Just 2 blocks away from the UC Berkeley campus, this popular day care center usually has a waiting list of 6 to 9 months. They offer care for 30 infants under 2 years and 58 children from 2 to 5 years.

Emeryville Child Development Center

1220 53rd St.
Emeryville
510-596-4343
www.ci.emeryville.ca.us/cdc

Ages: 18 months to kindergarten age

Child/caregiver ratios: 3:1 for under 12 months, 6:1 for 12-18 months, and 8:1 for 18 months to 5 years

Total number of children: 90

Owned and operated by the city of Emeryville, this day care center offers an infant program that has capacity for 13 babies who are less than 18 months old.

Mills College Children's School

See Ch. 10.

The Model School

2330 Prince St.
Berkeley
510-549-2711
www.themodelschool.org

Ages: 3 months to 5 years

Child/caregiver ratios: 3:1 for infants (3-14 months), 4:1 for toddlers (14-24 months), 5:1 for older toddlers (24-36 months), and 8:1 for pre-kindergarten ages

Total number of children: 90

The Model School is a leading day care and preschool. They embrace the teaching concepts of John Dewey and Maria Montessori, and parental participation is an important principle of the school. The child-to-caregiver ratios are considerably better than the standards set by the state of California.

Old Firehouse School

This center takes infants from 5 months and up. See Ch. 10.

Richmond Magic Years Children's Center

1221 Nevin Ave.
Richmond
510-970-7100

Ages: 3 months to 5 years

Child/caregiver ratios: 3:1 for infants (3-12 months), 4:1 for toddlers (13 months to 2 years), and 12:1 for preschoolers (3½-5 years)

Total number of children: 86

Magic Years is a nonprofit, private day care center offering day care for 16 infants under the age of 2 years, 12 toddlers ages 2-3 years, and 2 classrooms of 15 preschoolers, ages 3-4. A limited number of part-time spaces are available, and families employed by the federal government take priority.

Seedlings Preschool

This center takes infants from 6 months and up. See Ch.10.

St. John's Infant Center

22717 Garber St.
Berkeley
510-549-9342

Ages: 3 months to 3½ years

Child/caregiver ratios: 3:1 for 3-18 months, 4:1 for 18 months to 2½ years, and 5:1 for 2½-3½ years

Total number of children: 45

Largely subsidized by the church where it is housed, St. John's offers a popular child care program for up to 45 children, including 9 infants (up to 15 months old), and 15 "wobbly walkers," ages 15 months and up. They also offer early bird hours for an additional fee. Fees are both full pay and subsidized, with the subsidized fees being determined on a sliding scale, depending on a family's income. They often have a long waiting list of 12-18 months.

South Bay

Action Day Primary Plus

www.adnpp.com

Voted a "Family Favorite" by *Bay Area Parent* magazine in 2005, Action Day Primary Plus has been offering child care and educational services since 1968. Their philosophy features a "semi-structured" program, offering a variety of activities that mix play and learning in a nurturing environment. They have 10 infant and preschool centers located throughout Santa Clara Valley, including campuses accepting infants through the preschool years in Campbell, Mountain View, San Jose, Saratoga, and Willow Glenn. They also have a Santa Clara campus that accepts toddlers from age 18 months old and other campuses in Saratoga and San Jose for children who are at least 2 years old. For more information visit their website.

Bright Horizons Family Solutions

For full desciption, see under East Bay.

◆ **Bright Horizons at Cupertino**
10253 N. Portal Ave.
San Jose
408-366-1963
Ages: 6 weeks to pre-kindergarten
Child/caregiver ratios: 4:1 for infants 6 weeks to 2 years, 5:1 for 2-3 years, and 8:1 for 3 years through pre-kindergarten age
Total number of children: 24 infants (6 weeks to 24 months) and 72 children (ages 2 and up)
This center takes infants through preschoolers; the corporate sponsor here is Sun Microsystems.

◆ **The Tamien Childcare Center**
1197 Lick Ave.
San Jose
408-271-1980
Ages: 6 weeks to 12 years
Child/caregiver ratios: 7:2 for infants 6 weeks to 14 months, 4:1 for 14 months to 2 years, 6:1 for 2-3½ years, and 10:1 for ages 3½-5 and school-age children
Total number of children: 126
This center takes 111 infants through preschool ages; the remaining are school-age children. The corporate sponsor here is the Valley Transportation Authority.

California ChildCare Centers, Inc.

These day care centers are owned and operated by a parent company, Educational Pursuits Inc., which has been serving Bay Area parents since 1985. They possess memberships in the Professional Association of Child Educators (PACE), the National Association for the Education of Young Children (NAEYC), and the Child Care Coordinating Council.
www.educationalpursuits.com

◆ **Crystal Springs E.C.E. Center**
2145 Bunkerhill Dr.
San Mateo
650-572-1110
Ages: 2-5 years
Child/caregiver ratios: 12:1 for all ages
Total number of children: 36

◆ **Southgate Preschool**
1474 Southgate Ave.
650-755-8472
Daly City
Ages: 2-5 years
Child/caregiver ratios: 12:1 for all ages
Total number of children: 42

◆ **Community Preschool**
450 Chadbourne Ave.
Millbrae
650-652-4504
Ages: 2-5 years
Child/caregiver ratios: 12:1 for all ages
Total number of children: 43

◆ **Redwood Children's Center**
1445 Hudson St.
Redwood City
650-367-7374
Ages: 2-5 years

Child/caregiver ratios: 12:1 for all ages

Total number of children: 45

Children's Creative Learning Centers, Inc.

794 E. Duane Ave.
Sunnyvale
408-732-2288
www.cclcinc.com

Ages: Varies depending on site

Child/caregiver ratios: Varies depending on site

Total number of children: Varies depending on site

Founded in 1992, Children's Creative Learning Centers (CCLC) pride themselves on providing affordable quality child care to employers and families nationwide. They are based in Sunnyvale and serve the Peninsula and South Bay with sites in Palo Alto, Stanford, Los Altos, Sunnyvale, Redwood City, and San Jose. They also have corporate centers open only to families who are employees of Electronic Arts and Google.

The Children's Pre-School Center

4000 Middlefield Rd.
Palo Alto
650-493-5770
www.cpsccares.org

Ages: Newborn to 5 years

Child/caregiver ratios: 4:1 for infants and toddlers (under 2 years), 6:1 for older toddlers (2-3 years), and 9:1 for preschoolers (3-5 years)

Total number of children: 150

PARENT RATING: ☆ ☆ ☆ ☆ ☆

Since its opening in 1984 as the first corporate-sponsored day care program in the Bay Area, the Children's Pre-School Center has developed into a nationally accredited program serving more than 200 families. Priority is given to employees of corporate sponsors, including Roche, ALZA Corporation, Cooley Godward, and SAP, Inc. The Children's Pre-School Center offers care for infants to 5-year-olds. The Center usually has a substantial waiting list, especially for infants, as they take only 8 babies. The toddler program (1-2 years) consists of groups no larger than 12 children. Corporate-sponsored fees and part-time options are available.
Comment: "CPSC stood out as the most nurturing, well-run, happy, stimulating, and exciting environment we saw. . . . This is a wonderful environment for our daughter. She has been there since she was one year old and loves her teachers, her friends, the music program. . . . The teachers are caring and attentive. . . . I could go on and on."

Early Horizons

1510 Lewistown Rd.
Sunnyvale
408-746-3020
www.earlyhorizons.com

Ages: 2 months to 12 years

Child/caregiver ratios: 4:1 for infants under 2 years, 6:1 for 2-year-olds, 10:1 for 3- and 4-year-olds, and 14:1 for ages 5 and up

Total number of children: 210

Established in 1984, Early Horizons in Sunnyvale offers full- and part-time care, including 3-quarter days, half days, and a preschool session.

Child Care

Drop-In Child Care

What do you do when your primary child care arrangement is unavailable for a day or so? Perhaps your nanny is sick, the day care center is closed, or the weather is bad—if so, backup or drop-in care is what you need!

ChildrenFirst

- San Francisco
  Bank of America Building
  555 California St.
  415-392-7531
- Palo Alto
  3 Palo Alto Sq.
  3000 El Camino Real
  650-493-3777

PARENT RATING: ☆ ☆ ☆ ☆ ☆

Parents who work for participating companies can take advantage of a relatively new backup day care, run by ChildrenFirst, the only national company that exclusively specializes in backup child care. Exclusively corporate sponsored, ChildrenFirst offers care for well children from 12 weeks to 12 years of age. Parents must first register their children by bringing current medical records, photos of the family, and insurance and pediatrician information. Comments: "A very professionally run facility. . . .

I was impressed with the report of my son's day that I received when I picked him up. It told me exactly what he did, what activities and toys he played with, what he ate, how long he napped, and so on."

Core Group

See under Babysitting Services and Resources.

Marin Day Schools

Backup Relief Child Care
199 Fremont St.
San Francisco, 415-331-7766

This backup relief child care center, run by one of San Francisco's largest day care and preschools, works through corporate sponsorship. Participating companies purchase slots for their employees and their families. Please call for more information and to find out whether your or your spouse's company participates in this program.

Foster City Pre-School and Day Care Center

Charter Square Shopping Ctr.
1064F Shell Blvd.
Foster City
650-341-2041
www.fostercitypreschool.com/

Ages: 2-6 years

Child/caregiver ratios: 7:1 for 2-year-olds and 12:1 for 3- to 6-year-olds

Total number of children: 135

Serving the Foster City area since 1973, Foster City Pre-School and Day Care Center offers full-time care and part-time options of either 2 or 3 days a week. No infant care is available.

Hoover Children's Centers

2396 Evergreen Dr.
San Bruno
650-871-5025
www.hooverchildrenscenters.com

Ages: 2 months to preschool age

Child/caregiver ratios: 3:1 for infants 2-12 months, 4:1 for infants 12-18 months, 6:1 for toddlers 18 months to 2½ years, and 12:1 for preschoolers

Total number of children: 100

The Hoover Center is a large full-service day care center offering parents many scheduling options. They also have other locations in Millbrae, Redwood City, Daly City, and San Mateo. Visit their website for ages of children in each program. A $100 registration fee (which does not apply to the first month's tuition) must accompany your application.

Jewish Community Center of Silicon Valley

14855 Oak Rd.
Los Gatos
408-358-5939
www.sanjosejcc.org

As this book goes to press, the JCC plans to open a small child care center, for ages 18-30 months, for full-time care, geared to working parents. The ratio of caregiver to child will be 1:4, and they will have their own classroom with a play yard.

Marin Day Schools

See above under San Francisco.

◆ Redwood City Campus
403 Winslow Street
Redwood City

(650) 363-4939

Ages: 2 months to 5 years

Child/caregiver ratios: 3:1 for infants, 4:1 for toddlers

Total number of children: 92

◆ EFI Campus
301 Velocity Way
Foster City
(650) 357-4250

Ages: 2 months to 5 years

Child/caregiver ratio: infant 3:1; toddler 4:1; younger preschool 7:1, older preschool 10:1

Total number of children: 120

This campus is corporate sponsored by the company, EFI, but is also open to the community.

Palcare

945 California Dr.
Burlingame
650-340-1289
www.palcare.org

Ages: 3 months to 5 years

Child/caregiver ratios: 4:1 for infants, 6:1 for toddlers (ages 2-3 years), and 8:1 for preschoolers (ages 3-5 years)

Total number of children: 263

Palcare's flexible and unique hours cater to parents who have nontraditional or changing work schedules. Parents can request a customized schedule each month, rotating their days as their work schedule dictates. Fifty percent of Palcare's enrollment is reserved for families employed at the San Francisco Airport. Other special employers also have priority because of their annual contributions. Palcare offers care for 2 rooms of 16 infants each, 3-24 months. They also offer 2 rooms of 18 toddlers each, ages 2-3 years, and 3 large rooms of

20 to 30 preschoolers, ages 3-5 years. Palcare uses an unusual graduated rate system in which the hourly rates go down as you use more hours per month. Fees are based on your monthly hours and your child's age. In addition, there is an annual registration fee of $150 per child.

Palo Alto Community Childcare
3990 Ventura Ct.
Palo Alto
650-493-2361
www.paccc.com

This private nonprofit organization runs 17 day care centers in the Palo Alto area, 3 of which take infants. Each center has its own name and license to operate. Call or visit their website for information on specific centers.

Well Infant Care Center (part of Under the Weather)
2612 South El Camino Real
San Mateo
650-212-5439
See under Sick Child Care.

Sick Child Care

It's always smart to make arrangements for emergency and backup care before you really need it. Typically, you need to have visited and registered with a center to receive backup or drop-in care. Childcare Resource and Referral agencies in your county can help you find a family day care or day care center when you need temporary backup help with a sick child. Most nanny agencies also handle temporary sick child care. In addition, here are a few sick child care programs that we've heard about:

Wheezles and Sneezles
1108F San Pablo Ave.
Albany
510-526-SICK (7425)
Wheezles and Sneezles helps when your child has a mild illness that keeps her out of school or child care but is not serious enough to keep a parent home from work. The staff and an on-site nurse look after up to 10 children a day (from infants to 12 years old).

A registered nurse screens children as they come in each morning. A nurse on staff will administer the child's medication, offer him quiet activities, story time, and of course, a

scheduled nap. They also offer an in-home service for infants or children who are contagious or bedridden. Fees are reasonable and are on a sliding scale.

The "Get Well Room" at the Fairfax/San Anselmo Children's Center
199 Porteous Ave.
Fairfax
415-454-1811
www.fsacc.org
This day care center offers care for mildly ill children ages 3 months to 10 years who are enrolled in the center as well as for those who are not. Prior

registration and a visit to the center are prerequisites to using the service, as well as immunization records and a physician's report. All children who are not enrolled for child care at the center must be seen by their nurse or doctor each day that they attend the Get Well Room. To be seen, you need to call ahead and make an appointment during the period from 7:30 to 9:30 a.m., when the nurse is on call. You can call the day before or that morning to schedule the appointment. If your child is seen by his or her own pediatrician, they can be taken in at any time during the day on a space-available basis. Generally, enrollment in the Get Well Room is limited to 6 children. They are open September to June. Fees are $20 for a half-day and $40 for a full day.

Under the Weather

2612 South El Camino Real
San Mateo
650-212-KIDZ (5439)
866-455-5439
www.under-the-weather.com

This center, specifically designed for mildly ill children, welcomes children aged 2 months to 12 years. Children must be pre-registered. The center is designed to prevent cross-contamination of illnesses while keeping in mind the developmental needs of a variety of age groups. They have 3 rooms, each designed for specific illnesses and symptoms. The children are assigned to a room and then placed in a group with children of similar age. A pediatric registered nurse, on the premises at all times, assesses each child upon arrival and throughout the day. An individualized plan of care is developed and implemented for each child. After a child is accepted into care, a pager is assigned to each parent so they can be contacted if needed. Family memberships as well as corporate memberships are available. In early 2002, Under the Weather opened a Well Infant Care Center at the same address in San Mateo. It accommodates 8 infants ages 2 months to 2 years.

Hiring an In-Home Care Provider

Hiring someone to take care of your child in your home while you are at work is an overwhelming task, both emotionally and practically. Basically, you have 2 choices—conduct the search yourself or enlist the support of an agency. For a fee an agency will provide you with appropriate candidates and will do the initial screening such as confirming their legal status (that candidates are eligible to work in the United States) and ensuring that the candidates have previous professional experience, including checking references. Since nannies are typically women, in this book we refer to a nanny as a "she." Please note, however, that male nannies do exist—approximately 3% of the nanny work force in the Bay Area are males. They seem to be especially popular with families with boys.

CONDUCTING THE SEARCH YOURSELF

With in-home care, the search and selection process for the right caregiver is obviously critical. There are myriad books, experts, and other resources available (a few are mentioned in this chapter or listed in the bibliography). One source we found particularly helpful is *Finding a Nanny for Your Child in the San Francisco Bay Area* by Alyce Desrosiers.

We heard from many parents how they went about conducting their search for an in-home child care provider; these are some of the basic steps that they took. Of course, there are other ways to conduct a search too. And no matter how systematized many parents are about collecting and analyzing information about prospective candidates, many say that they really just "knew" when they found the provider who was right for them. The process is as much an art as a science. One mother described it as a kind of "gestalt," and another described it as akin to dating, and said "you know when you've met her." Even so, most parents will agree that while instincts are helpful, a well-planned strategy and search method will help you make your ultimate decision with confidence.

Writing a Job Description

If you decide to conduct the search yourself, you'll first need to write a job description. The job description should include care-giving responsibilities (including the age of your child or children and where you live), housekeeping responsibilities (if any), and hours, and list the salary range and benefits. You may also want to include specific qualifications such as training, education, and prior experience as well as legal status, languages spoken, CPR and first aid certification. Before writing the job description, you should assess your schedule and your child's daily routine (which of course will be changing from month to month if your child is an infant) to best articulate the requirements of the position. When writing the job description, be as specific as possible.

Announcing Your Job Opening

Get the word out through family, friends, and colleagues, and via newspapers, bulletin boards at local parenting organizations, local colleges, and various child and parenting centers. Some centers, such as Parents Place in San Francisco and Bananas in the East Bay, have entire walls devoted to bulletin boards for parents and potential nannies to place ads. You can also ask about placing your ad in churches and temples or schools, especially nursing schools. Be as specific as possible in your ad in terms of what you need (such as days, hours, language skills, and other qualifications). This may help reduce the volume of unqualified callers.

BULLETIN BOARDS AND BINDERS WITH CHILD CARE LISTINGS

The Bay Area has many child care bulletin boards and parenting centers that maintain binders, all of which provide the opportunity for parents seeking child care and child care providers seeking employment to connect with one another. Many offer bulletin boards as a public service while others charge a nominal fee for posting your ad. Be aware that most of the organizations that host such bulletin boards only do that—they offer no screening, recommendations, or referrals of the candidates. Still, if you are willing to do all the screening and reference checks, these information sources can be a parent's best friend:

San Francisco

Alliance Française
1345 Bush St.
415-775-7755
This well-known French language school hosts a bulletin board with a variety of items, including some child care ads, typically of bilingual nannies and babysitters.

DayOne
3490 California St., 2nd Fl., Ste. 203 (entrance on Locust)
415-440-Day1 (3291)
www.dayonecenter.com

This wonderful state-of-the-art parent resource center offers free referrals in binders for nannies, as well as other care providers, including childbirth and postpartum care doulas.

Natural Resources
816 Diamond St.
415-550-2611
PARENT RATING: ☆ ☆ ☆ ☆ ☆

Natural Resources is a pregnancy, childbirth, and parenting center that offers all sorts of resources, products, and services to parents, including a regular newsletter that includes some child care provider listings. Your best bet is to go there and look through the binders with current listings of nannies and babysitters seeking employment; parents say that they are great resources!

Parents Place

1710 Scott St.
415-359-2454
www.jfcs.org

PARENT RATING: ☆ ☆ ☆ ☆

Parents Place, a Jewish and Family Children's Services program, has the most extensive child care resource bulletin board in town! While over-whelming at first, a large board lists available nannies and babysitters seeking employment. For a nominal fee, you can place an advertisement on pre-printed index cards with your particulars (days and times needed, and the number and ages of your children). There is no screening of candidates, although some of the nannies have also joined up with nanny agencies. They also have an electronic bulletin board on their website. Comments: "Really hit or miss . . . our first nanny was great, not worthwhile since. . . . Good, but not always updated. . . . Great resources, but you have to filter through a lot of chaff and need to check references carefully."

Peek-a-Boutique

1306 Castro St.
415-641-6192

This popular children's resale shop hosts a community bulletin board containing some child care ads.

California Pacific Medical Center

Newborn Connections
3698 California St.
415-600-BABY (2229)

Newborn Connections has a resource binder that includes child care referrals.

North Bay

Marin Jewish Community Center

200 North San Pedro Rd.
San Rafael
415-479-2000

This center has a large bulletin board with postings of nannies looking for employment and parents looking for nannies.

Parents Place Marin

600 5th Ave.
San Rafael
415-491-7959
www.jfcs.org

Parents Place Marin moved into a new building in 2002, where they offer more services and programs, including a large bulletin board that features advertisements for nannies and babysitters. The aim is to have a similar size board with as many postings as their popular San Francisco location.

Canal Community Alliance

91 Larkspur St.
San Rafael
415-454-2640
415-454-3967 (fax)

The Canal Community Alliance, a social service organization that aims to help low-income residents in the Canal neighborhood of San Rafael, has a bulletin board that contains postings and notices for various employment opportunities. You may fax your posting to the number listed above.

Bananas

5232 Claremont Ave.
Berkeley
510-658-7101 (child care resources center)
510-658-0381 (child care referral)

PARENT RATING: ☆ ☆ ☆ ☆ ☆

Bananas is a nonprofit child care referral agency for Alameda County residents. You will get better information and be less frustrated if you visit Bananas rather than call. They have cards with each child care provider's information (such as address, schedule, and available space) that you can match up to maps, which they have there.

Peninsula Parents Place

410 Sherman Ave.
Palo Alto
650-688-3040
www.jfcs.org

They have a child care bulletin board that includes child care wanted and offered, including shared care opportunities. Preprinted index cards are provided for you to complete, describing the job, which are then posted. If you wish to place an ad, you need to go in person, as information is not taken over the phone.

YMCA

3412 Ross Rd.
Palo Alto
650-856-9622

They have a good bulletin board with ads for babysitters and nannies.

NEWSPAPERS

Newspapers are another great way to advertise your child care needs. Both nannies in need of work and parents in need of child care advertise in these papers. However, do your homework—screen carefully and check references thoroughly. If you decide to run an ad, be as specific as possible about the days of the week and times and the age(s) of your child or children. You might also set up a voice mailbox where you reiterate your specific criteria and urge people to leave a message only if they meet your criteria.

El Mensajero, 415-206-7230
France Today, Journal Français,
    415-921-5100
    www.discoverfrance.net
Hokubei Mainichi, 415-567-7323

Irish Herald, 415-665-6653
Marina Times, 415-928-0968
Noe Valley Voice, 415-821-3324
The Philippine News, 650-872-3000
Potrero View, 415-824-7516
San Francisco Chronicle,
    415-777-7777

Nannies

507

The Ark Newspaper, 415-435-2652 (Tiburon)

Classified Gazette, 415-457-4151 (San Rafael)

Family News, 415-492-1022

Marin Independent Journal, 415-883-8666 (Novato)

Marin Scope Newspapers (*Marin Scope, Mill Valley Herald, Twin City Times, Ross Valley Reporter, News Pointer*), 415-339-8510

Napa Valley Register, 707-226-3711

Pacific Sun Weekly, 415-383-4500

San Francisco Chronicle, 415-777-7777

East Bay

Contra Costa Newspapers (*Montclarion, Piedmonter, Berkeley Voice, Contra Costa Times, San Ramon Valley Times, West Coast Times, Oakland Hills El Cerrito Journal, Alameda Journal*), 510-339-8777

East Bay Express, 510-879-3700

The Daily Planet, 510-841-5600

The Oakland Tribune, 800-595-9595

UC Berkeley Daily Californian, 510-548-8300

Vallejo Times Herald, 707-644-1141

South Bay

El Observador, 408-938-1700

Los Altos Town Crier, 650-948-9000

Pacifica Tribune, 650-359-6666

Palo Alto Weekly, Mountain View Voice, and *The Almanac*, 650-326-8210

Palo Alto Daily News, 650-327-6397, ext. 301

San Jose Mercury News, 408-920-5111

San Jose Metro, 408-298-8000

San Mateo Daily Journal, 650-344-5200

San Mateo Times, 650-348-4459

Stanford Daily Newspaper, 650-723-2555

BEST WEBSITES FOR CHILD CARE SEARCHES

Bay Area Sitters

www.bay-area-sitters.com

This free message board for the Bay Area helps connect parents and nannies and babysitters.

Craigslist

www.craigslist.org

PARENT RATING: ☆ ☆ ☆ ☆ ☆

This is a free community-based bulletin board. Look under child care for job listings. Many parents report great success in finding child care, both live-in and live-out, on this website. Be aware, though, that like many internet sites, it does not screen candidates.

Department of Social Services, Community Care Licensing

http://ccld.ca.gov/docs/links.htm#childcare

This California Social Services Department website offers all sorts of valuable information about finding child care, including links to other sites that will provide you with names and numbers of day care and family day care centers in your area.

www.GoNannies.com

This national website offers a database of more than 3,000 candidates in the United States who are looking for domestic employment such as child care.

www.NannyLocators.com

This user-friendly website offers classified ads for nannies by state and locale.

www.Nannies4Hire.com

This website offers a searchable database of nanny candidates, complete with specifications such as full- or part-time, live-in or live-out, etc.

Parent Watch

www.parentwatch.com

This site helps child care providers and parents with child care needs find each other. It also has a search engine that locates day care centers by typing in a zip code.

Parents Place

www.jfcs.org

Parents Place offers an online child care bulletin board for families and caregivers. Caregivers can submit (for free) "position wanted" listings, and for $20 families can submit "caregiver wanted" listings. Both parents and caregivers can browse through listings already posted. Listings run for 30 days from the time they are posted. Parents Place does NOT run any form of background or reference checks on either the families or the caregivers who post listings on this bulletin board, nor do they confirm the accuracy of the information they post. Parents Place recommends that both families and caregivers run their own background and reference checks on any candidates that interest them. See also under Bulletin Boards and Binders with Child Care Listings—San Francisco.

UC Berkeley Parents Network

http://parents.berkeley.edu

PARENT RATING: ☆ ☆ ☆ ☆ ☆

This extensive site offers more advice and recommendations than you'll ever need on almost every aspect of parenting. You can sign up to receive the online newsletter, where you can post child care want ads on the parent-run e-mail list. Parents frequently post available caregivers that they personally recommend. Originally intended for parents who either work or are students at UCB, the list has grown to include many others who live in the Berkeley area.

4nannies

www.4nannies.com

Serving San Francisco, for a fee this service provides access to an online directory of hundreds of nannies looking for immediate employment. Candidates' resumes expire after 30 days. If you use this service, you arrange and run background checks yourself.

Legal Child Care Issues

Remember that if you hire in-home care, you may be deemed an employer and be subject to various federal and state laws. We have listed some things you should know as an employer, but be sure to check with a legal or tax professional before you hire—laws are always changing!

- California law requires you to pay an employee a minimum wage of $8.50 per hour.
- If you pay a single caregiver $1,400 or more in a calendar year (in 2005), you are considered an employer and are required by the IRS to pay federal and state employment taxes. (See IRS publication #926.)
- The Internal Revenue Service's Kit 942 includes everything you need for domestic employees. Call 800-TAX-FORM (800-829-3676).
  - Publication 503: Child and Dependent Care Expenses
  - Publication 923: Employment Taxes for Household Employees
  - Form 942: Employer's Quarterly Tax Return for Household Employees
  - Publication 15, Circular E: Employer's Tax Guide
  - Form 941 or 940 EZ: Federal Unemployment Tax
- Household employers are required to file IRS Schedule H with their personal income tax return. They can either make estimated tax payments using IRS 1040 ES estimated tax payment voucher, or they can elect to have additional federal income taxes withheld and file schedule H at the end of the year with their own personal income tax form.
- In-home employees may ask you to withhold state income taxes from their paychecks and forward it to their state. This is not a requirement but something you may discuss with your employee.
- An employee must be provided with a W-2 form for the previous year's earnings by January 31.
- As an employer, you must verify the identity and legal status of your employee and pay employment taxes. Both you and the caregiver are required to sign a Form I-9 from the U.S. Department of

Homeland Security's Bureau of U.S. Citizenship and Immigration Services (USCIS) verifying that the employee is eligible to work in the United States. These forms require that you, the employer, have your employee submit to you relevant documentation of her identity and employment eligibility in the U.S. You may obtain this form either by downloading it from the USCIS website at www.uscis.gov or by calling the USCIS at 800-870-3676. You may also want to obtain a copy of the Handbook for Employers (Form M-274) which includes Form I-9. (You may also download this form from www.uscis.gov or call the above toll-free number.) You will also need to contact the Internal Revenue Service and ask for Publication #926, the Household Employer's Tax Guide, at 800-TAX-FORM. You may also download this publication from the IRS website at www.irs.gov/publications/p926.

◆ All employers in the state of California are required to report information about new employees to the California New Employment Registry at 916-657-0529.

◆ The state of California requires that you provide your caregiver with worker's compensation insurance. (Contact your insurer about coverage under an existing homeowner's insurance or tenant's insurance policy. Alternatively, the California State Compensation Insurance Fund may be reached at 415-974-8000.) Also, talk to your insurer about potential liability if your caregiver is watching someone else's child in your home. If your caregiver will be driving, you'll need to confirm that she has adequate insurance coverage if she is using her car. (If driving your car, she'll need to be added to your policy.)

INTERVIEWING CANDIDATES AND CONDUCTING BACKGROUND CHECKS

The Telephone Interview

As you receive calls from prospective candidates responding to your ad, use the telephone to screen applicants. This will help save you from wasting invaluable time by meeting with inappropriate people. If possible, set aside a quiet time (when baby is napping) to return calls so that you can focus your attention on the applicants. As you speak with each one, describe the responsibilities, hours, and days needed to see whether these suit the applicant. Then ask the applicant about her qualifications, previous work experience, why she is looking for work right now (and why she left her most recent position), CPR and first aid certifications, and salary expectations. You may also want to ask whether or not she has tuberculosis and hepatitis screening certificates.

Some parents find it helpful to have a form that they have prepared in advance, and use it throughout the interviewing process, to help develop a profile on each candidate. Others are more comfortable just talking on the phone and taking notes as they go along. If you decide to use a form, it might include the following categories for you to fill in with the information you collect as you go through the interviewing process with each candidate:

- Name, address, telephone number, and e-mail address
- Education, experience, and training
- Legal status
- Health and safety certificates
- Description of last position and reasons for leaving
- Gaps in employment
- Jobs that didn't work and why
- Personality and fit with your child
- Understanding of children
- Ability to communicate with you
- Child care approaches and philosophies (for instance, whether she embraces feeding on demand or on schedule, how comfortable she is with handling breast milk, if applicable, how she handles a crying baby, how she feels about having your child nap on a regular schedule, and so on)
- Approach to discipline

If you are interested in an applicant, request the names of her 3 most recent employers. Unlike other jobs that you may have hired for, you will want to check references at the beginning of this process rather than at the end. If she cannot provide you with references, don't even consider her.

MEETING AND INTERVIEWING POTENTIAL CAREGIVERS

After the telephone interview and screening of potential candidates, and reference checks, schedule a round of initial interviews in person. Ask each candidate to bring copies of her resume, visa (if applicable), certificates, and licenses. Use this interview to evaluate each applicant's work experience, personality and character, and fit with your child. If your child is one year old or younger, you may want to consider having the first interview without your child so that you can focus your attention on the applicant. Invite back those candidates you are most comfortable with and impressed by for a second interview.

During the second interview continue your previous discussion. Have your candidates meet your child and observe their interaction. You may want your spouse or partner to meet the candidates at this time as well. After this interview, you should be down to one or 2 potential candidates. Invite them back for a third and final interview in which you continue to assess their overall match with your child. This interview may be a half-day working interview in which you offer to pay the applicants for their time.

CHECKING REFERENCES

Check references carefully. Make sure they are authentic. Also, if an applicant tells you that a recent employer has moved away or has an unlisted number, request other references from that job (such as a neighbor who may have known the family she worked for). For each reference get the following information:

- Full name
- How the applicant knows the reference
- Current address
- Current work and home telephone numbers

CONDUCTING BACKGROUND CHECKS

The TrustLine Registry
800-822-8490
www.TrustLine.org

Conducting a background check can confirm that a candidate is who she says she is and that she has no history of substantiated child abuse or neglect on record in California. TrustLine is the California state registry of in-home child care providers who have passed a background screening. The screening includes a review of records of criminal convictions and substantiated allegations of child abuse and neglect maintained by the California Department of Justice. It also screens for records of any federal crimes maintained by the Federal Bureau of Investigation. If nothing disqualifying comes up, the individual is listed as "cleared" and is placed on the TrustLine registry.

One of the shortcomings of this system is that, apart from records of federal crimes, the search of state court records is limited to those of the state of California. So, in theory someone with a prior conviction in another state could actually "clear" the TrustLine process. Also, TrustLine does not include a review of an applicant's driving record, unless something shows up in the criminal justice system review, such as a DUI.

Ideally, the TrustLine screening process would be completed before, or immediately after, the nanny has started work. Despite recent progress with expediting this process, it often takes longer than expected. Another of the shortcomings of the TrustLine process is that a nanny is registered and listed on TrustLine as soon as she clears the California checks which can take anywhere from 3 weeks to 3 months. Since the FBI check takes even longer, a nanny can initially clear the California portion of the screening and be TrustLine registered before the FBI check is completed.

In operation since 1989, TrustLine is managed by the California State Department of Social Services (CDSS). CDSS contracts with the California Child Care Resource and Referral Network to provide access to the database through a toll-free number, listed above. Roughly 10% of those undergoing background checks do not clear, some because of repetitive misdemeanors, but some because of very serious criminal convictions including murder and kidnapping. Staff at the TrustLine office will tell you only if your candidate doesn't clear the background check, not why, because of confidentiality laws. Since 1994, nanny agencies are required by California state law to initiate the TrustLine process upon placement of a nanny in a position. Some agencies pay for this service, which costs $124. If a nanny or potential nanny tells you that she is TrustLine registered, you should call 800-822-8490 for confirmation.

Nannies, au pairs, and babysitters hired outside a nanny agency are not required to register with TrustLine, but you may certainly ask your candidate to do so. Who pays for this service is negotiated between you and your nanny. The nanny or babysitter will need to complete a one-page application form and have her fingerprints taken. Call the Trustline registry to request the application form and to find out where your nanny can go to get fingerprinted. Applicants need a California driver's license, a California I.D. card, a photo I.D. card from a state other than California, or an Alien Registration Card (green card) to register.

PRIVATE BACKGROUND INVESTIGATIONS

There are also private companies that specialize in conducting background checks for nannies and other in-home caregivers. Be sure to obtain a candidate's driving record, even if you are not planning on having her drive your child.

PFC Information Services

6114 La Salle Ave., Ste. 638
Oakland
510-653-5061
www.pfcinformation.com
PARENT RATING: ☆ ☆ ☆ ☆ ☆

This public filing service works nationally with nanny agencies and parents to provide comprehensive background checks of caregivers. Owned by Lynn Peterson, a former owner of a nanny placement agency, the service is more comprehensive than the state-mandated TrustLine registry. They cover criminal records for felonies and/or misdemeanors in any jurisdiction or state; DMV reports for suspensions, license revocations, and moving violations (including DUIs); credit reports verifying an applicant's prior addresses and employment, and identifying excessive debts or collections; and a Social Security Scan, which verifies an applicant's Social Security number.

PFC Information Services, Inc. has a very strong reputation. They pride themselves on providing details that TrustLine does not. Their searches are done manually, which they believe is more thorough than a computer search. This check takes roughly 3 to 7 days to complete. Nannies must provide a signed authorization to run a background check. 5% to 7% of PFC's background checks for nannies come back showing significant negative items on a nanny's record.

Know Your Nanny

20 Oxford Rd.
Jackson, NJ 08527
888-692-2291
www.knowyournanny.com
Know Your Nanny assists parents all over the United States with the process of screening, hiring, and monitoring in-home child care providers, including offering background checks

and renting and selling surveillance equipment such as the "nanny cam" (these allow you to see how your nanny and child spend the day).

Paula Drake Investigations

P.O. Box 51622
Palo Alto
650-857-9465
www.siliconvalleypi.com

Paula Drake Investigations is a full-service agency that has been serving the Bay Area since 1994. It offers "unrivalled service throughout California and beyond for all your investigative needs," including thorough background checks for nannies as well as nanny camera surveillance.

Online Resources for Background Checks

www.USSearch.com

This website offers a range of background checks, including a nanny screening service for a flat fee.

www.ChoiceTrust.com

This website checks a proprietary criminal records database, court records, and Social Security numbers for a flat fee.

www.MyBackgroundCheck.com

This company does most of its background checks for Fortune 100 and 500 companies, and also offers background checks to individuals seeking employment. They pride themselves on their efficient and timely system which usually takes 1-3 days.

www.theapna.org

This is the website of the Alliance of Professional Nanny Agencies which includes current information about the nanny placement industry

www.nannynetwork.com

For a flat fee, this website offers background investigations that include a 7-year Social Security number trace and a single jurisdiction criminal records search. You may also include sex offender registries, national criminal records locator searches, aliases, and DMV records searches. Results are usually available in 2 to 3 working days. Parents are quite pleased with this service.

TIP: Many mothers' groups have active e-mail groups and informative newsletters for their members that contain useful classifieds for sitters, nannies, and other forms of child care. In most cases, other moms place the ads, recommending people who have worked for them. One of the best child care classified sections that we have seen among such newsletters is that of the *Neighborhood Parents Network* (formerly Neighborhood Moms), based in the East Bay. Call 510-527-MOMS to inquire about membership and their newsletter.

FINAL DETAILS

Once you have hired a caregiver, you are required by the INS to confirm your caregiver's identity and employment eligibility. In order to do this you will need Form I-9 from the INS (employment eligibility form), which explains what documents (e.g., passport, visas, and a driver's license) your caregiver needs to submit to you. See above under Legal Child Care Issues.

As a final step, you may want to draft and sign an agreement. Such an agreement clarifies roles, responsibilities, and expectations, and can prevent misunderstandings. It may also include a trial period, allowing either party to terminate the agreement within a certain period of time. Other things that you may include in such an agreement include the following:

◆ Term of employment (beginning date and ending date)
◆ Work schedule
◆ Specific duties
◆ Compensation and pay schedule
◆ Benefits (such as medical, vacation, and telephone use). Some parents find it to their benefit to provide health insurance for their caregivers, since it is often viewed as an incentive for caregivers to provide long-term care. Basic health insurance for caregivers can cost anywhere from $70 to $250 monthly.
◆ Conditions and terms for termination
◆ Confidentiality regarding personal and family information
◆ Performance review dates and frequency

Nanny Tax and Payroll Services

As an employer of an in-home child care provider, you are responsible for taking care of the related payroll and tax matters. You are responsible for complying with IRS and state tax laws, attending to payroll issues such as sick, vacation, and personal time tracking, and preparing and filing taxes for your care provider. Since these details can be time consuming, some families opt for professional assistance in this area. Here are a few resources that we've heard about:

Accuchex

365 Bel Marin Keys Blvd.
Novato
415-883-7733
www.accuchex.com

This company specializes in household payroll and tax services, and will do quarterly filings.

Breedlove and Associates

5300 Bee Caves Rd., Bldg. 1, Ste. 200
Austin, TX 78746
888-breedlove (888-273-3356)
www.breedlove-online.com

PARENT RATING: ☆ ☆ ☆ ☆ ☆

Breedlove is a national company specializing in nanny payroll tax services for household employers, processing about $100 million of payroll annually for busy families, including many in the Bay Area. They have been featured in *The Wall Street Journal, Forbes, Kiplinger's, The New York Times,* and *Business Week.*
Comment: "Extremely helpful, always call back and are available to answer questions."

California State Employment Development Department

www.edd.ca.gov

One of the largest departments in the state government of California, this agency has offices throughout the Bay Area. Visit their website to find your closest office. They offer free seminars on payroll and tax issues for domestic employers, and you may also obtain the state-required registration forms for new employees here, or download them from their website.

Crown Bookkeeping and Payroll Services

1733 Woodside Rd., #205
Redwood City
650-365-5005

This agency offers domestic employer tax and payroll services.

Essentia Software

888-999-1722 or 601-582-0669
www.essentia-soft.com

This company offers NannyPay 99, a Windows-based payroll program designed to calculate your nanny's taxes.

Gibbs Bookkeeping and Tax Service

344 20th St.
Oakland
510-893-8304

Greenberg and Greenberg

2090 Chestnut St.
San Francisco
415-775-9503

This is a small and successful local tax service whose clients are mainly neighborhood businesses and families.

GTM Associates

16 Computer Dr. W.
Albany, NY 12205
888-432-7972
www.gtmassociates.com

PARENT RATING: ☆ ☆ ☆ ☆ ☆

GTM provides household payroll and tax services all over the country and is a recognized leader in its field. They provide free over-the-phone advice and have a resourceful website that features a "nanny tax resource center."

Home/Work Solutions

2 Pidgeon Hill Dr., #210
Sterling, VA 20165
www.4nannytaxes.com

They are one of the nation's leading providers of household payroll and employment tax preparation services, specializing in nanny tax compliance. Parents rave about their website!

NannyTax, Inc.

51 East 42nd Street - Ste. 601
New York, NY
Tel: 888-NANNYTAX (626-69829)
www.nannytax.com

NannyTax, Inc. provides "complete tax compliance services, from assistance in obtaining federal identification numbers and Social Security numbers to quarterly and annual filings." Based in New York, they say that all the work can be done on the phone.

Internal Revenue Service

800-829-1040 (24-hour recording)
800-829-3676 (forms and publications)
www.irs.gov

The IRS publishes a Household Employers Tax Guide that provides all the forms you need for household employment tax matters. You can also download this publication from their website.

Legally Nanny

37 Trailwood
Irvine
714-336-8864
www.legallynanny.com

"All the legal and tax help you need to hire a nanny legally," is the motto of this one-stop solution for all your legal and tax needs related to hiring a nanny. They will fill out every federal and state form you need; advise you about registration, immigration, and insurance requirements; show you how to make tax payments and withhold taxes; and maximize your tax savings and more.

One Stop Payroll

620 Contra Costa Blvd., Ste. 215
Pleasanton
800-788-2088

This company offers domestic employer tax and payroll services.

SurePay

1880 Pleasant Valley Ave.
Oakland
877-787-3729

Although located in the East Bay, this company primarily serves clients in San Francisco, including domestic employers.

PayCycle

210 Portage Avenue
Palo Alto
866-PAYCYCLE (729-2925)
www.paycycle.com

This company started out offering household payroll products for families with nannies. Even though they now focus on small business owners, they still offer household services for a reasonable flat fee.

Nannies

519

Insurance and Financial Products for Nannies

Eisenberg Associates
1340 Newton Centre
Newton, MA 02459
617-964-4849 or 800-777-5765
www.eisenbergassociates.com
This official insurance representative of the International Nanny Association offers short-term and permanent health insurance, life insurance, disability coverage, and so on.

Nanny Agencies and Resource Centers

In return for a fee, agencies can take care of most of the search process for you. They typically ask you to provide them with information on your ideal caregiver by filling out a detailed questionnaire that includes job description details such as salary, responsibilities, and hours. Based on this information, they provide you with candidates that they prescreen. They may do basic research that includes background checks of criminal records, legal status, and language proficiency. They also usually contact references and may provide you with a set of written comments based on telephone interviews of the candidate's previous employers. Most agencies require their nannies to make at least a one-year commitment when placed with a family.

Many agencies also offer other related services, including accountants to handle nanny tax issues and advice on salaries, vacation policies, and other benefits. Be aware that agencies may present you with candidates who are unwilling to have their income reported to the IRS. While some agencies offer advice and work with nannies and parents to find a solution to these issues, others leave parents and nannies to work out the question of compliance with tax and employment laws. As an aside, we've been told that the San Francisco Bay Area has one of the highest percentages of parents who pay employment taxes on their nannies' salaries.

Basic registration fees to initiate a nanny search with an agency range from free up to $350. This fee, if any, starts the process along with the completion of the agency's detailed questionnaire and/or interview that assists the agency in providing candidates to you. You then interview the agency-supplied candidates. Salaries are typically negotiated between you (the employer, rather than the nanny agency) and the candidate. Agencies usually charge a flat referral fee when you hire one of their candidates. This fee may be based on a certain number of weeks of the nanny's salary, or a percentage of her salary (12.5% is the current rate). Typically, placement fees range from $3,000 to $3,600 in the Bay Area, depending on the agency and whether you are looking for full- or part-time help. Nanny agencies typically prefer exclusivity but cannot legally demand it. While it may be expensive to sign up with more than one agency, you will get a larger selection of candidates if you do so, although some may overlap.

Most agencies offer a trial period (which varies but is often one to 2 weeks) before parents make a hiring decision. If a parent hires a nanny and it doesn't work out for whatever reason (e.g., whether she leaves, or whether she is let go), most nanny agencies offer either a credit policy toward finding a replacement or a refund for a portion of the placement fee.

The nanny agency industry is unregulated. However, many of the larger nanny agencies are members of the member-run Bay Area Nanny Agencies Association (BANAA). BANAA seeks to ensure that members conduct their businesses ethically and work toward informing one another about issues pertinent to the child care industry. BANAA members need to be in business for at least 3 years and are voted in by fellow members based on their business practices. BANAA membership generally means that an agency takes its business seriously. There are also the International Nanny Agency Association (which any agency may join) and the Alliance of Professional Nanny Agencies. Both host an annual conference and have members nationwide.

The following agencies and centers can help locate live-in and live-out, permanent or temporary care. Please note that most nanny agencies service more counties than the one in which they are based. This is particularly true of the San Francisco-based agencies, many of which serve the entire Bay Area.

Aunt Ann's Agency (In-House Staffing)

2722 Gough St.
San Francisco
415-749-3650
www.inhousestaffing.com

Placements: A full range of domestic staff, including full- and part-time nannies, baby nurses, and postpartum care providers. They also place housekeepers, house managers, chefs, and personal assistants.

Registration fee: None.

Placement fee: For a permanent/long-term full-time nanny, 12.5% of a nanny's gross annual salary; the same for part-time nannies, with a $1,000 minimum. Baby nurse placement fees are 20% of their salary; all other temporary placements (short-term) are 35% of the salary.

BANAA member: Yes.

PARENT RATING: ☆ ☆ ☆ ☆ ☆

A well-established, private family-owned business, Aunt Ann's was founded in 1958 and offers a full range of domestic staffing including full-time or part-time nannies and baby nurses. Aunt Ann's serves the entire Bay Area, with their main office in San Francisco and satellite offices in Daly City, San Mateo, and Oakland. Aunt Ann's requires applicants to be experienced adults with at least one year of child care experience. Candidates are TrustLine registered upon placement, with no additional fee for this service. References are checked, and CPR training is offered. Aunt Ann's requires no registration fee (one of the very few that doesn't), as they believe that you shouldn't have to pay before a service is rendered. Nannies caring for one child typically get between $15 and $18 an hour in San Francisco, $13-18 in the East and North Bay, and $15-20 on the Peninsula and in the South Bay. Aunt Ann's has a refund policy that guarantees a prorated return of your placement fee should your needs change in the first 120 days of employment As an extra bonus, Aunt Ann's will gladly meet with you in person to discuss your child care needs. Comments: "Professional, reliable, first-class service. . . . They listened to my needs which were quite unique and only sent me candidates that fit my requirements. . . . Aunt Ann's presented me with 3 excellent candidates to interview. . . . I had such a hard time making a decision since they all seemed very impressive, each with their unique strengths, but all with a solid core set of skills. . . . The staff is easy to work with, and their follow-up was outstanding. . . . Sue Collins is very intuitive and helpful. . . . Helen Riley has great insight and is so enjoyable to work with!"

Bay Area 2nd Mom, Inc.

See description under South Bay.
415-346-2620
www.2ndmom.com

Bay SuperSitters

1621 Haight St.
PMB23
San Francisco
650-576-3296
www.baysupersitters.com

PARENT RATING: ☆ ☆ ☆ ☆ ☆

Initially a babysitting service, offering prescreened sitters, Bay SuperSitters also offers full-time/permanent or part-time nanny placements through-out the Bay Area. Owner Becky Meyer is well known for her personal touch! Also, she only charges you if she places someone with you. Her fee is a flat fee that parents say is very reasonable. Comment: "Becky found our last 2 nannies for us, both of whom have been totally fabulous!" See also under Babysitting Services and Resources.

Natural Resources

See description under Bulletin Boards and Binders with Child Care Listings—San Francisco.

PARENT RATING: ☆ ☆ ☆ ☆ ☆

This organization offers free referrals and resources for child care.

Town and Country Resources

- San Francisco
  1388 Sutter St., Ste. 904
  800-398-8810 or 415-567-0956
- Palo Alto
  425 Sherman Ave., Ste. 130
  800-457-8222 or 650-326-8570
www.tandcr.com

Placements: A full range of domestic staff, including live-in or live out, full- or part-time nannies, baby nurses, and postpartum care providers.

Registration fee: $150

Placement fee: 12.5% of the nanny's gross annual income, with the same fee for part-time help, although with a $1,500 minimum. For temporary or short-term help, 35% of the overall pay for that period.

BANAA member: Yes.

PARENT RATING: ☆ ☆ ☆ ☆

Offering service throughout the Bay Area since 1982, Town and Country is one of the city's largest nanny placement agencies. They pride themselves on building long-term relationships between families and nannies. Although they are a Bay Area standby, reviews about the qual-ity of nannies and staff were mixed, Comments: "I had great luck with Town and Country. . . . Expensive, but efficient, thorough, and gracious. . . . They are honest, thorough, and most importantly helpful when you hit road bumps." One respondent expressed disappointment at not get-ting the registration fee refunded when the search proved unsuccessful.

North Bay

Nannies of the Valley Placement Agency

3212 Jefferson St., #373
Napa
707-251-8035

Placements: Nannies only.

Registration fee: $250

Placement fee: $1,350 for full-time nannies and $1,000 for part-time.

BANAA member: No.

Nannies of the Valley offers compre-hensive nanny placement in Sonoma, Napa, and Marin counties. Prior to the interview of appropriate candidates, half of the placement fee is due, with the remaining fee due before a hired nanny starts work. This placement fee includes a free replacement should the nanny not work out in the first 90 days. Nannies of the Valley

Nannies

also offers on-call services that are designed to provide parents with quality nanny care for short-notice occasions such as illnesses, vacations, or other last-minute needs. A one-year subscription for access to prescreened nannies for on-call needs is $400 a year or $250 for 6 months, not exceeding 9 hours of care per week. (For care between 9 and 15 hours per week, a subscription fee is $600 per year or $450 for 6 months.)

Rent-A-Parent

1640 Tiburon Blvd.
Tiburon
415-435-2642
www.rentaparent.net

Placements: Temporary and permanent nannies and babysitters, including on-demand service.

Registration fee: None.

Placement fee: The placement fee for a full-time nanny equals 12.5% of the hired nanny's annual gross salary, with a minimum of $2,000 for full-time placements and $1,400 for part-time placements. For babysitters, the placement fee is 35% of the caregiver's total fee with a minimum fee of $20 per day for temporary or call-on-demand placement. There is also a $10 service charge for same-day placements.

BANAA member: Yes.

PARENT RATING: ☆ ☆ ☆ ☆ ☆

Serving Marin County since 1984, Rent-a-Parent offers a full refund plan within the first 3 months for any reason. Parent Comment: "They were helpful in narrowing the candidate pool. . . . They are responsive and send good, qualified, reliable sitters."

East Bay

A Nanny Connection

P.O. Box 1038
Danville
925-743-0587
www.nannyconnection.com

Placements: Full- or part-time, live-in or live-out, permanent or temporary nannies.

Registration fee: None.

Placement fee: Five weeks of the hired nanny's salary for full-time and part-time nannies.

BANAA member: No.

PARENT RATING: ☆ ☆ ☆ ☆ ☆

With nearly 20 years of experience in the child care business, A Nanny Connection offers professional customer service-oriented assistance in placing nannies in the East Bay. All nannies are experienced, CPR certified, tuberculosis certified, TrustLine registered upon placement, and have references. After you complete an application, they will set up interviews for you. Placements are guaranteed for 3 months, or you are entitled to another search free of charge or half of your money back.

Bay Area 2nd Mom, Inc.

6400 Hollis St., Ste. 8
Emeryville
510-595-1535
888-926-3666
See description under South Bay.

The Nanny Network, Inc.

712 Bancroft Rd. #216
Walnut Creek
925-256-8575
www.nannynet.net

Placements: In-home permanent, temporary, full-time, and part-time nannies in Contra Costa and Alameda counties.

Registration fee: None.

Placement fee: $1,800 for a full-time nanny (more than 25 hours a week) and $1,000 for a temporary nanny (working from one to 90 days, either part-time or full-time). Placement fees for a temporary nanny (working from one to 90 days, either part-time or full-time) are $15 a day for live-out and $25 a day for live-in.

BANAA member: No.

PARENT RATING: ☆ ☆ ☆ ☆ ☆

The owner started this business after her own experience of hiring a nanny in 1992. Parents love the fact that this agency makes house calls and can come to your home to explain their services and do the initial paperwork. Comment: "Fast, personalized service."

South Bay

Bay Area 2nd Mom, Inc.
872 San Antonio Rd.
Palo Alto
1-888-926-3666
650-858-2469 Peninsula/South Bay
www.2ndmom.com

Placements: Nannies and baby nurses.

Registration fee: $350

Placement fee: The placement fee for a full-time nanny is $2,500 (or 15% of the nanny's salary, whichever is greater), and $2,000 (or 15%, whichever is greater) for part-time nannies who work less than 25 hours a week.

BANAA member: Yes.

PARENT RATING: ☆ ☆ ☆ ½

Serving the entire Bay Area since 1987 with offices in Emeryville and Palo Alto, 2nd Mom offers screened and experienced nannies and baby nurses, including permanent full-time and part-time nannies; live-ins and live-outs; temporary nannies for one week to 3 months; on-call nannies for last-minute sick baby care, cancellations, newborn baby care, and weekends and overnights, as well as single-night occasions. This nanny agency received mixed reviews as to the quality of nannies and their staff. On-call service for well or sick child care is $18-33 per hour depending on the age and number of children. Their on-call sick child care services received excellent reviews.

California Nanny Network
4100 Moorpark Ave.
San Jose
650-321-6942 (Peninsula office)
408-260-9125 (South Bay office)
www.cananny.com

Placements: Nannies only.

Registration fee: $75

Placement fee: Placement fees for live-in and live-out nannies are 6 weeks of the nanny's gross salary. An additional placement fee for temporary help is $25 a day.

BANAA member: No.

Serving the South Bay through San Jose for live-in, live-out, and temporary care, the California Nanny Network offers comprehensive family and nanny matching with a one-year guarantee. They serve all of California for live-in help. All nannies undergo thorough background checks. The refund policy states that within the first 30 days a free replacement nanny is offered, or 50% of the fee is credited toward a new search. The registration fee for temporary care is $225, providing access to a pool of temporary nannies for a year.

Connie's Household Management

122 2nd Ave., Ste. 214
San Mateo
650-344-0111

Placements: Nannies and baby nurses.

Registration fee: None.

Placement fee: 80% of one month of the nanny's salary.

BANAA member: No.

Serving South San Francisco to San Jose, Connie's offers full-time nannies and baby nurses, including weekends and overnights.

South Bay Nannies and Nurses Registry

P.O. Box 28931
San Jose
408-236-3494

Placements: Nannies, nurses, and mothers' helpers.

Registration fee: $175

Placement fee: The referral fee for a permanent placement is $2,500 (or 12% of the nanny's total salary, whichever is greater), and for a temporary placement it is $2,000 (or 30% of the nanny's total wage, whichever is greater).

BANAA member: Yes.

In business for more than 30 years, South Bay Nannies and Nurses is a full-service placement agency for live-in and live-out nannies, nurses, mothers' helpers, and housekeepers,

and also offers occasional, temporary, and on-call placements, including sick child care. They place one-third of their nannies in permanent positions, one-third in temporary positions, and one-third in on-call jobs.

Stanford Park Nannies

1050 Chestnut St., Ste. 202D
Menlo Park
650-462-4580
www.spnannies.com

Placements: Nannies and baby nurses.

Registration fee: $150

Placement fee: 12% of a nanny's annual salary.

BANAA member: Yes.

PARENT RATING: ☆ ☆ ☆ ☆ ☆

Serving San Mateo and Santa Clara counties since 1990, Stanford Park Nannies offers exceptional nanny and baby nurse placement services. The owners have more than 17 years of combined nanny referral experience. All nannies must make a one-year commitment and have at least 2 years of experience. Nurses and nannies are available part-time or full-time, live-in or live-out. The agency does complete background checks, fingerprinting, and driving history and insurance checks. In the event of termination during the first 12 months of employment, a partial credit of the original fee is applied toward a future search.

Town and Country Resources

See description under San Francisco.

Au Pair Agencies

Au pairs are young adults from outside the United States who provide live-in child care in exchange for a stipend, room and board, and the opportunity to spend a year in the United States. They are an affordable option for in-home child care, and many parents appreciate exposing their children to a foreign culture and language. The U.S. State Department administers the au pair program and must approve candidates coming into the U.S. for visas. The State Department also administers other regulations of the program: Among other things, an au pair must be offered her own room and cannot work more than 10 hours a day and 45 hours a week. At the time this book goes to press, the weekly stipend for an au pair is $139.50 (in 2005).

Au pair agencies make placements with families, usually charging an application fee (between $250 and $300) for matching the family with a suitable au pair, and placement fees, which range from $5,100 to $6,100 (in 2005). Sometimes the au pair's flight from her home country to the United States is included in the placement fee, but not always. Parents also talk about hidden costs such as extra car insurance, or even having to purchase an additional car, if they plan on having the au pair drive. (And don't forget a little Driver's Ed—fender benders are not infrequent occurrences!)

While some au pairs are wonderful caregivers, most lack the experience and credentials of nannies and come to this country first and foremost for the cultural experience. For this reason, many professionals in the child care industry believe that an au pair is best used as a "support person" in a "busy" home (ideally where one parent does not work full time outside the home) and should not be intended for exclusive child care for extended periods of time. Of course, all of this depends on the particular family and the individual au pair. Agencies typically screen candidates, and parents often conduct telephone interviews to find the best match. Parents say that one of the hardest things about choosing an au pair is that while they get to speak to them and interview them over the phone, they don't get to meet them in person before they make their decision. In the words of one Bay

Area mom, "You have to be very comfortable with making this type of decision."

Parents report varying degrees of success with the au pair program. Many say that when it works, it's great, but when it is not a good match, it can be a disaster. Tips that parents shared with us in evaluating candidates include assessing their fluency in English; whether they can drive and have experience driving; and whether they are likely to abide by the "house rules," such as curfews, drinking, visitors, etc. Also consider whether you and your family have the right kind of personalities to have someone from outside your family living under your roof for a year. Families with separate living quarters (a separate floor or area of the house) seem happiest with their au pair experiences.

Au Pair Care
600 California St., 10th Fl.
San Francisco, CA 94108
800-4-AUPAIR or 415-434-8788
www.aupaircare.com

Au Pair In America
River Plaza
9 W. Broad St.
Stamford, CT 06902
800-727-AIFS (2437)
www.aifs.com

Go Au Pair
111 East 12300 South
Draper, UT 84020
800-287-2471
www.goaupair.com

Au Pair USA/InterExchange
161 6th Ave.
New York, NY 10013
800-287-2477 or 212-924-0446
www.interexchange.org

Culture Care Au Pair (and EF Au Pair)
One Education St.
Cambridge, MA 02141
800-333-6056 or 617-619-1100
www.efaupair.org
auapair@culturalcare.com

United States Department of State
Exchange Visitor Program Office
301 4th St., SW
Washington, DC 20547
202-203-5096

Babysitting Services and Resources

Even if you decide not to work outside the home, you will probably need some regular help. Moreover, you will, at least occasionally, want to have some life away from your child! A babysitter is a great option when a full-time nanny is too much for your needs or your budget.

Average hourly rates for sitters in the Bay Area range from $12 to $17 for one child and $14 to $20 for care for 2 or more children, depending on where you live and the sitter's experience and background. Many sitters and agencies have a 4-hour minimum.

There are many Bay Area babysitting resources. The most important things to remember are to check references and trust your instincts in hiring a mature individual who can handle your child's needs. Don't forget that many mothers' clubs offer babysitting co-op services; see Ch. 6 for more information.

BAY AREA BABYSITTING SERVICES AND RESOURCES

Throughout the Bay Area

BabySitterExchange.com
www.babysitterexchange.com
This free online service is helpful for coordinating and arranging babysitting co-ops.

Bay SuperSitters
1621 Haight St.
PMB23
San Francisco
650-576-3296
www.baysupersitters.com
PARENT RATING: ☆ ☆ ☆ ☆ ☆

Bay SuperSitters is a sitter/nanny referral service specializing in on-call, occasional, and part-time care. Part-time and full-time placements are also available. For a reasonable flat fee, they screen and interview candidates and provide you with a list of sitters in your area. Owner Becky Meyer works directly with Bay Area families, including meeting them in person to take careful note of their needs. They serve San Francisco, the East Bay, the Peninsula, and the South Bay.

Craig's List
www.craigslist.com
PARENT RATING: ☆ ☆ ☆ ☆ ☆

Many parents rave about this website and yes, even for child care. You post an ad specifying job particulars such as age and number of children, hours, and so on. As with any search that you are doing yourself, screening is totally up to you. Comment: "Great, but you have to weed out and have patience."

Good Connection
www.goodconnection.com (formerly bay-area-sitters.com)

Sitter City
www.sittercity.com
This large national parent-babysitter matching service is conducted online.

San Francisco

California College of Arts
1111 8th St.
415-703-9500
415-621-2396 (fax)
Fax your job description to the attention of Student Life, and it will be posted on the college's bulletin board for job opportunities.

Nannies

City College of San Francisco

Student Career Services
50 Phelan Ave.
415-550-4346
415-550-4400 (fax)
www.ccsf.org/career/employer

Mailed or faxed job announcements to the office of Cooperative Work are sent to the Child Development Department and all 9 campuses. You may also submit an ad via their website. Comments: "This office is well run and on top of things. . . . They posted my job in a timely fashion, and I received several calls from well-qualified candidates."

Core Group

415-206-9046
www.thecoregroup.org

PARENT RATING: ☆ ☆ ☆ ☆ ☆

In 1998 a business-savvy University of San Francisco graduate set up a personal concierge service offering child care among other services such as catering, cooking, party help, and computer assistance. The "core" of many San Francisco parents' babysitting services, its fees are $13 per hour for one child, $15 per hour for 2, and $18 for 3. They serve the entire Bay Area. Extra charges for driving time and tolls apply. Sitters are also available for overnight stays, which run $85 for a weeknight and $95 for a weekend night. The Core Group prides itself on offering babysitters who are college students or graduates with child care experience, and who are professional and reliable. In addition to the hourly rates, $50 per month allows you to use any service the group offers for that 30-day period. The cancellation policy requires

notice 24 hours in advance, or you pay a $25 fee. Comments: "Reliable service with stellar sitters. . . . I highly recommend them! . . . I found one of our favorite sitters through the Core Group—she's been babysitting for us now for several years. . . . Rose, the owner is great—she is always helpful and very up front . . . whenever I am in a pinch the Core Group seems to come through."

Enterprise for High School Students

200 Pine St., Ste. 600
415-392-7600
www.ehss.org

This well-respected organization places high school students in domestic and other jobs. All students are required to take a workshop to participate in the program. Students must show proof of a C average or better to qualify for the program and must provide a letter of recommendation from an academic teacher.

Natural Resources

See description under Bulletin Boards and Binders with Child Care Listings—San Francisco. They offer referrals for babysitters.

San Francisco State University Career Center

1600 Holloway Ave.
415-338-1111
415-338-2979 (fax)
recruit@sfu.edu
www.sfsu.edu/~career

This career center will post your job description on its MonsterTrak-run website and send it out to SFSU students and alumni. The fee for each listing is $17. Alternatively, for free, e-mail, fax, or mail your listing to be placed in the employment binders. Interested students will call you. The Career Center does not screen students.

University of San Francisco Career Services Center

2130 Fulton St.
415-422-6216
415-422-6470 (fax)

PARENT RATING: ☆ ☆ ☆ ☆ ☆

The Career Services Center will fax or mail you a current list of students interested in babysitting or part-time nanny positions. Requests are free and are generally processed that day. The Career Center does not do any screening. To post a job listing in their job binders, send your job description to careerservices@usfca.edu. Or, post your ad online for $25 for 30 days by calling 800-999-8725 (MonsterTrak). The USF School of Nursing also maintains a bulletin board on the first floor of Cowell Hall where students advertise their availability. The bulletin board is called "Students with Cars Looking for Work." You need to go there in person to get listings or to post an ad. Comment: "Fast turnaround, but you do the work of background checks and interviews."

North Bay

Dominican University

Student Development Office
50 Acacia Ave.
San Rafael
415-485-3283
415-257-1399 (fax)
www.dominican.edu

E-mail job postings to careerservices@dominican.edu or send a fax to the above number.

College of Marin, Career Center

835 College Ave.
Kentfield
415-485-9369 (Early Childhood Education Program)

Send written job descriptions with contact information to Peggy Dodge, Director of the Early Childhood Education Program, at the above number, or send her an e-mail at peggy.dodge@marin.cc.ca.us.

Nannies of the Valley Placement Agency

See description under Nanny Agencies and Resource Centers—North Bay.

Napa Valley Community College

2277 Napa Vallejo Hwy.
Napa
707-253-3050 (Career Re-entry and Job Placement)
707-253-3089 (fax, Attention: Jessica)
www.nvc.cc.ca.us

Novato Mothers Club

415-458-3203
www.novatomothersclub.com

PARENT RATING: ☆ ☆ ☆ ☆ ☆

This club offers various programs and playgroups for new mothers, including a babysitting co-op, which many parents rave about!

Rent-A-Parent

See description under Nanny Agencies and Resource Centers—North Bay. Almost half of their placements are on-call/on-demand placements in Marin.

Nannies

Sonoma State University
1801 E. Cotati Ave.
Rohnert Park
707-664-2196 (Career Services)
www.sonoma.edu/sas/crc
Post your job advertisement on their website.

Tamalpais High School, Student Career Services
700 Miller Ave.
Mill Valley
415-388-3292
415-380-3506 (fax)

Redwood High School, Student Career Services
395 Doherty Dr.
Larkspur
415-945-3600

East Bay

Bananas
See under Bulletin Boards and Binders with Child Care Listings—East Bay.

Bay Area Sitters Unlimited
See description under Sitters Unlimited—South Bay.

Contra Costa College
Career Placement Office
2600 Mission Bell Dr., RM H-10
San Pablo
510-235-7800 (ext. 4344, Job Placement Services)
510-231-0327 (fax)
Fax your job announcement to the above number, or send an e-mail to jchristensen@contracosta.edu.

Diablo Valley College
Job Placement Office
321 Golf Club Rd.
Pleasant Hill
925-685-1230, ext. 2206
925-691-7538 (fax)

Merritt Community College
12500 Campus Dr.
Oakland
510-531-4911
510-434-3825 (fax)
www.merritt.edu
Mail or fax babysitting job descriptions to the career services department, attention Catherine Thur.

Mills College
5000 MacArthur Blvd.
Oakland
510-430-2069
510-430-3235 (fax)
www.mills.edu
Mail or fax your job description to the career center. Your listing will be posted for free for 30 days.

Saint Mary's College
1928 St. Mary's Rd.
Moraga
925-631-4380
www.stmarys-ca.edu
PARENT RATING: ☆ ☆ ☆ ☆ ☆

Parents find the job board a great help for finding babysitting help. To post a child care job listing, log onto their website and complete their forms. Your job listing will be posted for 4 weeks on the SMCnet, the college's internal website, and in the Career Center's Job Placement Office. To cancel your ad, please call the above number. Students will contact you directly for an appointment or to apply.

Cañada Community College

Student Career Center
4200 Farm Hill Blvd.
Redwood City
650-306-3100
650-306-3457 (fax)
www.monstertrak.com

Job announcements can be faxed and placed in a binder or posted via www.monstertrak.com.

College of Notre Dame
Career Center

1500 Ralston Ave.
Belmont
650-593-1601
650-508-3715 (fax)
www.ndnu.edu

They have a bulletin board of jobs and a binder with child care opportunities for students. Fax your job description.

College of San Mateo

Career Services Center
1700 W. Hillsdale Blvd.
San Mateo
650-574-6161
650-574-6167 (fax)
www.gocsm.net

They will fax or send you a job description form. Completed forms are placed in an employment binder for one month at no charge.

Skyline College

Career Center
3300 College Dr.
San Bruno
650-738-4337
650-738-4260 (fax)
www.skylinejobs.omc

To post an advertisement on the school's electronic jobs website, visit www.skylinejobs.com. Ads received by fax or mail are placed in job binders for 30 days.

Stanford University
The Worklife Office

Main Quad (Building 310)
845 Escondido Rd.
Stanford
650-723-2660
www.stanford.edu/dept/ocr/worklife

This office has a physical bulletin board where you may post an advertisement. They also will fax or e-mail you a list of babysitters, primarily for weekends and evenings. If you happen to be a Stanford student or employee, be sure to visit the Worklife Office for child care resources and referrals.

Peninsula Sitters Agency

10370 Prune Tree Ln.
Cupertino
408-255-1291

In business for more than 30 years, Peninsula sitters offer babysitting services to the Peninsula and South Bay area on an on-call basis.

Sitters Unlimited

1286 Arnold Ave.
San Jose
408-452-0225
www.sittersunlimited.com

Sitters Unlimited is a national babysitting service with franchises across California and Hawaii. In business since 1979, the San Jose office caters to the out-of-town visitor who needs child care or has local occasional

Nannies

needs. Hourly rates are $12 per hour for one child (4 hours minimum). An additional dollar per hour is added for each additional child, up to 4. Clients must also pay the sitter's transportation charges, usually $3-6. There is an additional $10 fee for a temporary sitter home visit.

South Bay Nannies and Nurses

See description under Nanny Agencies and Resource Centers—South Bay.

Additional Helpful Websites on Child Care

www.iamyourchild.org (formerly the I Am Your Child Foundation, it is now the website for Parents Action for Children)

www.nccic.org (National Childcare Information Center)

www.zerotothree.org (parenting site for information on infants and toddlers)

www.commonsensemedia.org (great parenting site for movie reviews and more)

CHAPTER 10

CHOOSING A
PRESCHOOL YOU'LL LOVE
(and Getting In)

Given the competitiveness of the Bay Area preschool admissions process, we might have put this chapter at the beginning of the book. That way, the first thing you would do after your pregnancy test comes back positive would be to sign up your unborn child for preschool. In all seriousness, while the process is competitive, it's not quite that bad, and we do not want to create even more stress in a situation already too stressful. So we've chosen to put this chapter where it belongs, at the end of the book, after you have had some time to get to know your child and his or her needs (and yours). This chapter will answer the following questions and more:

- What are the different types of preschools?
- What should I look for in choosing a preschool?
- How do we get into the schools we want?
- Which preschools in my area do other parents recommend?

What Type of Program Should I Choose?

Here is a basic rundown of the different types of schools, but the best way to decide what is right for your child is to visit various schools and see for yourself how they work.

A **developmental** program focuses on play as a vehicle for learning. While not completely eschewing academics, these schools believe that it's too early for kids to absorb a heavy dose of reading, writing, and arithmetic. Instead, learning is accomplished through group play, with a sprinkling of the alphabet, numbers, colors, and science and nature thrown in where appropriate. Activity areas often include blocks, dramatic play (e.g., playing house), books, and arts and crafts. Programs for younger children are less structured than those for older kids, but all usually include a circle time for social interaction, music, and stories. These schools emphasize a low student-to-teacher ratio with a fairly small number of children in the classroom. Children are usually grouped by age. Probably the majority of preschools today espouse some variant of the developmental philosophy.

An **emergent** curriculum is developmentally based, but responsive to the needs and interests of the children. For example, the children may be studying trees and become interested in building a tree house. Rather than sticking to the daily curriculum plan, the teacher may allow the children to pursue that interest.

Two other variants on the developmental model include **High/Scope** and **Reggio Emilia**. In the Piaget "High/Scope" theory, teachers encourage children to plan and implement their own lesson plans for the day. Reggio Emilia, named for the Northern Italian region where the theory developed, refers to a project-based, child-centered curriculum in which children develop their own ideas for the innovative projects. The underlying philosophy of the Reggio Emilia approach profoundly respects children's interests and creativity. The result is a flexible, not "set," curriculum, with teachers shaping their work around children's ideas and children who are excited about learning because their curiosity is aroused.

It's best to visit a **Montessori** school to see the Montessori method in action. Montessori classrooms are set up very differently than developmental classrooms. When you walk in, you will notice the noise level is considerably lower. Materials are organized on shelves in an orderly manner, without a lot of clutter. Students are given opportunities to complete individual, self-directed projects at their own pace, and teachers provide lessons designed to take advantage of children's individual "sensitive periods" in which they are receptive to learning. Lessons range from practical life to sensory skills to language and math; all are designed to foster a good work ethic and individual growth. Classes are a mix of older and younger children, with the older children helping to teach the younger ones. Classes are usually larger, with a higher student-to-teacher ratio, than in developmental schools. (This is because the program is student-directed rather than teacher-directed.) Maria Montessori, an Italian educator working with underprivileged children in the early 1900s, originated the method. Modern Montessori schools are affiliated with either the American Montessori Society (AMS, see www.amshq.org) or the Association Montessori Internationale (AMI, see www.montessori-ami.org). AMS schools do not follow the original Montessori method as strictly as AMI schools. Note, however, that Montessori schools do not need to be affiliated with either organization, or any organization, to call themselves Montessori schools. As a result, schools are organized in many different ways, and it is best to visit each school to see how the philosophy is implemented. Montessori schools tend to be more expensive than developmental programs because children usually attend school 5 days per week, and the school day runs into the afternoon.

An **academic** preschool reflects its name: it focuses on instilling the basic academic subjects to prepare children for elementary school. The teacher usually initiates projects, children work in groups, and the atmosphere generally is structured and disciplined. This approach is popular in some foreign countries (France, for instance) and is used in a sprinkling of schools in the U.S. as well, though its popularity is waning in the U.S. as older preschool students sometimes burn out. Even developmental preschools include some academic aspects, however. Academic schools tend to be more expensive than developmental programs, particularly if they are part of a private elementary school.

A **Waldorf** school, based on the work of turn-of-the-century educator Rudolf Steiner, encourages creativity in young children as a vehicle for intellectual growth and development. Learning is hands-on rather than through academics. In addition, children are taught to respect their teachers, because Steiner believed that such admiration would motivate children to learn. Waldorf schools usually emphasize the arts, interaction with the natural environment, use of wooden rather than plastic toys, and little or no television at home. Classes are a mix of older and younger children.

A **cooperative** or parent-participation nursery school is not so much a theory of learning as a way of organizing and running a school. Parents run cooperative schools; they teach in the classroom (helped by a few professional teachers), maintain the school, administer policies, and so on. Generally, cooperative preschools incorporate a developmental philosophy since teachers are lay persons without formal training. Cooperative schools are also usually less expensive than other preschools, and most provide great community-building and parental-education opportunities. Parents must, however, be prepared to devote the necessary time to the school, which may be difficult for working parents or those with younger children at home.

Religious schools are affiliated with a particular church or synagogue. The curriculum may be developmental or academic with the addition of some religious traditions. Programs run the gamut from including compulsory chapel to teaching biblical stories to weekly shabbats to simply celebrating certain holidays or festivals. Be sure you are comfortable with whatever traditions are celebrated in a religious program (and with the possible lack of diversity among the students).

Foreign language schools seek to teach a second language to students at a very young age by either a partial or total immersion

HELPFUL WEBSITES FOR GENERAL INFORMATION ABOUT CHOOSING PRESCHOOLS

- ◆ iparenting.com website at http://preschoolerstoday.com/resources/daycarechecklist.htm (handy checklist and form for jotting notes about each school)
- ◆ Babycenter.com website at www.babycenter.com/general/6007.html (questions to ask each school)
- ◆ Babycenter website at http://parentcenter.babycenter.com/preschooler/ppreschool/index (preschool-related articles and advice)

method. Children are believed to be receptive to learning other languages during the preschool years. Schools vary in the amount of English taught; some include instruction in English for part of the day, while others exclude English entirely. These schools tend to have longer school days and place more emphasis on academics than traditional nursery schools.

Laboratory schools, based on college campuses, employ students as teachers, generally under the supervision of a professional director. Some programs also conduct child development research. Despite the constant teacher turnover, some of these programs have stellar reputations for innovative programs.

What to Look for in a Preschool Program

Here are some things to look for when you are evaluating different preschool programs:

- **Licensing requirements**. The California Department of Social Services licenses preschools and enforces minimum quality and safety standards. The licensing requirements are basically the same as for day care facilities. In fact, the state classifies preschools as "day care centers." To get a license, a preschool must meet the requirements listed in Ch. 9 for day care licensing: ample space, facilities, equipment, teacher and director qualifications, and so on. To check whether your preschool is licensed or to get a list of local licensed facilities, contact the California Department of Social Services' Community Care Licensing Division, listed in Ch. 9. Keep in mind that these standards are only minimums; generally the best programs greatly exceed them.
- **Accreditation**. The National Association for the Education of Young Children (NAEYC), the largest national organization of early childhood educators, conducts an extensive national voluntary accreditation process for early childhood education programs, including preschools. Accredited preschools must meet certain quality standards. Because the process is so rigorous, very few schools make the grade. To find out more about accreditation or to obtain a list of accredited preschools, contact:

NAEYC
1509 16th St., NW
Washington, DC 20036-1426
202-232-8777
www.naeyc.org

◆ **Ratio and teachers.** The NAEYC and the American Academy of
Pediatrics recommend that the ratio of students to teachers be no
more than 5:1 for 2-year-olds, 7:1 for 3-year-olds, and 8:1 for 4-
and 5-year-olds. Two- and 3-year-olds should be in groups of no
more than 10 to 14 children, and 4- and 5-year-olds should be in
groups of no more than 16 children. Look for teachers with at least
an associate's degree or higher in early childhood education, and a
low turnover of teachers from year to year. Make sure the relationship between the students and the teachers is positive and that
teachers are warm and nurturing.

◆ **Safe and nurturing environment.** Of course, we would all like our
preschools to have campuses the size of Stanford. To be realistic,
however, look for at least the space required for licensing (35
square feet of space per child in a classroom and a fenced outdoor
play area with 75 square feet of space per child). Facilities should
be clean, cheerful, and arranged at a child's eye level. Children
should be within a teacher's line of sight at all times. Diaper-changing facilities and bathrooms should be sanitary. Activities, equipment, and toys should be stimulating, inviting, and age appropriate.
The program should encourage self-direction and problem solving,
as well as communication between the children. There should be
time for both structured and unstructured activity. Ultimately, the
most important criterion in choosing a program is whether it is a
safe, loving environment. Ask yourself whether the school will nurture your child's self-esteem, encourage him or her to thrive and
develop in positive ways, and stimulate a love of learning.

◆ **Location.** The preschool day is fairly short (usually less than 3
hours in traditional programs), making location critical. If by the
time you get home from dropping your child at school, you need to
turn around and head out to pick him or her up again, the school is
too far away! Attending a local school also allows your child to meet

540

other neighborhood kids with whom he or she may attend kindergarten.

◆ **Extended care**. Working parents may need extended care in the early mornings or afternoons. If so, choose a flexible program, preferably one that allows you to sign up for such care at the last minute in case of emergency. Parents warn, however, not to expect a Harvard curriculum, or even one approaching the regular school day, during extended care hours. Accept it for what it is: glorified day care.

◆ **Potty training**. In general, schools only offering programs for children ages 2 years, 9 months and up require children to be potty trained because they are not usually licensed for diaper-changing facilities. Programs for younger children usually do not require children to be potty trained. Many Montessori programs are known for helping parents to potty train their toddlers.

◆ **Cost**. Preschool tuition varies greatly and depends on the type of school and number of hours your child attends. Cooperative schools tend to be the least expensive and averaged around $2,000-3,000 per school year (assuming a 10-month year) in 2005. Developmental, emergent, and religious schools with half-day programs tend to be mid-range in price, varying from $3,000 per year for 2-day programs to $6,000 or more per year for full-week programs. (That said, there are some half-day developmental programs in the city that greatly exceed this average!) Schools with extended day programs can be even more expensive, up to about $10,000 (or more) per year. At the top of the chart are Montessori and academic programs. Both tend to have long school days and full weeks, so the cost can be $10,000-14,000 or more per year.

◆ **Pre-kindergarten or transitional kindergarten programs**. To attend public school kindergarten in California, a child must be 5 years old by December 1 of the year of entry. For private schools, the official cutoff date is September 1. However, some schools have a different time frame in mind, especially for boys, recommending that they reach age 5 by late spring to early summer. A child's "readiness," more than anything else, determines when he or she begins kindergarten. As a result, children are entering kindergarten at various ages, with the trend even in public schools for parents to "hold" children with fall birthdays from entering kindergarten until the year they turn 6. Hence, the pre-kindergarten or transitional kindergarten year has become a popular solution for young 5-year-olds. The nomenclature gets a bit tricky here because the same terms are often used for different types of programs. Some schools call the final year before a student enters kindergarten the "pre-kindergarten" year, but the curriculum is the same as in the preschool program. Some schools have a special "pre-kindergarten" program for students with fall and winter birthdays, who are not yet ready or eligible for kindergarten, with more kindergarten preparation than they would get in the normal preschool program. And some schools have a version of kindergarten for children who are technically eligible but not yet ready for regular kindergarten, called "transitional kindergarten" or "junior kindergarten." The upshot? If your child's birthday falls between June and December, but particularly if you have a child with a late fall birthday, you may want to consider schools that have pre-kindergarten or transitional kindergarten programs.

QUESTIONS TO ASK WHEN VISITING PRESCHOOLS

- What is the school's philosophy?
- Is the school licensed? Accredited?
- Who are the teachers? What sort of training do they have?
- How do the teachers interact with the students? Are they actively engaged or supervising?
- Does the school have specialists (e.g., music or dance teachers)?
- What is the turnover of teachers each year? (Look for stability.)
- What is the student-to-teacher ratio? How large are the classes?
- Are students grouped by age or in multiple-age groups?
- What is a typical day's schedule? Are there opportunities for outdoor play? Creative play? Imaginative play? Are there routines?
- How much time do students spend in individual play and in group play?
- Is the day structured, or do students have a lot of free time?
- How does the school communicate with parents? Monthly calendars? Newsletters?

- Is extended care available?
- Does a child need to be toilet trained?
- Do parents meet with teachers to discuss students' progress? What areas do they evaluate?
- How do teachers evaluate whether a child is ready for kindergarten?
- How does the school handle discipline or set limits? How does it handle conflicts between children?
- How does the school handle children with separation issues?
- Are there outings or field trips?
- How are parents involved in the school? Do they engage in fund-raising? Work in the classroom?
- What is the security policy?
- What is the procedure for dropping off and picking up a child? Is parking or a drop-off zone available? (This is particularly critical in crowded areas of San Francisco and Oakland.)
- How and when does the school make its admissions decisions?
- (If relevant) What elementary schools do graduating students attend?
- Overall, what are the school's strengths and weaknesses?

The Admissions Process

So how do you get your child into a preschool? Though it can be a time-consuming process, it need not be the "nightmare" that many parents reported to us. Here is a synopsis of the Bay Area preschool admissions process from start to finish:

1. Make a list of schools. First, you need to decide where to apply. Make a list of criteria, and then a list of schools meeting your needs. Start by asking friends, neighbors, and colleagues where they send their children to school. The list of favorite preschools identified by parents completing our surveys (see below) also provides a starting point for finding a school. Additional resources for identifying schools include the following:

- The NAEYC website (www.naeyc.org) features a searchable database of accredited schools. No information about the schools other than addresses and telephone numbers is provided, but it's a place to start.
- In San Francisco and Marin, consult *Finding a Preschool for Your Child in San Francisco and Marin*, by Lori Rifkin, Vera Obermeyer,

Irene Byrne, and Melinda Venable. The book lists many city and Marin schools together with information provided by each school. There is no independent evaluation of each school, but it is another useful starting point.

◆ In the East Bay, check out *The Neighborhood Parents Network's Preschool Directory*, a detailed compilation of schools published annually. To order, go to www.npnonline.org or contact Neighborhood Parents Network, P.O. Box 8597, Berkeley, CA 94707, 877-648-KIDS (5437).

◆ East Bay Moms, a Berkeley-Oakland parents' group, publishes a *Preschool and Child Care Fair Program Directory* with a limited selection of schools. To order, go to www.eastbaymoms.com or write to East Bay Moms, 6000 Contra Costa Rd., Oakland, CA 94618.

◆ The online *East Bay Preschool Directory* (www.eastbaypreschools.com) covers the Contra Costa and Tri-Valley areas. Listings are advertisements from local preschools, not independent research, but it's a good place to find a school with openings.

◆ The Palo Alto Online website has a number of listings of local preschools and child care centers (www.paloaltoonline.com).

◆ Attend a **public preschool preview night** for your area, usually held in the fall or winter. Representatives from local preschools are available to answer parents' questions and provide brochures. (Sadly, some of the most popular San Francisco preschools are so oversubscribed that they don't attend.) **PARENT RATING:** ☆ ☆ ☆ ☆ ☆ Comment: "It's an opportunity to meet the directors in person, find out who has openings for the next year, and get all of the brochures at once without having to call around." The following organizations sponsor public preschool preview nights:

◇ **San Francisco**: Parents' Place San Francisco, a program of Jewish Family and Children's Services, hosts a San Francisco Preschool Preview Night in September or October, 415-359-2454 or www.parentsplaceonline.org. Parents' Place also periodically offers a class on choosing a preschool in San Francisco (**PARENT RATING:** ☆ ☆ ☆ ☆ ☆).

◇ **Marin**: Marin Childcare Coordinating Council (415-491-5775) and Parents' Place Marin (415-491-7959) host a Marin Schools

Night Fair in October. Parents' Place also periodically offers a class on choosing a preschool.

⬧ **Berkeley/Oakland**: Neighborhood Parents Network hosts a Preschool Fair in December, 877-648-5437, ext. 86. This one features parent speakers so is more valuable than some of the others.

⬧ **Contra Costa County**: Pleasant Hill/Walnut Creek Mothers' Club hosts a Contra Costa Preschool, Childcare and Parenting Fair in February, 925-939-6466.

⬧ **Lamorinda**: Lamorinda Moms' Club hosts a Preschool Fair in November, www.lamorindamomsclub.org.

⬧ **Livermore/Pleasanton/San Ramon**: The Amador Mothers' Club hosts a Tri-Valley Preschool Fair, www.amadormothersclub.com.

⬧ **San Mateo County**: The Peninsula Family YMCA in San Mateo hosts a preschool preview night in February, 650-286-9622 or www.ymcasf.org/peninsula.

⬧ **Palo Alto**: The Mothers' Club of Palo Alto and Menlo Park hosts a Preschool Fair in April, www.pampmothersclub.org. Parents' Place Palo Alto also periodically offers a class on choosing a pre-school, 650-688-3040.

◆ Attend your **local mothers' group's preschool preview night**, which is even better than a public preschool night. Fellow mothers will give you personal insights into local preschools. See Ch. 6 to contact the group in your area. **PARENT RATING:** ☆ ☆ ☆ ☆ ☆ Comment: "This is the kind of invaluable inside information you won't get from the preschools themselves!"

◆ In the East Bay, visit the UC Berkeley Parents Network's website, http://parents.berkeley.edu, for frank parent feedback about local preschools. **PARENT RATING:** ☆ ☆ ☆ ☆ ☆ Comment: "Great insider tips!"

◆ For a directory of parent cooperative preschools, check out the website of the California Council of Parent Participation Nursery Schools, www.ccppns.org.

◆ To find a Montessori school in your area, consult the North American Montessori Teachers' Association website, www.montessori-namta.org.

Do You Need Professional Help?

For most Bay Area parents, hiring an educational consultant to help with the preschool admissions process is probably overkill. (Fortunately, we do not live in Manhattan!) But for children with special needs, or parents who need a little extra guidance or don't have time to do the research themselves, consultants can be very helpful. A good consultant with a psychology background can help you sort out the million-dollar question: which school is the right "fit" for your child? Just make sure the person you hire has the requisite education (preferably a masters degree or above in education or psychology) and experience working with top-tier schools. Here are several consultants recommended to us by parents:

Sue Dinwiddie, MA

Palo Alto
650-325-3033
www.daise.com

A former head teacher at Bing Nursery School at Stanford, she now teaches, speaks, and counsels parents on school choice.

Little and Molligan

4040 Civic Center Dr., Ste. 200
San Rafael
415-492-2877
www.littleandmolligan.com

They do preschool, elementary, and secondary school placement throughout the Bay Area.

Diane Provo, MSEd

Larkspur
415-464-9040
www.dianeprovo.com

This psychologist and television commentator speaks to and counsels with parents on child development and educational placement topics.

Lori Rifkin, MSEd, PhD

• San Francisco, 2084 Union St.
• San Rafael, 2012 5th Ave.
415-485-1976

This psychologist and educational consultant specializes in preschool issues and co-authored the book *Finding a Preschool for Your Child in San Francisco and Marin*, see above.

Lee Ann Slayton, MS

Parents Place
1710 Scott St.
San Francisco
415-359-2473
E-mail: leeanns@jfcs.org

This educator consults with parents about making informed school choices and other educational issues.

A word on feeder schools: Do "feeder schools" exist and does your child really need to attend one? Yes and no. While some educational consultants will deny the existence of feeder schools, we have noticed that in San Francisco certain preschools send more of their graduates to certain private elementary schools than do other preschools. Those feeder preschools tend to be the ones with longer waiting lists and more competition for admission. That does not mean, however, that no children from other preschools get in to private elementary schools, or that you should simply choose the most popular school. We suspect that one reason children from a particular preschool tend to end up at the same elementary school is self-selection; what drove them to choose the same preschool—similar interests and values—may also steer them to the same elementary school. Moreover, you'll ultimately be happier with a preschool you like rather than one you choose simply to get your child into a particular elementary school. If you plan to send your child to a private elementary school, particularly in San Francisco, you should find out what preschools that elementary school's students attended. Check with friends who have children in private elementary school and find out where their kids went to preschool. (Elementary schools usually won't tell you. Some preschools will provide you a handout listing the elementary schools to which its recent graduates were admitted, while others may be a bit optimistic about their "in" status with elementary schools.) If you are planning to send your child to the local public elementary school, relax. Don't worry about going to the most popular preschool. Just find one that is safe, stimulating, and a good fit for your child.

2. Start the application process. Certain very popular schools have long waiting lists, particularly in San Francisco, but also a few in the suburbs. Many preschools, especially in the city, say they accept students based solely on the date of application and gender of the child. If you want your child to attend any of these schools, get on waiting lists as soon as you can. Sometimes, as ridiculous as this sounds, you can (and should) actually apply while you are still pregnant! Most schools, however, will not put a child on a waiting list until the child is born. It's a good idea to apply to all of the schools you are interested in as early

547

as possible to increase your chances of admission, if the application date is a basis for admission.

On the other hand, some schools don't look at the application date at all. Rather, they set a deadline to apply (usually in December before the year of entry), and accept students based on an application, sometimes a parent interview, and other criteria such as having diversity and a gender and age balance in a classroom, as well as enthusiasm and interest. (Reality check: Some suspect—and anecdotal evidence backs this up—that this "selective" admission process really boils down to whether the director likes you and "who you know." After all, it's difficult to interview 2-year-olds!) In Berkeley and some parts of San Francisco, for example, very few schools maintain waiting lists based on order of application. If these schools are your choice, apply as soon as your child is old enough to have a clearly defined personality and needs.

Still other schools (e.g., some parent cooperatives and publicly run schools) accept students by lottery. In that case, just make sure you submit your application by the deadline, then cross your fingers.

Another problem with the early application approach is that the programs to which you apply when your child is a baby may not end up being appropriate for your child as a preschooler. Perhaps, for example, you applied to schools with structured programs, but your child needs a more playful environment. Or (like us), you may move to a different neighborhood between birth and preschool, making your early applications moot. At a nonrefundable $50 fee per application, consider your applications carefully.

Call the schools to get brochures and applications. Write a letter to accompany each application, explaining why you want your child to attend the school. Some schools require a detailed written application in which you are asked everything from your educational plans for your child to how you handle discipline. Use the opportunity to your advantage. While many schools claim they base decisions solely on date of application, we have found that directors are more likely to give spaces to parents they like and children they know will attend the school if admitted.

3. Take a tour. Call the schools early in the fall of the year prior to your desired date of entry. Tour season is usually September through

January. A few schools provide tours only to parents of admitted students, but most offer public open houses or individual tours for interested parents. This may be your only chance to see a school in session, so take advantage of the tour and ask the director all your questions. Take time to observe a class in action. Do the students seem happy, engaged, and enthusiastic? Do the teachers provide appropriate stimulation and supervision? Is the facility clean and safe? If you toured the school while you were pregnant or when the child was first born, go back again to make sure you still like the school. Teachers come and go, facilities move, and curriculums get revised.

4. **Follow up.** After you have toured several schools, try to prioritize your list. We kept spreadsheets with information about each school so that we could easily compare choices and keep track of our contact with schools. If you have a favorite, write to the director and tell him or her that the school is your first choice. It's also a nice idea to write each of the directors a thank-you letter for providing the tour, especially if it was an individual tour. Call each school to ascertain your child's place on the waiting list and his or her chances of admission, particularly as admission time grows nearer. Convey your enthusiasm to the director. After all, many schools don't rely solely on the numbers in choosing whom to admit. Nonprofit schools, in particular, are always looking for signs that parents will actively participate in the school if their children enroll. And, of course, directors prefer to fill a class with children whose parents are committed. Finally, to gain a better perspective of what it's like to attend the school, talk to parents of students at the school—often the school will provide you a list of available parents, if you don't know any.

5. **Make a decision.** Most preschools notify applicants of admissions decisions between January and March for September admissions. Typically parents have only a week or 2 to decide whether to accept the spot (by putting down a hefty nonrefundable deposit). It is critical to prioritize your list of schools ahead of time, should you be so lucky as to get into more than one place. Ultimately, it comes down to choosing a school that fits with your family's needs and your child's personality and temperament. Parents have told us time and again that they were much happier when they followed their instincts rather

Preschool for All?

California is leading the way in making preschool available and affordable to every family.

Research shows that attending a quality preschool program can help children be more successful in elementary school and beyond. In response to this research, California voters in 1998 passed Proposition 10, creating the Children and Families Commission, known as "First Five California." Funded by a cigarette tax, and chaired by the proposition's author, film director Rob Reiner, this group works with First Five agencies in each county to improve school readiness and provide preschool opportunities for all children. Among other things, they have funded pre-kindergarten programs for children who never attended preschool. (See www.ccfc.ca.gov or www.f5ac.org.)

In San Francisco, "Preschool for All" Proposition H, passed in March 2004, establishes publicly funded preschool programs for all San Francisco 4-year-olds beginning in September 2005. Statewide, an advocacy group known as Preschool California is pushing for a similar state proposition, to be put on the June 2006 ballot, funding voluntary preschool for all 4-year-olds in California (www.preschoolcalifornia.org). If you are feeling the pinch of paying for preschool, stay tuned . . .

than the herd. Remember, even if you don't get into a school in March, openings often arise before the school year begins, as families move or change plans. Additionally, some families report having an easier time getting into a desirable program in the pre-kindergarten (or pre-k) year or even the "transitional kindergarten" year, because depending on their birthdays and readiness, some students go directly from preschool to kindergarten and leave spaces for new students in pre-k.

Favorite Local Preschools

While our parent surveys revealed a core group of parents' favorite preschools in each region of the Bay Area, the list below is far from comprehensive, and the fact that a certain preschool is not on the list is no indication of its quality. And be aware that some of the schools listed, especially in San Francisco, are so popular that they are very difficult to get into, given the number of applications and the small class sizes. As one parent dryly remarked, it was harder to get his child into certain preschools in the city than it was for him to get into graduate school. While this process can be trying, keep your sense of perspective by remembering: This is only preschool! Consider all of the schools that appeal to you, not just the most popular ones. There is a preschool out there for everyone. Location may be the most important criterion of all for busy families, so we've further subdivided the list into neighborhoods within each region. Note that the ratio listed after each preschool refers to the child-to-adult ratio for that school or class. Please also note that ages listed in decimal form, such as 2.9 years, means 2 years, 9 months and is often how schools express age eligibility for their classes. In addition, "full school day" means a traditional elementary school type of schedule (e.g., 8-9 a.m. to 2-3 p.m.).

PACIFIC HEIGHTS/COW HOLLOW/ MARINA/RUSSIAN HILL

Alta Plaza Preschool

2140 Pierce St.
415-928-6483
www.altaplazapreschool.com
Ages: 2.5-5.5 years
Schedule: Open 7:30 a.m.-6 p.m. year round. Schedule is flexible, ranging from 2 mornings to 5 full days.
Ratio: 6:1 (27 children with 4 teachers and director)
Philosophy/other: This nonprofit, developmental preschool focuses on social, emotional, and academic skills, particularly self-discipline, self-help, and self-esteem. Classrooms are mixed ages, but children separate into 3 age groups for age-appropriate activities during group times. They employ outside "resource" teachers for gymnastics, music, dance, and yoga programs during the school day. The school uses Alta Plaza Park, across the street, for outdoor time.

Admission: By application, considering not only the date of the application, but the child's gender, age, and "fit" with program. There is usually a one- to 2-year "waiting pool."

PARENT RATING: ☆ ☆ ☆ ☆

Parents praised teachers and the flexible hours. Graduates go on to private schools. Comments: "The atmosphere is cozy, very comforting, and welcoming to all children. Parental involvement is encouraged but not mandatory. . . . My son loves all the teachers and feels very safe and loved. . . . He has learned a tremendous amount and always comes home excited and happy about his day. . . . There has never been a morning where my son did not want to go to school . . . wonderful committed and caring community. . . . It's a loving environment in which to learn. . . . The school environment is small so that these young students do not get overwhelmed or overstimulated." We received only one negative comment; one parent felt that there was too much staff turnover.

Calvary Presbyterian Church Nursery School

2515 Fillmore St.

415-346-4715

Ages: 3-6 years

Schedule: Mornings, 5 days a week. Pre-kindergarten (pre-k) program has a slightly longer schedule until 1:30 p.m. Extended care available until mid-afternoon 2 days a week.

Ratio: 10:1 (preschool); 8:1 (pre-k)

Philosophy/other: Founded in 1955, the school offers a developmental curriculum in a church-affiliated preschool. Art and music abound. The play yard is on the roof. Students attend chapel once a week during the second year of school, but the school incorporates religious traditions of all types. The relatively new pre-k program is designed for 5- and 6-year-olds.

Admission: By date of application and observation of the child. There is a very long waiting list (at least 3 years) with preferences for siblings, legacies, and church members.

PARENT RATING: ☆ ☆ ☆ ☆ ☆

Parents love this well-established school, its art and music programs,

and its small size and close community, but they report it is difficult to get in unless you are a member of the church. They say the school is "very successful" in getting its children into kindergarten.

Circle of Friends Preschool and Pre-K

265 Moulton St.

415-345-9184

www.circleoffriendssf.com

Ages: 2.5-5.5 years

Schedule: Mornings or afternoons, 2 or 3 days a week. No extended care.

Ratio: 6:1

Philosophy/other: This small private preschool has a unique, art-based developmental program, with daily exposure to the French language and an environment filled with music. They also have a transitional kindergarten program. They seek to foster compassion, empathy, respect, and a lifelong love of learning in their students. They have a small outdoor area.

Admission: By date of application, with priority for siblings.

PARENT RATING: ☆ ☆ ☆ ☆ ☆

Parents say this school is "the best kept secret in town." Comments: "It is a structured, loving environment that teaches children to be confident and caring inside the classroom and out. The level of education is remarkable. My 4-year-old is reading, learning the piano, and singing in English and French. . . . My son comes home feeling proud of his work. . . . The kids really bond and are all close friends. . . . I cannot speak highly enough about the program. . . . Our son grew by leaps and bounds . . .

and found a love of art and music.
. . . The teachers are creative, fun,
and nurturing. . . . The teachers are
dedicated professionals. . . . The
French program is really impressive.
. . . The music teacher is also a jazz
musician. . . . Don't let the small size
of this school fool you. Your child will
receive significant personal attention,
enhanced through a range of activities not found in larger schools." The
school has an excellent track record
with private school admissions.

Cow Hollow Preschool

St. Mary the Virgin Episcopal
Church
2325 Union St.
415-921-2328
www.cowhollowpreschool.org

Ages: 2-5 years

Schedule: Mornings or afternoons, 2
to 4 days a week (schedule determined by age). No extended care.

Ratio: 3:1 for 2-year-olds; 4:1 for 3-
year-olds; 8:1 for pre-k

Philosophy: Founded in 2000 by a
group of parents, this parent-participation, nonsectarian preschool originally was designed for children too
young for many traditional preschool
programs. Now it has 3 programs (2-
year-olds, 3-year-olds, and pre-k).
The inquiry-based, child-directed,
developmental curriculum includes
socialization, skill development, creative activities, art, and music. They
also have outside specialists teaching
enrichment programs in gymnastics,
music/movement, Spanish, and art.
Parents co-op in the 2- and 3-year-
old programs, but not in the pre-k
program.

Admission: By date of application,
with preference for siblings and members of St. Mary's Church, and consideration to gender and diversity balance
of the class and the applicant's age.

PARENT RATING: ☆ ☆ ☆ ☆ ☆

Parents say this school's facilities are
"great" (they have access to a huge
great room for gymnastics and other
programs, and a lovely courtyard and
garden) and the professional teachers
"very involved." They love the small
class sizes (14-16 students).
Comments: "I love the school
because it has given my daughters
the opportunity to think of school as
a magical, safe, inspiring, social, and
curious experience. . . . This is the
hottest new preschool in San
Francisco right now and with good
reason; the teachers are fantastic, the
curriculum is thoughtful and inspiring,
and the children are stimulated and
engaged. . . . Cow Hollow has made
us better parents. . . . The inquiry-
based, experiential style capitalizes
effectively on a child's own curiosity
about the world. . . . We learned so
much as parents working alongside
the teachers. . . . The school has a
phenomenal and competent teaching
staff . . . the parents are involved in
the growing and learning processes of
their children."

Jewish Community Center of San Francisco

3200 California St. (Helen Diller
Family Preschool)
415-292-1283
www.jccsf.org

Other SF campuses: 655
Brotherhood Way and 325 Arguello
Blvd.

Ages: 2-6 years (including transitional kindergarten program)

Schedule: Mornings, 2 to 5 days a week. Extended care available.

Ratio: 6:1

Philosophy/other: This developmental, Reggio Emilia project-based curriculum is influenced by the Jewish heritage, incorporating Jewish values, customs, and holidays. Shabbat is celebrated weekly in each class, and parents are encouraged to participate. Music, drama, art, dance, gym, and storytelling specialists make regular visits. The new, state-of-the art facility designed specifically for the preschool has an outdoor science area, a large outdoor playground, and an art studio. Older children enjoy field trips.

Admission: By application date and other considerations (e.g., parental enthusiasm and interests).

PARENT RATING: ☆ ☆ ☆ ☆ ☆

The new facility is "beautiful," and they have a "great" art program and "professionally-run" school with an "active" director and "innovative curriculum." Parents emphasized that the school's "excellent afternoon enrichment programs" (ballet, sports, gymnastics, swimming, and art) are "especially convenient for working parents" as children are escorted by a preschool teacher to the extracurricular classes in the main JCC building. The parents' association is very strong and active. The school has been very successful in private elementary school admissions. Parents also appreciate the access to the adjoining JCC facility with its wonderful new fitness center!

Little Gators Preschool

3149 Steiner St.

415-346-8608

Ages: 2-5 years

Schedule: Mornings or afternoons, 2 or 3 days a week (schedule determined by age). No extended care.

Ratio: 6:1

Philosophy/other: This private preschool offers a developmental curriculum, including music, art, games, stories, cooking, dance, introduction to letters and numbers, social studies, science, computer, and motor skills. They focus on helping children develop a positive self-image. The school day is well structured and organized, with a balance of self- and teacher-directed projects, and a monthly calendar provided to parents. There is a small outdoor area.

Admission: By application, with priority to siblings. Admission is from a waiting pool, with emphasis on the interest level of parents and "fit" with the program.

PARENT RATING: ☆ ☆ ☆ ☆ ☆

Parents liked the "cozy" class size and loving feel of the school, and praised the "involved" director/founder, a San Francisco native. Comment: "Children move through fun and different projects in a smooth way." They say the parent community is "closely knit" owing to the large amount of parent involvement in the school and a number of social events for parents. The assistant teachers are "very energetic." The school has a great track record with private school admissions.

The Little School

1520 Lyon St.

415-567-0430

www.littleschool.org

Ages: 2-6 years (including transitional kindergarten program)

Schedule: Mornings or afternoons, 2 to 5 days a week (schedule determined by age). Extended care available.

Ratio: 7:1

Philosophy/other: This private non-profit school in Lower Pacific Heights has a developmental, child-centered philosophy. The curriculum includes music and movement, art, dramatic play, writing, woodworking, and free play. There is time for individual play and group activities. Children stay with the same group during their entire education at the school.

Admission: By application prior to deadline and attendance at an orientation meeting. Admission is very selective and diversity-oriented, with criteria such as gender, age, special needs, and ethnicity taken into consideration. The date of application no longer has any bearing on admissions, but siblings receive preference.

PARENT RATING: ☆ ☆ ☆ ☆ ☆

Parents reported this highly competitive school, one of the "best" in the city, takes early childhood education "very seriously," and it has even developed a video about its philosophy for other educators. The facility is "top-notch," with an innovative design featuring generous-sized outdoor and indoor play areas. Parents praised the "creative" play and "unusual" projects encouraged by the teachers. Parents are "very involved" with the school. They report it is very difficult for new families to get in, although there are sometimes openings in the transitional kindergarten program.

Marin Day Schools

Temple Sherith Israel Campus

2266 California St.

415-775-2211

www.marindayschools.org

Other SF campuses: Hills Plaza, 2 Harrison St.; Spear St., 220 Spear St.; Laurel Heights, 3333 California St.; City Hall, 1 Dr. Carlton B. Goodlett Pl.; Fremont St., 342 Howard St.; Fox Plaza, 1390 Market St. (infant-toddler only).

Ages: 2-6 years (other campuses accept younger children)

Schedule: Open all year. Mornings, afternoons, or all day with extended care available.

Ratio: 6:1 (2-year-olds); 8:1 (3-year-olds); 9:1 (4-year-olds)

Philosophy/other: The developmental curriculum incorporates play, math and reading, music and art, and motor skills, with different themes for each month. Other campuses in San Francisco include day care for younger children. The Sherith Israel campus offers a separate, optional Jewish curriculum component to its program for Temple members.

Admission: By date of application, with preference for siblings. Each campus gives preference to certain groups from whom they lease space or have corporate affiliations. At the popular Sherith Israel campus, members of the Temple and employees of CPMC receive priority in admissions.

Preschols

PARENT RATING: ☆ ☆ ☆ ☆

Parents were very pleased with the flexible scheduling (including accommodating last-minute requests for extended care), the school's "excellent" communication with parents and "professional" attitude (including a special annual presentation on kindergarten admissions), and the "theme" approach to the curriculum. The year-round program and extended care are tailored to working parents. See also Ch. 9 under Day Care Centers.

La Piccola Scuola Italiana

2616 Sutter St.

415-567-2663

www.lpsisf.org

Ages: 6-24 months (Italian play-group), 2-5 years (preschool)

Schedule: Mornings (with lunch) for ages 2-3 years, 3 to 5 days per week. Mornings (with lunch) or afternoons, 3 to 5 days per week, for ages 3-5 years. Afternoon playgroup for ages 6-24 months.

Ratio: 3:1 in playgroups (not including parents); 4:1 in preschool

Philosophy/other: Begun by a group of parents several years ago, this nonprofit cooperative school in a Lower Pacific Heights residence offers an Italian language immersion program with a Reggio-Emilia approach. The project-based curriculum includes art, music, drama, science, math, and sculpture/construction, and integrates pre-academic skills. The physical space is organized into "learning centers" (writing, house-keeping, blocks, and so on). Children are grouped by age, with one group for the 2 to 3.6-year-olds and another

for the 3.6 to 5-year-olds. The children help prepare the home-cooked, family-style, hormone- and antibiotic-free Italian lunches, using almost exclusively organic foods.

Admission: By application, due February 1 each year. They strive to create a group balanced in gender, Italian language skills, and disposition. Children do not need to speak Italian in order to enroll, but they prefer that children older than 18 months have previous exposure to the Italian language. Parents are asked to commit to speaking Italian as much as possible outside the classroom.

PARENT RATING: ☆ ☆ ☆ ☆ ☆

This very popular and reputable new school strives to create an authentic Italian culture and community among their children, many of whom have at least one European parent. Parents love the "talented" director, an American with extensive experience working in Italian preschools. They say there is "high demand" for the program, and the waiting list is lengthy. The school is actively looking for a bigger site.

Russian Hill School

2026 Divisadero St.

415-202-0525

www.russianhillschool.org

Ages: 3-6 years (includes transitional kindergarten)

Schedule: Mornings, afternoons, or full day, 5 days a week. Open year round.

Ratio: 4:1 (and parents may work in class, improving ratio)

Philosophy/other: This small non-profit developmental school has a unique, mixed-age, art- and music-based curriculum designed to promote academic readiness and self-reliance. Learning is "child-directed", with a balance between organized and free activity, and they can accommodate children with special needs. They have a private yard, and also take field trips to the neighborhood parks and library. The school was located in Russian Hill for 24 years before moving to its current location in Pacific Heights.

Admission: By tour, application, and observation of child. Admission is from a waiting list, and the school balances ages, genders, and ethnicities.

PARENT RATING: ☆ ☆ ☆ ☆

Parents say the school has an innovative curriculum and a good track record with private school admissions.

St. Luke's School

1755 Clay St.
415-474-9489
www.stlukespreschool.org

Ages: 2.6-5.9 years

Schedule: Mornings or afternoons, 3 to 5 days a week (schedule determined by age). No extended care.

Ratio: 9:1

Philosophy/other: This structured, NAEYC-accredited program balances between academic instruction, social interaction, and artistic expression. The school is located in St. Luke's Episcopal Church. The academic curriculum includes grace and courtesy, music and movement, art, cooking, ballet, gymnastics, French, social studies, reading, and stories.

Admission: By date of application and by interview, with preference for siblings. Tours are by invitation only. In recent years, only parents who applied very early (i.e., during pregnancy) or had ties to the school were able to get their children into this very competitive school.

PARENT RATING: ☆ ☆ ☆ ☆ ☆

Parents report that this well-established, top-tier, "traditional" school presents a "positive environment" where students are very "well-disciplined" and emerge ready for kindergarten, owing to the "academic" orientation. The school has a stellar reputation for getting its graduates into private elementary schools.

Tiny Giants Preschool and Child Care Center

1748 Clay St.
415-359-9499

Ages: Infant to age 5 for day care; 2-5 years for preschool

Schedule: Preschool is mornings or afternoons, 2 to 5 days a week (schedule determined by age). Preschool students may also enroll in the day care program for extended care.

Ratio: 5:1

Philosophy/other: Recently founded (2004), this Russian Hill neighborhood school offers both a preschool and a day care program. In the preschool, children are divided by age into 3 separate classes. They offer a developmental curriculum with a balance between play and structured time, including art, music, pre-math, and pre-writing. They have a large outdoor space.

Admission: By application, attendance at a January open house, and a family meeting with the director. Considerations include "fit" with the program and philosophy, as well as balance of genders and ages. Families enrolled in the day care program are guaranteed a spot in the preschool.

PARENT RATING: ☆ ☆ ☆ ☆

Parents say this school is "awesome! Really wonderful physical space, warm loving teachers, and great student-teacher ratios."

PRESIDIO/LAKE STREET/ RICHMOND/SUNSET

Lakeside Presbyterian Center for Children

201 Eucalyptus Dr.
415-564-5044

Ages: 2.6-6 years

Schedule: Mornings or afternoons; 2, 3, or 5 days a week (schedule determined by age). Extended care available.

Ratio: 6:1

Philosophy/other: NAEYC accredited, this developmental program has a Christian orientation and is affiliated with the Lakeside Presbyterian Church. The curriculum includes socialization, daily art projects, songs and games.

Admission: By interview visit with parents and child.

PARENT RATING: ☆ ☆ ☆ ☆

Parents report that classrooms are "large," outdoor equipment "great" and projects "creative." Most of the students' families "are not members of the church," and there is not a "heavy dose" of religion. Parents are expected to participate "quite a bit" in the school events.

Lone Mountain Children's Center

The Presidio
1806 Belles St.
415-561-2333

Ages: 2.7-5 years

Schedule: Mornings or afternoons; 2, 3, or 5 days a week (schedule determined by age). No extended care.

Ratio: 8:1

Philosophy/other: This private, nonprofit school offers a developmentally appropriate experience for each of its three age-segregated levels. The curriculum is theme-based and offers a range of hands-on learning experiences with lots of time for free play and self-direction. Children rotate through activities during the school day in small groups. The school moved to a refurbished building in the Presidio in 2001 and recently expanded its outdoor play area.

Admission: By date of application relative to the child's date of birth, with preference for siblings and children of alumni. All who apply while pregnant or within the first two months of their child's life are grouped at the top of the list and go into a lottery for admission, and the class is usually filled from this group. The school tries to achieve a gender balance. Parents are invited to visit the school when there is a space to offer.

PARENT RATING: ☆ ☆ ☆ ☆ ☆

Parents call this school "top notch," "extremely nurturing" and "focused" on the children. Children have the same group of teachers throughout their years at the school, so teachers "really get to know the children." Comment: "The teachers are all very professional, and some have been there for many years, including the director who is active in the classroom. . . . The team approach with all the teachers in the classroom makes for a great student-teacher ratio." Parents say "kids come out of the program very ready for a demanding elementary school experience," and the school has an "excellent" reputation for getting children into private elementary schools.

Montessori Children's House of the West Coast

25 Lake St.

415-922-9235

www.mchsf.com

Ages: 2.9-5.11 years

Schedule: Open all year, half or full days (schedule determined by age). Extended care available.

Ratio: 6:1

Philosophy/other: The nonsectarian, Montessori curriculum focuses on communication skills. Parents must volunteer 18 hours per year for the school. There is no outdoor space on site, but students take daily walks to nearby parks and regular field trips. There is a pre-k program in the afternoons.

Admission: By application and interview. Parents are encouraged to submit an application 12 to 24 months in advance of the expected date of enrollment.

PARENT RATING: ☆ ☆ ☆ ☆ ☆

Parents are very involved with the school and give it high praise. Comments: "Both the program and community are awesome. It's a traditional Montessori school, but they welcome parent volunteers in the classroom. . . . The afterschool program is great because of the enrichment classes like Spanish, art, music, and gymnastics. . . . The separate pre-k program emphasizes journal writing. . . . The teachers are very diverse and experienced."

Mother Goose School

334 28th Ave.

415-221-6133

Ages: 2-6 years

Schedule: Open 7 a.m.-6 p.m., year round. Mornings, afternoons, or full-day programs; 2, 3, or 5 days. Hot lunch provided.

Ratio: 8:1

Philosophy/other: Located in outer Richmond near Sea Cliff, this developmental preschool has an academic-based program, with a strong emphasis on social skills. The program includes music, phonics, letters, themes, numbers, and small motor skills. Children are grouped by age levels in separate classrooms, and enjoy 3 different play yards according to age.

Admission: Call to schedule a tour with your child. After touring, you may deposit a registration fee, guaranteeing your schedule and starting date. In 2005, the school was registering families 8-10 months before start dates.

PARENT RATING: ☆ ☆ ☆ ☆

Parents say the school is "very thorough" and provides "great feedback at the end of each day." There is

559

"very little teacher turnover." Parents appreciated the "flexible" scheduling and "academic, structured environment." The curriculum is "kindergarten level," and students are "writing their names and sentences by the time they graduate." Graduates go on to private (35%), parochial (35%), and public (30%) schools.

150 Parker Avenue School

150 Parker Ave.
415-221-0294
www.onefiftyparker.org
Ages: 2.9-6 years (includes kindergarten program)
Schedule: Mornings or afternoons, 5 days a week (schedule determined by age). Extended care available.
Ratio: 6:1
Philosophy/other: This nonprofit corporation is run by a board of parents and the director. Founded in 1954, the school features a developmental, experience-based curriculum with a focus on the natural environment, including fine and gross motor skills, music, creative arts, social skills, and preparation for academics. The school was recently renovated and is located in a historic red schoolhouse in the residential Laurel Heights neighborhood.
Admission: By application, "educational considerations and date of inquiry." The school seeks diversity in admissions.
PARENT RATING: ☆ ☆ ☆ ☆ ☆

This is a small, well-established, and well-regarded program with a "great" director and outdoor space. The school takes a "holistic" approach to the child and has a "fabulous" art program. Children can "float" to different areas of interest during free play periods.

Peter's Place Nursery School

227 Balboa St.
415-752-1444
www.petersplace.org
Ages: 2.9-5 years
Schedule: Mornings or afternoons; 2, 3, or 5 days a week (schedule determined by age). Lunch program but no extended care.
Ratio: 7:1 or 6:1 (no more than 20 students with 3 teachers)
Philosophy/other: This private nonprofit Richmond neighborhood school offers a developmental curriculum focusing on encouraging confidence and self-esteem in each child. The school has a small setting in a renovated building with an outdoor area in the backyard.
Admission: By application date with preference for continuing students, siblings, and children with special needs. The school tries to balance genders in each class.
PARENT RATING: ☆ ☆ ☆ ☆ ☆

Parents appreciate the small size of this highly regarded school and the "low teacher turnover rate," allowing teachers to focus on each child.

St. James Preschool

4620 California St.
415-752-8258
www.stjamessf.org
Ages: 2-5
Schedule: Mornings or afternoons, 5 days a week (2-year-olds can choose fewer days). Extended care available.

Ratio: 4:1 for 2; 6:1 for 3; 7:1 for 4

Philosophy/other: Founded in 1963, this NAEYC-accredited preschool is affiliated with the Episcopal Church, but operates nondenominationally. They have weekly chapel with stories and lessons from many different traditions. The curriculum is developmental and project-based, includes art, music, cooking, science, and stories, and focuses on personal confidence, social skills, and language development. They will assist families with toilet training, and they take frequent trips to Mountain Lake Park and the local library. The school is planning to expand its facility and increase the number of children it can accommodate.

Admission: By application, with preferences for siblings and active members of the church. They also consider diversity, and seek to balance genders and ages in their classes.

PARENT RATING: ☆ ☆ ☆ ☆ ☆

Parents call this "gem" of a preschool "warm, cozy, nurturing, and incredibly supportive. . . . They emphasize behavior and attitude, and among my child's peers in kindergarten those who went to St. James know how to treat others. . . . They do plenty of academics too, but it's not overly stressed. . . . My 3 children were all very ready for kindergarten." The school has a good track record with kindergarten admissions.

The Serra Preschool

The Presidio
7 Funston Ave.
415-561-2200
www.theserrapreschool.com
Ages: 2.9 to 5.9 years

Schedule: Mornings including lunch for 3-year-olds, afternoons for younger 4-year-olds, mornings for pre-k/transitional kindergarten class.

Ratio: 6:1 for preschool classes; 5:1 for pre-k class

Philosophy/other: This new preschool, opened in January 2005, offers an emergent, developmental curriculum "with a spiritual framework based on Roman Catholic traditions." Making use of its location in a restored Civil War-era officers' home in the Presidio, the school also has a science program, an art room, and a huge outdoor area. Children are divided into 3 classes by age.

Admission: They have a "wait pool" from which they accept students, balancing date of application, ages, and genders.

PARENT RATING: ☆ ☆ ☆ ☆

This new and respectable preschool has a "great facility." The "experienced director" has worked in the field for 30 years, including many years as an instructor at 150 Parker School.

Temple Emanu-El Preschool

2 Lake St.
415-751-2541, ext. 118
www.emanuelsf.org
Ages: 2.0-5.6 years

Schedule: Mornings, 5 days a week (except for young 2-year-olds who attend 3 mornings). Extended care available.

Ratio: 6:1

Philosophy/other: The developmental curriculum in this NAEYC-accredited school incorporates Jewish values and traditions. Children spend time with a mixed-age group for a part of the day, and then move to small groups. Additional programs include storytelling, music and movement, and Friday Shabbat. Outdoor play is held in an atrium area. They also offer parent-child programs for babies and toddlers; see Ch. 7 under Gym and Play Programs—San Francisco.

Admission: By date of application, with preference for siblings and Temple members.

PARENT RATING: ☆ ☆ ☆ ☆ ☆

There is a "strong" religious component to the program, with non-Jewish children welcome but only Jewish traditions taught. Parents report that the school has an "excellent" director, "extremely well-educated" teachers, and a very good reputation for getting children into private kindergartens.

WESTERN ADDITION/HAIGHT ASHBURY/COLE VALLEY

Chinese-American International School (CAIS)
150 Oak St.
415-865-6000
www.cais.org

Ages: 3 years to 12th grade

Schedule: Full school day, 5 days a week. Extended care available.

Ratio: 8:1

Philosophy/other: Located between the Civic Center and Western Addition, this private nonprofit independent school offers a bilingual immersion Mandarin Chinese/English Montessori program. Prior Chinese is not required. Students spend half of each day with an English teacher and half with a Mandarin Chinese teacher.

The curriculum includes Montessori lessons, everyday life skill experiences, auditory and speaking skills, storytelling, music, games, and after-school enrichment classes.

Admission: By tour, application, parent interview, and evaluation visit.

PARENT RATING: ☆ ☆ ☆ ☆

Parents seeking to send their children to CAIS for elementary school are encouraged to apply to the preschool program. Although more than 50% of the students are Asian-American, most of the students are from non-Mandarin-speaking households. Parents are "very involved" in the school. The full-day program "is great for working parents, in particular. . . . Our daughter began with no knowledge of Mandarin and now can converse in a language I can't even pronounce much less understand! The school performances, with songs in Mandarin, are not to be missed."

French-American International School (FAIS)
150 Oak St.
415-558-2060
www.fais-ihs.org

Ages: 4 years to 12th grade

Schedule: Full school day, 5 days a week. Extended care available.

Ratio: 10:1

Philosophy/other: On the same campus as CAIS, this private independent school offers a structured, bilingual French-English program beginning with the pre-k year; they do not offer a preschool. Prior French is not required. The curriculum meets French and State of California requirements. In the early grades, students spend 80 percent of their time with a French teacher and 20 percent with an English teacher.

Admission: By campus visit, application, and interview (with an emphasis on a child's auditory and language development skills and a shared philosophy of family and school).

PARENT RATING: ☆ ☆ ☆ ☆

Parents report the pre-k program is "excellent" and "more structured" and "intensive" than the average preschool. Parents seeking to enroll their child in the FAIS elementary school are encouraged to apply to the pre-k program. The school offers "great facilities," and it attracts a "very diverse" student population.

Lycée Français La Pérouse

- San Francisco
  755 Ashbury St.
  415-661-5232
- Corte Madera
  330 Golden Hind Passage
  415-924-1737
www.lelycee.org

Ages: 2.6 years to 12th grade

Schedule: Full school day, 5 days per week. A half-day program option is available in Corte Madera for the youngest students (under 3.9 years). Extended care available.

Ratio: 10:1

Philosophy/other: A French immersion program, the "Lycée" is a private school but part of a worldwide French educational network. It follows the French public school curriculum and is funded by the French government. The preschool, known as the "Maternelle," extends through kindergarten. The curriculum focuses on socialization, academics (pre-reading, pre-math, and pre-writing), and learning the language, and incorporates gymnastics, art, music, and theater. Preschool students spend 5 hours per week with an English-speaking teacher, and the remainder of the time speaking French. The day is "highly structured." About 50% of the families have at least one parent who speaks French. The Ashbury Heights campus was renovated recently.

Admission: By application, interview, and child observation session. Preschool applicants and their parents need not speak French to apply.

PARENT RATING: ☆ ☆ ☆ ☆ ☆

Parents say this "fabulous" school has a "strong sense of community" and a very "diverse" international student body, with many families from countries other than France. Comment: "The preschool program is structured and well thought out. I can see my daughter learning a lot there . . . in addition to French." Parents say they "get a lot of information about how children are doing through a 'cahier' ('log book') of activities." The Lycée system also works well for families who move from country to country because the program is the same worldwide.

Pacific Primary

1500 Grove St.
415-346-0906
www.pacificprimary.org

Ages: 2.5-6 years

Schedule: Flexible. Open all day, all year.

Ratio: 7:1 or 5:1, depending on age of child.

Philosophy/other: This developmental, open-ended, and thematic curriculum emphasizes creative arts and conflict resolution skills. The school celebrates diversity among its families and draws from the Western Addition/Panhandle neighborhood in which it sits. Designed to meet the needs of working parents, it serves breakfast, lunch, and snacks.

Admission: By application and interview (with preference for siblings). The school seeks a diverse population and welcomes children with special needs. Admission is very selective.

PARENT RATING: ☆ ☆ ☆ ☆

Parents raved about the active dramatic program that culminates in a school play at the end of the year. Parental involvement is required.

NOE VALLEY/MISSION/ SOUTH OF MARKET

Parents report that despite an influx of families to Noe Valley, the neighborhood remains tremendously underserved in terms of preschools. Many popular programs have closed or relocated in recent years. With demand so high, Noe Valley parents are advised to look early!

Big City Montessori School

240 Industrial St.

415-648-5777

www.bigcitymontessorischool.com

Ages: 2-6 (includes kindergarten)

Schedule: Full school day, 5 days a week, year round (except for the part-time toddler program for ages 2-3.5 years). Extended care is included in tuition (7 a.m.-6 p.m).

Ratio: 5:1 for toddlers; 8:1 for pre-k and kindergarten

Philosophy/other: The oldest family-owned and operated preschool in the city, this AMI-certified Montessori school located in Bernal Heights offers a full-time schedule tailored to working parents. Extracurricular classes include art, music, Spanish, gymnastics, drama, and cooking. They accept toddlers in diapers and will assist with toilet training, and they have a large playground and garden and a hot lunch program. The school does not require any parent participation.

Admission: By application, visit, and interview.

PARENT RATING: ☆ ☆ ☆ ☆

Parents say the students and teachers are very diverse, "there is virtually no teacher turnover," teachers are "very available" to help with development issues, and the school focuses on developing social skills.

Children's Day School

333 Dolores St.

415-861-5432

www.cds-sf.org

Ages: 3 years to 8th grade

Schedule: Full school day, 5 days a week. Extended care available.

Ratio: 6:1

Philosophy/other: This private non-profit independent school has an inquiry-based, project-based, multi-cultural curriculum. They focus on teaching respect for diversity and each child's individual needs and background. The curriculum includes environmental education and Spanish, and the school features a farm and organic garden on an acre of land, as well as specialists in art, music, and movement. Tuition is on a sliding scale for eligible families.

Admission: By application, interview, and visit to the school. Admission is selective, based on the applicant's "social, emotional, and cognitive development." Admissions are rolling, but applicants are encouraged to apply before mid-January for September entry.

PARENT RATING: ☆ ☆ ☆ ☆ ☆

It's a "unique" setting with a farm and garden on more than an acre of land in the heart of the Mission. Parents especially appreciate the school's "multicultural emphasis" and extended hours to accommodate working parents.

Eureka Learning Center

- 464 Diamond St., 415-648-0380
- 551 Eureka St., 415-821-3422

Ages: 2.6-5 years

Schedule: Mornings or full school day, 5 days a week. Early arrival care, but no care after 3 p.m.

Ratio: 5:1 (preschool); 8:1 (pre-k)

Philosophy/other: This NAEYC-accredited, developmental program is based on "real life" activities, including art, woodworking, dance, dramatic play, language, music, natural science, math, and field trips.

Admission: By date of application, with preference for siblings and consideration for gender balance and diversity. There is a several-year-long waiting list, so parents are encouraged to apply early.

PARENT RATING: ☆ ☆ ☆ ☆ ☆

The school has a reputation as "the best" in Noe Valley. Parents also appreciate the small class sizes (15 children) and outdoor play opportunities.

Katherine Michiels School

1335 Guerrero St.
415-821-1434
www.katherinemichielsschool.org

Ages: Infants through 5th grade. Preschool is ages 2-5.

Schedule: 7 a.m.-6 p.m., 5 days per week, with optional extended care to midnight each night.

Ratio: 8:1 for preschool

Philosophy/other: Founded in 1976, this nonprofit, developmental, child-centered school is located in a historic Mission District Victorian mansion. The non-traditional curriculum incorporates Piaget High/Scope and Reggio Emilio concepts, and children move freely through activity rooms known as "learning stations." Some of the school's unique features include an "untimed" curriculum, an organic vegetable garden, a "dirt mountain" in the play yard, an environmental awareness program where the children participate in composting, weekly field trips, wearing slippers indoors, and an on-site kitchen serving hot, organic, vegetarian meals.

Admission: By application, attendance at open house, and interview.

PARENT RATING: ☆ ☆ ☆ ☆

Parents, particularly working parents, praised this innovative program. They celebrate their multiethnic community. It can be difficult to get into the infants program, so it's best to apply when you are pregnant.

565

The Preschool

Baja Noe Valley

415-285-5327

www.ThePreschool.com

Ages: 2-6 years (most are ages 3-5)

Schedule: Mornings, 5 days a week. Lunch program, but no extended care.

Ratio: 15:3 (sometimes 15:4)

Philosophy/other: This NAEYC-accredited, developmental program with mixed-age groups includes art, music, dance, stories, cooking, gardening, Spanish, math, science, and nature.

Admission: By date of application, with preference for siblings and consideration of gender and age balance. The school contacts parents for tours when openings arise.

PARENT RATING: ☆ ☆ ☆ ☆

Parents appreciate the "nurturing" environment of this small school.

The San Francisco School

300 Gaven St.

415-239-5065

www.sfschool.org

Ages: 3 years to 8th grade (for preschool/kindergarten: ages 3-6)

Schedule: Full school day, 5 days a week. Extended care available.

Ratio: 36:4

Philosophy/other: The curriculum in this private, independent, nonprofit school is a mixture of developmental and Montessori philosophies. The school encourages diversity among students, and teachers are trained in the Montessori method. It also provides 2 preschool-kindergarten classrooms.

Admission: By tour, application, and a family interview.

PARENT RATING: ☆ ☆ ☆ ☆ ☆

This "structured" preschool program provides an entrée into the excellent elementary school. Admission is very selective. Commuting parents say the school's location near the 280/101 highways' interchange is "ideal."

Treehouse Preschool and Treehouse Pre-K

- Preschool
  75 Fountain St.
  415-641-8867
- Pre-K
  16 Agua Way
  415-661-4745

www.treehouseprek.com

Ages: 2-5 years (preschool); 3.5-5.5 years (pre-k)

Schedule: Full school day; 3, 4, or 5 days a week. Extended care available.

Ratio: 5:1 (preschool); 4:1 (pre-k)

Philosophy/other: These sister schools in Noe Valley and Miraloma Park offer developmental, thematic curriculums including pre-reading, math and science, dance, art, music, storytelling, dramatic arts, and gymnastics. The pre-k program is more structured than the preschool. Children are grouped by ages.

Admission: By application, with consideration to age, gender, and schedule desired. Call for a tour and submit an application in the fall before the year of entry.

PARENT RATING: ☆ ☆ ☆ ☆

Comments (all pertaining to the pre-k program): "Our children have come home happy from preschool every day. . . . It feels like a home away from home, where the children are loved, nurtured, appreciated for their individuality, and corrected when necessary. . . . The curriculum is well structured. . . . The director provides parents with a calendar with a theme for each month; the children do activities and projects about [the theme]. . . . It's a wonderful school that combines all the best of a larger preschool—music, art, athletics, and skill building—with the intimate small group feel that [preschoolers] crave and need. . . . Amy runs a wonderful operation with a stellar cast of college-educated teachers that will wow even the most discriminating parent. . . . The teachers are fabulous, enthusiastic, and patient, and [they] approach their jobs with joy, enthusiasm, and genuine affection for the kids."

Wind in the Willows Early Learning Center

713 Monterey Blvd.
415-333-7166
www.windinthewillows.org

Ages: 3-5 years

Schedule: Mornings or afternoons, 2 to 5 days a week. No extended care.

Ratio: 6:1 in morning; 5:1 in afternoon.

Philosophy/other: This long-time neighborhood nonprofit school moved from Noe Valley to Sunnyside in 2000. It offers a developmental program emphasizing creativity, socialization, play, and language development. Enrollment is limited to 18 children in each half-day session, and children are in a mixed-age grouping. Children who will be entering kindergarten the next year have a designated pre-k work time with emphasis on large and fine motor skills, pre-reading, writing, math, and science.

Admission: By date of application, but with consideration to gender, age, and diversity balance, and the child's developmental readiness. The waiting list opens one year prior to the fall start date. The parents and children attend an open house in the spring.

PARENT RATING: ☆ ☆ ☆ ☆ ☆

Despite the change in location, this school remains a favorite among Noe Valley parents, who love its small size and warm environment. Parents are encouraged to participate in the classroom and in fund-raising activities. Comment: "There is a lot of opportunity for dramatic play and art. . . . Not only did our child receive a well-rounded and memorable preschool experience, but our family made good friends through the school, friends who we continue to see years later, though our children have gone to different elementary schools."

North Bay

SOUTHERN MARIN

See also the Corte Madera schools listed under Central Marin, below, attended by many Southern Marin families.

Belvedere Hawthorne Nursery Schools

415-435-1661
• Belvedere
  1 Cove Road Pl. (Belvedere Nursery School)

567

- Tiburon
  145 Rock Hill Dr. (Hawthorne
  Pre-k)

Ages: 2.6 years to pre-k

Schedule: Mornings; 2, 3, or 5 days a week. Extended care available.

Ratio: 6:1

Philosophy/other: Founded in 1939 and recently accredited by the NAEYC, this nonprofit corporation is the oldest independent nursery school in Marin County. The curriculum includes social and motor skills, listening, following directions, problem solving, art and music, nature, science, math, crafts, puppetry, stories, and play. Pre-k students study sequential units of different topics. They also offer a "Time for Twos" program for young 2-year-olds with parent participation.

Admission: By date of application, with priority for siblings, legacies, and residents of the Reed Union School District.

PARENT RATING: ☆ ☆ ☆ ☆ ☆

Parents love this "very popular" and "traditional" school. They say "the teachers are very experienced, have been at the school for many years, and have an impressive set of credentials. . . . They use a team approach, with 7 teachers in the classroom with 38 children, making for a great student/teacher ratio." Parents are very involved in fundraising for the school. They advise applying as early as possible, as there is a long waiting list.

Kumara School
540 Marin Ave.
Mill Valley
415-388-5437
www.kumaraschool.com

Ages: 2.6-6 years

Schedule: Mornings or full school day, 3 to 5 days a week. Extended care available. Open year round except August.

Ratio: 8:1

Philosophy/other: This private "alternative" preschool and kindergarten offers a child-initiated, play-based curriculum. They believe that children will be excited about learning if they are allowed to explore and choose their own activities in an open, unstructured setting. Most of the day is spent in a mixed-age group, aside from a short "core group" time with children of similar ages. Children can choose from art, outside, large-motor, small-motor, and pre-kindergarten activities. Enrichment programs are available in music, Aikido, dance, and swimming.

Admission: By application and observation of child.

PARENT RATING: ☆ ☆ ☆ ☆

Parents say the program is "highly experiential, with lots of hands-on learning." Parent participation is not required.

Marin Day Schools
- Hillside
  80 Lomita Dr., Mill Valley,
  415-381-3120
- Mill Valley
  10 Old Mill Rd., 415-381-4206
- San Rafael
  1123 Court St., 415-453-9822

- St. Vincent's
  #1 St. Vincent's Dr., San Rafael,
  415-479-0531

See San Francisco listing. The Hillside campus (formerly in Tiburon) is particularly popular.

Marin Horizon School

305 Montford Ave.
Mill Valley
415-388-8408
www.marinhorizon.org

Ages: 2 years-8th grade

Schedule: Full school day, 3 to 5 days a week. Extended care available.

Ratio: 9:1

Philosophy/other: Founded in 1977, this private nonprofit independent school offers a child-centered, Montessori-inspired curriculum. Their "values education" emphasizes respect for diversity and the environment. They have a toddler program for ages 2-3, and a 3-year-cycle primary class culminating in kindergarten. The primary class curriculum includes reading, math readiness, world cultural studies, science, art, and music, in addition to the traditional Montessori practical life skills. Students begin to study Spanish in kindergarten.

Admission: By application, tour, and observation/assessment of child.

PARENT RATING: ☆ ☆ ☆ ☆ ☆

Parents say this "hidden gem" is a "great, Montessori-based but not rigid Montessori" preschool, with "a very nurturing environment." Academics are very strong, but the social development and values taught are also very important. They have "about as much demographic diversity as you can get in Marin." Parents say the teachers are "wonderful and all have different styles, and the school is good at matching children with the right teacher." They especially love the toddler program. The school is planning to renovate and expand its facility.

Mill Valley Nursery School

51 Shell Rd.
Mill Valley
415-388-9174
www.ccppns.org/mvns

Ages: 2.9-5 years

Schedule: Mornings, 5 days a week. Extended care available until 2:15 p.m.

Ratio: 5:1

Philosophy/other: Established in 1941, this small parent-cooperative school offers a play-based program. The theme-based curriculum includes art, cooking, stories, games, science, music, and field trips. Children enjoy free choice of indoor and outdoor activities.

Admission: By date of application, with consideration to gender balance. They would like parents to understand the level of involvement required by a cooperative school.

PARENT RATING: ☆ ☆ ☆ ☆ ☆

This well-established favorite is a "small family-oriented school" with "a strong sense of community," enrolling only 22 families per year. Comment: "What an amazing and unexpected experience. . . . Not only has our son blossomed in the play-based environment, but our entire family has made friend[ship]s that will last a lifetime."

Old Firehouse School

10 Olive St.
Mill Valley
415-388-1417
www.oldfirehouseschool.com

Ages: 13 months to 5 years

Schedule: Open all day, year round.

Ratio: 4:1 (16-24 months); 6:1 (2- and 3-year olds)

Philosophy/other: A branch of the eponymous school in Lafayette (see East Bay listing), this new location in downtown Mill Valley offers a similar Reggio Emilia-inspired, child-centered curriculum, with innovative project-based learning. There are 2 classrooms, and children are grouped by age, spanning about a year in each classroom. The children begin together as toddlers and stay in the same class, with the same teachers, throughout their tenure at the school until kindergarten. In 2005, about one-third of families were on a full-time schedule. They have a split-level outdoor play area and go on nature walks and field trips around Mill Valley. Old Mill Park is directly across the street.

Admission: By date of application, which can be submitted after attending an open house or tour. Families requesting a full-time schedule have preference in admission. Because the children begin as toddlers and stay together until kindergarten, openings generally do not arise until an entire class graduates or someone leaves the school. In 2005, the children ranged from 13 months to 2 years old.

PARENT RATING: ☆ ☆ ☆ ☆ ☆

Parents say the teachers, many of whom came from the Lafayette branch, are "experienced, awesome, sensitive, highly educated, professional, communicative, warm, nurturing, adored by their pupils, and work in teams with the parents. . . . It's a wonderful school with an enchanting quality apparent when you walk through the door. There is a lot of attention to detail in the care of the children, and they keep parents well informed about daily happenings and the child's progress. They have creative, stimulating, in-depth projects, often about subjects the kids see every day. . . . Because the projects are child-driven they are excited about what they are learning and constantly making new discoveries. . . . The stable class structure is unique. . . . The facilities are immaculate. . . . The school hosts invaluable complimentary parent education. . . . We have been thrilled with the care."

Strawberry Preschool/ Tamalpais Preschool

- Tiburon
  240 Tiburon Blvd., 415-388-4437
- Mill Valley
  410 Sycamore Ave., 415-388-4286

Ages: 2.9 to pre-k

Schedule: Mornings; 2, 3, or 5 days a week. Extended care available.

Ratio: 9:1

Philosophy/other: These "sister" non-profit nonsectarian preschools offer a developmental curriculum. The NAEYC-accredited programs include math and reading readiness, arts and crafts, sensory motor games, music, drama, cooking, carpentry, outdoor play, gardening, science, and nature study.

Admission: By date of application (with preference for siblings).

PARENT RATING: ☆ ☆ ☆ ☆ ☆

Parents appreciated the "excellent, spacious" facilities, "very enthusiastic" and "committed" teachers, "warm atmosphere," and the "traditional preschool" approach. They recommend applying early for this "very popular" program, as waiting lists often close several years in advance.

Sausalito Nursery School

625 Main St.
Sausalito
415-332-0174
www.sausalitonurseryschool.org

Ages: 2.6-4 years

Schedule: Mornings (including lunch); 2, 3, or 5 days a week (schedule determined by age). Extended care available.

Ratio: 4:1

Philosophy/other: Founded in 1939, this small nonprofit school (they accept only 12 students a year) is one of the oldest cooperative nursery schools in the country. The school is located on a double lot in the Old Town neighborhood. The developmental curriculum includes music, art, gymnastics, and storytelling.

Admission: By date of application, with priority to siblings and children of alumni.

PARENT RATING: ☆ ☆ ☆ ☆ ☆

Comments: "Since it is a cooperative, there is great parent involvement in the school, and the kids get to know all the parents and visa versa. It is very nurturing and a great way of strengthening the community in the most fundamental way." Parents say the long-time director is "wonderful" and the facility is "storybook picturesque with a great outdoor area." Parent participation is required only one day per month.

CENTRAL MARIN

Children's Cottage Cooperative Nursery School

2900 Larkspur Landing Cir.
Larkspur
415-461-0822
www.cccmarin.com

Ages: 2-4 years

Schedule: Mornings; 2, 3, or 5 days a week. Extended care available.

Ratio: 4:1

Philosophy/other: This cooperative preschool is located in a historic cottage built in 1891. The school was founded in 1949 and is NAEYC accredited. They have a developmental curriculum with both large-group, mixed-age activities and small-group time where children are grouped by age. Activities include art, music, science, nature, math, and reading. The summer sessions are open to non-cooperative members.

Admission: By date of application, with preference for siblings and alumni, and consideration to gender balance. Parents must visit the school to be put on the waiting list. The summer camps are quite popular, so contact the school as early as possible to be put on the camp waiting list.

PARENT RATING: ☆ ☆ ☆ ☆ ☆

Parents praised the low student-teacher ratio, "nurturing" teachers, and "relaxed, joyful atmosphere." The cottage and renovated play yard with surrounding gardens feature an abundance of fun activities for children, from costumes to water and sand play. "Kids are never bored" at this school, say parents. Though it is "a lot of work" for parents, they say they appreciate "knowing all about what our children are doing," "gaining important parenting skills," and the "extensive parent education program."

Kids on the Hill

5461 Paradise Dr.
Corte Madera
415-924-3033
www.kidsonthehillpreschool.org

Ages: 2.6-5 years

Schedule: Mornings, 2 to 5 days a week for ages 2-3 years, or 4 to 5 days a week for ages 4-5 years. Extended care available.

Ratio: 6:1 for youngest class; 8:1 for others

Philosophy/other: This nonprofit preschool is operated by the Hillside Community Church but with a nondenominational, developmental curriculum. The curriculum includes large- and small-motor activities, language arts, art, music, cognitive development, science, and life skills, as well as weekly Bible story classes, monthly values and themes, and monthly visits from outside specialists. They balance between teacher-directed and child-initiated activities, and large- and small-group times.

Admission: By date of application (earliest application date is 2 years before entrance date), with priority to siblings and members of Hillside Church.

PARENT RATING: ☆ ☆ ☆ ☆ ☆

Parents praised the "very educated, knowledgeable, and hands-on director" and small class sizes (the youngest group has only 6 children). They say the atmosphere is "warm and nurturing," and the school is operated "family style" with lots of parent involvement. They also appreciated the flexible extended-care policy, allowing for last-minute drop-ins.

Lycée Français La Pérouse

See listing under San Francisco.

Marin Day Schools (San Rafael campus)

See listing under Southern Marin.

Marin Enrichment

Bacich School Campus
25 McAllister Way
Kentfield
415-461-4395

Ages: 2.9-5 years

Schedule: Mornings; 2, 3, or 5 days a week. No extended care.

Ratio: 7:1

Philosophy/other: This school features an emergent developmental curriculum with arts, science, music, and storytelling, designed to prepare children for kindergarten. The students are divided by age into the preschool and pre-k groups. The school uses Bacich kindergarten's playground and also provides the extended-care program for Bacich kindergarteners.

Admission: By date of application and visit to the school.

PARENT RATING: ☆ ☆ ☆ ☆ ☆

Parents praised the "intimate" class size and excellent, "diverse" teachers who are "committed" to the children.

Marin Jewish Community Center

200 N. San Pedro Rd.
San Rafael
415-479-2000, ext. 8041
www.marinjcc.org

Ages: 2.11-5 years

Schedule: Mornings, 3 or 5 days a week. Extended care available.

Ratio: 10:1

Philosophy/other: The NAEYC-accredited school features an "enriching Judaic curriculum," including reading, math readiness, science, social studies, gymnastics, music, aquatics, art, drama, and cooking. Teachers are trained to "recognize each child as a unique individual." There is also a separate full-day care program, as well as parent-participation programs and playgroups for younger toddlers. See Chapters 9 (Child Care Centers) and 7 (Gym and Play Programs).

Admission: Registration begins on the first business day in January for the September session. Parents reportedly line up early in the morning to secure a spot, as the program is extremely popular. Priority enrollment is given to current students, siblings, and legacy families, then to JCC members, and then to the general public.

PARENT RATING: ☆ ☆ ☆ ☆ ☆

Parents laud the facility as "top-notch," with access to a pool and other JCC programs. Although the classes are large (40 children), parents think the program is "excellent."

Marin Montessori School

5200 Paradise Dr.
Corte Madera
415-924-5388
www.marinmontessori.org

Ages: 18 months to 8th grade

Schedule: Mornings or full school day, 5 days a week. Extended care available.

Ratio: 5:1 (toddler program ages 18 to 28 months); 12:1 (primary program ages 2.5 to 6 years)

Philosophy/other: Founded in 1960, this private nonprofit school features an AMI-accredited program with much "self-direction" and little "play" involved. The curriculum includes traditional Montessori subjects along with mathematics, language, geography, geology, botany, zoology, physical science, music, and art. There are also enrichment classes in many areas.

Admission: By application by January deadline, and interview with parent and child (with preference for siblings and children with previous Montessori experience). Parents must commit to keep their children in the program through kindergarten.

PARENT RATING: ☆ ☆ ☆ ☆ ☆

This well-respected school has "fabulous" facilities, with "spacious, clean" classrooms and a large "sunny" playground and garden right on the Bay. The "hands-on" academic program, in particular mathematics instruction, is "phenomenal." Comment: "They follow the Montessori philosophy very strictly." Admission is very selective, particularly for the small toddler program. Primary classes are larger. "Community building" is very important, and parents are very involved in the school, from fundraising to parent-education programs. The program is "well designed for working parents."

Marin Primary and Middle School

20 Magnolia Ave.
Larkspur
415-924-2608
www.mpms.org

Ages: 18 months to 8th grade

Schedule: Flexible, with minimum 10-15 hours a week. Open all day, all year.

Ratio: 6:1 (toddlers); 8:1 (preschool)

Philosophy/other: Founded in 1975, this nonprofit, independent school offers a developmental curriculum focusing on each child's best method of learning. There are specialists in art and music, field trips, and elective classes in gymnastics, piano, dance, and computer.

Admission: By application and interview with parents. The school seeks to balance classes by gender, birth dates, schedule desired, and "other pertinent information received from the parents." Preference is given to siblings and children of staff.

PARENT RATING: ☆ ☆ ☆ ☆ ☆

Parents like the small (6-month) age span in the younger classes to help "ease the transition" to school. They praise the school's "extensive" resources and facilities, including a library and spacious playground, as well as the "flexible" scheduling tailored to working parents' schedules.

The Mountain School

50 El Camino Dr.
Corte Madera
415-924-4661

Ages: 2.9-6 years

Schedule: Mornings; 2, 3, or 5 days a week. Extended care available.

Ratio: 10:1 or 12:1, depending on age of child.

Philosophy/other: This nonprofit, Waldorf-inspired preschool and kindergarten was founded by parents. The curriculum focuses on developing every child's imagination through songs, stories, and puppetry, as well as establishing a connection with nature.

Admission: By application, due in February. Admission is selective (not by date of application).

PARENT RATING: ☆ ☆ ☆ ☆ ☆

This is a very popular and well respected "alternative" school with a focus on art and drama.

Ross Recreation Preschool

St. John's Episcopal Church, 14 Lagunitas Rd. (school location)
Ross School (office)
Ross
415-453-6020
www.rossrecreation.org

Ages: 3-5 years

Schedule: Mornings (including lunch); 2, 3, or 5 days a week. Extended care available.

Ratio: 6:1

Philosophy/other: Run by the Ross Recreation Department, this small developmental preschool has a mixed-age classroom and focuses on kindergarten readiness. The curriculum includes art, music, stories, science and nature, seasonal activities, and pre-reading (letters) and pre-math (games) concepts. The school uses the Ross School kindergarten playground across the street.

Admission: By date of application, with priority for siblings.

PARENT RATING: ☆ ☆ ☆ ☆ ☆

Parents say this is a "traditional preschool with a loving, small-town, community feel." Teachers "really get to know the students," and many of the students go on to attend Ross School together.

Ross Valley Nursery School

689 Sir Francis Drake Blvd.
Kentfield
415-461-5150

Ages: 2.9 to pre-k

Schedule: Mornings or afternoons; 2, 3, or 5 days a week (schedule determined by age). No extended care.

Ratio: 6:1

Philosophy/other: Established in 1951, this nonprofit, NAEYC-accredited school offers a developmental curriculum. Activities include art, music, stories, science and nature, circle time, imaginative play, outdoor play, and cooking. Children break into smaller groups of 6 (by age/developmental level) with individual teachers for stories, games, and snack. The pre-k program is more structured and focuses on basic math and language concepts, sorting and sequencing, and pre-writing skills.

Admission: Strictly by date of application (with preference for siblings and legacies). Applications accepted from birth.

PARENT RATING: ☆ ☆ ☆ ☆ ☆

Probably the most popular developmental program in the Ross Valley, this school enjoys an excellent and long-standing reputation in the community. Currently parents must apply very early in a child's life to obtain admission. Parents praised the "warm" atmosphere, "excellent school-parent communication," and "involved" parents at this "traditional" nursery school. Projects are "innovative" and designed to "foster age-appropriate skills." The teachers are "experienced," "loving," "true professionals" who "deal well with different learning styles." "There is virtually no teacher turnover." The "wonderful" outdoor area was completely renovated in 2001.

San Anselmo Montessori School

100 Shaw Dr.
San Anselmo
415-457-3428

Ages: 2.10-6 years (includes kindergarten program)

Schedule: Mornings, 3 to 5 days a week. Kindergarteners have longer days. Extended care available.

Ratio: 10:1

Philosophy/other: Founded in 1971, this nonprofit Montessori preschool and kindergarten blends indoor traditional Montessori work with outdoor social play, circle time, and music. There are group and individual projects. The classroom is large, with a beautiful greenhouse and garden outside. The curriculum includes pre-academics, and enrichment such as bringing in outside storytellers and music instructors or going on field trips. The kindergarten program is smaller, with only 10 students, and focuses on academics.

Admission: By application and meeting with parents. They do not screen the children, but they take into account the date of the application, gender and age balance, and the family's fit with the program.

PARENT RATING: ☆ ☆ ☆ ☆ ☆

Parents say this "excellent" program is more "relaxed" than other "classic" Montessori programs, with a "nice balance of play and 'work.'" Teacher-student ratios are "considerably better" than at other Montessori schools, with 4 teachers for 40 or fewer students per day. All of the teachers are "fully qualified Montessori teachers, not aides." Parents are "very involved" in the school on a very "egalitarian basis," from fund-raising to fulfilling 25 service hours per year. Comment: "Communication between teachers and parents is excellent. . . . I get lots of feedback about how my child is doing every day."

San Anselmo Preschool

121 Ross Ave.
San Anselmo
415-453-3181
www.sananselmopreschool.org

Ages: 2.5 to pre-k

Schedule: Mornings or afternoons; 2, 3, or 5 days a week. Extended care available.

Ratio: 7:1

Philosophy/other: This nonprofit school offers a developmental curriculum focusing on science and the environment. There are numerous small live animals on the premises,

and a courtyard with a roof overhang for rainy days. Large classes divide into smaller groups for part of the day. The school is located in the First Presbyterian Church but is secular.

Admission: Applications are accepted up to one year in advance. After returning students reenroll, admissions begin by order of application.

PARENT RATING: ☆ ☆ ☆ ☆

Though the program is large, parents noted the ability of the children to "self-direct" their play in one of several adjoining rooms (e.g., science, art, or reading). Parents report that the staff is "diverse" and that they appreciate the "unique" science and nature approach.

San Domenico School

1500 Butterfield Rd.
San Anselmo
415-258-1990, ext. 1121
www.sandomenico.org

Ages: 4 (pre-k) through 12th grade

Schedule: Mornings, 5 days a week. Extended care available.

Ratio: 12:1

Philosophy/other: Founded in 1850, this private, independent Catholic school in the Sleepy Hollow neighborhood offers a pre-k program (not a preschool) for ages 4-5 years. The approach is very academic, and students rotate through language arts, mathematics, and art rooms. Music, religion, and values are components of the curriculum throughout the grades. The after-school enrichment program includes cooking, art, music, science, and social studies.

Admission: By tour, application by December, and formal child assessment.

PARENT RATING: ☆ ☆ ☆ ☆ ☆

The pre-k program has a stellar reputation for academic excellence, and also provides an entrée into the highly regarded elementary school. The school's music program (including a Music Conservatory for private lessons) is renowned.

Trinity Preschool and Kindergarten

333 Woodland Ave.
San Rafael
415-453-4526
www.trinitypreschool.com

Ages: 2.9-5 years (must be potty trained, and includes a transitional kindergarten program)

Schedule: Mornings, 2 to 5 days a week. An afternoon class for 4-year-olds 3 days a week is also available. Extended care available.

Ratio: 7:1 (3-year-olds); 10:1 (4-year-olds); 12:1 (pre-k)

Philosophy/other: This nonprofit school affiliated with the Lutheran Church offers a Christian-oriented developmental program. Students attend chapel one day a week and learn Bible stories and songs. The faith-based curriculum includes weekly themes, language skills, science, music, arts and crafts, and nature studies. An after-school program includes gymnastics, dance, music, French, and Spanish.

Admission: By date of application.

PARENT RATING: ☆ ☆ ☆ ☆ ☆

Parents call the teachers "fabulous," "proactive," and "tuned in" to each child's needs. The facility is "spacious, bright, and clean" with a nice view of the hills, and the shaded outdoor playground was completely renovated in 2001. Comment: "A loving Christian environment . . . affordable program, [with] supportive and engaged parents." Parents especially appreciated being able to choose which and how many days their children attend the school, as well as the "inexpensive and flexible" extended-care program allowing for last-minute drop-ins. The transitional kindergarten program is a popular choice for children with fall birthdays who are not ready for other kindergartens. Graduates do very well in admissions to local private Catholic and parochial schools.

Village Montessori

17 Arroyo Ave.
San Anselmo
415-457-1336

Ages: 18 months to 3 years

Schedule: Mornings, 3 or 4 days a week, including lunch.

Ratio: 6:1

Philosophy/other: Directed by the former head of Marin Montessori School, this small, home-based AMI Montessori program is designed for toddlers. The beautifully prepared indoor and outdoor environment is arranged specifically for toddlers, including a yard with tricycles and a garden. In addition to the traditional Montessori practical life skills, the curriculum includes music and art, and both individual and group time.

Admission: By parent tour of the school, application, and family visit to the school for child observation. The director tries to balance classes by ages, genders, and personalities, and also takes into account the family's interest in the Montessori approach.

PARENT RATING: ☆ ☆ ☆ ☆ ☆

Comment: "I can't say enough about this school. Jules Layman, the instructor and director, is amazing with toddlers—she is so in tune with the kids. I believe that children who participate in this one-year program get a head start on life!" Many graduates go on to the primary programs at the Marin Montessori and San Anselmo Montessori schools.

NORTHERN MARIN

Creekside Village School of Novato

1787 Grant Ave.
Novato
415-898-7007
www.creeksidevillageschool.com

Ages: 6 weeks to 5 years (child must be potty trained)

Schedule: Flexible. Open all day, all year.

Ratio: 4:1 (newborn-2 years); up to 12:1 for older children, but usually smaller.

Philosophy/other: This day care center and school offers a developmental program. There is a large outdoor area, and breakfasts, lunches, and snacks are included.

Admission: By application as space becomes available.

PARENT RATING: ☆ ☆ ☆ ☆

Parents appreciate the "flexible" hours and committed staff. See also Ch. 9 under Child Care Centers.

Good Shepherd Lutheran School

1180 Lynwood Dr.
Novato
415-897-2510
www.goodshepherdlutheran.org

Ages: 2 years to 5th grade

Schedule: Mornings; 2, 3, or 5 days a week. Extended care available.

Ratio: 5:1 (2-year-olds); 7:1 (3- and 4-year olds)

Philosophy/other: This NAEYC-accredited Christian school offers a developmental curriculum with many hands-on activities. Students attend chapel once a week, and Christian philosophy is part of the curriculum. The students sing in the chapel several times a year.

Admission: Church families and siblings of elementary school students enroll first, then returning preschool families. Open enrollment begins in March, and admissions are handled on a first-come, first-served basis. Parents must tour the school before applying.

PARENT RATING: ☆ ☆ ☆ ☆ ☆

This is the only NAEYC-accredited school in Novato.

Ice Cream and Shoe Preschool and Kindergarten

1055 Las Ovejas Ave., #4
San Rafael
415-492-0550

Ages: 2-5 years

Schedule: Mornings or full school day, 3 to 5 days a week. Extended care available. Open year round.

Ratio: 6:1

Philosophy/other: This small private preschool in Terra Linda offers an eclectic curriculum drawing from developmental, academic, and Waldorf traditions. They incorporate art, nature, creative movement, play, and kindergarten preparation. In the words of the director, "Children need both the joy and delight of ice cream and the shoe that fits properly." There are 3 age groups: toddlers (2-year-olds), preschoolers (3- and 4-year-olds), and pre-k/kindergarteners (4- and 5-year-olds). The school is located in a former public school and has an organic garden.

Admission: Interested families must visit the school before applying. Application is selective, with consideration to the applicant's readiness for preschool, and balancing genders and ages.

PARENT RATING: ☆ ☆ ☆ ☆ ☆

This popular school fills quickly by word of mouth and has a "peaceful, calm atmosphere" and beautiful indoor and outdoor space.

Marin Day Schools (St. Vincent's campus)

See listing under Southern Marin.

Montessori de Terra Linda

620 Del Ganado Rd.
San Rafael
415-479-7373
www.mdtl.org

Ages: 2-12 years

Schedule: Mornings, full school day, or all day, 5 days a week (except toddlers who may attend 3 to 5 days a week).

Ratio: 12:1 (primary); 10:1 (toddler)

Philosophy/other: Founded in 1970, this nonprofit AMI-affiliated Montessori preschool and elementary

school offers a toddler class for 2-year-olds, and mixed-age primary classes for ages 3-5. The primary class is a 3-year cycle, culminating in kindergarten, which is a full school day. They offer an innovative outdoor education program in the garden during the primary years. Enrichment classes include dance, music, science, chess, and gymnastics.

Admission: By tour, application (submitted by January 31 for priority), and classroom visit/observation of child.

PARENT RATING: ☆ ☆ ☆ ☆ ☆

Parents say this well-established school "adheres very closely" to Montessori principles, and is particularly good at "encouraging independent learning and teaching respect." They call the toddler program "fabulous" and the teachers "excellent . . . they love their jobs and treat each other like a family." The parents' association is "very strong" and many preschool parents are "very involved" in fund-raising.

Montessori School of Novato

1466 S. Novato Blvd.
Novato
415-892-2228

Ages: 2-6 years

Schedule: Flexible. Open all day, all year.

Ratio: 12:1

Philosophy/other: This AMI-accredited private school offers a traditional Montessori curriculum with practical life exercises, sensorial materials, and math and language.

Admission: By date of application, with preference for siblings. The school also tries to balance genders and ages.

PARENT RATING: ☆ ☆ ☆ ☆ ☆

Novato Parents Nursery School

1473 S. Novato Blvd.
Novato
415-897-4498
www.ccppns.org/npns

Ages: 2.6-5 years

Schedule: Mornings; 2, 3, or 5 days a week. Extended care available.

Ratio: 5:1 or less

Philosophy/other: This cooperative preschool offers a developmental curriculum with multi-age classrooms, focusing on positive discipline. Projects are open-ended, the program includes art and music, and they take field trips once a month. They also offer a Toddler Time playgroup for parents and children ages 18-33 months; see Ch. 7 under Gym and Play Programs—North Bay.

Admission: First-come, first-served, after touring the school. Returning students and siblings have priority.

PARENT RATING: ☆ ☆ ☆ ☆ ☆

A feature that makes this school more accessible than most cooperatives: they have a sibling room for children ages 2 and under while parents work in the classroom. They also offer drop-in child care in the afternoons.

St. Francis Preschool

967 5th St.
Novato
415-892-2597
www.stfrancisnovato.com

Ages: 2.9-5 years

Schedule: 2 or 3 mornings a week. Lunch program but no extended care.

Ratio: 7:1

Philosophy/other: This developmental nonprofit preschool is affiliated with the Episcopal Church, but the program does not include any religious teaching. The curriculum includes pre-reading, pre-math, art, literature, music, nature, science, and dramatic play. The school also offers a program for toddlers and parents.

Admission: By date of application, with preference for siblings and toddler program graduates.

PARENT RATING: ☆ ☆ ☆ ☆

SONOMA/NAPA COUNTIES

Brush Creek Nursery School

4687 Badger Rd.
Santa Rosa
707-539-1612
www.brushcreekschool.org

Ages: 2.9-5 years

Schedule: Mornings or afternoons; 2, 3, or 5 days a week. Extended care available.

Ratio: 8:1

Philosophy/other: This private, non-profit, NAEYC-accredited school offers a developmental curriculum with emphasis on the arts, sciences, social skills, and building self-esteem. Children are divided into 2 groups by age. The school is located on a beautiful 3-acre property surrounded by huge oak trees, and they have a woodworking barn.

Admission: The waiting list opens May 1 of each year for the school year that begins in 1.5 years (e.g., May 2005 for September 2006 entry), and parents may put their child's name on the list in the year their child reaches age 2.

Live Oak Preschool
75 W. Matheson St.
Healdsburg
707-433-1543
www.liveoakschool.com
Ages: 2.9-5 years

Schedule: Mornings or afternoons, 2 or 3 days a week (schedule determined by age). No extended care.

Ratio: 8:1

Philosophy/other: This private nonprofit preschool is NAEYC accredited. They have a developmental curriculum, with indoor and outdoor activities and circle time, designed to foster imagination.

Admission: By date of tour, with priority to siblings. The waiting list is always several years long, so it's best to apply early.

PARENT RATING: ☆ ☆ ☆ ☆ ☆

Parents rave about this fabulous, traditional school, considered the best in the area. Comment: "They focus on social and emotional development rather than strictly on letters and numbers, though academics are woven in. . . . The director, who has been with the school since its inception, embodies the philosophy."

St. Helena Cooperative Nursery School
1201 Neibaum Ln.
Rutherford
707-963-7212
www.sthelenacoop.org
Ages: 3-5 years

Schedule: Mornings or afternoons. No extended care.

Ratio: 3:1

Philosophy/other: NAEYC accredited, this nonprofit parent-cooperative school offers a developmental curriculum, focusing on social and emotional development. Classes are small (17 children) and ages are mixed. Students stay with the same teacher throughout their years at the school. Parents must attend 12 hours of parent education workshops offered in conjunction with the St. Helena School District. The school district owns and helps maintain the schoolhouse in which the cooperative is located. They also offer a morning toddler program with parent participation.

Admission: Enrollment begins on April 1 each year, with priority to current students, then siblings, then returning families, then alumni families, and then new families. If they have more demand than available spots, they hold a lottery.

East Bay

BERKELEY

Berkeley Hills Nursery School
1161 Sterling Ave.
Berkeley
510-849-1216
www.berkeleyhills.org
Ages: 2.6-5 years

Schedule: Mornings, 3 to 5 days a week. Extended care available.

Ratio: 7:1

Philosophy/other: This private, nonprofit preschool in North Berkeley offers a developmental curriculum with 2 classrooms, one for younger children (ages 2.6-4 years) who may attend 3 to 5 days a week, and one for older children (ages 4-5) who attend 5 days a week. A typical day involves 2 individual choice periods (one indoors and one outdoors) and a group time for ideas, songs, plays, and stories.

Admission: By date of application while balancing gender and age.

PARENT RATING: ☆ ☆ ☆ ☆ ☆

Located near a park in a woodsy residential area, this is a "traditional" nursery school with "experienced" directors and "nurturing" teachers.

Berkeley Montessori School

2030 Francisco St. (preschool campus)
Berkeley
510-665-8800, ext. 103 (admissions)
510-849-8340 (preschool)
www.bmsonline.org

Ages: 3 years to 8th grade

Schedule: Full school day, 5 days a week. Extended care available.

Ratio: 12:1

Philosophy/other: Founded in 1963, this AMS-affiliated school's curriculum includes traditional Montessori learning plus environmental education, music, art, and drama. The preschool has a separate campus from the elementary school.

Admission: By parent tour, application by January deadline, and student interview. Candidates are evaluated for academic, social, and emotional skills.

PARENT RATING: ☆ ☆ ☆ ☆

Parents say children at this longtime favorite are "polite" and "well-behaved" and can really "focus" on

individual projects. Teachers are "creative" with good ideas for projects. Alice Waters, of Chez Panisse fame, is a former teacher!

Child Education Center

2100 Browning St.
Berkeley
510-548-1414
www.childeducationcenter.com

Ages: 3 months to 5 years

Schedule: Flexible hours, 3 or 5 days a week. Extended care available.

Ratio: 3:1 to 8:1, depending on age of child.

Philosophy/other: This private nonprofit school and day care center offers a developmental curriculum, including art, music, motor skills, nature, walks, field trips, computers, dance and swim classes, cooking and drama. The program emphasizes language development.

Admission: By interview, tour, and date of application.

PARENT RATING: ☆ ☆ ☆ ☆

This school features a diverse, but "close-knit community of parents," with "lots" of parent involvement. "Great director, great teachers, supportive of kids and parents," said parents. See also Ch. 9 under Child Care Centers.

Dandelion Cooperative Nursery School

941 The Alameda
Berkeley
510-526-1735
www.dandelionnurseryschool.org

Ages: 2.9-5 years

Schedule: Mornings, 2 to 5 days per week. Extended care available.

Ratio: 4:1

Philosophy/other: This NAEYC-accredited, cooperative preschool offers a play-based curriculum. Parents work at the school the same number of days per month as the child attends school per week. Classrooms mix ages except at circle time.

Admission: Parents may submit an application after visiting the school in the fall prior to the year of entry. Admissions begin in February on a first-come, first-served basis.

PARENT RATING: ☆ ☆ ☆ ☆ ☆

Parents rave about this school and say they "become a real community" by working in the preschool. They report that the head teachers, who have been with the school since its founding, provide great consistency.

Duck's Nest Preschool

- Berkeley
  1411 4th St., 510-527-2331
- Oakland
  4498 Piedmont Ave., 510-428-0901

Ages: 2 years to pre-k

Schedule: Mornings; 3, 4, or 5 days per week. Extended care available.

Ratio: 6:1 to 9:1, depending on age of child.

Philosophy/other: This school offers a developmental curriculum with monthly themes. The program includes garden and animals, art, music, movement, and enrichment classes.

Admission: Attend open house in February and submit an application.

PARENT RATING: ☆ ☆ ☆ ☆ ☆

Parents "love it." They say teachers are "experienced" and kids "are

happy" and have "a lot of fun" while "actually learning" at the same time. The facilities are "clean and well-kept" and parents are "very involved."

The Gay Austin School

1611 Hopkins St.
Berkeley
510-526-2815

Ages: 2-4 years

Schedule: Mornings or afternoons; 2, 3, or 5 days. Extended care available.

Ratio: 5:1 to 8:1, depending on age of child.

Philosophy/other: Founded in 1956, this private school features a developmental curriculum, including art, music, math, science, and language. Classes are divided by age.

Admission: By date of application (priority deadline is the end of January for entry the following September).

PARENT RATING: ☆ ☆ ☆ ☆ ☆

Parents praised the "small" size of this "traditional" preschool with a "close-knit community of parents."

Hearts Leap School

2638 College Ave.
Berkeley
510-549-1422

Ages: 2-5 years (including a transitional kindergarten program)

Schedule: Full school day, 4 or 5 days a week. Extended care available.

Ratio: 6:1 to 9:1, depending on age of child.

Philosophy/other: This school has an emergent, developmental curriculum that includes play, creative arts, science, literacy, and motor skills. The multicultural program takes a problem-solving and conflict-resolution approach to discipline.

Admission: By application and tour. The school does not encourage a waiting list, but parents may apply early.

PARENT RATING: ☆ ☆ ☆ ☆

Parents praised the "enthusiastic" teachers and "great facilities" in the Julia Morgan Center, with spacious outdoor yard. Comment: "Not a day care-type facility . . . this is a real school."

Montessori Family School

1850 Scenic Ave. (preschool and kindergarten campus)
Berkeley
510-848-2322
www.montessorifamily.com

Ages: 3-12 years

Schedule: Mornings (youngest children) or full day (others), 5 days a week.

Ratio: 11:1

Philosophy/other: This AMS-affiliated nonprofit school features multi-age classes and a traditional Montessori curriculum with the addition of art, movement, music, and grace and courtesy. The 3-year cycle culminates in kindergarten. Special-interest classes are offered after school. The preschool and kindergarten have a separate campus from the elementary school.

Admission: By classroom observation, date of application, and student visit. The school tries to balance genders and ages in the classroom.

PARENT RATING: ☆ ☆ ☆ ☆

Parents say the school produces "well-disciplined" kids and has "trained, experienced" teachers. The founder/director is "very involved."

Step One Nursery School and Kindergarten

499 Spruce St.
Berkeley
510-527-9021
www.steponeschool.org

Ages: 2-6 years (including kindergarten)

Schedule: Mornings, 3 to 5 days a week. Extended care available.

Ratio: 5:1 (2-year-olds); 7:1 (3- and 4-year-olds); 12:1 (kindergarten).

Philosophy/other: This nonprofit school offers an emergent, developmental curriculum. Parents are expected to contribute 15 hours a year.

Admission: By date of admission (with preference for siblings, children of staff, and families of cultural and racial diversity). The school balances ages and genders.

PARENT RATING: ☆ ☆ ☆ ☆ ☆

"Great" facility and "experienced," "caring," "long-time" teachers with "diverse" student body, say parents. Teachers "really pay attention to each child. They truly know my kids and love them." The parent community is very strong. Parents recommend getting on the waiting list "very early" as the school is very popular.

OAKLAND

Duck's Nest Preschool

See listing under East Bay—Berkeley.

The Lake School

304 Lester Ave.
Oakland
510-839-4227
Ages: Not available.
Schedule: Mornings.
Ratio: Not available.
Philosophy/other: Located in a Victorian home, this developmental preschool program focuses on language development and conflict resolution. They have a spacious outdoor play area.
Admission: Not available.
PARENT RATING: ☆ ☆ ☆ ☆ ☆

Parents say this program is "excellent." For privacy reasons, the school does not provide information to the public, so interested parents should call the school for more information.

Lakeshore Children's Center

3534 Lakeshore Ave.
Oakland
510-893-4048
www.lakeshorechildrencenter.org
Ages: 2.9-6 years
Schedule: Full day, 5 days a week. Open all year.
Ratio: 8:1 or 10:1, depending on age of child.
Philosophy/other: Owned by a Baptist church, this nonsectarian school's developmental curriculum emphasizes conflict resolution and multiculturalism. Activities focus on developing social, emotional, creative, physical, cognitive, and life skills, and include a lot of free play. Outside teachers provide lessons in Spanish, gymnastics, music, dance, and sign language.

Admission: By parent visit and date of application.
PARENT RATING: ☆ ☆ ☆ ☆

Parents are "very enthusiastic" about the self-described "Peace Academy," a longtime school with "diverse" students, "consistent" faculty, and a "warm atmosphere."

Lakeview Preschool

515 Glenview Ave.
Oakland
510-444-1725
Ages: 2.9-5 years
Schedule: Open all year. Full school day, 2 to 5 days a week. Extended care available.
Ratio: 5:1
Philosophy/other: Founded in 1971, this private preschool has a multicultural emphasis with celebrations from around the world. The curriculum includes Spanish, music, science, movement, stories, art, and cooking.
Admission: By parent visit, application, and interview with child. Decisions are made on the basis of the child's age, gender, readiness, diversity, schedule desired, fit between the family's and the program's objectives, and the date of application.
PARENT RATING: ☆ ☆ ☆ ☆ ☆

Parents appreciated the "diversity" in students and program, and call this a "premier school" in the area.

Mills College Children's School

5000 MacArthur Blvd.
Oakland
510-430-2118
www.mills.edu/campus_life/
childrens_school/

Ages: 3 months to 5th grade

Schedule: Mornings or full days, 5 days a week.

Ratio: 1:1 and 2:1 (infants and toddlers); 4:1 (preschoolers)

Philosophy/other: This NAEYC-accredited laboratory school is staffed by a head teacher and student teachers from Mills College. The curriculum is developmental, and there are multi-age classrooms. Established in 1926, this is the oldest campus laboratory school on the West Coast. The science program benefits from a creekside outdoor classroom.

Admission: By tour and application, with priority to children of Mills College faculty, staff, and students, as well as to siblings of currently enrolled students. Admission is selective. "We strive for classrooms with a balance of boys and girls, a range of ages, and diversity."

PARENT RATING: ☆ ☆ ☆ ☆ ☆

Parents call this established school "excellent" and "fabulous," with "wonderful facilities." Head teachers have master's degrees and "tons" of experience. Students have access to Mills College facilities, including dance and swimming classes. It can be "highly competitive" to get in to the school if you are not affiliated with the college.

Montclair Community Play Center

5815 Thornhill Dr.
Oakland
510-339-7213
www.mcpckids.org

Ages: 3-5 years

Schedule: Mornings, 5 days a week. Extended care available 2 days a week.

Ratio: 4:1

Philosophy/other: Founded in 1933, this nonprofit, parent-owned cooperative offers a developmental curriculum based on parent involvement, antibias, and conflict resolution. The program is small, with 25 families. They also offer a toddler program with parent participation for ages 15-36 months; see Ch. 7 under Gym and Play Programs—East Bay.

Admission: By lottery in March, after attending January open house, taking February tour, and submitting application. The school strives to create diversity and a balance of genders and ages in admissions.

PARENT RATING: ☆ ☆ ☆ ☆

"Lots of work" for the parents, but a "tight-knit" community and an "excellent" program, say parents. The facility recently was renovated.

Temple Sinai Preschool

2808 Summit St.
Oakland
510-451-2821
www.templesinaipreschool.org

Ages: 2-5 years

Schedule: Mornings, 3 to 5 days a week. Extended care available.

Ratio: 4:1 or 8:1, depending on age of child.

Philosophy/other: This Reform Jewish preschool offers a developmental program with Jewish traditions. The school is open to children of all religions.

Admission: Current preschool families receive first preference in admissions, then Temple member families, and then non-Temple member families by date of application.

PARENT RATING: ☆ ☆ ☆ ☆

Parents had nothing but praise for the "longtime" staff and "kid-focused" program with its "well-equipped playground" and "supportive" parent community.

LAFAYETTE/MORAGA/ORINDA

The Child Day Schools

- Antioch
  112 East Tregallas Rd., 925-754-0144
- Lafayette
  1049 Stuart St., 925-284-7092
- Moraga
  372 Park St., 925-376-5110
- Pleasanton
  883 Rose Ave., 925-462-1866
- San Ramon
  18868 Bollinger Canyon Rd.
  925-820-2525

www.tcdschools.com

Ages: Infant to kindergarten (available programs may vary by campus)

Schedule: Half or full days, 5 days a week. Open all year.

Ratio: 4:1 to 10:1, depending on age of child.

Philosophy/other: This NAEYC-accredited private day care center and school features a High/Scope developmental curriculum. The rooms are organized into specific learning areas through which children rotate. Teacher-child interaction emphasizes teacher support rather than control.

Admission: First-come, first-served.

PARENT RATING: ☆ ☆ ☆ ☆ ☆

The campuses are individually run, so programs and ratings may vary.

Parents at the Lafayette campus had high praise for the director and appreciated the flexible scheduling. They say the school hires "great staff" who tend to stay.

Growing Tree Pre-School

1695 Canyon Rd.
Moraga
925-376-8280

Ages: 18 months to 5 years

Schedule: Mornings or full school days, 1 to 5 days a week. Extended care available.

Ratio: 4:1 to 12:1, depending on age of child.

Philosophy/other: This NAEYC-accredited school offers an emergent play-based curriculum. The youngest group focuses on cognitive learning, the middle ages rotate through activities, and the pre-k program introduces letters and numbers.

Admission: By date of application.

PARENT RATING: ☆ ☆ ☆ ☆ ☆

Parents praise the small classes, newer facilities, and relatively structured program. They say the codirectors are very involved, and advise parents to apply early as this is a very popular program.

Old Firehouse School

984 Moraga Rd.
Lafayette
925-284-4321
www.oldfirehouseschool.com

Ages: 5 months to 5 years

Schedule: Mornings or full days. Extended care available.

Ratio: 3:1 to 9:1, depending on age of child.

Philosophy/other: The individualized, emergent curriculum draws on the Reggio Emilia philosophy and emphasizes literacy. Recent projects have included creating a dinner party, a spaceship, a doll hospital, and a jungle video. Each child is assigned to the same teacher throughout his or her years at the school.

Admission: By application, with consideration of gender and age balances, schedule requested, and parental support of the school.

PARENT RATING: ☆ ☆ ☆ ☆ ☆

Located in an old fire station, the school gets high praise for its "innovative" curriculum and incentive bonus program to retain qualified teachers. The playground includes hills, a deck, a garden, a pagoda, an enchanted cottage, a tricycle track, and a sand and water play area.

The Orinda Preschool (TOPS)
10 Irwin Way
Orinda
925-254-2551
www.topsonline.org

Ages: 2-5 years

Schedule: Mornings; 2, 3, or 5 days a week. Extended care available.

Ratio: 5:1

Philosophy/other: Founded in 1938, this NAEYC-accredited parent-cooperative preschool and kindergarten in downtown Orinda has a developmental curriculum. The transitional kindergarten program includes math, science, and literacy activities.

Admission: By date of application (with preference for current and alumni families).

PARENT RATING: ☆ ☆ ☆ ☆

Parents say this school is "lots of fun" with a very "loving environment" and a "great music program." This is a popular program, so apply early.

St. Mark's Nursery School
451 Moraga Way
Orinda
925-254-1364

Ages: 2.9-4 years

Schedule: Mornings, 2 or 3 days a week. Lunch program but no extended care.

Ratio: 8:1

Philosophy/other: Founded in 1962, this Methodist Church-affiliated school offers a developmental program with a lot of free play and small-group time.

Admission: By date of application.

PARENT RATING: ☆ ☆ ☆ ☆

Parents praise this school's "warm" atmosphere, longtime staff, and "very traditional" program.

St. Stephen's Nursery School
66 Saint Stephen's Dr.
Orinda
925-254-3770
www.ststephensorinda.org/
NurserySchool/

Ages: 2-4 years

Schedule: Mornings, 2 or 3 days a week (schedule determined by age). Lunch program but no extended care.

Ratio: 4:1 (2-year-olds) or 8:1 (3- and 4-year-olds)

Philosophy/other: This school offers a developmental program with a structured schedule of free play and circle time. The school is affiliated with the Episcopal Church, but the curriculum does not include religious content other than holiday celebrations and saying grace.

Admission: By date of application, with priority registration for current families, siblings, and church members.

PARENT RATING: ☆ ☆ ☆ ☆ ☆

Parents praised the intimate size, longtime director and staff, "wonderful" art teacher, and involved families.

Saklan Valley School

1678 School St.
Moraga
925-376-7900
www.saklan.org

Ages: 2.9 years to 8th grade

Schedule: Half day or full day (to 2 p.m.), 3 to 5 days a week (preschool). Full school day, 4 to 5 days a week (pre-k). Extended care available.

Ratio: 6:1 (preschool); 10:1 or 12:1 (pre-k)

Philosophy/other: Established in 1954, this private, nonprofit, non-sectarian, coeducational day school occupies a new 2-acre campus. They have a developmental, High/Scope preschool focusing on each child's individual needs. Academics, such as language development and mathematical reasoning, are emphasized. Enrichment specialists come into classes to teach French, science, P.E./movement, and music. Preschoolers have access to school-wide resources such as a library.

Admission: By application and observation of child, with preference for siblings and those who are interested in the K-8 program.

PARENT RATING: ☆ ☆ ☆ ☆ ☆

Parents appreciated the small class sizes and structured, academic approach of this established school.

Seedlings Preschool

49 Knox Dr.
Lafayette
925-284-3870
www.lopc.org/seedlings.html

Ages: 6 months to 5 years

Schedule: Full school day, 2 or 3 days a week. Extended care available.

Ratio: 3:1 to 8:1, depending on age of child.

Philosophy/other: This NAEYC-accredited program is affiliated with, and located in, the Lafayette-Orinda Presbyterian Church. The developmental curriculum includes art, math, science, music, motor skills, language, and practical life skills, as well as Christian traditions.

Admission: First-come, first-served, with priority for current families, siblings, and members of the church.

PARENT RATING: ☆ ☆ ☆ ☆ ☆

"Great reputation" and "excellent facilities," say parents.

ALAMO/DANVILLE/PLEASANTON/ LIVERMORE

The Child Day Schools

See listing under Lafayette/Moraga/Orinda.

Creative Learning Center

120 Hemme Ave.
Alamo
925-837-4044
www.clcalamo.com

Ages: 2.9 years to kindergarten

Schedule: Mornings, afternoons, or full school days, 3 or 5 days a week. Extended care available.

Ratio: 5:1 to 8:1

Philosophy/other: Located in an old house surrounded by huge trees, the school offers a developmental curriculum, including art, language, drama, science, math, woodworking, music and movement, health, nature, social studies, computer, and field trips. Parent participation is encouraged.

Admission: By date of application.

PARENT RATING: ☆ ☆ ☆ ☆ ☆

Parents praised the school's philosophy of "socialization" rather than "strict academic drills," and "respectful" staff who "do a great job at resolving conflict and redirecting the children to more appropriate activities."

The Dorris-Eaton School

1286 Stone Valley Rd. (preschool)
Alamo
925-837-7248
www.dorriseaton.com

Ages: 3 years to 8th grade

Schedule: Mornings or afternoons; 2, 3, or 5 days a week. Extended care available.

Ratio: 10:1 (some classes are smaller)

Philosophy/other: This private school offers a developmental curriculum including basic reading and math, art, music, movement, and motor skills. The elementary school campus is located in Walnut Creek.

Admission: By date of application beginning a year in advance of entry, with priority for continuing families

and siblings. Interested families must tour the campus with the director.

PARENT RATING: ☆ ☆ ☆ ☆

"Warm, attentive, experienced staff."

Gingerbread Preschool

4333 Black Ave.
Pleasanton
925-931-3430
www.ci.pleasanton.ca.us/gbgeninfo.html

Ages: 3-5 years

Schedule: Mornings or afternoons, 2 to 4 days a week. No extended care.

Ratio: 8:1

Philosophy/other: Run by the City of Pleasanton, this longtime preschool offers a developmental curriculum of themed units, including music and movement, dramatic play, art, natural sciences, literature, and math.

Admission: By lottery, with priority for currently enrolled families, then Pleasanton residents, then non-residents.

PARENT RATING: ☆ ☆ ☆ ☆

Parents lamented that the program lasts for only 2 hours each day!

Shining Light Preschool

4455 Del Valle Pkwy.
Pleasanton
925-846-2588

Ages: 3-5 years

Schedule: Mornings or afternoons, 2 to 4 days a week. No extended care.

Ratio: 4:1 (3-year-olds) or 5:1 (4-year-olds)

Philosophy/other: This Christian, parent-cooperative preschool is affiliated with the Valley Community Church. The school also offers a limited number of non-cooperative spots. The developmental curriculum includes monthly themes and letters, building character and Bible time, special events and field trips, crafts, science, cooking, fine motor skills, and music and movement.

Admission: By date of application.

PARENT RATING: ☆ ☆ ☆ ☆ ☆

Parents praised the small classes and "fun way of teaching." Comment: "The director is excellent . . . my child has developed wonderful skills."

Stratford School

3201 Camino Tassajara
Danville
925-648-4900
www.stratfordschools.com

Ages: 2.9-5 years

Schedule: Mornings, afternoons, or full days; 2, 3, or 5 days a week. Extended care available.

Ratio: 10:1 or 12:1, depending on age of child.

Philosophy/other: This private, independent school offers an academic curriculum, including phonics, mathematics, music, art, and science. During SMART (Stratford Math and Reading Time), teachers use puppets and visual aids to teach the alphabet and numbers.

Admission: First-come, first-served, based on space available and grade-level readiness (with priority for siblings).

PARENT RATING: ☆ ☆ ☆ ☆ ☆

"A relative newcomer with a great reputation," say parents. Comments: "Very academic and very structured, and the program is very well-rounded. . . . Great preparation for kindergarten."

Sycamore Valley Day School

1500 Sherburne Hills Rd.
Danville
925-736-2181
www.sycamorevalleydayschool.com

Ages: 2-6 years

Schedule: Mornings or full school days; 2, 3, or 5 days a week. Extended care available.

Ratio: 10:1 (2-year-olds); 12:1 (3- and 4-year-olds); 14:1 (pre-k)

Philosophy/other: The developmental curriculum features art, reading awareness, science, math, small and large motor skills, physical fitness, field trips, and music.

Admission: By application and evaluation by the director.

PARENT RATING: ☆ ☆ ☆ ☆

South Bay

BURLINGAME/SAN MATEO/ HILLSBOROUGH

First Presbyterian Church Nursery School

1500 Easton Dr.
Burlingame
650-342-8326
www.burlpres.org

Ages: 2-4 years

Schedule: Mornings, 2 to 4 days a week. No extended care.

Ratio: 3:1 (2-year-olds); 6:1 (3-year-olds); 7:1 (4-year-olds)

Philosophy/other: Founded in 1964, this nonprofit cooperative preschool is affiliated with the church. The curriculum is play-based, and the school is NAEYC accredited.

Admission: By date of application, with priorities for church members, current families, siblings of graduates, and graduates of the toddler class.

PARENT RATING: ☆ ☆ ☆ ☆ ☆

Little Wonders

225 Tilton Ave.
San Mateo
650-348-0736
www.littlewonders.org

Ages: 9-33 months

Schedule: Two-hour classes meet once a week.

Ratio: 1:1 (parents must accompany children)

Philosophy/other: This nonprofit, nonsectarian cooperative school offers an unstructured program including free play, snack, discussion, and music. Children are grouped by age to foster age-appropriate discussion among parents.

Admission: Priority registration is for current and alumni families. New families must visit the school and register by the deadline (usually April) to be entered in a lottery for admission. After that, spaces are filled on a first-come, first-served basis.

PARENT RATING: ☆ ☆ ☆ ☆ ☆

Marin Day Schools

- Redwood City
  403 Winslow St.
  650-363-4939
- EFI Campus
  301 Velocity Way
  Foster City
  650-357-4250

www.marindayschools.org
See San Francisco listing.

Peninsula Jewish Community Center Preschools

800 Foster City Blvd.
Foster City
650-212-7522
www.pjcc.org

Ages: 2-5 years

Schedule: Mornings or full day. Extended care available.

Ratio: 7:1

Philosophy/other: The developmental, theme-based curriculum in this NAEYC-accredited school includes music, movement, art, and holiday celebrations. Shabbat is celebrated each week. Enrichment classes in music, cooking, ballet, swimming, drama and science are also available. There are also parent participation programs for younger children.

Admission: After reenrollment occurs in February for currently enrolled families and siblings, the general public is admitted on a first-come, first-served basis.

PARENT RATING: ☆ ☆ ☆ ☆ ☆

St. Matthew's Episcopal Day School

16 Baldwin Ave.
San Mateo
650-342-5436
www.episcopalstmatthew.org/
smeds.html/

Ages: 3 years to 8th grade

Schedule: Afternoons, 3 days a week (preschool); mornings, 5 days a week (pre-k). No extended care.

Ratio: 8:1

Philosophy/other: This private independent school offers a traditional, academic curriculum based on

Christian principles, with a particular emphasis on compassion.

Admission: Admission is selective and based on an application and interview. Priority is given to siblings, church members, and children of alumni.

PARENT RATING: ☆ ☆ ☆ ☆

St. Paul's Nursery School

405 El Camino Real
Burlingame
650-344-5409
www.stpaulsnurseryschool.org

Ages: 2.9-5 years

Schedule: Mornings, 2 to 5 days a week (schedule determined by age). Pre-k enrichment program and "lunch bunch" in afternoons.

Ratio: 4:1

Philosophy/other: Accredited by the NAEYC, this nonprofit, independent, parent-participation nursery school is located on the grounds of St. Paul's Episcopal Church but is nonsectarian. They offer a developmental curriculum, including art, music, dramatic play, math, language, and science. Resource instructors teach special cooking, music, and science activities. Children are grouped by age.

Admission: Interested families must visit the school for an entire morning. They begin taking appointments on November 1 for the following year's program, and will accept applications within one week after a visit. Registration priority is given to current members, then alumni, and then new families by date of visit and application, with consideration to gender balance.

PARENT RATING: ☆ ☆ ☆ ☆ ☆

PALO ALTO/MENLO PARK/ ATHERTON/REDWOOD CITY

Bing Nursery School

850 Escondido Rd.
Stanford
650-723-4865
www.leland.stanford.edu/dept/
bingschool/

Ages: 2-4 years

Schedule: Mornings or afternoons; 2, 3, or 5 days a week. Minimal extended care.

Ratio: 4:1 to 8:1, depending on age of child.

Philosophy/other: Founded in 1966, this NAEYC-accredited university laboratory school features a developmental curriculum, including art, music, language, computers, building, gardening, and animal care. Both professional instructors and Stanford students teach.

Admission: By date of application with priority to: current students and siblings; children of Stanford faculty, students, and staff; siblings of Bing alumni; and children of Stanford alumni. The school also strives to balance genders, ages, and ethnicities, and to accommodate special needs.

PARENT RATING: ☆ ☆ ☆ ☆ ☆

Probably one of the most well-known and prestigious preschools in the country, the school is housed in a 13,000-square-foot building on a 4-acre campus. Each light-filled preschool room has its own half-acre outdoor area, with covered patio areas for rain. Admission is "very competitive."

The Children's Pre-School Center

Palo Alto

See listing under Child Care Centers in Ch. 9.

First Congregational Church Nursery School

1985 Louis Rd.

Palo Alto

650-493-1915

www.fccpa.org

Ages: 2-5 years

Schedule: Mornings only.

Ratio: 5:1 (2-year-olds); 7:1 (3- and 4-year-olds)

Philosophy/other: This established nonprofit preschool is affiliated with the church but open to the public. Parents participate 9-12 times per year.

Admission: By application (with priority for siblings and church members).

PARENT RATING: ☆ ☆ ☆ ☆ ☆

Parents say "it's fantastic. I can't say enough good things about it." They have "loads of support and education for parents. . . . The director has been there for over 25 years and is very involved."

Kirk House Preschool (Menlo Park Presbyterian Church)

1148 Johnson St.

Menlo Park

650-323-8667

www.mppc.org

Ages: 2.9-5 years

Schedule: Mornings or afternoons, 2 or 3 days a week (schedule determined by age). No extended care.

Ratio: 6:1 or 7:1, depending on age of child.

Philosophy/other: Founded in 1953, this nonprofit preschool affiliated with the church offers a developmental, theme-based curriculum. The program includes Christian teachings and Bible stories, as well as art, science, and music.

Admission: By date of application (with priority for church members).

PARENT RATING: ☆ ☆ ☆ ☆ ☆

Ladera Community Church Preschool

3300 Alpine Rd.

Portola Valley

650-854-0295

www.ladera.org

Ages: 2-5 years

Schedule: Mornings or afternoons, 2 or 3 days a week. No extended care.

Ratio: 4:1 or 5:1, depending on age of child.

Philosophy/other: Founded in 1966, this NAEYC-accredited, nonprofit preschool is an outreach of the church but offers a developmental curriculum with no religious education in the classroom. Children are divided into separate classes by age.

Admission: By visit to the school and application. Priority is given to children of church members, then to currently enrolled families, then to alumni families, and then to date of application. The school tries to balance genders in each class.

PARENT RATING: ☆ ☆ ☆ ☆

This is a small program with wonderful outdoor space.

Menlo-Atherton Cooperative Nursery School

801 Middle Ave.
Menlo Park
650-322-7148
www.maco-op.org

Ages: 2.3-6 years

Schedule: Mornings or afternoons; 2, 3, or 4 days a week (schedule determined by age).

Ratio: 2:1 to 4:1 depending on age of child.

Philosophy/other: Founded in 1951, this parent cooperative is NAEYC accredited and has a developmental curriculum emphasizing free play. They moved to a new building in 1994 with a large, remodeled play yard. There is also a parent-toddler program one day a week for ages 21-30 months.

Admission: Priority registration for current class members, then members from the immediate preceding class, then siblings and alumni, and then new members by date of application.

PARENT RATING: ☆ ☆ ☆ ☆ ☆

Palo Alto Adult School/Palo Alto Unified School District

- Preschool Family
  4120 Middlefield Rd.
  Palo Alto
  650-856-0833
- Parents Nursery School
  2328 Louis Rd.
  Palo Alto
  650-856-1440
www.paadultschool.org

Ages: newborn to 5 years

Schedule: Mornings, 1 to 4 days a week. Parents attend once a week with their children, as well as meet 2 to 3 times per month for discussion classes. No extended care.

Ratio: 2:1 or 3:1, depending on age of child. Children under 2 are accompanied by parents.

Philosophy/other: A parent-education program of the school district, this NAEYC-accredited, cooperative preschool was founded in 1946 and offers a developmental curriculum.

Admission: After priority registration for currently enrolled students in March, public registration is held in April on a first-come, first-served basis.

PARENT RATING: ☆ ☆ ☆ ☆

Palo Alto Friends Nursery School

957 Colorado Ave.
Palo Alto
650-856-6152
www.pafns.org

Ages: 2.9-4 years

Schedule: Mornings or afternoons; 2, 3, or 5 days a week. No extended care.

Ratio: 5:1 to 8:1, depending on age of child.

Philosophy/other: This nonprofit, nonsectarian cooperative nursery school is sponsored by the Friends Meeting. The curriculum is play-based, involves free choice, and includes creative activities. The emphasis is on social and emotional skills rather than academics.

Admission: The waiting list opens 10 months prior to entry and interested families must call to put their name on the list. Admission is first-come, first-served, after priority for current students, siblings, and legacies. Other than one open house, there are no

Preschools

school visits until the applicant's name is at the top of the waiting list.

PARENT RATING: ☆ ☆ ☆ ☆ ☆

Playschool

- Atherton
  Holbrook-Palmer Park, 150
  Watkins Ave.
  650-325-1623
- Redwood City
  1835 Valota Rd.
  650-369-4151

Ages: 2.6 to 5 years (Atherton); 2.9 to 5 years (Redwood City)

Schedule: Mornings or afternoons. No extended care.

Ratio: 7:1 to 9:1 depending on age (in Atherton); 8:1 (in Redwood City)

Philosophy/other: This NAEYC-accredited school offers a developmental curriculum on 2 campuses. They have monthly themes, with academics worked into all activities, and they have an outside music teacher who comes in several times a week. It's a very literature-rich environment, and they have a special communication program designed to teach children skills like making eye contact, using names, sharing, and taking turns. The original Atherton location is in a beautiful park setting. At the Atherton campus, children are separated by age into classes. In Redwood City, classes mix ages. Both locations also have a "mommy and me" toddler program one afternoon a week.

Admission: They give preference to siblings, then to Atherton residents, and then to the public by date of application. Graduates of the toddler program are admitted to the preschool program and get priority in selecting schedules.

PARENT RATING: ☆ ☆ ☆ ☆ ☆

The school is in high demand, and expanded several years ago to accommodate more students. Insider tip: sign up for the afternoon program; it's not as popular as the morning program.

Stratford School

870 N. California Ave.
Palo Alto
650-493-1151
www.stratfordschools.com
See listing under East Bay—Alamo/Danville/Pleasanton/Livermore.

T'enna Preschool (Albert L. Schultz Jewish Community Center)

4000 Middlefield Rd.
Palo Alto
650-213-9316
www.paloaltojcc.org

Ages: 2-5 years

Schedule: Mornings; 2, 3, or 5 days. Extended care available.

Ratio: Not available.

Philosophy/other: The NAEYC-accredited, developmental curriculum features songs, music, art, and play. Students are divided into classes by age. The school celebrates Shabbat and Jewish holidays. Students may also take extracurricular enrichment classes. They also offer parent-participation classes for younger children.

Admission: First-come, first-served.

PARENT RATING: ☆ ☆ ☆ ☆ ☆

Trinity School

- 330 Ravenswood Ave. (lower campus, for ages 3-4)
- 2650 Sand Hill Rd. (upper campus, for junior kindergarten through 5th grade)

Menlo Park
650-854-0288, ext. 100
www.trinity-mp.org

Ages: 2.9 years to 5th grade

Schedule: Mornings, 5 days a week. Extended care for junior kindergarten and up.

Ratio: 8:1

Philosophy/other: This NAEYC-accredited, private Episcopal day school offers a developmental, project-based curriculum, including academics, music, and movement. Students attend chapel weekly. Preschool students are automatically admitted to kindergarten.

Admission: By application (due in January), student evaluation, and parent interview.

PARENT RATING: ☆ ☆ ☆ ☆ ☆

Admission is very selective to this "very popular" program.

Woodland Preschool

360 La Cuesta Dr.
Portola Valley
650-854-9068
www.woodland-school.org

Ages: 2 years to 8th grade

Schedule: Open all year. Flexible hours and extended care available.

Ratio: 6:1

Philosophy/other: This preschool is part of a private independent day school on a 10-acre campus. They offer an academic curriculum that

includes language arts, French, art, music, drama, and gymnastics.

Admission: By application and evaluation visit of child to school.

PARENT RATING: ☆ ☆ ☆ ☆

Woodside Parents' Nursery School

3154 Woodside Rd.
Woodside
650-851-7112
www.woodsideparents.org

Ages: 15 months to 6 years

Schedule: Mornings or afternoons, one to 5 days a week (schedule determined by age). Lunch program but no extended care.

Ratio: 1:1 (toddlers, parents participate); 4:1 (preschool, ages 3-4 years); 5:1 (pre-k)

Philosophy/other: This NAEYC-accredited, nonprofit cooperative preschool offers a developmental curriculum including art, science, reading, and music.

Admission: By date of application.

PARENT RATING: ☆ ☆ ☆ ☆ ☆

Reported to be "a lot of work" for the parents, but well worth it.

LOS ALTOS/SAN JOSE/ AND SOUTH

Jewish Community Center of Silicon Valley Preschool

14855 Oka Rd.
Los Gatos
408-358-5939
www.sanjosejcc.org

Ages: 2-5 years, with optional parent co-op for 2-year-olds

Schedule: Mornings; 2, 3, or 5 days for regular preschool. Extended care available.

Ratio: 5:1 (2-year-olds); 8:1 (3-year-olds); 9:1 (4-year-olds)

Philosophy/other: This developmental program features "hands-on" experiences in Judaic studies, science and math, art, music, movement, drama, stories, and cooking. Jewish culture and Shabbat are celebrated, but children of other religions are welcome. Afternoon enrichment classes are available. A new JCC facility, with a fitness center and café, is scheduled to open in Fall 2005 on the same site as the old facility.

Admission: By date of application.

Los Altos United Methodist Church Children's Center

655 Magdalena Ave.
Los Altos
650-941-5411
www.laumc.org

Ages: 2-5 years

Schedule: Mornings or afternoons; 2, 3, or 5 days a week. Extended care available.

Ratio: 5:1 to 8:1 depending on age of child.

Philosophy/other: This developmental program is Christian based and church affiliated but open to all.

Admission: First-come, first-served, with priority for returning students, siblings, and church members.

PARENT RATING: ☆ ☆ ☆ ☆ ☆

This is a new facility with a long waiting list.

Mariposa Montessori

- Los Gatos
  16548 Ferris Ave.
- San Jose
  1550 Meridian Ave.

408-266-LOVE (5683)
www.mariposamontessori.org

Ages: 2.5-6 years

Schedule: Mornings or afternoons; 2, 3, or 5 days a week. No extended care.

Ratio: 7:1 to 9:1, depending on age of child.

Philosophy/other: The campuses of this Montessori school are located on church property, but the program is nonsectarian. Classes are mixed-ages.

Admission: By date of application.

PARENT RATING: ☆ ☆ ☆ ☆ ☆

Montecito School

1468 Grant Rd.
Los Altos
650-968-5957
www.montecitoschool.com

Ages: 2-5 years

Schedule: Mornings or afternoons; 2, 3, or 5 days a week (schedule determined by age). Extended care available.

Ratio: 8:1

Philosophy/other: Founded in 1962, this private preschool offers a developmental curriculum emphasizing social skills, motor development, coordination, auditory and visual skills, following directions, and enhancing attention span. The school is part of the National Wildlife Federation's "Schoolyard Habitat" program.

Admission: By date of application, with priority to returning students, siblings, and alumni children, and then to students on the waiting list who did not get in the previous year.

The school does not maintain waiting lists longer than a year in advance of entry.

PARENT RATING: ☆ ☆ ☆ ☆ ☆

This is a longstanding parent favorite on a beautiful wooded campus with animals. There is a long waiting list, so apply early and get your name on the mailing list to be notified of an enrollment opening.

Mulberry School

220 Belgatos Rd.
Los Gatos
408-377-1595
http://mulberry.ca.campusgrid.net/home

Ages: 2.5 to 5th grade

Schedule: Mornings or afternoons; 2, 3, or 4 days a week (schedule determined by age).

Ratio: Not available.

Philosophy/other: This long-established nonprofit, nonsectarian parent participation school began as a preschool in 1963 and gradually expanded to the elementary years. The curriculum is experiential and multisensory, and emphasizes the whole child. They also have a "parent and me" class for toddlers (18-30 months) one day a week.

Admission: By classroom visit and application. Pre-k applicants must undergo a play-based assessment.

PARENT RATING: ☆ ☆ ☆ ☆ ☆

Saratoga Parent Nursery School

20490 Williams Ave.
Saratoga
408-867-9774
www.saratogaparentnurseryschool.org

Ages: 2-5 years

Schedule: Mornings or afternoons; 2, 3, or 4 days a week (schedule determined by age).

Ratio: 3:1 (2-year-olds); 4:1 (3-year-olds); 5:1 (pre-k)

Philosophy/other: Established in 1948, this parent cooperative school is NAEYC accredited. Parents attend a 3-hour parent education session monthly. The developmental curriculum features art, music, science, pre-math, and pre-reading. They also offer a "mommy and me" class for toddlers ages 18-36 months.

Admission: By application, with priority to returning students, siblings, and alumni children.

PARENT RATING: ☆ ☆ ☆ ☆ ☆

This newly remodeled school is spacious and bright, and the play yard is fabulous. They have a very strong parents' association.

St. Andrew's School

13601 Saratoga Ave.
Saratoga
408-867-3785
www.st-andrews.org

Ages: 4 years to 8th grade

Schedule: Mornings. Extended care available.

Ratio: 10:1

Philosophy/other: Located on a 6-acre campus, this is a private, coeducational Episcopal day school offering a pre-k and junior kindergarten program. They have a traditional, structured, academic curriculum with small class sizes and are NAEYC accredited. The program includes literature, creative dramatics,

Preschools

art, music, religion, reading readiness, math, and science.

Admission: By application (due in February) and assessment of child.

PARENT RATING: ☆ ☆ ☆ ☆ ☆

Stratford Schools
www.stratfordschools.com
- Fremont
  5301 Curtis St., 510-438-9745
- Los Gatos
  220 Kensington Way, 408-371-3020

- San Jose
  6670 San Anselmo Way
  408-363-2130
- Sunnyvale (DeAnza Park)
  1196 Lime Dr., 408-732-4424
- Sunnyvale (Washington Park)
  820 W. McKinley Ave.,
  408-737-1500

See listing under East Bay—Alamo/Danville/Pleasanton/Livermore.

Looking Ahead to Elementary School?

It's not too early to investigate elementary schools, particularly if you are considering private school or a move to a better public school district. Start with your local mothers' club for their insights, and in the East Bay be sure to check out the Berkeley Parents' (http://parents.berkeley.edu) and Neighborhood Parents' (www.npnonline.org) websites. Educational consultants, listed above, can also be helpful. Here are just a few of the many resources available to guide you in this process.

RECOMMENDED READING:

Private K-8 Schools of San Francisco and Marin, by Betsy Little and Paula Molligan

San Francisco Bay Area School Ratings, by Mark Mastracci

Picky Parent Guide: Choose your Child's School with Confidence (The Elementary Years, K-6), by Bryan Hassel and Emily Ayscue Hassel

USEFUL WEBSITES:

California Department of Education
www.cde.ca.gov/ta/
You can find school test scores and performance ratings here.

Great Schools
www.greatschools.net
This is a great website for test scores, parent ratings, and more.

Online Guide to Bay Area Private Schools
www.baprivateschools.com

Bibliography

CHAPTER 1

American College of Obstetricians and Gynecologists. *Planning for Pregnancy, Birth & Beyond.* 2nd Ed. New York: Penguin Books, 1997.

American Society for Reproductive Medicine. *Third Party Reproduction: A Guide for Parents.* American Society for Reproductive Medicine, pamphlet, 1996.

American Society for Reproductive Medicine website, www.asrm.org.

"Best Doctors." *San Francisco,* January 2003.

"Best Doctors 2005." *San Francisco,* January 2005.

California Employment Development Department website, www.edd.ca.gov.

California Employment Development Department. *Certified Nurse Midwives and Licensed Midwives.* California Occupational Guide No. 555, 1995.

California Employment Development Department. "Paid Family Leave." California Employment Development Department, Fact Sheet DE 8714CF Rev. 2, October 2003.

California Employment Law Center. *Family/Medical Leave.* Pamphlets, The Law At Work series.

California Employment Law Center. *Pregnancy Discrimination.* Pamphlets, Your Rights At Work series.

California Pacific Medical Center. *Information about Cord Blood Banking for Expectant Parents.* California Pacific Medical Center, pamphlet, November 1996.

Clapp, Diane N. "Selecting an Infertility Physician." RESOLVE, Fact Sheet 16, June 2000.

Disability Rights Education and Defense Fund website, www.dredf.org.

Dumcius, Gintautus. "Cord-Blood Coordination Is Urged." *Wall Street Journal,* 15 April 2005.

Eisenberg, Arlene, Heidi Murkoff, and Sandee Hathaway. *What to Expect When You're Expecting.* New York: Workman Publishing, 1996.

Equal Rights Advocates. "Californians Have Access to First Paid Family Leave Program in the U.S." Equal Rights Advocates website, www.equal-rights.org, press release dated 29 June 2004.

Equal Rights Advocates. *Family and Medical Leave and Pregnancy Issues.* Equal Rights Advocates, pamphlet.

Equal Rights Advocates. "Know Your Rights: Family and Medical Leave and Pregnancy Discrimination." Equal Rights Advocates website, www.equal-rights.org.

Held, Nancy, Teresa Corrigan, Jonna Schengel, Alison Horton, and Jeannie Karel Pimentel. *Healthy Pregnancy Guide*. San Francisco: California Pacific Medical Center, 1998.

Huang, Suein. "As 'Doulas' Enter Delivery Rooms, Conflicts Arise." *Wall Street Journal*, 19 January 2004.

Huang, Suein. "U.S. Adoptions Get Easier." *Wall Street Journal*, 28 September 2004.

Jeffers, Michelle. "Advocating for Disabled Children." *Bay Area Parent*, March 2003.

Johannes, Laura. "Alternatives to Amnio." *Wall Street Journal*, 26 January 2004.

Kapp, Diana. "Forever Fertile?" *San Francisco*, October 2003.

Knorr, Caroline. "Mandatory Hearing Test for Newborns." *Bay Area Parent*, March 2003.

Kramer, Jill. "Freezing Eggs." *Pacific Sun*, 19 January 2005.

Lehrman, Sally. "Surprise! It's An HMO!" *San Francisco*, January 2005.

Legal Aid Society-Employment Law Center. "Pregnancy Discrimination." Legal Aid Society-Employment Law Center website, www.las-elc.org.

Legal Aid Society-Employment Law Center. "Taking a Leave for Pregnancy, Prenatal Care, and/or Bonding with a New Child." Legal Aid Society-Employment Law Center website, www.las-elc.org.

Midwives' Alliance of North America website, www.mana.org.

National Adoption Information Clearinghouse. "Adoption: Where Do I Start?" National Adoption Information Clearinghouse website, Fact Sheet AB-0006A, www.calib.com/naic [now http://naic.acf.hhs.gov].

National Adoption Information Clearinghouse. "Intercountry Adoption." National Adoption Information Clearinghouse website, Fact Sheet AB-0009A, www.calib.com/naic, June 2000 [now http://naic.acf.hhs.gov].

National Adoption Information Clearinghouse. "Statistics on Cost of Adopting." National Adoption Information Clearinghouse website, http://statistics.adoption.com, May 2005.

National Adoption Information Clearinghouse website, http://naic.acf.hhs.gov.

Opdyke, Jeff. "Adoption's New Geography." *Wall Street Journal*, 14 October 2003.

602

Parker-Pope, Tara. "To Find a Good Doctor, Ask a Nurse: More Advice from Medical Insiders." *Wall Street Journal*, 10 February 2004.

RESOLVE. "Assisted Reproductive Technologies." RESOLVE, Fact Sheet 33, July 2000.

RESOLVE. "Overview of Adoption." RESOLVE, Fact Sheet 1, May 2000.

RESOLVE. "Regulation of Infertility Clinics and Laboratories." RESOLVE, Fact Sheet 32a, 1997.

RESOLVE website, www.resolve.org.

Shellenbarger, Sue. "Baby Blues: The Dangers of the Trend Toward Shorter Maternity Leaves." *Wall Street Journal*, 20 May 2004.

"Staying Healthy." *San Francisco*, January 2004.

U.C. Berkeley Parents Network website, http://parents.berkeley.edu.

U.S. Department of Labor, Employment Standards Administration. "The Family and Medical Leave Act of 1993." Fact Sheet No. 028.

U.S. Equal Opportunity Commission website, www.eeoc.gov.

Williams, Constance. "What's a Doula?: A Brief Discourse on the Latest Innovation in Birth Care." Birthways website, www.birthways.org.

CHAPTER 2

"Baby Steps: East Bay Trails to Enjoy with Babies on Board," Neighborhood Moms Home Pages 1996-1999 Era website, http://home.earthlink.net/~natashab/NMbabysteps.html.

Bay Area Moms website, www.plumsite.com/bayareamoms/outandabout/naturetrails/.

Byrne, Helen. *Exercise After Pregnancy, How to Look and Feel Your Best.* Berkeley, CA: Ten Speed Press, 2001.

East Bay Moms Newsletter. March 2000.

"Get in Shape with Kids in Tow." *Bay Area Parent*, January 2003.

Ginsburg, Marsha. "Stroll Through History." *San Francisco Examiner*, 18 July 2001.

Golden Gate Mothers' Group website, www.ggmg.org.

"Hit the Trail." *Get Up and Go*, Fall 2002.

Kukula, Kathryn. "Yoga For You." *American Baby*, December 2000.

Marie and Ron website, www.marieandron.com.

Martin, Don and Kay. *Hiking Marin.* 2nd Ed. San Anselmo, CA: Martin Press, 1999.

"On a Roll." *Marin*, April/May 2005.

Penny, Vicki. "Mommy and Me Workouts." Golden Gate Mothers Group Newsletter, October 2001.

San Francisco Bay Area Hiker website, www.bahiker.com.

Sherry Reinhardt's Support Services for Mothers website, www.supportgroupformothers.com.

"Take a Hike." *Bay Area Parent*, May 2000.

"Take a Hike or Stroll." *Parents Press*, February 2004.

Torassa, Ulysses. "Stretch and Deliver." *San Francisco Chronicle*, 13 January 2002.

U.C. Berkeley Parents Network website, http://parents.berkeley.edu.

CHAPTER 3

"Asset Management." *In Style*, February, April, and July 2003.

"Dressing for Two." *In Style*, May 2003.

Fields, Denise and Alan. *Baby Bargains*. 3rd Ed. Boulder, CO: Windsor Peak Press, 1999.

Lipman, Susan Sachs. "Second-Hand But First-Rate: The Ultimate Guide to Bay Area Children's Resale Stores." *Parents Press*, February 2000.

Lourosa-Ricardo, Cristina. "Baby Steps." *Wall Street Journal*, 16 September 2002.

Tien, Ellen. "An Early Lesson in Prada." *New York Times*, 27 February 2005.

CHAPTER 4

"Best of the Best 2005," *Bay Area Parent*.

Berrett, Dan. "These Days, It Has To Do a Lot More Than Roll." *New York Times*, 3 July 2005.

Brody, Jane. "Back to Basics: The Real Risks to Children." *New York Times*, 13 July 2004.

Carber, Kristine M. "Just for the Kids." *San Francisco Examiner Magazine*, 13 August 2000.

DeFao, Jamie. "Outgrown Shoes Find New Feet: Berkeley Mom Collecting Footwear for Kids in Need." *San Francisco Chronicle,* 15 July 2005.

Fields, Denise and Alan. *Baby Bargains*. 3rd Ed. Boulder, CO: Windsor Peak Press, 1999.

Higgins, Michelle. "Car Seats for Eight-Year-Olds." *Wall Street Journal,* 27 January 2005.

Kids in Cars website, www.kidsincars.org.

Lipman, Susan Sachs. "Second-Hand But First-Rate: The Ultimate Guide to Bay Area Children's Resale Stores." *Parents Press*, February 2000.

Mos, Leanne. "Chasing Baby." *San Francisco Chronicle*, 10 November 2001.

"New Laws Require Home Carbon-Monoxide Detectors." *Wall Street Journal*, 17 October 2002.

Oppenheim, Joanne and Stephanie. *Oppenheim Toy Portfolio*. New York: Oppenheim Toy Portfolio, Inc., 2002.

Reivich, Casey. "The Ultimate Spring Cleanup Guide." *San Francisco*, April 2005.

CHAPTER 5

American Baby website, www.americanbaby.com.

California Children and Families Commission website, www.ccsf.ca.gov.

California Pacific Medical Center website, www.cpmc.org.

Doulas of North America website, www.dona.org.

Dunnewold, Anne, PhD, and Diane G. Sanford, PhD. *Postpartum Survival Guide*. Oakland, CA: New Harbinger Press, 1994.

Kapp, Diane. "Mother's Little Helpers, Doulas Making Life Easier for Pre and Postpartum Women." *San Francisco Chronicle*, 18 November 2001.

Kleinman, Karen R., MSW, and Valerie D. Raskin. *This Isn't What I Expected*. New York: Bantam Books, 1994.

Myer, Michele. "Beyond the Baby Blues." *Parade*, 13 October 2002.

Placksin, Sally. *Mothering the New Mother: Your Postpartum Resource Companion*. New York: Newmarket Press, 1994.

Town and Country Resources website, www.tandcr.com.

"Understanding Postpartum Mood Disorders." *B.A.B.Y.*, Spring 2003.

Underwood, Anne, Ana Figueroa, Joan Westreich, and Tara Pepper. "Motherhood and Murder." *Newsweek*, 2 July 2001.

WIC website, www.wicworks.ca.gov.

Williams, Molly. "... Prepare for a Baby," *Wall Street Journal*.

CHAPTER 6

B.A.B.Y., Fall 2004 and Spring 2005.

Bay Area Parent, March 2001-February 2002.

Bay Area Parent, May 2005.

Bellafante, Gina. "Cover Baby's Ears: Mommy's Online." *New York Times*, 21 March 2004.

Parents Press website, www.parentspress.com.

Parents Press, February 2005.

CHAPTER 7

American Academy of Pediatrics. "Swimming Programs for Infants and Toddlers: Policy Statement." American Academy of Pediatrics website, www.aap.org, 4 April 2000.

American Orff-Schulwerk Association website, www.aosa.org.

Coff, Richard. "Suzuki Violin Versus Traditional Violin." Music Staff website, www.musicstaff.com, 1990.

Dalcroze Society of America website, www.dalcrozeusa.org.

Kodály Center for Music Education at Holy Names University website, http://kodaly.hnu.edu.

"Learning Second Language Changes Brain." MSNBC website, www.msnbc. com, 13 October 2004.

Organization of American Kodály Educators website, www.oake.org.

Suzuki Method Network website, www.suzuki-music.com.

U.C. Berkeley Parents Network website, http://parents.berkeley.edu.

Yamaha Music website, www.yamaha.com.

CHAPTER 8

Aaland, Rebecca Taggart. "Lawrence Hall of Science: From Animals to Zoetrope." *Parents Press*, March 2003.

Amador Mothers' Club website, www.amadormothersclub.com.

Bennett, Robin and San Francisco Mothers of Twins Club. *Play Around the Bay*. San Francisco: San Francisco Mothers of Twins Club, 2003.

Berger, Kevin. "The New Zoo Wants to Save the World." *San Francisco*, November 2002.

California State Parks website, www.parks.ca.gov.

Castro Valley Mothers' Club website, www.castrovalleymothersclub.com.

Corrigan, Patricia. "California Critters." *St. Louis Post-Dispatch,* 9 February 2003.

East Bay Regional Park District. *Educational Services of the East Bay Regional Parks*. East Bay Regional Park District, pamphlet.

East Bay Regional Park District. *Regional Parks*. East Bay Regional Park District, pamphlet.

East Bay Regional Park District. *Special Programs for Youth.* East Bay Regional Park District, pamphlet.

East Bay Regional Park District website, www.ebparks.org.

Golden Gate Mothers' Group website, www.ggmg.org.

Grant, Kay. "A Night Out With(out) the Kids." *Parents Press*, January 2005.

Jenkins, Amy. "WG Parks Offer a Variety of Choices." *Willow Glen Resident*, 23 April 2003.

Klein, Debra. "A Most Adult City has Plenty of Appeal for the Young, Too." *New York Times*, 1 May 2005.

Las Madres Neighborhood Playgroups website, http://lasmadres.clubexpress.com.

Marin Playgrounds website, www.justplaygrounds.com.

Marin Parents of Multiples Club website, www.mpomc.org.

MOMS Club of San Jose website, www.bayareamoms.org.

Neighborhood Parents Network website, www.npnonline.org.

Palo Alto and Menlo Park Mothers' Club website, www.pampmothersclub.org.

Redwood City Mothers' Club website, www.rwcmc.org.

Schiffman, Jean. "Animals, Activities, and the Arts Abound at the Randall Museum." *San Francisco Arts Monthly*, April 2003.

Serra, Joanell. "Raise a Conservationist." *Bay Area Parent*, February 2003.

Seshadri, Jana. "Park and Play: Take Advantage of the Bay Area's Recreational Offerings." *Bay Area Parent*, May 2000.

Shine, Marianne, and Richard Shiro. *Marin Playgrounds.* Shine & Shiro, 2003.

Skyvara, Suzanne. "Have Kids, Will Travel." Ross Valley Mothers' Club Newsletter, June/July 2005.

"Ten Fun Things to Do With Your Kids." Palo Alto Online website, www.paloaltoonline.com.

Thomas, Mike. "Overheard: Junior Birdmen Will Love It!" *Pacific Sun*, 19 January 2005.

U.S. Consumer Product Safety Commission, *Public Playground Safety Checklist*, Document #327, U.S. Consumer Product Safety Commission website, www.cpsc.gov/cpscpub/pubs/327.html.

CHAPTER 9

Adrade, Ana. *Infant to Five, A Comprehensive Guide for Parents Looking for Childcare*. The Wolf Pack Family Child Care, pamphlet, 1998.

Bananas, Inc., A Childcare Resource and Referral Agency. Pamphlets, Choosing Childcare series, 2001-2002.

Bay Area Parent, March 2001-February 2002; January 2003-June 2005.

California Childcare Resource and Referral Network website, www.rrnetwork.org.

California Department of Social Services. *Facts You Need to Know about Licenses for Childcare Facilities*. Pamphlet, 1999.

California Department of Social Services, Community Care Licensing Division website, http://ccld.ca.gov.

Children's Council of San Francisco. *Choices in Childcare*. Pamphlet, 2000.

Desrosiers, Alyce. *Finding a Nanny for Your Child in the San Francisco Bay Area*. San Francisco: Pince-Nez Press, 2001.

Desrosiers, Alyce. *Choosing In-Home Childcare, A Parenting Guide*. Pamphlet, 1999.

Eisenberg, Arlene, Heidi Murkoff, and Sandee Hathaway. *What to Expect the First Year*. New York: Workman Publishing, 1996.

Golden Gate Mothers' Group website, www.ggmg.org.

Go City Kids website, www.gocitykids.com.

Held, Nancy, Teresa Corrigan, Ann Kosistky-Haiman, and Diane Goldman, *Choosing Childcare Guide*. California Pacific Medical Center, pamphlet, 1998.

Raffin, Michele P. *The Good Nanny Book: How to Find, Hire, and Keep the Perfect Nanny for Your Child*. Berkeley, CA: Berkeley Publishing Company, 1996.

Shellenbarger, Sue. "When the Nanny Has a Past: Services That Offer Help Screening Babysitters." *Wall Street Journal*, 24 October 2002.

U.C. Berkeley Parents Network website, http://parents.berkeley.edu.

CHAPTER 10

American Academy of Pediatrics website, www.aap.org.

American Montessori Society website, www.amshq.org.

Association Montessori Internationale website, www.montessori-ami.org.

California Council of Parent Participation Nursery Schools website, www.ccppns.org.

California Department of Social Services, Community Care Licensing Division, *Facts You Need to Know About Licenses for Child Day Care Facilities.* Pub. 199, pamphlet, October 1996.

Deck, Cecilia. "Private School Snapshots: Sorting Out the Vocabulary." *Bay Area Parent*, February 2000.

Friedman, Mark. "Making the First Five Years Count." *San Francisco Chronicle*, 15 September 2004.

Huang, Suein. "Pre-K Prep: How Young is Too Young for Tutoring?" *Wall Street Journal*, 13 October 2004.

Hymes, James. "But Why A Co-op?" from *Notes for Parents*, reprinted in Children's Cottage Cooperative Newsletter, November 2003.

Kirp, David. "Life Way After Head Start." *New York Times Magazine*, 21 November 2004.

Molland, Judy. "What's Going on in Preschools Today?" *Bay Area Parent*, January 2003.

National Association for the Education of Young Children website, www.naeyc.org.

Neighborhood Parents Network. *Preschool Directory*. 2000-2001 Ed. Berkeley, CA: Neighborhood Parents Network, 2000.

"Picking An Early Childhood Program." *Bay Area Parent*, June 2003.

Preschool California website, www.preschoolcalifornia.org.

Rifkin, Lori, Vera Obermeyer, and Irene Byrne. *Finding a Preschool for Your Child in San Francisco and Marin.* San Francisco: Pince-Nez Press, 2000.

Roether, Barbara. "Spots for Tots." *San Francisco Bay Guardian*, 18 February 1998.

Rusch, Liz. "Preschool Prep." *Child*, February 2000.

Schrobsdorff, Susanna. "Finding the Right Preschool." *Parents*, January 2001.

Webb, Sarah Brody. "Co-op Preschools: All Together Now." *Bay Area Parent*, February 2003.

U.C. Berkeley Parents Network website, http://parents.berkeley.edu.

Yun, Dawn. "In Marin, An Early Scramble for Day Care." *San Francisco Chronicle*, 21 May 2004.

Index

About the Authors

Now a full-time mom, **Stephanie Lamarre** formerly practiced intellectual property law in several private and governmental positions. She is a graduate of Princeton University and Stanford Law School.

Stephanie moved to the Bay Area in 1989, and lived on the Peninsula and in San Francisco before moving to Marin County, where she lives with her husband, David, six-year-old son, Jack, and four-year-old daughter, Elise. She is an active member of various North Bay parenting groups, a former board president of Ross Recreation, and a supporter of Pixie Park, a children's cooperative park.

Michelle Keene was formerly a World Bank consultant, and executive with the U.S. Environmental Protection Agency, where she specialized in international pollution issues. She is a graduate of Bowdoin College and holds an MA from The Fletcher School of Law and Diplomacy at Tufts University.

Michelle has lived in San Francisco since 1998, relocating from the East Coast just three months before the birth of her first child. She lives with her husband, Mark, and three sons, six-year-old Michael, four-year-old Maximilian, and two-year-old Mattheus.

from left to right
front row: Michael, Maximilian, and Mattheus Tellini, and Elise and Jack Lamarre
back row: Michelle Keene and Stephanie Lamarre

Michelle and Stephanie met in 1999 as they struggled to adapt to life after their first babies were born. They quickly realized the need for a guide to parenthood in the San Francisco Bay Area, found there was none . . . and the idea for this book was born. They have spoken to Bay Area parents' groups about transitioning from professional life to life at home, entrepreneurial ideas for working from home, and the many Bay Area baby resources included in *Babies by the Bay*. As the first edition of *Babies by the Bay* quickly became a local best seller, they also have appeared on Bay Area television news programs and been featured in numerous publications, including the *San Francisco Chronicle*, the *Marin Independent Journal*, and *Bay Area Parent*.